ᴅUMBARTON OAKS
ᴍEDIEVAL ᴌIBRARY

Jan M. Ziolkowski, General Editor

LITERARY WORKS

ALAN OF LILLE

DOML 22

Literary Works

ALAN OF LILLE

Edited and Translated by

WINTHROP WETHERBEE

DUMBARTON OAKS
MEDIEVAL LIBRARY

HARVARD UNIVERSITY PRESS
CAMBRIDGE, MASSACHUSETTS
LONDON, ENGLAND
2013

Library of Congress Cataloging-in-Publication Data
Alanus, de Insulis, d. 1202.
   Literary works / Alan of Lille ; edited and translated by Winthrop
Wetherbee.
      pages. cm.—(Dumbarton Oaks medieval library ; 22)
      Includes bibliographical references and index.
      ISBN 978-0-674-05996-2 (alk. paper)
      1. Latin literature, Medieval and modern.
      I. Wetherbee, Winthrop, 1938–   II. Alanus, de Insulis, d. 1202.
Works. Selections. English. 2013.   III. Alanus, de Insulis, d. 1202.
Works. Selections. Latin. 2013.   IV. Title.   V. Series: Dumbarton Oaks
medieval library ; 22.
   PA8240.A5A2 2013
   871'.03—dc23   2012037856

Contents

Introduction   *vii*

"Sermon on the Intelligible Sphere"   1

"The Plaint of Nature"
(De planctu Naturae)   21

Anticlaudianus   219

"Undoing the Knot"
(Vix nodosum valeo)   519

"On the Incarnation"
(Rithmus de Incarnatione Domini)   535

"The Book of Creation"
(Omnis mundi creatura)   543

Note on the Texts   *548*
Notes to the Texts   *553*
Notes to the Translations   *569*
Bibliography   *603*
Index of Names   *614*

Contents

Introduction

Despite his fame and the importance of his writings, we know little about the life of Alan of Lille. He was born at Lille, possibly as early as 1120. His mastery of the liberal arts, for which he became known as *Doctor universalis,* was probably acquired at one or more of the cathedral schools of the Loire valley, and perhaps also at Chartres. He apparently taught at Paris, spent time in Provence, probably at Montpellier, and evidently returned to Paris toward the end of the century. He entered the Cistercian order in old age and died in 1202 or 1203 at Citeaux.[1] His epitaph, found in several thirteenth-century manuscripts, recalls his great learning:

> *Alanum breuis hora breui tumulo sepeliuit*
> *Qui duo, qui septem, qui totum scibile sciuit.*

> Our brief life has left Alan buried in a small tomb.
> He knew the two, he knew the seven, he knew all that is
>   knowable.

The "two" are presumably the Old and New Testaments. The "seven" are the liberal arts, which shaped the *totum scibile* for the twelfth-century *magister:* the *trivium,* Grammar,

Rhetoric, and Dialectic; and the *quadrivium,* Arithmetic, Music, Geometry, and Astronomy.

Perhaps the most important Latin poet of his day, Alan was also an innovative theologian and one of the founders of systematic theology, an apologist who attacked the Cathars and Waldensians and defended Christianity against Jews and Muslims, and the author of a treatise on preaching and a manual for confessors that are among the first of their kind. His diverse writings are unified by a theologian's concern with the relations between nature and the divine and with the problem of expressing these relations in language.[2] But while the focus of his work is finally theological, Alan's studies exposed him to the academic culture of the cathedral schools, where the study of rhetoric, logic, and law was becoming professional training, and the intellectual was emerging as a social type.[3] The evidence of his early writings suggests that his education was essentially that described in the *Metalogicon* of John of Salisbury (1159), and associated, largely on the basis of John's account, with the School of Chartres.[4] It is a program founded on a careful training in the verbal arts: grammar, which included close study of the ancient *auctores,* rhetoric, and dialectic. With this linguistic grounding, logic and the sciences could lead the mind to an understanding of a universe which was essentially that of Plato's *Timaeus,* as interpreted by Calcidius, Macrobius, and the anonymous author of the Hermetic *Asclepius.* Aspiring further, prompted by the *opuscula sacra* of Boethius, which used Aristotelian logic and Neoplatonist metaphysics to explore the relationship of the sensible world to God and the realm of divine ideas, pioneering thinkers like Gilbert of Poitiers (1085/90–1154) and Thierry of Chartres (d. after

1156), with both of whom Alan may have studied, were discovering new ways of bringing the arts and philosophy to the service of theology.

This worldview and the education it reflects are easily recognized in Alan's writings, but Alan was no mere disciple. His earliest works show him already distancing himself from the interest in cosmology and natural science that produced Thierry's commentary *secundum physicam* on the opening chapter of Genesis and led William of Conches (ca. 1085–1154) to repeatedly revise his glosses on Plato and Boethius in the light of newly available medical and astronomical texts.[5] Alan's model of the physical universe, though it reflects a sophisticated appreciation of the cosmological thought of his mentors, is in the end simple and conventional. His emphasis is on its moral and spiritual implications, and he keeps both ancient science and the Neoplatonism of the late antique interpreters of Plato at a distance. And though his frequent insistence on the "negative" relation of theology and its use of language to the practice of the liberal arts shows him aware of the visionary Neoplatonism of the Pseudo-Dionysius and Eriugena, he is equally cautious in appropriating their "supercelestial" theology.[6]

While Alan's methodological innovations were important for later theologians, the direct influence of his strictly theological writings was evidently short-lived. But the penitential manual and the *Ars praedicandi* were copied and recopied throughout the Middle Ages, and his major literary works, the *De planctu naturae* and *Anticlaudianus,* were hardly less well known; each survives in more than one hundred manuscripts, and they were read throughout medieval Europe.

2. ALAN'S LITERARY WORKS

The "Sermon on the Intelligible Sphere" and *De planctu Naturae* were probably written no later than the 1160s, when Alan was perhaps teaching in one of the cathedral schools.[7] Since the *Anticlaudianus* refers clearly to datable works by other poets, and the *homo novus* has been seen as an idealizing portrait of the young Philip Augustus, who ascended the French throne at fifteen in 1179,[8] it is assigned to the early 1180s.

The "Sermon on the Intelligible Sphere" is the work that most closely engages issues that concerned the scholars who were Alan's mentors, and it might be read as a valediction to the world of his early training. It raises epistemological questions that show Alan pondering the relations between philosophical and religious understanding with a freedom that closely recalls, and at times virtually parodies, the themes and aspirations of the Platonizing *magistri* of the previous generation, though the view it presents of the relations of the divine and natural orders is in the end conservative.

The cathedral schools promoted literary as well as philosophical studies, and the twelfth century saw a flowering of classically informed Latin poetry of many kinds. Alan's ambitious poems, the *De planctu Naturae* and *Anticlaudianus*, though strikingly original, can be placed in a tradition which includes Marbod of Rennes, Baudri of Bourgueil, and Hildebert of Lavardin and comes to full realization in the *Cosmographia* of Bernardus Silvestris (1147), the work in which Alan found his greatest inspiration and his greatest artistic challenge. From Bernardus, and from their great common exemplars, Boethius and Martianus Capella, Alan learned to cast complex intellectual issues in literary form, and his career as poet was largely defined by a sustained dialogue with the *Cosmographia*.[9] The two together set an artistic standard well documented in the *artes poeticae* of the later twelfth and thirteenth centuries, and their poems assumed classic status in the schools.[10]

We know almost nothing about Alan's teaching career, but his poetry shows him aware of his intellectual and social environment. The later twelfth century saw a vast outpouring of learned Latin satire, aimed not only at the rich and mighty but also at the pretensions of "new men," themselves products of the schools, who sought only such training as might enable them to set up as teachers of a superficial rhetoric or logic,[11] or satisfy their avarice and ambition as satellites of the powerful.[12] The *De planctu Naturae* considers the corruption of human language and sexuality from a cosmic perspective, but Nature interrupts her discourse at a certain point to incorporate extended and vivid attacks on gluttony, drunkenness, the love of money, and the meanness and hypocrisy to which social ambition gives rise. But Alan also demonstrates respect for true *courtoisie;* in the *Anticlaudianus,* where the formation of a *homo novus* requires the service of all the resources of the human mind and spirit, and an ascent to the very throne of God, the new man receives both a perfect soul and careful instruction in the social virtues that will enable him not only to remain immune to vice but also to conduct himself with the honor, generosity, and grace of a gentleman.

The two great poems[13] are markedly different in style. The *De planctu Naturae* is closely engaged with a world where

language itself and hence poetry as well have lost the power
to express natural love and the values implicit in the order of
nature. Poetic language conveys the effect of the corruption
of human nature in the form of bizarre rhetoric, obscene
puns, paradox, and ambiguity, and this crisis creates a corresponding crisis on the level of poetics. In the *Anticlaudianus*
such concerns are transcended. The verse no longer shows
the gnarling effects of vice, but maintains a pure conven-
tionality. The language of the *Anticlaudianus* recalls that of
the *De planctu Naturae* only when it aspires to express the
mystery of the divine, and its recourse to wordplay and paradox anticipates the "pure" rhetoric of the "Rhythmus on the
Incarnation."

3. The "Sermon on the Intelligible Sphere"

This strange work is an exhortation to mental and spiritual
discipline organized around a meditation on the life of form.
The only known witness to the text appears in an anonymous collection of sermons, and it resembles to some extent
the several sermons of Alan that take their texts from classical poetry.[14] But despite its broadly homiletic tone, it suggests a teacher's deliberately provocative address to his students rather than a sermon in any usual sense. Much of its
language and imagery appears also in the *De planctu Naturae*,
and it was probably written during the same period.

The cosmology of the Sermon, imaginative and occasion-
ally bizarre, is in effect a working model of the cosmology
attributed by John of Salisbury to Bernard of Chartres (d.
ca. 1130) and his followers. The quasi-hermetic formula, perhaps his own,[15] that is Alan's text is perhaps an attempt to

capture in a single image Boethius's description of providence, at once the center and the all-encompassing limit of
universal life.[16] In imputing spherical form to "the immensity of the divine essence," Alan recalls Boethius's definition
of the sphere as a unity *virtute et potestate* and the image from
Parmenides which completes Philosophy's cosmic vision in
Consolatio 3: God as a perfect sphere, unmoving as it turns
the *orbem mobilem* of creation.[17]

The organizing concepts of the Sermon are similarly
Boethian. Alan describes four spheres, each associated with
a mode of the existence of form, and each defined by a mode
of perception: "sensible," "imaginable," "rational," and "intelligible." These last are defined in the *Consolatio* by Philosophy:

> Sense assesses form as it is established in subject mat-
> ter, but imagination assesses only form apart from
> matter. Reason goes beyond this and considers in its
> universality the species that is present in individual
> things. The eye of intelligence is still higher: rising be-
> yond the bounds of the universe, it beholds pure form
> itself with the clear vision of the mind.[18]

In adapting this hierarchy of faculties to his hierarchically
ordered spheres, Alan follows his mentor Gilbert of Poitiers,[19] who in turn had based his metaphysics on the theory
of forms briefly detailed in Boethius's *De Trinitate*. Boethius
distinguishes between forms that are the ideas of things,
and exist wholly apart from matter, and the lesser forms
derived from these, which John of Salisbury calls "native"
forms.[20] In the "sensible" sphere, the physical universe,

INTRODUCTION

sense beholds the union of these secondary or native forms with matter; the forms in the "imaginable" sphere have descended to the material realm but not yet undergone the dreaded, alienating transformation of union with material substance. They yearn vainly to return to "true being" *(verum esse)* even as their ideal properties are undergoing translation into mortal ones. These secondary forms appear again in the "rational" sphere, which Alan identifies with the world soul. Here, freed from the contagion of matter, they revert to the pure condition of their origin and bask "amid the aroma of their own incorruptibility." In the "intelligible" sphere, the realm of the divine ideas, all difference is resolved into unity, and the contemplating mind, *intellectualitas,* exalted by the vision of the true natures of things in their ideal form, can scarcely imagine their mortal embodiments.

The one point at which the divine and natural orders can definitely be said to come together is in the creative activity of the sensible sphere, and even here Alan's language is hard to penetrate. The *ychones,* it seems clear, are material images of the divine ideas; their purple garments, which indicate their noble status as products of Nature,[21] are presumably the *formae nativae* that are made to inhere in them by the *geniale osculum,* the process of generation. Through this mediating process Nature administers each birth, ideal form determines created form, and *proprietas,* or true character, defines the creature. But the remoteness of the divine is clear from the two glimpses we are given of the imaginable sphere, where the *iconiae* "dwell in exile," banished by their primal parent, and the physical existence for which they are destined seems alien and threatening.

Alan's treatment of the *formae nativae* reflects both the

influence of Gilbert and a certain conservatism that sets him apart from the more speculative views of his predecessors and leads him to stress the absolute separateness of the divine and natural realms.[22] The mediating forms are in some sense emanations of divine ideas, and the sphere of the *anima mundi,* the world soul, in which we see them at rest, is the source of a perpetually sustaining vitality and illumination for universal life. Thus when Alan traces the journey of the soul, its experience in the rational sphere, "the palace of the world soul," is almost visionary. But though Alan vividly evokes the transcendent source of the world soul's illuminative power, he defines it only in its relation to the physical universe. It is a created entity, the engine of natural life, and will be effectively reborn as the goddess *Natura* of his major poems.[23] And human knowledge, its scope defined by the liberal arts, is precisely congruent with the sphere of Nature. Fully possessed of natural reason, man would realize the full capacity of his own nature, his *proprius status,* as the mirror and lord of the created universe,[24] but reason cannot empower him to see beyond the limits of the created universe, and it is perhaps to emphasize its finally subordinate position that Alan shifts, in the later stages of his narrative of the mind's ascending journey, from the metaphor of the chariot to that of the ladder.

The climactic vision in which the created universe is seen as the center of the intelligible sphere seems to verge on pantheism, and there is nothing comparable elsewhere in Alan's work. It must be understood as expressing the vision of a soul that has momentarily "become God" and sees the universe wholly as an expression of divine love. The metaphors that follow preserve something of the sermon's philosophical tone while reinterpreting it in orthodox terms, but the transition is inevitably awkward.

4. THE *DE PLANCTU NATURAE*

The *De planctu Naturae* is a dialogue between the poet-narrator and the goddess *Natura,* written, in imitation of Boethius's *Consolatio,* in alternating sections of verse and prose. Like the Sermon it plainly reveals Alan's debt to the intellectual tradition described by John of Salisbury. Its divine Nature is a largely autonomous power whose laws govern the reproduction of created life and provide a standard for social and moral order.[25] But while Alan's "goddess" has much to say about her authority, we learn that her power has been seriously compromised, by a human depravity that defies her laws. Despite the deep affinity of Alan's dialogue with the *Consolatio,*[26] he has created an authority figure who cannot, like Boethius's *Philosophia,* simply show her disciple the *via recta,* but must acknowledge the limits of her power to direct his life.

Alan's personified Nature is inherited from the *Cosmographia* of Bernardus Silvestris.[27] The first of the two books of this cosmological "epic," *Megacosmus,* describes the formation of the universe by *Noys,* the divine wisdom in its creative aspect,[28] in response to the appeal of Nature; the second book, *Microcosmus,* describes the creation of man. The *Cosmographia* is both a distillation of the work of the twelfth-century Platonists,[29] Bernardus's mentors as they were Alan's, and a self-conscious literary exercise, in effect an *ars poetica.*[30] Bernardus's account of the *ornatus elementorum* is an exercise in rhetorical *ornatus* and *dispositio,* charged with wordplay and images of the disciplining of an unruly *subiecta materia*.[31] Creation begins with a five-hundred-line poem on the emergence from *Silva,* or primal matter, of a universe of creatures, a display of creative energy with a life of its own, virtually independent of the activity of *Noys.* The complexity of human nature is anticipated in the near intractability of Silva, which threatens continually to disrupt or transgress the divine plan, as playful language resists the aspiration of human art to impose form and embody the ideal.

But beneath the waywardness of animated nature lurks *malignitas,* a more fundamental resistance to form and order that is effectively neutralized in the universe at large but remains inherent in the human microcosm. Human experience will always involve a tension between the integrating vision in which man realizes himself as mirror and lord of the universe and the aberrant, potentially subversive tendencies of *ingenium,* creative imagination. Yet these cannot be denied: intellectual and imaginative reach are essential to the fully realized humanity celebrated in anticipation by the goddesses of the *Cosmographia;* and desire too is essential. The *Cosmographia,* which opens with Nature's passionate demand that Noys grant form and order to Silva, ends by extolling the twin *genii* who guide the heroic work of the male genitalia, fighting to preserve humankind in the face of the threat of dissolution.

That the forces essential to human survival are capable of undermining human self-realization is the central issue in the *De planctu Naturae.* Nature's lament is an existential counterweight to the authoritarian idealism of Boethius's Philosophy, a sad answer to Philosophy's wish that the love that orders the heavens might govern the human spirit.[32]

The human scene she describes realizes the potential for disruption in human life present as an undertone in the *Cosmographia*. Bernardus's universe is a model of language in creative play, but the *De planctu Naturae* shows language reverting toward chaos. In place of the creation of man, shaped by and endowed with the formative power of the procreative *genii,* we will be shown the birth of *Jocus* through the adulterous union of Venus and *Antigenius.* The imaginative vision that would enable Bernardus's microcosmic man to realize the divine plan within his own mind and the sexual heroism that was to defend him against annihilation have been perverted.

The crisis of the *De planctu,* which will extend to all areas of human life, appears first as an epidemic of homoerotic behavior, represented metaphorically as a crisis of language. In the opening *metrum* the poet-narrator uses grammatical terms to describe a world of rampant sexual deviance: instead of the connections for which grammar offers legitimate metaphors, a kind of troping has emerged that violates the laws of grammar, physical and verbal, and the decorum that governs figurative language.[33] Procreative sexual intercourse and the generation of meaning through normal grammatical practice have been abandoned. He's become she's; a single male is made both subject and predicate. Such a man, Alan's proem declares,

> denies that he is a man, for he has become a barbarian in the art of Nature. The art [of grammar] does not satisfy him, only trope. But a translation of this kind cannot be called a trope; this figure is too readily reduced to a vice. (*DpN* 1.21–24)

Nature then appears, and vicious troping is replaced by a
luminous prose description of the goddess and her raiment,
but the tortured elegiacs of the proem have revealed a paradox that will become more obvious as the dialogue proceeds.
In establishing an equivalence between rhetorical trope and
homoerotic act, the Poet has implicated himself, for the linguistic *vitia* he condemns are of his own devising, and Nature herself cannot express her concern over the condition
of sinful mankind without employing them.[34] The healthy
"natural" rhetoric Nature demands is steadily displaced by
what she will later call *falsigraphia*. Once Nature has descended into the world and engaged the reality of sinful human desire, there is no longer a sure basis for discrimination,
for declaring one kind of language more legitimate, more
natural than another. And it can be argued that what is true
of language is true as well of sexual conduct, that in the *De
planctu,* homosexual as well as heterosexual behavior is a natural function of *cupido*.[35]

These concerns are set aside for a time as the Poet responds to the goddess. His account of the chaste beauty of
Nature is a prototype for the *descriptio puellae* that will become an important feature of the *artes poeticae*.[36] The survey
of her garments, a cascade of rich, naturalistic description
descending in a series of catalogs from the heavenly bodies
to earthly fauna and flora, has the vitality of the newborn
world of the *Cosmographia*. Though the vignettes of birds
and beasts, like those of Bernardus, include traits that re-
semble flawed human behavior, Nature and *ars poetica* seem
for the moment to be in rapport. The idealizing emphasis is
maintained as Nature, seeking to comfort the Poet, who has
been overwhelmed by the force of her presence, summons

forth "archetypal words" and gives a magnificent account of how she formed man on the model of the cosmic order, "so that in his nature, as in a mirror, one might see this natural order inscribed."[37] The Poet revives and offers his hymn of praise to "the child of God and mother of creation."

But Nature is weeping, and celebration soon gives way to anger. The goddess's language recalls that of the proem as she expresses her detestation of men reduced to "the shameless trafficking of the brothel."[38] The character of the dialogue changes further when the Poet, invited by Nature to question her freely, asks her to explain why, having condemned so emphatically the sexual transgressions of men, she has said nothing of those of the gods. Nature responds with a short treatise on poetics that, despite its orthodox ring, raises more problems than it solves.

Nature first notes the elaborate means by which poets seduce their audience into giving ear to false or dishonorable matter, then abruptly reverses herself: poets often employ an outer coating of falsehood, but beneath it the discerning reader will find "the mystery of a deeper truth" (*secretum intelligentie altioris*). This is standard critical doctrine, but Nature does not stop at this, and as she proceeds, her seemingly dogmatic assertions become less clear.[39] To create "a more elegant narrative pattern," poets often combine history and fable, "but when poets dream of a plurality of gods, or when the gods themselves are said to have submitted their hands to the rod of Venus, here the shadow of falsehood begins to shine forth (*falsitatis umbra lucescit*). Yet in such things the poet is not deviating from his proper character."[40]

The gods are dismissed as mere *sompnia,* then immediately become sufficiently real that they must be defended against the charge of promiscuity. The oxymoronic linkage of light with shadowy *falsitas* underlines the contradiction, and the assertion that such falsehoods are the essence of the poet's work *(sue proprietatis genere)* is Nature's last word on the subject. She shifts abruptly to an elaborate affirmation of the oneness of the true God, then reasserts the absolute falsity of stories which tell of many gods; these, she says, she will cover with "the cloud of silence" *(nube taciturnitatis).*

Nature has lost confidence in a fundamental principle of the hermeneutics practiced in the schools where Alan received his early training. She cannot guarantee that truth lies at the heart of the poetic text, beneath the veil of the *involucra* or *integumenta* presented by classical mythology,[41] and so cannot offer the defense of poetry that is needed at this point, because she is caught up in the very situation she condemns. She cannot avoid speaking of gods, yet she is herself implicated in their transgressive behavior. From her first appearance, ideally beautiful and clothed in imagery, she is herself a poetic text, and to read her is to engage in a kind of love-play. To the idealistic Poet, her virgin beauty seems to promise the pleasure of a love she herself would approve.[42] Nature herself can define such love only in theoretical terms, or as having existed *in illo tempore,* in a lost world like that of the *Cosmographia.* When she must speak directly about *Cupido,* sexual desire in all its aspects, withdrawing the "integumental covering" *(integumentali involucro)* with which the poets have veiled his enigmatic nature, she is at the same time unveiling herself as she exists for the fallen world, and what we discover is not "the sweeter kernel of truth," but near-chaos. Nature claims that Cupido shows no obedience to her laws, but she acknowledges that they are linked *quadam germanae consanguinitatis fibula*—"by the clasp of a certain consanguinity."[43] For all his complexity and danger, desire is integral to the process of generation, and in responding to it man follows Nature.

Nature complains that in speaking of Cupido she will be forced to "demonstrate something indemonstrable, and extricate the inextricable," and the long poem that follows is a distillation of horrors already described, a string of oxymora and paradoxes in which poetic language seems to assume a monstrous life of its own.[44] That Nature's most vivid poetry should be evoked by Cupido tells us that poetry itself is now a function of a new and ambiguous power, its rhetoric and imagery generated by the manifold forms in which natural love now manifests itself. From the pristine *descriptio* of the opening prose chapter through the empty dogmatism of Nature's attempts at theory, we have descended to a point at which Nature has abandoned her traditional role as a model, an arch-text. She is now a text that can be rewritten according to the desire of any lover-writer, but is the only means of representing the real state of affairs in the world of the poem.[45]

Nature's sad tale ends with the adulterous union of Venus and *Antigenius* and the birth of *Jocus*.[46] Of Antigenius we know only that his origins were of "scurrilous ignobility," and the arbitrary role of Jocus is made plain when his *vulgaritas* is compared to the graces of his half brother Cupido, who is abruptly transformed to an embodiment of urbane *civilitas* for the occasion.[47] The little episode can hardly bear the weight of irony: sexual transgression is now taken wholly for granted, and the stigma attaches, not to the sin, but to the social inferiority of the partner.

And this, as regards its plot, is where the *De planctu Naturae* leaves us. The Poet is the wholly nonparticipant narrator of the final pageant. Hymen and the Virtues appear, and Hymen is sent to summon Genius, Nature's alter ego and "priest," to pronounce the decree of excommunication foretold in the opening proem against all "who follow out their own desires in the constructions of Venus."[48] In the final words of the *De planctu,* we learn that it has been a dream, but of a type that the cluster of terms describing it—*imaginaria visio, extasis, insompnium, mistica apparitio*—makes it difficult to determine.[49]

The final recourse to an authority modeled on that of the Church is an acknowledgment that Nature lacks the power to control the sexual transgressiveness of men, that in them nature itself must be corrected or punished.[50] It also reveals what Nature's dominant presence in the dialogue has obscured, the dependence of her authority and agency on a higher "masculine" power.

When Nature first appears, descending "from the inner palace of the unchanging realm," a male figure *(homo),* in whose face appears "the mysterious quality of godhead," steers her chariot, "lending support to the weakness of her womanly nature by his gentle promptings."[51] This figure embodies the divine *ratio* to which the work of Nature must conform, and he is also the prototype of man in his original dignity, lord of the natural world, man as prophesied by the goddesses of Bernardus's *Cosmographia,* and as he once appeared on the now-torn portion of Nature's robe.[52] The apparition of Nature's charioteer reminds us that this primal dignity is a more-than-natural endowment; possessing it, man could realize himself in collaboration with Nature, making his mind the mirror of the cosmos, but in achieving this realization, he could know himself divine.

Nature is careful to emphasize her dependence on divine authority in all her work and dwells at length on her obedience to its dictates in regulating human sexual activity. It is her delegation of her own authority as *subvicaria* of God, which she herself describes as an abrogation, that opened the way to Venus's betrayal of Hymen and the torrent of sexual transgression that followed. But a vestige of her original role as an agent of divine authority survives in her relationship with Genius.

As priest, Genius speaks for a higher authority in pronouncing his decree of excommunication, though his condemnation even of sexual transgression is surprisingly perfunctory, one item in a list of formulaic censurings of vice. But Genius is also the formative principle, in nature at large and in the human organism, that preserves things in their "proper" or original natures, and it is in this sense that he is *Nature's* priest, among his other offices conferring a quasi-sacramental status on the union of male and female. There is a certain grotesque appropriateness in his excommunication of sexual sinners, for excommunication withdraws from the sinner the grace and protection of God, leaving him, in Peter Lombard's grim phrase, "free to rush into deadly sin."[53] The orientative function of Genius is the natural counterpart to that divine protection, and the suggestion of a religious element in his relationship with Nature is developed in other ways as the poem draws to a close.

Courtoisie and its values are a recurring theme throughout the poem. Man is by nature endowed with the courtly virtues; the art of Venus as instilled by Nature consists of "courtly precepts" which ensure lest the "nobility" of her handiwork "suffer diminishment of its glory"; and magnanimity and nobility are celebrated throughout,[54] culminating in the prominence given to *Largitas,* or Generosity, the true mark of *curialitas.* If Nature is inescapably linked to Cupido, her bond with Largitas is profound: through her "the far off times of the Golden Age live anew." The "Eternal Being," Nature tells us, brought forth Largitas "through generation by the eternal kiss of his Noys"; she is Nature's "womb sister," joined to her by "the chain of pure love."[55] Largitas is as close to *caritas* as natural virtue can attain. Her cult, "through which men pursue the rewards of gracious favor,"[56] is the most striking feature of the bond which makes the Virtues a "sacramental synod." She is in effect an emanation of the benevolence of the Creator, a natural counterpart to the Holy Spirit.

A similar suggestiveness surrounds the relationship of Nature and Genius. Genius is Nature's alter ego; in him she sees, as if in a mirror, the image of herself, and Genius declares that, "the exemplary notion of a single idea brought us to birth."[57] In effect Nature "thinks" Genius; in this metaphysical sense, as we learn rather surprisingly, he is her "son": *Veritas,* who assists Genius in creating the archetypal images of things, is the daughter of Nature and Genius, and her birth is described as the product of "the generative kiss of Nature and her son." If Alan's Largitas is in some sense a counterpart to the Holy Spirit, we may see in the cooperation of Nature and Genius a modeling of the roles of the first and second Persons of the Christian Trinity, considered as efficient and formal causes in the process of creation.[58] In an extension of this process, Hyle or matter is "saluted" by the eternal idea, and form and matter come together in a kind of incarnation, a moment which quietly evokes the angelic salutation to the Virgin and recalls a similar Marian echo in the words of the Noys of the *Cosmographia,* who addresses Nature as *uteri mei beata fecunditas,* "the blessed fruitfulness of my womb."[59]

This passage also reminds us that Genius is primordial, that he has been a formative presence in man from the beginning. The Genius of the *De planctu* is a synthesis of two types of genius who appear in the *Cosmographia.* I have referred to the twin *genii* of the *Microcosmus,* who govern the organs of generation. Earlier in the poem, Nature, searching through the heavens for Urania, who will create the human soul, encounters a Genius "devoted to the art and office of delineating and giving shape to the forms of things."[60] The sexual genii represent one aspect of this cosmic, form-bestowing genius: together they ensure that created beings will be fully realized, endowed with all the qualities appropriate to their kind. The role of Alan's Genius is to guide man to behavior that reflects his primal dignity. One aspect of this role is that of the genii of Bernardus, to direct sexual activity to the purposes of procreation.

The Genius of the *De planctu* is powerless to alter the behavior the poem describes; "natural" love has assumed forms he cannot understand. But his presence reminds us of the natural continuity beneath the chaotic surface of human life. In spite of all, marriages are made, the world is peopled, humanity endures. And the Genius, who attests the vestigial dignity of man, is also the genius who defines the nature of things in the larger universe. In a treatise on the celestial hierarchy, Alan clearly defines this larger role, contrasting our perception of transcendent reality through *theophania* with our understanding of created things through their *substantificos genios:*

> Through their substantific genii, that is, through their substantial natures. For the genius of a thing is its nature, or the god of its nature. Now this kind of manifestation is the object of natural philosophy, which deals with the natures of things . . . When we behold the beauty, grandeur, and order of things, we understand God not fully, but in a half-complete fashion: yet what is now imperfect in our understanding will be made perfect hereafter.[61]

The "beauty, grandeur, and order of things" include not only the magnificent universe brought to birth in the *Cosmographia* and celebrated by Alan's goddess Natura, but also the original dignity of man, depicted fleetingly on Nature's robe, still present *in potentia* in the noble virtues who form Nature's synod, and a Venus who instructs by courtly precept. There are literary modes that give expression to the idealism expressed in all of these conceptions, and like the "substantific" genii which give form to created things, bring the ideals of *courtoisie* into a form that can be fully realized in the light of a more perfect understanding. In the schools of twelfth-century France, it is often difficult to say what the "perfection" of our understanding will mean, as it can be difficult to define the precise relation of the virtues that inhere in us by nature to these same virtues as "animated" by Grace.[62]

There is a tendency in this period, in the face of the Augustinian view that redemption involves the elevation of humankind to a higher status than that enjoyed by Adam, to see it as essentially a return to the prelapsarian world, to the dominion of Nature and the original dignity of man.[63] The restoration of man to his original dignity, his *proprius status,* is the work performed, theoretically at least, in the *Anticlaudianus.*

5. THE *ANTICLAUDIANUS*

The *Anticlaudianus* engages its moral theme only in the most general terms. Rather than complaining of the sins of mankind, Nature herself now accepts responsibility for the imperfections of the human world. The poem opens with her summoning of a council of the Virtues, to whom she announces her resolve to atone for her errors by creating a new, perfect man. Advised by them, she commissions Providence *(Prudentia),* human understanding in its potentially transcendent aspect,[64] to ascend to heaven and petition God to create a soul for this *novus homo.* A chariot is created by the Liberal Arts, and Providence, drawn by the five senses with Reason as charioteer, ascends to the empyrean.[65] Reason and the senses can proceed no further, and Providence is now led forward by Theology and Faith to the throne of God. Her prayer granted, she descends again to earth, the New Man is created, and his regenerative role is dramatized by a battle in which the Virtues defeat the Vices, and the New Man inherits the earth.

The poem's full title, *Anticlaudianus de Antirufino,* alludes to the *In Rufinum* of the fourth-century poet Claudian, a powerful attack on the Praetorian Prefect of the East (392–395 CE), who was chief advisor to Emperor Arcadius in Constantinople. Claudian's poem opens with a council of infernal powers who, not daring to attack the gods, decide to inflict their protégé Rufinus on the world. After the disastrous effects of his ascendancy are described at length, he is lynched to universal rejoicing and consigned to deepest hell. The early portions of the *Anticlaudianus* are a reversal of the plot of Claudian's poem, and its influence is plain in the mustering of the forces of evil for the climactic battle.

Equally clear is Alan's debt to the *Psychomachia* of Claudian's Christian contemporary Prudentius, which describes the triumph of an army of Virtues over the forces of Vice. The war and its aftermath, the announcement by Faith and Concord of a new order, inform the later books of the *Anticlaudianus,* and the concluding erection of a temple in which the human soul encounters the Holy Spirit is a more explicitly religious counterpart to the redemption of human nature in Alan's New Man.

The effect of Alan's adaptation of Claudian and Prudentius is a matter of structure; once translated into the terms of his allegory, these models lose their distinctive character and with it any influence their poetry as such might exert. More significant is Alan's engagement with the *Cosmographia.* The influence of Bernardus's poem pervades the *Anticlaudianus,* but whereas the *De planctu* had only confirmed the *Cosmographia*'s forebodings about the precariousness of human existence, the *Anticlaudianus* is in effect a "super-Bernardus," a corrective reconsideration of his theme. Bernardus's heroine begins Alan's poem by confessing her failure to bring her order sufficiently to bear on the life of humankind and proposes the remedy of a wholly new creation, a microcosm without flaw. Again Nature seeks the aid of a higher power, but whereas Bernardus's goddess had herself ascended through the spheres to summon Urania, the wisdom figure who would create the human soul and set it on the path to cosmic understanding, Alan's Nature recognizes that only the Divine Wisdom can create a soul and that she lacks the capacity for self-transcendence that would enable her to appeal to God in her own right.

Another important model for the *Anticlaudianus* is Virgil. The journey of Providence, followed by war and the triumph of the New Man, corresponds to the pattern of the *Aeneid* as interpreted by medieval commentators. Virgil's first six books, full of trial and error but culminating in Aeneas's reunion with wise Anchises, and completed by a vision of cosmic order, were viewed as an initiation, preparatory to his victory in war and subsequent kingship. So well established was this reading that one commentator could view the *Aeneid* as the model for the Neoplatonic allegories so highly esteemed by the twelfth century: as Aeneas is guided by the Sibyl to his meeting with Anchises, so Boethius is led by Philosophy from falsehood to truth. Epic and philosophical vision, says the commentator, "express virtually the same idea."[66]

Such a reading obviously emphasizes the importance of the first half of the *Aeneid* at the expense of the later books, which in fact were given scant attention by medieval commentators. The *Anticlaudianus,* too, reflects this emphasis: Alan has clearly devoted far more care to the voyage of Providence, and what follows can seem mechanical, a separate poem robbed of dramatic energy by its adherence to the unalterable pattern of the *Psychomachia,* and culminating in a golden age which seems to bear no clear relation to the world of Alan and his readers. We are never shown how the experience of Providence influences that of the New Man, whose triumph seems to be entirely due to natural virtue, or what differentiates his soul from those of other men.[67]

The *Aeneid* provides a more satisfying model than Prudentius or Claudian, but its value can be seen to have limitations. The first half of the *Anticlaudianus* depicts the intellectual perfection attainable through the liberal arts and the origin of the soul. The second shows the development of human character to a state of natural perfection. The structural analogy of the *Aeneid* can account for such an ordering of the narrative, but James Simpson, on the basis of a penetrating reading of Alan's poem, has argued persuasively that reversing this order would establish a more functional relation between the natural and spiritual aspects of the New Man's experience.[68] Since the later books of the *Anticlaudianus* deal with the formation of his character on the level of the *vita activa,* they correspond to the earlier portions of the *Aeneid* as read by the commentators and thus ought to precede a celestial journey which would then be the culmination of all aspects of his education.

This reversal would correspond to the distinction made in one important commentary on the *Aeneid* between the "natural" and the "artificial" ordering of narrative. The "artificial" narrative begins with the sea storm instigated by Juno and the arrival at Carthage, and then reverts to the story of the war at Troy and Aeneas's subsequent wanderings; the "natural" (and moral or philosophical) narrative traces Aeneas's growth to the mature wisdom attained in his reunion with Anchises in Elysium.[69] In the case of the *Aeneid* such a reading leaves the final six books in an indeterminate relation to the pattern it defines. Alan's emphasis on the formation of the character of the New Man and the clear moral purpose of his warfare avoid this difficulty. Deficient as poetry, they lend themselves readily to their elementary role in the "natural" order of the poem. And by integrating the experience of the New Man with that of Prudence, they resolve the issue of whom we should regard as the true hero of the poem.[70]

Simpson's reading has the further advantage of doing full justice to the experience of Providence in the supercelestial realm. At the poem's center, where Providence encounters Theology, the poetry takes on a higher seriousness. The description of the heavenly maiden is almost impossibly charged with light, but still recognizable as a *descriptio puellae*. But the adornment of her robe takes us to the heart of Alan's theology:

> Picture proclaims what the tongue cannot utter: how language, being subject to Nature, is confounded when it tries to speak of things divine; it loses the power to communicate, and longs to retreat to old meanings; sound is struck dumb, scarcely capable of a stammer, and words lay aside any dispute about new meaning. (*Anticl.* 5.118–23)

No form, and hence no name, can truly predicate God. As Alan declares in his *summa "Quoniam homines,"* naming God can only be *transnominatio,*[71] wholly transcending natural usage. The effects when spelled out can seem like a bizarre, through-the-looking-glass counterpart to the linguistic horrors described in the *De planctu*.[72] Of course, the poem points beyond itself. Alan does not attempt to make his poetry perform the "translation" which a truly theological use of language requires.[73] Here and later, in describing the dual nature of Christ, he resorts to the rhetoric of paradox to express the mystery of the divine. But by incorporating a statement of complex theological principle he authenticates the experience of Providence and enhances the meaning of the poem as a whole.

But it is the creation of the soul of the New Man, the fulfillment of the mission of Providence, that is both beginning and end of the poem's "natural" order. The birth of the New Man's soul, and his moral development in the final books of the poem, should be understood to precede Providence's noetic journey. It is his intellectual development that the Liberal Arts perform, and the culmination of his development is Providence's vision of the origin of the soul, "the highest form of self-knowledge in Alan's intellectual world."[74]

The theological outburst of Book 5 is an isolated moment. The litanies of praise to Mary and Christ that follow are beautiful, but conventional. Even Providence's encounter with God is brought to life only by her rather brazen citing of Horace to suggest that God's interests as well as those of mankind are at stake in the crisis she describes[75] and by a brief outburst of divine anger at the sins of the world. The importance of this encounter is, however, made clear when God responds to Providence's initial prayer by raising her from her knees:

He draws her *erect* and orders her to stand and cease to be afraid, so that fear may not hinder her thoughts or their expression. The maiden draws *erect* and steadies her mind, and as her fear diminishes a little, her mind aligns itself with her body; her *erect* mind adopts the stance of her body. Now her subdued voice recovers its strength, and her words conform to the *erect* stance of her mind. (*Anticl.* 6.289–94)

The repeated emphasis on the "erectness" of Providence anticipates the renewal, the recovery of man's *status primae originis* that is to come.[76] But it also introduces the one moment in the poem when we hear Providence speaking assertively, and reminds us that the ascent to the vision of God is an inner journey, a process of self-discovery.[77]

Alan's sense of the importance of his undertaking is clear from his appeal, in the opening line of the verse prologue of the *Anticlaudianus,* for "the voice of an author *(auctoris stilum),* the trappings of a poet." For the twelfth-century schools, *auctor* signifies an ancient writer of classic stature, and the name of *poeta* is reserved for the poets of Rome. There is no medieval precedent for Alan's appropriation of these titles, and no later writer before Dante (who knew and admired the *Anticlaudianus*[78]) will make a comparable gesture. Later, as Providence is about to enter the celestial realm, a second authorial self-reflection redefines his role:

Wholly abandoning the lyre of the poet, I presume to claim for myself the new voice of a prophet. Earthly Apollo must give way to the heavenly Muse, the Muse herself to Jove (*Anticl.* 5.265–71)

Again no other poet before Dante assumes the role of prophet, or downplays the title of *poeta* that both he and Alan had so boldly claimed. The assertion in the prose prologue of the *Anticlaudianus,* that the poem, read correctly, will yield several levels of meaning, literal, moral, and allegorical levels of meaning, once again anticipates Dante, and the application of the terminology of biblical exegesis to the *Commedia* in the *Epistle* to Can Grande. The scheme it outlines remains theoretical, but its boldness makes plain the importance Alan assigned to his undertaking.[79]

But despite these claims, and the higher strain of the central episode, the *Anticlaudianus* is inescapably school poetry—programmatic, pedantic, encyclopedic. Its originality is theoretical, a matter of projection rather than embodiment. It aims more to teach than to inspire, to stabilize language and codify the poetic material that the *De planctu Naturae* had shown in disarray. Where the *Cosmographia* had stressed the collaboration of natural and divine powers in creation, Alan has narrowed his focus from cosmology and anthropology to psychology and ethics and emphasizes the limitations of Nature as moral and spiritual guide. His imagery, his references to planetary influence, and his many classical references are utterly conventional, devoid of the sense of mystery that pervades Bernardus's cosmogony. His inventiveness is a matter of stylistic ingenuity rather than quasignostic speculation. The *Anticlaudianus* presents the *idea* of a poem, the paradigm for a still unwritten Christian epic.

But if the poem is pedantic, its pedantry is deliberate, and in its way engaging. Only Alan could turn the Quadrivium into an actual chariot,[80] or provide a detailed equine description of each of the five senses that, in good Platonic fashion, draw it upward. Such quasi-parody recalls the great model of twelfth-century pedantry, the *De nuptiis Philologiae et Mercurii* of the late-antique *auctor* Martianus Capella.

This encyclopedic work consists of a set of manuals for each of the seven Arts,[81] prefaced by an elaborate allegorical narrative: Mercury, god of eloquence, elects to marry Philology, or earthly knowledge, who must be immortalized and ascend through the spheres to the hall of Jove, where the marriage is celebrated and each of the Arts then gives an account of herself. Mercury's eloquence is a mysterious power, capable of transforming human knowledge into something visionary, and the *De nuptiis* celebrates Philology's apotheosis in terms that anticipate the heavenly voyage of Prudentia. Alan's debt to the *De nuptiis* is plain, and what they have most in common is their theoretical character. The allegory of the *De nuptiis* amounts to an animated mythography and provides the program for a Neoplatonic reading of virtually any ancient poem. Alan clearly responded to this aspect of Martianus's work. His project is more austere and forward looking, a prospectus for poetry to come rather than a nostalgically conceived *summa* of ancient poetic and religious lore, but the *Anticlaudianus,* too, is a *summa,* one that seeks to establish a stable basis for the medieval *ars poetica,* order its materials, and suggest its proper mission.

The *Anticlaudianus* also has a certain political purpose. Alan clearly had in view a secular as well as a clerical audience, and his virtues and vices are those of the court rather than the confessional; the New Man is to be a gentleman as well as a hero. Though something more austere and spiritual is required of Providence as she prepares to enter heaven (5.62–69), the New Man triumphant is invested not only with Faith, Prudence, and Modesty, but also with Laughter, Charm, and Abundance. His nobility and generosity are those of the chivalric hero, and the poem as a whole has been characterized as a mirror for princes, in all likelihood conceived as a tribute to the young king of France, Philip Augustus.[82] Such a reading provides further grounds for seeing the *Anticlaudianus* as extending the tradition of the *Timaeus*, Macrobius's commentary on Cicero's *Somnium Scipionis*, and Boethius's *Consolatio*, all of which view the cosmic order as a model for the justly ordered society.

6. MINOR POEMS

The "*Rhythmus* on the Liberal Arts and the Incarnation" is attributed to Alan in an early thirteenth-century manuscript from Cîteaux, and in two early manuscripts a quotation from it is assigned to *Alanus Poryus*.[83] Again, internal evidence suggests an author aware of the work of Alan, in this case presumably the *Anticlaudianus*,[84] though there are no clear echoes of Alan's descriptions of the *artes*. The forbidding difficulty of the poem makes it hard to imagine its being performed beyond a clerical coterie, though one manuscript provides evidence that at least the first strophe was set to music.

The oft-quoted lyric "Omnis mundi creatura" (*De miseria mundi*) is attributed to Alan in a thirteenth-century manuscript from St.-Germain-des-Prés. The wordplay and bookish terminology make the attribution plausible.

Though the *Vix nodosum valeo* often follows the *De planctu Naturae* in the manuscripts, its attribution is by no means clear. The author knows the *De planctu* intimately, as confirmed by many verbal correspondences. The poem's first nine quatrains inveigh against the waste and cruelty of love in the manner of Nature's denunciation of Cupido.[85] But in line 37 a wholly new theme is introduced, the proposition that one should make love to a virgin rather than a matron. From this point forward a rhetoric that recalls the style of the *De planctu* is devoted to contrasting the innocent generosity of a virgin's love to the corrupting embrace of an avaricious and adulterous married woman.

It is hard to see how this theme could be related to that of the *De planctu*. The poet's zealous misogyny overpowers any moral force the poem might have, and later medieval readers manifest a certain confusion about its purpose. The verse epilogue of Brother Walter de Burgo, appended to the text in one manuscript, simply equivocates, arguing first that adultery with a married woman is the greater sin, and urging lovers to take the fair road rather than the muddy one, then urging chastity and inveighing against an unnamed "sodomite abbot" whom Walter holds responsible for the errors of his flock. None of this seems to redeem the poem or link it in any coherent way with the *De planctu Naturae*, and the possibility that Alan is its author, while plausible, must be left for further study.

7. FORTUNAE

By the early thirteenth century the *De planctu Naturae* and the *Anticlaudianus,* with Bernardus's *Cosmographia* and the *Alexandreis* of Walter of Chatillon, had attained the status of "masterpieces," in Douglas Kelly's phrase, works that set a standard of excellence in the composition of poetry and prose.[86] But the *De planctu Naturae* seems to have attained this status only gradually.[87] There are few early manuscripts, and it seems that the work's later wide circulation is due largely to its installation in the rhetoric curriculum.[88] In Latin literature the most noteworthy evidence of its influence is the slavish imitation in the fourteenth-century *De Consolatione rationis* of Peter of Compostella.[89]

The *Anticlaudianus* was treated more seriously than any other of the major Latin poems of the twelfth century. Walter's *Alexandreis* undoubtedly enjoyed a broader readership, due largely to the popularity of Alexander's legend and his importance as a political symbol, and Walter was vested with many of the trappings of an *auctor*. But despite the complex style of the *Anticlaudianus* and Alan's warnings about its difficulty, within a generation of his death it too had attained a virtually classic status. An elaborate commentary (ca. 1210–1215) by one "Radulphus," who declares his deep attachment to Alan and was probably his student, was followed over the course of the thirteenth century by several others, some accompanied by extensive programs of illustration.[90] Radulphus is mainly concerned to amplify Alan's descriptions of the Liberal Arts, and his work ends with Concordia's assembling of the chariot of Prudentia (*Anticl.* 4.77–78). The later commentaries, too, deal only with the earlier books of the poem, though some illustrators touch briefly on the creation of the New Man and the ensuing battle. The New Man is commonly seen as Christ, and there is an increasing tendency to render the work more explicitly and conventionally Christian.

Already within Alan's lifetime the Platonizing intellectual program of the twelfth century schools, grounded in the liberal arts and the study of ancient *auctores,* was being displaced by a far more complex curriculum, Aristotelian, "modern," and highly specialized. Within a generation of his death, the *Anticlaudianus,* while still widely read, had come to be seen as the product of an obsolescent intellectual culture, and the scope of its authority was perceptibly diminished. John of Garland, writing on the art of poetry in the 1230s, gives us a sense of the new situation. Matthew of Vendôme and Geoffrey of Vinsauf had composed their *artes poeticae* under the stimulating influence of the new wave of creativity in Latin poetry represented by the work of Alan and Bernardus. In contrast, John's *Poetria* is marked by an absence of quotations from earlier poetry and a predominant concern with fine points of rhetoric that reflects the growing influence of the practically oriented *ars dictaminis* in the schools. John knew and admired the *Anticlaudianus* and could declare Alan a poet "greater than Virgil and truer than Homer."[91] But he views Alan from a distance, and when in one of the specimen *rhythmi* of his *Poetria* he recalls the motif of the threefold *speculum rationis* from the *Anticlaudianus,* he adds that such "Platonic" thinking will seem outmoded to his audience.[92] The same sense of the passing of an era marks the *Bataille des vii Ars* of John's contemporary Henri d'Andeli (ca. 1240), which narrates the defeat of the forces of Grammar by the armies of Logic and Rhetoric—who, however, narrowly escape a final assault by a rear guard that includes Martianus Capella, Bernardus, and "Anticlaudien."[93] As late as the 1280s Hugh of Trimberg will include four *moderni,* Alan, Matthew of Vendome, Geoffrey of Vinsauf, and Walter of Chatillon among the *auctores* in grammar, but over the course of the thirteenth century, literary studies had clearly been diffused into new and more specialized channels and now played a smaller role in a far larger plan of study.

Nevertheless the continuing renown of the *Anticlaudianus* is confirmed by a number of adaptations. In the later thirteenth century the monk Ellebaut produced a Christianized version in French that departs from Alan's narrative at many points and breaks off as Reason and Providence, while returning to earth, are planning their campaign against the vices. The *Ludus super Anticlaudianum* of Adam de la Bassée (1279–1286) is an elaborate, highly selective retelling of Alan's narrative interspersed with hymns, moralizing songs (several of which include musical settings), invectives on clerical morality, and references to episodes in recent history. The *Ludus* omits most of Alan's theological discourse, though it thoroughly Christianizes his allegory. It was translated into French but seems not to have enjoyed wide circulation. More influential was the *Compendium Anticlaudiani* of an anonymous fourteenth-century writer that, despite its title, is not a mere digest but a highly original adaptation of Alan's narrative, in which Nature is reduced to *natura humana,* and divine grace mediated by *Misericordia* replaces Providence's indoctrination by Theology.[94] The *Compendium* circulated independently and inspired its own vernacular adaptations.

The influence of both the *De planctu* and the *Anticlaudianus* on vernacular literature was of course far greater than such emulation can suggest. With Bernardus's *Cosmographia,* Alan's two great allegories elevated imaginative literature to a new level, endowing it with a seriousness of purpose and depth of meaning that could require analysis of the sort previously reserved for a few classical *auctores* and for biblical exegesis.[95] The influence of the *De planctu* has been seen in the complex treatment of *Minne* in the *Tristan* of Gottfried von Strassburg, and its presence in later Middle High German poetry is clear.[96] Jean de Meun gave prominent roles to a lamenting Nature and a preaching Genius in his vast continuation of the *Roman de la Rose,* bequeathing both to Brunetto Latini and Guillaume de Machaut.[97] Chaucer names Alan and cites his "Pleynt of Kynde" to identify the Nature who conducts the avian debate in his "Parliament of Fowls," and the priestly Genius of John Gower's *Confessio Amantis* is recognizably descended from Alan's.[98]

The *Anticlaudianus,* too, exercised a significant influence on vernacular poetry. The structure of the poem has been seen as informing the romances of Chrétien de Troyes, and its importance for Gottfried von Strassburg seems undeniable.[99] It is a major source for the later portions of the *Roman de la Rose,* though Jean de Meun is perhaps mocking Alan's epic pretensions in making his climactic psychomachia a model for the siege of the Castle of Jealousy by the forces of *Amors* and Venus. Dante saw in Alan a literary self-consciousness much like his own. His allusions in the *Commedia* to his role as poet echo Alan's, and he shares Alan's sense of the challenge posed by a poetic undertaking which must not only meet but transcend the standard set by the great *auctores.*[100]

In preparing this volume I have been most fortunate in being able to call on the aid of Danuta Shanzer and David Townsend, both of whom have gone carefully through much of my work and offered many valuable corrections. My friend Jeanne Krochalis walked with me through drafts of my text and translation of the *De planctu Naturae,* and both are the better for her criticisms. Milena Minkova busy with a new baby nonetheless found time to offer help with *loci vexati* in the *De planctu.* At Cornell, Scott McDonald helped me make sense of Alan's engagements with dialectic, and Andrew Hicks guided me through his treatments of music. Shane Bobrycki, *Doctor Scrupulosus,* forced my usage to submit to the stern code of the Chicago Manual and shed light on a number of difficult passages as he did so. Jan Ziolkowski, that genial presence, saw deeply into Alan at an early age, and in addition to reading carefully through my texts and translations, he has been a valuable source of advice and encouragement throughout. But I could never have learned to appreciate Alan if I had not had the great good fortune, fifty years ago, to meet and work with Paul Piehler.

I am grateful to have been able to work with texts prepared by Father Nicholas Häring and Marie-Thérèse d'Alverny and a text of the *Anticlaudianus* that is owed almost entirely to Danuta Shanzer. The pioneering translations of *Anticlaudianus* and *De planctu Naturae* by Father James Sheridan have helped me over many rough patches,[101] but I alone must take responsibility for the *falsigraphiae* that remain.

Notes

1 See d'Alverny, *Alain de Lille,* 11–29.

2 On the self-consistency of Alan's *opera* as a whole, Evans, *Alan of Lille,* 1–14. On the consistency of his literary writings with his theological writings, Bartola, "Filosofia, teologia, poesia," 238–48; "Lachrymae," 148–55; Arduini, "'. . . et ratio . . .'"

3 Le Goff, *Les intellectuels,* 9–59; Murray, *Reason and Society,* 215–33.

4 See d'Alverny, *Alain de Lille,* 20–22, 165–80. John's famous account of the teaching of Bernard of Chartres appears in *Metalogicon* 1.24.

5 See Lemoine, "Alain de Lille et l'école de Chartres."

6 On Alan's knowledge of the pseudo-Dionysius, and its limits, see Neuberger, "Les écrits dionysiens"; on his use of Eriugena, d'Alverny, *Alain de Lille,* 93–94, 179. Erismann, "Alain de Lille, La métaphysique érigénienne," 27–46, shows that Alan, following Gilbert, rejected ideas of Eriugena adopted by Thierry and others.

7 Wollin, "'Floridus Aspectus,'" 384–87, noting that the *Dpn* is closely imitated in a *descriptio cuiusdam nemoris* by Peter Riga, which she tentatively dates 1155–1160, suggests that the *Dpn* may have been written in the early 1150s. D'Alverny, *Alain de Lille,* 34, dates the *DpN* to the 1160s.

8 Wilks, "Alan of Lille and the New Man."

9 I see no basis for the view of Godman, *Silent Masters,* 296–300 (compare Köhler, "'Aus der Herrin wird eine Dienstmagd,'" 471–73), that Alan viewed Bernardus with hostility, though his approach to their common material is more conservative.

10 Kelly, *Arts of Poetry,* 57–59; Tilliette, *Des mots à la parole,* 128–29; Woods, *Classroom Commentaries,* 47–49.

11 John of Salisbury, *Metalogicon* 1.3–4.

12 Murray, *Reason and Society,* 71–86, 102–109.

13 Since "prosimetrum" is a cumbersome term, I will refer to the *De planctu Naturae* and the *Cosmographia* of Bernardus Silvestris as "poems."

14 Siri, "I classici e la sapienza"; Dronke, "Metamorphoses," 27–31.

15 That the formula is Alan's is suggested by Dronke, *Fabula,* 145. It appears verbatim as *Regula* 7 in Alan's *Regulae.* Later authors attribute the maxim to "Trismegistus," but Albert, skeptical about its antiquity, speaks of having found it in "some book of Master Alan," and Thomas cites Alan as having commented on it (Häring, ed. *Regulae,* 100–101). If it is not Alan's, a likely source is the anonymous *Liber XXIV philosophorum,* apparently a product of the "Porretan" school with which Alan was associated. There and elsewhere the sphere is not "intelligible" but "infinite."

16 See *Consolatio* 4.pr.6.12–17.

17 See *SIS* 3; Boethius, *De arithmetica* 2.30; *Consolatio* 3.pr.12.37.

18 *Consolatio* 5.pr.4.28–30. Philosophy goes on to discuss the psychological processes in the work of the different faculties in 5.pr.5. On this hierar-

chy of faculties in Alan's other works and in other twelfth-century authors, Bartola, "Lachrymae," 174–75; d'Alverny, *Alain de Lille,* 181–83.

19 Whether or not Alan studied under Gilbert, his discipleship is clear. Manuscripts of the *Regulae* and *Ars praedicandi* identify the author as "Alanus Porretanus," "Alanus Poriensis," or simply "Porretanus," with many variants (Raynaud de Lage, *Alain de Lille,* 36–37; Häring, ed. *Regulae,* 105–11). The label refers to the "vicus Poretarum" or "ad Poretas" on Mont Ste. Genevieve in Paris, where Gilbert taught before becoming bishop of Poitiers (Gibson, Shanzer, and Palmer, "Manuscripts," 909). On Gilbert's "school" see Landgraf, *Histoire de la littérature théologique,* 112–29.

20 Boethius, *De Trinitate* 2. See *Metalogicon* 4.35, where the use of this term is apparently attributed to Gilbert.

21 At *DpN* 6.4, Nature describes the matter of the human body as "adorned with the noble regalia *(purpuramentis)* of its natural attributes."

22 See Rodriguez, "Nature et connaissance de la nature," 182–190; Speer, "Kosmisches Prinzip," 115–19, 126–28.

23 This development is traced by Gregory, *Platonismo medievale,* 122–50.

24 In *SQH* 2.4.177, Alan suggests that only "bodily dullness" prevents man from possessing knowledge of the liberal arts "in accordance with the state of his primal origin," an idea which recalls Eriugena; see Roques, *Libres sentiers,* 45–98. On the arts and self-knowledge, see Luckner, "'Prudentia,'" 124–35.

25 On the development of the idea of nature in the twelfth century, see Chenu, *La théologie,* 19–51; Post, *Studies in Medieval Legal Thought,* 499–524; Gregory, *Platonismo medievale,* 122–50; all three assign a prominent role to Alan, and for Chiffoleau, "*Contra naturam,*" 290–92, he is the first medieval author to fully express the "majesty" of Nature, her sovereign, all-powerful role. On the literary tradition of the "goddess" Nature and Alan's fundamental role in it, see Economou, *Goddess Nature,* 72–103; White, *Nature, Sex, and Goodness,* 84–101.

26 Pabst, *Prosimetrum,* 1.484–508.

27 Both authors recall the Nature of Claudian, *De raptu Proserpinae* 3.33–45, who complains to Jupiter of the suffering of mankind caused by his ending the Saturnian golden age.

28 Wetherbee, trans. *Cosmographia,* 39 and nn. 146–47.

29 Whitman, "Twelfth-century allegory," 105–110.

30 Kelly, *Arts of Poetry and Prose*, 57–65.

31 Lomperis, "From God's Book to the Play of the Text"; Tilliette, *Des mots à la parole*, 49–59; Méla, "'Poetria Nova.'"

32 *Consolatio* 2.metr.8.28–30.

33 Ziolkowski, *Grammar of Sex*, provides the fullest treatment of Alan's metaphorics of grammar. See also Alford, "Grammatical Metaphor," 750–55; Green, "*De planctu Naturae*," 660–61; Bartola, "Lachrymae," 156–59.

34 In *DpN* 8.12 Nature acknowledges employing *prophanas nouitates* to describe impious conduct that others may be warned. Later, in *DpN* 8.26, preparing to tell how human love became corrupted, she says first that she will "gild" her foul subject with high style, but then acknowledges that style should conform to matter.

35 For versions of this argument, and discussion of the problematic implications of Alan's style, Scanlon, "Unspeakable Pleasures," 218–22; Jordan, *The Invention of Sodomy*, 67–91; Johnson, "Reading the Sex out of Ovid." A related question is the extent to which sodomy is at issue in the poem. Häring ("Manuscripts," 99), cites six French manuscripts of the *De planctu* which append the colophon "Explicit Alanus, pereat sodomita prophanus," and his list includes two English manuscripts in which the *De planctu* is said to have been directed against sodomy. But while "natural," procreative sexuality, in the *DpN* as in Bernardus's *Cosm.*, epitomizes the rightly ordered relation of man to Nature, and any deviation from this is seen as "unnatural," it remains unclear to what extent sodomy in particular is implicated; Nature's censure comes to encompass illicit sexual conduct of all kinds, and finally sin in general. Like the sin with which Dante charges Ser Brunetto in *Inferno* 15, the accusation may convey a cultural message we can no longer read.

36 Maffia Scariati, "La 'descriptio puellae'," 439–45.

37 *DpN* 6.2; 6.6.

38 *DpN* 8.12.

39 The conventional doctrine and its uncertain application are noted by Meier, "Zum Problem der allegorischen Interpretation," 266–67.

40 *DpN* 8.18.

41 On these terms, and their role in validating the study of ancient texts,

see Chenu, "Involucrum"; Jeauneau, "L'usage de la notion d'*integumentum*"; Dronke, *Fabula,* 13–67.

42 *DpN* 2.2–3.

43 *DpN* 10.1.

44 Here too Alan may have begun a rhetorical tradition. Glendenning, "Eros, Agape, and Rhetoric," traces the history of oxymoronic poetry on love only via the *artes poeticae,* but as with the *descriptio puellae,* Alan must have been influential. Wollin, "Werkchronologie," 329–37, suggests that Alan himself was perhaps influenced by the *Ars versificatoria* of Matthew of Vendôme, which may have been circulating by 1165; but see Wollin, "'Floridus Aspectus,'" 386 and n. 62.

45 As Maureen Quilligan observes, *Language of Allegory,* 159–60, Alan's treatment of sexual perversity "must necessarily become literary criticism," because poetic language is the only means of defining the relation of sexuality to culture.

46 *DpN* 10.10–12.

47 *DpN* 10.11–12.

48 *DpN* 16.26.

49 The *insomnium,* according to Macrobius (*In somnium Scipionis* 1.3.3) a dream caused by mental or physical distress, has no prophetic significance. *Extasis,* as defined by Alan in *Regula* 99, is a departure from the *thesis* or *proprius status* of one's nature, whether through ascent into contemplation or descent into vice; Bartola, "Filosofia, teologia, poesia," 240–42. *Mistica* need mean no more than "metaphorical" or "allegorical."

50 Scanlon, "Unspeakable Pleasures," 230–42.

51 *DpN* 4.2.

52 *DpN* 2.28.

53 *Sententiae* 4.18.6 ad fin., cited by Scanlon, "Unspeakable Pleasures," 238.

54 On Venus's "courtly" teachings and their purpose, see *DpN* 10.3. On *curialitas* in the poem's system of values, see Huizinga, "Über die Verknüpfung des Poetischen mit dem Theologischen," 52–56.

55 *DpN* 18.2.

56 *DpN* 18.2. Alan's promotion of *largitas* seems to have been proverbial: Peraldus reports that at Montpellier, when asked by a group of knights

what was the highest form of chivalrous conduct *(maxima curialitas),* Alan replied, "to give" *(De vitiis* 6.3.29).

57 *DpN* 16.25; 18.14.

58 Jean Jolivet, "La figure de Natura," 134–37.

59 *Cosmographia* 1.2.1.

60 *Cosmographia* 2.3.10.

61 "Hierarchia Alani," ed. d'Alverny, *Alain de Lille,* 228.

62 On this distinction see Alan, *Regulae* 88; *SQH* 2.2.151; Delhaye, "La vertu et les vertus," 19–21. Alan clearly distinguishes *naturalia* from *gratuita* but insists on a *naturalis dilectio,* "whereby we are born with the inclination to love God for Himself, and our neighbor for the sake of God," and which joins with grace to form religious virtue: "just as in the earth there is a certain natural force through which, together with moisture that descends from above, seed is made productive, so in the soul free will is a kind of natural force, and the supervenient grace of faith is like dew, and from these arises a kind of motion which is called belief" *(De virtutibus et vitiis* 1.3).

63 Chenu, *La théologie,* 293–97.

64 *Prudentia* is glossed, if not fully explained, by John of Salisbury, *Metalogicon* 4.17: "When providence, who is concerned with earthly things and loves reason, ascends to the hidden realm of pure truth and things divine, she is transformed into wisdom, and is to a certain degree exempt from the limits of mortality." See also Arduini, "'. . . et ratio . . . ,'" 30–39, on the role of reason in Alan's theology.

65 On the chariot, cf. Boethius, *De Arithmetica* 1.1, where the mathematical sciences are seen as "the chariot in which those must travel whose superior minds are drawn away from the senses which all possess by nature to the more certain truths of intellect."

66 Westra, *Commentary on Martianus Capella,* 47.

67 On the problem of the character of the New Man, see Deug-Su, "'Novus homo.'"

68 James Simpson, *Sciences and the Self,* 57–91.

69 Ibid., 77–79.

70 On the various answers to this question, see Meier, "Zum Problem der allegorischen Interpretation," 252–53; Simpson, *Sciences and the Self,* 65, 118.

71 *SQH* 1.1.9b; cf. 1.1

72 Cf. Nature's complaint about the difficulty of describing Cupido, *DpN* 8.34, with the description, on the robe of Theology, of things beyond the power of "natural" language, *Anticl.* 5.115–27. The *locus classicus* for what theological language must be and do is the prologue to Alan's *Distinctiones*, PL 210.687B–88C.

73 See Meier, "Zum Problem der allegorischen Interpretation," 272–73 n. 57a.

74 Simpson, *Sciences and the Self*, 79.

75 With *Anticl.* 5.314, cf. Horace, *Epistle* 1.18.64.

76 See Wetherbee, *Platonism and Poetry*, 217; Meier, "Zum Problem der allegorischen Interpretation," 291–92.

77 See Luckner, "'Prudentia,'" 124–35.

78 See Ciotti, "Alano e Dante"; Dronke, *Dante*, 8–14; Vasoli, *Otto saggi*, 39–40.

79 The prose prologue is not found in the earliest manuscripts, but the style and diction, as well as the lofty tone, seem clearly to be Alan's.

80 The chariot and its construction are a prominent motif in the illustrated manuscripts of the *Anticlaudianus;* see Meier, "Die Rezeption des Anticlaudianus," 529–34, 541–45, 549.

81 Music is not given separate treatment in Martianus's scheme; instead, the presentation of the Arts concludes with the semi-mystical discourse of Harmony.

82 See Wilks, "Alan of Lille and the New Man"; Marshall, "The Identity of the 'New Man'"; Simpson, *Sciences and the Self*, 291–92.

83 D'Alverny, *Alain de Lille*, 40–41. "Poryus" and "Poro" are perhaps corruptions or abbreviations of "Porretanus" or "Poriensis." See above, n. 19.

84 See, e.g., *Anticl.* 6.147–56, 170–84.

85 The verbal correspondences are examined by Thomas Gärtner, "Der Eros-Exkurs." He considers the *Vix nodosum* a work of Alan's immature years (61–62).

86 Kelly, *Arts of Poetry*, 57–64; Woods, *Classroom Commentaries*, 47–49.

87 See Raynaud de Lage, *Alain de Lille*, 35–42; Häring, "Manuscripts," 98; Minkova, "Textual Suggestions," 180–81. On the work's likely circulation among a clerical elite, see Penny Eley, "Sex and Writing," 97–99.

88 See Woods, *Classroom Commentaries,* 223–31; Krochalis, "Alain de Lille: *De planctu Naturae.*"

89 On the date, see Gonzalez-Haba, *La Obra 'De Consolatione Rationis,'* 11–24.

90 See Jung, *Études,'* 89–90; Meier, "Die Rezeption," 415–34; on Radulphus, 468–71, 484–88; on the three illustrated manuscripts, 415–67; 471–80; 499–505; reproductions of their serial illustrations of the poem, 527–49.

91 *De triumphis Ecclesiae* 6.13.

92 *Parisiana Poetria* 7.690–93.

93 *La Bataille des vii ars,* 316–54.

94 Ochsenbein, "Das Compendium Anticlaudiani"; Meier, "Die Rezeption," 480–84.

95 See Meier, "Zwei Modelle"; "Wendepunkt der Allegorie," 51–57'; von Moos, "Was galt im lateinischen Mittelalter," 440–51.

96 See Huber, *Aufnahme und Verarbeitung;* Krayer, *Frauenlob;* Finckh, *Minor Mundus Homo,* 326–420. On Gottfried and the *De planctu,* Ganz, "Minnetrank und Minne," 68–71, and the cautious remarks of Huber, 127–35.

97 See Rossi, "La tradizione allegorica," 143–79; Leach, *Machaut,* 96, 100.

98 Wetherbee, "Latin Structure and Vernacular Space."

99 See Pollmann, *Das Epos,* 64–67; Luttrell, *Creation,* 47–53, 69–79; Jaeger, *Medieval Humanism,* 39–54, 142–48.

100 Dronke, *Dante,* 8–13; Vasoli, *Otto saggi,* 83–102.

101 In the notes to *DpN* and *Anticl.,* references to "Sheridan" are to footnotes on the corresponding passages in his translations.

SERMON ON THE
INTELLIGIBLE SPHERE

Deus est spaera intelligibilis cuius centrum ubique, circumferentia nusquam.

Attendite, commilitones karissimi, qualiter huius auctoritatis thesauro ditatur Hebraeus quo spoliatur Aegyptius. Haec est enim altiloqua philosophi tuba, quae terrenorum naturam dedignans balbutire, altioris theologiae ausa est secreta intonare. Hic enim est magnus retor Tullius, qui sicut humanae eloquentiae flore praenituit, sic altioribus theologiae verbis intonuit dicens: Deus est spaera int. etc.

2. Cui aptius quam diuinae essentiae spaericae formae aptatur proprietas, quae est alpha et omega, principium et finis, principio carens et fine? Unde Martianus in Epithalamico suo Aeternitati diadema ascribens ait: Iupiter detraxit diadema a capite primogenitae filiae suae Aeternitatis et impressit capiti Choes, filiae Endelichiae et Solis. Circlus est Aeternitatis diadema, quasi "duo demens," principium et finem, quia ab aeternitate principii origo relegatur, et fini posteritas absentatur. Hoc diadema Iupiter, id est universalis pater, Deus scilicet, dedit Choe, id est humanae animae, non integrum, sed potius impressit dimidium. Humana etenim anima, quamvis perpetuitatis nobilitetur honore, principii tamen non privatur origine.

God is an intelligible sphere whose center is everywhere, whose circumference nowhere.

Consider, my most dear fellow soldiers, how the Hebrew is made rich by this precious wisdom stolen from the Egyptian. For this is the sounding brass of a philosopher who disdains to stammer about the nature of earthly things, and dares proclaim the deeper secrets of theology. This is Tullius the great rhetorician who, just as he outshone all humanity in the beauty of his rhetoric, also gave voice to the more profound language of theology, saying: "God is an intelligible sphere whose center is everywhere, whose circumference nowhere."

2. To whom could the property of spherical form be attributed more aptly than to the divine essence, which is alpha and omega, beginning and end, though lacking beginning or end? Thus Martianus in his marriage fable, assigning a diadem to Eternity, says: "Jupiter removed the diadem from the head of his firstborn daughter Eternity, and placed it on the head of Choe, daughter of Endelechia and the Sun." The diadem of Eternity is a circle, in that it "subtracts two things," beginning and end; for no point of origin is ascribed to eternity, and nothing can exist posterior to its end. Jupiter, the universal father, namely God, did not give the complete diadem to Choe, the human soul, but rather crowned her with half. For the human soul, though it is ennobled by the honor of perpetuity, does not lack a point of origin.

3. Disquisitius etiam intueamur qualiter immensitas divinae essentiae formam induat spaerae, ut legitur in Boetio: Spaera est semicirculi circumductio. Si quis etenim ad idem punctum a quo processit semiciclum intelligibiliter circumducat, necesse est ut spaericam formam inveniat. Circlus autem est aeternitas, tempus semiciclus, quia aeternitatis pars. Unde Tullius in Rethorica Inventionum ait: Tempus est pars aeternitatis. Tempus etenim ab aeternitate progreditur et in aeternitatem regreditur. Unde Mercurius temporalitatem dicit ad eundem fontem regredi a quo verum est ipsum progredi. Aeternitas igitur, quia tempus in se reflectens circumducit, id est, circulariter ducit, merito ut semicicli temporalitatis aeternitas circumductio esse dicatur, et ita, spaera.

4. Sed notandum quod spaerarum alia sensilis, alia ymaginabilis, alia rationalis, alia intelligibilis.

5. Mundus iste sensilis, quia circulari motu circumducitur, et sensus indagini obnoxius esse tenetur, recte spaera sensilis nuncupatur.

6. Primordialis vero materia, quae orbiculari formarum reciprocatione circumfertur, et ymaginationis fantasia concipitur, merito spaera ymaginabilis esse censetur.

7. Mundana vero anima, quae indefessa rationis orbiculatione volvitur, et eiusdem investigatione comprehenditur, iure spaera rationabilis perhibetur.

3. Let us consider more closely in what way the immensity of the divine essence assumes the form of a sphere. As described by Boethius, "a sphere is the continuation of a semicircle; for if one possessed of understanding draws a semicircle around to the same point from which it started, he will necessarily produce a spherical form." Now the circle is eternity, and time, being a portion of eternity, is the semicircle. Thus Tullius says in his *De Inventione:* "time is a portion of eternity." For time sets forth from eternity and returns to eternity. Thus Mercury says that temporal existence returns to the same source from which it truly proceeds. Therefore, because eternity, reflecting time in itself, draws it around, that is, draws it in a circular path, eternity is the completion of the semicircle of temporality, and thus is rightly called a sphere.

4. But it must be observed of the spheres that one is sensible, another imaginable, another rational, another intelligible.

5. This sensible world, because it is drawn in a circular course by its circular motion, and is subject to the scrutiny of the senses, is rightly called the sensible sphere.

6. Primal matter, which is driven about by the circulation of forms as they come and go, and is conceivable only by an act of imagination, is rightly considered to be the imaginable sphere.

7. The World Soul, which is made to revolve by the tireless circling of reason, and is understood through the inquiry of that same faculty, is rightly named the rational sphere.

8. Divinae vero essentiae immensitas, cuius numine rerum universitas movetur, quae etiam excellentiori intellectualitatis indagine consideratur, consequenter spaera intelligibilis esse dicitur.

9. Harum spaerarum prima est formalis, secunda deformis, tertia conformis, quarta informis; prima mobilis, secunda immobilis, tertia instabilis, quarta stabilis. In his autem spaeris quasi in quibusdam palatiis variae rerum species suas collocant mansiones. In prima habitant ychones, in secunda ychoniae, in tertia ychomae, in quarta ydeae.

10. In prima regnant ychones, id est, subiecta suarum formarum, purpuramentis ornata, quae dicuntur ychones, id est, ymagines, quia ad similitudinem aeternorum exemplarium que ab aeterno fuerunt in mente divina, in veritatem essendi sunt producta.

11. In hoc palatio celebrantur nuptiae Naturae et nati, Formae et formae nati, proprietatis et subiecti. Forma etenim geniali inherentiae osculo subiectum osculatur, ex quo variae prolis fecunditas propagatur. Hoc etenim compositionis osculum tres parit filias; possibilitatem, essentiam et veritatem. His nuptiis Logica veritatis naturalium declarativa suo assistens praeconio, propositionum terminorumque organis citarizat.

12. In secunda vero exulant yconiae, quae a suae dignitatis virtute degeneres, fluitantis materiae contagio fluctuantes esse caligantes umbratili de suae caligationis fuligine conquerentes, ad verum esse conantur reverti. Ibi idem

8. The immensity of the divine essence, by whose power the created universe is moved, is contemplated through the exercise of a superior intellectuality, and thus is said to be the intelligible sphere.

9. The first of these spheres is formal, the second deformed, the third conformed, the fourth unformed; the first mobile, the second immobile, the third unstable, the fourth stable. In these spheres, as if they were palaces, the various images of things establish their dwellings. In the first reside the icons, in the second the iconiae, in the third the icoms, in the fourth the ideas.

10. In the first [sphere] rule the icons, the material images of their forms, adorned with royal robes. They are called "icons," or images, because they are brought forth into actual existence in the likeness of the eternal exemplars that have eternal being in the mind of God.

11. In this sphere is celebrated the marriage of Nature and what comes to be, of form and the form of new being, of property and substance. For form bestows on substance the "genial" kiss of formation, through which abundant progeny of the various kinds are propagated. This constitutive kiss gives birth to three daughters: possibility, essence, and truth. Logic is present at these nuptials, proclaiming the truth of natural process, and playing a celebratory song on the Organum of propositions and terms.

12. In the second sphere the iconiae dwell in exile. They have declined from their inherent dignity, driven to and fro by the influence of unstable matter. Lamenting that they are blinded by the murky gloom of their dark condition, they strive to return to true being. Here same becomes

diversum, individuum dividuum, caeleste caducum, ydos ycos, immortale fit caducae proprietatis mortalitas.

13. In tertia vero spaera principantur ychomae, id est formae a subiectis divisae, quae ad propriam suae immortalitatis revertentes originem, in subiecti dedignantur adulterari materiem, quae minime faeces corruptibilium ordocantes gratulantur, suae incorruptionis odore viventes. Ibi primitivum suae nativitatis retinentes ortum, nesciunt materiae fluitantis occasum. Ibi, suae perpetuitatis virginitate florentes, nulla adulteratione rei corruptibilis deflorantur.

14. In quarta vero spaera irradiantur ydeae, id est exemplares rerum formae que suae puritatis lumine fulgurantes diem pariunt contemplationis aeternae. Extra harum solium habitans volat ingenium, quod rerum proprietates circumvolans, caducas vix earum valet sompniare naturas. Ibi ad unitatem pluralitas, ad identitatem diversitas, ad consonantiam dissonantia, ad concordiam discordia proprietatum revertitur.

15. Quatuor vero potentiae animae ancillantur, quibus quasi quibusdam gradibus ad praedictarum spaerarum contubernia patet accessus, scilicet sensus, ymaginatio, ratio, intellectualitas. Hae sunt quatuor rotae, ex quibus quadriga humanae animae fabricatur, qua ascendens nobilis auriga philosophus recta aurigationis ductu ad aeterna deducitur. Harum rotarum duae sunt antecedariae: sensus, ymaginatio, quae circa caducorum inferiora umbratiliter volitant, nec ad solium eternorum aspirant.

different, individual becomes divided, heavenly becomes subject to death, idea becomes image, immortal becomes mortality, whose nature it is to die.

13. In the third sphere the rulers are the icoms, forms separate from substance. Returning to the true origin of their immortal nature, they disdain to be disgracefully joined to a material subject. They rejoice that the filth of perishable life does not befoul them, and they live amid the aroma of their own incorruptibility. Here, secure in their original birthplace, they know nothing of the ruinous course of unstable matter. Here they flourish in the virginity of their perpetual state, and no adulterous assault from the world of corruption deflowers them.

14. In the fourth sphere shine the ideas, the exemplary forms of things which, glowing in the light of their purity, bring forth the bright day of eternal contemplation. Dwelling outside the court of these forms, active intelligence hovers; flitting about among the true properties of things, it has only a dreamlike sense of their mortal natures. Here plurality returns to unity, diversity to identity, dissonance to consonance, discord to a concord of properties.

15. Four powers serve the soul, by which, as if by a kind of stairway, one gains access to the sites of the aforementioned spheres, namely sense, imagination, reason, and intellect. These are the four wheels with which is constructed the chariot of the human soul, in which the noble philosopher, ascending with the assurance of a skilled charioteer, is brought to know things eternal. Two of these wheels are elementary: sense and imagination, which hover in a shadowy way over the lower world of mortal things, and do not aspire to the eternal throne.

16. Per sensum vero, quasi primum huius scalae gradum, anima humana mundum ingreditur, in quo, quasi in quodam libro, sensus, inquisitione subiectorum, lituras, id est corruptibilium maculas, quasi quasdam litteras speculatur, et haec est prima scala in qua humana anima exercitatur.

17. Per ymaginationem vero, quasi per secundum huius scalae gradum, humana anima in habitaculum primordialis materiae defertur, ubi formas quasi de dampno suae informitatis lacrimantes, subsidia subiecti melioris postulantes, imaginabiliter intuetur. Ibi videt deformari formarum conformitatem, denobilitari earum nobilitatem.

18. Per rationem vero quasi per tertium huius scalae gradum, anima humana ad mundanae animae regiam ascendit, ubi vivificum fomitem, indefessum fontem, perpetuum solem, id est mundanam animam aspicit, quae mundanae machinae tenebras luce suae vegetationis illuminat, et quasi quodam oculo interiori clarificat.

19. Per intellectualitatem quasi per quartum huius scalae gradum ad penitiorem ydearum thalamum humana anima aurigatur, ubi aeterna rerum exemplaria in suae aeternitatis flore virentia contemplatur.

20. His quatuor praetaxatis potentiis humana anima regitur, et nisi per istarum viarum orbitam ab orbita veritatis exorbitaverit, ad superna dirigitur. Per sensum et ymaginationem fit anima homo; per rationem fit anima humana spiritus; per intellectualitatem fit anima humana deus. Per sensum et ymaginationem est circa se; per rationem apud se;

16. Through sense, as if on the first step of this ladder, the human soul enters the world, in which, as if in a kind of book, sense, exploring material things, examines the blottings, the stains of mortal corruptibility, as if they were a kind of writing. And this is the first step on which the human soul is trained.

17. Through imagination, as if on the second step of this ladder, the human soul is borne into the abode of primal matter, where it gains an imaginary vision of forms that seem to weep over the disaster of their misshaping, and demand the support of better material. Here it sees the conformity of forms deformed, their nobility rendered ignoble.

18. Through reason, as if on the third step of this ladder, the human soul ascends to the court of the world soul, where it beholds the life-giving spark, the unfailing fount, the perpetual sun—the world soul which illumines with the light of its enlivening power the dark places of the cosmic structure, and as if by a kind of inner vision makes them clearly visible.

19. Through intellect, as if by the fourth step of this ladder, the human soul is carried to the inner chamber of the ideas, where it contemplates the eternal exemplars of things flourishing in the beauty of their eternal state.

20. The human soul is guided by the four powers here described, and if it does not stray from the road of truth in following their paths, it is led to know heavenly things. Through sense and imagination the soul becomes human; through reason the human soul becomes spirit; through intellect the human soul becomes God. Through sense and imagination it lives outside itself; through reason it lives

per intellectualitatem supra se. Per sensum et ymaginationem indulget anima virtutibus politicis, per rationem phisicis, per intellectualitatem exemplaribus sive noeticis.

21. Cavendum, fratres karissimi, ne quis vestrum per has, vel in hiis viis deviaverit. Ingrediamur mundum sensu et ymaginatione, non ad concupiscendum, non ad indulgendum mundanis, sed ad legendum supremum auctorem in rebus caducis; ascendamus curriculum rationis, non ad sapiendum plus quam oportet in mundanae sapientiae ebrietate, sed ad sapiendum iuxta quod oportet in sobrietate. Ascendamus thorum intellectualitatis, non tumore superbiae, sed caritatis ardore. Per deviationem enim sensus et ymaginationis fit homo pecus; per exorbitationem rationis fit homo paetus; per alienationem intellectualitatis fit anima humana diabolus. Deviatio sensus et ymaginationis animam offendit; anima, rationis exorbitatione, cadit; alienatione intellectualitatis, ruit. Per offensam primarum anima laeditur; per casum rationis, infirmatur; per ruinam intellectualitatis, moritur.

22. Inter has praedictas spaeras cuiusdam prerogativae monarchiam optinet spaera intelligibilis, cuius centrum ubique, circumferentia nusquam. O huius spaerae ad alias spaeras similis dissimilitudo, dissimilis similitudo! Ceterarum spaerarum centrum immobile, circumferentia mobilis; ceterarum spaerarum centrum nusquam, circumferentia alicubi; huius spaerae centrum ubique, circumferentia nusquam. Quid est huius spaerae centrum, nisi opus mundanum, id est

within itself; through intellect it lives above itself. Through sense and imagination the human soul practices the political virtues, through reason the physical virtues, through intellect the exemplary or noetic virtues.

21. Take care, brothers most dear, lest any of you be led astray through these faculties, or on these paths. Let us enter the world through sense and imagination not for the sake of desire, not to indulge worldly appetites, but to read the [signs of] the supreme author in the world of mortal things. Let us ascend the chariot of reason not in order to know more than is right, made drunk by the wisdom of this world, but to know in accordance with what is right, in sobriety. Let us ascend the marriage bed of intellect, not in the arrogance of pride, but in the ardor of charity. For through the straying of sense and imagination the soul becomes bestial; by leaving the orbit of reason the soul becomes blinded; through the turning away of his intellect man's soul becomes devil. The straying of sense and imagination troubles the soul; through reason's abandoning its orbit the soul falls; through the turning away of intellect it perishes. By the offense of the first powers the soul is injured; by the fall of reason it is sickened; through the downfall of intellect it dies.

22. Among these spheres the intelligible sphere, whose center is everywhere, whose circumference nowhere, holds a sort of royal authority. O the similar dissimilitude, the dissimilar similitude of this sphere to the other spheres! In the other spheres the center is unmoving, the circumference moves. Their center is nowhere, their circumference is anywhere. The center of this sphere is everywhere, its circumference nowhere. What is the center of this sphere if not the

universitas rerum quae ab amplitudine divinae essentiae quasi a quadam circumferentia aequalem et ita quodammodo linearem suae essentiae unitatem trahens, in machinam deducit mundialem; et ita omnes lineae ab hac circumferentia usque in centrum ductae sunt equales.

23. Omnia enim quae a Dei immensitate in mundum per creationem venerunt aeque bona sunt: vidit enim Deus cuncta quae fecerat, et erant valde bona. Huius spaerae centrum ubique est, quia universitas rerum gratia sua proprium omnem optinet locum; circumferentia nusquam, quia immensitas divina extra cuncta non exclusa, intra cuncta non inclusa; huius spaerae centrum mobile, quia creatura mutabilitati obnoxia; circumferentia immobilis, quia ab immensitate Dei omnis mutabilitas est relegata.

24. Cum autem ceterae spaerae apud philosophos naturales nec quadrari nec triangulari possunt, in hac spaera cuiusdam aequilateri trianguli reperitur proprietas, id est, personarum Trinitas. In hoc autem aequilatero triangulo omnia latera reperiuntur aequalia, omnes etiam anguli recti, qui non solum duobus rectis, sed uni inveniuntur aequales. Tres etenim personae sibi invicem sunt aequales, quae consequenter possunt dici anguli, quasi sicut anguli in contactu et quodam osculo linearum consistunt, sic tres personae unitate divinae essentiae se quodammodo osculantur. Isti etiam anguli censentur recti, quia nec generationis obtusione, nec corruptionis acumine deviant a rectitudine unitatis essentiae. Isti tres anguli non solum duobus rectis, sed

cosmic order, the created universe, which derives from the fullness of the divine essence, as if from a kind of circumference, the equal, and thus in a sense the linear, unity of its own essence, and fashions it into a cosmic structure? And for this reason all lines drawn from this circumference to the center are equal.

23. For all things which have come from the immensity of God into the world through creation are equally good: for God saw all the things that he had made, and they were very good. The center of this sphere is everywhere because through his grace the created universe claims all space as its own. Its circumference is nowhere because the divine immensity is neither excluded from the cosmos, nor contained within it. Its center is mobile because creation is subject to change; its circumference is unmoving because all change is controlled by the immensity of God.

24. Moreover, while other spheres, according to natural philosophers, cannot be squared or triangulated, in this sphere can be found the property of a certain equilateral triangle, a Trinity of persons. In this equilateral triangle all the sides will be found equal, and moreover all the angles right angles. These will be found equal not only to two right angles, but also to one. For the three persons are equal with one another, and for this reason can be called angles, in the sense that just as angles consist in a touching and a sort of kissing of lines, so the three persons in a certain manner kiss one another within the unity of the divine essence. These angles are deemed right angles because they do not deviate through the bruisings of birth or the stings of corruption from the perfect rightness of the divine essence. These three angles are found to be equal not only to two right angles, but

uni inveniuntur aequales, quia et tres personae uni et una tribus, et una uni reperiuntur aequalis.

25. De hoc triangulo dicit Claudianus in libro de Anima: Deus triangulum suum impressit mundo. Vere mundo Deus impressit triangulum, quia in eo Trinitatis resultat vestigium. Mundanorum enim perseverans essentia potentiam Patris loquitur; mundanorum pulcritudo praedicat sapientiam Prolis; mundanorum ordo depingit benignitatem Flaminis.

26. Praetaxati autem trianguli non ex alio procedit primus angulus; ex primo nascitur circulariter secundus; ex utroque orbiculariter tertius. Pater enim a nullo; a Patre Filius; ab utroque Spiritus Sanctus.

27. Hermes Mercurius, in libro qui dicitur Logostileos, ait: O Asclepi, tres deos profitemur aeternos, primus a nullo, secundus a primo, tertius ab utroque; cuius verba retractans Augustinus in libro Contra V hereses ait: o quam eleganter Hermes Mercurius de Trinitate esset locutus, nisi incircumciso lapsu sermonis diceret: deos.

28. Hunc triangulum menti imprimamus. Habeamus potentiam resistendi vitiis, sapientiam in moribus ordinandis, benignitatem in sustinendis molestiis. Praedictae autem spaerae circulus in mentibus fidelium quodammodo quadratur, cum eiusdem auctoritate in fidelibus quatuor cardinalium virtutum quadratura efficitur, quae quadratura quantum ad hoc quod ad immensitatem aeternitatis reflectitur, quodammodo circulatur.

to one, because the three persons are equal to one, and the one to three, and the one to one.

25. In his book "On the Soul" Claudian says of this triangle: "God imprinted His triangle on the world. And indeed God did print a triangle on the world, for on the world there appears the imprint of the Trinity. For the enduring essence of the universe declares the power of the Father; the beauty of the universe proclaims the wisdom of the Son; the order of the universe shows the benevolence of the Spirit."

26. The first angle of this triangle is not derived from another. From the first the second is born in a circular manner; and from the two in a circular way the third. For the Father is born of no one; the Son of the Father; the Holy Spirit of both.

27. In the book that is called "Logostileos," Hermes Mercury says: "O Asclepius, we acknowledge three eternal gods, the first [born] of no one, the second of the first, the third of both." Augustine, reflecting on these words in his book "Against Five Heresies," says: "Oh, how elegantly Hermes Mercury would have spoken about the Trinity, had he not, in the flawed speech of the uncircumcised, said 'gods.'"

28. Let us imprint this triangle on our minds. Let us have power to resist vices, wisdom in regulating our conduct, goodwill in enduring troubles. The circle of the aforementioned sphere is in a certain way squared in the minds of the faithful, since by its authoritative presence in the faithful the square of the four cardinal virtues is created, and this square, inasmuch as it reflects the divine immensity, is in a certain manner encircled.

29. Nos igitur, in centro huius spaerae existentes, a centri motu tendamus in circumferentiae quietem; ab huius instabilitate ad illius stabilitatem; ab huius tempestate ad illius pacem, non per linearem motum sensualitatis, non per retrogradationem ymaginationis, sed per orbicularem motum rationis, ut intellectualitatis ductu, ad divinae circumferentiae tranquillitatem perveniamus, quod nobis prestat . . .

29. Let us, then, dwelling at the center of this sphere, strive to pass from the movement of this center to the stillness of the circumference, from the instability here to the stability there, from this storm to that peace, not through the linear movement of sensuality, not through the retrograde movement of imagination, but through the circular movement of reason, so that with the guidance of intellect we may attain the tranquility of the divine circumference, because . . . offers to us . . .

THE PLAINT OF
NATURE

In lacrimas risus, in luctus gaudia verto,
    in planctum plausus, in lacrimosa iocos,
cum sua Naturae video decreta silere,
    cum Veneris monstro naufraga turba perit;
5   cum Venus in Venerem pugnans illos facit illas,
    cumque sui magica devirat arte viros.
Non fraus tristitiem, non fraudis fletus adulter
    non dolus, immo dolor, parturit, immo parit.
Musa rogat, dolor ipse iubet, Natura precatur,
10   ut donem flendo flebile carmen eis.
Heu, quo Naturae secessit gratia, morum
    forma, pudicitiae norma, pudoris amor?
Flet Natura, silent mores, proscribitur omnis
    orphanus a veteri nobilitate pudor.
15   Activi generis sexus se turpiter horret
    sic in passivum degenerare genus.
Femina vir factus sexus denigrat honorem,
    Ars magicae Veneris hermafroditat eum.
Praedicat et subicit, fit duplex terminus idem,
20   grammaticae leges ampliat ille nimis.
Se negat esse virum, Naturae factus in arte
    barbarus. Ars illi non placet, immo tropus.
Non tamen ista tropus poterit translatio dici;
    in vitium melius ista figura cadit.

Chapter 1

My laughter turns to weeping, my joy to sorrow, rejoicing
becomes lamentation, jests give way to tears, when I see that
the decrees of Nature are silent, when multitudes perish,
their vessel wrecked by a monster of Venus: when Venus, 5
warring against Venus, makes he's become she's, and unmans
men with her magical art.

No deception produces this sadness, nor the counterfeit
tears of fraud; it is not guile, but grief that labors and now
even gives birth. The Muse begs, grief demands, Nature
prays that amid my tears I present them a tearful song. 10

Alas! Whither has fled the fair form of Nature, the pattern of conduct, the rule of chastity, the love of modesty?
Nature weeps, morality is silenced; modesty, an orphan, is
wholly banished from her once noble station. The active sex 15
is horrified that it thus falls disgracefully into the passive
role. Man become woman demeans the dignity of his sex;
the art of a Venus turned sorcerer renders him hermaphrodite. He is both predicate and subject; a single term assumes a double role, and extends the rules of grammar too 20
far. He denies that he is a man, for he has become a bar-
barian in the grammar of Nature. The art itself does not satisfy him, only troping. But a translation of this kind cannot be called a trope; this figure is better defined as a vice.

25 Hic nimis est logicus, per quem conversio simplex
    Artis Naturae iura perire facit.
Cudit in incude quae semina nulla monetat;
    horret et incudem malleus ipse suam.
Nullam materiem matricis signat idea,
30   sed magis in sterili litore vomer arat.
Sic pede dactilico Veneris male iambicat usus,
    in quo non patitur sillaba longa brevem.
Quamvis femineae speciei supplicet omnis
    forma viri, semper huius honore minor;
35 quamvis Tindaridi vultus famuletur Adonis,
    Narcisique decor victus adoret eam;
Spernitur ipsa tamen, quamvis decor ipse peroret,
    et formae deitas disputet esse deam
qua Iovis in dextra fulmen langueret, et omnis
40   Phoebi cessaret otia nervus agens;
qua liber fieret servus, propriumque pudorem
    venderet Ypolitus, huius amore fruens.
Virginis in labiis cur basia tanta quiescunt,
    cum reditus in eis sumere nemo velit?
45 Quae mihi pressa semel mellirent oscula succo,
    quae mellita darent mellis in ore favum.
Spiritus exiret ad basia deditus ori
    totus, et in labiis luderet ipse sibi,
ut dum sic moriar, in me defunctus, in illa
50   felici vita perfruar alter ego.
Non modo Tindaridem Frigius venatur adulter,
    sed Paris in Paridem monstra nefanda parit.

The man for whom a simple conversion destroys the laws of 25
Nature's art is too much the logician. He strikes an anvil that
mints no seed; the very hammer detests its anvil. No idea
sets its seal on the matter of the womb; instead the plow 30
makes furrows in barren ground. Thus the dactylic practice
of Venus becomes a crude iambic, in which the long syllable
does not accept the short.

Though all male beauty bows down before the beauty
of woman, always less honored; though the face of Adonis 35
submits to that of the daughter of Tyndareus, and the fair
form of Narcissus, defeated, worships her, Helen is now
spurned, despite the appeal of her beauty; though her divine
form declares her a goddess before whom the thunderbolt
in the hand of Jove would lose its force, and the music of 40
Phoebus would wholly cease, the strings fall still; for whom
a free man would become a slave; in the enjoyment of whose
love Hippolytus would sell his very chastity.

Why do so many kisses lie dormant on virgin lips, and
none wish to claim them as reward? These lips, pressed to 45
mine, would give kisses of moist, honeyed sweetness, honeyed kisses that would bestow the honeycomb itself on my
mouth. My spirit, wholly committed to my mouth, would
issue forth in response to such kisses, and delight itself in
playing about her lips. Hence, though I should thus die,
once dead to myself I should enjoy a happy life, a new being, 50
in her.

But no longer does the adulterous Phrygian stalk the
daughter of Tyndareus; instead, Paris, an anti-Paris, gives
birth to abominable monsters. No longer does Pyramus seek

Non modo per rimas rimatur basia Thisbes
Piramus; huic Veneris rimula nulla placet.
55   Non modo Pelides mentitur virginis actus,
ut sic virginibus se probet esse virum;
sed male Naturae munus pro munere donat
cum sexum lucri vendit amore suum.
A Genii templo tales anathema merentur,
60   qui Genio decimas et sua iura negant.

2

Cum haec elegiaca lamentabili eiulatione crebrius recen-
serem, mulier ab impassibilis mundi penitiori delapsa palatio ad me maturare videbatur accessum; cuius crinis non
mendicata luce sed propria scintillans, non similitudinarie
radiorum repraesentans effigiem sed eorum claritate nativa
naturam praeveniens, in stellare corpus caput effigiabat
puellae; quem duplex tricatura diffibulans, superna non de-
serens, terrae non dedignabatur osculo arridere. Quoddam
vero liliosi tramitis spatium sub obliquitate decusata crinis
dividebat litigium. Nec illa, inquam, obliquitas vultus detri-
mento praeerat, sed decori. Crinale vero aureum, in legitimi
ordinis choream crinis aurum concilians, vultum mirabatur
invenisse conformem. Fantasia etenim coloris aurum consequentis utrumque paralogismum visui concludebat.

the kisses of Thisbe through a crevice; no little crack of
Venus gives him pleasure. No longer does the son of Peleus 55
feign the behavior of a maiden, so that he may prove himself a man to the maidens. Instead he gives up the gifts of
Nature in return for gifts, for he sells his sex in his love of
money.

May such men, who refuse to pay Genius's tithes and observe his laws, be banished from the temple of Genius. 60

Chapter 2

While I was repeating these elegiac verses again and again
in tones of mournful lamentation, there appeared a woman,
descended from the inner palace of the unchanging realm,
making her way toward me. Her hair, shining with no borrowed luster but with its own, and presenting the effect
of radiance not by mere resemblance but by a native gleam
that surpassed that of nature, gave the maiden's head the appearance of a celestial body. Separated into two braids, it
neither abandoned its high place nor disdained to grant the
earth a smiling kiss. A slight parting, a lilywhite path slanting crosswise through her hair, prevented any dispute. And
this slanting path, I assure you, was not a detriment to her
appearance, but an enhancement. The golden comb that
gathered the gold of her hair into a regular and harmonious
order marveled to find its appearance the same. By a wondrous effect of color, the gold of the two consequents concluded in a visual paralogism.

2. Frons vero in amplam evagata planitiem lacteo liliata colore lilio videbatur contendere. Supercilia vero, aureo stellata fulgore, non in pilorum evagantia silvam nec in nimiam demissa pauperiem, inter utrumque medium optinebant. Oculorum vero serena placiditas, amica blandiens claritate, gemelli praeferebat sideris novitatem. Naris utraque, odore inbalsamata mellito, nec citra modum humilis nec iniuste prominens vultui, quiddam praesentabat insigne. Oris nardus naribus delicatas odoris epulas offerebat. Labra modico tumore surgentia Veneris tirones invitabant ad oscula. Dentes quadam sui coloris consonantia eboris faciem exemplabant. Genarum ignis purpureus, rosarum succensus murice, dulci flamma faciem amicabat; candore namque glaciali amicam sentiebat temperiem, purpura vultus sindoni maritata. Menti expolita planities, cristallina luce conspectior, argenteum induebat fulgorem.

3. Colli non iniusta proceritas sub gracilitate moderata cervicem maritari humeris non sinebat. Mamillarum vero pomula gratiosae iuventutis maturitatem spondebant. Brachia ad gratiam inspectoris perspicua postulare videbantur amplexus. Laterum aequata convallatio, iustae moderationis impressa sigillo, totius corporis speciem ad cumulum perfectionis eduxit.

4. Cetera vero quae thalamus secretior absentabat meliora fides esse loquatur. In corpore etenim vultus latebat beatior cuius facies ostentabat praeludium. Ut ipse tamen

2. Her forehead extended to an ample breadth, and its milky lily-whiteness seemed to rival the lily. Her brows, shining like starry gold, were not overgrown thickets of hair, and did not dwindle into sparseness, but preserved a mean between the two. The peaceful serenity of her eyes, charming in their friendly brightness, gave the rare effect of twin stars. Her nose, embalsamed with a honeysweet odor, was neither disproportionately small nor unduly prominent, but exhibited a certain elegance. Her mouth's sweet breath offered a choice feast of odors to the nostrils. Her modestly swelling lips were a summons for Venus's young recruits to kiss her. Her teeth, in the uniformity of their color, presented the appearance of ivory. The bright glow of her cheeks, suffused with the color of roses, lent favor to her face with its sweet fire. Its purple, joined with the white linen of her face, underwent a congenial tempering by its snowy gleam. The smooth surface of her chin, more striking than the brilliance of crystal, wore a silvery glow.

3. The unexcessive length of her moderately slender neck did not allow its nape to be joined too closely to her shoulders. Her breasts, like small apples, attested the maturity of her youthful grace. Her arms, clearly visible for the delight of the beholder, seemed to insist on an embrace. The smooth curve of her waist, marked by the seal of just measure, brought the beauty of her whole body to the height of perfection.

4. Those other parts that a more secret chamber kept apart, may confidently be declared fairer still. For on her body there lay hidden a still more beautiful face of which her visible face gave promise. And yet, as her countenance

vultus loquebatur, non Dionaea clavis eius sigillum reserave-
rat castitatis.

5. Et quamvis tanta esset pulcritudinis laetitia, huius tamen risum decoris fletus inextinguibilis exstinguere conaba-
tur. Ros namque furtivus ex oculorum scaturigine derivatus
fluxum doloris praedicabat interni. Ipsa etiam facies in terram casto pudore demissa ipsi puellae illatam quodammodo
loquebatur iniuriam.

6. Regalis autem diadematis corona rutilans, gemmarum
scintillata choreis, in capitis supercilio fulgurabat; cuius non
adulterina auri materies ab ipsius honore degenerans, luce
sophistica oculos paralogizans, sed ipsius nobilitas ministrabat essentiam. Miraculoso vero circuitu aeternaque volu-
tione ipsum diadema, ab oriente peregrinans in occidens,
reciprocando crebrius ferebatur in ortum. Idemque perhen-
niter exercendo ex nimia eiusdem petitione principii quasi
nugatoria motio videbatur.

7. Praedictarum vero gemmarum aliae ad tempus novi
diei miracula novo sui luminis sole visibus offerebant. Ad
tempus vero suae coruscationis eclipsi videbantur ab ipsius
diadematis exulare palatio. Aliae insertae solio suae scin-
tillationis vigiliam perhennantes perhennes fiebant excubiae. Inter has circulus elucens ad Zodiaceae obliquitatis
similitudinem, pretiosorum lapidum stellatus monilibus, si-
dereae contiguitatis oscula sincopabat. In quo cohors duodena gemmarum, suae quantitatis processu privilegialique
splendore, inter alias praerogativam poscere videbatur.

attested, the key of Dione had not broken the seal of her chastity.

5. But despite the joyous effect of her beauty, unquenchable tears strove to extinguish her smile. For a furtive moisture, drawn from the spring of her eyes, gave notice of a flood of grief within. Her face, too, turned toward the ground in chaste modesty, declared that the maiden had somehow suffered an injury.

6. A glowing crown, a royal diadem, sparkling with a circle of gems, shone forth high on her head. Its material was no impure substitute for gold, demeaning her dignity and misleading the eye with its sophistical sheen; the nobility of gold itself provided its substance. This diadem, turning perpetually in a wondrous circle, traveled from its rise in the east to its setting in the west, and was then ceaselessly brought back to its rising point by a reciprocal path. Continuously performing the same circuit, its movement, a ceaseless quest to return to the same point of origin, seemed rather pointless.

7. At times certain of the aforementioned gems, radiant as a new sun, presented to the sight the miracle of a new day. But at other times, when their brilliance was eclipsed, they seemed to have been banished from the palace of the diadem. Other gems, fixed on their thrones, and maintaining a vigil of continual sparkling, were made perpetual sentinels. In their midst a shining circle resembling the slanting Zodiac, and decorated with a necklace of precious stones, interrupted the kissing of closely placed stars. In this circle a company of twelve gems, by the stately progress of their number and their superior splendor, seemed to claim a privileged status among the others.

8. In anteriori namque ipsius diadematis parte tres pretiosi lapides audaci suae radiationis superbia reliquis novem anthonomasice praefulgebant. Lapis primus lumine noctem, frigus incendio pati iubebat exilium. In quo, ut faceta picturae loquebantur mendacia, Leonis effigiata fulminabat effigies. Lapis secundus, a priori non secundus in lumine, in praefatae partis audaciori loco praefulgurans, quasi ex quadam indignatione reliquos lapides deorsum aspicere videbatur. In quo, prout veritatis simia pictura docebat, sub imitatoria confictione progrediendo retrogradus, incedendo recedens, Cancer post se incedere videbatur. Lapis tertius oppositi lapidis splendorem pauperculum habundantibus suae claritatis recompensabat divitiis. In quo, sicut picturae veritas praedicabat, umbratilis Ledaea proles sibi mutuo amplexu congratulans incedebat.

9. Ad hunc modum tres secundae dignitatis honore pollentes thronum in contradictoria parte locaverant, quorum primus, sudoris guttulis lacrimas exemplando, quodam imaginario fletu contristabat aspectum. In quo, prout curialis sculpturae fantasia imaginando docebat, Idaei adolescentis urceolus fluentem singultabat torrentem. Lapis secundus a suo regno caloris alienans hospitia glaciali torpore hyemem sibi hospitam vendicabat. In quo ex caprinae lanae adulterino vellere Capricorno tunicam pictura texuerat. Lapis tertius, vultum lucis induens cristallinae, vexillo sui frigoris hyemis prophetabat adventum. In quo assidua sui arcus

8. For on the forward part of the diadem three precious stones outshone the nine others by the boldness and pride of their radiance, in keeping with their names. The first stone demanded that darkness suffer banishment by its light, and cold by its fiery heat. On this stone as the elegant deceptions of decoration gave it voice, the pictured image of a Lion roared. The second stone, not second to the first in brightness, and flashing forth in a higher position in the aforementioned place, seemed to look down on the other stones with a certain disdain. On this stone, as art, the ape of truth, set it forth with imitative invention, a Crab, turned backward as he traveled forward, withdrawing as he moved ahead, seemed to be advancing behind himself. The third stone made up for the meager radiance of its opposing sign by its abundant wealth of brilliant light. On this stone, as truthful depiction proclaimed them, the shadowy forms of the sons of Leda moved forward, gladly joined in a mutual embrace.

9. In the same way three stones whose honor and dignity were of the second rank had established their thrones in the opposing position. The first of these, imitating tears by little drops of moisture, presented a sad appearance with this imaginary weeping. On this stone, as the courtly fantasy of sculpture set it forth in image, the pitcher of the youth of Ida sobbed forth a torrential flow. The second stone, excluding from its domain any visitation of heat, claimed winter as its chosen guest by its icy chill. On this stone art had woven, with the counterfeit wool of goat's hair, a tunic for Capricorn. The third stone, its surface enveloped in crystalline light, by its signs of chill foretold the arrival of winter. On

inflexione senex Haemonius vulnera minabatur, nunquam tamen minis recompensabat effectum.

10. Alteri vero lateri, lumine blandienti lasciviens, trium gemmarum benigna oculis gratiabatur serenitas, quarum prima rosei coloris flammata murice rosam visibus praesentabat. In qua Taurus suae frontis insignia praeferens sitire proelium videbatur. Alia, suae lucis privilegiata temperie, benignitatis gratia sororum beabat collegia. In qua Aries suae frontis honore superbiens gregis postulabat dominium. Tertia vero, viriditatem praeferens smaragdinam, refocillationis oculorum in se gerebat antidotum. In qua sub imaginario flumine Pisces suae naturae nando exercitium frequentabant.

11. In contradicenti latere trini lapidis siderea pulcritudo iocundo scintillabat applausu. Horum lapidum primus, suae fulgurationis aureo sole meridians, indefessae pulcritudinis gratiam efferebat. In quo, sicut sculpturae tropica figuratio demonstrabat, quadam sui praerogativa fulgoris astris contendebat Astraea. Secundus, non superfluo splendore luxurians nec penuriosi splendoris mendicans scintillulas, flamma moderata gaudebat. In quo sub aequo examine, iuxta artis pictoriae normam, Libra ponderum spondebat iudicia. Tertius, vultus alternando vicarios, nunc serenitatis benivolentiam spondens, nunc obscuritatis nubes induebat. In quo resultans facies Scorpionis, vultu risum, fletum caudae minabatur aculeo.

this stone the Old Man of Thessaly, eagerly drawing his bow, threatened wounds, but the event never made good his threats.

10. On another side the gentle serenity of three stones that reveled in their soothing light gave pleasure to the eyes. The first of these, its glowing color a deep red, offered a rose to the viewer. On it a Bull, thrusting forward the regalia of his forehead, seemed to thirst for battle. Another, distinguished by its temperate light, favored the company of its sisters with its gracious kindness. In it Aries, glorying in his forehead's marks of honor, claimed dominion over his flock. But the third, putting forth a light of emerald green, harbored in itself a remedy that could renew one's eyesight. On it the Fish, swimming in an imaginary river, pursued their natural activity.

11. On the opposing side the starry beauty of a trio of stones sparkled in happy applause. The first of these, at ease amid the golden sunlight with which it shone, gave forth a gift of unceasing beauty. On it, as the figurative devices of sculpture displayed her, Astraea, assuming a certain privilege by virtue of her brilliance, sought to rival the stars. The second stone, neither wantoning in excessive splendor nor begging for little sparks of meager light, rejoiced in its moderate flame. On it, carefully considered in accordance with the rules of pictorial art, Libra vouched for the justness of her weighings. The third stone, shifting from one appearance to another, at one moment gave promise of tranquil benevolence, at the next wrapped itself in cloudy darkness. On this stone the shining figure of Scorpio, though his face invited laughter, threatened to bring tears with the sharp sting of his tail.

12. Sub hiis autem duodecim lapidum domiciliis, septena gemmarum pluralitas, motum circularem perhennans, miraculoso ludendi genere choream exercebat plausibilem. Nec ipsi choreae sua deerat suavitas armoniae, nunc semitoniis lasciviens, nunc mediocri tonorum sonoritate iuvenescens, nunc maturiori tuba in diapasoneum melodiama procedens, quae, sua timpanizatione nostrarum aurium excitando libidinem, nostris oculis offerebat dormiendi praeludia. Sed quoniam audiendi parcitas auris deprecatur offensam, prodigalitas educat fastidium, ex superhabundanti audiendi copia fastidita auris elanguit.

13. Hii septem lapides, quamvis nullis iuncturarum ligaturis ipsi diademati tenerentur obnoxii, numquam tamen sui absentatione superiorum lapidum orphana faciebant collegia. Lapis autem superior adamas erat qui, motu ceteris avarior, prodigalior in desidia, in ampliori sui circuli peragratione nimia temporis morabatur expensa. Qui tanti frigoris gelicidio senescebat ut ipsum ex Saturnino sidere genitum genialis naturae probaret conformitas.

14. Secundus achates erat qui, dum sui cursus vicinia ceteris fiebat familiarior, quorundam inimicitias transformabat in gratiam, quorundam benivolentiam puerilem imperiali suae virtutis potentia reddebat adultam, quem propinqua naturae cognatione Ioviali sideri familiarem esse gracialis disputabat effectus.

15. Tertius astrites erat in quo, calibis principatu castrametante, quadam proprietatis continuitate Martii sideris legebatur effectus qui minaci suae fulgurationis vultu terribilis ceteris minabatur perniciem.

12. Below the houses of these twelve stones, a sevenfold group of gems, moving in ceaseless circles, performed a pleasing dance with a wondrous kind of playfulness. Nor was the sweetness of harmony absent from their dancing: now it wantoned in semitones, now grew stronger in the sonority of middle tones, now advanced to the trumpet call of the melodious diapason which, arousing the desires of our ears by its rhythmical beat, offered our eyes a prelude to sleep. But since to listen sparingly prevents irritation of the ear, [but] overindulgence leads to distaste, the ear was annoyed and grew weary after a too abundant amount of listening.

13. Although these seven stones were not held in subjection to the diadem by any connective bonds, they never left the company of the higher stones bereft by absenting themselves. The highest of these seven was a diamond which, more sparing of motion and more lavish of inactivity than the others, expended too much time in its longer journey through its orbit. It was hoary with a coat of frost so frigid that the close resemblance of its inherent nature made clear that it stemmed from the star of Saturn.

14. The second stone was an agate. When the proximity of its orbit brought it closer to the others, it transformed the hostility of certain of these to favor, and brought the childlike goodwill of others to maturity by the effect of its royal power. This benign influence was proof that it was intimately bound to the star of Jove by a close natural affinity.

15. The third stone was an asterite, in which, since the dominion of steel had established itself here, a close correspondence of character manifested the power of the star of Mars. Terrifying in the menacing appearance of its fiery glow, it threatened destruction to the others.

16. Quartus erat carbunculus, qui Solis gerens ymaginem, suae radiationis cereo noctis proscribens umbracula, fratrum lampades soporabat eclipticas, nunc ceteros regali suae maiestatis auctoritate deviare praecipiens, nunc quietam agitationi tribuens potestatem.

17. Cum saphiro vero iacinctus, eius insistendo vestigiis, ipsi velut asseclae ancillando praefati luminis nunquam fraudabantur aspectu. Brevique interiecta distantia circa eius orbem currunt pariter aut sequuntur, aut una subsequens stella alteri praeeundi concedit obsequia. Horum duorum lapidum alter suae naturae congruentia Mercurialis stellae, reliquus vero Dionaei sideris redolebat effectum.

18. Lapis ultimus margarita erat quae, rutilantis coronae margini citima, luce lucens aliena a carbunculo luminis mendicabat suffragia. Quae aliquando, lumini vicina praefato proficiens sive deficiens in crescendo, radios sui luminis quasi carbunculum venerata submittit, ut fraternis ignibus rursus ornata renovata sui splendoris ornamenta circumferat, nunc supplementis solempnibus attriti orbis nutriens dampna, nunc propriis orphanata luminibus iacturam propriae conquerens maiestatis; quae cristallino inargentata fulgore lunaris sideris respondebat effectui. Hiis omnibus lapidum splendoribus praefati diadematis serenata nobilitas in se firmamenti repraesentabat effigiem.

19. Vestis vero ex serica lana contexta, multiphario protheata colore, puellae pepli serviebat in usum, quam discolorando colorans temporum alteritas multiplici colorum

16. The fourth stone was a ruby that bore the image of the Sun. Banishing the shadows of night by the radiance of his flame, it caused the lamps of its brothers to sleep in eclipse. At one moment, by the regal authority of its majestic presence, it bade the others stray from their paths; at the next it granted them the power to move undisturbed.

17. An amethyst, together with a sapphire, followed closely in the Sun's footsteps, and like attentive servants they were never deprived of its light. With a short distance separating them from the Sun they move together with it, or follow behind, or one star, following, grants to the other the office of preceding it. One of these two stones by the similarity of its nature reveals the influence of the star of Mercury, the other that of the star of Dione.

18. The final stone was a pearl. Closest to the rim of the Sun's shining crown, and shining with light not its own, it begged an allowance of light from the ruby. At times, when it is close to this source of light and either gaining or dwindling in size, it dims its radiance as if in homage to the ruby, so that when once again adorned with this brotherly light, it may display the beauty of renewed radiance. Now it nurses the injuries of its diminished orb with supplies duly provided; now, bereft of its own light, it laments the loss of its dignity. Gleaming like silver in its crystalline light, it was subject to the influence of the Moon. With the manifold splendors of all these stones, the serene majesty of the diadem was in itself a representation of the firmament.

19. The maiden's dress, woven of silken thread and protean in its array of different colors, served as her robe of office. The changing of the seasons caused its color to change, altering its appearance with many colors. At first it met the

facie alterabat. Quae primitus candoris lilio dealbata offendebat intuitum. Secundo velut paenitentia ducta, quasi laborans in melius ruboris sanguine purpurata splendebat. Tertio ad cumulum perfectionis viroris smaragdo oculis applaudebat. Haec autem nimis subtilizata, subterfugiens oculorum indaginem, ad tantam materiae tenuitatem devenerat ut eius aerisque eandem crederes esse naturam. In qua, prout oculus in picturae imaginabatur sompnio, aerii animalis celebrabatur concilium.

20. Illic aquila primo iuvenem, secundo senem induens, tertio, in statum reciprocata priorem, in Adonim revertebatur a Nestore. Illic accipiter, civitatis praefectus aeriae, violenta tirannide a subditis redditus exposcebat. Illic milvus, venatoris induens histrionem, venatione furtiva larvam gerebat accipitris. Illic falco in ardeam bellum excitabat civile, non tamen aequali lance divisum; non enim illud pugnae debet appellatione censeri, "ubi tu pulsas, ego vapulo tantum." Illic structio, vita saeculari postposita, vitam solitariam agens, quasi heremita factus, desertorum solitudines incolebat.

21. Illic olor, sui funeris praeco, mellitae citharizationis organo vitae vaticinabatur apocopam. Illic in pavone tantum pulcritudinis compluit Natura thesaurum ut eam postea crederes mendicasse. Illic phoenix, in se mortuus, redivivus in alio, quodam Naturae miraculo se sua morte a mortuis suscitabat. Illic ciconia prolem decimando Naturae persolvebat tributum. Illic, passere in athomum pigmaeae humilitatis relegato, grus ex opposito in giganteae quantitatis

gaze with the gleaming whiteness of the lily; next, as if drawn to repentance and striving to do better, it was stained with blood of glowing purple; third, the height of perfection, it greeted the eye with an emerald green. So subtly woven was this garment, moreover, that it evaded the scrutiny of sight, and had attained such a fineness that you might think it was of the same nature as air. On this garment, as the eye was held in reverie by the dreamlike effect of art, a council of the creatures of the air was taking place.

20. Here the eagle, assuming first the appearance of youth, then that of age, then again returning to his earlier state, reverted from Nestor to Adonis. Here the hawk, governor of the airy realm, demanded tribute from his subjects with tyrannical violence. Here the kite, playing the role of hunter, appeared in his stealthy hunting like the ghost of the hawk. Here the falcon stirred up civil war against the heron, but not on equal terms. For that cannot be called by the name of battle "where you alone strike blows, and I only receive them." Here the ostrich, leaving the secular world behind, and living a solitary life as if he had become a hermit, dwelt in the solitude of the desert.

21. Here the swan, herald of his own death, foretold the ending of his life with sounds of honeyed musicality. Here Nature had poured such a treasury of beauty on the peacock that you would suppose her to have been a beggar henceforth. Here the phoenix, having died in one life and been reborn in another by a kind of natural miracle, by dying raised himself from the dead. Here the stork paid her tribute to Nature by decimating her brood. Here, while the sparrow was assigned the minute body of a lowly pigmy, the crane, in contrast, rose to the height of an oversized giant.

evadebat excessum. Illic phasianus, natalis insulae perpessus angustias, principum futurus deliciae, nostros evolabat in orbes. Illic gallus, tanquam vulgaris astrologus, suae vocis horologio horarum loquebatur discrimina. Illic gallus silvestris, privatioris galli deridens desidiam, peregre proficiscens, nemorales peragrabat provincias.

22. Illic bubo, propheta miseriae, psalmodias funereae lamentationis praecinebat. Illic noctua tantae deformitatis sterquilinio sordescebat ut in eius formatione Naturam fuisse crederes sompnolentam. Illic cornix, ventura pronosticans, nugatorio otiabatur garritu. Illic pica, dubio picturata colore, curam logices perhennabat insompnem. Illic monedula, laudabili latrocinio reculas thesaurizans, innatae avaritiae argumenta monstrabat. Illic columba, dulci malo inebriata Diones, laborabat Cipridis in palaestra. Illic corvus, zelotipiae abhorrens dedecus, suos fetus non sua esse pignora fatebatur, usque dum nigri argumento coloris hoc quasi secum disputando probabat.

23. Illic perdix nunc aeriae potestatis insultus, nunc venatorum sophismata, nunc canum latratus propheticos abhorrebat. Illic anas, cum ansere sub eodem iure vivendi, hiemabat in patria fluviali. Illic turtur, suo viduata consorte, amorem epilogare dedignans in altero, bigamiae refutabat solatia. Illic phsitacus in sui gutturis incude vocis monetam fabricabat humanae. Illic coturnicem, figurae dictionis ignorantem fallaciam, imaginariae vocis decipiebant sophismata.

Here the pheasant, having endured the privations of his native island, took flight to our world, to become the delight of princes. Here the cock, the people's astronomer, called out the turning of each hour with his voice for a clock. Here the woodcock, scorning the idleness of the domestic cock, roamed abroad and explored forested regions.

22. Here the horned owl, prophet of misfortune, sang foreboding psalms of funereal lamentation. Here the night owl, made foul by filth, displayed such ugliness that you might suppose Nature to have been drowsy when fashioning her. Here the crow, foreteller of things to come, idled away her time in trivial chatter. Here the magpie, with her plumage of uncertain color, persisted in her tireless devotion to argument. Here the jackdaw, accumulating knickknacks with commendable skill in thievery, gave clear evidence of her innate avarice. Here the dove, intoxicated by the sweet evil of Dione, struggled in the arena of the Cyprian. Here the raven, shunning the indignity of rivalry, would not acknowledge that his young were his own brood until he had proved it by the argument of their blackness, as if in disputation with himself.

23. Here the partridge shunned, now the attacks of powers of the air, now the wiles of hunters, now the ominous barking of dogs. Here the duck, living with the goose under a common rule of life, passed the winter in their native stream. Here the turtle dove, bereft of her spouse but refusing to add to their love the epilogue of love for another, rejected the consolations of bigamy. Here the parrot stamped out the coinage of human speech on the anvil of his throat. Here the quail, unaware of the falseness of feigned speech, was deceived by the trickery of an imitative voice. Here the

Illic picus, propriae architectus domunculae, sui rostri dola-
bro casulam fabricabat in ylice. Illic curuca, novercam
exuens, materno pietatis ubere alienam cuculi prolem adop-
tabat in filium. Quae tamen, capitali praemiata stipendio,
privignum agnoscens filium ignorabat.

24. Illic yrundo, a sua peregrinatione reversa, sub trabe
nidi lutabat hospitium. Illic philomena, suae deflorationis
querelam reintegrans, armonica tympanizans dulcedine,
parvitatis dedecus excusabat. Illic alauda, quasi nobilis cy-
tharista, non studii artificio sed Naturae magisterio musicae
praedocta scientiam, citharam praesentabat in ore, quae to-
nos in tenues subtilizans particulas, semitonia usque in gum-
phos invisibiles dividebat. Illic vespertilio, avis hermafrodi-
tica, cifrae locum inter aviculas obtinebat. Haec animalia,
quamvis ibi quasi allegorice viverent, ibi tamen esse videbantur ad litteram.

25. Sindo, in virorem adulterato candore, quam puella in-
consutiliter, ipsa postmodum dicente, texuerat, non plebea
vilescens materia, artificio subtili lasciviens, pallii gerebat
officium. Quae, multis intricata implexionibus, colorem
imaginabatur aquatilem. In qua super animalis naturam
aquatilis, multipharias particulatam in species, fabula com-
mentabatur picturae.

26. Illic cetus, rupibus contendens, suae scopulo quantitatis turriti corporis incursu, navium arietabat oppidula. Illic canis marinus, cum latrabili sui nominis significationem

woodpecker, architect of his own little home, fashioned his cottage in an oak with the pickaxe of his bill. Here the hedge sparrow, rejecting stepmotherly behavior, in motherly compassion adopted the child of another, the cuckoo. She was rewarded, however, with cruel wages: she acknowledged the stepson, but did not know her own.

24. Here the swallow, returned from her travels, coated with mud her home, a nest beneath the eaves. Here the nightingale, renewing her lament at her defloration, and pulsing rhythmically with the sweetness of harmony, absolved the indignity done to her small body. Here the lark, like some courtly harpist, but one whose knowledge of music has been gained, not by study of the art, but through the teaching of Nature, made her throat her harp; subtly separating each tone into finer parts, she divided the semitones into imperceptible elements. Here the bat, the hermaphrodite bird, occupied the position of a cipher among the little birds. These creatures, though their existence here was a kind of allegory, seemed nonetheless to be literally present.

25. A muslin garment, its whiteness changed to green, performed the office of a cloak. The maiden (as she later declared) had woven it without seam. Rather than seeming worthless because of its humble material, it playfully displayed the subtlety of her artistry. It was covered with intricate embroidery, and its color gave the impression of water. On its surface fanciful painting had inscribed the many kinds of water-dwelling creatures, arranged by species.

26. There the whale, rivaling the cliffs in his craggy immensity, battered ships, the villages of the sea, by attacking them with his well-fortified body. There the sea dog, confuting the suggestion of barking in his name with equivocating

aequivocationis bivio praeconfundens, nullis indulgendo latratibus, sui generis lepores maris venabatur in saltibus. Illic
sturgio, sui nobilitate corporis individualis, sui corporis
benedictionem mensis offerebat regalibus. Illic allec, piscis
generalissimus, ampla sui communitate pauperum solabatur
ieiunia. Illic plais, sui corporis dulcoratis saporibus, in qua-
dragesimali austeritate carnis redimebat absentiam. Illic
mulo dulcibus suae carnis irritamentis palata seducebat gus-
tantium. Illic trucula, sinus marinos ingrediens, in aequore
baptizata, salmonis nomine censebatur. Illic delphines suae
apparitionis prooemio maris invectiones futuras navibus
predicebant. Illic in Sirenum renibus piscis, homo legebatur
in facie. Illic Luna, proprio lumine pauperata, quasi invidens
in conchilia propriam vindicabat iniuriam, quae, quasi sui
corporis novilunio laborantia, lunae luebant pauperiem.

27. Hiis marinae regionis incolis pallii portio concessa
fuerat medialis. Reliqua vero clamidis portio pisces peregri-
nos habebat qui, diversis fluctibus evagantes, in dulcioris
aquae patria sedes posuerant. Illic lucius, exactione tyran-
nica, non exigentia meriti, subditos proprii corporis incar-
cerabat ergastulo. Illic barbulus, non minori sui corporis
dignitate famosus, cum plebecula piscium familiarius habi-
tabat. Illic alosa, tempus comitata vernale, cum veris deliciis
sui saporis delicias offerens, sui corporis adventu gustus sa-
lutabat humanos. Illic murena, multiplici fenestrata fora-
mine, febrium introductiones lectitabat prandentibus. Illic
anguilla, colubri naturam imaginans, quadam proprietatis

ambiguity, since he never gives vent to barks, hunted the hares of his own element in the thickets of the sea. There the sturgeon, exceptional in the nobility of his body, offers that body to bless the tables of kings. There the herring, most common of fish, eased the hunger of the poor with his abundant shoals. There the plaice made up for the absence of meat in the austere season of Lent by the rich taste of his body. There the mullet seduced gourmets with the sweet enticement of his flesh. There the trout made his way to the ocean inlets, and having been baptized by the sea was accorded the name of salmon. There dolphins, by their prefatory appearance, foretold coming attacks on ships. There one observed in Sirens the bodies of fish, but a human face. There the Moon, deprived of its own light, as if in envy avenged its own loss on the oysters, who, as if their bodies were experiencing a new moon, paid a price for the moon's impoverishment.

27. To these natives of the ocean the middle portion of her cloak had been assigned. The remaining portion of the garment held pilgrim fish who, roaming through different streams, made their homes in the region of fresh water. There the pike, by tyranny rather than the demands of justice, condemned his subjects to the prison house of his own body. There the barbel, no less renowned for the excellence of his flesh, lived on friendlier terms with the lower orders of fish. There the shad, companion of the vernal season, offering amid the pleasures of spring the pleasure of his own flesh, greeted human palates with the arrival of his body. There the lamprey, windowed with many pores, often provided the introduction to feverish feasting. There the eel, from his close resemblance to the serpent and a certain

similitudine neptis credebatur esse eiusdem. Illic perca, spinarum iaculis loricata, aquatilis lupi minus abhorrebat insultus. Illic capito quod in inferioris corporis paucitate perdebat strumoso recuperabat in capite. Haec picturae tropo eleganter in pallio figurata sculpturae natare videbantur miraculo.

28. Tunica vero polimita, opere picturata plumario, infra se corpus claudebat virgineum. Quae, multis stellata coloribus, in grossiorem materiam conglobata, in terrestris elementi faciem aspirabat. In huius vestis parte primaria homo, sensualitatis deponens segnitiem, directa ratiocinationis aurigatione caeli penetrabat archana. In qua parte tunica, suarum partium passa discidium, suarum iniuriarum contumelias demonstrabat. In reliquis tamen locis partes, eleganti continuatione concordes, nullam divisionis in se sustinebant discordiam. In quibus quaedam picturae incantatio terrestria animalia vivere faciebat.

29. Illic elephas, monstruosa corporis quantitate progressus in aera, sibi corpus a Natura creditum multiplici faenore duplicabat. Illic camelus, strumosi corporis scrupulositate deformis, quasi servus emptitius hominum usibus ministrabat. Illic cornua, vicem cassidis usurpando, bubali frontem videbantur armare. Illic taurus, terram pedibus vexando, mugitibus intonando, sui duelli fulmina praecinebat. Illic boves, taurorum recusantes militiam, quasi rustici servilibus negotiis inhiabant.

30. Illic equus ferventi provectus audacia, suo insessori conmilitans, hastam frangebat cum milite. Illic asinus,

similarity in behavior, was held to be the serpent's grand-child. There the perch, armor-plated with sharp spines, had little fear from the attack of the sea wolf. There the capito made up with its swollen head for what it lacked in the small-ness of its lower body. These creatures, elegantly depicted on the cloak by artful imagery, through a miracle of sculp-ture appeared to swim there.

28. A damask tunic, decorated with embroidery, confined within itself the maiden's body. Brightened by many colors, but giving shape to coarser material, it sought to present the appearance of earthly life. On the most prominent part of this garment Man, casting off the dulling effect of sensu-ality, probed into the mysteries of heaven, borne along a straight path by his rational faculty. But in this part the tu-nic had been torn apart, and clearly revealed the abuse it had suffered. Elsewhere, however, its parts were joined in ele-gant and unbroken harmony, and suffered from no divisive misalignment. On this garment the enchantment of art gave life to earthly creatures.

29. There the elephant, raising into the air the monstrous bulk of his body, doubled the body entrusted to him by Na-ture with compound interest. There the camel, ugly in the roughness of his swollen body, served the purposes of men like a bondservant. There the horns on the forehead of the buffalo, taking the place of a helmet, seemed like armor. There the bull, tearing at the earth with his hoof and bel-lowing loudly, gave notice of his fierceness as a fighter. There oxen, rejecting the belligerence of the bull, gaped like peas-ants while performing their humble tasks.

30. There the horse, urged on by impetuous boldness, joined his rider in fighting and shattered spear and warrior

clamoribus aures otiosis fastidiens, quasi per antifrasim organizans, barbarismum faciebat in musica. Illic unicornis, virginali soporatus in gremio, ab hostibus mortis sompnium incurrebat in sompno. Illic leo, rugitus carmina auribus natorum inmurmurans, mira naturae incantatione in illis vitae suscitabat igniculum. Illic ursa, per portas narium fetus enixa deformes, ipsos stilo linguae crebrius delambenti monetans, meliorem deducebat in formam.

31. Illic lupus, latitando furis usurpans officium, furcarum itinere exaltari merebatur aerio. Illic pardus, apertiori latrocinio neronizans, pecudum vulgus non solum in vestibus, verum etiam in propria praedabatur substantia. Illic tigris pecualium civium rempublicam crebra innocentis effusione sanguinis violabat. Illic onager, asini exuens servitutem, Naturae manumissus imperio, montium incolebat audaciam. Illic aper, dentis armatura fulmineus, mortem propriam canibus multiplici vendebat in vulnere. Illic canis auras fantasticis vexando vulneribus, aera dentium importunitate mordebat.

32. Illic cervus et dama, pedum velocitate volantes, vitam praeeundo lucrantes, subsequentium canum morsus defraudabant iniquos. Illic caper, lana vestitus sophistica, nares fastidire quatriduano videbatur odore. Illic aries, tunica nobiliori trabeatus, uxorum pluralitate gavisus, matrimonii defraudabat honorem. Illic vulpecula, idiotiam bruti exuens animalis, ad meliorem hominis anhelabat astutiam. Illic

alike. There the ass, annoying the ear with useless brayings, the very opposite of organ tones, created a barbarous kind of music. There the unicorn, grown drowsy in a maiden's lap, met the nightmare of death at the hands of his enemies as he slept. There the lion, murmuring a growling music into the ears of his young, kindled the spark of life in them through Nature's wondrous magic. There the she-bear, after emitting her young unshapen from the portals of her nostrils, imposed a better form, shaping them by the exercise of her constantly licking tongue.

31. There the wolf, stealthily adopting the role of thief, earned exaltation to the airy height of the gallows. There the leopard, Nero-like in his open thievery, preyed on the herd not just in disguise but in his true form. There the tiger did violence to the citizens of the nation of cattle by continual shedding of innocent blood. There the wild ass, freeing himself from asinine servitude, set free by the authority of Nature, dwelt on the heights of the mountains. There the boar, gnashing his armament of teeth, exchanged his own death for countless wounds to the hounds. There the dog, snapping at the air with his savage teeth, harassed the breeze with imaginary wounds.

32. There stag and doe, in swift-footed flight, purchasing life by leading the way, disappointed the wicked jaws of the pursuing hounds. There the goat, clad in pretended wool, seemed to trouble the nostrils with a fourth-day odor. There the ram, invested with a nobler garment, rejoiced in his multitude of wives, and betrayed the honor of marriage. There the small fox, rejecting the ignorance of a brute beast, aspired to the greater acuity of man. There the hare, possessed

lepus, melancolico arrepticius timore, non sompno sed timoris sopore perterritus, canum sompniabat adventum.

33. Illic cuniculus, pelle nostri frigoris iram temperando, carne propria nostrae famis debellabat insultum. Illic scisimus, dedignans panno nubere viliori, eleganti suturae matrimonio purpurae iugabatur. Illic castor, ne ab hostibus totius corporis patiatur diaeresim, corporis partes apocopabat extremas. Illic linx tanta luminis limpiditate vigebat, ut eius respectu lippire cetera animalia viderentur. Illic martrix cum sabelo semiplenam palliorum pulcritudinem eorum postulantem subsidia suarum pellium nobilitate deducebat ad plenum. Has animalium figuras hystrionalis figurae representatio quasi iocunditatis convivia oculis donabat videntium.

34. Quid vero in caligis camisiaque in superioribus vestibus consepultis picturae sompniaret industria, nulla certitudinis auctoritate probavi. Sed tamen, ut quaedam fragilis probabilitatis remedia docuerunt, opinor in herbarum arborumque naturis ibi picturae risisse lasciviam: illic arbores nunc tunicis vestiri purpureis, nunc comis criniri virentibus, nunc florum parturire redolentem infantiam, nunc in fetum senescere potiorem. Sed quoniam solius probabilitatis lubrico, non certitudinis fide, huius seriem picturationis agnovi, hanc sub silentii pace sepultam praetereo. Calcei vero, ex alutea pelle traducentes materiam, ita familiariter pedum sequebantur ideas, ut in ipsis pedibus nati ipsisque

by chronic fear, dreamed in terror of the onset of the hounds, not in sleep but in a fearful stupor.

33. There the rabbit, who moderates fierce cold for us with his pelt, defended us against the attack of hunger with his very flesh. There the squirrel, disdaining to wed any meaner cloth, was married by elegant tailoring to a purple robe. There the beaver cut off the private parts of his body, lest he suffer the dismemberment of the whole body by his enemies. There the lynx enjoyed such clarity of vision that other animals seemed bleary eyed in comparison. There marten and sable, by the fineness of their coats, made complete the beauty of the half-finished robes which sought their aid. The representational power of imitative art presented these animal figures to the eye of the viewer like a delightful feast.

34. I could not establish with certainty what the artist's skill might envision for the shoes and underclothing that were concealed beneath her outer garments. However, as certain promptings, possible but tentative, suggested, I suspect that on these lively decoration made merry with the varieties of plants and trees; that the trees were at one moment decked in purple garments, then in a coat of green leaves; that they then gave birth to sweet-smelling infant buds, and at last grew old as their fruit matured. But since my knowledge of the plan of these images is only random conjecture, not confident certainty, I leave the matter to rest in quiet peace. But her shoes, which took soft leather as their material, traced the form of the feet so intimately that they might have been born there, inscribed on the feet

mirabiliter viderentur inscripti. In quibus, vix a vera degenerantes essentia, sub picturae ingenio flores amoenabantur umbratiles.

3

Illic forma rosae picta fideliter,
a vera facie devia paululum,
aequabat proprio murice purpuram
telluremque suo sanguine tinxerat.
5 Concludens sociis floribus affuit
flos illic redolens gratus Adonidis,
Argentoque suo nobile lilium
praeditabat agros imaque vallium.
Illic ore thimum dispare disputans
10 certabat, reliquis floribus invidens.
Narcisi socio flore iocantia
ridebant tacito murmure flumina.
Vultu florigero flos aquilegius
florum praenituit Lucifer omnium.
15 Vernalisque loquens temporis otia,
stellabat violae flosculus arbuta,
picturae facies plena favoribus.
Hic floris speciem vivere iusserat
quae regalis erat cartula nominis,
20 scribentisque tamen nescia pollicis.

themselves in a wondrous way. To these the images of flowers, scarcely inferior to flowers truly alive, lent their beauty through the painter's skill.

Chapter 3

There the form of the rose, faithfully rendered and differing very little from the true flower, matched that flower's purple with its own color, and stained the earth with its blood. The 5 pleasing flower of Adonis, sweet smelling, was included in the floral company, and the noble lily bestowed its silver on the fields and deep valleys. There thyme, less fair of face, vied 10 with the other flowers in envious dispute. Playful streams, with the flower of Narcissus as their companion, smiled with a gentle murmur. The columbine, its face in full bloom, foremost of all flowers, shone like Lucifer. And the little vio- 15 let, a reminder of the idle hours of springtime, shone star-like amid the wild strawberries, its face abounding in the graces of painting. Here Nature had ordered to flourish that flower which is inscribed with a royal title, though it has 20 never known a writer's hand.

Hae sunt veris opes et sua pallia,
telluris species et sua sidera,
quae pictura suis artibus edidit,
flores effigians arte sophistica.
25 Hiis florum tunicis prata virentibus
veris nobilitat gratia prodigi.
Haec bissum tribuunt, illaque purpuram,
quae texit sapiens dextra Favonii.

4

Haec vestium ornamenta, quamvis suae plenis splendiditatis
flammarent ardoribus, eorundem tamen splendor sub puellaris decoris sidere patiebatur eclipsim. In latericiis vero ta-
bulis, arundinei stili ministerio, virgo varias rerum picturali-
ter suscitabat imagines. Pictura tamen, subiacenti materiae
familiariter non cohaerens, velociter evanescendo moriens,
nulla imaginum post se relinquebat vestigia. Quas cum saepe
suscitando puella crebro vivere faciebat, tamen in scripturae
proposito imagines perseverare non poterant.

2. Virgo etiam, ut praetaxavimus, a celestis regiae emer-
gens confinio, in mundi passibilis tugurium curru vitreo ferebatur. Ipse vero Iunonis alitibus nullius iugi magisterio
disciplinatis sed sibi spontanea voluntate coniunctis, trahe-
batur. Homo vero, virginis capiti curruique supereminens,
cuius vultus non terrenitatis vilitatem sed potius deitatis

These are the riches and robes of spring, stars on the fair face of the earth, which the skills of the artist brought forth, imaging the flowers with subtle skill. The kindness of prodigal spring ennobled the meadows with these flourishing floral garments. Some contribute the whiteness of linen, others a purple robe, woven by the knowing hand of Favonius. 25

Chapter 4

While the decorative images on her robe shone with a full and splendid brilliance, their splendor was nevertheless eclipsed by the girl's own starlike beauty. On clay tablets, with the aid of a reed pen, the maiden was giving life to the pictured forms of various creatures. But her imagery, rather than adhering closely to this material surface, soon died and disappeared, leaving behind no trace of its forms. Though the girl was constantly restoring them to life, their forms were not able to survive in this inscriptional fashion.

2. The maiden, coming forth, as we have said, from the inner recesses of the heavenly realm, was borne downward to the lowliness of the world of change in a chariot of glass. It was drawn by the birds of Juno who, with no yoke to govern them, were joined together by their own spontaneous desire. But a man, standing over the maiden and her chariot, guided the chariot's descent, lending support to the

redolebat archanum, inpotentiam sexus supplendo feminei, modesto directionis ordine currus aurigabat incessum. Ad cuius pulcritudinis dignitatem investigandam, dum tamquam manipulos oculorum radios legarem visibiles, ipsi tantae non audentes maiestatis obviare decori, splendoris hebetati verberibus, nimis meticulosi ad palpebrarum contubernia refugerunt.

3. In praefatae vero virginis adventu, quasi suas renovando naturas omnia sollempnizare crederes elementa. Firmamentum vero, quasi suis cereis virgineum iter illuminans, ut solito plenius radiarent suis imperabat sideribus. Unde et ipsa lux diurna tantam eorum mirari videbatur audaciam, quae in eius conspectu quasi nimis insolenter viderat apparere. Phoebus etiam, solito vultum induens laetiorem, in occursu virginis totas sui luminis effundebat divitias. Sororem etiam, quam sui splendoris depauperaverat ornamentis, ei veste iocunditatis reddita, reginae venienti iubet occurrere. Aer vero, vultus nubium exuens lacrimosos, sereni vultus benivolentia virgineis arridebat incessibus. Qui primum aquilonaris irae vexatus vesania, nunc in Favonii favorali gremio quiescebat. Aves vero, quadam Naturae inspiratione, alarum ludo plausibili ioculantes, virgini venerationis faciem exhibebant. Iuno vero, quae iampridem Ioviales tactus fuerat dedignata, tanta fuit inebriata laetitia ut crebro oculorum praeludio maritum ad venereas invitaret illecebras.

4. Mare vero, prius tumultuosis fluctibus debachatum, nunc puellaris adventus feriando sollempnia, tranquillitatis pacem spondebat perpetuam. Aeolus namque tempestatis

weakness of her womanly nature by his gentle promptings. His face showed no trace of earthly baseness, but rather the mysterious quality of godhead. Though I sought to keep the rays of my eyesight as steady as a troop of soldiers, to assess her noble beauty, they were afraid to encounter an elegance so majestic; dimmed and intimidated by the force of her radiance, they retreated to the tents of my eyelids.

3. At the approach of this maiden, you would have thought that the elements were renewing their native powers in celebration. For the firmament, as if to light the maiden's path with its candles, commanded its stars to give forth a more than normal radiance, such that the very light of day seemed to marvel at their great boldness, when it saw them appear with such seeming insolence in its sight. Phoebus, too, assuming a more joyful aspect than is his wont, poured forth all his wealth of light as the maiden approached, and ordered his sister, whom he had deprived of her adorning splendor, to come forth, her charming dress restored, to greet the arriving queen. The very air, casting off its sorrowful, cloudy appearance, smiled upon the maiden's arrival with a face of calm benevolence. Once tormented by the mad rage of Aquilo, it now lay quiet in the bosom of kindly Favonius. And the birds, inspired in some way by Nature, merrily beating their wings in playful applause, plainly expressed their veneration of the maiden. Juno, too, who had long since repudiated the caresses of Jove, was overcome by such joy that she sought to entice her husband to the pleasures of Venus with frequent promising glances.

4. The sea as well, once maddened by tumultuous surges, now acknowledged the festive event of the maiden's coming by embracing the tranquility of perpetual peace. For Aeolus

ventos, ne in conspectu virginis plusquam civilia bella moverent, in suis vinculavit ergastulis. Pisces vero, in aquarum superciliis enatantes, in quantum sensualitatis patiebatur inertia, quadam hylaritatis festivitate suae dominae praeconabant adventum. Thetis etiam, nuptias agens cum Nereo, Achillem alterum concipere destinabat. Puellae vero, quarum pulcritudo non solum suam rationem homini furaretur, verum etiam caelestes suae deitatis cogeret oblivisci, locis fluvialibus emergentes, quasi tributariae venienti reginae pigmentarii nectaris praesentabant munuscula. Quibus favoraliter susceptis a virgine, iugi complexuum innexione crebraque repetitione osculi virgo virginibus suum intimabat amorem.

5. Terra vero, iampridem hiemis latrocinio suis ornamentis denudata, a veris prodigalitate purpurantem florum tunicam usurpabat, ne vestibus pannosis ingloria adolescentulae indecenter compareret aspectui. Ver etiam, quasi artifex peritus in arte textoria, ut virgineis beatius applauderet incessibus, vestimenta texebat arboribus, quae demissione comarum encletica sub quadam adorationis specie, quasi flectendo genua, virgunculae supplicabant. E quibus egressae virgines, suae pulcritudinis die materialis diei locupletantes divitias, ex anthonomasicis herbarum speciebus confecta in cedrinis vasculis ferebant aromata, quae tamquam suos redditus puellulae persolvendo, eius favorem suis emebant muneribus.

6. Napaeae vero, gremia floribus saturantes, reginae currum aliquando roseis floribus sanguinabant, aliquando florum foliis liliabant albentibus. Flora vero camisiam bissinam,

held the storm winds chained in his prison, lest they stir up "wars more than civil" in the maiden's presence. Even fish, swimming upward to the surface of their waters, proclaimed the arrival of their mistress with as much festive gaiety as the sluggishness of their sensory nature allowed. Thetis, too, performing the nuptial rites with Nereus, resolved to conceive a second Achilles. Girls whose beauty would not only rob a man of his reason, but cause even celestial beings to become forgetful of their divinity, emerged from their streams and offered little gifts of spiced nectar as tribute to the coming of their queen. These gifts were graciously accepted by the maiden, who expressed her love for the maidens with close embraces and repeated kisses.

5. The earth, too, long since left bare of her adornment by the thievery of winter, acquired a richly colored garment of flowers through the prodigal generosity of spring, lest she appear unsightly in the eyes of the young lady, disgraced by ragged clothing. And spring, like a craftsman skilled in the weaver's art, in order to greet the arrival of the maiden more joyfully, also wove robes for the trees, which, as if genuflecting, humbly honored the maiden by lowering their boughs in a reverent fashion. Maidens emerging from the trees increased the richness of the natural day by the daylight of their beauty. They brought scents produced from the varieties of herb for which they are named, in little cedar cups, as though paying tribute to the maiden, and by their gifts they gained her favor.

6. The nymphs of the vales, filling their laps with flowers, at one moment made the queen's chariot bloodred with rose blossoms, at the next gave it the glow of the lily with white-petaled flowers. Prodigal Flora presented to the maiden a

quam marito texuerat ut eius mereretur amplexus, prodiga-
liter virgini praesentavit. Proserpina vero, mariti thoro fastidita Tartarei, ad superna repatrians, suae imperatricis noluit
defraudari praesentia. Terrestria etiam animalia, nescio qua
docente natura, iocantibus indulgendo lasciviis, virginalem
didicere praesentiam. Sic rerum universitas, ad virginis fervens obsequium, miro certamine laborabat sibi virginis gratiam comparare.

5

Floriger horrentem Zephyrus laxaverat annum,
    exstinguens Boreae proelia pace sui.
Grandine perfusus florum pluit ille ligustra,
    et pratis horum iussit inesse nives.
5   Ver, quasi fullo novus, reparando pallia pratis,
    horum succendit muricis igne togas.
Reddidit arboribus crines quos bruma totondit,
    vestitum reparans quem tulit illa prius.
Tempus erat quo larga suis expandit in agris,
10   applausu Driadum, gratia veris opes;
quo dum maior inest virtus, infantia florum,
    altius emergens, matre recedit humo;
quo violae speculum, terrae cunabula linquens,
    aeris afflatus postulat ore novo.
15   Tempus erat quo terra, caput stellata rosarum,
    contendit caelo sidere plena suo;

linen gown which she had woven for her husband that she might be found worthy of his embrace. Proserpina, weary of the bed of her husband, lord of Tartarus, returned to her home in the upper world, unwilling to be denied the presence of her empress. Even the beasts of the field, indulging in wanton sports at the prompting of who knows what natural impulse, responded to the maiden's presence. Thus universal creation, eager to do homage to the maiden, strove with wondrous energy to gain her favor.

Chapter 5

Zephyr, bringer of flowers, had calmed the fierceness of the year, quelling the assaults of Boreas by his peaceful influence. Brimming with a storm of blossoms he rained down flowers, and commanded their snows to cover the meadows. Spring, a fuller of a new kind, refurbishing the garments of 5 the fields, set their robes ablaze with glowing purple. He gave back to the trees the tresses which winter had cut short, and restored the garments which she had snatched away.

It was the season when spring graciously diffuses its rich abundance through the fields, while the Dryads make merry; 10 when the infant blossoms, as their strength increases, come forth and draw away from the nurturing soil; when the glowing violet, forsaking earth, its nursery, lifts its fresh face to seek the breeze.

It was the season when earth, a stellar crown of roses on 15 her head, seeks to rival heaven with this abundance of stars;

quo vexilla gerens aestatis amigdalus ortum
   praedicat, et veris gaudia flore notat;
quo vitis gemmata sinus amplexa maritos
20   ulmi, de partu cogitat ipsa suo.
Proscribit brumae solaris cereus umbram,
   cogens exilium frigora cuncta pati,
multis bruma tamen latuit fantastica silvis,
   quam silvae foliis fecerat umbra recens.
25 Iam flori puero Iuno dedit ubera roris,
   quo primum partus lactet alumpna suos.
Tempus erat Phoebi quo mortua gramina virtus
   suscitat et tumulis surgere cuncta iubet;
quo mundum facies Iovialis laeta serenat,
30   et lacrimas hiemis tergit ab ore suo,
aeris ut fidei se flos committere possit,
   nec florem puerum frigoris urat hiems;
quo mundum Phoebus hiemis torpore gementem
   visitat et laeta luce salutat eum;
35 pristina quo senium deponit temporis aetas,
   et mundus senior incipit esse puer;
quo noctem Phoebus propriis depauperat horis,
   pigmaeusque dies incipit esse gigas;
quo parat hospitia Phoebo solvendo tributum
40   frixeum, gaudens hospite sole, pecus.
Quo Philomena sui celebrat sollempnia veris,
   odam melliti carminis ore canens,
in cuius festo sua gutturis organa pulsat,
   ut proprio proprium praedicet ore deum,
45 quo dulci sonitu citharam mentitur alauda
   cum volat ad superos colloquiturque Iovi.

when the almond tree, bearing the badges of summer, foretells proclaims his coming, while his blossoms attest the joys
of spring; when the budding vine, embracing the breast of
its husband elm, thinks of giving birth. The sun's candle ban-   20
ished the shadows of winter, forcing all cold to submit to
exile, yet in many groves a phantom frost still lurked, because of the shade created by the trees' new leaves. Now   25
Juno suckled the infant flower with dew, that she, as foster
mother, might be the first to nurse the newborns.

It was the season when the strength of Phoebus quickens
the dead fields, and bids all things rise from their tombs;
when the happy countenance of Jove smiles on the world,
and wipes away the wintry tears from her face, that the   30
flower may entrust itself to the protection of the air, and no
wintry frost blight the tender blossom; when Phoebus revis-
its a world lamenting the lassitude of winter, and greets it
with his joyous light; when the fresh youth of the season   35
casts off old age, and a world grown old begins a new boyhood; when Phoebus deprives the night of hours that were
his, and dwarfish day begins to be a giant; when Phrixus's   40
ram does homage to Phoebus by offering hospitality, rejoicing to have the sun as guest.

It was the season when Philomela celebrates her rites of
spring, giving voice to her honey-sweet lyric song: she plays
on her vocal instrument in this ritual way, that her voice may
proclaim a divinity of its own; when the lark imitates the   45
lyre with her sweet song, and flies into the heavens to hold
converse with Jove.

Splendor lascivos argenteus induit amnes
    in fluviisque suum iusserat esse diem.
Discursus varii fontis garrire videres,
50   prologus in sompnum murmur euntis erat.
Splendorisque sui facie fons ipse rogabat,
    ut sua defessus pocula sumat homo.

6

Hac igitur amoenante temporis iuventute, nullis rerum exhilarata favoribus priorem virgo potuit temperare tristitiem; sed currum in terram humilians, propriis humum ve-
nustando vestigiis, ad me pudico pervenit incessu. Quam
postquam michi cognatam loci proximitate prospexi, in faciem decidens, mentem stupore vulneratus exivi, totusque
in extasis alienatione sepultus, sensuumque incarceratis virtutibus, nec vivens nec mortuus inter utrumque neuter labo-
rabam.

2. Quem virgo amicabiliter erigens, pedes ebrios susten-
tantium manuum confortabat solatio, meque suis innec-
tendo complexibus, meique ora pudicis osculis dulcorando,
mellifluoque sermonis medicamine a stuporis morbo cura-
vit infirmum. Quae postquam mihi me redditum intellexit,
mentales intellectus materialis vocis mihi depinxit imagine,
et quasi archetipa verba idealiter praeconcepta vocaliter
produxit in actum.

A silvery splendor enhanced the playful streams, and caused the rivers to give off a daylight of their own. One could behold the running chatter of a shimmering fountain, and the murmur of its flow was a prologue to sleep. The 50 fountain itself, by its splendid appearance, seemed to beg that the weary man drink its waters.

Chapter 6

Thus the youthful season was flourishing, but the maiden was not cheered by the acclamation of her creatures, and could not restrain her earlier sorrow. Bringing her chariot down to earth, and adorning the ground with her footsteps, she came toward me at a modest pace. When I saw that she had drawn close to me, I fell on my face, stricken by stupor, abandoned consciousness and sank into total disorientation. My sensory powers suspended, I was neither living nor dead, but reduced to a neutral state between the two.

2. The maiden, kindly drawing me erect, assisted my drunken footsteps with the support of her comforting hands. As she held me in her embrace, the sweetness of her chaste kisses on my lips and the healing power of her honey-sweet words cured her patient of his afflicting stupor. Once she recognized that I was restored to myself, she painted the workings of intellect with the shapes of material language, and in effect translated archetypal words, preconceived in the realm of ideas, into actual speech.

3. "Heu," inquit, "quae ignorantiae caecitas, quae alienatio mentis, quae debilitas sensuum, quae infirmatio rationis, tuo intellectui nubem opposuit, animum exulare coegit, sensus hebetavit potentiam, mentem compulit aegrotare, ut non solum tuae nutricis familiari cognitione tua intelligentia defraudetur, verum etiam, tanquam monstruosae imaginis novitate percussa, in meae apparitionis ortu tua discretio patiatur occasum? Cur a tua memoria mei facis peregrinari notitiam? In quo mea munera me loquuntur, quae te tot beneficiorum praelargis beavi muneribus? Quae a tua ineunte aetate, Dei auctoris vicaria, rata dispensatione legitimum tuae vitae ordinavi curriculum? Quae olim tui corporis materiem, adulterina primordialis materiae essentia fluitantem, in verum esse produxi?

4. "Cuius vultum miserata deformem, quasi ad me crebrius declamantem, humanae speciei signaculo sigillavi, eamque, honestis orphanam figurarum ornamentis, melioribus formarum vestibus honestavi. In qua ad corporis clientelam diversas membrorum ordinans officinas, in eadem sensus quasi corporeae civitatis excubias vigilare praecepi, ut quasi externorum hostium praevisores corpus ab exteriori importunitate defenderent, ut sic totius corporis materia, nobilibus naturarum purpuramentis ornata, ad nuptias gradiens, marito spiritui gratius iugaretur, ne maritus, suae coniugis turpitudine fastiditus, eius refutaret coniugia.

5. "Tuum etiam spiritum virtualibus insignivi potentiis, ne corpore pauperior eius successibus invideret. Cui ingenialis virtutis destinavi potentiam, quae, rerum venatrix subtilium

3. "Alas," she said, "what blind ignorance, what disorientation of mind, what defect of perception, what weakness of
reason has imposed this cloud on your intellect, driven your
mind into exile, dulled the power of your senses, caused your
thought to become so diseased that not only has your understanding been robbed of its intimate acquaintance with
your nurse, but your rational powers succumb to darkness
at my very appearance, as though shocked by some strange
monstrous form? Why have you caused recognition of me to
depart from your memory, you in whom my gifts declare me
the one who has blessed you with so many lavish bestowals
of benefits? Who from the beginning of your existence have
been commissioned, as the vicar of God the creator, to guide
your life along its rightful course? Who first drew the material of your body forth from the fundamental impurity of
primordial matter into true being?

4. "Pitying the shapeless face which so often seemed to
cry out to me, I stamped it with the seal of humanity, and
dignified what was bereft of dignifying features with the
clothing of a nobler form. With regard to bodily service,
in assigning the different functions of the members, I instructed the senses to stand guard as watchmen of the
bodily city, so that, like sentinels alert to enemies without,
they might defend the body from external intrusions. Thus
the entire material body, processing to marriage adorned
with the noble regalia of its natural attributes, might be happily united with the husband spirit, and the husband not refuse to marry her, offended by the baseness of his bride.

5. "I also equipped your spirit with valuable powers, lest it
be poorer than the body and envy its accomplishments. I assigned to it the power of active intelligence, which pursues

in notitiae indagine, easdem intellectas concluderet. Cui etiam rationis impressi signaculum, quae suae discretionis ventilabro falsitatis inania a seriis veritatis secernat. Per me etiam tibi memorialis ancillatur potentia, quae in suae recordationis armario nobilem censum scientiae thesaurizat. Hiis ergo utrumque beavi muneribus, ut neuter vel suam gemeret paupertatem, vel de alterius affluentia quereretur. Sicut ergo praefatae nuptiae meo sunt celebratae consensu, sic pro meo arbitrio eadem cassabitur copula maritalis.

6. "Nec in te solo particulariter, verum etiam in universis universaliter meae potentiae largitas elucescit. Ego illa sum quae ad exemplarem mundanae machinae similitudinem hominis exemplavi naturam, ut in ea velut in speculo ipsius mundi scripta natura compareat. Sicut enim quatuor elementorum concors discordia, unica pluralitas, consonantia dissonans, consensus dissentiens, mundialis regiae structuram conciliat, sic quatuor complexionum compar disparitas, inaequalis aequalitas, difformis conformitas, diversa idemptitas, aedificium corporis humani compaginat. Et quae qualitates inter elementa mediatrices conveniunt, eaedem inter quatuor humores pacis sanciunt firmitatem. Et sicut contra ratam firmamenti volutionem motu contradictorio exercitus militat planetarum, sic in homine sensualitatis rationisque continua reperitur hostilitas.

7. "Rationis enim motus ab ortu caelestium oriens, occasum pertransiens terrenorum, considerando regiratur in caelum. Econtrario vero, sensualitatis motus planetici

difficult matters in its search for knowledge and holds them fast once understood. I also impressed upon it the seal of reason, which with the winnowing fan of its discernment distinguishes empty falsehood from serious truth. It is also through me that the power of memory is at your service, which stores in the chest of remembrance the noble wealth of knowledge. Thus I blessed both body and spirit with my gifts, so that neither might lament its poverty, or complain of the affluence of the other. And just as the marriage I spoke of is celebrated with my consent, so this same marital bond will be annulled in accordance with my judgment.

6. "The generous exercise of my power shows forth not just in you alone, but in the whole created universe. I am she who modeled the nature of man in imitation of the model of the cosmic order, so that in his nature, as in a mirror, one might see this natural order inscribed. For just as the concordant discord of the four elements, a uniform plurality, a dissonant consonance, a dissenting consensus, holds together the structure of the cosmic realm, so the compatible incompatibility of four temperaments, an unequal equality, a dissident conformity, a differing identity, holds together the edifice of the human body. And the same qualities that act as mediators between the elements also solemnize the stable bond of peace among the four humors. And just as the army of the planets marches on a course contradictory to the fixed revolution of the firmament, so there is found in man an unceasing hostility between reason and sensuality.

7. "For the movement of reason, arising from a celestial source, and passing through the fallen state of earthly life, returns to heaven in contemplation. But in a contrary manner the planetlike movements of sensuality, opposing the

contra rationis firmamentum in terrestrium occidens obli-
cando labuntur. Haec mentem humanam in vitiorum occasum deducit ut occidat. Illa in orientem virtutum ut oriatur
invitat. Haec hominem in bestiam degenerando transmutat.
Illa hominem in deum potentialiter transfigurat. Illa contemplationis lumine mentis noctem illuminat. Haec concu-
piscentiae nocte mentis lumen eliminat. Illa hominem facit
disputare cum angelis. Haec eundem cogit debachari cum
brutis. Illa in exilio docet hominem patriam invenire. Haec
in patria cogit hominem exulare.

8. "Nec in hac re hominis natura meae dispensationis potest ordinem accusare. De rationis enim consilio tale contradictionis duellum inter hos pugiles ordinavi ut, si in hac
disputatione ad redargutionem sensualitatem ratio poterit
inclinare, antecedens victoria praemio consequente non ca-
reat. Praemia enim victoriis comparata ceteris muneribus
pulcrius elucescunt. Munera enim empta laboribus iocun-
dius omnibus clarescunt gratuitis. Maioris enim laudis meretur praeconia qui laborando munus recipit quam qui repe-
rit otiando. Labor enim antecedens, quandam consequenti
praemio infundens dulcedinem, maiori favore praemiat la-
borantem. In hiis ergo amplioribusque Naturae muneribus
mundus in homine suas invenit qualitates.

9. "Attende qualiter in hoc mundo velut in nobili civitate
quaedam reipublicae maiestas moderamine rato sancitur. In
caelo enim, velut in arce civitatis humanae, imperialiter residet Imperator aeternus, a quo aeternaliter exiit edictum, ut

firmament of reason, sink downward to the dark end of earthly things. These draw the human mind into the sunset of vice that it may die. The other summons it into the sunrise of virtue that it may be renewed. One by its degenerative power turns a man to a beast. The other has the power to transform a man into a god. One illumines the darkness of the mind with the light of contemplation. The other drives away the light of the mind with the dark night of concupiscence. One enables man to hold discourse with angels. The other compels him to debauch himself with beasts. One teaches man in his exile to find his homeland. The other drives man to live as an exile within his homeland.

8. "And human nature cannot blame my ordering and management of all this. For it is on the advice of reason that I ordained such a war of contradiction between these two antagonists, so that if Reason is able to force sensuality to yield to refutation in this dispute, the antecedent victory will not lack its consequent reward. For rewards obtained by victories shine more brightly than other gifts. Gifts bought with labor give off a more pleasing light than those freely given. For he who receives a gift in return for his labor deserves to be heralded with greater praise than one who receives it while sitting idle. Antecedent labor, imparting to the consequent reward a certain sweetness, rewards the laborer with greater approbation. In these ways, then, and in the still greater gifts of Nature, the universe discovers its own qualities in humankind.

9. "Observe how, in this universe as in a noble city, a kind of majestic civil order is ensured by well considered governance. For in the heavens, as in the citadel of the human city, the eternal Emperor dwells in imperial state. From him

singularum rerum notitiae in suae providentiae libro scribantur. In aere vero, velut in urbis medio, caelestis angelorum exercitus militans administratione vicaria suam homini adhibet diligentem custodiam. Homo vero, velut alienigena habitans in mundi suburbio, angelicae militiae obedientiam non denegat exhibere. In hac ergo republica Deus est imperans, angelus operans, homo obtemperans. Deus hominem imperando creat, angelus operando procreat, homo obtemperando se recreat. Deus rem auctoritate disponit; angelus actione componit; homo se operantis voluntati supponit. Deus imperat auctoritatis magisterio, angelus operatur actionis ministerio, homo obtemperat regenerationis misterio.

10. "Iam nimis nostrae ratiocinationis series evagatur, quae ad ineffabile deitatis archanum tractatum audet attollere. Ad cuius rei intelligentiam nostrae mentis languescunt suspiria. Huius ergo ordinatissimae reipublicae in homine resultat simulacrum. In arce enim capitis imperatrix Sapientia conquiescit, cui tamquam deae ceterae potentiae velut semideae obsequuntur. Ingenialis namque potentia potestasque logistica, virtus etiam praeteritorum recordativa, diversis capitis thalamis habitantes, eius fervescunt obsequio. In corde vero velut in medio civitatis humanae Magnanimitas suam collocavit mansionem, quae sub Prudentiae principatu suam professa militiam, prout eiusdem imperium deliberat operatur. Renes vero tanquam suburbia cupidinariis voluptatibus partem corporis largiuntur extremam quae, Magnanimitatis obviare non audentes imperio, eius

eternally the edict has gone forth that knowledge of all things must be inscribed in the book of his providence. In the air, as in the center of the city, the ranks of the heavenly army of angels in their delegated role watch diligently over mankind. Man, dwelling like a foreigner on the outskirts of the universe, does not refuse to show obedience to the angelic host. In this state, then, God is the ruler, the angels his agents, man his obedient subject. God creates man by his command, the angels carry out the work of creation, man through obedience recreates himself. God by his authority orders creation; the angels by their activity fashion creation; man, a creature, submits himself to the will of these operative powers. God commands in the majesty of his authority; the angels perform an active ministry; man, through the mystery of regeneration, obeys.

10. "But the course of our thinking strays too freely when it dares to raise our discourse to the ineffable mysteries of the divine; our mind sighs wearily as it seeks to understand these things. The image of this perfectly ordered state, then, is clearly seen in man. For in the citadel of the head resides the empress Wisdom, to whom the other faculties show obedience as if she were a goddess and they were demigoddesses. For ingenuity, and the logical faculty, and the power to record things past, dwelling in different chambers of the head, obey her eagerly. In the heart, as the center of the human city, Magnanimity has established her dwelling; having pledged herself to serve under the command of Providence, she acts in accordance with her commander's decisions. The loins, as it were the outskirts of the city, concede this lowest region of the body to physical desire. Not daring to go against the authority of Magnanimity, they obey her will.

obtemperant voluntati. In hac ergo republica, Sapientia imperantis suscipit vicem; Magnanimitas operantis similitudinem, Voluptas obtemperantis usurpat imaginem.

11. "In aliis etiam humani corporis forma mundi furatur effigiem. Sicut enim in mundo solaris caloris beneficium rebus medicatur languentibus, sic in homine calor a cordis fundamento procedens humani corporis partes vivificando exhilarat. Sicut etiam luna in machina mundiali multi humoris mater existit, sic epar in homine membris humorem impartitur conformem. Et sicut luna solis lumine defraudata languescit, sic vivificante cordis solatio virtus epatis viduata torpescit. Et sicut aer solis absentatione obscuritate vestitur, sic sine cordis beneficio vitalis potentia spiritus inanitur.

12. "Praeter haec vide qualiter mundus variis temporum Protheatus successibus, nunc veris lascivit infantia, nunc aestatis iuventute progreditur; nunc virilitate maturescit autumpni; nunc hiemis senectute canescit. Compar vicissitudo temporis eademque varietas hominis inmutat aetatem. Cum enim humanae aetatis aurora consurgit, ver homini oritur matutinum; cumque vitae curriculum metas aetatis perficit longiores, homo iuventutis meridiatur aestate. Sed, cum vita prolixior quasi nonam aetatis horam compleverit, homo in autumpnum virilitatis evadit; aetateque in occidens inclinata, iam vitae vesperam senio nuntiante, hyemale gelicidium senectutis hominem suis cogit albicare pruinis.

In this state, then, Wisdom, occupies the position of ruler, Magnanimity can be compared to a minister, and Desire claims the role of obedient subject.

11. "In other respects, too, the form of the human body bears a hidden resemblance to the universe. For just as in the universe the sun's beneficent heat has a curative influence on whatever is languishing, so in man the heat that proceeds from the heart at the center renews the extremities of the human body by its vital power. And just as in the universal system the moon is the mother of many humors, so in man the liver sends equivalent humors into the limbs. And just as the moon grows pale when deprived of the light of the sun, so the power of the liver grows listless when bereft of the heart's vital comfort. And just as air, when the sun is absent, is veiled in darkness, so without the kindly influence of the heart the vital power of the spirit is reduced to nothing.

12. "Besides all this, consider how the universe, Protean in its changing sequence of seasons, first plays in the infancy of springtime, advances through the youth of summer, gains the maturity of autumn manhood, and grows gray in wintry old age. A comparable changing of seasons and similar alterations transform the life of man. For when the dawn of human life arises, man's spring morning is beginning. And when the course of his life has passed through a further stage, the man is at his ease in the midsummer of youth. But an extended life has, so to speak, completed its ninth hour, the man passes into the autumn of manhood. And as it descends into the west, and debility is already announcing the evening of life, the wintry chill of old age covers the man with its white frost.

13. "In hiis omnibus meae potentiae ineffabiliter resultat effectus, sed tamen plerisque meae potestatis faciem palliare decrevi figuris, defendens a vilitate secretum, ne si eis de me familiarem impartirem scientiam, quae apud eos primitus ignota vigerent, postmodum iam nota vilescerent. Ut enim vulgare testatur proverbium, 'Familiaris rei communicatio contemptus mater existit.' Aristotelicaeque auctoritatis tuba proclamat quia 'Ille maiestatem minuit secretorum qui indignis secreta divulgat.'

14. "Sed ne in hac meae potestatis praerogativa Deo videar quasi arrogans derogare, certissime Summi Magistri me humilem profiteor esse discipulam. Ego enim operans operantis Dei non valeo expresse inhaerere vestigiis, sed a longe quasi suspirans operantem respicio. Eius enim operatio simplex, mea operatio multiplex; eius opus sufficiens, meum opus deficiens; eius opus mirabile, meum opus mutabile. Ille innascibilis, ego nata. Ille faciens, ego facta. Ille mei opifex operis, ego opus opificis. Ille operatur ex nichilo, ego mendico opus ex aliquo. Ille suo operatur in numine, ego operor illius sub nomine. Ille rem solo nutu iubet existere, mea vero operatio operationis est nota divinae. Et respectu divinae potentiae meam potentiam impotentiam esse cognoscas, meum effectum scias esse defectum, meum vigorem vilitatem esse perpendas.

15. "Auctoritatem Theologicae consule facultatis, cuius fidelitati potius quam mearum rationum firmitati dare debes assensum. Iuxta enim ipsius fidele testimonium homo mea actione nascitur, Dei auctoritate renascitur. Per me a non

13. "In all of this the ineffable effect of my powers is clear. Nevertheless I have seen fit to veil the face of my authority from the many with figures, to protect my mysteries from debasement. If I should grant them intimate knowledge of myself, what at first was esteemed by them because unknown would lose its value once it became known. For as the common proverb declares, 'the revealing of a private matter is the mother of contempt.' And the trumpet of Aristotelian authority proclaims that 'he who divulges mysteries to the unworthy robs the mysteries of their dignity.'

14. "But lest I should seem to arrogantly disparage the power of God in thus asserting my own, I most certainly declare myself a humble disciple of the supreme teacher. For my work is not capable of following closely the footsteps of the work of God; instead I sigh as I behold his work from afar. His working is simple, mine is manifold. His is complete, mine is incomplete. His is miraculous, mine is changeable. He is unborn, I was born. He is the maker, I was made. He is the artisan of my work, I am the work of the artisan. He produces his works from nothing, I beg my works from another. He works through his own divinity, I work in his name. He commands a thing to exist by his mere nod; my workings are a mere trace of the workings of the divine. Understand that in relation to divine power my power is impotence; know that my successes are failures; consider my strength to be as nothing.

15. "Be guided by the authority of the teachings of Theology. It is to their grounding in faith rather than to the firmness of my reasonings that you should give assent. For according to their faithful testimony man is born through my agency, but reborn through divine authority. Through me he

esse vocatur ad esse; per ipsum ab esse in melius esse producitur. Per me homo procreatur ad mortem, per ipsum re-
creatur ad vitam. Sed ab hoc secundae nativitatis misterio
meae professionis ministerium relegatur, nec talis nativitas
tali indiget obstetrice; sed potius ego Natura huius nativitatis naturam ignoro, et ad haec intelligenda mei intellectus
hebet acumen, meae rationis confunditur lumen. Intelligentia non intellecta miratur, insensibilibus sensus confunditur.
Et cum in his omnis naturalium ratio langueat, sola fidei firmitate tantae rei veneremur archanum.

16. "Nec mirum, si in hiis Theologia suam michi familiari-
tatem non exhibet, quoniam in plerisque non adversa sed
diversa sentimus. Ego ratione fidem, illa fide comparat rationem. Ego scio ut credam, illa credit ut sciat. Ego consentio
sentiens, illa sentit consentiens. Ego vix visibilia video, illa
inconprehensibilia conprehendit in speculo. Ego vix minima
metior intellectu, illa immensa ratione metitur. Ego quasi
bestialiter in terra deambulo, illa caeli militat in secreto.

17. "Et cum de praedictis tractare mei non sit officii, tamen ad hoc sermonem evagari permisi, ut respectu superla-
tivae Dei potentiae meam potentiam diminutivam esse
non dubites. Sed quamvis meus effectus divinae potentiae
deficiat comparatus, tamen humanae potentiae proficit
coaequatus. Et sic in quodam comparationis triclinio, tres

is summoned from nonexistence into existence, through him he is raised from existence into a better state. Through me man is procreated unto death; through him he is recreated unto life. But from this mystery of a second birth the ministry I perform is excluded; such a birth has no need of a midwife such as I. Thus I, Nature, know not the nature of this nativity; in seeking to understand these things the acuteness of my understanding is dulled, the lamp of reason is disturbed. The intellect marvels at things beyond its intelligence; sense is confounded by things inaccessible to sense. And since in these matters all natural reasoning is powerless, it is only on the firm basis of faith that we may venerate so great a mystery.

16. "And it is no wonder that in these matters Theology does not reveal to me her intimate knowledge, since in many ways our purposes, though not opposed, are different. I by reasoning prepare the way for faith; she by faith supplements reason. I know that I may believe, she believes that she may know. I assent to what I understand, she understands by assenting. I scarcely see what is visible, she in a mirror comprehends what is beyond understanding. My intellect can barely assess the smallest thing; her reason measures things immeasurable. I wander about the earth like a beast; she soldiers in the hidden depths of heaven.

17. "Though it is not my office to discourse about these matters, I have nonetheless allowed my discourse to stray in this way that you may have no doubt that in respect to the superlative power of God my own power is diminutive. But though my capability falls short when compared with divine power, it gains in stature when set beside the powers of man. Thus in a kind of three-sided comparison we can speak of

potestatis gradus possumus invenire, ut Dei potentia super-lativa, Naturae comparativa, hominis positiva dicatur.

18. "Haec omnia sine omni scrupulo quaestionis, de me tibi familiarem largiuntur notitiam. Et ut familiarius loquar, ego sum Natura, quae meae dignationis munere te meae presentiae compotivi, meoque sum dignata beare colloquio."

19. Dum per haec verba michi Natura naturae suae faciem develaret, suaque ammonitione quasi clave praeambula cognitionis suae mihi ianuam reseraret, a meae mentis confinio stuporis evaporavit nubecula. Et per hanc ammonitionem, velut quodam potionis remedio, omnes fantasiae reliquias quasi nauseans stomachus mentis evomuit. A meae mentis igitur peregrinatione ad me reversus ex integro, ad Naturae devolutus vestigia, salutationis vice pedes osculorum multi-plici impressione signavi, postque me explicans erigendo, cum reverenti capitis humiliatione, velut maiestati divinae ei voce viva salutis obtuli libamentum.

20. Consequenter vero ad excusationis asilum confugiens, precibus humilitatis melle conditis eius benivolentiam exo-rabam, ne vel meae temeritatis assignaret errori, vel indigna-tionis supercilio deputaret, vel ingratitudinis venenis ascri-beret, quod eius adventui nullam hilaritatis festivitatem persolveram, sed potius eius apparentia, velut monstruosi fantasmatis anomala apparitione percussus, adulterina exta-sis morte fueram soporatus; dicens non esse mirandum si in tantae deitatis praesentia meae umbra mortalitatis expalluit, si in tantae maiestatis meridie meae discretionis

three levels of power, and say that God's power is superlative, Nature's is comparative, and man's is positive.

18. "All this information has granted you, without the slightest hesitation, an intimate knowledge of me. And let me speak more familiarly still: I am Nature, and by the gift of my favor I have allowed you to partake of my presence and deigned to bless you with my discourse."

19. While Nature with these words was unveiling for me the face of her nature, and through her instruction, as if with a preambulatory key, was opening the door to my recognition of her, the cloud of dullness evaporated from within my mind. Through her teaching, as if by means of some curative potion, my mind's stomach, as if nauseous, vomited forth all traces of fantasy. Thus wholly restored to myself after my mind's journeying, I fell at Nature's feet and, by way of greeting, stamped them with the impression of many kisses. Then drawing myself erect, and with my head reverently bowed, I offered to her, as if to divine majesty, a libation of welcoming speech.

20. After this I fled to the shelter of excuses, and sought to win her to kindness with prayers steeped in honeyed humility, lest she attribute to a mistaken rashness, impute to haughty disdain, or ascribe to poisonous ingratitude my having made no festive display of joy at her arrival; instead I had been stricken at her appearance as if by the uncanny apparition of some monstrous phantasm, and succumbed to the false death of alienation of mind. I declared that it was not to be wondered at if in the presence of so great a divinity my shadowy mortality grew pale, if amid the noonday brilliance of such majesty the little beam of my understanding

radiolus in vesperam exorbitationis evanuit, si in tantae felicitatis apparentia meae pannositas infelicitatis erubuit, cum humanae fragilitati ignorantiae tenebrosa caligo, admirationis impotens hebetudo, frequensque stuporis concussio quodam germanitatis foedere socientur, ut ex horum sociali contubernio humanae naturae fragilitas, quasi a disciplina convictus suos mores informans, in novorum primitiis, in magnorum stupendis et ignorantia tenebrari et stupore percuti et admiratione soleat vulnerari.

21. Dum haec excusationis via reginae auditum michi pararet favoralem, eiusque gratiam favoralius mereretur, insuper michi conpararet audiendi maiora fiduciam, cuiusdam meae dubitationis ambiguum quae nimiae inquietationis impulsu meae mentis concutiebat hospitium, eius exponens examini, in haec verba quaestionis exivi:

7

"O Dei proles genitrixque rerum,
vinculum mundi stabilisque nexus,
gemma terrenis, speculum caducis,
    lucifer orbis.
5 Pax amor virtus regimen potestas
ordo lex finis via dux origo
vita lux splendor species figura
    regula mundi.

vanished to wander in darkness, if in the presence of such great felicity my ragged wretchedness blushed with shame. For the dark shadows of ignorance, the enfeebled dullness of uncomprehending wonder, the constant shock of stupefaction are joined to human frailty by a kind of sibling bond, and it is owing to this close companionship with them that frail human nature, modeling its behavior on theirs as if conforming to a law of conduct, is apt to be clouded by ignorance, stricken by dullness, and smitten with amazement when confronted with some new thing.

21. Since this line of excuse was gaining me a favorable hearing from the queen and winning her gracious goodwill, and made me increasingly confident of hearing still greater things, I presented for her scrutiny an unclear matter that was causing me a certain uncertainty and disturbing the quiet of my mind with attacks of anxiety. I brought forth my question in these words:

Chapter 7

"O child of god and mother of creation, linkage and firm bond of the universe, bright gem for earthly life, mirror for mortal creatures, daystar for the world.

Peace, love, strength, rule, power, order, law, end, path, 5
leader, source, life, light, splendor, beauty, form, universal law.

Quae tuis mundum moderans habenis,
10   cuncta concordi stabilita nodo
nectis, et pacis glutino maritas
      caelica terris.

Quae, Noys puras recolens ideas,
singulas rerum species monetas,
15   rem togans forma, clamidemque formae
      pollice formans.

Cui favet caelum, famulatur aer,
quam colit tellus, veneratur unda,
cui, velut mundi dominae, tributum
20   singula solvunt.

Quae diem nocti vicibus cathenans,
cereum solis tribuis diei,
lucido lunae speculo soporans
      nubila noctis.

25 Quae polum stellis variis inauras,
aetheris nostri solium serenans,
siderum gemmis varioque caelum
      milite complens.

Quae novis caeli faciem figuris,
30 Protheans, mutas, aviumque vulgus
aeris nostri regione donas,
      legeque stringis.

Cuius ad nutum iuvenescit orbis,
silva crispatur folii capillo,
35 et sua florum tunicata veste,
      terra superbit.

Quae minas ponti sepelis et auges,
sincopans cursum pelagi furori,
ne soli vultum tumulare possit
40   aequoris aestus.

You who, guiding the world with your reins, impose sta- 10
bility on all things in binding agreement, and unite heavenly
to earthly in the closeness of peace;

who, contemplating the pure ideas of Noys, coin the several kinds of creatures, clothing matter with form and with 15
your hand shaping the mantle of form;

whom heaven loves, whom the air serves, whom earth
worships and water reveres, to whom, as to the mistress of
the universe, all things pay tribute; 20

who, linking day to night in alternation, assign the candle
of the sun to day, and make the clouds of night drowsy with
the glowing mirror of the moon;

who gild the vault with an array of stars, illumining our 25
ethereal domain, and fill heaven with starry gems and a varied soldiery;

who in Protean fashion change the face of the sky with 30
new shapes, granting to the throngs of birds the regions of
the air and confining them there by your law;

at whose nod the world grows young, the woods bristle
with curling foliage, and the earth waxes proud, clad in its 35
garment of flowers.

Who lay the threatening seas to rest and cause them to
swell, curbing the flow of the raging ocean lest its seething 40
tides bury the face of the land.

Tu viae causam resera petenti!
Cur petis terras, peregrina caelis?
Cur tuae nostris deitatis offers
    munera terris?
45   Ora cur fletus pluvia rigantur?
Quid tui vultus lacrimae prophetant?
Fletus interni satis est doloris
    lingua fidelis."

8

Praefata igitur virgo, huius quaestionis solutionem in vestibulo excubare demonstrans, ait: "An ignoras quae terreni
orbis exorbitatio, quae mundani ordinis inordinatio, quae
mundialis curiae incuria, quae iuris iniuria ab internis penetralibus caelestis archani in vulgaria terrenorum lupanaria
me declinare coegit? Si affectuoso mentis affectu colligeres
et in pectoris armario thesaurizares quae dicerem, tuae dubitationis laberinthum evolverem."

2. Ad haec ego, sub castigato vocis moderamine, respon-
sionis reddidi talionem: "Nihil," inquam, "o Regina caelestis,
affectuosiori desiderio quam huius quaestionis enodatio-
nem esurio."

3. Tunc illa: "Cum omnia lege suae originis meis legibus
teneantur obnoxia, michique debeant ius statuti vectigalis
persolvere, fere omnia tributarii iuris exhibitione legitima
meis edictis regulariter obsequuntur. Sed ab huius universa-

But reveal the reason for your journey to your petitioner! Why have you come to earth, forsaking heaven? Why do you proffer the gift of your divinity to the world?

Why does a rain of tears water your face? What does your 45 tearful countenance portend? Tears are surely a certain sign of inner sorrow."

Chapter 8

Then the maiden, making plain that the answer to this question was waiting at the entrance, replied: "Do you not know what dislocation of the earthly sphere, what disruption of universal order, what disregard for the world's governance, what injury to justice has compelled me to descend from the inner chambers of celestial mystery to the common brothels of this world? If you would receive what I should say with a mind kindly disposed, and store it in the treasury of your breast, I would unwind the labyrinth of your uncertainty."

2. To this, in a voice chastened and subdued, I gave a fitting reply: "O heavenly Queen, I long for nothing with more heartfelt desire than for the untangling of this question."

3. Then she began: "Since by the law of their origin all things are held subject to my laws, and are obliged to render to me the duty of an established tribute, nearly all are unfailingly obedient to my edicts in duly performing their tribu-

litatis regula solus homo anomala exceptione seducitur, qui pudoris trabea denudatus, impudicitiaeque meretricali prostibulo prostitutus, in suae dominae maiestatem litis audet excitare tumultum, verum etiam in matrem intestini belli rabiem inflammare. Cetera, quibus meae gratiae humiliora munera commodavi, pro suarum professionum conditione subiectione voluntaria meorum decretorum sanctionibus alligantur. Homo vero, qui fere totum mearum divitiarum exhausit aerarium, Naturae naturalia denaturare pertemptans in me soloecisticae Veneris armat iniuriam.

4. "Attende quomodo fere quidlibet iuxta mei promulgationem edicti, prout ratio nativae conditionis expostulat, michi iuris statuta persolvat. Firmamentum cotidiana circumactione circinans universa iuxta meae disciplinae doctrinam, non nugatoria volutionis idemptitate unde procedit regreditur et quo vadit progreditur. Stellae vero, ad ipsius firmamenti fulgurantes honorem, ipsum suis ornatibus vestiendo, breves sui itineris dietas explentes, varia giratione eiusdem spatia metiendo meae militant maiestati. Planetae vero, prout a me meae dispositionis exivit edictum, firmamenti impetum refrenantes ad ortum nisu contrario peregrinant, postque ad suam occasus regionem repatriant.

5. "Aer vero, meis disciplinatus doctrinis, nunc aura benivola gratulatur, nunc nubium fletibus quasi compatiens lacrimatur, nunc corrixationibus ventorum irascitur, nunc

tary duty. But from the rule of this universal order man alone has been drawn away, an unaccountable exception. Stripped of the robe of modesty, prostituting himself in the whorish brothel of unchastity, he dares to stir up tumultuous strife against the majesty of his mistress—to kindle the madness of domestic warfare against his very mother. Other creatures, whom I have graced with more modest resources, are bound in voluntary submission to the requirements of my decrees in accordance with the terms of their ordained role. But man, who has nearly emptied my entire treasury of its riches, seeks to put the natural gifts of Nature to an unnatural use and wounds me with the weapons of a solecistic Venus.

4. "Observe how almost any creature performs its lawful duties to me in accordance with the edicts I have promulgated, as the principle of its nature requires. The firmament, turning about the universe in its daily revolution, returns to the place whence it sets forth and sets forth from the place to which it travels, not in some uselessly repetitious pattern, but according to the dictates of my teaching. The stars, honoring the firmament with their gleam and clothing it with their adornment as they complete their brief day's journey, do service to my majesty as their rotation moves them through their several courses. The planets, as decreed by me in the setting forth of my edict, resist the impetus of the firmament, traveling by an opposing impulse toward their rising, and later return home to the region of their setting.

5. "The air, instructed by my teaching, now pleases us with kindly breezes, now, as if in sympathy, sheds tears from its clouds, now seethes with the quarrels of the winds, now

coruscationibus illuminatur, nunc tonitrus minaci mugitu concutitur, nunc clibano caloris decoquitur, nunc austeritate frigoris asperatur. Aves vero variis sigillatae naturis, meae directionis regimine sub alarum remigio fluctus aeris transfretantes, praecordialiter meis inhiant disciplinis.

6. "Meae vero meditationis interventu aequor terrae firmis amicitiae nexibus glutinatum, coniuratae fidei sacramentum sorori violare non audens, ultra definitae evagationis terminum in terrae domicilia evagari formidat. Ad meae tamen voluntatis arbitrium nunc tempestatis stomachatur in iram, nunc in tranquillitatis pacem revertitur, nunc tumoris superbia in montis evadit ymaginem, nunc in aequatam lineatur planitiem. Pisces vero voto meae professionis astricti reformidant mearum regularum canonibus derogare.

7. "Meae etiam edictionis imperio, quodam nuptiali complexu terris pluviae maritantur, quae prolis laborantes ad fabricam, indefessa parturitione varias rerum species parentare non desinunt. Terrestria vero animalia sub meae dispositionis examine diversas suorum obsequiorum profitentur militias. Terra vero nunc pruinarum albescit canitie, nunc florum crinitur caesarie. Silva vero nunc frondium crinibus capillatur, nunc acuta hiemis novacula decalvatur. Hiemps etiam semina sepulta gremio terrae matris inviscerat, ver inclusa decarcerat; aestas decoquit messes, autumnus suas exhibet ubertates.

8. "Et quid per singula meae narrationis curriculum evagari permitterem? Solus homo, meae modulationis citharam aspernatus, sub delirantis Orphei lira delirat: humanum namque genus a sua generositate degenerans, in constructione generum barbarizans, venereas regulas invertendo

is struck by the menacing roar of thunder, now grows rough with the harshness of frost. The birds, too, bearing the marks of their several kinds, crossing the airy waves with their wings as oars according to my plan, respond with eager instinct to my teachings.

6. "The sea, fast bound to the earth by strong bonds of friendship through my intervention as mediator, and not daring to violate the pledge of faith sworn to his sister, fears to stray beyond the limits set to his encroachment on the domain of earth. As my will determines, however, he swells into stormy wrath at one moment, then returns to peaceful tranquility, then again, swollen with pride, rises up like a mountain, then extends into a level plain. Fish, bound by the vows of my order, fear to disregard the standards of my rule.

7. "The rains, too, by my imperial edict, are wedded in a kind of marital embrace to the land, which labors to produce offspring, and never ceases to bring the various species of creatures to birth in tireless parturition. The animals of the earth proffer the different services to which they are pledged. The earth itself first becomes white with a covering of frost, then puts forth a rich coat of flowers. The forest trees are now topped with leafy hair, now left bald by winter's keen razor. Winter stores seeds in the womb of mother earth; spring releases them from prison; summer heats the crops; autumn displays their abundance.

8. "But why should I let the course of my narrative stray into these matters? Man alone, scorning the music of my harmonious governance, is deluded by the lyre of a delirious Orpheus. For the human race, fallen away from its noble origin, is barbarous in its construction of gender, and

nimis irregulari utitur metaplasmo. Sic homo, Venere Tire-siatus anomala, directam praedicationem per compositio-nem inordinate convertit. A Veneris ergo orthographia deviando recedens sophista falsigraphus invenitur. Conse-quentem etiam Dionaeae artis analogiam devitans, in anas-trophen vitiosam degenerat. Dumque in tali constructione me destruit, in sua synaeresi mei themesim machinatur.

9. "Paenitet me tot venustatum praerogativis hominum plerumque privilegiasse naturas, qui decoris decus abusione dedecorant, qui formae formositatem Veneris informatione deformant, qui pulcritudinis colorem fuco adulterini cupidi-nis decolorant, qui formae florem in vitia efflorendo deflo-rant.

10. "Cur decore deifico vultum deificavi Tindaridis, quae pulcritudinis usum in meretricationis abusum abire coegit, dum regalis thori foedus defoederens foede se Paridi foede-ravit? Pasiphe etiam, yperbolicae Veneris furiis agitata, sub facie bovis sophisticae cum bruto bestiales nuptias concele-brans, paralogismo sibi turpiori concludens, stupendo bovi conclusit sophismate. Mirra etiam, mirticae Cypridis acu-leis stimulata, in patris dilectione a filiae amore degenerans, cum patre matris exemplavit officium. Medea vero, proprio filio novercata, ut inglorium Veneris opus construeret, glo-riosum Veneris destruxit opusculum. Narcisus etiam sui um-bra alterum mentita Narcisum, umbratiliter obumbratus,

practices a most irregular metaplasm that inverts the rules of Venus. Thus a male, Tiresias-like in his strange practice of love, transforms direct predication into composition of an irregular kind. Abandoning the orthography of Venus in his truancy, he shows himself a writer of sophistic falsehood. Evading the natural, analogous path of the Dionean art, he falls into the vice of anastrophe. He works my destruction by such constructions, and his combinations threaten to divide me.

9. "It shames me that I have favored the nature of man with such special beauties and so many privileges; he has debased his dignity by abusing his honored status, has deformed his formal beauty by his disfigured practice of love, tainted his beautiful coloring with the paints of the false lover, deflowered the flower of beauty with an efflorescence of vice.

10. "Why did I deify with godlike beauty the face of the daughter of Tindareus, who made the attraction of her beauty submit to the disgrace of harlotry when, dishonoring the pledge of the royal marriage bed, she foully pledged herself to Paris? Pasiphae, too, driven by a grossly excessive love, in the deceiving likeness of a cow celebrated a bestial union with a brute beast. Concluding for herself by this disgusting paralogism, she concluded for the bull with a bewildering sophism. And Myrrha, goaded by the sting of Venus's myrtle, abandoned daughterly love in her desire for her father, and performed with her father the office of her mother. Medea, a stepmother to her own son, destroyed a wonderful little product of love that she might accomplish a terrible work of love. Narcissus, too, when his reflection feigned another Narcissus, was left in darkness by this

seipsum credens esse se alterum de se sibi amoris incurrit periculum. Multi etiam alii iuvenes mei gratia pulcritudinis honore vestiti, siti debriati pecuniae, suos Veneris malleos in incudum transtulerunt officia.

11. "Talis monstruosorum hominum multitudo totius orbis amplitudine digressorie degrassatur, quorum fascinante contagio ipsa castitas venenatur. Eorum siquidem hominum qui Veneris profitentur gramaticam alii solummodo masculinum, alii femininum, alii commune sive genus promiscuum familiariter amplexantur. Quidam vero, quasi etherocliti genere, per hyemem in feminino, per aestatem in masculino genere irregulariter declinantur. Sunt qui, in Veneris logica disputantes, in conclusionibus suis subiectionis praedicationisque legem relatione mutua sortiuntur. Sunt qui vicem gerentes suppositi praedicari non norunt. Sunt qui solummodo praedicantes subiecti termini subiectionem legitimam non attendunt. Alii etiam, Diones regiam ingredi dedignantes, sub eiusdem vestibulo ludum lacrimabilem commentantur.

12. "Contra hos omnes conqueruntur iura, leges armantur, et ultore gladio suas affectant iniurias vindicari. Non igitur mireris si in has verborum prophanas exeo novitates, cum prophani homines prophanius audeant debachari. Talia enim indignanter eructuo ut pudici homines pudoris caracterem vereantur, impudici vero ab inpudentiae lupanaribus commerciis arceantur. Mali enim cognitio expediens est ad

shadow. Believing himself to be this other self, he brought upon himself through himself a perilous love. And many other young men, endowed with glorious beauty through my favor, but drunk with the thirst for wealth, have converted their hammers of Venus to perform the function of the anvil.

11. "Such is the multitude of monstrous human beings who rampage over the length and breadth of the entire world, by whose bewitching infection chastity herself is threatened. Of those men who practice the grammar of Venus, some are inclined to embrace only those of masculine gender, others those who are feminine, others those whose gender is common. Certain ones indeed, as if heteroclite, are declined irregularly: during winter in the feminine, during summer in the masculine gender. Others, disputing in the logic of Venus, render arbitrary in their conclusions the law that governs the mutual relationship of subject and predicate. There are some who perform the role of the "subject," but are unable to admit predication. And some, who only predicate, have no regard for the appropriate subjection of the subject term. Still others, disdaining to enter the court of Venus, engage in a deplorable game outside her door.

12. "Against all these right protests and law takes up arms, eager to avenge its wrongs with the punishing sword. You should not wonder, then, if I resort to such novel and profane language, when profane men dare to run riot so profanely. I belch forth such words in anger, that men of pure life may revere the standard of purity, and the impure may be warned to shun in their trafficking the brothel of shamelessness. For the recognition of evil is useful as a warning: it

cautelam, quae culpabiles nota verecundiae cauteriatos puniat et cautelae armatura immunes praemuniat.

13. "Iam meae solutionis lima tuae quaestionis scrupulum elimavit. Ideo enim a supernis caelestis regiae secretariis egrediens, ad huius caducae terrenitatis occasum deveni, ut de execrabilibus hominum excessibus tecum, quasi cum familiari et secretario meo, querimoniale lamentum deponerem, tecumque decernerem tali criminum oppositioni qualis debeat poenae dari responsio, ut praedictorum facinorum morsus coaequata punitio poenae talione remordeat."

14. Tunc ego: "O omnium rerum mediatrix, nisi vererer mearum quaestionum copiam tuae benevolentiae fastidium educare, alterius meae dubitationis tenebras luci tuae discretionis exponerem."

15. Tunc illa: "Immo, omnes tuas quaestiones non solum adolescentes, verum etiam vetustatis antiquatas rubigine audientiae nostrae conmunices, ut nostrarum solutionum stabili firmitate tuarum dubitationum tranquilletur impulsus."

16. Tunc ego: "Miror cur poetarum commenta retractans, solummodo in humani generis pestes praedictarum invectionum armas aculeos, cum et eodem exorbitationis pede deos claudicasse legamus. Iupiter enim, adolescentem Frigium transferens ad superna, relativam Venerem transtulit in translatum. Et quem in mensa per diem propinandi sibi praefecit propositum, in thoro per noctem sibi fecit suppositum. Bachus etiam et Apollo, paternae cohaeredes

can punish the guilty by branding them with the mark of shame, and fortify the unoffending with the armor of caution.

13. "Now the file of my explanation has smoothed away the anxious concern of your question. It was for this reason that I came forth from the lofty and secret places of the heavenly court and descended to the darkness of this perishable earthly world, to deliver to you, as my intimate confidant, my lamentation and plaint, and determine with you what sort of penalty ought to be assigned in response to so many criminal charges, so that the punishment, determined by the law of retribution, should bite back at the fierceness of the crimes I have described."

14. Then I said, "O mediatress of all, if I did not fear that the abundance of my questions might cause annoyance to your good nature, I would expose the shadows of another of my uncertainties to the light of your discernment."

15. She replied, "Nay, convey to our hearing all your questions, not only those still fresh, but those coated with the rust of old age, that the pressure of your uncertainty may be soothed by the firm certainty of my explanations."

16. Then I said, "I wonder why, when you recall the writings of the poets, you aim the darts of the invective you have delivered only at the ills of humankind, when we read that the gods, too, have limped on the same aberrant foot. For Jupiter, bearing the Phrygian youth up to heaven, transformed a relational love into something else. By day he conferred on the boy the office of pouring his wine at table; but in bed at night he made him his subject. Bacchus, too, and Apollo, coheirs of their father's lechery, pervertedly turned

lasciviae, non divinae virtutis imperio, sed superstitiosae Veneris praestigio, verterunt in feminas pueros invertendo."

17. Tunc illa, autenticae severitatis vultum vultus vultuositate figurans, ait: "An interrogationem quae nec dubitationis faciem digna est usurpare quaestionis quaerendo vestis imagine, an umbratilibus poetarum figmentis quae artis poeticae depinxit industria fidem adhibere conaris? Nonne ea quae in puerilibus cunis poeticae disciplinae discuntur, altioris discretionis lima senior philosophiae tractatus eliminat? An ignoras quomodo poetae sine omni palliationis remedio auditoribus nudam falsitatem prostituunt, ut quadam mellitae delectationis dulcedine velut incantatas audientium aures inebrient? Aut ipsam falsitatem quadam probabilitatis ypocrisi palliant, ut per exemplorum imagines hominum animos inhonestae morigerationis incude sigillent? Aut in superficiali litterae cortice falsum resonat lira poetica, interius vero auditoribus secretum intelligentiae altioris eloquitur, ut exterioris falsitatis abiecto putamine, dulciorem nucleum veritatis secretae intus lector inveniat?

18. "Poetae tamen aliquando hystoriales eventus ioculationibus fabulosis quadam eleganti sutura confoederant, ut ex diversorum conpetenti iunctura ipsius narrationis elegantior pictura resultet. Sed tamen, cum a poetis deorum pluralitas sompniatur, vel ipsi dii venereis ferulis manus

boys into women, not at the command of divine power, but through the trickery of a pseudo-religious Venus."

17. Then she, exhibiting a countenance of true severity, through the disapproving expression of her face, replied: "In asking this are you clothing in the likeness of a question an inquiry which does not deserve to lay claim to the appearance of uncertainty? Or are you attempting to claim credibility for the cloudy fictions of the poets, which the efforts of the art of poetry have depicted? Does not the more mature study of philosophy rub away with the file of deeper understanding those things which one learns in the childish cradles of poetic studies? Or do you not know how poets prostitute naked falsehood to their audience with no protecting garment, that they may make drunk the ears of the listener with the pleasure of a certain honeyed sweetness, as if by enchantment? Or clothe falsehood itself with a kind of hypocritical probability, so that through their exemplary images they may stamp the minds of men on the anvil of dishonorable emulation? Or that if we consider only the surface coating of literal meaning, the poetic lyre gives off a false sound, but inwardly it proclaims the mystery of a deeper truth to the listener, and thus by casting aside the outer rind of falsehood the reader may discover the sweeter kernel of truth hidden within?

18. "Poets often join historical events to their own playful fabulations by a sort of elegant stitching, in order that from the artful conjoining of these diverse materials a more elegant narrative pattern may emerge. But when poets dream of a plurality of gods, or when the gods themselves are said to have flinched before the rods of Venus, here the

subduxisse dicuntur, in hiis falsitatis umbra lucescit. Nec in hoc poeta a suae proprietatis genere degener invenitur.

19. "Cum enim iam Epicuri soporentur insompnia, Manichaei sanetur insania, Aristotilis arguantur argutiae, Arrii fallantur fallaciae, unicam Dei unitatem ratio probat, mundus eloquitur, fides credit, Scriptura testatur. In quem nulla labes invehitur, quem nulla vitii pestis aggreditur, cum quo nullus temptationis motus congreditur. Hic est splendor nunquam deficiens, vita indefesse non moriens, fons semper scaturiens, seminale vitae seminarium, sapientiae principale principium, initiale bonitatis initium.

20. "Quia ergo ut poetae testati sunt plerique homines praedicamentalibus Veneris terminis ad litteram sunt abusi, narratio vero illa quae vel deos esse vel ipsos in Veneris gignasiis lascivisse mentitur in nimiae falsitatis vesperascit occasum; ista nube taciturnitatis obduxi, illa vero in lucem verae narrationis explicui."

21. Ad haec ego: "Iam meam quaestionem, mater, agnosco redolere nimiae ruditatis infantiam, sed si alia paupercula quaestio, quae tamen michi spondet aliquantulam dignitatem, tuae audientiae auderet comparere conspectui, a te vellem quiddam conquaerendo quaerere, non querendo."

22. Ad haec illa: "Nonne iam pridem sine omni meae refrenationis obstaculo liberas quaerendi habenas exposui?"

23. Tunc ego: "Miror, cur quaedam tuae tunicae portiones, quae texturae matrimonio deberent esse confines, in ea parte suae coniunctionis patiantur divortia in qua hominis imaginem picturae repraesentant insompnia?"

shadow of falsehood begins to shine forth. Yet in such things the poet is not deviating from his proper character.

19. "For when the troubled dreams of Epicurus are soothed and the madness of the Manichaean is cured, when the subtleties of Aristotle are made clear and the fallacies of Arius exposed, reason proves, the universe declares, faith believes, Scripture attests the unique oneness of God, against whom no fault is charged, whom no plaguing vice afflicts, whom no power of temptation can engage. He is a never-failing splendor; an inexhaustible, undying vitality; an ever-flowing fountain; the seed of the seedbed of life; the chief principle of wisdom; the ultimate origin of goodness.

20. "Because many men, as the poets attest, have misused the predicating terms of Venus in a literal way, stories that pretend either that gods exist or that they have wantoned in Venus's gymnasium descend into the darkness of sheer falsehood. The latter I have left beneath the cloud of silence. The former I have brought forth into the light of truthful narration."

21. To this I replied, "Now, Mother, I recognize that my question was tainted by childish ignorance. But if another poor little question—yet one which promises to be of no little value to me—might dare to present itself for your consideration, I would like to ask you about a thing regarding which I seek to learn, not by complaining, but by inquiring."

22. To this she answered, "Have I not long since granted free rein to your questioning without any restriction on my part?"

23. Then I said, "I wonder why certain portions of your tunic, which should be held together by the marriage of weaving, suffer divorce in that area of their conjoining where the painter's imaginings display the image of man."

24. Tunc illa: "Iam ex praelibatis potes elicere quid misticum figuret scissurae figurata parenthesis. Cum enim, ut praediximus, plerique homines in suam matrem vitiorum armentur iniuriis, inter se et ipsam maximum chaos dissensionis firmantes, in me violentas manus violenter iniciunt et mea sibi particulatim vestimenta diripiunt, et quam reverentiae deberent honore vestire, me vestibus orphanatam quantum in ipsis est cogunt meretricaliter lupanare. Hoc ergo integumentum hac scissura depingitur quod solius hominis iniuriosis insultibus mea pudoris ornamenta discidii contumelias patiuntur."

25. Tunc ego: "Iam mearum dubitationum fluctus, tuarum solutionum serenitate sedati, meae menti impellendi largiuntur indutias. Sed si tuo conplaceret affectui, affectuose affectarem agnoscere quae irrationabilis ratio, quae indiscreta discretio, quae indirecta directio ita in homine obdormire rationis coegit scintillulam ut homo, letaeo sensualitatis poculo debriatus, in tuis legibus apostata fieret, verum etiam tuas leges illegitime debellaret?"

26. Tunc illa: "Si sementitiam huius pestis originem velis agnoscere, altius mentis accendas igniculum, appetentius intelligendi repares appetitum. Hebetudinem ingenii depellat subtilitas, cogitationum fluctus attentionis conpescat stabilitas. Ab altiori etenim sumens initium, excellentiorique stilo meae volens seriem narrationis contexere, nolo ut prius plana verborum planitie explanare proposita, vel prophanis verborum novitatibus prophanare prophana, verum

24. She replied, "Now from what you have already heard you can deduce what symbolic meaning the parenthesis represented by this tearing represents. For when, as I have said, many men assail their mother with the injurious weapons of the vices, and create between themselves and her an utter chaos of discord, it is on me that they are violently laying their violent hands; they tear apart my garments, and do all they can to compel me, me whom they should invest with honor and reverence, to present myself, bereft of clothing, in the lewd fashion of a prostitute. This then is the hidden meaning represented by this tear: it is through the injurious assaults of man alone that the rich vestments of my modesty suffer the abuse of being torn."

25. Then I said, "Now the surge of my doubts is stilled by the calming effect of your explanations, and grants my mind a respite from its pounding. But if it were pleasing to your goodwill, I would be eagerly desirous to know what reckless reasoning, what ill-judged judgment, what unguided guidance caused the little spark of reason in man to become so dim that he became drunk on the deadly draft of sensuality and not only became an apostate from your laws, but even warred unlawfully against them."

26. Then she replied, "If you wish to learn the seminal origin of this plague, quicken the fire of your mind, let your appetite for knowledge feel a new hunger, let acuteness banish sluggish understanding, and steady thinking restrain the fluctuations of your attention. As I am beginning from a higher place and wish to fashion the course of my narrative in a finer style, I will not, as before, set forth my explanations in plain and simple words, or profane profane topics

pudenda aureis pudicorum verborum faleris inaurare, variis-
que venustorum dictorum coloribus investire. Consequens
enim est praedictorum vitiorum scorias deauratis locutioni-
bus purpurare, vitiorumque fetorem odore verborum inbal-
samare mellifluo, ne si tanti sterquilinii fetor in nimiae promulgationis auras evaderet, plerosque ad indignationis
nauseantis vomitum invitaret. Sed tamen aliquando, ut su-
perius libavimus, quia 'rebus de quibus loquimur cognatos
oportet esse sermones,' rerum informitati locutionis debet
deformitas conformari. In sequenti tamen tractatu, ne locutionis cacephaton lectorum offendat auditum vel in ore
virginali locum collocet turpitudo, praedictis vitiorum
monstris euphonia orationis volo pallium elargiri."

27. Tunc ego: "Iam mei intellectus esuries, ingenii flagran-
tis acies, mentis inflammatae flagrantia, attentionis stabilitae constantia, ea postulant quae promittis."

28. Tunc illa: "Cum Deus ab ydeali internae praeconcep-
tionis thalamo mundialis palatii fabricam foras voluit evo-
care, et mentale verbum, quod ab aeterno de mundi consti-
tutione conceperat, reali eiusdem existentia velut materiali
verbo depingere, tanquam mundi elegans architectus, tanquam aureae fabricae faber aurarius, velut stupendi artificii
artificiosus artifex, velut admirandi operis operarius opifex,
non exterioris instrumenti laborante suffragio, non materiae praeiacentis auxilio, non indigentiae stimulante flagitio,
sed solius arbitrariae voluntatis imperio, mundialis regiae

by speaking in novel profanities, but instead will adorn shameful matters with the gilt trappings of modest speech, and the varied adornments of graceful language. For it is appropriate to decorate the dross of the vices we have named with gilded terms, and to sweeten their vicious foulness with the scent of honeyed words, lest the stench of this great dung heap be spread too far abroad by the breeze, and cause many to vomit in nauseous indignation. At times, however, as we suggested earlier, since 'it is fitting that our speech be akin to that of which we speak,' the distortion of our language must correspond to the deformity of its subject. But in the discourse which follows I intend to spread a mantle of sweet-sounding speech over these monstrous vices, lest coarseness of speech offend the reader's ear, or foul words find a place on virgin lips."

27. Then I said, "Already the hunger of my intellect, the keenness of my quickened understanding, the ardor of my excited mind, the firmness of my steady concentration demand what you have promised."

28. Then she began: "When God willed to summon forth from the ideal marriage bed of his inner preconception the structure of the cosmic palace, and to represent in actual existence, as a material idea, the mental idea of the creation of the universe which he had conceived eternally—like an elegant cosmic architect, like a goldsmith creating a work of gold, like the highly gifted artist of an astonishing piece of art, like the skilled producer of an admirable work—he fashioned the wondrous beauty of his universal kingdom not with the assistance of any exterior instrument, nor by making use of preexisting matter, not driven by any shameful sense of need, but wholly at the command of his own will

ammirabilem speciem fabricavit. Deus igitur mundiali palatio varias rerum species ascribendo, quas discrepantium generum litigio disparatas legitimi ordinis congruentia temperavit, leges indidit, sanctionibus alligavit. Sicque res generum oppositione contrarias, inter quas locus ab oppositis locum posuerat, cuiusdam reciprocae habitudinis relativis osculis foederando, in amicitiae pacem litem repugnantiae conmutavit. Subtilibus igitur invisibilis iuncturae cathenis concordantibus universis, ad unitatem pluralitas, ad idemptitatem diversitas, ad consonantiam dissonantia, ad concordiam discordia, unione pacifica remeavit.

29. "Sed postquam universalis artifex universa suarum naturarum vultibus investivit, omniaque sibi invicem legitimis proportionum connubiis maritavit, volens ut nascendi occidendique mutuae relationis circuitu per instabilitatem stabilitas, per finem infinitas, per temporalitatem aeternitas rebus occiduis donaretur, rerumque series seriata reciprocatione nascendi iugiter texeretur, statuit ut expressae conformationis monetata sigillo, sub derivatae propagationis calle legitimo ex similibus similia ducerentur.

30. "Me igitur tanquam pro-deam, tanquam sui vicariam rerum generibus sigillandis monetariam destinavit, ut ego in propriis incudibus rerum effigies conmonetans ab incudis forma formatum deviare non sinerem, sed mei operante sollertia ab exemplaris vultu nullarum naturarum dotibus

and judgment. Then God distributed throughout the cosmic palace the various orders of creatures, whom, though set at odds by the incompatibility of their differing kinds, he reduced to an acceptance of regular order, imposing laws and binding ordinances. And thus he converted from hostile conflict to peaceful friendship things conflicting by the opposition of their natures, whose very placement had set them in opposed positions, uniting them by a mutual kiss in a coexistence acceptable to both. Thus as all things were brought into concord by the subtle cords of an invisible bond, plurality returned to unity, diversity to identity, dissonance to consonance, discord to concord, in peaceful union.

29. "But after the universal creator had clothed all things in the outward forms proper to their natures, and joined all things to one another by performing the marriage of their congruent properties, he willed that by means of a reciprocally balanced cycle of birth and death stability be granted to mortal existence through instability, life without end through an ending of life, the eternal through the temporal; and that the serial life of creatures be ceaselessly maintained through a compensatory series of births. He decreed that like creatures, stamped with the seal of manifest resemblance, should be produced from like through the regular process of generative procreation.

30. "For this purpose he appointed me his agent-goddess, his vice-regent, coiner of the distinctive likenesses of the several kinds of creatures, to stamp out the images of things, each on its own anvil. I was never to allow what was formed to deviate from the form imposed at the forge, but through my diligent efforts the form of the copy would be derived directly from that of its exemplar, and it would be deprived

defraudata exemplati facies dirivaret. Imperantis igitur imperio ego obtemperans operando, quasi varia rerum sigillans numismata ad exemplaris rei ymaginem, exempli exemplans effigiem, ex conformibus conformando conformia, singularum rerum vultus reddidi sigillatis. Ita tamen sub divinae potestatis misterio ministerium huius operationis exercui ut meae actionis manum dextera supremae auctoritatis dirigeret, quia meae scripturae calamus exorbitatione subita deviaret nisi supremi Dispensatoris digito regeretur.

31. "Sed quia sine subministratorii artificis artificio suffragante tot rerum species expolire non poteram, meque in aethereae regionis amoenante palatio placuit commorari, ubi venti rixa effaecatae serenitatis pacem non perimit, ubi accidentalis nox nubium aetheris indefessum diem non sepelit, ubi nulla tempestatis saevit iniuria, ubi nulla debachantis tonitrus minatur insania, Venerem in fabrili scientia conpertam meaeque operationis subvicariam in mundiali suburbio collocavi, ut ipsa sub meae praeceptionis arbitrio, Ymenei coniugis filiique Cupidinis industria suffragante, in terrestrium animalium varia effigiatione desudans, fabriles malleos suis regulariter adaptans incudibus, humani generis seriem indefessa continuatione contexeret, ne Parcarum manibus intercisa discidii iniurias sustineret."

32. Dum in hoc narrationis contextu de Cupidine mentio nasceretur, praefatae narrationi meorum verborum parenthesi sincopatae tenorem huius quaestionis inserui, dicens:

of none of its natural attributes. Thus, obeying the command of the commander in my work, stamping the different coins of creation with likenesses of exemplary reality, modeling the likeness of the model, assimilating similar to similar, I rendered the aspects of individual creatures according to their exemplars. Yet my performance of this office was so far subject to the mystery of divine power that the hand of the supreme author directed my actions. For the pen with which I write would veer into sudden transgressions were it not guided by the finger of the supreme governor.

31. "But because I was not capable of creating so many kinds of creatures without the supportive efforts of an assistant artisan, and it was my pleasure to sojourn in the delightful palace of the ethereal region—where quarreling winds do not destroy the peace of perfect serenity, where no misfortune of cloudy darkness covers the sky's unending day, where no violent storms rage, where the madness of riotous thunder never threatens—I established Venus, who was well versed in the work of the forge, as the assistant overseer of my work on the outskirts of the universe, so that under my instruction and guidance, with the aid of her spouse Hymenaeus and their son Cupid, striving to shape the various forms of earthly creatures, matching the craftsmen's hammers to her forges in the correct fashion, she might weave the serial life of the human race in unflagging continuation, lest it suffer a ruinous cleavage, severed by the hand of the Fates."

32. When in the course of this narration a reference to Cupid emerged, I inserted into this narration, as an abrupt parenthesis of my own words, the following question:

"Ha, ha, nisi iniuriosa tuae locutionis sincopatione mearumque quaestionum venatione timerem tuae benignitatis offensam incurrere, vellem Cupidinis naturam, de quo aliquantulum mentionem tua praelibavit oratio, pictura tuae descriptionis agnoscere. Quamvis enim plerique auctores sub integumentali involucro aenigmaticam eius naturam depinxerint, tamen nulla certitudinis nobis reliquere vestigia. Cuius in humano genere tanta per experientiam legitur potentialis auctoritas ut nullus, vel nobilitatis sigillo signatus, vel sapientiae privilegiantis venustate vestitus, vel fortitudinis armatura munitus, vel pulcritudinis clamide trabeatus, vel aliarum gratiarum decusatus honoribus se valeat a generalitate cupidinariae dominationis excipere."

33. Tunc illa, cum temperato capitis motu, verbisque increpationem spondentibus, ait: "Credo te in Cupidinis castris stipendiarie militantem quadam internae familiaritatis germanitate eidem esse connexum. Inextricabilem etenim eiusdem laberinthum affectanter investigare conaris, cum potius meae narrationi sententiarum locupletatae divitiis mentis attentionem attentius adaptare deberes.

34. "Sed tamen antequam ad sequentia meae orationis evadat excursus, quia tuae humanitatis inbecillitati compatior, tuaeque ignorantiae tenebras pro meae possibilitatis modestia teneor extirpare; insuper tuarum quaestionum solutionibus ex voto promissionis astringor; sive certa descriptione describens, sive legitima definitione diffiniens, rem indemonstrabilem demonstrabo, inextricabilem extricabo, quamvis ipsa nulli naturae obnoxialiter alligata, intellectus indaginem non expectans, nullius descriptionis posset signaculo sigillari. Ergo, incircumscriptae rei haec detur

"Aha! Were I not fearful of offending against your kindness by rudely interrupting your discourse with the harassment of my questions, I would like to learn from your description the nature of this Cupid of whom your speech gave a brief foreshadowing. For though many authors have represented his enigmatic nature beneath the veil of an integument, they have left us no definite information. We read that his authority among the human race is so powerful that no man, whether stamped with the seal of nobility, or invested with the dignity of the prerogatives of wisdom, clad in the armor of fortitude, decked in the stately mantle of beauty or adorned by the tribute of some other grace can exempt himself from the universal dominion of Cupid."

33. Then she, shaking her head a little, and in words which promised rebuke, said, "I believe that you too are serving for hire in Cupid's army, and that you are bound to him by a kind of brotherhood born of intimate familiarity. For you are eagerly seeking to explore his insoluble labyrinth, when you should rather be attentively directing your attention to my discourse with its rich abundance of wise advice.

34. "Nevertheless, before the course of my discourse proceeds to what follows, because I pity your human frailty, and am obliged to purge the shadows of your ignorance to the best of my modest ability; because, moreover, I am bound by a promissory vow to provide answers to your questions, whether describing with clear description or defining with appropriate definitions, I will demonstrate something indemonstrable, and extricate the inextricable, though it is a thing bound by no obedience to the natural order, will not allow the scrutiny of intellect, cannot be stamped with the seal of a single definition. Let this then be taken as the

descriptio, inexplicabilis naturae haec exeat explicatio; haec
de innoto habeatur notitia, haec de non scibili comparetur
scientia, stili tamen altitudine castigata:

9

"Pax odio, fraudique fides, spes iuncta timori
    est amor, et mixtus cum ratione furor;
naufragium dulce, pondus leve, grata Caribdis,
    incolumis langor, insatiata fames.
5   Esuriens saties, sitis ebria, falsa voluptas,
    tristities laeta, gaudia plena malis;
dulce malum, mala dulcedo, sibi dulcor amarus,
    cuius odor sapidus, insipidusque sapor;
tempestas grata, nox lucida, lux tenebrosa,
10   mors vivens, moriens vita, suave malum.
Peccatum veniae, venialis culpa, iocosa
    poena, pium facinus, immo suave scelus.
Instabilis ludus, stabilis delusio, robur
    infirmum, firmum mobile, firma movens;
15   insipiens ratio, demens prudentia, tristis
    prosperitas, risus flebilis, aegra quies.
Mulcebris infernus, tristis paradisus, amoenus
    carcer, hiemps verna, ver hiemale malum.

description of a thing uncircumscribed, let it appear the explication of an inexplicable nature, perception of the unperceived, knowledge of what can not be known—controlled, nonetheless, by a loftiness of style.

Chapter 9

"Love is peace linked with hostility, trust with deceit, hope with fear, and madness mixed with reason. It is a blissful shipwreck, a light burden, a delightful whirlpool, a healthy weakness, an insatiable hunger, a famished satiety, a drunken 5 thirst, a treacherous pleasure, a happy sorrow, joy filled with woes, a sweet pain, a painful sweetness, a deliciousness bitter to itself, sweet to smell but not sweet to taste; a pleasant storm, a sunny night, a day of darkness, a living death, a dy- 10 ing life, a soothing pain, a sin of indulgence, a sin indulged, cheerful hardship, pious misdeed, nay, tender crime; giddy game, constant confusion, uncertain strength, solid instability, unstable solidity; foolish reason, mindless prudence, sad 15 prosperity, tearful laughter, feverish rest; a pleasant hell, a sorrowful paradise, a charming prison, a springlike winter, a cruel, wintry spring.

Mentis atrox tinea quam regis purpura sentit
20   sed neque mendici praeterit illa togam.
Nonne per antifrasim miracula multa Cupido
    efficiens, hominum protheat omne genus?
Cum sint opposita monachus moechator eidem
    Haec duo subiecto cogit inesse simul.
25 Dum furit iste furor, deponit Sylla furorem,
    Et pius Aeneas incipit esse Nero.
Fulminat ense Paris, Tideus mollescit amore,
    fit Nestor iuvenis, fit Melicerta senex.
Thersites Paridem forma mendicat, Adonim
30   Davus, et in Davum totus Adonis abit.
Dives eget Cressus, et Codrus habundat egendo,
    carmina dat Bavius, musa Maronis hebet.
Ennius eloquitur Marcusque silet. Fit Ulixes
    insipiens; Aiax desipiendo sapit.
35 Qui prius Anthaeum solvendo sophismata vicit,
    vincitur hoc monstro, cetera monstra domans.
Quodlibet in facinus mulier discurrit et ultra,
    eius si mentem morbidet iste furor.
Nata patrem fratremque soror vel sponsa maritum
40   Fraude necat, fati praeveniendo manum.
Sicque per afferisim male sincopat illa mariti
    corpus, furtivo dum metit ense caput.
Cogitur ipsa parens nomen nescire parentis,
    in partuque dolos, dum parit ipsa parat.
45 Filius in matre stupet invenisse novercam
    inque fide fraudes, in pietate dolum.

"Love is a foul, gnawing worm in the mind, which the king's purple robe well knows, but neither does it neglect the cloak of the beggar. Does not Cupid perform countless antiphrastic miracles, and transform men of every kind? Though 'monk' and 'adulterer' are contradictory terms, love forces both to exist together in the same subject. When this rage is raging, Scylla casts off her rage, and the good Aeneas begins to become a Nero, Paris brandishes his sword, Tydeus is made tender by love, Nestor becomes youthful, Melicerta grows old, Thersites begs for the beauty of Paris, Davus for that of Adonis; and Adonis turns wholly into Davus. Wealthy Croesus is poor, and Codrus in his need is wealthy. Bavius gives forth poems, and the muse of Maro grows dull; Ennius waxes eloquent and Marcus is silenced. Ulysses becomes a fool; Ajax in his foolishness is wise. He who once conquered Antaeus by solving his riddles, though victorious over others, is defeated by this monster.

"A woman, if this madness once infects her mind, will rush to commit any sort of crime: a daughter will treacherously kill a father, a sister her brother, a wife her husband, anticipating the hand of fate. Thus a wife by a cruel aphaeresis, abbreviates her husband's body, when with hidden blade she cuts away the head. Even a mother is driven to deny the name of mother, and lays traps for her offspring as she gives them birth. A son is amazed to have found his mother a stepmother, her devotion deceptive, her kindness treacherous.

Sic in Medea pariter duo nomina pugnant,
   dum simul esse parens atque noverca cupit.
Nesciit esse soror vel se servare sororem,
50   dum nimium Cauno Biblis amica fuit.
Sic quoque Mirra suo nimium subiecta parenti,
   in genitore parens, in patre mater erat.
Sed quid plura docebo? Cupidinis ire sub hasta
   cogitur omnis amans iuraque solvit ei.
55 Militat in cunctis. Ullum vix excipit huius
   regula. Cuncta ferit fulminis ira sui,
in quem non poterit probitas, prudentia, formae
   gratia, fluxus opum, nobilitatis apex.
Furta doli metus ira furor fraus impetus error
60   tristities huius hospita regna tenent.
Hic ratio rationis egere, modoque carere
   est modus, estque fides non habuisse fidem.
Dulcia proponit, assumit amara. Venenum
   infert, concludens optima fine malo.
65 Allicit illiciens, ridens deridet, inungens
   pungit, et afficiens inficit, odit amans.
Ipse tamen poteris istum frenare furorem,
   si fugias; potior potio nulla datur.
Si vitare velis Venerem, loca, tempora vita,
70   et locus et tempus pabula donat ei.
Prosequitur, si tu sequeris. Fugiendo fugatur.
   Si cedis, cedit; si fugis, illa fugit."

Thus in Medea two names are at war, since she seeks to be at once mother and stepmother. Byblis could not be a sister, or confine herself to a sister's role, for she was too much a friend to Caunus. And Myrrha, too submissive to her parent, became a parent by her begetter, a mother by her father. [50]

"But why should I give further examples? Every lover is subject to the wrath of Cupid, and submits to his laws. He is at war everywhere, and his rule exempts scarcely any. The fury of his thunderbolt strikes everyone, and good character, wisdom, beauty, abundant wealth, lofty nobility are powerless against him. Theft, guile, fear, rage, madness, treachery, violence, folly, sorrow dwell as guests in his kingdom. Here it is reasonable to be devoid of reason, restraint is unrestrained, and it is honest to be wholly dishonest. Cupid promises sweetness, but the result is bitter; he instills poison and brings high hopes to a cruel conclusion. His attraction is entrapment, his smile is mockery, his balm carries a sting; his affection is infection, his love is hatred. [55] [60] [65]

"And yet you have the power to resist this madness if you flee from it; there is no surer antidote. If you wish to shun the power of Venus, shun her times and places. Both time and place provide her with fuel. If you approach, she will pursue you; if you flee she too is put to flight. If you withdraw, she withdraws; if you flee, she flees." [70]

IO

"Iam ex hoc meae doctrinae artificio tibi cupidinariae artis elucescit theorica; per librum vero experientiae tibi practicam poteris conparare. Nec mirandum si in praetaxata Cupidinis depinctione notulas reprehensionis intersero, quamvis ipse michi quadam germanae consanguinitatis fibula connectatur. Non enim vel detractoriae malignitatis caliginosa rubigo, vel incandentis odii fervor foras egrediens, vel invidiae tyrannus extra desaeviens ad has invectivas accusationis punctiones educit, sed ne veritatis per se loquentis evidentiam silentio videar strangulare. Non enim originalem Cupidinis naturam inhonestatis redarguo, si circumscribatur frenis modestiae, si habenis temperantiae castigetur; si non genuinae excursionis limites deputatos evadat, vel in nimium tumorem ipsius calor ebulliat. Sed si eius scintilla in flammam evaserit, vel ipsius fonticulus in torrentem excreverit, excrementi luxuries amputationis falcem expostulat, exuberationis tumor solatium medicamenti desiderat, quoniam omnis excessus temperatae mediocritatis incessum disturbat, et habundantiae morbidantis inflatio quasi in quaedam apostemata vitiorum exuberat.

2. "Praedicta igitur theatralis oratio ioculatoriis evagata lasciviis tuae puerilitati pro ferculo propinatur; nunc stilus, paululum ad pueriles tuae infantiae fescenninas digressus, ad seriale praefinitae narrationis propositum revertatur. Ut

Chapter 10

"Now the theory of the art of Cupid is clear to you from this artistic contrivance of my teaching. You can learn the practice of the art for yourself from the book of experience. And it should not be surprising that in the description of Cupid given above I have inserted some small marks of censure, though he is joined to me by a certain clasp of fraternal consanguinity. For it was not the gloomy festering of carping malice, or a furious outburst of blazing hatred, or the tyrannical raging of envy that gave rise to these darts of accusatory invective; it is rather that I would not give the appearance of suppressing by my silence the evidence of a truth which speaks for itself. For I do not bring the charge of dishonorable conduct against Cupid in his original nature, if he were curbed by the bridle of modesty, controlled by the reins of temperance; if he did not transgress the designated boundaries of natural behavior, and his heat did not become a seething swell. But if his spark expands to flame, or his small stream grows into a torrent, his wanton excess calls for the pruning knife, the overflow of his swelling passion requires a soothing medicine. For all excess disrupts the moderate pace of the temperate life, and the infection of unhealthy abundance breaks out into virtual ulcers of vice.

2. "The theatrical declamation just presented, digressing with the wantonness of the jongleur, is offered as a first course appropriate to your immaturity. Now, after this little digression into such puerile low comedy as befits your childish state, let my pen return to the orderly presentation of the narrative already begun. As I have explained briefly

supra praelibando docui, terrestrium animantium materiandae propagini Venerem destinavi, ut varias materias in rebus materiandis excudendo substerneret, ego vero in naturarum picturatione multiplici operibus manum supremae expolitionis apponerem. Et ut instrumentorum fidelitas pravae operationis fermentum excluderet, ei duos legitimos malleos assignavi, quibus et Parcharum inaniret insidias resque multimodas essentiae praesentaret. Incudum etiam nobiles officinas eiusdem artificio deputavi, praecipiens ut eisdem eosdem malleos adaptando rerum effigiationi fideliter indulgeret, ne ab incudibus malleos aliqua exorbitatione peregrinare permitteret. Ad officium etiam scripturae calamum praepotentem eidem fueram elargita, ut in competentibus cedulis eiusdem calami scripturam poscentibus, quarum meae largitionis beneficio fuerat conpotita, iuxta meae orthographiae normulam rerum genera figuraret, ne a propriae descriptionis semita in falsigraphiae devia eumdem devagari minime sustineret.

3. "Sed cum ipsa, genialis concubitus ordinatis complexionibus, res diversorum sexuum oppositioni dissimiles ad exequendam rerum propaginem connectere teneretur, ut in suis connectionibus artis gramaticae constructiones canonicas observaret, suique artificii nobilitas nullius artis ignorantia suae ferret gloriae detrimentum, curialibus praeceptis sub magistrali disciplina eam velut discipulam instruendam docui quas artis gramaticae regulas in suarum constructionum

above, I delegated to Venus the propagation of earthly life in its material aspect; she was to distribute the various kinds of matter, hammering them out in forming material creatures, while I, through the complex depiction of their natures, would apply the final refining touch to her work. And to ensure that the precision of the instruments prevented any taint of flawed workmanship, I assigned her two reliable hammers, with which she might render vain the wiles of the Fates and prepare the many kinds of creatures for existence. I also designated splendid anvil forges for the performance of this work, instructing her that in applying the hammers to the forming of creatures she should be sure to allow only these to strike those anvils, and not allow hammer to diverge from anvil through any transgressive impulse. For the purpose of inscription I bestowed upon her a most powerful pen, that she might depict the different kinds of creatures, according to the rules of my orthography, on pages, provided through my kind generosity, that were prepared to await the inscriptions of this pen, so that she might never permit its writing to stray from the path of truthful description into the sidetracks of false writing.

3. "But since Venus was required by the ordained constitution of generative coition to bring the dissimilar parts of the differing sexes into an opposing connection, to ensure the generation of creatures, I taught her, with a magisterial course of hallowed precepts, that in her connections she should follow the canonical constructions of the art of grammar, that the nobility of her handiwork might suffer no diminishment of its glory through ignorance of this art. I taught her, as one instructing a pupil, which rules of the art of grammar she should adopt in fashioning the unions she

unionibus artificiosis admitteret, quas velut extraordinarias, nullius figurae excusatione redemptas, excluderet. Cum enim, attestante gramatica, duo genera specialiter, masculinum videlicet et femininum, ratio naturae cognoverit (quamvis et quidam homines, sexus depauperati signaculo, iuxta meam oppinionem possint neutri generis designatione censeri), tamen Cypridi sub intimis ammonitionibus minarumque immensis iniunxi tonitruis, ut in suis coniunctionibus ratione exigentiae naturalem constructionem solummodo masculini femininique generis celebraret.

4. "Cum enim masculinum genus suum femininum exigentia habitudinis genialis adsciscat, si eorundem generum constructio anomale celebretur, ut res eiusdem sexus sibi invicem construantur, illa equidem constructio nec evocationis remedio vel conceptionis suffragio apud me veniam poterit promereri. Si enim genus masculinum genus consimile quadam irrationabilis rationis deposcat iniuria, nulla figurae honestate illa constructionis iunctura vitium poterit excusare, sed inexcusabili soloecismi monstruositate turpabitur.

5. "Praeterea Cipridi mea indixit praeceptio ut ipsa in suis constructionibus, suppositiones appositionesque ordinarias observando, rem feminini sexus caractere praesignitam suppositionis destinaret officio; rem vero specificatam masculini generis intersignis sede collocaret appositi, ut nec appositum in vicem suppositi valeat declinare, nec suppositum possit in regionem appositi transmigrare. Et cum utrumque exigatur ab altero, appositum sub adiectiva proprietate,

would construct, and which she should exclude as irregular and unredeemed by any excuse on figural grounds. For since, as grammar bears witness, natural reason has recognized two genders, namely masculine and feminine (though certain men, deprived of the marks of their sex, might in my opinion be assigned to the neuter category), I nevertheless charged the Cyprian, with friendly advice and with mighty, thunderous threats, that in consideration of necessity she should sanction in her conjoinings only the natural relationship of the masculine and feminine genders.

4. "For since the masculine gender takes the feminine to itself by the necessity of the inclination to procreate, if the coupling of identical genders in an irregular way were performed, such that creatures of the same sex were conjoined to one another, this construction could not claim my indulgence either by recourse to evocation or by right of conception. For if the masculine gender, by some outrageous act of irrational reasoning, should demand a gender similar to itself, the construction of this union will be unable to justify this vice by any respectable figure, but will be defiled by a monstrous and inexcusable solecism.

5. "Moreover my instructions made plain to the Cyprian that in her conjoinings she should observe the duly ordained suppositions and appositions, assigning that part distinguished by the mark of the female sex to the role of supposition, and placing the part identified by the emblems of masculinity in the apposite position. Thus the apposite would not be able to stray into the role of the supposite, nor the supposite transfer itself to the place of apposition. And since each is required by the other, the apposite, assuming the property of the adjective, is by the laws of grammar attracted

supposito substantivae proprietatis proprium retinenti, exigentiae legibus invitatur.

6. "Praeter hoc adiunxi, ne Dionaea coniunctio intransitivae constructionis habitum uniformem vel reciprocationis circulum vel retransitionis anfractum, reciperet, solius transitionis recta directione contenta, vel alicuius etiam degrassantis gratiae nimia extensione sufferret, ut genus activum in passivum valeat usurpativa assumptione transire, vel idem in activum suae proprietatis depositione redire, vel sub passivi litteratura activi retinendo naturam, sibi legem generis deponentis assumere. Nec mirandum si pleraeque maximae titulo gramaticae facultatis ascriptae a Venereae artis domicilio patiantur repulsam, cum ipsa eas quae suae praeceptionis regulis obsequuntur in sinus suae familiaritatis admittat, eas vero quae eloquentissimae contradictionis insultibus eius leges expugnare conantur aeterni anathematis exclusione suspendat; cum philosophicae assertionis auctoritas maximarum plerasque diversis facultatibus fateatur esse communes, quasdam vero ultra suarum disciplinarum domicilia nullam habere licentiam excursandi.

7. "Sed quia contra Parcarum argutas oppositiones Venerem novi agonisticae disputationis ingressuram conflictum, ne alicuius tergiversatione fallaciae Venus ab Atropos coartantes conclusionis sustineret argutias, ipsam disciplinam edocui iuxta quae disertivae disciplinae praecepta suarum argumentationum formas excuderet, et quomodo in adversariorum argumentationibus fraudulentis fallaciae latibulum inveniret, ut disputationis agoniam contra adversariae partis insidias posset securius celebrare, et per instantiarum

to the supposite, which claims for itself the properties of the noun.

6. "I also required that the Venereal union should admit only the rightly directed transitive act, and not allow the undeveloped condition of an intransitive construction, or a reflexive circularity, or a transitive that turns back on itself. Nor should it too freely grant the opportunity to digress, whereby the active might cross over into passive, taking over the receptive role; nor allow passive to render itself active by casting off its natural property, or claim for itself the function of the deponent type, preserving its active nature beneath passive forms. It is no wonder if many precepts identified by the name of the art of grammar suffer rejection from the halls of the art of Venus, for she admits to her intimate embrace those who obey the rules she teaches, but those who seek to combat her laws with assaults of eloquent counterargument she halts, exiling them with eternal anathema. For the authorities in philosophical argument declare that many of its precepts are common to several branches of study, but some have no license to travel outside the confines of their own disciplines.

7. "But because I knew that Venus would be engaging in a war of strenuous disputation against the subtle opposition of the Fates, lest through some fallacious subterfuge she should suffer the shrewd entrapment of a conclusion at the hands of Atropos, I instructed her in that discipline, teaching her through which precepts of the art of disputation she might shape the forms of her arguments, and how she might discover the hidden trace of fallacious fraud in the arguments of her adversaries, so that she might engage more confidently in disputatious combat against the hidden stratagems of the adversary party, and refute her opponents'

similia oppositionum argumenta refellere. Iniunxi etiam ut sillogistica eius conplexio, duorum terminorum contenta conpendio, nulli Aristotelicarum figurarum obnoxia, trium propositionum ordinatione congrua texeretur: ita tamen, ut in singulis propositionibus maior extremitas praedicationis fungeretur officio, minor vero subiciendi legibus teneretur. In prima vero propositione nullo verae inherentiae modo, sed sola ratione contactus extrinseci, quasi terminus de termino praedicetur, subiecto inhaereat praedicatum. In assumptione vero relativorum osculorum reciprocis impressionibus expressius minori maior annectatur extremitas. Sed in conclusione expressissimae inhaerentiae vinculo veriori subiecti praedicatique carnalis celebretur connexio.

8. "Hoc etiam mei fuit consilii, ut nullius conversionis retrogradatione pestifera Venereae conplexionis termini, analogicae praedicationis iura servantes, suarum vices sedium alternarent. Et ne consequentis fallacia ex similium conformatione progenita posset industriam Veneris impedire, terminos specialibus specificavi signaculis, ut familiari liberae agnitionis intuitu evidenter agnosceret quos terminos subiectionis gradus inferior, quos vero praedicationis apex superior ex suae habitudinis iure deposceret, ne si complexio terminorum inconsequens proportionatam habitudinem non teneret, inconcinnae nugationis uniformis deformitas nasceretur.

9. "Sicut autem quasdam gramaticae dialeticaeque observantias inimicantissimae hostilitatis incursu volui a Veneris anathematizare gignasiis, sic methonomicas rhetorum

arguments with similar counterinstances. I also instructed her that her syllogistic constructions, though fashioned by the normal arrangement of three propositions, should not be subject to the Aristotelian paradigms, but be content with abridgement to two terms; yet in such a way that in each proposition the major extreme should perform the function of predication, and the minor be bound by the laws governing the subject. In the first proposition, as when one term is predicated of another, predication would inhere in the subject not by any kind of actual inherence, but only as the result of external contact. In the partaking of mutual kisses the major extreme is connected more strongly to the minor by reciprocal influence. But in the conclusion a carnal connection of subject and predicate is celebrated by a true bond of the most intense inherence.

8. "I also advised her that the terms of the Venereal connection should not, by adhering to the rules of analogous predication, render their positions interchangeable by a pernicious, retrograde conversion. And lest the fallacy of the consequent, born of the close resemblance of similar things, should hinder the work of Venus, I took special care to mark the terms with special signs, so that she would clearly recognize, in a free and natural way, which terms belonged to the lower rank of subject, which by the law of their condition the higher eminence of the predicate required. For if an illogical combination of terms failed to preserve rightly ordered relations, the result would be the formless deformity of an inelegant absurdity.

9. "And just as I wished to wholly expel from the schools of Venus certain practices of grammar and dialectic, by attacking them with the utmost hostility, so too I proscribed

positiones, quas in suae amplitudinis gremio Rethorica mater amplectens multis suas orationes afflat honoribus, Cypridis artificiis interdixi, ne, si nimis durae translationis excursu a suo reclamante subiecto praedicatum alienet in aliud, in facinus facetia, in rusticitatem urbanitas, tropus in vicium, in decolorationem color nimius convertatur.

10. "Hiis apparatuum nobilitata praesignibus Venus terrestris incolatus cessit in patriam. Quae cum suis suffraganeis instrumentis ad humanae geneseos seriem contexendam desudando laborans, Parcarumque manibus intersecta subtili acu resarciens subtilius renodabat. Sicque aliquandiu stipendiariae administrationis iura michi officiosissima curiositate persolvit. Sed quoniam ex matre satietatis idemptitate fastiditus animus indignatur, cotidianique laboris ingruentia exequendi propositum appetitus extinguitur, unitas operis totiens repetita Cytheream infestavit fastidiis, continuataeque laborationis effectus laborandi seclusit affectum. Illa igitur magis appetens otiis effeminari sterilibus quam fructuosis exerceri laboribus, serialis operationis exercitatione negotiali postposita, nimiae otiositatis enervata desidiis coepit infantiliter iuvenari.

11. "Et quoniam apud quem desidiae torpor castrametatur, ab eo omnis virtutis militia relegatur, otiique sterilitas pravae sobolis solet fecunditate praegnari; potus etiam inundans diluvium in nimias despumat libidines, cibique effrenis

from the art of the Cyprian those metonymical maneuvers of the rhetors that Mother Rhetoric clasps in the amplitude of her bosom to puff up their declamations with many flourishes; I did so lest by straying into a too difficult metaphor the predicate, alienated from its protesting subject, turn to something else; lest elegance turn to villainy, urbanity to rusticity, trope to vice, and too much color end in discoloration.

10. "Ennobled by this distinctive equipment, Venus entered into possession of her earthly domain. Laboring strenuously with the aid of these instruments to continue the sequence of human generation, she carefully rejoined what was had been severed by the hands of the Fates, mending repeatedly with fine needlework. And in this way for some time she performed for me with the most scrupulous care the duties of the office assigned to her. But since the mind, wearied by sameness, the mother of satiety, grows disdainful, and eagerness to carry out one's undertaking is quenched by the relentlessness of the daily labor, the monotony of a task so often repeated infected Cytherea with boredom, and the effect of continual working took away her desire to work. Preferring, then, an effete life of sterile idleness to the exertion of fruitful labor, ignoring her responsibility for the work of maintaining the continuity of life, enervated by the sloth of too great idleness, she lapsed into childish indiscretion.

11. "And since soldierly virtue is rejected by those with whom the dullness of sloth has pitched camp, and the sterility of their idle state is apt to become pregnant with the fecundity of a degenerate progeny; since drink, too, swelling to a flood, foams into lustful excess, and an unrestrained

ingurgitatio consimiles nauseas superfluitatis eructuat; Venus, his furiis aculeata letalibus in suum coniugem Hymeneum, thori castitatem peste adulterationis incestans, cum Antigenio coepit concubinarie fornicari, suique adulterii suggestionibus irretita letiferis, liberale opus in mechanicum, regulare in anomalum, civile in rusticum inciviliter inmutavit, meumque disciplinare inficiata praeceptum, malleos ab incudum exhaeredans consortio, adulterinis dampnavit incudibus.

12. "Ipsae etiam incudes nativae, suorum malleorum deplorantes absentiam, eosdem lacrimabiliter videntur deposcere. Et quae gladio Atropos universa metenti solebat clipeum defensionis opponere, iam eidem stabilitae conciliationis mutuo foedere ligabatur, fatique falcem in messem humani generis nimium excursare permittens, dampnum nulla novi seminis rediviva pensabat origine; sed potius se gramaticis constructionibus destruens, dialeticis conversionibus invertens, rethoricis coloribus decolorans, suam artem in figuram, figuramque in vitium transferebat. Dumque fornicariis excessibus cum adultero perpetuat concubinatus illecebras, ab eodem prolem suscipiens pro filio spurio compotitur, qui, dum nullius delectationis amoenitate gauderet, nullius iocositatis vellet meridiari deliciis, ut quasi per antifrasim 'Iocus' a iocositate dicatur, ei nomen usus impressit.

13. "Dyonae igitur duo dati sunt filii, discrepantia generis disparati, nascendi lege dissimiles, morum titulis discrepantes, artificii disparitate difformes. Ymeneus namque

devouring of food belches forth a vomit corresponding to
the excess; Venus, goaded by these deadly furies to reject her
husband, Hymenaeus, polluted the chastity of her marriage
bed with the plague of adultery. She joined in fornication
with Antigenius, as his concubine, and ensnared by the
deadly urgings of her adulterous acts, she rudely transformed
a noble work into base labor, legitimacy into anomaly, civilized conduct into coarseness. She destroyed the purpose of
my teaching: Depriving the hammers of the companionship
of their anvils, she condemned them to adulterine anvils.

12. "The natural anvils, bemoaning the absence of their
hammers, seemed to weep in protest. And she who had once
held up a protective shield against the sword of Atropos
which cuts short all life, was now bound to that same power
by a mutual bond of firm agreement; she allowed the scythe
of fate to attack the human race in a continual reaping, and
provided no revivifying growth of new seed to compensate
for this destruction. Instead, destructive in her grammatical
constructions, perverse in her dialectical conversions, using
rhetorical colors only to discolor, she turned art into figure,
figure into vice; for she persisted in the whorish excesses of
lustful concubinage with her adulterer, and becoming pregnant by him was rewarded with a bastard instead of a son.
Since this child took no joy in any delightful pursuit, and
would not be entertained by the delights of any sort of jok-
ing, he was called 'Joker' by a kind of antiphrasis, and custom imposed this name upon him.

13. "Thus two sons were born to Dione, distinguished by
the discrepancy of their origin, dissimilar in legitimacy of
birth, different in moral character, different in form because
of the disparity in their creation. For Hymenaeus is joined

uterinae fraternitatis michi affinis confinio, quem excellentioris dignitatis extollit prosapia, ex Venere sibi Cupidinem propagavit in filium. Antigenius vero, scurrilis ignobilitatis genere derivatus, adulterando adulterinum filium Iocum sibi ioculatorie parentavit. Illius nativitatem matrimonii excusat sollempnitas; istius propaginem divulgati concubinatus accusat vulgaritas. In illo paternae civilitatis elucescit urbanitas; in isto paternae suburbanitatis tenebrescit rusticitas. Ille albis inargentatos nitoribus argenteos fontes inhabitat; iste loca perhenni ariditate dampnata indefesse concelebrat. Illi vallis complacet nemorosa; iste in deserta planitie figit tentoria. Ille in tabernaculis indesinenter pernoctat; iste sub divo dies noctesque continuat. Ille aureis venabulis vulnerat quem venatur; istequem ferit ferreis iaculis lanceatur. Ille suos hospites nectare debriat subamaro; iste suos absinthii potu perimit acetoso.

14. "Iam mea oratio cartulae tuae mentis inscripsit qualiter otii dampnosa pernicies Venerem educavit emphaticam; qualiter diluviosi potus inundatio Venereum patravit incendium; qualiter ex cibi ingurgitatione ducens originem plerosque luxuriae elephantica lepra percussit.

15. "Ecce, super hominibus acuta Veneris febre languentibus aerumpnosae lamentationis carmen cecini querulosum; nunc super aliis, quos aliorum vitiorum morbida turba conturbat, sub cantu elegiaco querimoniosae orationis cytharam temperemus. Multi etenim, dum Caribdis ingluviosae hiatus voraginosos subterfugiendo devitant, in Scillae malignantis abysso inopinata periclitatione miserabiliter

to me by the brotherly bond of confinement in the same womb; a lineage of the utmost dignity exalts him, and he begot Cupid as his son by Venus. But Antigenius, sprung from origins of scurrilous ignobility, fathered his illegitimate son Jocus in adulterous mockery. The solemnity of marriage justifies the birth of the former; the lowliness of debased concubinage accuses the begetting of the latter. In the one shines forth the urbanity of a civilized father; the other is shadowed by the coarseness of his father's rusticity. The one dwells among silvered fountains, their gleaming waters silvery white; the other dwells in regions relentlessly cursed by perpetual aridity. Shaded valleys delight one; the other has pitched his tents on the desert plain. One passes both day and night in the open air; the other spends night after night in taverns. One wounds those whom he pursues with darts of gold; the other pierces those whom he strikes with iron javelins. One dizzies his guests with a nectar only slightly sour; the other destroys them with a potion of bitter absinthe.

14. "Now my discourse has inscribed on the page of your mind how the terrible bane of idleness brought forth an emphatic Venus, how a torrential flood of drink created a Venereal conflagration, how the elephantine leprosy of lust, taking its origin from the unrestrained devouring of food, attacks so many.

15. "Lo, I have sung a plaintive song of misery and lamentation for mankind, enfeebled by the raging fever of Venus. Now let us tune our lyre to elegiac notes and sorrowing speech for those assailed by the deadly host of the other vices. For many who by some clever stratagem have avoided the gaping whirlpool of voracious Charybdis, are miserably shipwrecked by unforeseen disaster in the abyss

naufragantur. Plerique etiam, dum impetuosi torrentis occursus ruinosos evadunt, pigritantis stagni avida limositate viscantur. Alii, dum dependentis montis praecipitia cautela consulente declinant, in coaequata planitie praecipitatione spontanea colliduntur.

16. "Ea igitur quae disseram tuae menti clavo memoriae tenacis affigas, animique vigilantia sompnum torporis excutias, ut mecum maternis excitatus visceribus, periclitantium hominum naufragiis compatiendo condoleas, et praeambulae ammonitionis clipeo loricatus, monstruoso exercitui vitiorum occurras, et si qua pravi seminis herba in horto tuae mentis audeat pullulare, falce maturae sectionis extirpes."

17. Tunc ego: "Iam pridem mea mens, exhilarata tuae disciplinationis conpendio, tuis correctionibus libentissimam aurem inclinat."

Tunc illa:

II

"Heu, quam praecipitem passa ruinam
virtus sub vitio victa laborat!
Virtutis species exulat omnis,
laxantur vitio frena furoris.
5   Languet iustitiae Lucifer; huius
vix umbrae remanet umbra superstes
extinctumque sui sidus honoris

of unforgiving Scylla. Many, too, though they escape the perilous onset of the impetuous surge, become mired in the greedy slime of a stagnant pool. Others, guided by caution, turn away from the steeps of the craggy mountains, but collide on the level plain through their own desire to make haste.

16. "Keep fixed in your mind under the key of retentive memory the things which I will tell you, and drive out sleepy dullness with vigilant awareness; be moved by a mother's tender feelings, and join with me in compassion and pity for the disasters that threaten mankind. Thus, armed with the shield of advance warning, you may encounter the monstrous army of the vices, and if any growth from an evil seed should dare to sprout in the garden of your mind, you may cut it away with the scythe of timely pruning."

17. Then I said, "My mind has long since been heartened by your valuable teaching, and will give a most willing ear to your admonitions."

Then she sang:

Chapter 11

"Alas, what a headlong fall virtue has suffered, overcome by the weight of vice! All the beauty of virtue is banished; the madness of vice is given free rein. The star of justice grows 5 faint; scarcely a shadow of its shade remains; bereft of light, engulfed in darkness, it weeps that the sign of its honor is

deflet, lucis egens, noctis habundans.
Dum fulgur scelerum fulminat orbem,
10 nox fraudis fidei nubilat astrum
virtutumque tamen sidera nulla
istius redimunt noctis abissum.
Incumbit fidei vespera mundo
nocturnumque chaos fraudis habundat.
15 Languet fraude fides, fraus quoque fraudem
fallit fraude, dolo sic dolus instat.
Mores moris egent moribus orbi
leges lege carent, iusque tenoris
perdunt iura sui. Iam sine iure
20 fit ius omne, viget lex sine lege.
   "Mundus degenerat, aurea mundi
iamiam degenerant saecula, mundum
ferri pauperies vestit; eundem
olim nobilitas vestiit auri.
25 Iam non ypocrisis pallia quaerunt
fraudes nec scelerum fetor odorus,
ut pravo clamidem donet odori,
virtutum sibimet balsama quaerit.
Non urtica rosis, alga iacinctis,
30 argento scoria, murice fucus,
formae pauperiem palliat, ut sic
interni redimat crimina vultus.
Sed crimen phaleras exuit omnes
nec se iustitiae luce colorat.
35 Nam sese vitium glosat aperte.
Fit fraus ipsa sui lingua furoris.

extinct. While the thunderbolt of crime strikes the world, the night of fraud clouds over the star of trust, and no lights of virtue offset the deep darkness of this night. The sunset of trust descends on the world and the nocturnal chaos of fraud prevails. Trust gives way to fraud, fraud indeed deceives fraud itself by fraud, so that guile becomes a threat to itself. The customs of the world are lacking in customary morality; laws are ungoverned by law, rights have lost their right of tenure. For every claim is made without just claim, law is imposed unlawfully.

"The world is degenerating. The golden age of the world has long since decayed, and the pauper's cloak of iron now covers the same world that the nobility of gold once adorned. Now the deceptions of hypocrisy do not seek a cover, nor does the foul stench of crime seek for itself the balsam of virtue to provide a cloak for its vile odor. The nettle does not cover the meanness of its appearance with roses, the seaweed with hyacinth, dross with silver, rouge with royal purple, to make up for the defective appearance of what is hidden. Instead crime puts off all trappings and does not adorn itself with the glow of justice. For it openly defines itself as vice. Fraud itself declares its own mad designs.

"Quid tuti superest, cum dolus armat
ipsas in propria viscera matres?
Cum fraternus amor fraude laborat
40   mentiturque manus dextra sorori?
Censetur reprobum ius probitatis
observare probos; et pietatis
lex est impietas. Esse pudicum
iam cunctis pudor est, absque pudore
45   humanos hominis exuit usus
non humanus homo. Degener ergo
bruti degeneres induit actus
et sic exhominans exhominandus."

12

Ad haec ego: "Quoniam in area generalitatis huius intellectus excursor oberrat, intelligentiae vero praefinita speciali-
tas amicatur, vellem, ut vitia quae in quodam generalitatis
implicas glomicello specialissimarum specierum interstitiis
discoloribus explicares."

2. Tunc illa: "Quoniam tuae postulationis rationem eme-
ritam indecens est adimpletionis merito defraudari, tibi
singula vitia aequum est singillatim notulis singularibus an-
notari. Quia ergo iam dictum est quomodo totus orbis in nativae Veneris fere generali periclitatur incendio, nunc restat

"What safety remains when treachery makes even mothers take up arms against their own offspring? When brotherly love works falsehood and the right hand deceives its sister? The duty of righteousness, to show respect to the righteous, is now considered unrighteous; the law of piety is now impious. To be chaste is now held shameful by all, and without shame man, no longer human, rejects the human customs proper to a man. Now, degenerate, he assumes the degenerate behavior of a brute beast, thereby unmanning himself, and worthy to be unmanned." 40 45

Chapter 12

To this I replied, "Since the intellect wanders uncertainly in an area of such broad generality, while specific definition commends itself to the understanding, I wish that you would lay out, in terms of the distinguishing shades of difference of each particular kind, those vices which you have wound together in a sort of tangled mass."

2. She answered, "Since it would be improper not to reward your reasonable and worthy request with the fulfillment it deserves, it is right that I describe each of the vices for you with its distinguishing marks. Because it has already been explained how the entire world is imperiled by a nearly all-consuming fire through the natural power of Venus, it

dicendum qualiter idem generalissimo gulositatis naufragatur diluvio, quoniam gulositas est quasi quoddam Venereae executionis prohemium, et quasi quoddam ad consequens Venereum antecedens.

3. "Nota ergo quasdam filias Ydolatriae veteris, olim medullitus extirpatae, in praesentia instanti suae matris inperium reparare conari, et eam quibusdam prestigiosis carminibus redivivam a mortuis excitare. Quae meretricali officio vultu phantasticae delectationis faciem dealbantes suos amasios alliciendo fraudulenter illiciunt. Quae sub tristi laetitia, sub amica saevitia, sub hostili amicitia, tanquam Sirenes usque in exitium dulces delectationis melodiam facie tenus praeferentes, suos amatores ad Ydolatriae perducunt naufragium.

4. "Quarum una, ut ficticio loquar vocabulo, congruentia proprietatis 'Bachilatria' poterit nuncupari. Haec suo amasio rationis furans igniculum, eundem tenebris brutae sensualitatis exponit, suum etiam more meretricio in tantum debriat amatorem, ut idem Bachum nimis enfatice affectare cogatur, in tantum quidem ut potator, Bacho nimiae dilectionis vinculo cathenatus, eidem divini cultus maiestatem exhibere credatur. Unde homo Bachilatra plerumque Bachum tanquam sui sancti reliquias locali interstitio a se alienari non perferens, in alienis vasculorum capsulis suum deum diu perhendinare non patitur, sed ut sibi eiusdem dei familiarius assistat divinitas, Bachum dolio sui ventris includit. Sed quia plerumque stomachi capsula tanti hospitis divinitatem sustinere non potest, idem deus aut per orientalis portae polum articum aut per occiduae regionis antarticum turpiter evaporat.

remains to tell how this same world is shipwrecked by the universal deluge of gluttony. For gluttony is a kind of prologue to the work of Venus, an antecedent to the venereal consequent.

3. "Know then that certain daughters of ancient Idolatry, who has long since been thoroughly uprooted, are at the present moment attempting to restore their mother's dominion and raise her up from the dead, reborn, by means of certain conjuring songs. Playing the role of prostitutes, painting their faces with a look of imaginary pleasure, they attract lovers with false enticements. But with their bitter joy, their friendly cruelty, their hostile hospitality, like Sirens, sweet unto death, offering a melody superficially sweet, they draw their lovers to the shipwreck of Idolatry.

4. "One of these Sirens, if I may use a fictive term in keeping with her character, could be called 'Bacchilatry.' Robbing her lover of the spark of reason, she exposes him to the darkness of brute sensuality, and in her whorish fashion so intoxicates him that he is driven to devote himself far too strongly to Bacchus—so far, indeed, that the drinker chained to Bacchus by such a bond of devotion believes himself to be offering the god the high honor of divine worship. Thus the Bacchilator, as if he could not endure that the relics of his saint be separated from him by any intervening space, does not allow his god to remain long set apart in a goblet; that his divinity may be more intimately present to him, he stores Bacchus in the cask of his belly. But because often the container of the stomach cannot bear the divine presence of so great a guest, this same god disgracefully wafts forth again, either through the north pole of the eastern gate or the south pole of the western region.

5. "Multotiens etiam Bachi cultor in capsulis ciphorum materiae honore pollentibus Bacchi architectatur hospitium, ut eiusdem divinitas divinius in aureo vase praefulgeret. Unde idem, aethereis nitoribus claritate concertans et smaragdinis viroribus viriditate contendens, plerosque sapores sui saporis maiestate praecellens, potationum filios suarum proprietatum divinitatibus irritat sophisticis, ut illi Bachum tanquam ineffabilis divinitatis archanum ineffabili amore concelebrent. Illi itaque, ne illius divinitatis aliquid remaneat inexhaustum, usque ad faeces Bacchum deglutiunt, sicque suum deum ad Tartaream abyssum ventris cogunt inhoneste descendere. Dumque sic ad genus generalissimum potationis deveniunt, superlativum gradum ebrietatis ascendunt.

6. "Haec pestis non solum plebeae vulgaritatis inimicatur hominibus, verum etiam praelatorum superciliosas sibi facit inclinari cervices. Quibus Bachi gratiae non sufficiunt quas in eum gratia Naturae perfundit, verum etiam arundineam usurpantes attractionem, nunc Bachum ex rosarum connubio gratulantem, nunc floris alterius fragrantiam respirantem, nunc ex hisopi consortio sibi quoddam privilegium arrogantem, nunc aliarum rerum dotibus locupletatum extrinsecis impetuosa gulae Caribdi deglutiunt; in tantum quidem, ut sine mari naufragium, sine tristitia fletum, sine infirmitate letargum, sine sopore sompnium ebrietatis incurrant. Qui dum ebriationis energia percussi operam psalmodiis inpendunt, versus nimia interscalatione interrumpentes crapulae Boream importunum interserunt.

5. "Oftentimes, too, the worshipper of Bacchus con-structs a guest chamber for Bacchus in vessels ennobled by the dignity of their material, that his divinity may shine forth more divinely in a golden bowl. As he vies with the splendor of the heavens in radiance, and his lively color ri-vals the vivid green of emerald, he surpasses all flavors with the nobility of his flavor, and so stimulates the disciples of drink with his allegedly divine properties that they worship Bacchus with a love beyond words, like some mysterious un-namable divinity. Then lest any trace of their deity remain unconsumed, they swallow Bacchus down to the very dregs, thus forcing their god to descend disgracefully to the Tartar-ean abyss of the belly. And as they arrive at this most com-prehensive kind of drinking, they ascend to the superlative degree of drunkenness.

6. "This plague threatens not only men of the vulgar throng, but causes even prelates to bow their haughty necks to it. For them the charms that Nature has showered upon Bacchus do not suffice; adopting the drawing power of a reed, and with the ravenous throat of a Charybdis, they swallow down a Bacchus now joyously wedded to roses, now breathing in the fragrance of some other flower, now claim-ing for himself a certain privilege by consorting with hyssop, now endowed with external riches of other kinds, to the point at which they encounter shipwreck though not at sea, tears without sorrow, weakness without disease, drunken slumber without sleep. When, struck by the elation of drunkenness, they devote themselves to singing psalms, they intersperse the unwelcome blast of drunken excess, in-terrupting their verses with overlong interpolations.

7. "Nec solum praetaxata potus cupiditas, verum etiam plerosque cibi canina inescat aviditas, quorum voluntates inordinariae, cogitationes inconsonae cibi sompniant apparatus. Qui dum cotidianum exactori escae debitum nimis habundanter exsolvunt, exactor superhabundans suo cogitur reddere debitori. Isti quidquid possident in archa stomachi thesaurizant. Et quamvis illud conmissum nec rubigo corrosionis dente demordeat nec vulpeculantis furis sophisma surripiat, ipsum tamen decoquentis caloris turpiori latrocinio turpius evanescit. Isti bursam ad nummorum vomitum, archam marcharum invitant ad nauseam, ut exactori stomacho possint accuratius adulari. Interius ventrem ciborum locupletant divitiis, exterius in nuda et pura et sola positi paupertate.

8. "Haec pestilentia, non vulgari humilitate contenta, profundius se porrigit in praelatos, qui salmones, lucios, ceterosque pisces aequipollenti generositate praesignes, variis decoctionum cruciatos martiriis, baptizandi adulterantes officium, sacri piperis fonte baptizant, ut ex tali baptismate baptizati multiformem saporis gratiam consequantur. In eadem mensa terrestre animal piperis inundatione submergitur, piscis natat in pipere, avis eiusdem viscositate ligatur. Dumque tot animalium genera uno ventris ergastulantur in carcere, aquatile animal secum pedestre aeriumque genus in eodem sepulcro tumulari miratur. Quibus si detur licentia exeundi, egressui vix portae sufficit amplitudo.

7. "Not only this desire for drink but a doglike eagerness for food lures many men whose unruly desires and ill-ordered thoughts dwell on the preparation of meals. When they are too lavish in paying to the collector their daily debt of food, the collector, too richly supplied, is compelled to pay back to his debtor. Whatever they possess, they store in the treasure chest of the belly. And although rust does not gnaw at this deposit with its corrosive tooth, and the trickery of the foxlike thief does not steal it, it vanishes all the same, in a more shameful way, by the foul thievery of the heat of digestion. They urge their purses and coffers to vomit their silver and gold, invite their chests of coin to suffer nausea, that they may honor the demanding stomach with more elaborate flattery. Within they endow the belly with a wealth of food; outwardly they are reduced to sheer, naked, lonely poverty.

8. "This pestilence, not content with the humble crowd, is more widespread among prelates, who, defiling the rite of baptism, baptize, at the font of holy pepper, salmon, pike, and other fish distinguished by an equally imposing nobility, which are tortured with various forms of martyrdom as they are cooked, so that from this baptism the newly baptized may attain a manifold grace of flavor. On the same table a land animal is submerged by an inundation of pepper, a fish swims in pepper, a bird is caught in the birdlime of this same pepper. And when so many types of animal are imprisoned in the jail of a single belly, the water creature is astonished to see the walking and aerial kind buried in the same sepulcher; if permission to go forth were granted them, the breadth of the doorway would hardly suffice for their exit.

9. "Hae praefatae pestes pontem faciunt per quem ad luxuriae lupanaria devenitur. Hae sunt introductiones per quas quis furandi artem ingreditur. Hae morbos pariunt, seminant paupertates. Hae sunt nutrices discordiae, sorores insaniae, intemperantiae matres, immunditiae venatrices. Per has humanum genus modestiae limites excedit, temperantiae frena postponit, castitatis sigilla confringit, meae largitionis gratiam non attendit. Cum enim mea largitas tot hominibus fercula spargat, tot fercula conpluat, ipsi tamen gratiarum ingrati nimis illicite licitis abutentes, frena gulae laxantes, dum comedendi mensuras excedunt, lineas potationis in infinitum extendunt. Qui palata salsorum seducentes acumine, ut saepe et multum bibant, saepius sitire coguntur.

10. "Est et alia Ydolatriae filia, quam (si nominis proprietas suae significationis germanitatem in voce retineat) consequenti vocabulo consequens est 'Nummulatriam' nuncupari. Haec est Avaritia, per quam in animis hominum deificatur pecunia, nummo divinae venerationis exhibetur auctoritas; per quam ubi nummus loquitur Tulliani eloquii tuba raucescit; ubi nummus militat Hectoreae militiae fulgura conticent; ubi pugnat pecunia virtus expugnatur Herculea. Si quis enim armatur pecunia, tanquam loricis argenteis, torrentis impetum Tulliani, fulgur incursus Hectorei, robur virtutis Herculeae, versipelles Ulixeae calliditatis floccipendit argutias. In tantum etenim habendi fames

9. "These plagues form a bridge by which one arrives at the brothel of lechery. These are the introductory stages by which one enters on the art of thieving. These give rise to diseases, sow the seeds of impoverishment. These are the nursemaids of discord, the sisters of madness, the mothers of intemperance, the huntresses of impurity. Through these the human race transgresses the limits of modesty, casts off the reins of temperance, breaks the seal of chastity, becomes unmindful of the gifts I have bestowed. For although my generosity spreads forth for men so many choice dishes, showers them with such bounty, they are not grateful for my favors, and abuse what is granted them in unlawful ways. Giving free rein to the gullet, they exceed all measure in consuming food, and extend the limit of their drinking to infinity. They tease the palate with the sharp taste of salty things, so that they may drink often and copiously, and are more often made thirsty.

10. "There is another daughter of Idolatry who might appropriately be assigned 'Nummilatry' as a suitable name, if the meaning of a name should convey some of its significance in its sound. This is Avarice, through whom wealth is made a god in the minds of men, and the high dignity of divine veneration is offered to money. Because of her, when money speaks, the trumpet of Tullian eloquence sounds hoarse; when money goes to war, the brilliance of Hector's soldiery is stilled; when money fights, the strength of Hercules is overcome. If a man is armed with money, as if with a breastplate of silver, he views with scorn the onset of the Tullian torrent, the lightninglike assault of Hector, the oaken strength of Hercules, the shape-changing subtleties of shrewd Ulysses. For the hunger for gain has grown so

incanduit ut dialeticae muta sit subtilitas, rethoricae languescat civilitas. Ubi nummorum perorat pluralitas iam Tullius sui monetam vendit eloquii, sui pudoris monilia in auri pretium conmutat Lucretia, Penelope suae mercenaria castitatis pudorem deponit in pretio. Ypolitus etiam, si nummi preces audiat susurrantis, suae novercae non vult precibus novercari. Nam si in aure iudicis susurret pecunia Orphei lira, carmen Amphionis, musa Virgilii voce pecuniae suffocatur. Iam dives divitiarum naufragans in profundo ydropicae sitis incendiis tantalizat. Pauper etiam, quamvis materialem avaritiam realiter exercere non valeat, intus tamen archetypam retinet parcitatem.

11. "Proh pudor! Metallorum onera largiuntur honores, ad metalli pondera ponderatos. Iam non Caesar sed nummus est omnia, qui ab individualibus usque ad generalissima honores singulos tanquam mediator excurrit. Nam nummus patriarcha noster existit, qui quosdam archiepiscopatus inthronizat in apicem, quosdam episcopalis fastigii erigit in honorem, hos archidiaconalibus adaptans officiis, alios aliarum pedestrium dignitatum coaequans negotiis. Quid plura? Nummus vincit, nummus regnat, nummus imperat universis.

12. "Quid prodest cum Ptolomeo subterfugientis astronomiae fugas consequi subtilitatis curriculo; stellarum prophetias, spontaneos investigare planetarum errores; cum Euclide geometrichorum aenigmatum secreta penitiora scrutari; in profundum maris intellectu descendere, caeli altitudinem intelligibilibus mensuris attingere; cum Milesio musicarum proportionum consonantes amicitias invenire;

intense that the subtlety of dialectic falls silent, the persuasive power of rhetoric grows faint. Where a sum of money has stated its case, Tullius sells the treasure of his eloquence; Lucretia converts the jewel of her virginity to their price in gold; Penelope, marketing her chastity, casts off modesty for a price; even Hippolytus, should he hear the whispered appeals of money, will not respond like a stepmother to the prayers of his stepmother. For if money whispers in the ear of a judge, the lyre of Orpheus, the melody of Amphion, the muse of Virgil will be stifled by money's voice. The rich man, already shipwrecked in the depths of his wealth, tantalizes himself with the fever of his dropsical thirst for more. Even the poor man, though he cannot actually practice material avarice, maintains inwardly a kind of archetypal miserliness.

11. "For shame! Heaps of coin bestow preferment proportionate to the metal's weight. Now not Caesar but money is all, quick to negotiate every title, from the private to the most prominent. For money is our patriarch, who enthrones certain men at the summit of the archepiscopacy, raises some to the dignity of episcopal rank, assigns others to the office of archdeacon, and matches still others to the business of other more pedestrian offices. What more need I say? Money conquers, money rules, money is lord of all the world.

12. "What does it profit one to pursue the elusive secrets of astronomy in the chariot of Ptolemy, to explore the prophecies of the stars, the independent wanderings of the planets? To examine with Euclid the deeper mysteries of geometrical enigmas, to descend in thought to the depth of the ocean, to attain the height of heaven by mental calculation? To discover with the Milesian the consonant relations

cum Pithagora pugnas numerorum virtute multiplicationis inspicere; cum Tullio, orationem rethoricis colorum stellare sideribus; cum Aristotile ancipiti dialeticae gladio a veris falsa dividere; cum Zenone falsitatem probabilitate tunicare sophistica; cum Donato in accidentium congruentia nectere dictiones; cum Sapientia nostris temporibus nullius fructus praemietur stipendiis, nullius famae eam aura favoralis extollat, ipsa vero pecunia honoris titulos, laudis emat praeconia?

13. "Sola tamen Sapientia super omnem possessionem praeeminet, generosa possessio quae sparsa colligitur, erogata revertitur, publicata suscipit incrementum; per quam nobilis conscientiae thesaurus secretis penetralibus mentis innascitur, fructus internae delectationis acquiritur. Haec est sol per quem mens diescit in tenebris, cordis oculus, deliciosus animi paradisus. Haec in caeleste terrenum, in immortale caducum, hominem in deum deificae imitationis auctoritate convertit. Haec est unum tuae peregrinationis remedium, solum humanae calamitatis solatium, humanae noctis Lucifer singularis, tuae miseriae redemptio specialis; cuius aciem nulla aeris caligo confundit, non densitas terrae operam eius offendit, non aquae altitudo despectum eius obtundit.

14. "Haec igitur, quamvis apud multos qui sensuali bestialitate brutescunt nimia langueat vilitate, apud illos tamen qui in ignem originalem rationis redegerunt scintillulam

of the musical scale? To examine with Pythagoras the battling of numbers through the power of multiplication? With
Tully to stellify an oration with the starry colors of rhetoric?
To divide true from false with Aristotle, by means of the
double-edged sword of dialectic? With Zeno to cloak falsehood with sophistical probability? To connect words with
Donatus so that their accidents are congruent? For Wisdom
in our time is fruitless; she is granted no reward, no favoring
breeze of renown extols her. It is money that purchases the
dignity of high office, money that buys the proclamations of
praise.

13. "Nevertheless Wisdom alone is superior to all other
possessions, the possession of a noble spirit. Spread abroad
it remains intact; when paid out it repays itself; shared with
many it becomes greater. Through wisdom a noble treasure
of understanding is born in the hidden chambers of the
mind, and one gains fruit for inner delight. Wisdom is the
sun through which there is daylight amid the shadows of the
mind, the eye of the heart, the spirit's paradise of delight.
Wisdom transforms earthly into heavenly, mortal into immortal, human into divine through her authoritative power
to imitate the work of God. She is the sole remedy for your
condition of exile, the sole consolation for the calamitous
state of humankind, the morning star in the dark night of
human life, the unique redemption from your misery. No
clouding of the air defeats her keen vision; the hardness of
earth does not hinder her work, nor the depth of water resist her searching gaze.

14. "Though Wisdom suffers from her utter degradation
at the hands of those who live the brutish life of sensual bes-
tiality, she is still not deprived of resounding fame among

praeconantis famae munere non fraudatur. Quamvis enim Prudentia fantasticae adulationis plausibiles dignetur applausus, tamen quia verae Famae haec est gloriosa proprietas, ut appetitores sui contempnat, appetat contemptores, Famam fugiendo consequitur, quam perderet insequendo. Igitur si apud quosdam regnare pecuniam, iacere Prudentiam, militare divitias, Sapientiam videas exulare, ignava tamen opum pondera animo victori calcata subicias, et intestino affectionis amore Prudentiam consecteris, ut penitius Sapientiae matris cubiculum inoffenso intuitu valeas intueri."

15. Tunc ego: "Vellem ut, laxatis reprehensionis habenis, praecordialius Avaritiae filios impugnares."

Tunc illa, ad acerrimas invectionis demorsiones girans suae narrationis incessum, ait:

13

"Postquam sacra fames auri mortalia pungit
pectora, mens hominis nescit ieiuna timere.
Laxat amicitias, odium parit, erigit iras,
bella serit, nutrit lites, bellumque renodat
5 ruptum, nodata dirumpit foedera. Natos
excitat in patres, matres in viscera, fratres
dat fratrum nescire togas; et sanguinis omnes

those who have brought the little spark of reason back to the flame of old. For while Prudence scorns the elaborate applause of feigned adulation, nevertheless, since it is the glorious property of true fame that it scorns those who hunger for it and hungers for those who scorn it, she gains through flight that fame which she would lose by pursuing it. Thus if you see that for some people money rules and Prudence is cast down, that wealth holds sway and Wisdom is exiled, you must cast down and trample on the lifeless heap of riches in a spirit of victory, and pursue Prudence with an inclination born of deep love, so that you may be able to behold with unobstructed gaze, the inner dwelling place of mother Wisdom."

15. Then I said, "I wish that you would slacken the reins of censure and attack the sons of avarice still more vehemently."

Then she, turning the thrust of her discourse to the most bitter and biting invective:

Chapter 13

"Once the cursed hunger for gold has pierced the heart of mortal man, his hungering mind knows no fear. This hunger undoes friendships, breeds hatred, arouses wrath, sows war, raises quarrels, renews battles broken off, and breaks 5 the bonds of truce. It arouses sons against fathers, mothers against their young, lets a brother ignore his brother's robe of peace; and all those whom a common blood unites a

unio quos unit, furor hos male dividit unus.
Dum stomachum mentis ydropicat ardor habendi,
mens potando sitit, et Tantalus alter in ipsis
ardet aquis, viresque siti dat copia census.
Esurit ergo satur, sitit ebrius, optat habundans.
Unus cuncta cupit ipsaque cupidine pauper
efficitur; divesque foris, manet intus egenus.
      "Nil habet ergo miser, cum nil se credit habere.
Divitiis dum pauperiem sua vota repensant,
hospitium cordis et moenia mentis avarae
invadunt hostes multi, multoque tumultu
totam sollicitant humani pectoris arcem.
Nam timor aggreditur mentem, pariterque cupido
concutit, et totam mentis depauperat urbem.
Curarum geminus turbo sic turbat avarum,
cumque timenda timet, mens sompniat ipsa timores;
saepe novos fingitque metus, dampnique timore
dampna luit dampnique malum formidine pensat.
Sic casus varios terroris sompnia monstrant
uxoris fraudes furisque sophismata terror
nuntiat, insultus hostis; iuguloque minantes
mentitur gladios et fulmina dira potentum;
nunc ignis pestes recolit, nunc concipit iras
Oceani, soloque metu iam naufragus extat.
      "Divitis in nummo mens philosophatur, in archa
dum nummum sepelit, nummusque sepultus avari
usibus emoritur; illum non ille sed illa
possidet et totum nummi sibi vendicat usum.
Ut loculis varia nummorum fercula donet,
iniungit proprio dives ieiunia ventri.
Horret avaritiam venter, propriosque negari

common madness drives apart. When the ardent desire for
gain afflicts the stomach of the mind, the mind thirsts as it   10
drinks; a second Tantalus burns in the midst of water, and
an abundance of wealth only intensifies the thirst. Sated,
he hungers; drunk, he thirsts; amid abundance he longs for
more. One man desires all things, and by this very desire
is reduced to a pauper; outwardly rich, he remains poor
within.

"Thus the wretched man possesses nothing, since he be-   15
lieves that he has nothing. When his prayers compensate his
poverty with riches, a host of enemies invade the dwelling
place of his heart and the ramparts of his greedy mind, and
with a great uproar shake the whole citadel of his human
breast. For fear attacks, and desire strikes with equal force,   20
laying waste the entire city of the mind. Thus a twofold mob
of worries disturbs the greedy man: while he fears fearful
things, his mind is imagining fears; he is ever creating new
terrors, suffers ruin by fearing ruin, and measures his mis-   25
fortune by his fear of it. Thus his fearful dreams reveal various disasters: fear tells of a wife's treachery, the cleverness of
a thief, the assault of an enemy; it imagines swords menacing his throat, and the fearful weapons of the mighty; now   30
he dwells on the ravages of fire, now imagines the raging of
the ocean, and already, through fear alone, he becomes shipwrecked.

"The rich man's mind thinks deeply about his money as
he buries it in his coffer, and once buried the money is dead
to his miserly purposes: not he, but the chest possesses the   35
money and claims the use of it for itself. In order to bestow
a full menu of coin on his coffers he imposes fasts on his
own stomach. The belly lives in fear of avarice, astonished

miratur reditus; loculi suffragia quaerit,
40   sed ventri loculus surdas accommodat aures.
Pabula visus habet, et convivatur ocellus
solus in argento, sed venter philosophari
cogitur, et longo patitur ieiunia voto.
    "Non lacrimae, non mella precum, non ipsa perorat
45   pauperies hominis, quin faenore dives egenum
devoret, et tenuem miseri facit esse crumenam.
Pauperis in lacrimis ridet, miserique labore
pascitur, et poenam sibimet facit esse quietem.
Hunc dolor, hunc risus, iocus hunc, maeror manet illum.
50   Hic gemit, hic ridet, dolet hic, dum dedolet ille.
    "Omnis in affectum nummi laxatur avari
divitis affectus. Nec enim datur ulla voluntas
menti, qua possit alias deflectere vultum.
Divitias non dives habet, sed habetur ab ipsis.
55   Non est possessor nummi, sed possidet ipsum
nummus, et in nummis animus sepelitur avari.
Hos colit ille deos, haec ydola ditat honore
divini cultus, et nummus numina donat.
Sic hominis ratio, calcata cupidine, carni
60   servit, et ancilla famulari cogitur illi.
Sic oculus cordis, carnis caligine caecus,
languet, et eclipsim patiens agit otia solus.
Sic iubar humani sensus male palliat umbra
carnis, fitque nimis ingloria gloria mentis.
65   "Divitiis vel divitibus non derogat iste
sermo, sed vitium potius mordere laborat.
Non census, non divitias, non divitis usum

that its due income is withheld; it calls on the coffer for aid, but the coffer grants the belly only a deaf ear. There is food for sight, and the eye alone is feasted with silver, but the belly is forced to be philosophical and suffer starvation while hope grows old. 40

"Neither tears nor honeyed prayers, not a man's very pov- 45 erty can dissuade the rich man from devouring the beggar through interest, making lean the purse of the unhappy man. He laughs at the pauper's tears, thrives on the wretch's hardship, and makes the other's pain a source of comfort for himself. Suffering is the lot of one, mirth of the other, for one there is jesting, for the other sorrow. One weeps, the 50 other laughs, one grieves while the other has done away with grief.

"All affection in the rich miser has given way to his affection for money. For his mind is no longer endowed with the will that could direct his gaze elsewhere. The rich man does not hold his riches, but is held by them. He is not the pos- 55 sessor of money, but money possesses him, and his miserly spirit lies buried among his coins. These are the gods he serves, these are the idols to whom he pays the tribute of divine worship, and money endows him with divine favor. Thus human reason, trampled by desire, becomes the slave of the flesh, and is forced to serve as its handmaid. Thus the 60 eye of the heart, blinded by the obscuring flesh, grows dim, suffers eclipse, and in isolation becomes inactive. Thus the shadow of flesh covers over the radiance of human understanding to evil effect, and the glory of the mind becomes inglorious.

"This discourse does not disparage rich men or their 65 wealth, but strives rather to attack vice. I do not condemn property, or riches, or the practices of the rich, if the mind,

dampno, si victor animus, ratione magistra,
subiectas sibi calcat opes, si denique census
70 nobilis auriga ratio direxerit usum.
Nam cunctas si spargat opes, si munera fundat
dives, et in laudem spiret temptetque favorem
munere lucrari, tamen huius muneris auctor,
ductor et auriga, nisi sit discretio, nullus
75 fructus erit, quoniam laudem non dona merentur,
sed potius merchantur eam, nisi facta decenter
discrete fuerint. Pro munere namque frequenter
laus datur ypocrita, famae simulatio falsa,
symia laudis, honor umbratilis, umbra favoris."

14

"Ecce habes quomodo tenacis avaritiae viscus humanae mentis alis auferat libertatem. Nunc intuendum qualiter insolentis arrogantiae ampullosa ventositas humanas mentes erigat in tumorem, cuius infirmitatis contagione funesta vitiata hominum multitudo, dum se supra se insolenter extollit, infra se ruinosa descendit, sibi derogans arrogando, se deiciens erigendo, se sibi auferens efferendo. Horum hominum aut verborum sollempnis pompositas, aut suspicionis mater taciturnitas, aut quaedam actus specificatio, aut insolens gestus exceptio, aut nimia corporis comptio exterius interiorem mentis glosat superbiam.

victorious, with reason as its guide, keeps riches firmly subject to itself, and if it is reason, the noble charioteer, who   70
finally determines the use of property. For if a rich man
spreads all his wealth abroad, though he pours forth bounty,
is eager for praise, seeks to purchase favor with his gifts,
nevertheless, if discretion is not the origin, the guide and
charioteer of these gifts, they will yield no fruit, since the   75
gifts do not earn praise but rather purchase it, unless they
are made with modesty and discretion. For often what is offered in return for a gift is hypocritical praise, a false pretense of renown, an aping of praise, a shadowy honor, a
shadow of gratitude."

Chapter 14

"Thus you see how the birdlime of grasping Avarice denies
free movement to the wings of the human mind. Now we
must consider how the windy bombast of insolent arrogance
causes the human mind to become swollen. A great many
men are tainted by the deadly contagion of this disease;
when they haughtily seek to rise above themselves they
tumble and fall beneath themselves, diminishing themselves
by their arrogance, defeating themselves by their self-
promotion. The solemnly pompous speech of such men, or
that taciturnity which is the mother of suspicion, a certain
affectation of manner, unusually exaggerated movement or
too-careful grooming is an external gloss on the pride of the
mind within.

2. "Alii namque quos servilis conditionis demittit humilitas augustam iactitant libertatem; alii vero dum scurrilis generis vilitate plebescunt verbotenus se sanguinis insignitate praesigniunt; alii, dum in artis gramaticae vagientes cunabulis eiusdem lactantur uberibus, Aristotilicae subtilitatis apicem profitentur; alii, dum leporinae timiditatis gelicidiis intorpescunt, solo verbositatis remedio animositatem efferunt leoninam. Sunt alii qui ea quae internae indignationis supercilium claudit interius exteriori evidenter eloquuntur silentio. Nam aliis, vel inferiori morum gradu iacentibus, vel eis probitatis parilitate comparibus, vel etiam elatiori fastigio dignitatis pollentibus, mutuae collocutionis communicare participium dedignantur. A quibus si quis interrogationis suffragio verbum expostulet, tanta taciturnitatis intercapedine a quaestione dividetur responsio, ut eidem eadem nulla cognatione videatur affinis.

3. "Alii, suos actus specificare gaudentes, in multitudine singulares, in generalitate speciales, in universalitate adversi, in unitate diversi omnifariam esse laborant. Dum alii namque exercentur colloquiis, isti indulgent silentiis; dum alii lasciviis solvuntur, isti seriis implicari videntur; dum alii serialibus applicantur negotiis, isti otiantur lasciviis. Dum alii quadam hylaritatis festivitate serenantur in facie, isti in vultu quandam malivolae severitatis praeferunt tempestatem. Alii interiores superbiae gestus exterioris gestus exceptione figurant, qui tanquam terrena despiciant caelestia

2. "For some whom the humbleness of a servile condition keeps down boast of a noble liberty. Others, though their plebeian lineage is coarse and worthless, speak of themselves as distinguished by nobility of blood. Some, while still squalling in the cradle of the art of Grammar and nursing at her breasts, lay claim to the height of Aristotelian subtlety. Others, though numbed by the icy chill of harelike timidity, endow themselves with a leonine fierceness solely through the special power of talk. There are some who plainly declare by their outward silence what the haughtiness of a hidden scornfulness conceals within. For they disdain to take part in common discourse with those who lie at a lower social level, or with those who are of a respectability equal to their own, or even with those who possess dignity of a more exalted rank. If one should make inquiry of some of these people and seek an answer, the response will be separated from the question by so great an interval of silence that the one will seem to bear no relation to the other.

3. "Others, who delight in giving their actions a special character, strive to be unique among the many, particular amid the general, opposed amid universal agreement, differing amid unity. While others engage in conversation, they prefer silence. While others are abandoned to wanton delights, they appear to be engaged with serious matters. While others apply themselves to the orderly conduct of business, they play in wanton idleness. While the faces of others are bright with festive merriment, the faces of these exhibit a certain gloom, a hostile severity. Some illustrate the inner workings of pride by the inhibition of their outward behavior: throwing themselves back, they gaze toward heaven, as though they despised things earthly; they turn

supinati suspiciunt, oculos indignanter obliquant, supercilia habundanter exaltant, mentum superciliose supinant, brachia in arcus exemplant. Horum etiam pedes terram sola articulorum contactione delibant. Alii vero sua corpora femineis comptionibus nimis effeminant, qui suorum capillorum concilium pectinis subsidio in tanta pace conciliant, ut nec lenis aura in eis possit suscitare tumultum. Luxuriantis etiam supercilii fimbrias forpicis patrocinio metunt, aut ab eiusdem silva superflua extirpando decerpunt. Pullulanti etiam barbae crebras novaculae apponunt insidias, ut nec eadem paululum audeat pullulare. Brachia manicarum angustias conqueruntur; pedes in angustis calceorum ergastulis carcerantur.

4. "Heu! homini unde iste fastus, ista superbia, cuius aerumpnosa nativitas, cuius vitam laboriosa demolitur poenalitas; cuius poenalitatem poenalior mortis concludit necessitas; cui esse momentum, vita naufragium, mundus exilium: cui vita aut abest aut spondet absentiam, mors aut instat aut minatur instantiam?

5. "De Superbia vero filia nascitur, quae maternae malignitatis haereditate potitur. Haec est Invidia, quae continuae detractionis rubiginosa demorsione hominum animos demolitur. Hic est vermis cuius morsu morbidata mentis sanitas contabescit in saniem, mentis sinceritas conputrescit in cariem, mentis requies liquitur in laborem. Hic est hospes qui apud suum hospitem inhospitaliter hospitatus, sui hospitis labefactat hospitium. Haec est possessio pessime suum possidens possessorem, quae dum alios detractionis latratibus vexat, sui possessoris animum intestino morsu profundius inquietat.

their eyes disdainfully aside, raise the eyebrows ostenta-
tiously, aggressively thrust the chin forward, set the arms
akimbo. Even their feet taste the ground only by the slight
contact of the toes. Others effeminate their bodies by overly
feminine grooming; with the aid of the comb they convene
the council of their hair so peacefully that no light breeze
could possibly create a disturbance in it. They trim the fi-
bers of the luxuriating eyebrows with the controlling aid of
the scissors, or pluck out by the roots what is superfluous in
this forest. They assign the razor frequent ambushes on the
burgeoning beard, lest it dare to sprout even a little. Their
arms complain of the tightness of their sleeves. Their feet
are imprisoned in shoes like narrow prison cells.

4. "Alas, whence this arrogance, whence this pride in man?
His birth is difficult; painful labor destroys his life; the still
more painful necessity of death is his final penalty; existence
is for him a moment, life a shipwreck, the world a place of
exile. Life has either abandoned him or is sure to do so;
death is either at hand or an imminent threat.

5. "A daughter is born of Pride who inherits her mother's
malice. This is Envy, who ravages the spirits of men with the
corrosive gnawing of ceaseless slander. This is the worm
through whose bite the health of the mind becomes diseased, withers, and decays; purity of mind becomes corrupt
and rotten; peace of mind gives way to distress. This is the
guest who, once hospitably received, abuses the laws of hospitality and seeks to bring down the house of its host. This
is the possession that wickedly takes possession of its possessor, and while it harasses others with the barking of slander, troubles the spirit of its possessor more deeply with its
inward gnawing.

6. "Haec est Invidia quae in illos quos vitiorum absorbet infernus, a quibus corporis dotes ratio Naturae proscribit, quos in paupertatem insania fortunae evomit, indignantis suae detractionis facit aculeos otiari. Sed si quis in torrente divitiarum natat cum Croeso, opes spargit cum Tyto, in specie disputat cum Narciso, cum Turno tonat animositate, Herculi concludit in robore, cum Homero pegaseo nectare debriatur, cum Platone philosophiam facie ad faciem speculatur, cum Ypolyto castitatis signaculo sigillatur, in hunc omnes suarum detractionum acervos expendit. Nam audaciam furori temeritatis assignat, prudentiam aut in fraudis versutias aut in verbositatis ampullositatem obliquat. Per hanc etiam pudor in ypocrisis deaurationem detrahendo degenerat.

7. "Haec Invidiae tabes plerosque tabificat qui, dum alienae famae nitorem conantur deterere, prima suae probitatis sentiunt detrimenta. His aliena prosperitas adversa, aliena adversitas prospera iudicatur. Hii in aliena gratulatione tristantur, in aliena tristitia gratulantur. Isti suas in aliena paupertate divitias, suam paupertatem in alienis divitiis metiuntur. Isti aut alienae famae serenitatem detractionis nubilo nubilare conantur, aut eiusdem gloriam sola taciturnitate furari. Isti aut puram alienae probitatis sinceritatem fermentant, aut veris falsitatis fermenta maritant.

8. "Pro dolor, invidia quid monstruosius monstrum, quid dampnosius dampnum, quae culpabilior culpa, quae poenalior poena? Haec est erroneae caecitatis abissus, humanae mentis infernus, contentionis stimulus, corrixationis aculeus. Qui sunt invidiae motus nisi humanae tranquillitatis hostes, mentalis depraedationis satellites, animi laborantis

6. "This is Envy, which makes the darts of its angry slander strike feebly against those whom the hell of vice has engulfed, to whom the plan of Nature has denied bodily endowments, or whom the madness of Fortune has cast into poverty. But if one swims in the tide of riches with Croesus, spreads wealth abroad with Titus, competes with Narcissus in beauty, roars with the fierceness of Turnus, challenges Hercules in strength, becomes drunk with Homer on Pegasean nectar, with Plato contemplates philosophy 'face to face,' is stamped, like Hippolytus, with the seal of chastity— upon such people she exhausts all her storehouse of slander. For she attributes valor to reckless madness, and distorts wisdom into deceitful cunning or bombastic verbosity. Through her slanders modesty itself degenerates into gilded hypocrisy.

7. "The taint of Envy stains many who, when they seek to rub away the glow of another's reputation, first become aware that their own good name is being damaged. Another's prosperity is to them adversity, while they thrive on another's misfortune. They sorrow at the rejoicing of others, rejoice at others' sorrow. They measure their own wealth by another's poverty, their poverty by other men's wealth. They strive to darken the clear sky of another's reputation with the clouds of slander, or to rob him of glory by mere silence. They either contaminate the wholesome purity of another's good character, or mingle corrupting falsehood with truth.

8. "For shame! What monster is more monstrous than envy, what injury more injurious, what crime more criminal, what pain more painful? It is an abyss of hapless blindness, a hell of the human mind, a cause of strife, a goad to quarrels. What are the forces of envy but enemies of our peace, agents of mental pillage, the hostile watch kept by a troubled mind

vigiliae hostiles, alienae felicitatis excubiae? Quid prodest
alicui si ei serenitas fortunae prosperantis applaudat, corpus
etiam purpuramento pulcritudinis hylarescat, mens etiam
sapientiae splendore praefulgeat, cum liventis invidiae latro-
cinium, mentis depraedans divitias, fortunae prosperantis
serenitatem adversitatis vertat in nubila, decoris aurum turpitudinis demittat in scoriam, prudentiae gloriam degloriet
livor inglorius?

9. "Si quis tamen livoris rubiginem, invidiae tineam a
mentis thesauro velit proscribere, in alieno dolore suum dolorem inveniat condolendo, alienum gaudium suum faciat
congaudendo, in alienis opibus suas penset divitias, in aliena
pauperie suam lugeat paupertatem. Si alienam probitatem
famae videas solempniis celebrari, festum praeconii diem
nulla facias detractione profestum, sed tuae declarationis
meridie alienae probitatis lucerna in commune deducta pulcrius elucescat. Si quos in titulos alienae famae detractionum latratibus videas indulgere, te a grege latrantium canum
excipias, aut ammonitionis obiectu hebetes linguas, latratus
inanias, corrosionis conteras dentes, detractionum demor-
deas morsiones.

10. "Huic praetaxato vitiorum simbolo Adulatio suae malignitatis portionem annectit. Huius pestis pestilentia per-
cutiuntur principum laterales, palatini canes, adulationis artifices, fabri laudis, figuli falsitatis. Hii sunt qui magniloqua
commendationis tuba in divitum auribus citharizant, qui
mellitae adulationis favos foras eructuant; qui ut emungant

to spy on the happiness of others? What does it profit a man if the fair face of prosperous fortune favors him; if his body rejoices in the beauty of purple robes; if his mind glows with the light of wisdom; when the thievery of black envy may despoil him of the mind's riches, turn the fair weather of prosperous fortune into the cloudy darkness of hardship, and reduce golden beauty to foul dross? When inglorious jealousy can defile the glory of wisdom?

9. "But if one wishes to banish the rust of jealousy, the moth of envy, from the treasury of the mind, let him through compassion discover his own pain in the pain of another; let him make another's joy his own by rejoicing with him; let him find his own wealth in the prosperity of others, and lament his own impoverishment where others are poor. If you see that the good character of another is honored with the rites of fame, do not make the festive day unfestive by any invidious comment on the celebration, but let the lamp of the other's excellence, now brought into open view, appear more fair in the light of your testimonial. If you see anyone engaging in howls of slander against another's claim to renown, withdraw yourself from the mob of barking dogs, or by offering a warning, dull their tongues, make vain their yelping, blunt their gnawing teeth, defang their slanderous jaws.

10. "To the foregoing roster of vices Flattery adds her portion of malice. Afflicted with the contagion of this plague are the companions of princes—the palace dogs, the crafters of flattery, the forgers of praise, the shapers of falsehood. It is they who sound the great-voiced trumpet of approbation in the ears of the prince, who belch forth the honey of mellifluous flattery, who to snatch rewards anoint the rich

munera caput divitis oleo adulationis inungunt, praelatorum auribus pulvinaria laudum subiciunt; qui ab eorundem palliis aut ficticium excutiunt pulverem aut vestem sophistice deplumant implumem. Isti divitum actus in quos favor famae conspuit indignantis suffragiis laudum redimunt mendicantis. Isti penes munera laudes, penes dona favores, penes pretium praeconia famae blandientis constituunt. Nam si in dono divitis prodigalitatis torrens eniteat, adulator in prodigalitatem laudis totus effunditur; si vero hyemalis avaritiae torporem divitis munus redoleat, adulator avarus in laude commendationis algescit in munere. Sed si muneris anthonomasia videatur laudum tympana postulare, adulationis poeta stilo commendationis turget altiloquo. Si vero muneris pauperies famae mendicat suffragia, humiliori stilo famae depauperat dignitatem, quoniam ubi perorat muneris altitudo, adulator ypocritas laudes, famas umbratiles, leves periurias de thesauro sui cordis eructuat.

11. "Nam si ille pro quo munus eloquitur tanta turpitudinis fuerit tempestate deiectus ut in eo vix naturalium donorum fragmenta resultent, ei pulcritudinis praerogativam adulationis poemata sompniabunt. Pigmaeas etiam pusillanimis cordis angustias magnanimitatis mentientur esse palatia; humiles etiam torpentis avaritiae latebras prodigalitatis efferent in excessum; humilitatem etiam plebescentis generis titulo Caesareae nobilitatis mentientur augustam.

12. "Quid amplius? Si apud aliquem nulla virtute a vitiis excusatum castrametetur scelerum plenitudo, dum munus

man's head with the oil of flattery, place the pillow of praise beneath the prelate's ear; brush away nonexistent dust from his robe, or pretend to pluck down from a down-free garment. They redeem with the support of their praise beggarly actions of the rich man at which the voice of fame has sputtered in indignation. They make praise depend on reward, favors on gifts, proclamations of flattering reputation on a fee. For if the gift of the rich man is a glittering torrent of prodigality, the flatterer pours himself forth in prodigal praise. But if the rich man's payment gives off the chill of wintry avarice, the flatterer, miserly with his praise, is cold in his reciprocating encomium. If a gift almost beyond description seems to call for thunderous praise, a poet of flattery grows tumid with grandiose compliments. But if a meager gift begs the support of good repute for the giver, the poet demeans the worth of what he reports by a more humble style. For it is only where the loftiness of the gift makes an eloquent plea that the flatterer belches forth hypocritical praises, shadows of renown, facile perjuries from the treasury of his heart.

11. "For even if the man's whose gift speaks eloquently be fallen into such a tumultuous course of disgraceful living that scarcely even fragments of his natural endowments survive in him, flattering poems will envision for him a claim to beauty. Their lies will declare the dwarfish confines of his cowardly spirit to be a palace of magnanimity; they will elevate the lowly maneuverings of his listless avarice into extreme prodigality, and falsely ennoble the humbleness of his plebeian origin with the noble title of a Caesar.

12. "What more is there to say? Even though every form of wickedness should take up residence with a man whom

mediator occurrit, laudum mercenarius adulator superficiali
commendationum tunica vitiorum tenuiter colorat aspectum. Econtrario vero, si totius decoris meridies alicuius hylarescat in facie, lingua argenteis eloquentiae resplendeat
margaritis, mentis thalamus virtutum fulguret ornamentis,
tamen si adulationis artifex muneris gratiam non expectat,
tantae honestatis luci cum vitiorum fastidiis nebulas inmis-
cere laborat.

13. "Quid igitur Adulationis inunctio, nisi donorum
emunctio; quid commendationis allusio, nisi praelatorum
delusio; quid laudis arrisio, nisi eorundem derisio? Nam cum
loquela fidelis intellectus interpres, verba fideles animi picturae, vultus voluntatis signaculum, lingua mentis soleat esse
propheta, adulatores a voluntate vultum, ab animo verbum,
a mente linguam, ab intellectu loquelam amplo dissensionis
intervallo diffibulant. Plerisque etenim forinseca dealba-
tione laudis arrident quos interna mentis subsannatione de-
rident. Plerosque exterius plausibiliter applaudendo collau-
dant quos interius contradictoria derisione defraudant.
Foris vultu applaudunt virgineo, intus scorpionis pungunt
aculeo. Foris adulationis mellitos conpluunt imbres, intus
detractionis evomunt tempestates."

14. Tunc ego, continuae narrationis aurigationem refrenans, dixi: "Vellem ut rationabilibus tuae disciplinationis
propugnaculis contra furiales istorum vitiorum exercitus
meae mentis roborares oppidulum."

Tunc illa:

not a single virtue redeems from his vices, if money is present as intermediary, a mercenary flatterer will lightly color over the surface of his vices with a superficial coating of approbation. But if, on the other hand, the fair day of every grace should shine forth in a man's face, if his tongue should sparkle with silvery pearls of eloquence, and the chamber of his mind be bright with the adornments of virtue, nevertheless, if the artisan of flattery cannot look forward to the favor of a gift, he will strive, with vice-ridden scorn, to intermingle clouds with the light of such honor.

13. "What then is unctuous Flattery but a means of extorting gifts? What is the game of high praise for, if not to delude prelates? What is the happy sound of praise but a mockery of such men? For though speech is properly the faithful interpreter of understanding, words a clear representation of the mind, the face a sign of the will, the tongue the prophet of thought, flatterers separate face from will, word from mind, tongue from thought by a wide breach of disagreement. They show favor outwardly with the whitewashing of their praise to many whom they deride with inward mockery. They praise many men outwardly with most acceptable applause, but inwardly betray them by derisively contradicting it. Outwardly they applaud in virgin innocence, inwardly they strike with the sting of the scorpion. Outwardly they pour down showers of honeyed adulation, inwardly they belch forth storms of slander."

14. Then I, curbing the headlong course of this extended discourse, said, "I wish that you would prepare the little city of my mind to withstand the furious armies of the vices with the rational bulwarks of your instruction."

She began:

15

"Ne te gulosae Scilla voraginis
mergat profunda nocte libidinum,
praebe palato frena modestiae,
ventri tributum solve modestius.

5   "Imbrem Liaei semita gutturis
libet modeste; Bachica pocula
pota parumper, ut quasi poculis
bachi putetur os dare basia.
Frangat Liaei limpha superbiam,
10 Bachi furorem flumina temperent;
nuptam Liaeo se Thetis offerat,
frenet mariti nupta tirannidem.

    "Plebeia, simplex, rara comestio
carnis superbae murmura conterat,
15 ut te tyrannus parcius urgeat
semper in ista carne superbiens.
Lentus Cupido sic aget otia.

    "Frenentur in te frena Cupidinis,
languens stupescet carnis aculeus,
20 ancilla fiet sic caro spiritus.

    "Largire visus pessula ianuae,
frenans ocellos, ne nimis improbe
venetur extra luminis impetus,
praedamque menti nuntius offerat.

25   "Si quos habendi fervor inebriat,
exire cogant mente pecuniam,
mentis triumphum sentiat ambitus,
victi premantur colla Cupidinis.

Chapter 15

"Lest the Scylla of the abyss of gluttony draw you down to the deep darkness of lust, apply the rein of moderation to the palate, pay the belly a more modest tribute.

"Let your throat be temperate in drinking the Lyaean 5 stream; be brief in drinking the goblets of Bacchus, that your mouth may be thought to merely kiss Bacchus's cup. Let water break the pride of Lyaeus, let the river temper 10 Bacchus's madness. Let Thetis offer herself as Lyaeus's bride, let the bride curb the tyranny of her spouse.

"Let a humble, plain, and sparing meal beat down the murmurs of the haughty flesh, that the tyrant who claims 15 pride of place in this flesh may press you more sparingly. Thus will tenacious Cupid be stilled.

"Let the reins of Cupid within you be firmly held; let the pricking of the flesh grow weak and dull. Thus will flesh be- 20 come the handmaid of spirit.

"Place bolts on the portals of vision, controlling the eyes, lest their lamps feel the wanton impulse to hunt abroad, and provide the mind with report of game.

"If the rage for possession makes men drunk, let them 25 drive money from their minds; let ambition experience the triumph of reason, and the neck of conquered Cupid be bowed down.

"Non in crumenis ipsa pecunia
30 clausa moretur, pigraque dormiat
nulli vacando, sed magis excubet,
custos honoris, divitis usibus.
Si tempus assit, si locus exigat,
surgat sepultae massa pecuniae,
35 nummos crumenae funditus evomant.
Quaevis honori munera militent.
    "Calcare si vis colla superbiae,
flatus tumoris, fulmina spiritus,
pensa caducae pondus originis,
40 vitae labores, mortis apocopam."

16

Cum in hanc specialis disciplinae semitam oratio Naturae
procederet, ecce vir subitaneae apparitionis miraculo, sine
omni nostrae praeconsiderationis vexillo, suam praesentiam
nostris conspectibus praesentavit. Qui cum nullius aetatis
legi videretur obnoxius, nunc iuvenilis vere pubescebat aetatis, nunc maturioris aevi facies seria loquebatur, nunc vultus
senectutis sulcis videbatur arari. Qui sicut multimodae aetatis vicaria facie fluctuabat, sic eius staturam ancipitem nunc
quantitas castigatior humilius dimittebat, nunc aequilibra-
tae mediocritatis libramina staturae ampliabant inopiam,
nunc audaci proceritate quantitatis evadens giganteis contendebat excessibus.

"Let not money remain shut up in purses and idly slum- 30
ber, of service to none; instead let it keep watch as the guardian of honor in the service of the man of wealth. When the
time is right and the occasion demands it, let the mass of
buried money arise, let the purse wholly empty itself of coin. 35
Let every gift serve the cause of honor.

"If you wish to tread on the neck of pride, to put down
swollen vanity and the vauntings of the spirit, think on the
burden of your mortal condition, the hardships of life, the 40
final severance of death."

Chapter 16

While Nature's speech was proceeding along this path
of particularized instruction, behold, a man made himself
present to our sight by a miraculously sudden apparition,
with no advance signal that we might recognize. Since he
seemed subject to the condition of no one age, at one moment he was flourishing in the springtime of youth, at another his face spoke of the serious concerns of more mature
years, or appeared riven by the furrows of old age. Just as he
kept changing in appearance, substituting one age for another, so at one moment a strictly limited measure kept his
fluctuating stature at a humble level; at the next, the deter-
mination of a balanced mean augmented his deficient size;
again, boldly extending his height, he rivaled the tallest of
giants.

2. Huius in facie nulla femineae molliciei resultabant vestigia, sed sola virilis dignitatis regnabat auctoritas. Huius facies nec fletus imbribus conpluta nec risus erat lasciviis serenata, sed ab utroque feriata, modestius magis aspirabat in lacrimas. Caesaries tamen inducias adepta litigii artificiosi pectinis fatebatur industriam. Moderatae tamen comptionis libramine iacebat ornata, ne si comptionibus vagaretur anomalis, in femineam degenerare videretur molliciem. Et ne frontis aream comae sepeliret nubecula, forpicis morsum capillorum sensit extremitas.

3. Huius facies, prout virilis dignitas exposcebat, a nulla pulcritudinis gratia deviabat. Huius mentum nunc primam germinabat lanuginem, nunc idem barba fimbriabat prolixior, nunc luxurianti barbae vellere silvescere videbatur, nunc novaculae severitas barbae castigabat excessum.

4. Annuli vero lapidum gemmati sideribus, manus fulguratione serenantes eximia, solem reddebant novicium. Vestes vero nunc grossioris materiae vulgari artificio plebescere, nunc subtilioris materiae artificiosissima contextione crederes superbire. In quibus picturarum fabulae nuptiales sompniabant eventus. Picturatas tamen ymagines vetustatis fuligo fere coegerat expirare. Ibi tamen sacramentalem matrimonii fidem, connubii pacificam unitatem, nuptiarum indisparabile iugum, nubentium indissolubile vinculum, lingua picturae fatebatur intextum. In picturae etenim libro umbratiliter legebatur quae nuptiarum initiis exultationis applaudat sollempnitas, quae in nuptiis melodiae sollempnizet

2. In his face there appeared no hints of feminine softness; only the authority of manly dignity reigned there. His face was neither watered by showers of tears nor brightened by playful laughter, but while withdrawn from both, it was slightly more inclined toward tears. His hair, however, had obtained a truce with unruliness that attested the work of the skillful comb. It lay in order through the rite of a moderate combing, for if it were to go astray through an unusual coiffure he might appear to be degenerating into feminine softness. And lest he bury the expanse of his forehead with a cloud of hair, the tips of the hairs had felt the bite of the scissors.

3. His face, as manly dignity demanded, lacked no attribute of beauty. His chin was at one moment sprouting its first down, then a fuller beard fringed it, then it seemed to be thicketed with a beard of luxuriant fleece, then the sternness of the razor disciplined the beard's excess.

4. Rings, adorned with starlike stones, brightened his hands with an extraordinary gleam like that of a new sun. At one moment you would think his clothes were those of the common man, simply fashioned of coarse material; at the next you would find them proudly displaying the most delicate material, tailored with the utmost skill. On these garments pictured stories imagined the circumstances of marriage, though the darkening of age had almost caused the images depicted to fade away. Nevertheless pictorial language described the sacred trust of matrimony, the peaceful connubial union, the inseparable nuptial bond, the indissoluble joining of the wedded couple. In this book of pictures could be read in a shadowy form the exultant celebration that greets the beginning of a marriage; the sweetness of the

suavitas, quae connubiis convivarum arrideat generalitas specialis, quae matrimonia Cithereae concludat iocunditas generalis.

5. Organicorumque artificum decuriata pluralitas praedicti hominis decusabat incessum. Ipsi vero artifices in se sui magistri tristitiam figurantes, suis silentium indixerant instrumentis. Unde instrumentorum officinae, quas silentii torpor faciebat elingues, aspirare videbantur in gemitum.

6. Igitur postquam Naturae vicinitati eum localis vicinavit affinitas, illa illum signans ex nomine cum salutis libamine ei osculi libamen apposuit. Ex proprii igitur nominis signaculo ceterarumque circumstantiarum loquentibus signis Ymeneum qui venerat recognovi, quem Natura sua locans in dextera suae dexterae dignitate donavit.

7. Dum inter Naturam Ymeneumque quaedam colloquii celebraretur festivitas, ecce virgo, suae pulcritudinis aurora blandiens universis, repentina inopinati eventus praesentia sui directione itineris ad nostram aspirare videbatur praesentiam. In cuius pulcritudine tanti artificii resultabat sollempnitas ut in nullo Naturae claudicaret digitus polientis. Huius facies nullius adventicii coloris mendicabat ypocrisim, sed rosam cum lilio disputantem in facie insitione mirabili Naturae plantaverat dextera praepotentis. Oculi vero. simplicitatis disciplinati modestia, nullius petulantiae lasciviebant excursibus. Labra vero, proprii retentiva vigoris, nec exhausta suaviis nec osculis Veneris videbantur sensisse praeludia. Huius tamen faciem desudantem in lacrimas lacrimarum flumine crederes naufragari. Sertum vero materiatum ex liliis decusatae insertionis connubio fibulatis suis

melody that accompanies the marriage ceremony; the special gathering of celebrants who rejoice at the wedding; the larger happiness of Venus that completes the marriage.

5. An orderly company of musicians lent dignity to the entrance of this man, but these artists, displaying in themselves the sadness of their master, imposed silence on their instruments, so that their function, which listlessness rendered mute, seemed to be reduced to sighing.

6. When affinity of place brought this man close to the vicinity of Nature, she greeted him by name, and as a rite of greeting bestowed on him the offering of a kiss. From the indication of his name, and from other eloquent signs in his appearance, I recognized that it was Hymen who had come. Nature, placing him on her right, bestowed on him the honor of her right hand.

7. While a joyful communion was being celebrated by Nature and Hymen, behold, a maiden whose dawning beauty made all things glad was suddenly and unexpectedly present, and seemed, by the direction of her path, eager to enter our presence. In her beauty there shone forth so great a formal artistry that Nature's refining hand had failed in no respect. The face of this maiden required none of the hypocrisy of borrowed coloring, for the hand of all-powerful Nature, by a wondrous grafting, had planted in her face the rose vying with the lily. Her eyes, disciplined by a simple modesty, made none of the impudent side-glances of wantonness. Her lips, retaining their native vitality, were not wearied of kisses, and seemed not to have been introduced to the kisses of Venus. Yet you would suppose that her face, dissolving into tears, might drown in such a flood of tears. A garland, fashioned from lilies joined together by a marriage of interweaving,

capiti arriserat ornamentis. Cignei tamen crinis candor dedignatus liliorum supplicare candoribus contradictoriam iactitabat albedinem.

8. Vestes etiam suis nivibus praedictorum albedini argumentis verioribus conclusissent, nisi pictura varios commentata colores earum fefellisset albedinem. In his etenim sub conmento picturae videbatur intextum qualiter Ypolyti castitas muro vallata constantiae novercalis luxuriae oppositionibus institit refellendo. Illic Daphne, ne virginalis serae fracturam pessula sustineret, fuga Phoebi fugabat illecebras. Illic Lucretia fracti pudoris dispendium mortis excludebat conpendio. Illic in speculo picturae castitatis Penelope speculum poteram speculari. Et ut brevi narrationis tramite subterfugientia picturae multiloquia conprehendam, nullam Castitatis filiam suo commendationis ferculo depictionis industria defraudavit.

9. Aurei vero sigilli nobilitas, quod iaspidum stellabat syderea multitudo, praefatae virginis diescebat in dextera. Super sinistram vero residens turtur sub facie elegiaci carminis calamitosis eiulationibus suae vocis citharam coaptabat. Adolescentularum vero cohors quarum nulla videbatur in palaestra Veneris lascivisse, quae ad itineris solatium ad obsequiale ministerium venerat, eius adhaerebat vestigiis. Quam postquam Natura prospexit sibi locali proximitate vicinam, sollempni occursu ei obviam veniens, salutis proemio, osculi praeludio, conplexus connubio mentalem foris depinxit affectum. Cumque praedictae virginis in salutis

favored her head with its adornment. But the gleam of her swan-white hair, disdaining to seek aid from the sheen of lilies, asserted a countering whiteness.

8. Her snow-white garments would have answered with more truthful arguments the aforementioned claims to whiteness, were it not that art, employing various colors, had obscured their whiteness. In these pictures could be seen, wrought by the inventiveness of artistry, how the chastity of Hippolytus, defended by the rampart of constancy, stood firm, repelling the assaults of a stepmother's lust. There Daphne, that the lock of her virgin portal might remain unbroken, by fleeing defeated the enticements of Phoebus. There Lucretia canceled the cost of her lost chastity by the compensating gain of death. There in the mirror of a picture I was able to contemplate the exemplary chastity of Penelope. And to sum up in brief narrative fashion the manifold subtleties of this artistry, the work of portrayal had denied to none of the daughters of Chastity their portion of commendation.

9. The splendor of a golden seal, adorned with a starry multitude of gems, shone like sunlight on the maiden's right hand. Seated upon her left, a turtledove adapted the instrument of her voice to bemoanings of misfortune in the form of elegiac song. A band of adolescent girls, none of whom appeared to have wantoned in the arena of Venus, had come to lighten her journey and provide obedient service, and followed close behind her. When Nature observed that the maiden was near to her in local proximity, she came forward in formal welcome, and openly displayed her inner affection by the proem of a greeting, the prelude of a kiss, and the union of an embrace. And when the name of the maiden

praefatione nomen enituit, praesentialem agnovi Castitatis adventum.

10. Cumque Natura eidem festivitate collocutionis applauderet, ecce matrona, regulari modestia disciplinans incessum, ad nos videbatur sui itineris tramitem lineare. Huius statura mediocritatis erat circumscripta limitibus. Aetas vero meridianam vitae tendebat ad horam, vitae tamen meridies in nullo pulcritudinis obviabat aurorae. Pruina etiam senectutis crinem suis nivibus temptabat aspergere, quem ipsa virgo humerorum spatio inordinaria fluctuatione non permiserat iuvenari, sed fili disciplina eius cogebat excessum.

11. Vestes vero nec nobilis materiae gloria superbire nec eiusdem vilitatis iacturam videbantur deflere, sed mediocritatis obedientes canonibus nec nimiae brevitatis decurtatione truncatae a terrae superficie peregrinantes evaserant, nec portionibus superfluis terrae faciem tunicabant, sed eam brevi osculi degustatione libabant. Zona namque tunicae moderando decursum enormitatem revocabat in regulam. Monile vero sinus excubando vestibulis manui negabat ingressum. In vestibus vero pictura suarum litterarum fidelitate docebat quae in hominum verbis debeat esse circumcisio, quae in factis circumscriptio, quae in habitu mediocritas, quae in gestu serenitas, quae in cibis refrenatio oris, quae in potu castigatio gutturis.

12. Praefatam igitur virginem, pedissequarum paucitate vallatam, festinae obviationis applausu Natura suscipiens, multiplici osculorum epilogo, specificataeque salutationis auspicio, suae dilectionis cumulum figuravit, expressaque nominis proprii expressio Temperantiae favoralem expressit adventum.

became clear in the prefatory greeting, I recognized the actual presence of Chastity.

10. And while Nature was welcoming her in joyful conversation, behold, a matron, governing her progress by the rule of modesty, could be seen directing her path straight toward us. Her stature was contained within the limits of the mean. Her age seemed close to the noontime of life, but life's midday was in no respect a hindrance to her dawnlike beauty. The frost of old age sought to scatter its white over her hair. This she had not permitted to fall girlishly in disordered waves over her shoulders, but controlled its straying with the discipline of a ribbon.

11. Her garments seemed neither to glory pridefully in noble material, nor to weep at the humiliation of material too coarse, but adhered to the standard of the mean. They neither strayed upward from the ground, cut short by an amputation too great, nor cloaked the face of the earth with unnecessary additions, but touched it with a fleeting kiss. For a belt, controlling the length of her tunic, called its expanse to order. A necklace, keeping watch over the forecourt of her bosom, denied entry to the hand. On her garments images, with their own truthful form of writing, taught what care for cleanness should be present in men's speech, what self-control in their actions, what modesty in their appearance, cheerfulness in their behavior, restraint in eating, strict limits in drinking.

12. Nature came forward quickly, glad to receive this maiden, who was accompanied by only a few attendants. She displayed her great affection with an epilogue of many kisses and the auspicious gift of a special greeting, and the clear utterance of the maiden's proper name indicated the happy arrival of Temperance.

13. Cumque amicae salutationis munere Natura Temperantiae initiaretur praesentiam, ecce mulier, cuius pulcritudinis adiuta fulgore materialis dies serenioris vultus speciem iactitabat, iter festinando maturans, ad nos sui gressus lineas visa est ordinare. Huius statura, natu dedignata pauperiem, humanae staturae regulam regulariter evadebat. Huius caput non in terram humiliando degenerans faciem faciebat encliticam, sed erecta cervice ad superna suspendens intuitum ad altiora visus legabat excursum. Huius speciem Natura lima tantae expolitionis exsculpsit ut in ea sui artificii industriam posset admirari.

14. Diadema vero, non operis insignitatae materiae redimens paupertatem, nec eiusdem nobilitate materiae vilitatem recuperans, sed in utroque singularem praeferens monarchiam, sine morsu peremptoriae proprietatis ardebat in capite. Aureus tamen crinis, gratiori igne flammantior, aureo diademati indignanter videbatur praestare subsellia. Qui nec forpicis apocopatus industria nec in tricaturarum manipulos colligatus, sed digressoria excursione luxurians, limites humerorum transgrediens, terrae videbatur condescendere paupertati.

15. Brachia vero, non brevitatis dampnata pauperie sed proceritatis excursu fluentia, non retro reciproca sed in anteriora esse crederes transitiva. Manus vero, nullius conplosionis arcuatione reciprocae sed largae expansionis explicatione productiles, largiendi affectabant officia. Vestes etiam ex aureis sericisque filis insertionis osculo coniugatis

13. While Nature was solemnizing the presence of Temperance with the gift of her friendly greeting, behold a woman such that the very light of day, augmented by the radiance of her beauty, boasted a fairer aspect, was seen, hastening to end her journey, and directing the course of her steps toward us. Her stature was disdainful of natural limitation, and while maintaining due proportion, exceeded the norm of human height. Her head did not demean itself by bowing toward the ground and directing her face downward, but with neck erect and fixing her gaze on the heavens, she sent her vision forth to higher things. Nature had given shape to her beauty with a skill of such refinement that in her one could marvel at the power of Nature's artistry.

14. On her head shone a diadem that neither made up for poor workmanship by the excellence of its material nor compensated for inferior material by distinguished workmanship, but displayed a distinct nobility in both respects, yet without any harsh hint of proprietary pride. Her golden hair, glowing brighter than a kindly fire, seemed indignant at having to provide a seat for the golden diadem. It had neither been trimmed by the busy scissors nor gathered into braided tresses, but delighted to flow forth unrestrained. Descending below her shoulders, it seemed to graciously acknowledge the lowly earth.

15. Her arms were not impaired by demeaning shortness, but easily reached out at length; you might imagine them not as drawing back, but as extending forward. Her hands were not drawn tightly together, but drawn open in generous expansiveness, and devoted to the duty of giving. Her garments drew their material from gold and silken threads wedded by the kiss of weaving; and lest the delicacy of the

materiam sortientes, ne a materiei generositate operis dege-
neraret subtilitas, tanti artificii gratulabantur insignibus ut
non materialem, verum etiam supercaelestem manum operi
crederes insudasse. In quibus imaginaria picturae probabili-
tas sophistico picturationis suae praestigio homines notorio
avaritiae crimine laborantes anathematis dampnabat obpro-
brio, Largitatis vero filios famae praeconiis titulatos bene-
dictionis gratia conpotire.

16. Praefata igitur mulier solo asseclarum vallata ternario,
cum sui maturationi gressus insisteret, ecce Natura, celebri
occursu illius amicans incessus, osculum salutatione dimi-
dians, salutationem osculo sincopabat. Et cum formae
specialis insignitas, habitus specificati civilitas, gestus indi-
vidualitas Largitatis promulgarent adventum, nomen in salutatione resultans eiusdem rei fidem a nube dubitationis
excepit.

17. Dum Natura Largitati primitivae salutationis amicae-
que applausionis iura persolveret, ecce puella lentitudine
pigritantis gressus morosior, columbini vultus placiditate
serenior, modicitate staturae castigatioris humilior, ad nos
divertere suam testudinei gressus modestiam videbatur.
Staturae tamen humilitati gratia pulcritudinis venerat patrocinium. Quae non mecanicis humani artificii usurpata
fallaciis, sed vivo fonte Naturae scaturiens, totum corpus
decoris afflaverat ornamento. Huius crinis tanta fuerat forpicis demorsione succisus, ut apocopationis figura fere in
vitium transmigraret. Capillos vero quodam exorbitationis

workmanship prove inferior to the excellence of the material, the cloth enjoyed the marks of such artistry that you might believe that a hand not material but supercelestial had labored at the task. On these garments the plausible imagery of art, with the subtle trickery of its picture-making, condemned to the disgrace of anathema men burdened with the notorious crime of avarice, while the sons of Generosity, distinguished by the heralding of fame, were granted the gift of a blessing.

16. As this woman, attended by only a trio of servants, was vigorously quickening her pace, Nature, advancing swiftly to acknowledge her arrival, interspersed kisses with greetings, and interrupted greetings with kisses. And when the unique elegance of her beauty, the particular dignity of her bearing, the distinctiveness of her movements, plainly announced the arrival of Generosity, the sound of her name as she was welcomed drew forth my belief in this from the cloud of uncertainty.

17. While Nature was performing for Generosity the rites of the initial greeting and warm friendship, behold a girl, slower in the lingering pace of her weary steps, milder in the calmness of her dovelike face, humbler in her restricted, middling stature, could be seen directing her modest figure toward us with tortoiselike steps. The charm of her beauty came to the defense of her humble stature. It had not been borrowed from the false contrivances of human artifice, but flowed forth from the living fountain of Nature, and suffused her whole body with its graceful adornment. Her hair had been so cut back by the biting of the scissors that apocope had nearly turned from a figure into a vice. You would think that the hairs, straying in unruly irregularity

diversiclinio devagantes, inexplicabili intricatione conpli-
citos, inter se crederes litigare. Caput vero, demissione profunda deiectum, humiliter encleticabat in terram.

18. Vestes vero, non a nativo materiae colore appositivi
coloris adulteratione degeneres, suburbanae materiae vulga-
ritatem artificiosae operationis defendebant subsidio. Ibi
fabulosis picturae conmentis legebatur inscriptum qualiter
in virtutum cathalogo Humilitas insignitatis praefulgeret
vexillo, Superbia vero a sacramentali virtutum synodo, excommunicationis suspensa caractere, extremae relegationis
dampnaretur exilio.

19. Huic igitur adventanti Natura enixiori festinatione
veniens in occursum, salutationis suae ferculum osculorum
melliens condimento, vultum dilectionis exhibuit medulla-
tae. In specificatis vero personae ydiomatibus michi Humilitatis resultavit adventus.

20. Dum Hymeneus praetaxataeque virgines in Naturae
facie intestinae conquestionis faciem exemplarent, interni-
que doloris ideas in forinsecae lacrimationis icones produ-
cere molirentur, ecce Natura verbis verba praeveniens, ait:
"O sola humanae tenebrositatis luminaria, occidentis mundi
sydera matutina, naufragorum tabulae speciales, portus
mundialium fluctuum singulares, radicatae cognitionis ma-
turitate cognosco quae sit vestri conventus ratio, quae adventus occasio, quae lamentationis causa, quae doloris exor-
dia.

21. "Homines etenim, sola humanitatis specie figurati, interius vero belluinae infirmitatis deformitate deiecti, quos
humanitatis clamide doleo investisse, a terrenae inhabita-

and thrown together in an inextricable tangle, were quarreling among themselves. Her head, deeply downcast, was turned humbly toward the ground.

18. Her garments had not been alienated from the natural color of their material by the contamination of any applied coloring, but answered for the inferiority of their rustic material by recourse to the work of the artist. Here, inscribed in the fabling commentary of pictures, one could read how in the catalog of the virtues Humility bears the shining mark of excellence, but Pride, barred from the sacred company of the virtues by the brand of excommunication, is condemned to banishment into final exile.

19. Coming forward in eager haste to meet the arriving maiden, Nature displayed her deep affection, sweetening the feast of her greeting with the spice of kisses. And from her distinctive personal traits the arrival of Humility became clear to me.

20. While Hymen and the above-named maidens, taking their example from the face of Nature, were assuming faces expressive of inward lamentation, and striving to reproduce the ideas of inner sorrow in images of outward weeping, Nature spoke, anticipating their words with her own: "O sole bringers of light to the darkness of human life, morning stars in a failing world, special planks for the shipwrecked, best havens from the tides of worldly life, I understand, in the fullness of my profound knowledge, the reason of your convening, the occasion of your coming, the cause of your lamentation, the origin of your grief.

21. "For mankind, fashioned with only the outward appearance of humanity, and inwardly disgraced by the deformity of a bestial instability, men whom I grieve at having invested with the garment of human form, are attempting to

tionis patrimonio vos exheredare conantur, sibi terrestre
funditus usurpando dominium, vos ad caeleste domicilium
repatriare cogentes. Quoniam ergo res mea agitur cum familiaris paries inflammatur incendio, vestrae passioni conpa-
tiens, vestro dolori condolens, in vestro gemitu meum lego
gemitum, in vestra adversitate meum invenio detrimentum.

22. "De contingentibus igitur nichil omittens, in me finem proprium consecuta, prout valeo brachium meae potestatis extendere, eos vindicta vitio respondente percu-
tiam. Sed quia excedere limitem meae virtutis non valeo,
nec meae facultatis est huius pestilentiae virus omnifariam
extirpare, meae possibilitatis regulam prosecuta homines
praedictorum vitiorum anfractibus irretitos anathematis
cauteriabo charactere.

23. "Genium vero qui michi in sacerdotali ancillatur officio decens est sciscitari, qui eos a naturalium rerum cathalogo, a meae iurisdictionis confinio, meae iudiciariae potestatis assistente praesentia, vestrae assentionis convivente
gratia, pastorali virga excommunicationis eliminet. Cuius
legationis Himeneus erit probatissimus executor, penes
quem stellantis elocutionis astra lucescunt, penes quem exa-
minantis consilii locatur armarium."

24. Tunc astantes, a suae conquestionis lacrimis feriantes,
profunda capitum demissione submissi, gratiarum actiones
Naturae habundanti profusione solverunt. Himeneus vero,
in presentiali Naturae conspectu sese genibus arcuatis humilians, destinatae legationi sese fatebatur obnoxium. Tunc

disinherit you of your ancestral home on earth, usurping to themselves dominion over the entire world and forcing you to return to your celestial home. Since my own interest is at stake when a neighbor's wall is threatened by fire, I feel compassion for your suffering, I share your grief, in your sighing I hear my own, in your misfortune I discover harm to myself.

22. "Accordingly, disregarding nothing relevant, and pursuing my own ends in my own person, to the extent that I am able to extend the arm of my power, I will smite mankind with a punishment corresponding to their sin. But because I cannot exceed the limit of my power, and I do not have the capacity to wholly root out the poisonous cause of this pestilence, I will follow the rule by which I am enabled, and apply the burning brand of anathema to men entangled in the tortuous snares of these vices.

23. "It behooves me to consult Genius, who serves me in the office of priest, and who, supported by the presence of my judicial authority, and with your gracious company lending its assent, will eliminate these men from the catalog of natural creatures by the pastoral instrument of excommunication. The most appropriate agent of this embassy will be Hymen, in whom the beams of starry eloquence shine, to whose care the treasury of well-considered counsel is entrusted."

24. Then the company emerged from their tearful lamentation, and submissively, with heads deeply bowed, offered to Nature profuse gestures of abundant gratitude. Hymen, humbly presenting himself before Nature on bended knee, accepted responsibility for his assigned mission. Nature

illa cedulam papiream huius epistolaris carminis inscriptione arundinis interventu signavit:

25. "Natura, Dei gratia mundanae civitatis vicaria procuratrix, Genio sibi alteri salutem, eique per omnia serenantis fortunae blanditias amicari.

"Quoniam similia cum dissimilium aspernatione, similium sociali habitudine gratulantur, in te velut in speculo Naturae resultante similitudine inveniendo me alteram, tibi nodo dilectionis praecordialis astringor, aut tecum in tuo profectu proficiens, aut in tuo defectu aequa lance deficiens. Quare circularis debet esse dilectio, ut tu talione dilectionis respondens nostram fortunam facias esse communem.

26. "Patrati sceleris evidentia clamoris gerens imaginem humani generis naufragium tibi habundanter eloquitur. Vides enim qualiter homines originalis naturae honestatem bestialibus illecebris inhonestent, humanitatis privilegialem exuentes naturam, in bestias morum degeneratione transmigrant, Veneris in consequentia affectus proprios consequentes, gulositatis vorticibus naufragantes, cupiditatis vaporibus aestuantes, alis superbiae ficticiis evolantes, invidiae morsibus indulgentes, adulationis ypocrisi alios deaurantes.

27. "Hiis vitiorum morbis nullus medicinalibus instat remediis; hunc scelerum torrentem nullus obice defensionis castigat; hos facinorum fluctus nullus portus stabilitate refrenat. Virtutes etiam tantam hostilis conflictus ingruentiam sustinere penitus non valentes, ad nos tanquam defensionis asilum vice remedii confugerunt.

then took up a reed pen and inscribed on a sheet of paper this epistolary formula:

25. "Nature, by the grace of God vicar and protector of the earthly city, sends greetings to Genius, her second self; may the kindness of happy fortune favor him in all ways.

"Since similars rejoice in sharing the condition of similars, while rejecting the dissimilar, I find in you another self, as if my likeness were reflected in the mirror of Nature; I am bound to you by a bond of heartfelt devotion, so that I am successful through your success, or, in like manner, suffer failure when you fail. Thus our love should be circular, so that you, answering with reciprocal affection, would make our fortunes a common concern.

26. "The evidence of the crime committed, which seems almost to cry out, has made abundantly clear to you the shipwrecked state of the human race. For you see how men disgrace the dignity of their original nature with beastly temptations; casting off the privileged status of humanity, they transform themselves to beasts in the degeneracy of their behavior, following out their own desires in the constructions of Venus, drowning in the whirlpools of gluttony, seething with the heat of desire, soaring on the false wings of pride, submitting to the gnawings of envy, gilding others with the hypocrisy of flattery.

27. "There is none who attacks these vicious diseases with curative remedies, none who curbs this torrent of crime with a defensive barrier. No harbor offers stability by holding back this sea of wickedness. Even the Virtues are wholly powerless to endure the onslaught of such hostile violence, and have fled to us, as though to a sanctuary, for protection rather than remedy.

28. "Quoniam ergo res nostra communi degrassatione vexatur, te precibus melliens, tibi obedientiae virtute precipiens, et iubendo moneo et monendo iubeo quatinus omni excusationis sophismate relegato ad nos matures accessum, ut mei mearumque virginum assistente praesentia, abhominationis filios a sacramentali ecclesiae nostrae communione seiungens, cum debita officii solempnitate severa excommunicationis virga percutias."

29. Post haec illa epistolam sigillari signaculo consignatam, in quo nomen imaginemque Naturae peritia artificialis exculpserat, legato tradidit delegandam. Tunc Hymeneus, sollempniori vultu laetitiae gratiarum actiones epilogans, legationem destinatam initians, suosque a sopore pigritiae excitans consodales, iussit ut suis invigilantes organicis instrumentis a sompno silentii eadem excitarent, et ad armonici melodiomatis modulos invitarent. Tunc illi sua allicientes quibusdam prooemiis instrumenta, vocem diformiter uniformem, dissimilitudine similem, multiformi modulo picturabant:

17

Iam tuba terribili bellum clangore salutans
intonuit, congnata loquens praeludia belli,
mugitu simili similem signando tumultum.
    Aera laedebat mendaci vulnere cornu.
5   Devia vox huius, vox huius anomala nescit

28. "Our situations are imperiled by a common onslaught. Therefore, combining the sweetness of prayer with instruction on the duty of obedience, I advise you by my command, and command you by my advice, that you abandon all subtle excuses, and hasten to come to us, so that with me and my maidens present as witnesses, and in accordance with the sacred authority of your office, you may smite these sons of abomination with the stern rod of excommunication, excluding them from the sacred communion of our church."

29. After this Nature handed over the epistle, signed and stamped with a seal on which skillful artistry had impressed her name and likeness, to be delivered by her ambassador. Then Hymen, offering a final expression of gratitude with his more customary appearance of joy, began his assigned mission by arousing his companions from their sluggish dozing. He ordered them to look to their musical instruments, awaken them from their silent slumber, and draw from them the strains of a harmonious melody. Then [the musicians,] coaxing their instruments with a few preliminary notes, put forth a sound joining different tones into one, making consonance out of dissonance, a single melody out of many.

Chapter 17

Now the trumpet, heralding battle, gave forth its terrible blaring, uttering a warlike prelude to war, its roar the image of the roaring of war itself.

The horn assailed the air with a feigned wound; its wavering voice, its formless voice gave no obedience to the modes 5

organicis parere modis, artique favere
spernit, et effrenem miratur musica cantum.
　Grataque vox citharae sirenans gratius istis
mellitae tribuit auri convivia vocis,
10　quae cantus varii faciem variando colorans,
nunc lacrimas in voce parit, mentita dolorem,
nunc falsi risus sonitu mendacia pingit.
　Et lira, quae semper cantu philomenat amoeno,
dulcius alliciens, oculisque prooemia somni
15　lectitat, et sepelit offensae murmura mentis.
　Fistula, quae noctu solers vigil excubat, immo
excubiis voce conpensat dampna soporis,
auribus arrisit; per quam fit cerea cordis
saxea durities, mentisque liquescere durae
20　cogitur asperitas, propriumque fugare rigorem.
　Hunc vocis cursum, cantusque volucris acumen
obtusae vocis tardabant tympana gressu,
nec tamen omnino cantus fraudantur honore,
verbere si quis ea subtili verberet, ictu
25　suscitet, atque manus tractu delibet amico.
　Aeris exhausti tractu satiata profundo,
cum dulci strepitu ructabant organa ventum;
dividitur iuncta, divisaque iungitur horum
dispar comparitas cantus, concordia discors,
30　unio dissimilis, similis dissensio vocum.
　Plebeo sonitu, mendica voce sonabant
cymbala, quae nostris numquam clamando perorant
auribus, auditus hominum vix digna mereri.

of music and scorned to show kindness to art; music wondered at such uncontrolled song.

The charming Siren voice of the lute sings more gracefully than these, and bestows on the ear the feast of its honeyed note, which by its changes gives color to the face of 10 changing song: now it brings forth vocal weeping, pretended sorrow, now by its tone it creates the illusion of feigned laughter.

And the lyre, which, like Philomena, always warbles a charming song, sweetly summoning to the eyes the prelude of slumber, understands and lays to rest the murmurings of 15 the troubled mind.

The pipe, which keeps watch at night, alert and wakeful, and indeed compensates the watchman for his loss of sleep with its song, gladdens the ear; through its music stony hardheartedness becomes as wax, and the severity of the cruel mind is compelled to melt and banish its normal rigidity. 20

The drums slowed the flow of sound and the delicate movement of winged song with the plodding of their dull beat, yet they are not wholly deprived of the dignity of music, if one strikes them with a gentle stroke, arousing them with the blow and then quieting them with a friendly touch 25 of the hand.

The organs, stuffed by a profound intake of air for their pumps, belched forth wind with a sweet rumble. The unequal equality of their music, its discordant concord, the dissimilar unison and similar dissonance of its sounds is divided in its interconnection, interconnected in its division. 30

The cymbals gave out an inferior sound, a meager voice. They never win our favor by clanging in our ears, and are scarcely worthy to be granted a human audience.

Nullus erat maior, melior, vel mollior illo,
35   quo concludebat praedictis cantibus unus,
dulcis pentafonae cantus, vestigia cuius,
cuius adorabat vocum plebs aemula cantum.
  Et quae cum cythara discordi disputat ore,
psalterii condita favo, mellita sapore,
40   insonuit vox grata ferens munuscula cantus.
  Sistra puellaris tactum poscentia dextrae,
linguae feminei Martis, bellique prophetae
vocis inauditae miracula voce canebant.

18

Igitur Ymeneo misticae legationis ministeriis indulgente, Natura, aerumpnosae conquestionis elegiacam orationem contexens, illorum recensebat iniurias, quorum ingruente flagitio suae reipublicae maiestas profundi detrimenti habundantem senserat laesionem. Inter quos unum prae ceteris accuratius stimulis reprehensionis agebat, qui prae aliis incurialius decuriatam Naturae curabat dedecorare naturam. Cui quamvis gratia nobilitatis blandiretur Fortuna, suo munere immo suis muneribus amicaretur Prudentia, eumque Magnanimitas erigeret, Largitas erudiret, tamen, quia universa massa modici fermenti asperitate laborat, unius virtutis occidens ceterarum virtutum orientem funditus

No song was grander, finer, or more gentle than that with which the sweet pentaphone, unaccompanied, concluded 35 the music of the others. The common people, so critical of others' music, follow it in adoration, worship its song.

And the pleasing voice of the psaltery sounded forth, honeyed, sweet and delicate, answering the cithara with its distinctive note and offering its little gift of song. 40

Sistra, calling for the touch of the hand of a girl, for the tongue of a female Mars, a prophetess of war, gave the voice of song to wonders of a voice unheard.

Chapter 18

While Hymen was devoting himself to the duties of his mystical legation, Nature, fashioning an elegiac speech of painful lamentation, reviewed the wrongdoing of those through whose outrageous violence the majesty of her commonwealth had suffered such deep and extensive damage. Among these evildoers there was one to whom she applied the goad of reproof more than the rest, who sought to disgrace his nature, already banished from the court of Nature, more grossly than all the others. Though Fortune favored him with the grace of nobility, Prudence bestowed the gift, nay gifts, of her friendship, Magnanimity raised him and Generosity was his teacher, nevertheless, because "the whole mass suffers the sharp effect of a little yeast," the sunset of a single virtue wholly clouded over the sunrise of the nubilabat, unius probitatis eclipsis ceterarum probitatum sidera mori recessu cogebat ecliptico.

2. Cumque Largitas ad suum alumpnum ista spectare videret convicia, non audens defensionis pallio eiusdem vitia colorare, cum humiliati capitis demissione decidua ad lacrimarum confugit remedia. Natura vero perpendens quid capitis demissio, quid lacrimarum figuraret emissio, ait: "O virgo, cuius architectatione praesigni humana mens virtutum destinatur palatium; per quam homines favoralis gratiae praemia consequuntur; per quam Aetatis Aureae antiquata saecula reviviscunt; per quam homines sese glutino amicitiae praecordialis astringunt; quam aeterna Usia aeternali suae Noys osculo generando producens, michi sororem largita est uterinam: non solum te michi nativae consanguinitatis zona confibulat, verum etiam pudici amoris nexio concatenat. Unde a meae voluntatis examine tuae discretionis libra tuam voluntatem non patitur aberrare: tanta enim unio conformitatis immo unitas unionis fideli pace nostras mentes conciliat, ut non solum illa unio simulatoria unitatis vestiatur imagine, verum etiam unitionis fantasia deposita ad idemptitatis aspiret essentiam. Quare in neutram alicuius iniuria debachatur quae non degrassetur in alteram, neutri alicuius illecebra novercatur quae non novercetur et alteri.

3. "Quare qui impudicae patrationis clamante blasfemia meae dignitatis titulum effeminare laborat, iniuriosae vexationis instantia tuo honori derogare conatur. Ille enim qui excedentis prodigalitatis effluxu Naturae donis abutitur

others; the eclipse of a single good quality caused the stars of the other qualities to withdraw into the eclipse of death.

2. When Generosity saw that these censures pertained to her foster child, she did not dare to gloss over his vices with a cloak of defense, but with her head bowed downward in humiliation, she sought the relief of tears. But Nature, pondering what the bowed head and outpouring of tears might signify, spoke to her: O maiden through whose splendid architecture the human mind is made the palace of the Virtues, through whom men pursue the rewards of gracious favor, through whom the far off times of the Golden Age live anew, through whom men join together in the bond of heartfelt affection; whom the eternal Being brought forth through generation by the eternal kiss of his Noys, and granted to me as a womb sister; not only does the band of natural kinship bind you to me, but we are linked by the chain of pure love. Thus your sure judgment will not permit your will to deviate from the determinations of mine. For such a union of agreement, nay such a unity of union brings our minds together in trusting peace that our union is not just clothed with an imitative likeness of unity, but rejects the fantasy of mere uniting and aspires to an essential identity. Hence no man's madness can attack either of us that does not assail the other; no jealous lust can threaten one without threatening the other.

3. "Therefore whoever strives to belittle my claim to dignity by unchaste acts of flagrant blasphemy is also seeking to diminish your honor with the force of his damaging harassment. For he who abuses the gifts of Nature by an outpouring of prodigal excess strips himself of the gifts of

Fortunae muneribus dampno nimiae dilapidationis exuitur. Sicque Prodigalitatis meretricata communitas mentiendo Largitatis profitetur honorem, divitiarum torrens paupertatis derivatur in aridum, sapientae splendor fatuitatis deviat in occasum; magnanimitatis rigor laxatur in temeritatis audaciam. Quadam igitur admiratione fatigor, cur in dampnatione illius qui nos ceteris dampnosius dampnare contendit, lacrimarum diluvium non valeas refrenare."

4. Tunc Largitas, tersionis remedio a regione vultus rivulum lacrimarum absentans, capitisque demissionem revocans ad superna, ait: "O nativorum omnium originale principium! O rerum omnium speciale subsidium! O mundanae regionis regina! O supercaelestis principis fidelis vicaria, quae sub imperatoris aeterni auctoritate fidelem administrationem nulla fermentatione corrumpis; cui universitas mundialis originalis iustitiae exigentia obedire tenetur, prout intimae congnationis expressa parilitas expetit, me tibi aurea dilectionis catena connectit.

5. "Ille igitur qui suam naturam abhominationis damno venumdans te insultu eximiae rebellionis impugnat michi coaequatae concussionis inportunitate repugnat. Qui quamvis umbratili credulitatis deceptus imagine meis se credat conmilitare conmerciis, hominesque istrionali prodigalitatis figuratione decepti in eo Largitatis odorent vestigia, tamen a nostrae amicationis beneficio longa relegatione suspenditur. Sed quia nostrum est erroneae devagationis anfractibus conpati condolendo, in eius insensatae voluntatis exorbitatione pestifera non valeo non moveri."

Fortune by this ruinous squandering. Thus Prodigality's meretricious sense of community falsely claims to do honor to Generosity: the torrent of his wealth flows into the desert of poverty; his brilliant wisdom strays into the darkness of foolishness; the strength of his magnanimity gives way to reckless bravado. Thus I am troubled as to why you are unable to restrain the flowing of your tears at the condemnation of one who has striven more harmfully than all the others to cause us harm."

4. Then Generosity, removing the stream of tears from the area of her face by recourse to wiping, and raising her bowed head again toward the heavens, said, "O originating principle of all natural life, O essential protector of all creatures, O queen of the universe, O faithful vice-regent of the supercelestial prince, who by the authority of the supreme ruler perform your faithful governance with no fermenting corruption; you whom the entire universe is bound by the necessity of primordial justice to obey; a golden chain of love joins me to you, as the clear equality of our close kinship requires.

5. "He who offers his nature for sale by his ruinous abominations, and wars against you in assaults of rebellious excess, attacks me with a violence equally shocking. Though he is deceived by the shadowy imagining of credulity, and believes himself a comrade in my enterprises, and men deceived by the miming gestures of Prodigality sense traces of Generosity in him, he is nevertheless held at a great distance from the benefit of our friendship. But because it is our duty to pity and condole the wanderings of aimless error, I am unable to remain unmoved by the diseased rambling of his hapless will."

6. Dum inter has virgines dragmaticae collocutionis interscalaris celebraretur collatio, ecce Genius, organicorum instrumentorum applaudente laetitia, nova apparitionis resultatione conparuit. Cuius statura, mediocritatis canone modificata decenter, nec diminutione quaerebatur affaeresim nec de superfluitatis prothesi tristabatur; cuius caput pruinosis canitiei crinibus investitum hiemalis senii gerebat signacula; facies tamen iuvenili expolita planitie nulla erat senectutis exaratione sulcata.

7. Vestes vero, opere sequente materiam, huius vel illius nescientes inopiam, videbantur nunc inflammari purpura, nunc serenari iacincto, nunc colore succendi coccineo, nunc bisso expressius candidari; in quibus rerum ymagines momentanee viventes totiens expirabant, ut a nostrae cognitionis laberentur indagine. Ille vero calamum papireae fragilitatis germanum nunquam a suae inscriptionis ministerio feriantem manu gerebat in dextera; in sinistra vero morticini pellem novaculae demorsione pilorum caesarie denudatam, in qua stili obsequentis subsidio imagines rerum, ab umbra picturae ad veritatem suae essentiae transmigrantes, vita sui generis munerabat; quibus deletionis morte sopitis, novae nativitatis ortu alias revocabat in vitam.

8. Illic Helena, suo decore semidea, enfasi suae pulcritudinis mediante, "Pulcritudo" poterat nuncupari. Illic in Turno fulmen audaciae, vigor regnabat in Hercule. Illic in Capaneo gigantea ascendebat proceritas; in Ulixe vulpina

6. While this interval of dramatic conversation was taking place between these maidens, behold, Genius became visible, in a new manifestation of his appearance, amid the joyful applause of the musical instruments. His stature, governed by the standard of the mean, neither complained about the aphairesis of shortness nor lamented superfluous elongation. His head, covered with hair of frosty gray, bore the marks of wintry age, yet his face, shining with the smoothness of youth, had been furrowed by none of age's plowing.

7. His garments, whose workmanship was suited to their material, were deficient in neither respect. They seemed now to be aflame with purple, now to be fair with hyacinthine blue, now to blaze with scarlet, now to shine with the clearer white of linen. On these garments the images of creatures, momentarily living, faded so soon that they evaded our attempts to recognize them. In his right hand he held a pen, near kin to fragile papyrus, which never rested from its office of inscription. In his left he held the skin of a dead animal, scraped bare of its growth of hair by the bite of a knife, on which, with the aid of the obedient pen, he granted to images of creatures the life proper to their kind, making them pass from painted shadow to the truth of their essential nature. As these were laid to rest by the death of deletion, he recalled others to life in the rising of a new nativity.

8. There Helen, in her loveliness half goddess, might, with the vivid effect of her beauty speaking for her, have been given the name of "Beauty itself." There fiery boldness was dominant in Turnus, strength in Hercules. There in Capaneus a giant's height arose, in Ulysses the cunning of the fox

vigebat calliditas. Illic Cato pudicae sobrietatis nectare de-
briabatur aureo, Plato ingenii splendore rutilabat sidereo.
Illic stellata cauda Tulliani pavonis ridebat. Illic Aristotiles
sententias enigmaticarum locutionum latibulis involvebat.

9. Post huius inscriptionis sollempnitatem, dexterae manui continuae depictionis defatigatae laboribus, sinistra manus tanquam sorori fessae subveniens picturandi officium
usurpabat, manu dextera pugillaris latione potita. Quae ab
orthographiae semita falsigraphiae claudicatione recedens
rerum figuras, immo figurarum larvas umbratiles semiplena
picturatione creabat. Illic Thersites turpitudinis pannosi-
tate vestitus peritioris fabricae solertiam postulabat. Illic
Paris incestuosae Cipridis frangebatur mollitie. Illic Sinon
sinuosae locutionis latebris armabatur. Illic Ennii versus a
sententiarum venustate ieiuni artem metricam effreni trans-
grediebantur licentia. Illic Pacuvius nesciens narrationis
modificare curriculum in retrograda serie sui tractatus initium locabat.

10. Hiis igitur picturae solertiis Genio sollempniter operam impendenti, Veritas tamquam patri filia verecunda an-
cillatione obsequens assistebat. Quae non ex pruritu Affro-
dites promiscuo propagata, sed ex solo Naturae natique
geniali osculo fuerat derivata, cum Ylem formarum speculum mendicantem aeternalis salutavit Ydea, eam Iconiae in-
terpretis interventu vicario osculata. Huius in facie divinae
pulcritudinis deitas legebatur, nostrae mortalitatis aspernata

was alive. There Cato became drunk on the golden nectar of chaste sobriety. There flourished the starry tail of the Ciceronian peacock. There Aristotle enfolded his knowledge in the hidden depths of enigmatic utterances.

9. After this ceremonial act of inscription the left hand, as if coming to the aid of its weary sister, took over the office of picture-making from the right hand, which was fatigued by the labor of continual depiction, while the right hand took possession of the tablet. The left hand, abandoning the path of orthography for a limping pseudography, created the shapes of creatures, or rather the vague outlines of their shapes, in half-finished pictures. There Thersites, clad in the raggedness of his foul condition, demanded the cleverness of more skillful workmanship. There was Paris, broken by the enervating effect of an incestuous love. There Sinon was armed with the deceptions of sinuous language. There the verses of Ennius, devoid of elegance of thought, violated the laws of metrics with unbridled freedom. There Pacuvius, incapable of keeping the progress of a narrative in sequence, placed the beginning of his work in reverse order.

10. While Genius was devoting serious attention to the artistry of his painting, Truth, like a father's dutiful daughter, served as his obedient handmaid. She had not been spawned by the lustful itch of Aphrodite, but had spring from the pure genial kiss of Nature and her son, when the eternal Idea gave salutation to Hyle as she begged for the mirror of the forms, and impressed its kiss upon her through the mediating agency of the interpretative Icon. In the countenance of this maiden the divine beauty of godhead was revealed, repudiating the condition of our mortality.

naturam. Vestes vero caelestis artificis dexteram eloquentes, indefessae rutilationis splenditatibus inflammatae, nullis poterant vetustatis tineis cancellari; quae virgineo corpori tanta fuerant conexione iugatae, ut nulla exuitionis diaeresis eas aliquando a virginali corpori faceret phariseas. Aliae vero, tanquam adventiciae Naturae precedentibus appendices, nunc oculis visus offerebant libamina, nunc oculorum sese furabantur indagini.

11. Ex opposito vero Veritati Falsitas inimicans stabat attentior, cuius facies turpitudinis nubilata fuligine, nulla in se Naturae munera fatebatur, sed senectus faciem rugarum vallibus submittens eam universaliter in plicas collegerat. Caput vero nec crinis vestimento videbatur indutum nec pepli velamento excusabat calvitiem, sed panniculorum infinita pluralitas, quos filorum iungebat pluralis infinitas, ei texuerat vestimentum. Haec autem, picturae Veritatis latenter insidians, quidquid illa conformiter informabat, ista informiter deformabat.

12. Natura igitur suo gressui laxiores concedens habenas, sollempnem occursum sollempniter exhibendo, oscula nullo illicitae Veneris fermentata veneno, sed promiscui significativa cupidinis amplexus, etiam misticae dilectionis concordiam figurantes, Genio exhibuit adventanti.

13. Mutua ergo gratulatione expletionis termino consummata, Genius indixit, manu postulante, silentium. Consequenter vero in hanc locutionis formam suae vocis monetavit materiam: "O Natura, non sine internae inspirationis afflatione divina a tuae discretionis libra istud inperiale processit edictum, ut omnes qui abusiva desuetudine nostras

Her garments declared themselves the work of a heavenly artist; they were aflame with the splendor of an unfailing redness that could never be consumed by the moths of age. They were so closely fitted to the maiden's form that no dieresis of divestment would ever make them separate Pharisaically from her virgin body. Other garments, seemingly added to the previous ones as Nature's afterthoughts, at one moment offered brief glimpses to the eyes, at the next fled the scrutiny of vision.

11. On the other side Falsehood, no friend to Truth, stood waiting. Her face, clouded over with ugly soot, bore witness to none of the gifts of Nature, but submitted to the deep wrinkles of old age, and gathered itself everywhere into folds. Her head did not appear clad in a coat of hair, nor did it shelter its baldness by covering it with a robe. Instead an infinite quantity of rags, stitched together by a multiple infinity of threads, had fashioned her garment. She waited, secretly intending to attack the painting of Truth, and whatever the other informed with its true form, Falsehood reduced to formless deformity.

12. Nature, granting freer rein to her steps, came solemnly forward to this solemn meeting. On Genius's arrival she offered him kisses untainted by any poison of lawless Venus, but rather symbolic of a desire shared in common, and embraces representing the concord of mystical love.

13. When the mutual greetings had been carried through to the point of satisfaction, Genius by a gesture of his hand imposed silence, then stamped the material of his voice into this form: "O Nature, not without an inbreathing of divine inspiration did this imperial edict issue from your balanced judgment, decreeing that all who seek to render our

leges obsoletas reddere moliuntur, non in nostrae sollemp-
nitatis feria feriantes, anathematis gladio feriantur. Et quia
lex huius promulgationis legitimae legem iustitiae non
oppugnat, tuique examinali libra iudicii meae discretionis
sedet examini, tuae editionis maximam ocius roborare ma-
turo.

14. "Quamvis enim mens mea, hominum vitiis angustiata
deformibus, in infernum tristitiae peregrinans, laetitiae nesciat paradisum, tamen in hoc amoenantis gaudii odorat primordia, quod te mecum video ad debitae vindictae suspirare
suspiria. Nec mirum, si in nostrarum voluntatum unione
conformi concordiae reperio melodiam, cum unius ideae
exemplaris notio nos in nativum esse produxerit, unius of-
ficialis administrationis conformet conditio, cum nostras
mentes non superficiali dilectionis vinculo amor iungat ypocrita, sed penitiora animorum nostrorum latibula casti amoris pudor inhabitet."

15. Dum hoc verborum compendio Genius suae orationis
frenaret excursum, suae exclamationis quasi aurora nas-
cente, tristitiae tenebras paulisper absentans, salvo suae dignitatis honore Natura Genio gratiarum iura persolvit.

16. Tunc Genius post vulgaris vestimenti depositionem
sacerdotalis indumenti ornamentis celebrioribus honestius
infulatus, sub hac verborum imagine praetaxatam excommunicationis seriem a penetralibus mentis forinsecus evo-
cavit, hoc locutionis procedens curriculo:

laws obsolete through abuse and neglect, and who do not honor the festivals of our hallowed tradition, be struck with the sword of anathema. And because the law here promulgated does not contradict the law of legitimate justice and, by virtue of your scrupulously balanced judgment, satisfies the scrutiny of my own discernment, I hasten to enforce the authority of your edict.

14. "For though my mind, straitened by the ugly vices of men, and straying into a hell of sorrow, no longer knows the paradise of delight, yet here it scents the first beginnings of a renewal of joy, for I see that you are at one with me in longing for the well-deserved punishment. Nor is it strange that I should discover the melody of concord in the intimate union of our wills, since the exemplary notion of a single idea brought us to birth, since our condition as administrators of a single office conforms us, since no false love binds our spirits with the spurious bond of pleasure, but the purity of chaste affection dwells in the innermost chambers of our souls."

15. While Genius was bringing the course of his speech to a halt with this collection of words, dispelling a little the darkness of sorrow by the newborn day of his eloquence, Nature, with due respect for her dignity and honor, performed for Genius the rites of grace.

16. Then Genius, after laying aside his common garments, and robed with more dignity in the honorable adornment of his priestly vestments, summoned forth from the inner chambers of his mind the promised speech of excommunication, following this course as he spoke:

17. "Auctoritate superessentialis Usyae eiusque Notionis eternae, assensu caelestis militiae, coniunctae Naturae etiam ceterarumque officialium virtutum ministerio suffragante, a supernae dilectionis osculo separetur, ingratitudinis exigente merito, a Naturae gratia degradetur, a naturalium rerum uniformi concilio segregetur omnis qui aut legitimum Veneris obliquat incessum, aut gulositatis naufragium aut ebrietatis sentit insomnium, aut avaritiae sitientis experitur incendium, aut insolentis arrogantiae umbratile ascendit fastigium, aut praecordiale patitur livoris exitium, aut adulationis amorem comitatur ficticium.

18. "Qui a regula Veneris exceptionem facit anomalam Veneris privetur sigillo. Qui gulositatis mergitur in abisso mendicitatis erubescentia castigetur. Qui ebrietatis letaeo flumine soporatur perpetuatae sitis vexetur incendiis. Ille in quo sitis incandescit habendi perpetuatas paupertatis egestates incurrat. Qui in praecipitio arrogantiae exaltatus spiritum elationis eructuat, in vallem deiectae humilitatis ruinose descendat. Qui alienae felicitatis divitias tinea detractionis invidendo demordet, primo se sibi hostem inveniat. Qui adulationis ypocrisi a divitibus venatur munuscula, sophistici meriti fraudetur in praemio."

19. Postquam Genius huius anathematis exterminio finem orationi concessit, huic imprecationi applaudens virginum assistentia festino confirmationis verbo Genii roboravit edictum. Lampadesque cereorum in manibus virginum

17. "By the authority of the superessential Being and his eternal Idea; with the assent of the heavenly host, and the approval of the government of my partner Nature and her attendant Virtues: let all those be denied the kiss of heavenly love who obstruct the lawful channel of Venus; who undergo the shipwreck of gluttony or the nightmare of drunkenness; who know the heat of thirsting avarice, scale the illusory heights of insolent arrogance, suffer the ravaging of envy deep within, become familiar with the feigning love of flattery. As the necessary reward for their ingratitude, let them be declared unworthy of the grace of Nature, banished from the united community of the natural order.

18. "May he who pursues irregular exceptions to the rule of Venus be deprived of the seal of Venus. May he who is immersed in the abyss of gluttony be punished by the humiliation of beggary. May he who is drenched in the Lethean flood of drunkenness be tormented by the fires of perpetual thirst. May he who burns with the thirst for possession incur the endless wants of poverty. May he who is set high on the precipice of arrogance and puffs forth his prideful spirit undergo a ruinous fall into the valley of downcast humbleness. May he who gnaws enviously with the worm of slander at the wealth of one more fortunate discover that he is first an enemy to himself. Let him who pursues gifts from rich men through hypocritical flattery be deceived by a prize of deceptive worth."

19. After Genius had brought an end to his speech with this anathema of banishment, the attendant company of maidens applauded his imprecations and reinforced his edict with words of approval. Then the flames of the candles in the maiden's hands, whose light shone bright as noon,

suis meridiantes luminibus, in terram cum quadam aspernatione demissae extinctionis videbantur sopore deiectae.

20. Huius imaginariae visionis subtracto speculo, me ab
exstasis excitatum insompnio prior misticae apparitionis
dereliquit aspectus.

were dropped to the ground with a certain disdain, and seemed to dwindle in the slumber of extinction.

20. When the mirror of this imaginary vision was withdrawn, the sight of the previous mystical apparition left me awakened from my strange ecstatic dream.

ANTICLAUDIANUS

Prologus

Cum fulminis impetus vires suas expendere dedignetur in virgulam, verum audaces provectarum arborum expugnet excessus, imperiosa venti rabies iras non expendat in calamum, verum in altissimarum supercilia rerum vesani flatus invectiones excitet furiosas, per vitiosam nostri operis humilitatem invidiae flamma non fulminet, nostri libelli depressam pauperiem detractionis flatus non deprimat, ubi potius miseriae naufragium misericordiae portum expostulat quam felicitas livoris exposcat aculeum. In quo lector non latratu corrixationis insaniens, verum lima correctionis emendans, circumcidat superfluum et compleat diminutum quatenus illimatum revertatur ad limam, impolitum reducatur ad fabricam, inartificiosum suo referatur artifici, male tortum propriae reddatur incudi.

2. Sed quamvis artificii enormitas imperitiam accuset artificis, in adulterino opere imperitiae vestigium manus relinquat opificis, opus tamen sui veniam deprecatur erroris, cum tenuis humanae rationis igniculus multis ignorantiae obnubiletur erroribus, humani ingenii scintilla multas erroris evanescat in nebulas. Quare ad hoc opus non nauseantis animi fastidio ductus, non indignationis tumore percussus, sed

Prose Prologue

Since the thunderbolt disdains to expend its force on a mere sapling, and rather assails the bold projection of full grown trees; since the tyrannical fury of the wind does not vent its wrath on a reed, but pits the furious onslaught of its raging blast against the loftiest summits; let not envy hurl its fiery bolt at the many faults of our humble work; let the storm of detraction not bear down on the lowly poverty of our little book, where no happiness of style invites the stings of envy, but instead a miserable shipwreck is in urgent need of the safe harbor of compassion. Let the reader not rage against it with quarrelsome snarling; let him rather emend it with the file of correction, trimming what is superfluous, filling out what is insufficient; let what is rough be subjected again to the file, what is imperfect be sent back to the workshop, what is unskillfully done be returned to the artisan, what is badly forged be placed again on his anvil.

2. But though the great failings of the artifact point to the artisan's lack of skill, though the hand of the workman leave traces of his lack of skill in his ill-conceived production, his work nonetheless begs indulgence of its mistakes. For the flickering flame of human reason is obscured by the many failings of ignorance; the spark of human genius easily vanishes into many clouds of confusion. Therefore let no reader approach this work who is guided by the fastidiousness of a spirit too ready to declare itself sickened, or afflicted with

delectatione novitatis illectus, lector accedat, ut quamvis liber vernantis eloquii purpuramento non floreat, et fulgurantis sententiae sydere non clarescat, tamen in fragilis calami tenuitate mellis possit suavitas inveniri et arescentis rivuli modicitate sitis ariditas temperari.

3. In hoc tamen nulla vilitate plebescat, nullos reprehensionis morsus sustineat, quod modernorum redolet ruditatem, qui et ingenii praeferunt florem et diligentiae efferunt dignitatem, cum pigmaea humilitas excessui superposita gigantaeo, altitudine gigantem praeveniat, et rivus a fonte scaturiens in torrentem multiplicatus excrescat.

4. Hoc igitur opus fastidire non audeant qui adhuc nutricum vagientes in cunis inferioris disciplinae lactantur uberibus. Huic operi derogare non temptent qui altioris scientiae militiam spondent. Huic operi abrogare non presumant qui caelum philosophiae vertice pulsant. In hoc etenim opere litteralis sensus suavitas puerilem demulcebit auditum, moralis instructio perficientem imbuet sensum, acutior allegoriae subtilitas proficientem acuet intellectum. Ab huius igitur operis arceantur ingressu qui, solam sensualitatis insequentes imaginem, rationis non appetunt veritatem, ne sanctum canibus prostitutum sordescat, ne porcorum pedibus conculcata margarita depereat, ne derogetur secretis si eorum maiestas divulgetur indignis.

the swelling of disdain. Let him rather be drawn by the pleasure of novelty, so that even though the book is not adorned by the purple patches of lively eloquence, or shining with the starry glow of brilliant thought, a honeyed sweetness may still be discovered in the tenuous sound of its fragile pipe, and parching thirst be allayed by the small trickle of a stream nearly dry.

3. And yet this work must not be dismissed for its vulgarity or be subjected to the bite of faultfinders because it exhibits the rude workmanship of those modern writers who cherish blossoming ingenuity, and proclaim the dignity of hard work. For the lowly pigmy, set atop the tallness of a giant, surpasses the giant in height; and a small stream that flows from a spring becomes larger and swells into a rushing river.

4. Therefore let none dare to scorn this work who are still squalling in the nurse's cradle, still being suckled at the breasts of the lesser arts. Let none attempt to discredit this work who have committed themselves to the combat of higher learning. Let not even those who assail heaven from the lofty peaks of philosophy presume to dismiss this work. For in this work the sweetness of the literal sense will give pleasure to a youthful audience; moral doctrine will lend itself to the developing mind; the keener subtlety of allegory will sharpen the proficient intellect. Therefore let those be forbidden entry to this work who seek only the sensory appeal of imagery and have no appetite for the truths of reason, lest what is sacred be prostituted and defiled by dogs; lest a pearl be lost, trodden beneath the feet of swine. Mysteries are dishonored if their majesty is revealed to the unworthy.

5. Quoniam igitur in hoc opere resultat grammaticae syntaseos regula, dialecticae lexeos maxima, oratoriae reseos communis sententia, arismeticae matheseos paradoxa, musicae melos, anxioma geometriae, gramatis theorema, astronomicae ebdomadis excellentia, theophaniae caelestis emblema, infruniti homines in hoc opus sensus proprios non impingant, qui ultra metas sensuum rationis non excedant curriculum, qui iuxta imaginationis sompnia aut recordantur visa aut figmentorum artifices commentantur incognita. Sed hii qui suae rationis materiale in turpibus imaginibus non permittunt quiescere, sed ad intuitum supercaelestium formarum audent attollere, mei operis ingrediantur angustias, certa discretionis libra pensantes quid sit dignum in aures publicas promulgari vel silentio penitus sepeliri. Sicut enim quorundam genuinos detractionis insultus non timeo, sic favorabilem commendationis auram ab aliis non expecto. Non enim tumor superbiae intus eructuans ut exiret in publicum me huius operis coegit ad fabricam, vel favor popularis applausus insolentem invitavit ad operam, sed ne meus sermo contraheret de curae raritate rubiginem aliorumque profectibus labore mei studii desudarem.

* * *

5. In this work may be heard the rules of grammar, the terms of dialectic, the commonplaces of rhetoric, the paradoxes of arithmetic, the harmonies of music, the axioms of geometry, the linear theorems, the surpassing dignity of astronomy, the maxims of divine theophany. Therefore let not senseless persons impose their own understanding on this work, who cannot extend the course of reason beyond the boundaries of the senses, who either study things seen in dreams of the imagination, or produce unreality by commenting on things they cannot fathom. But those who do not permit the substance of their reasoning to be limited to crude imaginings, but dare to rise to the contemplation of supercelestial form, may enter the narrow portal of my work, and weigh on the scale of sound judgment what deserves to be offered to a popular audience, or should be laid to rest in total silence. For as I do not fear the inevitable onslaught of detraction from some, neither do I expect the favoring breeze of approval from others. For what led me to produce this work was no upsurge of hidden pride ready to burst forth in public, nor did the promise of popular applause persuade me to take up this unfamiliar task, but concern lest my literary powers grow rusty from infrequent exercise, and lest I should exhaust myself in scholarly labor only for the benefit of others.

* * *

Prologus

Autoris mendico stilum falerasque poetae,
ne mea segnitie Clio deiecta senescat,
ne iaceat calamus scabra rubigine torpens.
Scribendi novitate vetus iuvenescere carta
5   gaudet, et antiquas cupiens exire latebras
ridet, et in tenui lascivit harundine musa.
Fonte tuo sic, Phoebe, tuum perfunde poetam,
ut compluta tuo mens arida flumine, germen
donet, et in fructus concludat germinis usum.

Liber Primus

Ut sibi iuncta magis Naturae dona resultent,
et proprium donet donis mixtura favorem,
sollers Naturae studium, quae singula sparsim
munera contulerat aliis, concludit in unum.
5   Cudit opus per quod operi concluditur omni:
pristina sic operum peccata repensat in uno,
ut quod deliquit aliis compenset in isto.
Supplicat huic operi famulans opus omne decoris,
et tanta cupiens vestiri dote favoris,
10   incudis deposcit opem. Sed fessa laborat
incus, quae tantos vires expendit in usus.

Verse Prologue

I appeal for the voice of authority, the trappings of a poet, that my Muse may not grow old overcome by sloth, and my pen lie idle, coated with rust. My long neglected page finds the joy of youth in a new form of writing, laughs in its eager- 5
ness to emerge from the shadows of the past, and inspiration frolics in my slender reed. Phoebus, pour forth your waters on your poet, that his dry mind, watered by your stream, may become fertile, and bring the growth of the seed to fruition.

Book 1

That Nature's gifts, combined together, may better declare themselves; that the combination may bestow upon them a charm of its own; she, who had distributed all her gifts hither and thither among her other creatures, now gives her tireless energy to a single work that will contain them all. She forges a work which will be the consummation of all 5
her work, a single work whereby she atones for the flaws of her original creation, so that what is lacking in her other creatures may be made good in this. To aid in this task she calls on every kind of beauty; then, eager that her work be dressed out with this abundance of charm, she seeks the 10
help of her forge. But the anvil which has lent its strength to so many tasks now labors in exhaustion.

Ultra se se posse studet Natura suumque
supra se metitur opus. Sic vincere fertur
artifices alios, quod se superare fatetur.

15　Nec subitos animi motus perpessa, repente
currit ad haec opera, sed adhuc deliberat utrum
possit, et ad libram rationis singula pensat.

Protinus ergo suas vocat in sua vota sorores
a quibus emeriti descendat tramite recto

20　regula consilii mentisque coherceat aestum,
ut sic, freta suae scalpro rationis, in ipsos
effectus operum mentis deducat ydeas,
aut lima meliore diu concepta recidat.

Ergo consilii non aspernata rigorem,

25　concilium caeleste vocat. Peregrinat ab alto
militiae caelestis honor terramque serenat
luce sua, dignatus humum vestire beatis
gressibus, et nostri tolerans fastidia mundi;
a splendore suo descendit regia caeli.

30　Dum lumen proprium terrae concedit ad horam,
iam nova miratur tellus vestigia ferre;
gaudet onus, sed vis oneris pensatur honore.

Pacis alumna movet primos Concordia gressus,
et pleno cuncta perfundens Copia cornu,

35　et Favor, et multo perfusa Favore Iuventus,
et Risus nostrae proscribens nubila mentis,
et Pudor, et certo contenta Modestia fine,
et Ratio, mensura boni, quam semper adhaerens
felici gressu felix comitatur Honestas,

40　et Decus, et cuncta trutinans Prudentia libra,

Nature strives to attain what exceeds her powers; she
sets herself tasks that are beyond her. She is reputed to triumph so far over other artisans, that she is said to have surpassed even herself. Allowing no impulsive thought to move   15
her, she does not rush hastily to this task, but still ponders
whether she can accomplish it, weighing each idea in the
scale of reason.

Then she calls her sisters to aid her, that from them the
guidance of wise experience may descend by a straight path   20
and quiet her anxious mind; that by thus trusting to the
keenness of her reason she may bring the ideas in her mind
to the concrete realization of the work; or that with this
finer file she may refine her long-held plans.

Therefore she does not disdain their stern counsel, but
convenes a celestial council. The honored ones of the heav-   25
enly legion journey forth from on high, and illumine the
earth with their light. Deigning to adorn the ground with
their blessed footsteps and suffer the distastefulness of our
world, the royalty of heaven descend from their splendid
home. While they for a time grant their radiance to the   30
world, the earth is amazed to feel these new footsteps; it rejoices in this burden, but the weight of the burden is compensated by the honor.

Concord, nursling of Peace, is the first to step forth; then
Abundance, pouring all good things from her full horn; and
Grace, and Youth, whom Grace most imbues; and Mirth,   35
who banishes the dark clouds from our minds; and Shame,
and Modesty, whom definite bounds make happy; and Reason, the measure of well-being: blessed Honesty is ever her
close companion, and matches her own blessed footsteps
to hers. Glory, and Prudence, on whose scale all things are   40

et Pietas, et vera Fides, quae fraudis in umbra
nobis ypocritum mentiri nescit amorem,
et virtus quae spargit opes, quae munera fundit,
quam penes ignorat ignavam gaza quietem,
45   nec dormire potest thesauri massa sepulti,
sed mutat varios totiens peregrina magistros.
    Ultima Nobilitas, et formae laude secunda,
a longe sequitur harum vestigia. Quamvis
nescioquid praesigne gerat, tamen huius ad unguem
50   non poterat reliquis facies aequare decorem;
munere Fortunae melior sed parcius ipsa
gratia Naturae dotes effundit in illa.
Haec superum soboles gressus maturat in arcem
Naturae proprioque domum chorus afflat honore.
55   Est locus a nostro secretus climate tractu
longo, nostrorum ridens fermenta locorum.
Iste potest solus quicquid loca cetera possunt;
quod minus in reliquis melius suppletur in uno.
Quid praelarga manus Naturae possit et in quo
60   gratius effundat dotes, exponit in isto,
in quo, pubescens tenera lanugine florum,
sideribus stellata suis, succensa rosarum
murice, terra novum contendit pingere caelum.
Non ibi nascentis expirat gratia floris
65   nascendo moriens; nec enim rosa mane puella
vespere languet anus, sed vultu semper eodem
gaudens aeterni iuvenescit munere veris.
Hunc florem non urit hyems, non decoquit aestas,
non ibi bacchantis Boreae furit ira, nec illic
70   fulminat aura Nothi, nec spicula grandinis instant.
Quicquid depascit oculos vel inhebriat aures,

weighed; and Compassion, and Good Faith who never feigns a hypocritical love for us under the shadow of fraud; and that virtue who spreads her riches abroad, who showers us with gifts: in her hands wealth never knows ignoble rest, and no mass of buried treasure is allowed to sleep; instead it goes abroad, continually changing masters. 45

Last comes Nobility; her beauty merits less praise, and she follows in the footsteps of the others at a distance. Though she displays a certain distinction, her appearance cannot perfectly match the beauty of the others; she is bet- 50 ter endowed with the gifts of Fortune, but the true favor of Nature bestows its gifts on her more sparingly. All these children of the gods direct their steps to the palace of Nature, and the throng infuse the house with their own glory.

There is a place, a retreat far distant from our own region, 55 which laughs at the tumult of our world. This place alone can produce whatever all other places produce; whatever is scarce elsewhere is in good supply here. All that the generous hand of Nature can achieve, and in which she bestows 60 her gifts most freely, she brings forth here. Here, showing the first signs of adolescence with a delicate sprinkling of flowers, gleaming with stars of her own, alight with the purple of the rose, earth strives to paint a new heaven. Here the beauty of the newborn flower does not expire, dying even 65 as it blooms; the maiden rose of morning does not become evening's weary old woman. With face ever the same she remains young, rejoicing in the gift of an eternal springtime. Winter does not blast these flowers, nor summer parch them. The wrath of frenzied Boreas does not rage here, the breath of Notus brings no thunder, nor do shafts of hail ha- 70 rass them. Whatever feasts our sight, intoxicates our ears,

seducit gustus, nares suspendit odore,
demulcet tactum, retinet locus iste locorum.
Iste parit, nullo vexatus vomere, quicquid
75   militat adversum morbos nostramque renodat,
instantis morbi proscripta peste, salutem.
Non rerum vulgus, verum miracula gignens
sponte, nec externo tellus adiuta colono,
Naturae contenta manu Zephirique favore,
80   parturit et tanta natorum prole superbit.

    Flore novo gaudens, folio crinita virenti,
non demorsa situ, non iram passa securis,
non deiecta solo, sparsis non devia ramis,
ambit silva locum, muri mentita figuram.
85   Non florum praedatur opes foliique capillum
tondet hyems, teneram florum depasta iuventam.
Exilium patitur arbor quaecumque tributum
germinis et fructus Naturae solvere nescit,
cuius mercari fructu meliore favorem
90   contendens aliasque suo praecellere dono,
quaelibet et semper de partu cogitat arbor.

    Syrenes nemorum, citharistae veris, in illum
convenere locum mellitaque carmina sparsim
commentantur aves, dum gutturis organa pulsant.
95   Pingunt ore liram, dum cantus imbibit istos
auditus, dulces offert sonus auribus escas.

    In medio lacrimatur humus fletuque beato
producens lacrimas, fontem sudore perhenni
parturit et dulces potus singultat aquarum.
100   Exuit ingenitas faeces argenteus amnis,
ad puri remeans elementi iura, nitore
fulgurat in proprio, peregrina faece solutus.

seduces our palate, entrances our nostrils with its odor, is smooth to the touch; this place of all places contains it. Undisturbed by the plow, this land bears whatever wars against disease and restores our health, banishing the contagion of threatening disease. Bearing spontaneously not common plants, but rather miraculous ones, unaided by any attendant husbandman but content with the hand of nature and the favoring breeze, the earth gives birth, proud of so great a progeny.

A wood surrounds the place, assuming the likeness of a wall. It rejoices in an ever new flowering, decked with verdant foliage, neither ravaged by decay nor prey to the angry ax, not felled to the ground or rendered pathless by fallen branches. No winter preys on its wealth of blooms and coat of foliage, devouring the tender youth of its blossoms. Exile is the lot of any tree that cannot offer its tribute of growth and fruit to Nature. Striving to gain Nature's favor with finer fruit, and to rise above the others by its special gift, every tree is perpetually concerned with bearing fruit.

Sirens of the grove, spring's choristers, the birds congregate in this place, practicing their honeyed song all around, as their piping throats give it forth. Their voices imitate the lyre, and as the hearer drinks in these sounds, their melody brings to his ears a sweet repast.

At the center of the glade the earth is weeping. Producing a blessed stream of tears it gives rise to an ever-flowing fountain, and it sobs forth sweet drafts of water. The silvery stream has rid itself of any inherent taint; returning to a state of elemental purity, it shimmers in its true brightness, purged of foreign waste. This draft stirs the womb of the

Praegnantis gremium telluris inebriat iste
potus et ad partus invitant vota parentis.
105 Arboribus similes tellus non invida potus
donat et affectum pariendi suggerit illis.
    In medio nemoris evadit in aëra montis
ardua planities et nubibus oscula donat.
    Hic domus erigitur Naturae, si tamen isto
110 nomine censeri fas sit, cum numine possit
sidereas superare domos superumque penates,
nec sibi dignetur conferre palatia regum.
A nostris laribus excepta beatior aula
aëra metitur, altis suspensa columnis.
115 Sidere gemmarum praefulgurat, ardet in auro
nec minus argenti proprio donatur honore.
Non ibi materies quae sit demissior istis
iura tenet propriaque potest plebescere forma.
    Hic hominum mores picturae gratia scribit.
120 Sic operi proprio pictura fideliter heret,
ut res picta minus a vero deviet esse.
O nova picturae miracula! Transit ad esse
quod nihil esse potest picturaque simia veri,
arte nova ludens, in res umbracula rerum
125 vertit et in verum mendacia singula mutat.
Sic logicae vires artis subtiliter huius
argumenta premunt logicaeque sophismata vincunt.
Haec probat, ista facit; haec disputat, impetrat ista
omne quod esse potest: sic utraque vera videri
130 falsa cupit, sed ad haec pictura fidelius instat.
    Illic arma parat logico logicaeque palestram
pingit Aristoteles. Sed eo divinius ipsa
somniat arcana rerum caelique profunda

pregnant earth, and parental prayers summon forth new births. The ungrudging earth grants similar drafts to the trees, and instills in them a desire to bear fruit. 105

In the midst of the grove the steep face of a mountain rises into the air and offers kisses to the clouds. Here rises the dwelling of Nature—if indeed it be right to assign it such a name; for in divine majesty it can claim to surpass the starry dwellings and the abodes of the heavenly powers, and it would scorn comparison with the palaces of kings. Far removed from our human dwellings, this blessed hall rises into the air, supported by lofty columns. It gleams with star-like gems, glows with gold, and is no less endowed with the dignity of silver. No material that is inferior to these, or whose appearance might render its beauty commonplace, can claim a place here. 110 115

Here the charm of painting depicts the characters of men. So faithfully does this painting pursue its task that the painted object scarcely differs from the real. O the new miracles of painting! What cannot exist comes into existence, for painting, the ape of truth, sporting with rare skill, turns the shadows of things into the things themselves, and changes each falsehood into truth. Thus the arguments of this art prove stronger than the powers of logic, and conquer logic's sophisms. That art offers proofs, this creates; that disputes, this realizes whatever can come to be. Thus while both arts seek to make things false appear true, painting attains this end more truthfully. 120 125 130

Here Aristotle prepares the weapons of the logician, and lays out the wrestling hall of logic. But Plato, a spirit more divine, dreams in profound thought the hidden mysteries of

mente Plato, sensumque Dei perquirere temptat.
135 More suo Seneca mores ratione monetat,
optimus excultor morum mentisque colonus.
Divitis ingenii vena Ptholomeus inundans,
devectus superas curru rationis in arces
colligit astrorum numeros, loca, tempora, cursus.
140 Verbi pauperiem redimit splendore colorum
Tullius et dictis ornatus fulgura donat.
Virgilii musa mendacia multa colorat
et facie veri contexit pallia falso.
    Hic vigor et sensus aequali munere lance
145 pensant: Alcidem vigor armat, sensus Ulixem.
Ne mentem fermentet opum convictus, habunde
fudit opes Titus et munera cogit abire.
Militat instantis fervens audacia Turni,
ense tonans, ignara metus et prodiga vitae.
150 Ypolitique pudor Veneris subductus habenis
gaudet et excepto luget Cytherea pudore.
    Has species rerumque tropos et sompnia veri
regia picta tenet, tanto festiva decore.
Sed minus in vultu gestans insigne decoris
155 postremos subtristis habet pictura penates,
ut lusisse parum, vel saltem somnia passam
credas, vel tenues irae sensisse procellas,
vel magis oblitam facti praesentis in illa
Naturam pecasse putes: delira videtur
160 picturae facies meliorem poscere formam.
Sed neque gemmarum radius splendore diescens,
nec nitor argenti, nec fulgure gratius aurum

earth and heaven, and strives to see into the mind of God.
As is his custom, Seneca, best of moral teachers and culti- 135
vators of mind, stamps morality with the seal of reason.
Ptolemy, a mother lode of the riches of understanding, is
borne up to the vaults of heaven by the chariot of reason,
and sets down the numbers of the stars, their houses, seasons, and courses. Tully redeems the poverty of language 140
with the colors of rhetoric, and bestows on his words the
brilliance of artful order. The Muse of Virgil gives color to
many lies, and weaves for falsehood a garment with the appearance of truth.

Here strength and astuteness weigh their powers in a
scale that shows them equal: Strength is Alcides's weapon, 145
astuteness that of Ulysses. Lest feasting on riches corrupt
his mind, Titus pours out his abundant wealth, and casts
abroad his bounty. The bold fury of impetuous Turnus wages
war with clashing sword, ignorant of fear and with no care
for his life. Hippolytus's purity rejoices to have avoided the 150
reins of Venus, and Cytherea mourns the escape of one so
chaste.

Such forms, exemplary figures and imaginings of truth
the painted palace displays, joying in such beauty. But painting more troubled appears in the newer chambers; its ap- 155
pearance exhibits fewer marks of beauty, so that you would
think Nature had been merely playing, or at the least was
vexed by dreams, or had felt the faint stirrings of anger. You
might think, indeed, that Nature had failed here, forgetful
of the task at hand, for the crazy appearance of the painting 160
seems to show a need for better workmanship. But neither
the radiance of jewels, splendid as the light of day, nor polished silver, nor the still finer gleam of gold can excuse the

excusare potest picturae crimen adultum
quin pictura suo languens pallescat in auro.
165   Illic pannoso plebescit carmine noster
Ennius et Priami fortunas intonat. Illic
Mevius in caelos audens os ponere mutum
"gesta ducis Macedum" tenebrosi carminis umbra
pingere dum temptat, in primo limine fessus
170 haeret et ignavam queritur torpescere musam.
Illic praecipiti Nero fulmine concutit orbem;
indulgens sceleri, cogit plus velle furorem,
quam furor ipse velit; quicquid distillat ab illo
nequitiae totum sese partitur in orbem.
175 Illic dives eget, sitit aurum totus in auro
Midas, nec metas animo concedit habendi.
Militis excedit legem plus milite miles
Aiax militiaeque modus decurrit in iram.
Fractus amore Paris, Veneris decoctus in igne,
180 militat in Venerem; dum militis exuit actus,
damnose compensat in hac quod perdit in armis.
In Davo propriam miratur noctua formam
et vultus peccata sui solatur in illo.
    Ergo Naturae quicquid munuscula plene
185 percipit aut eius modicam subterfugit artem,
inscriptum calamis picturae fabula monstrat.
    Singula decernens sensu Natura profundo,
sedibus his sua iura tenet, legesque figurat
provida, quas toto sparsim promulgat in orbe.
190 Scrutatur rerum causas et semina mundi:
quis chaos antiquum vultu meliore redemit,
dum formae melioris opem vultusque decorem

consummate badness of such art: even when set with gold such a painting seems weak and sickly.

Here our modern Ennius fashions patchwork verse in a 165
low style, bellowing about the fortunes of Priam. There Maevius, daring to lift his mute face toward the heavens as he labors to depict "the deeds of the ruler of Macedon" in a pale shadow of dismal verse, halts, exhausted on the very threshold, and complains that his lazy muse is becoming 170
useless. There Nero shakes the earth with his reckless thunderbolts; abandoned to crime, he drives his madness to demand more than madness itself would demand; whatever wickedness he exudes spreads through the whole world. Here wealth is needy; Midas, surrounded by gold, thirsts for 175
gold, and accepts no limit to his desire to possess. Ajax, more warlike than any warrior, abandons the warrior's code, and measure in warfare turns to rage. Paris, made feeble by love, boiled away by the fire of Venus, wars against Venus: while 180
he abandons the role of soldier, she is the ruinous compensation for his failures in battle. In Davus the night owl marvels at an appearance like his own, and consoles himself with this for the ugliness of his face.

Thus the fiction of painting reveals with its descriptive pen creatures granted a full measure of the gifts of Nature, 185
and others that have evaded her tempering art.

Nature, who judges all things with profound understanding, is the ruler in this place; farseeing, she designs laws which she then proclaims throughout the world. She ex- 190
plores the causes of things and the seeds of the universe: she sees what power redeemed ancient chaos with a fairer appearance, when primal matter, bemoaning its tumultuous condition, begged for the gift of a nobler form, a beautiful

quaereret atque suum lugeret silva tumultum;
quis fidei nexu civilia bella refrenans,
195 et fratrum rixas, elementis oscula pacis
indidit et numeri nodo meliore ligavit.
Terrarum motus, mugitum fulminis, iras
oceani, ventorum proelia mente fideli
conspicit, et certa sollers indagine claudit
200 temporis excursus; cur contristata pruinis
luget hyems cana, ridet ver, aestuat aestas,
effluit autumnus rerum torrente profundo,
vel cur terra sedet, fluit amnis, profluit aër,
flamma volat reliquisque fidem non invida servat;
205 non audens violare fidem cur foedera terris
labilis unda tenet, certo contenta meatu.

    Postquam caelestis aurata sedilia coetus
implevit tantaque nitens deitate refulsit
ipsa domus, tanti lucem mirata diei,
210 concilii stetit in medio Natura, parumper
in terram demissa caput, concepta severis
vultibus exponens dextraque silentia dictans,
suspendensque animos, voces exivit in istas:
    "Saepe, diu, multum sollerti mente retracto
215 singula quae nostrae pinxit sollertia dextrae,
sed nihil invenio quod in omni parte beate
vivat, quin multas nobis deferre querelas
possit, si nostram velit accusare Minervam.
Sed nostras erasse manus, quia paenitet, error
220 haud nocet et nostros denigrat parcius actus.
Nec tamen haerentes maculas abstergere possum,
quas habitus firmi praescriptio longa tuetur.

face; what power by a pact of trust curbed civil war and fraternal strife, bestowing on the elements the kiss of peace, 195 and joining them together with the better bond of harmony. She beholds with steadfast mind the tremblings of the earth, the deep roar of thunder, the raging sea, the warring winds, and carefully confines the course of the seasons to a fixed 200 cycle. She sees why hoary winter mourns, sorely afflicted by frost, while spring is happy; why summer grows hot, while autumn overflows with the vast torrent of its fruits; why the earth is stable, water flows, air moves freely, why fire flies upward, and ungrudgingly keeps faith with the others; why 205 ever-moving water holds to its pact with the land, never daring to break faith, and content with its assigned course.

When the heavenly throng have taken gilded chairs, and the house itself, glistening, reflects the brilliance of their divine presence, dazzled by the light of so great a day, Nature 210 stands forth in the midst of the council. She bows her head toward the ground for a moment, revealing her thoughts by her grave expression, and motioning with her hand for silence. Keeping their minds suspended, she brings forth these words:

"Often, long, and with much force of mind have I reviewed everything which the skill of our hand has set forth, 215 yet I find nothing whose life is so blessed in every way that it would not be able to bring many complaints against us, if it wished to cast blame on our wisdom. But because we repent the errors our hands have made, the fault does no 220 harm, and scarcely discredits our work. Yet I am unable to eliminate these fast-clinging stains; the longstanding excuse of a confirmed habit protects them. For medicine falls silent

Nam medicina silet, ubi morbi causa senescit,
nec morbi veteres molimina tarda requirunt.
225   "Unica coniecto tantae solatia pestis,
quae tamen effectu describere nolo, priusquam
norma iudicii vestri mens nostra probetur.
Hoc in mente diu scriptum mihi sedit, ut omnes
et simul instanter, caute, sollerter ad unum
230   desudemus opus, in quo tot munera fundat
quaelibet, ut post has dotes videatur egere.
Nostrorum crimen operum redimatur in uno;
unius probitas multorum crimina penset;
unaque quamplures exterminet unda litturas.
235   "Non terrae faecem redolens, non materialis
sed divinus homo nostro molimine terras
incolat et nostris donet solatia damnis.
Insideat caelis animo, sed corpore terris;
in terris humanus erit, divinus in astris.
240   Sic homo sicque deus fiet, sed factus uterque
quod neuter, mediaque via tutissimus ibit;
in quo nostra manus et munera nostra loquantur;
sit speculum nobis, ut nos speculemur in illo
quae sit nostra fides, quae nostra potentia, virtus
245   quae sit et in quantum melius procedere possit.
     "Si labor accusat nostros in munere tanto
defectus onerique manus succumbere nostro,
hoc decus excusat, solvens obiecta laboris.
Si natura negat, animi succurrere robur
250   debet et affectus effectu claudere nostros.
Nam, quod nulla valet per se, supplebit in unum
coniurata manus, ut quae non singula prosunt,
multa iuvent collecta simul; nam plurimus amnem

when the cause of the illness grows old; ancient illnesses do not ask for treatments applied too late.

"I have conceived a unique means of relief from so great a 225 plague, but I will not speak of its implementation before our thought is tested by the standard of your judgment. This idea has long been inscribed in my mind: that all of us together should apply ourselves, in earnest, carefully and skillfully, to a single work, on which each should bestow so many 230 gifts that after this donation she herself will seem to be in need. Let the fault of our works be made good in one single work; let the worthiness of one compensate for the faults of many; let a single wave wipe away these blots, many though they be.

"Let a man who does not reek of earthly foulness, a man 235 not material but divine, dwell on earth though our efforts, and console us for our injuries. Let his mind dwell in the heavens, his body on earth; on earth he will be human, among the stars a god. Thus he will be created a man, and 240 thus a god, yet so made each that he is neither, and will pursue the middle way with full assurance. In him let our skill and our gifts declare themselves; let him be a mirror for us, that we may see reflected in him our good faith, our power, our worth, and how well they can prove themselves. 245

"If the difficulty of so great an undertaking exposes our weakness, and our hands give way to our heavy burden, the beauty of our plan is our excuse, absolving our work from criticism. If nature denies us, strength of will must sustain us, and ensure the realization of our desires. For what none 250 can accomplish by herself, our skills, conspiring for a single purpose, will achieve; where the effort of one cannot avail, many joined together will aid her. For many swollen streams

243

rivulus excrescens gignit, scintillaque flammam
255 multa parit, multusque lapis concludit acervum.
    "Heu! pudeat nostrum totiens errasse laborem
et totiens fructum male respondisse labori!
Heu! pudeat nostra terris decreta silere,
quod nostri languescit amor, quod fama tepescens
260 torpet et a toto viles proscribimur orbe,
quod laxas mundo sceleris concedit habenas
Thesiphone, nostraque sibi de gente triumphans
gaudet, et a nostro suggit sibi gaudia luctu.
Vincimur et victas pedibus summittit Herinis
265 et gravibus nostras castigat colla catenis."
    Sic Natura suo mentem sermone figurans,
fine dato verbis, orantis fine perorat.
Gaudet et assentit Naturae curia, votum
laudat et a voto non distant vota sororum.
270   Surgit ad haec placidi vultus gestusque modesti
circumscripta modum Prudentia. Colla pererrat
aurea caesaries, sed acus mediata refrenat
litigium crinis et regula pectinis instat.
Ordo supercilii, iusto libramine ductus,
275 nec nimis exhaustus nec multa nube pilorum
luxurians, sese geminos exemplat in arcus.
Luminis astra iubar, frons lilia, balsama naris,
dens ebur osque rosam parit offert reddit adaequat.
Spirat in ore color vivus nec candor adulter
280 turpiter effingit tanti phantasma decoris.
Siderei vultus castigavere ruborem
lilia nupta rosis et, ne palloris obumbrent
nubila candorem, defendit flamma ruboris.
Clarior argento, fulvo conspectior auro

create a river; many sparks produce fire; many stones end up   255
as a pile.

"Alas! Be it our shame that our efforts have so often failed,
that the fruits of our labor have so often been a poor reward!
Alas! Let it shame us that our decrees are not heard on earth,
that love of us has grown feeble, our reputation has diminished and lost its power, and we are ignominiously banished   260
from the world; that Tisiphone has given free rein to evil in
the world, glories in her triumph over our race, and sucks joy
for herself from our suffering. We are conquered: Erinys
holds us defeated beneath her heel, and burdens our necks   265
with heavy chains."

Thus Nature, having expressed her thoughts in speech
and made an end of speaking, brings her speech to its conclusion. Nature's court gives its joyous assent; the sisters
commend her appeal, and their own desires do not differ
from hers.

Now Providence rises, she of the gentle face and manner,   270
keeping always within the bounds of modesty. Her golden
hair falls around her neck, but a pin parting her hair in the
middle prevents disagreement, and a comb imposes its rule.
The line of her eyebrows is drawn with perfect symmetry;
they are neither too sparse nor reveling in a great cloud of   275
hairs, and they form themselves into twin arcs. Her starry
eyes give forth light, her forehead shows lily-white, her nose
has the scent of balsam, her teeth are like ivory, her mouth
like a rosebud. Living color plays over her face; no counterfeit glow produces base imitation of such beauty. Lilies wed-   280
ded to roses chasten the glow of her starry face, and the
warmth of a blush prevents the clouds of pallor from over-
shadowing its brilliance. Brighter than silver, more striking

245

285 lucidior glacie, cristallo gratior omni,
menti planities roseo non derogat ori.
Non male colla sedent, humeris non insidet alta
cervix sed spatio surgit distincta modesto.
Poma mamillarum, modico suspensa tumore,
290 nulla mollitie dependent fracta, sed ipsa
duritie proprii describunt signa pudoris.
Explicat explicito tractu iunctura lacertos
amplexusque suos deposcere bracchia credas.
Imaque conciliat summis extremaque primis
295 convallis laterum, modulo submissa decenti.
Cetera quis nescit meliora latere sub istis
quorum sola gerunt placidi praeludia vultus?
Canone sub certo dimensio nulla retardat
corporis excursum vel certo fine refrenat.
300 Nunc magis evadens caelestia vertice pulsat,
nunc oculos frustrans caelestibus insidet, ad nos
nunc redit et nostra sese castigat habena.
  Vestis erat filo tenui contexta, colorem
non mentita suum, nulloque sophismate visum
305 decipit, immo rubor nativus inebriat illam.
Non ibi materies formae suffragia quaerit
nec formae peccata sibi velamina quaerunt
materiae; neutra succumbit, neutra sorori
cedit et ex aequo certant utra vincere possit.
310   Somniat hic rerum species pictura resultans,
quas tamen ex parte iubet expirare vetustas,
et formae veteris vestigia pauca supersunt.
Sed tamen in partes vestem diffibulat istam
in variis scissura locis; lugere videtur
315 vestis et illata sibimet convicia flere.

than tawny gold, clearer than ice, finer than any crystal, the 285
smooth surface of her chin does not dishonor her rosy lips.
Her neck is not set awry; the upright nape does not cling to
her shoulders, but rises only to a seemly extent. The apples
of her breasts, descending to a gentle swelling, do not hang 290
drooping and flaccid, but by their very firmness are a manifest sign of her inherent purity. From the shoulder her arms
extend with an unhindered movement, and you might suppose that they sought an embrace. The inward curve of her
waist, submitting itself to an appropriate restraint, joins 295
lower parts to higher, the least to the greatest. And who does
not know that other and better parts lie hidden below these,
parts to which her quiet beauty serves as prelude? No standard measure limits her body's height to a fixed size, or confines her within fixed boundaries. Now rising on high she 300
strikes her head against the heavens, now eluding our eyes
she sits among the heavenly beings, now returns and submits herself to our rein.

Her garment, woven of fine thread, does not falsify its
color, or deceive our sight with trickery; instead a natural, 305
blushing red suffuses it. Its material does not seek the support of form, nor do any faults of form seek to veil themselves in its material; neither succumbs, neither yields to her
sister, and they compete on equal terms to see which will
prevail.

Here painting dreams the reflected forms of creatures, 310
though old age has caused them to grow somewhat faint,
and mere traces of the original shapes survive. However
tears in several places have divided her robe into pieces; the
garment seems to mourn, and weep at the insults inflicted 315

Dextra manus librat trutinam quae singula pensat
in numero, forma, mensura, pondere, causa.
　His ornata modis, isto festiva paratu,
verba parat sollers Prudentia cuius ab ore
320　curia dependet. Currunt instanter ad illam
visus et auditus, sed voto dispare certant:
visus, ut in specie tanta convivia quaerat
auditusque favos verborum suggat ab ore.
His igitur verbis mentem Prudentia pingit,
325　dum tenet intentas attentio tanta sorores:
　"Nil nisi divinum sapit haec sententia, tanti
provida consilii, quae sic rationis in igne
decoquitur quod nulla manent vestigia faecis.
Non fluidum redolent animum, non mentis obesae
330　segnitiem loquitur. Subitis non motibus instat
a summis exputa labris, sed mentis ab alto
prominet et nostris offert medicamina morbis.
Trans hominem mens ista sapit, condita sapore
divinae mentis, de cuius fonte profundo
335　rivulus emanat, animi discretio vestri.
Non igitur iacet exanimis, non indiga recti;
non rationis inops, non mens effrenis oberrat,
non agitur casu tanto suffulta patrono.
Quae tantam mentem detractio mordeat, aut quis
340　urgeat invidiae stimulus, quis nubila livor
misceat aut odium, cum limes regius illam
dirigat et recto producat calle viantem?
　"Ne vestrae faciat conceptio mentis aborsum,
ne res tanta ruat, ne lux moriatur in umbra
345　sed magis exposita praefulgeret, exeat istud
in commune bonum; melius sub luce patebit.

upon it. Her right hand holds suspended a scale, which determines the number, form, measure, weight, and cause of each creature.

Adorned in this way, festive in such a costume, Providence earnestly prepares her speech as the assembly hangs 320 on her words. Sight and hearing fly eagerly toward her, but they race toward different goals: sight seeks to feast on her great beauty, hearing to suck honeyed words from her lips. Then, while keen attention holds her expectant sisters, Providence sets forth her thoughts in these words: 325

"This plan, carefully formed with utmost deliberation, has in it nothing that is not divine; it has been so refined by the fire of reason that no traces of impurity remain. It has not the scent of an unstable mind, nor does it bespeak the dullness of sluggish thought. It is not the urging of a sud- 330 den impulse, spewed from the mouth alone, but comes forth from the depth of the mind, and offers a remedy for our disease. This idea has a quality beyond the reach of men, it is imbued with the savor of the divine mind, that deep well from which flow, like a stream, your powers of discernment. 335 Thus your mind does not lie lifeless, in need of direction, bereft of reason; it does not wander unguided, nor is it controlled by chance, upheld as you are by such a patron. What slander can gnaw at such a mind, or what sting of envy pro- 340 voke it? What spite or hostility can overshadow it, when a royal highway shows the way, and leads the traveler forward along a straight path?

"But so that the plan your mind has conceived may not miscarry, a project so grand not go to ruin; so that light may not succumb to shadow, but rather shine the brighter for 345 having been revealed, let it emerge for the good of all: it will

Namque bonum quod saepe latet splendore minori
degenerat; lucetque magis si luce fruatur.
Sic flos in fructus, in flumen rivus inundans
350   ibit et in messem pinguis procedet arista.
Quid melius sperare potest, quid maius et ultra,
quid poterit velle conceptus mentis honestae?
Si bonus est, hucusque licet, defigat in illo
gressus proposito nec longius ire laboret.
355   "Sed tamen hoc superest quod mentem concutit, obstat
proposito, vexat animum, concepta retardat:
quod tanti vires operis tot pondera rerum
tantum nescit opus, operas suspirat ad istas
nostra manus, quae sic hominem conducit ad esse,
360   quod non perducit; facit hunc, nec perficit ipsum;
semper ad esse movet, sed numquam promovet illum;
eius ad esse valet nec ad eius praevalet ortum.
    "Dispar natura, distans substantia, forma
discors, esse duplex hominis concurrit ad esse.
365   Una sapit terras, caelum sapit altera; caelis
insidet haec, illa terris, mortique tributum
cogitur ista dare, mortis lex excipit illam.
Haec manet, illa fluit; haec durat, deperit illa.
essendi nomen gerit haec, gerit altera numen;
370   corpus habet terras, caelestia spiritus; ergo
terram terra tenet, retinent caelestia caeli.
    "Incudem nostram corpus mortale fatetur,
artifices nostros et nostram postulat artem.
Artifices alios animae natale requirit,
375   artificis melioris opem caelestis origo

show itself more fully in the light. For often a good that lies hidden, its splendor diminished, loses its force; it will shine more brightly if it is given light. Thus the flower turns into fruit, a flowing stream becomes a river, and ripening grain 350 comes to the harvest. What better destiny can the issue of a noble mind desire? What greater, what higher could it seek? If the plan is good, it is right to proceed so far; but let it plant its steps with this proposal, and not labor to go further.

"This concern, however, remains; it troubles my mind, 355 presents an obstacle to what is proposed, disturbs my thinking and impedes my thoughts: that our hands lack the strength for so great a work, for the burden of so much responsibility, for such a task; they are exhausted by such labor. They bring a man to the threshold of a being which they 360 cannot achieve; they can make him, but not perfect him; they constantly move him toward being but never accomplish it; they have the power to bring him into existence, but not to bring him to life.

"In this man a twofold being, different in nature, distinct in substance, dissonant in form, comes together in a single being. One smacks of earth, the other of heaven; one dwells 365 in the heavens, the other on earth; one is compelled to pay death his tribute, while death's law exempts the other. One remains when the other passes away; one is enduring, the other mortal. One bears the title of being, but the other possesses its sacred power. The body claims the earth, the 370 spirit the heavenly realm; for earth cleaves to earth, while the heavens preserve things heavenly.

"His mortal body will display the work of our forge; it requires artisans like us, and all our skill. But giving birth to his soul requires another artistry; a heavenly origin 375

postulat et nostram fugit eius forma monetam;
divinique loquens operis miracula, nostrum
spernit opus, ridens artis vulgaria nostrae.
Qualiter ex nihilo, sine forma semine causa
380   materia motu sensu ductore ministro
ingenitum simplex animabile mobile purum
prodeat exterius, nullo mediante patrono,
sola Dei novit prudentia, cuius ab alto
pectore procedit quicquid procedit in esse.
385   Hic elementa silent, languescunt semina rerum,
sidus hebet, Natura iacet virtusque planetae
deficit et propria miratur iura silere.
   "Ergo cum nostra genituram regula talem
nesciat et tantam stupeat pictura figuram
390   occasumque manus talem patiatur ad ortum,
non video, non concipio, non iudico memet
scire modos causas rationes semina formas
instrumenta quibus, nostra mediante Minerva,
ortus caelestis animae ducatur ad ortum.
395   Ergo consilii super his libramina ferre
nescio; non valeo dubito desisto retardor;
consilio ratione, fide mea causa iacebit
orphana, nec certo claudetur fine voluntas,
singula ni Ratio trutina meliore repenset,
400   quam penes obscurum fluitans mutabile cassum
ignotum mendax nihil est, cui singula lucent,
cuncta patent dubiumque nihil, non alta videntur
astra nec obscurus aer pelagusque profundum;
Sol animi, mentis oculus lumenque vianti

demands the resources of a better artist, and its form is beyond our power to mint. His miraculous being, eloquent of the work of God, would put our handiwork to scorn, mocking our plebeian art. How a being that is simple, endowed with soul, capable of motion, pure, is engendered from nothing, without form, seed, cause, matter, motion, sense, 380 guide or teacher; how it comes to exist without the aid of any patron; this only the providence of God can know, she from whose deep bosom issues everything that comes to be. Here the elements fall silent, the seeds of created life lose 385 their powers, the stars grow faint, Nature lies prostrate, the influence of the planets fails, and they wonder to find that their powers have no effect.

"Since, then, our principles tell us nothing of such a natal horoscope, since the painter can only gape at so fine a pattern, and his skill is eclipsed by such a dawning, I do not see, 390 I cannot conceive, I do not deem myself capable of understanding the means, the causes, the principles, seeds, forms, the tools whereby, through the agency of our wisdom, the creation of a heavenly soul might be brought to birth. Hence 395 I cannot weigh these matters in the scale of judgment; I am ignorant, unable, doubtful, reluctant, hindered; my operative power will be orphaned of counsel, reason and confidence; my will will not be directed to a clear goal, unless Reason weighs all these matters in a better scale. For to the eye of Reason nothing is obscure, indefinite, changeable, 400 without purpose, unknown or deceiving. To her all things are clear, all lie open and there is no doubt. To her the stars do not appear far off, the air murky or the ocean deep. She is the sunlight of thought, the eye of the mind, guiding light

405 proscripti patria, mortis solamen, origo
iustitiae, virtutum regula, linea recti.
"Subducat dubia certis mendacia veris;
in certo figat animum dubiumque recidat.
Erroris tergat tenebras verique serenet
410 luce diem mentis et falsi nubila pellat.
Menti concussae dubiorum fluctibus aura
gratior applaudat Rationis flamine leni
concilians aestus animi fluctusque retardans.
"Segnitiemque meam non tanti massa laboris
415 accusare potest; non tanto victa labore
cedo nec ignavae mendico quietis asylum.
Aggrediar quicquid Ratio dictaverit, immo
iusserit atque nihil de contingentibus ipsa
transgrediar, finem proprio pro posse secuta.
420 Sed quia principia nullo concludere fine,
vel dare principiis fines aliunde profectos,
ut primo medium, medio non consonet imum,
censetur turpe fluitans mutabile stultum,
cedere principiis malo quam cedere fini."
425 Sic ait et tanto dubiorum turbine tota
curia concutitur, turbataque turba sororum
fluctuat in dubiis, alta cum voce fluentes
suspendens animos; et murmura sola pererrant.
Qualiter aura fremit, fluit aer, fluctuat unda,
430 quam primo Zephirus complanat flamine leni,
si maris excutiat borealis turbo soporem,
vel maris instantes cogit vigilare procellas,
sic animi fluitant et mentes mentibus instant;
quas Natura prius leni perflaverat aura,
435 perflat maiori flatu Prudentia mentes.

for the traveler, homeland of the exile, solace of mortality, 405
first principle of justice, standard of the virtues, path of rectitude.

"Let Reason purge our deceitful doubts with certain
truths; let her ground the mind in certainty and cut away
doubt. Let her clear away the darkness of error, brighten the
day of the mind with the light of truth, and banish the clouds 410
of falsehood. Let the favoring breeze of Reason give encouragement to the mind battered by the seas of doubt, calming
its turbulence with her gentle breath, and stilling the waves.

"The weight of so great a task cannot show me guilty of 415
laziness; I do not yield defeated by such labor, nor do I beg
the asylum of ignoble sloth. I will undertake whatever Reason proposes, or indeed commands; and I will omit nothing
the task requires, but aim to complete it as far as I am able.
But since I do not wish to cut off these beginnings with a 420
conclusion, and since to assign them objectives more suited
to other purposes, such that middle would be at odds with
beginning, end with middle, is rightly considered base, aimless, unstable, and stupid, I prefer to yield at the beginning
rather than fail at the end."

Thus speaks Providence, and the whole court is seized by 425
a great whirlwind of uncertainty; the anxious throng of sisters vacillates amid doubts. But they curb thoughts which
rush with a great noise, and only murmurs escape them, just
as the breeze whispers, air trembles, water ripples when 430
Zephyrus first soothes it with his gentle breath; but as if the
turbulent north wind were to strike the slumbering sea or
compel the menacing sea storms to stir themselves, thus
their minds are troubled, and thought wars with thought;
minds which Nature had first soothed with a gentle breeze
Providence now strikes with a greater blast. 435

Erigitur Ratio poscitque silentia nutu
voce manu facie; pacis tranquilla meretur
vultus et ad nutum morientia murmura nutant.
Virginis in facie Prudentia plurima vultu
440   paret et expressi sequitur vestigia vultus.
Suntque relativae facies: gerit altera formam
alterius seseque sibi conformat in illa.
Una sibi facies faciem presentat utramque.
Vultus diversi, facies diversa duarum,
445   non adversa tamen, quales decet esse sororum.
Par facies habitusque pares, par gestus in illis,
par modus atque decor, sed dispar vultus in annis.
Nam potior Ratio senii vexilla gerebat,
plenior aetate, plenis maturior annis.
450   Dextra manus speculi triplicis flammata nitore
splendet et in triplici speculo triplicata resultat
vitrea mollities, quae tactus abdicat omnem
insultum digitique leves vix sustinet ictus.
Unius speculi sese concedit in usum
455   attente Ratio. Speculo speculatur in isto
causarum seriem, rerum scrutatur abyssum,
subiecti formaeque videt connubia, cernit
oscula quae miscet concretio, quaeve propinat
unio nativa, formis subiecta maritans;
460   subiecti quae forma facit, quae perficit esse,
quae rem conducit vel quae perducit ad esse;
quae generat, quae mutat eam, quae servat in esse;
quid sit vel quanta, qualis vel quomodo sese
res habeat reliquosque status perquirit in illa.
465   Argenti facies, faeces exuta metalli,
infra se splendore diem stellasque relinquens,

Reason rises, and calls for silence by her nod, word, gesture, bearing; her placid countenance gains silence; whisper-
ing dies away in response to her nod. In the maiden's appearance there is much of Providence, and her face bears traces   440
of the other's expression. Their bearing is similar, in that
each displays the form of the other, each conforms herself
to the other. The appearance of each brings the other's appearance to mind. The faces of the two differ, and they differ in bearing, yet there is no discord, as befits those who are   445
sisters. They are alike in bearing, alike in dress, alike in carriage, alike in manner and beauty, but their faces differ in
age. For Reason, the stronger of the two, shows the signs of
old age. She is greater in age, mature through the fullness of
time.

Reason's right hand is brightened by the flamelike gleam   450
of a triple mirror, and in the glassy smooth surface of this
triple mirror, which rejects any rudeness of touch, can
scarcely bear the light tap of a finger, a tripled reflection
shines forth. Reason devotes herself attentively to the use of
one of these mirrors: in this mirror she studies the system of   455
causes, probes the depths of creation, views the marriage of
form and matter, discerns the kiss their coalescence effects,
the pledge of their natural union, marrying subjects to their
forms. She sees which form creates, and which completes   460
the being of the subject; which constructs the creature and
which guides him to full being; what generates the creature,
what makes it grow, what sustains its life. She observes in
this mirror what a thing is, its quantity and quality, in what
way it subsists, and the rest of its defining attributes.

A surface of silver, free of any adulterating metal, and re-   465
joicing to leave the sun and stars beneath it in splendor,

exultat, speculi formam vestita secundi.
Hic subiecta videt formis viduata reverti
ad Chaos antiquum propriamque requirere matrem

470 inque statu proprio puram iuvenescere formam
nec sua degeneris subiecti taedia flere;
quomodo forma suo gaudens requiescit in esse,
nec varios fluctus subiecti naufraga sentit;
qualiter ad proprium peregrina revertitur ortum

475 subiecti fugit occasus et funera vitat;
subiecti senio non deflorata iuventus
formarum, formas semper facit esse puellas.
Cernit inoffenso vultu mentisque profundo
quomodo compositum simplex, caeleste caducum,

480 diversum fit idem, gravidum leve, mobile certum,
obscurum lucens, pretiosum vile, iocosum
flebile, perpetuum mortale, volubile fixum.
    Auri nobilitas, auro decoctior omni,
vixque suum dignata genus speciemque fateri

485 in speculi transit speciem, quae tertia rerum
umbras mentiri nescit, sed singula monstrat
certius et specie meliori cuncta figurat.
Hic rerum fontem, mundi genus, orbis ydeam,
exemplar speciem causam primordia finem

490 conspicit et certis metitur singula causis:
qua ratione quibus causis, cur quomodo quando
instabilis genitus fluitans mutabilis iste
mundus ab ingenito stabili certoque figuram
esse statum speciem vitam contraxit et ortum;

495 quomodo terrestrem formam caelestis ydea
gignit et in nostram sobolem transcribit abyssum;
mittit in exilium formas quas destinat orbi;

clothes the form of the second mirror. Here she beholds subject matter, bereft of form, returning to seek its original mother in ancient chaos; and form, in its own state of being, 470 pure, rejuvenated, shedding no tears over the foul state of degenerated matter. She sees how joyous form rests in its own being, a vessel untroubled by the stormy fortunes of matter; how, like a pilgrim, it returns to its true home, flee- 475 ing the disaster of matter and avoiding its grim fate. For the youthful purity of the forms is not violated by the senescence of matter, and ensures them a perpetual maidenhood. She sees with unobstructed sight and profound thought how the composite can be simple, the celestial perishable, how the different is the same, the heavy light, the movable fixed, 480 darkness bright, the precious worthless, the comic a cause for tears, the perpetual mortal, the revolving stationary.

The nobility of gold, yet more refined than any gold, and hardly deigning to acknowledge its genus and species, spreads over the surface of the third mirror, which cannot 485 offer deceiving shadows of things, but shows all things more exactly, and causes them to appear more clearly. Here Reason looks on the wellspring of creation, the origin of all things, the idea of the cosmos, its model, its kind, its cause, beginning and end, and determines the true causes of all 490 things. She sees by what plan, through what causes, how, why, and when this universe—unstable, created, fluctuating, everchanging—derived from an uncreated, stable, unchanging source, its pattern, being, condition, kind, life and origin. She sees how a heavenly idea gives birth to an earthly 495 form, and translates the abyss into the progeny of our world; how it sends into exile the forms which it destines for the

a patre degenerat proles faciemque paternam
exuit, antiqui vultus oblita parentis;
500   qualiter in mundo fantasma resultat ydee,
cuius inoffensus splendor sentitur in umbra;
qualiter a fonte formarum rivus aberrans
ingenitum perdit subiecti labe nitorem;
quid cogat fatum, quid casu defluat aut quid
505   arbitrii possit medio librata potestas.

    Se totam Ratio speculis expendit in istis,
sed magis ad praesens visus indulget, habenis
mentem sollicitat, animum diffundit ut intus
hauriat a speculis aliquid ratione probatum,
510   quod digne ferri tantas mereatur ad aures.

Liber Secundus

Regia tota silet; expirat murmur in altum.
Cum visu placidos delegat curia vultus,
cum visu currit animus visumque volantem
anticipare cupit visus auriga voluntas.
5   Evocat ergo foras mentem Rationis inundans
eloquium sermoque modum decurrit in istum:
  "Plus quam posse meum possit me posse iubetis,
dum vestram cogor indocta docere Minervam.
Sic mirti praesunt lauris, oleaster olivis,
10   sic saliunca rosis, vilis sic alga iacinctis
praefertur gemmisque lutum violisque cicuta;

world, how the child degenerates from its father and puts off the paternal likeness, forgetting the face of the ancient parent. She sees how in this world the ghost of an idea is re- 500 flected, whose untroubled splendor can be sensed in this shadowy form; how the stream that flows from the fountain of forms loses its original splendor in the degradation of material life. She sees what fate determines, what happens by chance, and what the power of our will, suspended between 505 them, can effect.

Reason devotes herself wholly to these mirrors, but for the moment she gives still freer rein to sight, goads her mind and pours forth thought, that she may draw from the mirrors something her reasoning can approve, something she 510 deems worthy to be offered to such auditors.

Book 2

The entire court is still; murmuring dies away. With calm faces the assembly raise their eyes; thought keeps pace with sight, and will, charioteer of sight, strives to anticipate sight's swiftness. Now flowing eloquence summons forth the 5 thoughts of Reason, and her speech proceeds in this way:

"You bid me be capable of more than my ability can accomplish, when I, uninstructed, am required to instruct your wisdom. Thus myrtle outranks laurel, the oleaster the olive, the wild nard the rose, the lowly weed the hyacinth; 10 clay is preferred to jewels, the hemlock to the violet. Thus

sic ovis a capra mendicat velleris usum,
sic tumidus torrens a rivo postulat undam;
sic solet a Davo Narcissus quaerere formam;
15 sic addit lucem candelae flamma diei.
    "Sed quantum cogit iubet instat vestra voluntas
ut super his quae vestra modo discretio movit
mendicata mei tandem suffragia dentur
consilii; plene vestris obsistere votis
20 nolo, sicque mea vobiscum velle voluntas
incipit ut tandem cupiat quodcumque necesse est.
Defaecata minus aliamque rogantia formam,
consilii secreta mei deponere vobis
malo quam votis vulgata fronte repugnem,
25 aut mea coniectent suspecta silentia fastum.
Ergo precor veniam, veniae non tarda sequatur
gratia delictum, relevet compassio morbum,
si minus excoctas rationes verba propinent,
vel rationis inops ieiunus sermo laboret.
30 Nec stupor invadat vestrae munimina mentis,
si sibi sermo meus maculas erroris adoptat:
error in humanis comes indefessus oberrat.
Denigrare solet fermenti copia quicquid
humanus sermo vel mens humana volutat.
35 Si tamen officio finis respondeat alter
non orantis erit error, non culpa medentis,
si primus finis fraudetur fine secundo.
Non ferit assidue telum quodcumque minatur,
non semper medicus sanat, non ipse perorat
40 rhetor non logicus ad metam pervenit, immo
saepe iacens calle medio defessus anhelat.

the sheep begs fleece from the goat, or a swollen river asks
for water from a stream. Thus Narcissus is wont to seek
the beauty of Davus. Thus a candle's flame augments the 15
light of day.

"But since your will compels, commands, importunes me
to offer the beggarly contribution of my advice regarding
this matter which your discerning minds propose, I will not
wholly oppose your wishes. My will is beginning to so con- 20
cur with yours that it is now eager for whatever is necessary.
I prefer to entrust to you my inner thoughts, though imperfectly refined and in need of a better form, rather than reject your wishes with base obstinacy, or let my suspect si- 25
lence be construed as scorn. Thus I beg your indulgence; let
kindly tolerance follow quickly on my failings, and compassion soothe my unease, if my words produce thoughts insuf-
ficiently prepared, or my meager discourse is labored and
lacking in reason. Let not amazement assail the bulwarks of 30
your minds if my address shows the stains of error. Error is
the tireless, lurking companion of human endeavor; much
corruption is apt to blacken whatever human speech or the
human mind contrives. However, if a different proposal re- 35
sults from my contribution, if the first proposal is called into
question by the second, it will not be an error on the speak-
er's part, the fault of her who offers aid. A javelin does not
invariably strike the target at which it aims; the doctor does
not always produce a cure, or the orator a peroration, nor
does the logician always arrive at a conclusion; indeed he of- 40
ten falls only halfway there, panting and exhausted.

"Discretum prudens cautum laudabile tutum
utile consilium Nature iudico, votum
approbo, propositum laudo, molimen adoro,
45 ut novus in mundo peregrinet Lucifer, in quo
nullius labis occasus nubilat ortum.
Solis in occasu sol alter proferat ortum,
sol novus in terris oriatur, cuius in ortu
sol vetus occasus proprios lugere putetur.
50 Possideat solus quicquid possedimus omnes;
omnis homo sic unus erit, sic omne quod unum,
unus in esse suo, sed erit virtutibus omnis.
Sit contra vitia quae nos extinguere temptant
tutor defensor iudex athleta patronus:
55 a nostris laribus cum nos exterminet orbis,
hic noster thalamus, nostrum firmetur asylum.

"Non tamen infitior uterinae verba sororis
quae tanti limam sapiunt examinis, immo
verius haec eadem possunt examina dici,
60 cum nostrum fateatur opus nostramque requirat
incudem fluitans humanae machina molis.
Corpus ad esse suum vocat artis regula nostrae;
excipit haec hominis animam, quae semper ab istis
legibus excipitur, meliore pollice ducta.
65 Non tamen a tanto debet secedere voto
instans propositum nec citra proelia vinci;
quamvis ad tantas operas tantumque laborem
Naturae suspiret opus citraque residat,
supplebit tamen ipsa manus divina quod infra
70 perfecti normam Naturae norma relinquet.
Quod Natura facit divinus perficit auctor:
divinum creat ex nihilo, Natura caducum

"I consider Nature's advice discerning, farsighted, careful, praiseworthy, sound, useful. I approve her wish, I applaud her proposal, I honor her endeavor that a new Lucifer 45 may walk forth in the world, one whose birth will be clouded by no fatal flaw. As this sun sets let a new sun be brought forth, a new sun arise on earth, at whose rising one may suppose the old sun setting in sorrow. Let him alone possess 50 whatever all of us possess; thus one man will be all men, all will be resolved into one. Though he is one in his being, he will possess the powers of all. Against those vices which threaten our extinction, let him be a sure defender, judge, champion, patron. When the world drives us from our 55 homes may he be our dwelling, and provide us sure asylum.

"But I would not contradict the words of my sister by birth, words which show the marks of much planning; indeed these very words may rightly be called a plan, inasmuch 60 as the unstable structure of the human body is plainly our task, and requires our forging; the principles of our arts bring his body into being. They do not include the human soul, which is wholly exempted from our laws, produced by a more skillful hand. Yet one must not retreat from a task 65 urged with such great hope, or surrender before the battle. Though Nature sighs at the prospect of such a task, so much labor, and the work is halted before it has begun, the very hand of God will make good whatever Nature's standard 70 leaves short of the standard of perfection. What Nature makes the divine creator perfects: from nothing he creates divinity; from something Nature produces mortality. God

procreat ex aliquo. Deus imperat, illa ministrat;
hic regit, illa facit; hic instruit, illa docetur.

75 Ergo si nostris quae sunt indigna favore
votis aspirat, suspiria nostra relaxans,
plenius applaudet istis que sola perorant,
nec candore precum vestiri cultius orant.

"Vota tamen precibus nostris mellita mereri
80 plus poterunt tali melius condita sapore.
Ergo vota preces animos fundamus in illum,
ut nostris faveat votis, ut vota secundet,
qui solus complere potest, nec tarda sequetur
mens divina preces, si mens legaverit extra
85 quam non rhetoricis oratio picta figuris,
non ignavus opum cumulus, non musa Maronis,
non amor ypocrita, nec honor venator amoris
demulcet, sed sola precum dulcedo perorat,
si tamen a fonte cordis deducta madescat.

90 "Restat in ambiguo nec certa luce patescit
quae nostrum, quibus auxiliis, quo calle viarum
in superas devecta domos, donetur honore
legati, quae vota Deo praesentet et instans
imbre precum, precibus divinas compluat aures.
95 Sed tamen, ut propriae mentis sentencia dictat,
nulla potest melius istius muneris usum
amplecti quam nostra soror Prudentia, cuius
debellare nequit virtutem turba laborum;
cuius iter gressus obstacula nulla retardant,
100 non strepitus, non ira maris, non vallis abyssus;
non iuga, non celsi praeceps audacia montis
asperitasque viae saxis callosa, nec ipse
limitis ambages desertaque nescia gressus;

commands, Nature serves, he rules, she acts, he teaches, she is taught. If, then, he gives approval to appeals of ours that 75 are unworthy of his favor, and relieves us from our sighing, he will approve still more of these, which only make a case, and do not beg to be clothed in the finer white robe of prayer.

"And yet a petition honeyed by our prayers will be better 80 rewarded when imbued with this sweeter taste. Let us therefore pour out our wishes, our prayers, our spirits to him, that he may favor our prayers and lend them his aid, he who alone can fulfill them. For the divine mind will not be slow in responding to our prayers, if our minds also dispatch an ambassador, one whom no oration adorned with the figures of 85 rhetoric will commend, no lifeless heap of riches, no Virgilian muse, no false display of love, no favor-seeking deference. The sweetness of prayer alone will convey our appeal, if only it be brought forth dripping from the fountain of the heart.

"It remains uncertain, it has not yet been made clear, 90 which of us, with what assistance and by what path, will be borne up to the heavenly seat, who will be granted the honor of this embassy, what appeal she will offer to God, urging it with an outpouring of prayer, filling the divine ears with prayers. But the prompting of my own mind tells me that 95 none is more capable of assuming this office than our sister Providence, whose strength no multitude of labors can make weary. No obstacles along the way will hinder her progress, no roaring storm, no angry sea, nor the deepest valley, no 100 hill, no daunting steep of lofty mountain, not the roughness of a rock-strewn road, not even the windings of her path, or

non rabies venti, non imbribus ebria nubes,
105   non tonitrus horrenda lues, non nubilus aër,
quin superos adeat, quin visitet astra Deique
imbibat arcanum, divino fonte madescens.
    "Cernit in arcanis superum quis conditor orbis,
quid deus ipse velit, quid mundo praeparet aut quid
110   praevideat vel provideat, vel destinet orbi:
quid possint caeli secreta, quid astra loquantur,
cur caeli cursus motu nugetur eodem,
semper in occasum vergens, contraque planeta
militet adverso motu caelumque refrenet;
115   morbida Saturni quid mundo stella minetur
quamve salutis opem Iovialis gratia mundo
nuntiet, aut Martis sidus quae bella prophetet;
quo duce, qua causa, quo fomite quove patrono
temperie motu vita splendore meatu
120   providet applaudit blanditur consulit orbi
Sol oculus mundi, fons vitae, cereus orbis;
quas Venus illecebras, quae tristia gaudia, tristes
laetitias, mala dulcia, pocula fellea terris
offert et felle mellito compluit orbem;
125   quo nexu, qua lege meant, quo foedere iuncti
Lucifer et nostri Cyllenius assecla Solis
nascentis, vexilla gerunt, famulantur eunti
alternantque vices, sibi quas partitur uterque;
alter in alterius usum transcribitur; alter
130   Solis in occasu splendescit, Solis in ortu
alter, et alterni sibi mutua nomina donant:
Hesperus occasum comitatur, Lucifer ortum;
quo modo mendicat alienum Luna decorem,
cur a luce sua Phoebe demissa parumper

deserts which no foot has trod, or the raging wind, or clouds
drunken with rain, not the awful crash of thunder or a low- 105
ering sky. Rather will she attain the heights, move among
the stars, imbibe the hidden wisdom of God, bathed by the
divine fount.

"In the hidden realms above she discerns him who created the universe; what God wills, what he holds in store for
the world, what he foresees or foreordains or destines, what 110
the secret powers of the heavens can effect, what the stars
declare, why the revolution of the firmament is trivial in its
unchanging movement, always tending toward the western
horizon, while the planets march along an opposing path
and control this movement. She sees how the unwholesome 115
star of Saturn menaces the world; what a wealth of good for
the world the kindly influence of Jove portends; what wars
the star of Mars foretells; by what guidance, cause, quickening, or sponsor the Sun, the world's eye, source of life, candle of the universe, provides, favors, delights, cares for the 120
world by its temperate warmth, its motion, its vital energy,
its splendor, its course. She knows what enticements, what
woeful joy, what unhappy happiness, what sweet evils, what
bitter drafts Venus proffers, showering the world with honeyed poison; by what law or linkage, through what pact Lu- 125
cifer and Cyllenius, the attendants of our rising Sun, journey
together; why they bear the Sun's banners, follow him as he
sets, and alternate in the duties they share together. For each
is transferred to the office of the other; one shines at the 130
setting of the sun, the other at his rising, and they bestow
their shared names on one another by turns: Hesperus attends at sunset, Lucifer at sunrise. She sees how the Moon
solicits the beauty of another; why Phoebe, drawn away

135 detrimenta suae deplorat lucis, at infra
plenius exhausta, totius luminis amplam
iacturam queritur, sed rursus fratris in igne
ardescens, nutrit attriti damna decoris,
perfectos tandem circumfert plena nitores;
140 quis ligat in nube pluviam, cur mugiat aër,
quis pariat ventos, quis eorum seminet iras,
cur in tot facies exit substantia nubis,
nunc pluviae plena lacrimis, nunc cana pruinis,
nunc vestita nivis facie, nunc grandinis arma
145 suscipit et caeli miratur terra sagittas.
    "Ergo quae melius legati munus inibit
quam Fronesis, cui cuncta Dei secreta loquuntur?
Ergo si nostris vult condescendere votis,
omnia provenient, ut lex deposcit et ordo
150 postulat et certis claudentur singula metis.
Nec puto quod tanta rerum molimina, tantos
conatus animi, tanti momenta favoris
defraudare velit tantosque refellere quaestus.
Nil dubii superest, his concurrentibus; omnes
155 aggrediamur opus, melior fortuna sequetur.
Dimidium qui coepit habet, finisque beati
gratia principiis semper respondet honestis."
    Sic animos captat Ratio mentesque sororum
allicit et turbam cogit plus velle volentem,
160 sed tamen assensum Prudentia sola minorem
donat seque parem tanto negat esse labori.
Cogitur, illa negat meruitque negatio cogi;
fluctuat haec, se nolle negat nec velle fatetur,
inter utrumque volat, nec vult et nolle veretur.

from her source of light for a time, bewails the diminish- 135
ment of her light; but later, more nearly extinguished, laments the prolonged disappearance of all light; and yet, once
again glowing with her brother's fire, nurses the remains of
her wasted beauty; then, full at last, displays a perfect radiance. She knows what confines rain in the clouds, why the 140
air rumbles, what gives rise to the winds, what instills them
with rage, why the stuff of clouds appears in so many characters: now brimming with rainy tears, now white with frost,
now clad in a covering of snow, now it takes up arms of hail,
and earth is amazed by arrows from heaven. 145

"Who, then, will perform the office of ambassador better than Fronesis, to whom all the mysteries of God declare
themselves? If she is willing to accede to our wishes, all will
come to pass as law requires and order demands; everything 150
will be brought to a sure conclusion. And I do not think she
will betray an enterprise so great, such efforts of mind, an
opportunity so favorable, or deny such an appeal. No doubt
can remain when all these circumstances concur. Let us all
take up the task; success will follow. He who has begun has 155
done half the work; the blessing of a happy ending will always reward a worthy beginning."

Thus Reason wins her sisters' goodwill, persuades their
minds, and makes the willing company still more willing.
But Providence alone offers less than full assent, declaring 160
herself unequal to so great a task. Pressed, she refuses, and
her refusal is rewarded with further pressure. She vacillates,
denies that she is unwilling but will not say that she is willing; she hovers between the two, not willing yet afraid to refuse.

165   Dum sic in dubio mens pendet fluctuat heret
in medium cuncta medians Concordia sese
profert, in cuius facie deitatis ymago
splendet et humani fastidit taedia vultus.
Pacem sponte tenet crinis flammantior auro,
170 se sibi conciliat nec opem sibi pectinis optat;
sed sibi sufficiens in tanta pace quiescit
ut nec perflantis Boreae suspiria crinem
sollicitare queant litisque creare tumultum.
Forma figura modus numerus mensura decenter
175 membris aptatur et debita munera solvit.
Sic sibi respondent concordi pace ligata
membra, quod in nullo discors iunctura videtur.
    Unius vultus, uno contenta colore
vestis in ornatum membrorum transit, eisdem
180 sic foris aptata quod eis inscripta putetur.
Illic arte sua vitam pictura secundam
donat eis quos castus amor, concordia simplex,
pura fides, vera pietas coniunxit et unum
esse duos fecit purgati foedus amoris.
185 Nam David et Ionathas ibi sunt duo, sunt tamen unum:
cum sint diversi, non sunt duo mente sed unus;
dimidiant animas, sibi se partitur uterque.
Ut sibi Pyrithoüs se reddat, redditus orbi,
Theseus inferni loca monstra pericula temptat;
190 vivere posse negat in se nisi vivat in illo.
Tydeus arma rapit, ut regnet Tydeus alter,
in Polinice suo pugnat, seseque secundum
dum regnare cupit, sibi poscere regna videtur.
Alter in Eurialo comparet Nisus et alter
195 Eurialus viget in Niso; sic alter utrumque

While her doubtful mind ponders, vacillates, holds back, 165
Concord, who mediates in all matters, presents herself before the company. In her face the divine image shines forth,
scorning the taint of the human countenance. Her hair,
more glowing than gold, keeps itself in order, arranges itself 170
and never calls for the aid of a comb; instead, self-sufficient,
it lies in such peace that not even the gusting breath of
Boreas can disturb a hair, or give rise to a tumultuous tangle.
Form, shape, poise, number and measure dispose her limbs 175
with grace, and each duly performs its function. The limbs
are joined in such harmonious agreement that nowhere can
any disproportion be seen.

An unadorned garment, content with a single color, en-
wraps and adorns her body, so fitted to her form as to seem 180
inscribed on it. There the art of painting bestows a second
life on those whom chaste love, guileless agreement, pure
trust, true devotion join together, so that a pledge of perfect
love causes two to become one. For here David and Jona- 185
than are two, and yet one: though they are separate, in mind
they are not two but one; they divide their souls, and each
shares himself with the other. Theseus braves the depths,
monsters, perils of the underworld, that Pirithous, once restored to the world, may be reunited with his other self, for
he feels he cannot live himself unless he lives in him. Tydeus 190
takes up arms that a second Tydeus may be king; he too
fights in the person of his loved Polynices, and though he
desires that this second self may rule, he seems to seek
the kingdom for himself. Another Nisus exists in Euryalus,
and another Euryalus lives in Nisus; thus each reflects the 195

reddit et ex uno comitum pensatur uterque.
Atride furit in furiis eiusque furorem
iudicat esse suum Pilades patiturque Megeram,
ne patiatur idem Pilades suus alter et idem.

200   Haec pictura suis loquitur mysteria signis;
nec res ipsa magis, nec lingua fidelius umquam
talia depingit, talique sophismate visum
decipiens oculis, rerum concludit in umbra.

Qui praeco solet esse boni pacisque figura,
205   virginis in dextra, foliorum crine comatus,
flore tumens, fructus expectans, ramus olivae
pubescit, nec matris humi solatia quaerit;
quo mediante vices nexus et vincula rerum
foedus amicitiam pacem Concordia nectit.

210   Ad virgae nutum pacem sibi postulat illa
verborumque votis succurrens, nutibus illis
prodit et haec verbique sonum sententia ditat:

"Si mea iura, meas leges, mea foedera mundus
olim servasset vel adhuc servaret amoris
215   vincula, non tantis gemeret sub cladibus orbis.
Non cenam fratrum, non cenae flesset abusum
Phoebus et errantis Naturae crimina lugens,
noctis abusivae tenebras legasset in orbem.
Non rex Thebanus, Polinicis frater et hostis,
220   exutus fratrem, sese mutasset in hostem.
Non Progne commenta dolos, exuta parentem,
pro pietate scelus redolens, pro matre novercam,
in sua degenerem vertisset viscera dextram,
[Nec furor armasset contra sua viscera matrem.]

other; from one of these comrades one may imagine the other. Pylades raves in the raving of Atrides; he considers the other's madness to be his own, and confronts Megaera lest *his* Pylades, both other and one with him, should suffer.

This painting reveals mysteries with its images: the thing 200 itself does not exhibit itself more clearly, nor can language describe such things so well; such art, deceiving the eyes with its subtlety, convinces our sight with mere shadows of reality.

In the maiden's right hand flourishes that which is wont to be the herald of good tidings, the sign of peace: an olive 205 branch crowned with foliage, its swollen buds giving promise of fruit, yet having no need of the tender care of mother earth. By its mediating power Concord creates relations, linkages, bonds among created things, covenant, friendship, and peace. Motioning with this wand to reinforce her verbal 210 appeal, Concord calls for peace. She prevails by her gesturing, and these thoughts enrich the sound of her words:

"If the world of old had observed my decrees, my laws, my compacts, if it still acknowledged the bond of love, it 215 would not now bewail such disasters. Phoebus would not have wept, lamenting the brothers' feast, and what was consumed at the feast, the crime of Nature gone astray, nor would he have brought upon the world the darkness of unnatural night. The Theban king, brother and enemy of Polynices, would not have cast off brotherhood and become 220 an enemy. Procne would not have planned her treacherous act, rejecting parental love, showing wickedness in place of devotion, the stepmother instead of the mother; never would she have turned inhuman hands against her own flesh and blood, [nor would madness have made the mother

275

225 Troiae nobilitas, Troiae decus, inclita Troiae
fama vireret adhuc nec laudis flore careret.
Non auri potum sitiens, non ebrius auro
aurum potasset Crassus, male potus in auro.
Non olim civile nefas, non Caesaris arma,
230 non pueri regis animum, non foedera regni,
non mortis servile genus servosque probasset
Magnus et exanimis truncatus nudus honore
funeris in nuda solus iacuisset harena.
Post tantos belli strepitus, post fulmina Martis,
235 post gladii furias, post tot discrimina Caesar
non fraudes pugnamque stili sensisset inhertem.
Caesaris insultus belli momenta furorem
fortunae casusque vices Antonius olim
de facili posset vitasse nec uxor adoptans
240 mammis serpentes, colubros lactasset et ipsos
uberibus potans, potasset in ubere mortem.
    "Ni stabili nexu, concordi foedere pace
perpetua vicibusque meis elementa ligassem,
intestinus adhuc strepitus primordia rerum
245 dissona concuteret germanaque bella moveret:
officiis excepta suis, ignara meatus,
scabra situ, confusa locis, permixta figuris,
fortuitis agitata modis elementa iacerent.
Et nisi sponte meis obnoxia legibus essent
250 astra poli caelique vices septemque planetae
ordine pace fide numero nexuque ligati,
omnia fortuitis fluerent incerta ruinis.
Ni mea corporibus animas iunctura ligasset,
dedignans habitare casas, ergastula carnis,

attack her own offspring.] The nobility, the honor, the glori- 225
ous fame of Troy would be living still, and would not be denied the garland of renown. Crassus, thirsting for gold, made
drunk by gold, would not have drunk gold, drunk ruin in the
form of gold. Pompey long ago would not have attempted
the impiety of civil war, braved the arms of Caesar, tested 230
the spirit of the boy king and his kingdom's treaties; would
not have put down the slaves, nor met a slave's death. He
would never have lain, lifeless, mutilated, denied the honor
of a funeral, alone on the bare strand. Caesar, after the din of
so many campaigns, after the thunderings of Mars, after the 235
mad clash of arms, after so many crises, would not have
fallen prey to deceit, and the dagger's cowardly warfare. An-
thony would easily have avoided the scorn of Caesar, the
tides of war, the madness of Fortune, the vicissitudes of fate;
never would his wife have clasped serpents to her bosom 240
and nursed them, and as she suckled them suckled death
as well.

"Had I not by my conciliatory power bound the elements
with a stable bond, a pact of agreement, a perpetual peace,
internal clashes would still be throwing the primal sources
of creation into opposition, and provoke war among kin- 245
dred powers. The elements would lie scattered as if dismissed from their duties, ignorant of their purpose, rusty
from inaction, dislocated, confused, unrecognizably min-
gled, buffeted in random ways. And were the fixed stars, the
moving heavens, the seven planets not willingly obedient 250
to my laws, and governed by order, peace, constancy, number and relation, all would fall haplessly into random destruction. Had not my jointure fastened souls to bodies, the
spirit, refusing to dwell in the house, the prison house, of

255 spiritus egrediens proprios remearet in ortus.
Haec probat, haec fatur, haec disputat, edocet, instat,
ostendit Ratio: quod nil servatur in esse,
quod servare meas leges et iura recuset.

"Nos ergo liget unus amor, liget una voluntas,
260 unum velle liget, liget unum nolle sorores.
Caetera si pacis normam servare tenentur,
nos magis ad quarum nutum disponitur orbis,
quas penes arbitrium ius est et regula mundi.
Quis nexus, quis verus amor, quod foedus amoris,
265 quae pietas, quae pura fides, quae linea recti
in rebus reliquis saltem vestigia pacis
servabit, si nostra manet concordia discors?
Deffluet in membra capitis iactura dolentis;
deffluet in ramos vitium radicis amarae;
270 deffluet in rivos tabes cognata fluento.

"Quis lunae splendor, si solis lumen oberrat?
Quis rivi fluctus, si copia fluminis aret?
Quis grani fructus, si torpens languet arista?
Si nostram pacem discordia dissuit, immo
275 rumpit, nostra perit virtus, nam stare negatur
occasum patiens in se divisa potestas.
Cum nobis donet consensus robur adultum,
dissensus noster vires exhauriet istas.
Effectus medicina suos divisa recusat;
280 quem sibi distribuunt rivi minus amnis inundat,
vel divisa minus candescit flamma camini.

"Acrior insultus vitiorum pugnaque maior
nobis incumbet, si nos diviserit error;
postquam cementi rumpit discordia muros,
285 hostili pugnae muros exponit inhermes;

278

the flesh, would go forth and retrace its path to its true   255
home. All this Reason confirms, declares, argues, teaches,
demands, makes plain: that nothing can be kept in existence
which refuses to obey my laws and decrees.

"Let a single love unite us, then, a single purpose, a single   260
yea, a single nay, sisters as we are. If the rest of creation is
bound to observe the rule of peace, all the more are we, at
whose bidding the universe is ordered, in whose charge are
the governance and guidance of the world. What bond, what
true or plighted love, what devotion, what simple trust,   265
what pattern of conduct will preserve even the vestiges of
peace in creation at large, if our concord remains discordant? An accident that harms the head affects the body; bitterness at the root will pass into the limbs; poison that in-   270
fests the river will flow into the streams.

"What splendor has the moon, if the sun's light should go
astray? What water will flow in the stream, if the river runs
dry? What fruit will grow from the seed, if the stalk is
blighted and weak? Should discord unstitch our peace, or,
worse, destroy it, our strength fails, for power divided   275
against itself cannot endure, but suffers ruin. Since it is
agreement that grants us full power, dissent among us will
diminish that strength; a diluted medicine withholds its effect. The river which streams distribute among themselves   280
has a lesser flow; the fire of a furnace glows less hot when it
is divided.

"A fiercer attack by vice and a larger war will be forced
upon us if error divides us. When badly mixed mortar causes
a fracturing of the walls, it lays the useless ramparts open to   285

acrius insultat saevitque profundius ensis,
consertae partes ubi nulla repagula donant,
nec series harum conserta recalcitrat ensi;
acrius in volucrem Iovialis fulminat ales,
290 cum plebem volucrum venientis disgregat horror;
uberius torrens effunditur obice nullo
defendente viam fluvioque negante meatum.
      "Ergo concordes votum curramus in unum
quod Natura petit, Ratio commendat, Honestas
295 approbat, immo cupit, Pietas deposcit et optat.
Nec Fronesis sola distans contraria discors
nos omnes pacis conformi lege iugatas
dividet in partes ut amoris vincla relaxet,
sed potius constans congaudens consona concors
300 in nostram veniet mentem, ne victa labore
cedere credatur citra praeludia luctae,
vel tumido flatu perflare superbia mentem,
vel sibi livor edax animi mordere recesssus.
An quae sola solet bona poscere, sola recidet
305 hoc commune bonum, nostrum decus, utile votum,
nos omnes quae sola libens et sponte monere
in tantum deberet opus tantumque favorem,
si flammata minus torperet nostra voluntas
nec tantum vellet animus conscendere noster?"
310   His verbis accensa magis Prudentia mentem
sistit et in certo figit vestigia mentis.
Tempestas animi moritur fluctusque recedunt,
velle suum commune facit cum velle sororum.
Cogitat exquirit studet invenit eligit ergo
315 quae via, quis callis, quae semita rectius ipsam
deferat ad superos arcanaque regna Tonantis.

enemy attack. A sword strikes more sharply and inflicts a deeper wound when no closed ranks offer resistance, and close engagements do not thwart its blows. The bird of Jove strikes another bird more fiercely when fear of his descent 290 has scattered the flock. A torrent pours down more abundantly when no obstacle so bars its course that the river rejects its channel.

"And so let us draw together, united by the common aim which Nature urges, Reason commends, Honesty approves, 295 indeed desires, which Duty demands and expects. Fronesis will not keep herself apart, contrary and dissenting, nor create division among us who are united by a common commitment to peace, loosening our bond of love. Instead she will join in our plan, steadfast, joyous, in full agreement, in 300 peaceful harmony, lest it be supposed that she may give way, defeated by the task, before the conflict has begun; or that pride inflates her mind with its tumid breath, or that envy, which feeds on itself, gnaws at the recesses of her mind. Will she, who is often the only one to urge a good thing, will she alone refuse this good which all will enjoy, which honors us 305 all, this beneficial goal? She, who would most gladly and willingly urge us all to this great task, this great opportunity, if our will, grown less intense, should flag, and our spirits no longer wish to rise to such a height?"

Inspired by these words Providence settles her thoughts, 310 and sets the footsteps of her mind on firm ground. The tempest of her thoughts dies away, the waves recede, and her will makes common cause with the will of her sisters. She ponders, inquires, studies, and so discovers and settles on the road, the path, the way that will bear her up most directly 315 to the heavens, and the hidden realm of the Thunderer. And

Utque minus possit gressus vexare viantis
limitis asperitas, pes scandala nesciat, immo
ut citius possit munus complere quod instat,
320   in quo percurrat caelum mare sidera, currum
imperat excudi Sapientia. Nec pede lento
affectum sequitur effectus, sed simul instant.
Nascitur effectus cum nascitur ipsa voluntas;
sic matri prolique simul conceditur ortus.

325   Cautae prudentes pulcrae similesque puellae
septem, quae vultum sub septem vultibus unum
reddunt, quas facies genus aetas forma potestas
una tenet, tenet una fides, tenet una voluntas,
assistunt Fronesi. Fronesis decreta sequuntur,
330   eius in obsequio semper fervere paratae.
Tot dotes in eas effundunt dona Sophyae
quod sese totam Prudentia fundit in illas,
se partitur eis; sibi thesaurizat in illis.
Sic divisa tamen manet integra sparsaque tandem
335   colligitur, diffusa redit cum faenore multo.
Delegans vultus in eam mentisque latebras,
in vultu velut in speculo chorus iste sororum
conspicit attendit discit notat atque docetur
quicquid carta tenet, quicquid mens concipit, audet
340   lingua loqui. Tantamque bibit sine fine sophiam,
quid manus artificis, pictoris gratia, fabri
dextera, sculptoris sollers industria poscit.
Ut Zeuxis pingit chorus hic, ut Milo figurat,
ut Fabius loquitur, ut Tullius ipse perorat,
345   ut Samius sentit, sapit ut Plato, quaerit ut Hermes,
dividit ut Socrates, ut Zeno colligit, instat
ut Brisso, studet ut Crisias, speculatur ut Argus,

that the roughness of the path may hinder less the traveler's
steps, that her feet may encounter no stumbling block—in
short, that she may accomplish more quickly the impending
mission, Wisdom orders that a chariot be fashioned, in
which she may traverse the heavens, the sea, the stars. Re- 320
sult follows on intention at no slow pace; they occur simul-
taneously. The result is realized when the wish is expressed;
thus the moment of birth is the same for mother and child.

Seven maidens, careful, foresighted, beautiful, much 325
alike, attend on Fronesis. In their seven faces they display a
single face; a single appearance, lineage, age, form and power
unites them, a common integrity, a common will. They carry
out the decrees of Fronesis, always ready and eager to obey 330
her. The bounty of Sophia has showered them with so many
gifts that Providence pours her entire being into them; she
divides herself among them; they are her treasury. Yet divided in this way she remains intact; though dispersed she is
still whole. Given away, she returns with much interest. 335
Turning their faces and minds toward her, this chorus of sisters perceives in her face, as if in a mirror, considers, learns,
observes, is taught all that written pages contain, all that
mind has conceived, or tongue has dared to utter. Such wis- 340
dom they endlessly imbibe; whatever the artisan's skill, the
painter's gift, the hand of the craftsman, or the mindful labor of the sculptor requires. This sisterhood paints like
Zeuxis, sculpts like Milo, speaks like Fabius, pleads like Cicero himself. They have the understanding of the Samian, the 345
wisdom of Plato, the insight of Hermes. They make Socrates's distinctions, Zeno's conclusions, have Bryson's perse-
verance, the zeal of Critias, the vision of Argus; order the

temporis excursus ut Caesar cogit, ut Atlas
sidera perquirit, ut Zetus pondera librat,
350 tamquam Crisippus numerat, metitur ut alter
Euclides, canit ut Phoebus, cytharizat ut Orpheus,
circinat ut Perdrix, ut Daedalus erigit arces,
fabricat ut Cyclops, ut Lemnius arma monetat,
instruit ut Seneca, blanditur ut Appius, urget
355 ut Cato, succendit ut Curio, velat ut alter
Persius, ut Crassus simulans, ut Iulius alter
dissimulans, ut Sollius implicat, explicat idem
ut Naso, vernat ut Statius, ut Maro dictat
concipit exponit imitatur gestat adimplet
360 Mercurii sensus, nostri Demosthenis iras,
Ovidii flumen, Lucani fulmen, abyssum
Virgilii, morsus satyrae, Solonis asylum.
　　Ergo Minerva videns tanto splendore Sophiae
tot donis tantisque datis splendere sorores,
365 ordinat iniungit iubet imperat orat ut instans
quaelibet istarum comitum, comitante Sophia
corpore mente fide studeat desudat anhelet
instet et efficiat ut currus currat ad esse,
quo terrae spatium mare nubila sidera caelum
370 transeat et trini superato cardine caeli
scrutetur secreta Noys sensusque profundos
hauriat et summi perquirat velle magistri.
Vix satis expressit votum, cum vota iubentis
certatim complere student seseque sorores
375 accingunt operi. Non mens discordat ab actu,
non a mente manus, sed eam delegat in actum
affectus mentis, manus ergo praedicat extra

course of time like Caesar; explore the stars like Atlas; weigh
alternatives like Zethus; compute like Chrysippus, measure   350
like a second Euclid. They sing like Phoebus, play like Orpheus, form circles like Perdix, build great halls like Daedalus, forge like the Cyclops, shape armor like the Lemnian,
teach like Seneca, charm like Appius, insist like Cato, in-   355
flame like Curio. They veil meaning like another Persius —
coining similes like Crassus, disguising their purpose like
another Julius —, condense like Solius, expand like Naso,
flower like Statius, compose like Maro. They conceive, ex-
pound, imitate, carry out, perfect the astuteness of Mercury, 360
the wrath of our Demosthenes, Ovid's great river, Lucan's
thunderbolt, the depth of Virgil, the bite of the satirist, the
clemency of Solon.

Now Minerva, seeing that the sisters shine with so much
of Sophia's splendor, so many of her gifts and attributes, or- 365
dains, enjoins, orders, commands, prays that all these companions, in company with Sophia, earnestly dedicating body
and mind, apply themselves, exert themselves, strive, press
on, and bring the chariot quickly into being. In it she will
cross the wide earth, the sea, the stars, the heavens and,
when the pole of the threefold heavens is attained, look on   370
the mysteries of Noys, take in their deep significance, and
seek the will of the master of all. Scarcely has she made her
wish known when the sisters move eagerly to fulfill the wish
of her who commands, and gird themselves for the task.   375
There is no disharmony between thought and action, nor
between mind and hand: the mind's purpose sets the hand
to work, the hand proclaims outwardly what the mind

quod mens intus habet. Sic mentis lingua fidelis
fit manus et proprio mentem depingit in actu.
380   Harum prima studet ut themo, preambulus axis
et quasi venturi quaedam praefatio currus,
prodeat, ut tanti sit pars primaeva laboris.
Illa vigil studiosa libens attenta laborans
indulgens operi, mentem deducit in actum.
385 Non habitu vilis nec vultu sordida, gestu
degener, incompta verbis vel barbara factis,
sed tamen in vultu perscribit signa laboris
pallor—sed modicus, qui non proscribit ab ore
purpureos ignes niveique coloris honorem.
390 Cum flos virgineus non defloretur in illa,
nec proprium frangat Veneris fractura pudorem,
sunt tamen in multo lactis torrente natantes
mammae, subducti mentitae damna pudoris.
Dum suspirat adhuc lactantis ad ubera matris,
395 infantem cibat iste cibus liquidoque fovetur
quem solidus non pascit adhuc; dum pocula lactis
lactea delibat aetas potuque sub uno
et cibus et potus in solo lacte resudat.
    Asperat illa manum scutica qua punit abusus
400 quos de more suo puerilis combibit aetas.
Verberibus sic asperat ubera, verbera mollit
uberibus. Facto pater est et mater eodem;
verbere compensat patrem, gerit ubere matrem.
Officio scalpri servit manus altera, dentes
405 liberat a scabie, dum buxum dentis in ipsum
vertit ebur rursusque suo candore venustat;
vel si dens aliquis aliorum de grege solus
deviet, excessum sub iusta lance recidit.

harbors within. Thus the hand becomes the faithful interpreter of the mind, and portrays the mind in its own action.

The first of the sisters works zealously to bring forth the   380
tongue, the preamble to the axle, and, as it were, a kind of
preface of the chariot to come, as the first fruit of their great
labor. Alert, eager, willing, attentive, industrious and devoted to her task, she applies her mind to the work. She is   385
not poorly dressed, nor is her face unclean, her bearing ignoble, her speech inelegant or her actions rude, though pallor inscribes on her face the signs of her toil—but a slight
pallor, which does not banish from her face the rosy warmth
or the glory of the snow-white complexion. The flower of   390
her virginity has not been plucked, nor her chastity broken
by the intrusion of Venus, yet her breasts run with a great
flow of milk, falsely suggesting the misfortune of chastity
seduced. While the infant still longs for the milk of the
mother's breast, this is his food, and he whom solid food   395
does not yet sustain is nourished with liquid; for in his suck-
ling years he enjoys his milky drafts of milk, and in the form
of this one drink, in milk alone, both food and drink come
forth.

A lash lends harshness to her hand, with which she pun-
ishes the misbehavior to which boyhood is naturally in-   400
clined. Thus her nurture is made harsh by whippings, and
these in turn she soothes with her breasts. In this role she is
at once father and mother: with her lash she fulfills a father's
duty, with her breast a mother's. Her other hand does its
work with a file, and frees the teeth from filth, restoring the   405
boxwood of the tooth to its proper ivory, and adorning it
once again with its true gleam. And should a single tooth
stray from the others' flock, she reduces the aberration to

Infantes docet illa loqui linguasque ligatas
410 solvit et in propriam deducit verba monetam.
    Candida Niliaco vestis contexta papyro
vestit eam; formae non detrahit illa nec illi
forma nocet; cultus formae connubia grata
nectunt et sese proprio venerantur honore.
415 Vestibus his inscripta manent, descripta resultant,
artis grammaticae virtus natura potestas
ordo materies pars finis nomen et actor,
officium species genus instrumenta facultas.
Illic imperium datur arti, regula regnat,
420 exilium patitur vitium veniamque mereri
nescit Grammaticae, patiens sine fine repulsam.
Defendens sese propria ratione Figura
excubat ante fores artis veniamque precatur.
Ars admittit eam, veniam largita precanti,
425 nec fovet in gremio sed tamen sustinet illam.
Hic docet ars, monstrat ratio, doctrina fatetur
littera cur simplex, cur indivisa vocetur,
cur sibi mendicet elementi littera nomen,
vel tropice soleat elementum littera dici;
430 quae pingant elementa notae, quae nomina signent,
quis claudat numerus, quis congruit ordo, potestas
quae sit, et has species certo sub canone claudit;
cur tenui deiecta sono poscentia vocem
cetera mutescant, verum vocalis aperte
435 clamitet et reliquis vocis spiracula donet;
qua ratione, quibus causis H littera non sit,
cum sibi praetendat scripturam, nomen et usum,
sed cifri loca possideat solaque figura
ius sibi deffendens, elementi praeferat umbram;

288

even order. She teaches infants to speak, frees their fettered
tongues, and guides their words into the proper form.   410

A white robe clothes her, woven of the papyrus of the
Nile; it does not detract from her beauty, nor does her form
dishonor the robe. Its adornment has made a pleasing marriage with her body, and each does due homage to the other.
On her robe are inscribed, and vividly depicted, the value,   415
nature, power of the art of Grammar, its order, matter, parts,
purpose, name, and teachers, its purpose, species, genus,
tools, and efficacy. Here an empire is granted to this art, here
rule governs, vice is exiled, finds no sympathy in Grammar,   420
and suffers a banishment without end. Figure, claiming an
appropriate function for itself, camps before Grammar's
doors, and begs for mercy. Grammar admits her, granting
mercy to the suppliant; does not clasp her to her bosom, but   425
grants her sustenance. Here art teaches, reason demonstrates, doctrine professes: why the letter is declared simple
and indivisible; why letters claim for themselves the name of
"element," or are commonly called elements metaphorically;
what shapes represent these elements; what names denote   430
them; what number contains them; what order disposes
them; what is their purpose; and confines them in a fixed
canon. Why the other letters are mute, reduced to a thin
sound, and begging for a voice, whereas the vowel rings clear,   435
and grants its vocal breath to the others. On what basis, for
what reason "H" is not a letter, though it can claim for itself
a shape, a name, and a function, but occupies the place of a
cipher, justifying itself by shape alone, and displays only the

440   qualiter in metro secum rixata liquescat
       vocalis, vocisque suum deperdat honorem;
       qualiter in metro nativas littera vires
       perdit et ad tempus languet proscripta potestas;
       qualiter in metro vires et iura duarum
445   vindicat una sibi, redimendo damna sororum;
       quomodo diversas species vox induit una,
       quam gravis accentus infra demittit, acutus
       erigit, in gyrum fert circumflexus eandem;
       quidve sibi proprium defendit littera, quidve
450   sillaba, quid proprii iuris sibi dictio servat;
       quid proprie proprium nomen sibi vindicat, aut quid
       appropriat verbum, sibi quid pronomen adoptat;
       quid reliquae partes proprio sibi iure reservant;
       quid nomen proprie designat, quid peregrine
455   insinuat, quid verba notant, pronomina signant
       cum subiecta notent; cur sic pronomina formae
       dedignantur opem, quod demonstratio sola
       subveniat formaeque vicem compenset in illis;
       qua ratione regat pars partem quave regatur,
460   cur nomen substans aliis, vel cetera pingens,
       materiae gerat officium formamue figuret;
       verbi cur redeat in se, vel transeat actus;
       foedus amicitiae cur verbis nomina servent,
       et verbo iunctum solvat sua debita nomen,
465   quae nisi conveniant, oratio muta iacebit,
       nec plenos sensus vox decurtata loquetur;
       cur, partem capiens ab utroque, rependat utrimque
       dictio quod debetur ei, sic reddit utrumque
       quod neutrum, mediumque tenens mediatur utrimque;

shadow of an element. How in metrical verse a vowel, at   440
odds with itself, may melt away, and lose its distinguishing
sound; how in meter a letter loses its natural force, and its
power, outlawed for a time, lies idle. How in meter a single
letter claims for itself the force and rights of two, making   445
good a sister's loss; how a single vowel can assume different
characters, when a grave accent shortens it, an acute length-
ens it, a circumflex gives it roundness. What property a letter claims as its own, and what a syllable, what a word keeps   450
as its own by right, what a noun rightly guards as its own, or
what a verb claims for itself; what role the pronoun adopts;
what the other parts of speech reserve for themselves by inherent right. What a noun properly denotes, and what it
may imply when it strays from this role; what verbs refer to,   455
what pronouns signify, when they denote subjects; why pronouns may be so disdainful of declension that only demonstration can help them, fulfilling the role of declension for
them. By what rule one part of speech may govern another
or be governed by it; why a noun, standing for something   460
else or representing it, performs the role of matter or describes a form; why the action of a verb turns on itself, or is
transitive; why nouns preserve a bond of friendship with
verbs, and a noun fulfills its function when joined to a verb,
but unless the two agree, speech will be reduced to silence,   465
and the words, broken off, will not declare their full meaning. Why a word that derives its function from both verb
and noun grants to both its own function, and thus renders
both what neither is by itself, keeping to a middle position

470 cur reliquae partes istas venerentur et istis
sese summittant nec eis servire recusent.
　　Haec artis series seriatim picta propinat;
delicias oculis et menti fercula donat,
nam pictor praedoctus eam descripserat, immo
475 plus pictore potens, picturaque clamitat illum.
　　Aggrediens proprium virgo praefata laborem,
non oneris concussa metu, non fracta labore,
ad proprium desudat opus multumque rebellis
materies tandem sequitur superata volentem.
480 Nam praedicta iacent ad tempus et otia servant
instrumenta quibus pueriles excolit annos,
et mentita fabrum, fabrilibus utitur armis,
materiae fluxum superat cogitque negantem
materiam servire sibi lignique rigorem
485 edomat et lignum themonis ymagine vestit.
　　Hic ortu sculptura novo vitaque recenti
Grammaticae locat artifices et vivere cogit.
Illic Donatus rector patronus et heres,
Grammaticae precepta docens vitiumque recidens,
490 doctrina verbis studio ratione figura
ampliat extollit ditat defendit honestat
Grammaticam, nomenque sibi speciale meretur,
ut non grammaticus dicatur, at emphasis ipsam
"Grammaticam" vocat hunc, signans sub nomine numen.
495 Noster Aristarcus donaria fundit in artem
grammaticam, cuius thesauros ampliat, auget
divitias viresque suas mensurat in illa.
Partes Grammaticae dissutas cogit in unum

and mediating between the two; why the other parts of 470
speech honor these two, submit themselves to them, and
are never unwilling to serve them.

These things the sequence of paintings proffers, one by
one, granting delight to the eyes and a feast to the mind. For
the most learned of painters had depicted them; indeed, the 475
power of the painting declares him more than a painter.

Having thus announced her special role, the maiden
comes forward. Untroubled by any fear of her burden, un-
wearied by labor, she goes vigorously to work, and at length
her material, though very resistant, is conquered and obeys
her will. For the tools described above, those with which 480
she cultivates the years of boyhood, are laid aside for a time,
and remain idle. Now playing the role of artisan, she em-
ploys the artisan's weapons, conquers her unformed material, and compels unwilling matter to obey her; she tames
the stubbornness of wood and endows a log with the form of 485
a beam.

On this beam sculpture sets the practitioners of grammar, and by a new birth compels them to live a renewed life.
Here Donatus, guide, patron and master, teaching the
precepts of grammar and trimming away barbarism, with
learning, instruction, practice, rule and paradigm, expounds, 490
honors, enriches, preserves and dignifies grammar, and earns
for himself a special title: for he is not only called a grammarian, but hyperbole calls him "Grammar" itself, signifying
his great authority by this name. Our Aristarchus enriches 495
the art of grammar; he augments its treasure of words, increases its wealth, and makes it the measure of his own
worth. Didymus draws together tattered pieces of grammar,

Didymus et propriis describit singula formis.
500 Grammaticae tractus pertractat apostata noster,
pigrius in dictis torporis somnia passus;
in scriptis errans propriis, aut hebrius esse,
aut magis insanus, aut dormitare putatur.
Claudicat ille fide, ne fama claudicet eius
505 tractatus, venditque fidem, ne praemia libri
depereant, erratque fides, ne rumor aberret.
   Solos artifices quos fama beavit adulta
laude nec a fama discessit gloria facti,
haec sculptura tenet, minime dignata fateri
510 grammaticos humiles, qui sola cortice gaudent,
quos non admittit intus pinguedo medullae:
sed foris exposcunt fragmenta, putamine solo
contenti, nuclei nequeunt libare saporem.

Liber Tertius

Latius inquirens sollers studiosa laborans
virgo secunda studet; intrat penetralia mentis
sollicitatque manum. Mentem manus excitat, urget
ingenium, sensus proprios invitat, ut axis
5 effigiet speciem multoque secundet honore,
ut nec materiae nec formae laude secundus,
cum themone suo contendens disputet axis,
immo praecellens specie concludat eidem.
Et decor et species afflasset virginis artus,
10 sicut praesignis membrorum disserit ordo,

and describes each part with its proper forms. Our apostate   500
busies himself with a grammatical treatise, wearily letting a
sleepy lethargy invade his words. His mind wanders as he
writes: you would think he was drunk, or even mad, or that
he was falling asleep. He falters in faith that the fame of his
treatises may not falter; sets a price on his religion lest the   505
price of his book should dwindle; his faith is lost, that his
reputation may not be.

The carving includes only those teachers whom fame has
blessed with full praise, and whose work does not fall short
of their fame. It disdains to acknowledge those lesser gram-   510
marians, who are pleased with the mere rinds of language, to
whom the richness of the meat within is denied; they ask
only for the outer peelings, content with the husk alone, and
cannot know the savor of the fruit.

Book 3

Wide ranging, skillful, assiduous and industrious, the second maiden eagerly sets to work, enters the inner chambers
of her mind and readies her hand. Her hand arouses her
mind, stirs her imagination, musters her faculties to model
the form of an axle, and bestow on its shape such beauty that   5
the axle may challenge comparison with the beam, and be
no less praised for its matter and form—or even conclude by
surpassing the beam in beauty. Dignity and beauty would
completely suffuse the maiden's form as the perfect pro-   10
portioning of her body argues, were it not that her face is

ni facies quadam macie respersa iaceret.
Vallat eam macies, macie vallata profunde
subsidet et nudis cutis ossibus arida nubit.
Haec habitu gestu macie pallore figurat
15 insomnes animi motus vigilemque Minervam
praedicat et secum vigiles vigilasse lucernas.
Quomodo litigio contendens, crinis in ima
deviat et secum pugnans rixatur inepte.
Non pecten castigat eum, non forcipis urget
20 morsus, tonsurae non mordet apocopa finem.
Dum stellis oculi certant, ardere putantur;
subcumbunt aquilae visus et lincis adorant
intuitus oculos tales seseque fatentur
devictos et eis sese conferre verentur.
25 Dextra manus floris donatur honore, sinistram
scorpius incendens caudae mucrone minatur;
mel sapit ista manus, fellis gerit illa saporem;
haec spondet risum, fletu concluditur illa;
haec capit, illa fugat; haec ungit, pungitur illa;
30 haec ferit, hec mulcet; haec afficit, inficit illa.
Non sordis squalore iacens, non luce superba
vestis erat medium retinens, utrimque redacta.
Illic arte nova pictor novus, histrio veri,
monstrat elenchorum pugnas logicaeque duellum:
35 qualiter, ancipiti gladii mucrone coruscans,
vis Logicae, veri facie tunicata recidit
falsa, negans falsum veri latitare sub umbra;
cur pseudologicus, artis fur, artis adulter,
falsus et ypocrita, furtivus praedo, sophista,
40 mentitur Logicae vultum fretusque quibusdam
prodigiis, temptat pro vero vendere falsum;

marked by a certain leanness. Leanness entrenches it, so deeply that it is sunken, and the dry skin clings to the very bones. Her dress, bearing, leanness and pallor suggest the restless activity of her mind, proclaiming that her wakeful 15 wisdom keeps long vigils, with wakeful lamps at hand. Her hair is long and straggling, and seems engaged in an argument, at odds with itself and quarreling gracelessly. No comb chastens it, no biting clip restrains it, no abbreviating ton- 20 sure cuts off its ends. When her eyes vie with the stars they seem to burn; the eagle's sight yields to her, and the keen vision of the lynx reveres such eyes; they confess themselves defeated and fear to compare their sight with hers.

Her right hand is adorned with a flower, and a scorpion, 25 inflaming her left, threatens with the sharp sting of his tail. One hand smells of honey, the other gives off the smell of gall; one promises laughter, the other ends in tears; one attracts, the other repels, one anoints, by the other one is stung; one strikes, the other soothes, one graces, the other 30 corrupts.

Her dress is neither demeaned by filth nor pridefully brilliant, but keeps within modest bounds, distant from either extreme. On it, with a new art, a new painter, a portrayer of truth, displays the battling of syllogisms, the duel of logic: how, with the gleaming blade of its two edged sword, the 35 force of logic, clad in the livery of truth, cuts through falsehoods, refusing to let the false conceal itself in the mask of truth. Why the pseudologician—thief and corruptor of the art, false and hypocritical, skulking robber, sophist—imi- 40 tates the appearance of logic and, relying on a few curious tricks, tries to pawn off falsehood as truth. What in logic is

quid locus in Logica dicatur quidve localis
congruitas, quid causa loci, quid maxima, quid sit
vis argumenti, manans a fonte locali;
45   cur argumentum firmet locus, armet elenchum
maxima, quae vires proprias largitur elencho;
quomodo materia vel forma peccat elenchus
et sola facie larvam pretendit elenchi;
cur ex praemissis conclusio nata, loquendo
50   quod praemissa velint, vultu signetur eorum;
cur liget extremos medius mediator eorum
terminus et firmo confibulet omnia nexu;
cur decurtati species nascatur elenchi,
quando vel affaeresis vel sincopa curtat elenchum;
55   qualiter usurpans vires et robur elenchi,
singula percurrit inductio, colligit omne,
sed tamen inferior sese summittit elencho;
qualiter exemplum de se parit, immo recisa
parte sui curtata parens sibi pignora gignit;
60   qualiter est munita locis ars ipsa localis,
nec tamen est conclusa loco, cum non loca quaerat,
immo locum, capiatque locos, ignara locorum;
quomodo diffinit partitur colligit unit
singula quae gremio complectitur illa capaci;
65   quomodo res pingens descriptio claudit easdem
nec sinit in varios descriptum currere vultus;
quid genus in species divisum separat aut quid
dividit in partes totum rursumque renodat
quae sunt sparsa prius, divisaque cogit in unum;
70   qualiter ars Logicae, tamquam via ianua clavis
ostendit reserat aperit secreta Sophiae;
qualiter arma gerit et in omni militat arte

called a "topic," what is the suitability of topics, what is the
basis of a topic, what a maxim is, and what is the force of a
counterargument that has its source in a topic; why a topic   45
strengthens an argument, and a maxim, which freely lends
its own powers to a syllogism, strengthens the syllogism.
How a syllogism may be flawed in matter or form and produce, in its structure alone, the shell of a syllogism; why a
conclusion derived from premises, by expressing what the   50
premises demand, is stamped with their likeness; why the
middle term links the extremes as their mediator, and binds
together the whole with a sure bond. Why a type of abbreviated syllogism is created when either aphaeresis or syncope shortens it; how induction, usurping the powers and   55
strength of the syllogism, goes through all its stages, and
brings them to completion, yet acknowledges itself inferior to the syllogism. How induction produces an example
from itself; when a part of it is cut off, the diminished parent generates its offspring. How the art of using topics is it-   60
self strengthened by topics, but is nevertheless not limited
to a place, since it seeks not places but a topic, and grasps
topics with no regard for places; how it defines, divides, collects and unifies individuals which it gathers to its capacious
bosom. How description, depicting things, confines these   65
same things, and does not allow the thing described to assume other features. What separates a divided genus into
species or divides a whole into parts, and then reunites again
what had first been dispersed, making the divided parts become one. How the art of Logic, like some road, door, or   70
key, leads to, unlocks, opens up the secrets of Sophia; how
Logic bears arms, and does service in every art; how she

ascribitque sibi causas et damna sororum;
qualiter haec reliquas defendit, ditat egentes,
75   roborat infirmas, elingues instruit, ornat
incomptas, torpentes excitat, armat inhermes;
qualiter haec purgat vitium faecemque repellit,
si quid inest faecis, vitium ne deroget arti;
qualiter incudem servat, ne falsa monetet
80   argumenta sibi furtiva fraude sophista.
Haec expressa tenet inscriptio vestis ut artem
et proprios pugiles et luctam poscere credas.
    Hunc habitum gestum formam speciemque puella
praetaxata gerit, sed florem dextra resignat
85   ad praesens aliisque vacat, serpensque sinistram
exit et ad maius urget manus utraque votum.
Virginis ergo manus ne torpor inhebriet, adsunt
instrumenta fabri, manibus quae Lemnius ipse
commodat et propriis illi deservit in armis.
90   Ergo se totam concedens virgo labori
duritiem ferri temptat mollire, rigorem
flectere, torporem delere, fugare stuporem,
ut ferri delicta domans exemplet in axem
materiem ferri, vultu meliore figurans;
95   nunc ignis demollit eam, nunc malleus ipsam
flectit et ad cultum ferri suspirat uterque;
sic ferrum ferro contendit, ut excolat illud,
ut socium venerans sese veneretur in illo.
Post multum sudoris opus, post proelia luctae,
100   insultum ferri vincit labor improbus, aufert
nequitiam motumque ligat rixamque retundit:
materiam ferit informem vestitque figura.
Et quae iam fuerat discors rudis hispida torpens

takes responsibility for the suits and damages of her sisters, how she defends the others, makes good their deficiencies, strengthens the weak, equips the unskilled, adorns the un- 75 kempt, rouses the diffident, arms the helpless. How she purges defect, and eliminates waste, if any should be present, lest imperfection discredit her art; how she watches over her anvil, lest any sophist fashion false arguments for 80 himself by hidden fraud. The decoration of her robe presents these things so vividly that you would think she sought a contest and champions to fight for her.

Such are the dress, the bearing, the face and figure of the aforementioned maiden. But her right hand surrenders its flower for a time to devote itself to other matters; the ser- 85 pent abandons her left, and both hands are now ready for her greater task. And lest dullness should make her hand unsteady, ready at hand are the tools of the smith, tools that the Lemnian has prepared for her, and he himself eagerly assists her with tools of his own.

Now, giving herself wholly to her task, the maiden at- 90 tempts to soften the hardness of iron, to make its rigidity bend, to end its inertia and banish its stolidity, so that by controlling the refractory iron she may give it the form of an axle, working the raw metal into a more attractive shape. Now the fire makes it softer, then the hammer bends it, and 95 both together strive to mold the metal. Thus iron struggles with iron in an attempt to work it, so that by honoring its comrade it may thereby do honor to itself. After much sweat and toil, after a fierce struggle, brute labor overcomes the 100 defiance of the metal, drives away what is base, curbs its resistance, beats back its hostility. hammers at its shapeless substance and clothes it with form. Now what had been

temperiem formam cultum motumque resumit
105 materies axisque gerit formata figuram.
    Picturae series cum fama praedicat illic
auctores Logicae, quos donat fama perhenni
vita, nec sepelit illos quos terra sepultos
velat, sed recolens defunctos suscitat orbi.
110 Illic Porfirius directo tramite pontem
dirigit et monstrat callem quo lector abyssum
intrat Aristotelis, penetrans penetralia libri;
illic Porfirius archana resolvit, ut alter
Edipodes nostri solvens aenigmata Spingos.
115 Verborum turbator adest et turbine multos
turbat Aristotiles noster gaudetque latere;
Sic Logicam tractat, quod non tractasse videtur,
non quod aberret in hac, sed quod velamine verbi
omnia sic velat quod vix labor ista revelet;
120 qui tamen idcirco vestit sua dicta latebris,
ne sua prostituat secreta suumque relinquens
arcanum, vulgo tandem vilescere cogat;
nam sua secreti maiestas vilet et omni
privatur splendore sui, si publica fiat.
125 [Nam maiestatem minuit qui mistica vulgat,
nec secreta manent quorum fit conscia turba.]
Nam res vulgatae semper fastidia gignunt;
ex re vulgata contemptus nausea surgit.
    Zeno, pugil logicus, Logices athleta, Sophiae
130 rex et ductor adest, Logicae sibi proelia quaerens;
illius nudat latebras imosque recesssus,
in lucem tenebrosa refert, nova ducit in usum,
excusatque tropos, in normam schema reducit.
Exserit ambiguum Severinus, quo duce linquens

confused, crude, rough, unresponsive assumes proportion, form, elegance, and motion: now formed, that material exhibits the shape of an axle. 105

A series of illustrations proclaims the glory of the authorities in logic, those to whom fame has granted enduring life. For fame does not bury these who lie buried in the earth, but remembers the dead and restores them to the world. Here Porphyry, leading the way forward, creates a 110 bridge, and points out the road whereby the reader may enter into the depths of Aristotle, making his way to the inner chambers of his writings. Here Porphyry solves deep problems, like a second Oedipus solving the riddle of our Sphinx. Our own Aristotle, the confuser of language is here; he confuses many with his wordplay, and he delights in concealment. He practices logic in such a way that he seems not to be doing so; it is not that he does so wrongly, but that he veils everything in such a cloak of verbiage that hard work can scarcely uncover it. However, he veils his words in 120 shadow for this reason, lest he should debase his profound learning by giving up its secrets to all the world, and cause it finally to become worthless. For the dignity of deep learning is cheapened, and robbed of all its luster, if it is made public; [for he who divulges a mystery demeans its majesty, and 125 what the mob comes to know cannot retain its deep meaning.] For matters made widely known breed contempt; a thing widely known gives rise to scornful revulsion.

Zeno, logic's boxer and wrestler, Sophia's king and commander, is here, looking for logic bouts. He lays bare the 130 hidden places of logic, its uttermost depths, brings obscurities into the light, introduces new methods, defends the use of figures, and brings schemata under a rule. Severinus clarifies what is uncertain; at his bidding the power of logic,

135　natalem linguam nostri peregrinat in usum
　　sermonis Logicae virtus ditatque latinum.
　　　Non cultu facieque minor, non arte secunda,
　　tertia virgo suo non fraudat munere currum.
　　Evocat exterius mentem, studioque vocatam
140　destinat, atque manus animo ducente gubernat
　　supremasque manus apponit, opusque sororum
　　perficit atque semel factum perfectius ornat.
　　Excolit illa gradu supremo quae positivo
　　facta gradu fuerant, sed non augmenta superni
145　finis contigerant, gradibus contenta secundis.
　　Nec mirum si facta prius perfectius ornans
　　perficit et factum cultu meliore venustat,
　　cui magis arridet species et gratia formae,
　　quae comites multa pictoris praevenit arte,
150　totam pictoris artem sub pectore claudens.
　　　Exemplans auri speciem miraque politus
　　arte iacet crinis, investit colla capillus
　　in vultuque natat color igneus, ignis in ore
　　purpureus roseo vultum splendore colorat,
155　sed partim vultus candor peregrinus inheret
　　nativoque suum certat miscere colorem.
　　Nunc vario fluctu lacrimarum vultus inundat,
　　nunc vultum varii risus aurora serenat,
　　abstergens fletus lacrimas; nunc virgo severos
160　praetendit vultus cum maiestate rigoris,
　　nunc oculus sursum lumen delegat in altum;
　　nunc cadit huius apex, nunc totum lucis acumen
　　in latus obliquans, anfractus quaerit et umbram.
　　　In dextra gerit illa tubam cornuque sinistram
165　donat et in cornu signat praeludia belli.

abandoning its native language, has found its way into ours, 135
and granted its wealth to Latin.

A third maiden, not inferior in dignity and beauty, no less
adept at her art, does not cheat the chariot of her special
gift. She calls up her thoughts and directs them, once
brought forth, to their task. She submits her hands to the 140
direction of her mind, and finally puts them to work. She
completes the work of her sisters, perfecting what has already been produced. She brings to the highest degree of
perfection work that had been accomplished to a positive
degree but had not attained the final stage of development, 145
content to remain at the second level. And it is no wonder if
she completes what had already been made, making it more
beautiful, and bestows on it a greater refinement, for beauty
and graceful form show her special favor; she surpasses her
sisters in the many skills of the painter, for in her spirit 150
dwells the whole art of painting.

Her hair, which gives the appearance of gold, and is arranged with wondrous skill, covers her neck, and in her face
a fiery color plays, a purple flame on her rosy mouth that
splendidly enhances her beauty. Yet a gleam of a foreign kind 155
also lurks in her face, and seeks to blend itself with her natural color. Her face is at one moment flooded with a sudden burst of tears; at the next the sunrise of a sudden smile
makes it fair, wiping away the flowing tears; now the maiden
offers a severe expression, majestically stern; now her eye 160
directs its beam toward the heights; now it is aimed lower;
now turning aside the full keenness of her sight, she tries digression and obscurity.

In her right hand she wields a trumpet, and a horn graces
her left, and on this horn she sounds a call to arms. The robe 165

Claudit eam vestis, quae picturata colore
multiplici, ridet varios induta colores.
Hic pictoris ope splendet pictura coloris
rhetorici, sic picturam pictura colorat.

170 Hic velut in libro legitur quis finis et auctor
forma vel officium, quae causa, quis ordo, quid artis
Rhetoricae proprium, quae virtus, qualiter instans
nunc tonat illa minis, nunc verbi luce coruscat,
nunc pluit illa preces, nunc laudibus imbuit aurem:

175 quid causae genus efficiat, quo tendat et ad quem
deveniens finem deliberet utile, iustum
iudicet, affirmet rectum, demonstret honestum;
quae partes artis, quis earum texitur ordo;
qualiter in primis ars invenit ipsaque tandem

180 ordinat eloquitur memorat pronuntiat, ut sic
ordine legitimo sibimet respondeat ordo;
quas vel quot partes oratio rhetoris in se
contineat, vel qua serie texantur in illa;
quomodo principium mentem movet, erigit aurem,

185 excitat auditum, cor iudicis apparat illi,
quo magis attentus, docilis magis atque benignus
redditur auditor et mentem dedicat auri;
quomodo sub brevibus verbis narratio verum
explicat, aut latitans veri sub imagine falsum;

190 qualiter in summa partitio colligit omne
quod sequitur, dispersa legens, diffusa coartans;
qualiter in partem faciens assertio nostram
argumenta notat probat exprimit astruit infert;

that clothes her is decorated with many colors and rejoices
to be decked with their variety. Here through the painter's
bounty there gleams a portrayal of the colors of rhetoric;
thus what is painted lends its colors to the painting. Here   170
one may read, as if in a book, the aim of rhetoric, its in-
ventors, its kinds and their functions, its means, its procedures: what the art of rhetoric comprises, its power, and
how, at one moment importunate, it resounds with threats,
at the next shines with brilliant language, now pours forth
prayers, now fills the ear with praise. What sort of argument   175
achieves its effects, how it develops, to what goal it moves as
it weighs advantage, delivers justice, supports the cause of
good, explains what is honorable. What are the divisions of
the art and what order weaves them together; how at the
first stage the orator invents, then arranges, chooses suit-   180
able language, commits to memory, and speaks, in such a
way that his discourse conforms to an appropriate design.
What and how many parts the oration of a rhetor contains,
and in what sequence they are connected. How the opening
stirs the mind of a judge, makes his ear alert, arouses his in-   185
terest and engages his feelings; in this way the audience are
rendered more attentive, more easily persuaded, more fa-
vorably disposed, and devote their minds to listening. How
the narration explains the true facts in a few words, or de-
ceitfully presents a false account concealed by the likeness
of truth. How the division summarizes everything that is to   190
follow, deciding on the various points and making them
more concise. How the presentation of our case, in making its arguments, identifies them, offers proof, lays them
out, builds on them, draws inferences from them. How the

qualiter oppositam ferit infirmatio partem,
195   destruit infirmat dissolvit dissipat urget;
quomodo concludens conclusio singula fine
legitimo claudit, sistens sermonis habenas;
quod factum factive genus nomenve requirat
quaestio, diversis rationum nixa columnis;
200   quae lis de facto certet, quae quaestio iuris,
quae vel quot species, quae simplex quaeve relata
quaeve relativae partes; cur astruat illa
criminis obiectum, haec transferat, illa repellat,
comparet haec aequa librans incommoda lance;
205   qualiter assumat contentio robur utrimque,
cum lex rixatur sociae contraria legi,
vel contra scriptum discors sententia pugnat,
vel parit in scripto dubium sententia duplex,
vel quando nomen describi possit ut ipsum
210   nominis ambiguum descriptio certa resignet,
vel cum iure loci personae temporis ipsa
quaestio transfertur, alios motura tumultus;
vel si contendat contentio, nescia certae
legis, et a simili rationis robora sumat;
215   quomodo personis accomoda roboris arma
dant argumentis, sed falso robore nutant
nomen natura victus fortunaque vultus
praetendens dubios habitus, affectio, fallax
consilium, studia, casus, oratio, factum;
220   eventus quae contineant, quid quaestio facti
obtineat, facto quae sint adiuncta vel ipsum,
ut res deposcit, solito de more sequantur;

refutation strikes at the opposing position, destroys it, un- 195
dermines it, tears it apart, sweeps it away, inveighs against it.
How the peroration, in closing, brings everything to an appropriate ending, and draws the discourse to a halt. What
deed, what type of deed, or what definition a question requires, when it depends on several lines of argument; what is 200
at issue in a dispute about fact, or a question of law. What
and how many are the kinds of issue, what makes an issue
simple, or complex, and what issues involve extraneous matters. Why one constructs objections to the charge, another
requires a change of plea or venue, still another denies that a
law has been broken, a fourth compares, balancing two of-
fenses on the scale of justice. How the arguments of either 205
side may be strengthened when a law is shown to contradict
a related law, or a dissenting opinion conflicts with the written law, or an ambiguity in the written law gives rise to doubt;
or when a crime can be named in such a way that a precise
definition only shows the ambiguity of the name; or when, 210
on grounds of place, person, or time, the trial itself is transferred, to breed confusion elsewhere; or if a claim is urged to
which no law clearly applies, and which bases the strength
of its argument on comparison. How the attributes of per- 215
sonal character lend strong arms to an argument, whereas
name, nature, way of life and fortune, a face suggesting
doubtful character, temperament, uncertain judgment, avo-
cations, accidents, manner of speaking, actions, all rely on
the false appearance of strength. What the circumstances 220
comprise, what the performance of the deed includes, what
things are adjunct to the deed, or follow upon it, as the case
requires, according to normal procedure. What was the

quis modus in facto vel quae complexio facti,
quis locus aut tempus occasio causa facultas.
225   Hanc artis gerit effigiem pars unica vestis
sed tamen artificum loquitur pars altera formas.
Illic Rhetoricam sibi soli Marcus adoptat,
immo parit, quare Ciceronis filia dici
ars merito poterit, quam gignit Tullius, a quo
230   ars ortum ducens censeri "Tullia" posset.
Illic multiplici praesignit carmina flore
sermonisque notas Ennodius effricat omnes.
Quintilianus adest, quadam sub imagine veri,
causarum velans umbras; litesque novellas
235   fingit et in litem cogit sine lite venire.
Symmachus in verbis parcus sed mente profundus,
prodigus in sensu, verbis angustus, habundans
mente, sed ore minor, fructu non fronde beatus,
sensus divitias verbi brevitate coartat.
240   Illic Sidonii trabeatus sermo refulgens
sidere multiplici splendet gemmisque colorum
lucet et in dictis depictus pavo resultat;
nunc tenuem gracili meditatur harundine musam,
nec tamen exsanguis sermo ieiunia luget,
245   nunc mediam, nec in ima ruens, nec in ardua turgens,
nunc tonat altiloquis describens seria verbis,
nunc tamen inflato tumidus crepat ille boatu.
    Hoc cultu festiva suam non detrahit artem
virgo, sed in cultus eius factura redundat.
250   Gemmis stellatam speciem themonis inignit,
argento sparsim themonem vestit et ipsi
ligni materiae, quae pollet honore minori,
externus succurrit honor redimitque minorem.

310

manner of the deed, what did it involve, what were the place, time, occasion, motive, and circumstances.

One part of the garment displays this representation of 225 the art itself. Another portion shows the forms of its practitioners. Here Marcus adopts rhetoric for himself alone, indeed gives birth to it, so that the art can rightly be called the child of Cicero, whom Tullius begot; taking its origin 230 from him, the art may be deemed "Tullia." There Ennodius adorns his songs with flowers of all kinds, and rubs out every blemish from his discourses. Quintilian is at hand, cloaking imaginary cases with the appearance of real ones; he invents new trials, and bids us engage in litigation without a case. 235 Symmachus, sparing of words, but profound of mind, rich in understanding but austere in speech, abounding in thought but poor in expression, more blessed with fruit than foliage, makes the wealth of his understanding fit the brevity of his speech. Here the discourse of Sidonius, resplendently robed, 240 shines with myriad stars, and gleams with gems of color, and the image of the peacock is reflected in his words. Now he woos the tender muse with delicate piping, yet it is no bloodless utterance, downcast and meager; now he sounds a mid- 245 dle note, neither plunging to the depths nor struggling toward the heights; now depicts serious matters in high-sounding words, yet his grandiosity bursts forth in a windy bellow.

Thus gaily arrayed, the maiden does not withhold her art, but in her work her artistry abounds. She makes the shining 250 surface of the beam flash with gems, and coats it here and there with silver; this outer dignity enhances its wooden substance, which is of a lesser dignity, and redeems its lowli-

Ligni primaevos ortus omnesque querelas
255 splendor adoptivus sepelit lignique vetustas
exulat et primos sic obliviscitur ortus.
Ergo themonem gemmarum sidus inaurat,
immo diem verum reddit lux ista diesque
materialis hebet, nam lux nativa diei
260 lumen adoptivum tantum miratur adorans.
A simili variis inscribit floribus axem
virgo, flore novo cogens iuvenescere ferrum;
et quamvis ferrum soleat torpere rigore
frigoris et brumae soleat redolere pruinam,
265 hoc hyemem nescit, frigus natale relinquens,
usurpatque sibi risus et gaudia veris,
et faciem prati praetendit imagine florum.
    Dum sic themonem gemmis et floribus axem
exhilarat virgo, cumulum largita decoris,
270 pingentis calamo cedit tuba, dat loca celti
cornu, sicque duo sumunt sibi iura duorum.
    Quarta soror sequitur; quartae rota prima sororis
est opus. Huic operas operose dedicat illa
et, quamvis haec quarta foret, tamen esse secundam
275 se negat, in facto contendens prima vocari.
Ergo decora decens gracilis subtilis acuta
pollet et in vultu monstratur copia mentis.
(Nam vultus noster liber est et littera cordis,
nuncius, interpres verax animique figura.)
280 Solliciti vultus, animum prudentis, honesti
cultus, attenti speciem formamque modesti
haec gerit et sexum transcendit mente virili.
Non eius roseos color incolit advena vultus,

ness. This acquired splendor conceals the primitive origins of the wood, and silences all complaints; the ancient state of the wood disappears, and it forgets its first beginnings. Now a starry heaven of gems gilds the beam; its light, indeed, so resembles that true light of day that the actual day grows dim; the daylight of nature adores in amazement an artificial radiance so bright. In a like manner the maiden decorates the axle with flowers of different kinds, making the iron experience a new, flourishing youth; and though iron is usually inert and stiff with cold, and exudes an atmosphere of frosty winter, this iron knows no winter; leaving behind its native coldness it claims for itself the smiling joys of spring, and presents the appearance of a flowering meadow.

While the maiden enlivens the beam with jewels and the axle with flowers, lavish of her abundance of beauty, the trumpet yields to the brush of the painter, the horn gives way to the engraver's tool, and these two assume the rights of the others.

The fourth sister next comes forward; the first wheel is the fourth sister's task. To this she devotes painstaking effort, and although she is fourth, she denies that she is inferior, striving by her actions to be acclaimed as first of all. She shows herself beautiful, well-formed, graceful, subtle and astute, and the richness of her mind appears in her face. (For the face is the book, the writing of the heart, the messenger, faithful interpreter and image of the mind.) The maiden displays a serious face, a careful mind, a dignified bearing, an attitude of attention and a discreet manner, and in manly force of mind she rises above her sex. No foreign tint dwells

255

260

265

270

275

280

sed color indigena regnat nec purpura vultus
285   secum furtivi patitur fermenta coloris.
Demittit caput in terram nec lubrica sensus
venatur; menti cedens agit otia visus.
    Mensam Pythagorae, quae menti pabula donat,
delicias animi sapiens, non corporis escas,
290   sustinet una manus. Pugnas manus altera monstrat:
agmina disponit numerorum, proelia fingit,
indicat insultus varios numerosque rebelles,
tandem subtili concludit bella triumpho.
    Ex bysso contexta, suo vestita decore,
295   vestis sidereos investit virginis artus.
Materies subtilis erat; subtilius ipsam
materiam praecellit opus; sic praevenit usus
Naturae vires Naturaque vincitur arte.
Hic pictura loquens scripto clamansque figuris,
300   muta tamen, totam numerandi praedicat artem:
quae numeri virtus, quae lex, quis nexus et ordo,
nodus amor ratio foedus concordia limes;
quomodo concordi numerus ligat omnia nexu,
singula componit, mundum regit, ordinat orbem,
305   astra movens, elementa ligans, animasque maritans
corporibus, terras caelis, caeleste caducis;
quomodo nascenti mundo rebusque creandis
principium finis exemplar forma sigillum
hic erat, ad cuius formam deitatis ydea
310   impressit rebus formas mundoque figuram;
quomodo principium numeri fons mater origo
est monas, et numeri de se parit unica turbam;
quomodo virgo parit, gignens manet integra, simplex
sese multiplicat, de sese gignit et in se

314

on her rosy face; her native color holds sway, and its purple   285
allows with itself no rash of alien color. She bows her head
toward the ground, and her senses pursue no elusive object;
giving place to mind, sight takes its rest.

One hand bears the table of Pythagoras, which provides
sustenance to thought, delicacies for the mind, not food for
the body. The other hand appears ready for war: it deploys   290
ranks of numbers, and stages a mock battle, planning different assaults, noting rebel numbers, then at length brings the
war to an end with triumphant subtlety.

A robe woven of cotton, adorned with its own beauty,
clothes the maiden's glowing limbs. The material is delicate,   295
but a handiwork more delicate still surpasses its material;
thus practiced skill outdoes the powers of Nature, and Nature yields to art. Here painting, speaking through writing
and calling out with images, yet making no sound, shows   300
forth the whole art of numeration: the power of numbers,
their law, their connection and order, their jointure, their
sympathy, purpose, agreement, harmony, limit. How number joins all creation with a bond of harmony, arranges all
things, governs the universe, orders the world, regulating   305
the stars, uniting the elements, marrying souls to bodies,
earth to heaven, celestial to mortal. How in the birth of the
universe and the making of creatures number was the first
principle, the end, the model, the form, the image in the
likeness of which the divine Idea imposed form on crea-   310
tures, and a pattern on the universe. How the monad is the
beginning of number, its fount, mother, origin, and of itself
alone gives birth to the host of numbers. How a virgin gives
birth, and in so doing remains intact, is pure yet reproduces
herself, brings forth life from herself, yet herself remains

315 incorrupta manet, partus imitata parentis;
quis numerus numerans censetur, quis numeratus,
quis repetit, quis distribuit, quis colligit, aufert
addit et a primo radices extrahit ortu;
quo iuris merito vel qua ratione vocetur
320 femina par numerus, impar mas, virgo Minerva;
cur animam caelum rationem gaudia vitam
impare sub numero prudentum dogma figuret;
cur corpus terram sensum lacrimabile mortem
par numerus signet peioraque fata loquatur;
325 quis numerus punctum, quis linea, quisve figura
plana vel aequorum laterum, quis sphaera vocatur,
quis quadrus vel quis solidus, quis piramis, aut quis
ciclicus est, a se qui circumflectitur in se;
quis numerus propriis completur partibus aut quis
330 vel partes superat, vel ab his superatus abundat;
quae numerum numero concordia nectit et unde
provenit ut vicibus mediis extrema ligentur;
cur duo quadrati medio nectantur in uno
vel solidos nectat mediis iunctura duobus.

335   Hoc igitur cultu virgo praeculta laboris
pondera non fugiens, ne pondere pondus honoris
effugiat, dum vitat onus ne vitet honorem,
robur virgineum cumulo virtutis et arte
transgrediens, superat vir sensu, femina sexu;
340 sic vir, sic mulier, animo non illa sed ille est.
Nec motu subito quod concipit exprimit actu,
nec quod mens gignit subitos deducit in actus,
nam si conceptum pariat mens ipsa priusquam
formam suscipiat conceptus mentis in alvo,

inviolate as she imitates a mother's parturition. Which num- 315
bers are understood as "counting," and which as "counted,"
which doubles, which distributes, which collects, subtracts,
adds, or extracts the root at its first rising. By virtue of what
rule or for what reason an even number is called "female," an 320
uneven one "male," the virgin number "Minerva." Why the
teachings of the wise represent the soul, the heavens, reason, joy, and life itself by an uneven number; why an even
number signifies the body, earth, sense, sorrow, death, and
speaks of ill fortune. Which number is called a "point," 325
which a line, which a plane figure or equilateral, which a
sphere, which a square, which a solid, which a pyramid and
which a circular body, which bends around, away from itself
and back to itself. What number is equaled by the sum of its
parts, which exceeds that sum, which is exceeded by it. 330
What harmony joins number to number, and whence it happens that extremes are joined together by middle terms.
Why two squared numbers are united in a single mean; why
the linkage that joins solids involves two means.

Adorned in this way, the highly gifted maiden does not 335
evade her weighty task, lest great honor should escape her
along with the great deed; lest in refusing this burden she
should deny herself honor. Surpassing the powers of a
maiden by her abundant vigor and skill, she has a man's superior understanding, though in sex a woman. Thus, man 340
and woman both, in purpose she is not "she" but "he." She
does not reveal by any sudden action the plan she has conceived; she does not begin abruptly to enact what her mind
has produced; for if the mind should give birth to its conception before this conception has taken shape in the womb

345 vel firmum capiat mentis matrice sigillum,
nutritumque diu rationis fomite vivat,
fetus abortivus subito decurret ad ortum,
nec vita dignus proprio morietur in ortu,
vel vivens saltem lugebit crimina formae;
350 ergo legitimo ne partus mentis ab ortu
deviet et nullam ducat de matre querelam,
mens gignit, nutrit ratio, quod parturit actus;
fabricat in thalamo mentis mentale priusquam
materiale foras opus evocet. Ergo labore
355 mentis et artificis animi studiique favore
erigitur rota mentalis, post materiali
effigie describit eam; sic mente priorem
concipit ut pariat, actu parit illa secundam.
    Instrumenta prius manibus praefata relinquens,
360 ingreditur latomi studium. Domat arte rigorem
marmoris et primum partes complanat ad unguem;
Scrupulus in planum descendit, surgit in aequum
vallis et in curvum demittitur angulus, orbis
planiciem claudit planumque reducit in orbem.
365 Sed tumor in medio surgens supereminet, immo
sic in supremum tendens non deserit imum.
Partibus in curvum, ferro mediante, redactis
exhaurit partes virgo marmorque fenestris
distinguens, totum spaciis intersecat orbem;
370 Collocat in medio centrum mediumque coronat
multiplici radio quem latus circinat orbis.
    Hic pictura docet auctores qui numerandi
invenere vias, artem docuere, latentem

of the mind, before it has received its defining stamp in the   345
matrix of the mind, and lived through long nurture by the
heat of reason, an abortive creature will be brought too
quickly to birth, not fit to live, and will die at the moment of
its birth, or, should it live, will at the least lament its mis-
shapen state. Therefore, lest the bringing forth of her idea   350
should differ from normal birth, and give rise to complaints
against the mother, the mind conceives and reason nurtures
what performance will produce; the maiden fashions it men-
tally in the inner chamber of her mind before the task brings
it into material existence. Thus a mental wheel is con-   355
structed by mental labor and creative thought, the reward
of study; later she will depict it in material form; thus she
conceives the first version in her mind so that she may give
birth, then brings forth the second, actual version.

First laying aside the aforementioned instruments, she
begins the work of a stonecutter; she skillfully overcomes   360
the hardness of the marble, and first planes the sides perfectly smooth. What protrudes is planed down, depressions
are brought even with the surface, and each corner is turned
into a curve; roundness encloses the level stone, and shapes
it into a circle. But a swelling rises up in the center, yet in   365
thrusting outward it does not separate from the surface below. When the edges have been rounded off with the aid of
a file, the maiden draws out portions, piercing the marble
with windows, cutting through the entire wheel at intervals.
She positions the hub in the center, and crowns this center   370
with many radiating spokes, which the edge of the wheel encircles.

Here painting shows us the authors who discovered the
paths of numeration, taught others their art, brought to

produxere foras, fama coluere iacentem.

375 Illic Nicomachus praedicta ludit in arte
et quasi per numeros rerum secreta prophetat.
Illic castra tenet et eadem miles in arte
Gilbertus saltu fallaci transilit artem.

Pythagoras propriae menti convivia donans,
380 non carni satians, animos non corpora pascens,
certis ascribit numerorum legibus ortus,
esse vices causas motus et vincula rerum.
Indulget numeris tanto Crisippus amore
eius ut in verbo numerus factisque resultet
385 semper et in somnis illum numerare putares.

      Quinta soror quartae similis gerit ore priorem;
pingit eam cultu factoque recurrit in illam,
nec vacat a simili studio sequiturque sororem;
in studiis exemplat eam factumque sororis
390 respiciens eius facto sua facta sigillat.
Et quam iamdudum fecit Natura sororem
fit soror in facto, cumulans ius omne sororis.
Namque docet ratio, ius postulat, exigit ordo
ut fateatur opus id quod Natura fatetur.

395   Pro speculo vultum gerit haec preclara tuenti,
nam quicumque videt vultum se visus in illo
cernit et in speculo vultus epulatur ocellus.
Dum citharam manus una gerit, manus altera cordas
sollicitat dulcemque soni parit illa saporem,
400 auri dans epulas oculisque proemia somni;
quo cantu lapides mollescere, currere silvas,
flumina stare, feras mitescere, cedere lites
iussit Traicius vates, fractoque rigore,
compulit Eumenides lacrimis Ditemque coegit

light hidden knowledge, adorned the dormant science with fame. Here Nicomachus revels in this art, and seems through 375 numbers to foretell things hidden. Here Gerbert, a campaigner in this same art, has his camp, and leaps over certain points of the art by the leap of deception. Pythagoras, providing feasts for his mind, but not indulging the flesh, feed- 380 ing thought, not the body, ascribes to the fixed laws of number the birth, existence, growth, causes, motion, bonds of created life. Chrysippus enjoys arithmetic so much that numbers resound through all his speech and actions, and 385 one may imagine that he counts in his sleep.

The fifth sister is like the fourth, and bears the other's face in her own; she copies the other in her dress, and depends on her in her work; she continually pursues similar studies, following her sister; she models her studies on the other's, always aware of her sister's work, and her own work 390 bears the mark of the other's. And she whom Nature long ago made the sister of Arithmetic becomes her sister in act, claiming for herself all her sister's rights; for reason teaches, right demands, order requires that her work should express what Nature expresses.

This remarkable maiden presents her face to the beholder 395 as a mirror, for whoever beholds her face sees himself reflected in it, and the eye feasts on the mirror of her face. While one hand holds a lyre, the other plucks its strings, and it brings forth a sweet and elegant sound, providing a feast 400 for the ear and the promise of sleep for the eyes. With such a song the Thracian bard caused rocks to soften, trees to run, rivers to stay their flow, wild beasts to grow gentle, wars to cease; subduing the cruelty of the underworld, he reduced the Eumenides to tears, forced Dis himself to feel pity, and

405   esse pium Furiasque suum nescire furorem;
        quo cantu Tyrios montes in moenia vertit
        Amphion, sic saxa domans, quod nulla securis
        edomuit rigidas cautes, quas sola domare
        vox citharae meruit, tenuitque silentia ferrum.
410   Insigni vestita toga se Pacis alumnam
        esse puella docet nec quaerere fulgura belli.
        Illic picturae ridens lascivia ludit
        schemate sub vario monstrans quid Musica possit:
        quae sint vincla, quibus compaginet omnia nodis,
415   quae species artis, quae musica colligit horas,
        distinguit menses, locat anni tempora, cogit
        excursus, elementa ligat, iungitque planetas,
        astra movet variatque vices; quae Musica nectit
        corporis humani partes mundumque minorem
420   ordinat et specie mundi melioris honorat.
        ut sic pigmaeus fraterculus esse gigantis
        maiorisque minor mereatur ymagine pingi;
        quae partes animae sociat, quae foederat illam
        carni confirmatque fidem; quae Musica voces
425   dividit et numeris variat discrimina vocum;
        quae ratio cur omne melos dulcesque sonorum
        cantus non gignit vox una sed unio vocum,
        dissimilis similisque sonus, diversus et idem,
        unicus et simplex duplex difformis et alter;
430   quomodo mutato se mutat Musica cantu,
        cum lacrimis risus, cum ludis seria texens:
        nunc enarmonice resonat, nunc tristia fingens
        ditonico cantu luget, nunc cromate ludit;
        quae vox ad vocem fit dupla vel in diapason
435   quis resonet cantus, vel quis sesqualter ad illum

made the Furies forget their savagery. With such a song Am-   405
phion turned Theban mountains into walls, so taming the
boulders that when no ax could overcome their rocky hardness, the voice of the lyre alone was able to govern them,
and the iron fell silent.

Clad in a splendid robe, the girl declares herself the foster   410
child of Peace, not one who seeks the clashing of war. Over
this robe the merry wantonness of painting plays, showing
by various means what music can achieve, what are its bonds,
with what knots it joins all together, what are its kinds: 415
which music counts the hours, divides the months, determines the seasons of the year, controls their progression,
links the elements, regulates the planets, moves the stars,
and varies their activity. Which music connects the parts of
the human body, governs this lesser universe, and honors it   420
with a form like that of the greater universe, so that a pigmy
is permitted to be the little brother of a giant, the lesser to
be adorned with the likeness of the greater. Which music
joins the parts of the soul, which unites it with the flesh, and
ensures their good faith. Which music distinguishes pitches,
and marks the several intervals between pitches with num-   425
bers. What is the reason why not a single pitch but a union
of pitches give rise to every melody and sweet song, a sound
both like and unlike, diverse and yet the same, single and
simple, double, different, and other. How music, by altering   430
its song, alters itself, mingling laughter with tears, the solemn with the merry; now it resounds enharmonically, now,
feigning sadness, it mourns in diatonic song; now sports
chromatically. Which pitch becomes double relative to another, or what harmony resounds in the diapason, or what   435
sound will be a sesquialter in relation to this, or sound in

sit sonus aut illi concors sonet in diapente;
quae vocum iunctura parit diatessaron, in qua
cum tribus una sonans vox litigat, immo iocatur;
qua ratione toni pars altera semper habundet,
440　transgrediens partem reliquam, ne possit in aequas
distribui partes tonus integer, immo parumper
excedat pars una toni superetque minorem
et proprio vincat pars altera commate limma,
nec tamen aequali sectas libramine partes
445　in duo divisum diastemata comma recuset.
　　Hoc igitur splendens habitu cultuque decoris
virgo nitens, usum citharae deponit ad horam,
dum subit officium fabri lapidemque caloris
imperio convertit in aes, ex aere secundam
450　fabricat illa rotam, quae formae laude priorem
demonstrans, primae se predicat esse sororem.
Et quamvis diversa foret quae dividit illas
materies, has forma tamen facit esse gemellas.
　　Illic artifices quos musica gaudet habere
455　consortes, vel quos proprii dignatur honore
nominis amplecti, scripturae fama perhennat.
Mellitae vocis Milesius exerit usum
et veluti quaedam cantus exenia donat
auribus et tali mentes effeminat arte.
460　Alter ab opposito cantus fastidia lenti,
obtusae vocis rixam cantusque rebelles,
qui magis impugnant aures quam voce salutent
invenit et nostras offendit cantibus aures.
Navigat in medio partemque relinquit utramque
465　Gregorius noster, refugitque pericula vocum,
cantus Syrenum fugiens vitansque Caribdim.

harmony with it in the diapente. What combination of
voices produces the diatessaron, in which one voice strives,
or rather plays, with three. For what reason one part of a
tone is always fuller, encroaching on the other part, so that   440
the whole tone cannot be divided into equal parts, but instead one part quickly exceeds and surpasses the lesser, and
the other part dominates the lemma by its comma, yet the
comma, divided into two diastemata, does not reject parts   445
divided in equipoise.

Resplendent in dress, and dazzling in her refined beauty,
the maiden lays her lyre aside for a time, undertakes the
work of a smith, turns stone to bronze through the power of
fire, and from this bronze fashions a second wheel which,   450
displaying the beautiful shape of its predecessor, declares itself the sister of the first. And though differing materials
distinguish them, their beauty makes them twins.

There the glory of inscription keeps alive those artists
whom music rejoices to have as her partners, and those on   455
whom she has deigned to confer the honor of her own name.
The Milesian draws out the sound of his honeysweet voice,
bestows something like an offering of song on the ear, and
by his art effeminates the mind. Another, opposing him,   460
makes songs that are tediously slow, the bawling of a dull
voice, angry songs which assail the ears instead of address-
ing them kindly; he troubles our hearing with such songs.
Our Gregory sails a middle course, separate from either ex-   465
treme, and so avoids the perils of song, fleeing the harmonies of the Sirens, and shunning Charybdis. Music rejoices

Musica laetatur Michalo doctore suosque
corrigit errores, tali dictante magistro.
    Instat sexta soror operi; se funditus urget
470   ad studium, studio reliquis studiosius haerens.
Certatim gestus habitus decor huius honorem
accumulant pariter, eius pro laude loquentes.
Encleticum gerit illa caput, nec corporis ullam
iacturam patitur, sed lumen legat in unum,
475   ut quibus insideat mens, enclesis ipsa loquatur:
exponit mentem facies animumque fatetur.
    Virgam virgo gerit, qua totum circinat orbem,
qua terrae spatium metitur, qua mare claudit
limitibus certis, qua circinat ardua celi.
480   Et quamvis eius vestis respersa minuti
pulveris imbre foret, non denigratur honestas
materiae formaeque decor, sed grammate multo
picturata nitet multoque superbit honore.
    Hic artem totam picturae lingua recenset:
485   quae mensurandi doctrinam fundit et usum
edocet, immensum claudit, spatiosa refrenat
parvaque consequitur, metitur magna, profundum
scrutatur, valles habitat, conscendit in altum.
Hic legitur quid sit punctum, quae linea curva,
490   recta vel aequalis, quae circumflexa vocetur
quaeve superficies plano contenta, profundum
ignorans altoque carens, decurrit in aequum;
quid sit tetragonus, quid forma triangula, quid sit
mensura triplici clausum; quid sterion aut quid
495   circumducta sua describat linea centro;
cur centrum sedet in medio, cur angulus omnis
aut obtusus hebet, aut sursum tendit acutus

in Doctor Michal, and with such a master to teach her, corrects her faults.

The sixth sister stands to her task; she applies herself wholly to study, being more studiously devoted to study than 470 the others. Her bearing, dress, and beauty alike are eager to bestow honor upon her, sounding her praises. She bends her head downward; her body does not allow itself to bend, but her eye is directed to a single point, so that the angle of her 475 head itself makes plain what occupies her thoughts; her face reveals her mind, and expresses what she is thinking.

The maiden bears a wand, with which she encircles the world, measures the expanse of earth, contains the ocean within fixed limits, circles the vaults of the heavens. And though her robe is strewn with a fine scattering of dust, the 480 excellence of the material and the beauty of its arrangement are not dishonored, for it shines, adorned with many markings, and shows her pride in her great dignity.

Here the language of painting sums up the whole of her art, which sets forth the theory of measurement and teaches 485 its practice, contains immensity, curbs the vastness of space, takes note of small things, takes the measure of great things, sees into the depths, dwells in valleys, scales the heights. Here one may read what a point is, what a line — curving, straight, or continuous (which may be called circular); or 490 what a surface is: content with its plane, knowing nothing of depth and lacking height, it remains level as it extends. What a tetragon is, what is the shape of a triangle, what is defined by a triple measure. What a solid is, and what term denotes a line drawn out in a circular path around a point. 495 Why the center is set in the middle, why every angle either spreads, obtuse, or, acute, points forward, or is a right angle,

obtusove minor sit rectus, maior acuto;
cur iuxta leges artis normamque datorum,
500 supra gramma datum procedens tramite recto,
aequorum laterum trigonus describitur, in quo
sese prosternens partem data linea donat;
qualiter a puncto ducatur linea compar
propositae reddensque datam; cur linea maior
505 de se producat absciso fine minorem;
cur huius tyrones artis eleufuga terret
atque prius cogit illos exire profundum
quam subeant labique priusquam in arte laborent;
qua rationis ope sibi forma triangula formam
510 repperit aequalem; cur linea partibus aequis
scinditur aut simili distinguitur angulus arte
inque duos unum divisio dividit una.
   Hac igitur veste virgo nitet, immo virago
glossat in hac mentem. Virgae dans otia, fabrum
515 induit et sparsam mentem componit in unum.
Mente manu studiis invadit, corrigit ipsam
materiem plumbi, quam crebro malleus urget,
imprimit ad placitum formam. Vetus exit et intrans
forma recens plumbi veteres excusat abusus.
520 Nascitur ex plumbo rota tertia, nata priores
reddit et in vultu formam gerit illa priorum.
   Illic artifices pictoris littera clamat,
qui rerum tractus mensuras pondera fines
limite sub certo claudentes aëra caelum
525 astra fretum terras simili ratione tuentur.
Hic geometra Thales sine motu praeterit orbem
aërii tractus, sine pennis transvolat aequor,
oceani spatium sine remige transit, in astra

less than the obtuse, greater than the acute. How, in accordance with the rules of the art and the pattern of the data, by lines extending upward from a given line, an equilateral triangle is delineated, in which the given line contributes itself as a part, becoming the base. How a line extending from a point can be equal to a preestablished line, mirroring the given one. Why a longer line cut off at one end produces from itself a shorter line. Why "the flight of the wretched" terrifies beginners in this art, forcing them to abandon it before they have plumbed its depths, to fall before they have labored in the art. By what rational process a triangular form discovers another form equal to itself. Why a line is cut into equal parts, or an angle divided in a similar manner, and a single division divides one into two. 500 505 510

The maiden—indeed woman warrior—shines in this garment, and it enables us to read her mind. Laying down her wand, she becomes a smith, and focuses her wide-ranging mind on a single object. With thought, hand, and purpose she attacks and reshapes her leaden material with many hammer blows, and imposes the desired form. The old shape is gone, and the newly assumed form atones for the lead's former faults. A third wheel emerges from the lead; the newborn resembles those made earlier, and displays their outward shape. 515 520

Here the text of the painter applauds the masters who, confining within fixed bounds the extent, the size, the weight, the limits of all things, consider the air, the heavens, the stars, sea and land by a single standard. Here the geometrician Thales, without stirring rises beyond the aerial sphere, without wings flies over the plain, crosses the vast ocean without oars, climbs to the stars without a ladder, 525

absque gradu graditur, sine tactu tangit Olimpum.
530 In seriem precepta ligans artemque retexens,
Euclides partes artis locat ordine iusto,
quas veluti quodam rationis fune ligatas
nectit ut ex una reliquas exire putares.

Liber Quartus

Ultima subsequitur virgo, quae prima decore,
cultu prima, gerit primam sub pectore mentem.
Non morbo, non tristitia, non mente magistra,
degenerat caput in terram, sed vultus in astris
5 haeret et arcanum caeli causasque fugaces
venatur visus; mentis preambulus illi
nunciat et crebro mentem docet assecla mentis.
Ori fulgor adest, qui tanto fulgore nostrum
verberat intuitum, dum visus fulgur adultum
10 devitans, oculi tunicas exire veretur.
    Implet sphaera manum, sphaerae tamen umbra videri
haec melius posset, quae solam suscipit umbram,
nec proprium sphaerae retinens consurgit in altum,
sed iacet in plano, nullo promota tumore.
15 Vestis inardescit gemmis auroque superbit
et splendore suo stellas aequare videtur.
Hic viget, hic loquitur, hic instruit, hic docet, immo
dat praecepta suis picturae dote facultas
quae docet astrorum leges loca tempora motus
20 signa potestates discursus nomina causas.

scales Olympus without setting foot upon it. Euclid, fixing his theorems in sequence, revealing the laws of the art, organizes the components of the art in proper order, connecting them as if bound by a sort of rope of reasoning, so that you might suppose all the rest were derived from the first. 530

Book 4

Now follows the last of the maidens; foremost in beauty, foremost in dress, she bears within her breast the foremost mind. She does not bow her head toward the ground in illness, in sorrow, or when prompted by thought; instead her face is always fixed on the stars. Her gaze seeks out the hidden workings of the heavens and their elusive causes; leading the way for the mind, it informs her about them, and this servant of the mind frequently becomes its teacher. There is a brightness in her face which strikes our sight with such brilliance, that our vision, fleeing its full power, fears to emerge from the covering of the eye. 5 10

A sphere rests on her hand, but it might well seem the shadow of a sphere, for it preserves only the shape of its shadow; it does not possess the character of a sphere, for it does not raise itself upward, but lies flat, enlarged by no rotundity. Her robe glows with gems, and waxes proud in gold, and in its splendor it seems to rival the stars. Here, the skill which teaches the laws of the stars, their places, their times, their motions, signs, powers, vacillations, names and causes, through the gift of painting lives, speaks, informs, instructs, even gives rules to its students. 15 20

Hic legitur quae sit caelestis sphaera, quis axis
in partes sphaeram distinguat, quis polus axem
terminet, aut sursum tendens, aut mersus in imo;
cur mundi sit forma teres mundusque ligetur
25   quinque parallelis cinctus zonisve quibusdam
sectus, in extremis rigeat, medio tenus aestu
torreat atque duas laterales temperet harum,
excessu duplici castigans frigore flammam;
cur decurtatus concludat utrumque colurum
30   circulus et neuter ad puncta priora redire
possit, sed nomen abscisio donet utrique;
cur obliqua means, declivi limite ducta,
linea signiferi duodeno sidere caelum
pingat et hospitium peregrino grata planetae
35   donet et ipsius proprium communicet illi;
qua ratione meant stellae; qua lege planeta
directum metitur iter, qua lege retrorsum
aufugit aut certa fixus statione moratur;
qua ratione meant obliquo signa meatu;
40   cur signum proprios directius exit in ortus
opposito, furans nascendi tempora, tempus
perdit in occasu quod plus expendit in ortu;
quis lunae motus, quae solis sphaera, quis orbis
Mercurii, Venerisque semita, quae via Martis;
45   quae mora Saturnum retinet; quo limite currit
stella Iovis motusque vagos quis circulus equat;
quis sursum tendens egressa cuspide terram
exit et in terra nescit defigere centrum.

Here one may read what the celestial sphere is; what axis divides this sphere into parts, at what pole the axis terminates when rising upward, or when sunk to the depths. Why the shape of the universe is round, and why this cosmos is bound by five parallels, or segmented into several zones; why 25 in the outermost of these the earth is frozen, about the middle it suffers blazing heat, and in the two between these it is temperate through a double excess, countering fire with wintry chill. Why each of the colures terminates in a broken circle, and neither can return to its starting point, so that 30 the two are granted the name of "cut off." Why the line of the Zodiac, drifting slantwise and drawn toward its lower boundary, adorns the heavens with its twelve signs, graciously offers hospitality to the journeying planet, and im- 35 parts to it its own property. For what reason the stars wander; by what law a planet travels a straight course, by what law it retreats backward, or remains fixed in a particular position. For what reason the signs of the Zodiac wander in a slanting path; why a sign emerges in its rising more quickly 40 than its opposing sign, stealing from its rising time; or why it loses time in setting because it spends more in its rising. What is the Moon's movement, what is the sphere of the Sun, what is the orbit of Mercury, the path of Venus, the road of Mars; what delay slows the pace of Saturn, along 45 what path the star of Jove runs. What orbit regulates erratic movements; what orbit, tending upward as its center shifts, leaves the earth behind, and does not locate its center in the earth.

Ergo puella gerens tanti solemnia cultus
50   non animum sepelit nec pigra per otia sese
distrahit aut animi vires effeminat, immo
exercet studiis totam cum corpore mentem.
Exit sphaera manum, quoniam manus ipsa vocatur
ad nova, quae cudens fabri sibi vindicat artem.
55   Dum manus excudit aurum massamque figurat
nascitur ex auro rota quarta, decoris honore
haec comites vincens, primas facit esse secundas.
Illic scripturae facies applaudit et illos
colligit in scripto, qui ducti remige mentis,
60   in superas abiere domos secretaque caeli
scrutati, meruere sibi deitatis honorem.
Illic astra polos caelum septemque planetas
consulit Albumasar terrisque reportat eorum
consilium, terras armans firmansque caduca
65   contra caelestes iras superumque furorem.
Astraque sustentat, dum sustentatur ab astris
Atlantis virtus, caeli sine pondere pondus
gestat, fert caelum, dum fertur dumque ferendo
sideribus cedit, cedenti sidera cedunt.
70   Has igitur currus partes, ut norma requirit,
ordo petit, poscit Ratio, Prudentia dictat,
cudit et excudit facit immo perficit ornat
exornatque simul lima meliore sororum
praetaxata cohors, nullumque relinquit in illis
75   enormis formae vultum maculaeve querelam.
Apponensque manum supremam, fine beato
concludens operam, sparsas Concordia partes
ordine lege loco confoederat unit adaequat.
Ergo iunctura clavis gumfisque ligatae

This maiden, then, skilled in the practice of such an art, does not conceal her thoughts, nor distract herself with lazy 50 idleness, or dissipate her strength of purpose; instead she applies her entire mind to her plan, together with her body. The sphere leaves her hand, since that hand is summoned to new tasks; laboring at the forge, it claims for itself the skills of the smith. As her hand hammers out and shapes a mass of 55 gold, a fourth wheel of gold is born; surpassing its companions in dignity and beauty, it makes the first become second.

Here the inscribed surface praises and recalls in writing those who, driven forward by the oar of the mind, went 60 forth to the mansions above, explored the secrets of the heavens, and earned for themselves the honor owed to a god. There Albumazar consults the stars, the poles, the celestial sphere and the seven planets, and brings their wisdom back to earth, arming the world, giving mortals the strength to withstand the wrath of heaven, the fury of the powers 65 above. The strength of Atlas supports the stars, while he is himself sustained by them; he bears the weight of a heaven which has no weight; he holds up the heavens while being borne upward, and while, as their bearer, he serves the stars, the stars yield their secrets to their servant.

Thus the band of sisters, with surpassing skill, has forged, 70 shaped, made, nay perfected, polished and adorned the parts of the chariot, as rule required, as order asked, as Reason demanded and Providence ordered. They have left no trace of unshapeliness, nor any objectionable flaw. Concord, set- 75 ting her hand to work at last, bringing the work to a happy conclusion, joins the several parts in due order, unites them as required, fits them into place. Bound together now by

80   partes effigiant currum qui luce decoris
        praeradians, facie propria demonstrat in ipso
        divinam sudasse manum superumque Minervam.
         Tunc Ratio monitu Naturae docta docentis
        quinque sibi praesentat equos, quos foederat illa
85   foedere complacito, concordi pace, fideli
        connexu, cogitque iugo servire iugales
        indomitos, primis quos enutrivit ab annis
        gratia Naturae, quae sic instruxit equinos
        mores, his animi quaedam vestigia donans
90   ut, quamvis bruti, tamen hi venerentur alumnam.
        Insuper in quantum patitur Natura, iugalis
        horum quisque suae naturae munera iactat.
        Nil cultus formaeque nihil peregrinat ab illis
        quod plene possit speciem cumulare iugalis.
95   Primus equus cultu forma cursuque sodales
        praevenit et reliquos proprio summitit honori.
        Cultus forma color species audacia cursus
        ditat eum nec in hoc patitur sibi damna quod illum
        respersus candore color subrufus inaurat.
100   Non meat, immo volat, nec enim discrimine passus
        inscribit terram nec gramen curvat eundo,
        sed celeri cursu terram delibat euntis
        passus, et in terra vestigia nulla relinquit.
        Sed levis aura suos stupet invenisse volatus
105   miraturque suum Boreas torpescere cursum.
        Aura cadit, lentescit avis, volucrisque sagittae
        cursus hebescit, equi lentescunt omnia cursu.
        Anticipat monitum calcaris sponte meatum
        aggreditur facilique tamen frenatur habena.

jointure, nail, and ironware, the parts form a chariot which, 80
shining forth the light of beauty, makes it clear by its appearance that a divine hand and the wisdom of higher powers have labored over it.

Then Reason, instructed by a sign from the instructress, Nature, presents her with five horses, whom she joins in an agreeable pact, a peaceful harmony, a mutual trust; she 85
causes these untamed yokefellows to submit to the yoke, these creatures whom kindly Nature has cared for from their earliest years, so guiding their equine conduct and endowing them with certain signs of intellect that, brute 90
beasts though they are, they nevertheless revere their mistress. Moreover, insofar as Nature allows, each member of the team boasts his own natural gifts. No trait of shape or breeding is absent in them that could consummate the beauty of a horse.

The first horse surpasses his companions in breeding, 95
shape and swiftness, and makes the others yield him pride of place. Breeding, shape, color, bearing, boldness and speed distinguish him, and it cannot be considered a defect in him that a reddish coloring intermingled with white gilds him. He does not amble, indeed he flies; his hooves leave no imprint on the ground, nor is the grass bent down where he goes; his hooves barely taste the earth and leave no trace in the soil as he races swiftly along. The lively breeze is astounded to discover a swiftness like its own, and Boreas 105
marvels that his own onrush now seems slow. The breeze fails, the flight of birds is slower, the speed of the winged arrow flags; all are made slow by the swiftness of this horse. He anticipates the prompting of the spur, and spontaneously begins to run, yet can be governed by a light rein.

110 Praeterea dotes nativas aggerat ipsa
nobilitas generis; Pyroum namque parentem
iactat et in speculo prolis pater ipse resultat.
Hunc dedit in munus Iovialis gratia matri
Naturae, cuius grates dantisque favorem
115 accumulat doni meritum, quo munere maius
nil potuit tantus tantae conferre parenti.
His igitur, velut ipsius natura requirit,
nobilitatur equi species.
                              Infraque secundus
pollet equus, minor in specie cultuque minori
120 cultus et inferior, cursuque remissior illo.
Et quamvis minor a primo formaque secundus,
est tamen in reliquis maior primusque decoris
munere, sed reliquos superans, superatur ab uno.
Etsi non aequo passu contendere primo
125 possit equo, non aura tamen fugitiva secundum
praevenit, immo pari cursu contendit eidem.
Se varians nullo praescribitur ille colore,
sed vultum proprii mentitur saepe coloris.
Intonat ille fremens, hinnitibus aëra crebris
130 verberat et tenuem sine vulnere vulnerat auram.
A collo suspensa sonos crepitacula dulces
reddunt et multo perfundunt aëra cantu.
In vultu gerit ille patrem, dum reddit Eoum
gestibus huncque suum forma probat esse parentem.
135 Muneribis praelarga suis, hoc munere Iuno
Naturae cumulavit opes meruitque favorem
numinis et proprium dono descripsit amorem.
    Tertius a tanta speciei luce parumper
obliquatur equus nec enim sibi dona priorum

Moreover the nobility of his pedigree augments his natural 110
attributes; for he can proudly claim Pyrois as his sire, and
the father himself is reflected in the mirror of his son. Jove
graciously presented him as a gift to mother Nature; and the
excellence of the gift augments her gratitude and the bounty 115
of the giver; there is no greater gift that such a father might
confer on such a mother. With such qualities, then, as his
nature requires, this horse is ennobled.

The second horse is of lesser worth, smaller in size, less
handsome, of inferior stock, and slower paced than the 120
other. Although he is smaller than the first, and less beautiful, he is larger than the others, and first among them in
beauty; but while he surpasses the others in quality, he is surpassed by the first. Yet even if he is not able to match the
pace of the first horse, no fleeting breeze can outstrip the 125
second, or even challenge him with equal speed. He is confined to no single color, varying his appearance so that he
often falsely appears to have a color of his own. He snorts
loudly, assails the air with constant neighing, and inflicts 130
harmless wounds on the gentle breeze. Little bells hanging
from his neck give out sweet sounds, and fill the air with
music. In his appearance he reveals his father, for he resembles Eous in his behavior, and his beauty proves that Eous
was his sire. Juno, bountiful in her gifts, increased the wealth 135
of Nature, earned the goddess's gratitude with this gift, and
in offering it demonstrated her own love.

The third horse is somewhat put off by such dazzling
beauty, for he cannot lay claim to the attributes of the first

140 vindicat, immo minus retinens suspirat ad illos.
Et quamvis huius species tenebrescat eorum
respectu, tamen ad reliquos collata nitorem
exserit et proprio non est fraudata decore.
Et quamvis agili cursu vincatur ab illis
145 de quibus exivit sermo, tamen ipse triumphans
in reliquis victor gaudet reliquosque volatu
vincit, et in proprio motu concludit eisdem.
Subtilis respergit eum mixtura coloris,
sed fugiens oculos visum color ipse recusat.
150 Conserti floris series quasi veste decenti
induit hunc, et ei proprios inspirat odores:
flos violae perfundit eum, rosa debriat auras
affines, narisque thymi satiatur odore.
Nescia nativi coitus, aequa flamine solo
155 edidit hunc, ignara maris, contenta mariti
aëris afflatu, Zephiro gravidata marito.
Hoc dono Zephirus Naturae matris amorem
mercatus, proprium vectigal solvit eidem.
    Degenerat polletque minus, lentescit abunde
160 quartus equus, formaque iacet cursuque tepescit,
praedictis famulans, illos quasi pronus adorat.
Ancillatur eis nec se negat esse clientem
horum, sed tamquam dominis ut verna ministrat,
non tamen omnino Naturam sentit avaram;
165 immo dote sua qua se tueatur habundat
in nullo patiens eclipsim muneris huius
quo de more solet Natura beare iugalem.
Nec violae marcent, quamvis rosa floris honore
splendeat aut cultus componat lilia candor;
170 non omnis delirus erit cui sensus Ulixis

two; indeed, being less well endowed, he sighs at the sight 140
of them. But although his appearance is overshadowed by
theirs, he is strikingly handsome when compared with the
others, and has not been denied a beauty of his own. And although in liveliness of gait he is defeated by those we have 145
described, he yet rejoices as victor, triumphant over the others, bests them in swiftness, and by his own pace defeats
them. A subtle mixture of coloring spreads over him, but the
color eludes the eye, and refuses to be clearly seen. A chain 150
of interwoven flowers clothes him like a comely garment,
and breathes its odors upon him. The odor of violets envel-
ops him, the rose makes drunk the neighboring breezes, and
his nose is suffused with the scent of thyme. Heedless of
natural intercourse, his dam bore him through the wind 155
alone, having known no sire, content to be wedded to the
breathing air, great with child by no husband but Zephyrus.
With this gift Zephyrus acquired the love of mother Nature,
yielding up what was his own as tribute to her.

Less noble and less powerful, the fourth horse lags well 160
behind, inferior in beauty and slower of gait, yet of service
to his betters, to whom he virtually prostrates himself in adoration. He attends on them, and does not deny that he is
their dependent, but although he serves them as a slave
serves his master, he does not find Nature altogether miserly; indeed he has an abundance of her gifts with which to 165
hold his own, and in no respect does he suffer an eclipse of
that generosity with which Nature, in her fashion, had favored his yokefellows. Violets do not wither, though the rose
shines in the glory of its blooms, or gleaming beauty set off
the lily; not everyone who lacks the intelligence of Ulysses is 170

deficit, aut mutus quem nescit musa Maronis;
non nitor argenti livet, si fulgurat aurum,
non minus arma rapit Hector, si plenius Aiax
fulminat: a simili non omnis gloria quarto
175 absentatur equo. Quamvis gradus ille negetur
emphaticae laudis, in qua Natura priores
sistit equos, non iste tamen deiectus ab omni
munere Naturae queritur, sed gaudet in illa
fortuna qua dives eum Natura beavit.
180 Glaucus ei color arridet, respergit eundem
imber et irriguo ros compluit imbre iugalem.
Hoc speciale sibi retinet propriumque reservat:
quod celer ad potum non obliviscitur escam,
potibus indulget pro cunctis, solus ad esum
185 currit, et in potu defectus supplet equorum.
Hunc genuit Tritonis equus iurisque paterni
heredem statuens, sese descripsit in illo.
Naturae Triton dans intersigna favoris
contulit hoc munus, donans cum munere mentem.
190   Vix speciem defendet equi formamque tenebit
quintus equus, si quis tempet conferre priores
isti, nam deponet equum larvaque iugalis
vestitus sapiet asinum, deiectus eadem
segnitie, plene mores exutus equinos.
195 Si tamen ad reliquos collatio nulla redundet
huius equi, sed eum proprio scrutemur in esse,
non erit a propriis exclusus dotibus eius
cultus et in nullo formae patietur abusum.
Quintus equus quartum redolet partimque figurat,
200 sed tamen in modico quintus demittitur, in quo
parcius arrisit praedicto forma iugali,

therefore mad, nor is he mute whom the muse of Maro does not visit; the shine of silver does not become leaden if gold glitters; Hector is no less a man of arms because Ajax roars more loudly; so too all trace of glory is not withheld from the fourth horse. Though he be denied the degree of enthu- 175 siastic praise to which Nature has entitled the other horses, yet he does not complain of having been wholly deprived of her generosity, but rejoices in that condition which bounteous Nature has bestowed upon him. His color is a shining 180 gray; rain pours down upon this horse, and an abundant stream of dew bathes him. He possesses this special attribute and reserves it to himself: that while eager to drink, he is not forgetful of food. He partakes of drinking on behalf of all, he alone is quick to eat, and in drinking he makes good 185 the deficiency of the other horses. The horse of Triton begot him, and established a father's claim to his heir, for in him he produced a copy of himself. Triton, offering to Nature a token of mutual affection, conferred this gift upon her, and accompanied the gift with generous thoughts.

The fifth horse scarcely preserves the appearance or re- 190 tains the form of a horse, if one should seek to compare the others to him; for he has cast off his horse's nature, and clad in the spectral likeness of a horse he behaves like an ass; afflicted with the same lethargy, he has wholly abandoned the ways of a horse. Yet if no similarity to the others appears in 195 this horse, let us consider him for what he is; he will not be denied attractive qualities of his own, and he will by no means suffer insult on the score of beauty. The fifth horse has something of the fourth, and partly resembles him, yet 200 the fifth is somewhat downcast; beauty has smiled more

qui nimis in terram sese demittit eundo,
nec satis ad plenum caput erigit, immo caduco
declinans vultu, visus descendit in imum.
205 Vestit eum color obscurus quem possidet ipsa
nigredo, nullum secum passura colorem.
Nec plebeia iacet generis fortuna, sed Aethon
hunc genuit, qui Solis equos se gaudet habere
fratres et fratrum sese defendit honore.
210 Ops superum genitrix, in signum foederis isto
Naturam donavit equo, quo nodus amoris
firmior effectus illarum vota ligavit.

Predictos Ratio propria ratione magistra
sub iuga cogit equos, themoni foederat, urget
215 effrenes, ligat indomitos frenatque vagantes.
Primum sternit equum, stratum conscendit habenis,
corrigit excursus, in virga visitat, instat
verbere voce minis. Illum vix illa quietum
reddit, sed tandem superatus vincitur, illi
220 paret et ad nutum Rationis fessus anhelat.
Sic primum componit equos auriga Sophiae
ne, si quadrigam Fronesis conscendat, eisdem
indomitis, spatientur equi normamque relinquant,
devia sectentur, laxent iuga, vincula solvant,
225 cuncta fluant, nutet currus, compago vacillet,
cingula solvantur, laxetur nexus, habenae
depereant et tota labet substantia currus.
Postquam compositus ordo per singula currens
singula composuit, Fronesis conscendere currum
230 disponens, talem sese componit in usum.
Assidet applaudit congaudet complacet illi

sparingly on this horse, who holds himself too close to the ground as he goes, and does not raise his head to its full height, but turns away with his face lowered, and his eyes directed to the ground. A dusky color covers one whom blackness itself has claimed, allowing him no true color. Yet the misfortune of a plebeian origin does not depress him, for Aethon begot him, who rejoices to have the horses of the Sun as his brothers, and covers himself with his brothers' dignity. Ops, mother of the gods, bestowed this horse on Nature as a token of covenant, whereby the bond of love was made stronger, and linked their aspirations. 205 210

Reason draws the horses beneath the yoke, guiding them by the exercise of reason, joins the yoke to the beam, drives the unbridled, harnesses the untamed, reins in the unruly. She saddles the first horse, mounts him once saddled, and with the reins curbs his resistance, rebukes him with the whip, threatens him with lash, command, and threat. She quiets him with difficulty, but at last, subdued, he acknowledges defeat, obeys her, and pants wearily at her command. In this way Sophia's charioteer controls the horses, for if Fronesis were to ascend the chariot with the team still untamed, the horses would scatter, refuse to be ruled, run in different directions; shake off the yoke, break free from the harness; all would be confusion, the chariot would totter, its joints would be weakened, the bridles would be broken, the girths would go slack, the reins would lose control, and the very structure of the chariot would collapse. After orderly consideration has reviewed everything and set it in order, Fronesis, preparing to ascend the chariot, readies herself for this new experience. The whole court is at hand; they 215 220 225 230

curia tota simul, multoque favore recessum
virginis exhilarat, reditusque felicius omen
orat et eventus reditu meliore serenos.

235 Oscula multiplicat repetens et in ore sigillans
imprimit expresse; complexu bracchia nectens,
colla ligans animoque simul cum voce salutans,
illam congeminans iterat repetitque salutem.

Tunc monitu Rationis adest Prudentia; currum
240 conscendit currusque decor cumulatus habundat
plenius et roseo flammatur sidere vultus.
Instat equis Ratio; virga dictante iugales
aggrediuntur iter. Currus subtollitur, exit
terras et tenuem currens evadit in auram.

245 Aëris ingrediens tractus Prudentia caute
singula disquirit animo quae vindicat aër
ipse sibi, scrutatur eum penetratque fugacem.
Inquirit quae materies, quae nubis origo,
quomodo terra madens proprio sudore resudat
250 in nubes, caeloque suos componit amictus;
cur Phebus sitiens aestuque caloris anhelus
haurit ab Oceano potus, sua pocula vertit
in nubes, crasso suspendit in aëre nimbi
vasa, scyphos imbris varii pluviaeque lagenas;
255 qualiter ignis hebet moriens in nube paritque
fulmina, dum moritur, sic morte nocivior instat
quam vita, vivusque nequit quod mortuus infert;
unde trahunt ortum venti, quae semina rerum
inspirent motum ventis causasque movendi;
260 cur Auster pluvias, pluvii pincerna, propinat

applaud, share her joy, congratulate her, and by their great goodwill make her departure a festive occasion. They pray that the omens for her return may be favorable, that the event will be made happy by a higher reward. They give her 235 innumerable kisses, repeatedly and firmly impressing these tokens on her face, taking her in their arms in an embrace, clinging to her neck, wishing her well with both heart and voice, weeping together with her, they repeat this gesture again and again.

Then at a sign from Reason Providence comes forward; she ascends the chariot, and its sumptuous beauty increases 240 still more, illumined by the rosy glow of her face. Reason urges the horses forward, and at the command of the whip the team begins its journey. The chariot is borne upward, leaves the earth behind and swiftly moves forth into the subtle air.

As she enters the airy regions, Providence carefully and 245 thoughtfully examines everything that the air claims as its own, and her scrutiny probes its fleeting substance. She seeks to know the material and the origin of cloud, how the earth, abounding in waters of its own, exhales them to form clouds, and creates in the sky a garment for itself. Why 250 Phoebus, thirsty and panting in fiery heat, draws drink from the ocean, then pours his goblet into the clouds, hangs bowls in the dense air of the raincloud, goblets of wet weather, flagons of rain; how fire grows dull, dying in the clouds, and 255 as it dies produces thunderbolts, and thus shows itself more dangerous in death than in life, for what the dead fire inflicts living fire cannot. Whence the winds take their origin, what seminal principles inspire the movement of the wind and the causes of its movement. Why Auster, butler of the rain, 260

terris et plene largitur pocula mundo;
qualiter austrinos Boreae sitis ebibit imbres
emundatque vias pluviis quasi scopa viarum;
qualiter agricola Zephyrus sine vomere terram
265 excolit et florum segetes extollit in hortis;
cur volucris celeri pennarum remige tuta,
plumas in remos, alas in carbasa fingens,
transmeat aërium pelagus quasi navis imago
et sine naufragio talem pertransit abyssum
270 tuta, nec in tali pelago timet illa Caribdim.
    Aëris occultos aditus, secreta latebras
altius inquirit Fronesis sensuque profundo
vestigans, videt intuitu meliore vagantes
aërios cives, quibus aër carcer, abyssus
275 poena, dolor risus, mors vivere, culpa triumphus;
quorum mens humili livoris laesa veneno,
in genus humanum virus transfundit, ut ipsum
consimili sanie morboque laboret eodem.
Hi sunt qui semper in nos armantur, inhermes
280 deiciunt, vincunt armatos. Rarius ipsi
cedunt, sed victi nequeunt iterare duellum;
qui velut aërio vestiti corpore, nostram
mentiti speciem, multo phantasmate brutos
deludunt homines, falsi verique sophistae.
285 In tenebris lucem simulant, in lite quietem,
abscondunt sub pace dolos, in felle figurant
dulcia, sub specie recti vitiata propinant.
    Hos deus esse deos fecit, quos lumine vero
vera dies perfudit, quos ab origine prima
290 vestivit deitatis honos; qui luce relicta

toasts the earth with showers, and generously invites the world to drink; how thirsty Boreas drinks up the southerly showers, and clears the roads of water as if sweeping them clean; how farmer Zephyrus tills the earth without a plow, and raises up crops of flowers in our gardens. Why a bird, 265 relying on its swift feathered oarsmen, making its feathers seem like oars, its wings like sails, crosses the deeps of the air as if imitating a ship, passes over this great abyss in safety, immune to shipwreck, and has no fear of Charybdis in such 270 a sea.

Fronesis probes further into the hidden chambers, the mysterious depths, the caverns of the air, examining them with deep interest. With clearer insight she sees the wandering denizens of the airy realm, for whom the air is a prison, its depths their punishment, their laughter grief, their life a 275 death, their triumphs guilty. Their minds, afflicted with the base poison of envy, transmit this pestilence to the human race, that it too may be corrupted and suffer from the same disease. It is these who are always ready to attack us, who 280 cast down the helpless and conquer the strong. Rarely do they surrender, though once defeated they are unable to make war again. Having assumed a sort of airy body, deceptively taking our shape, they delude dullwitted mankind with manifold illusion, cleverly mingling falsehood with truth. In their darkness they feign light, in their restless 285 anger, repose; they cover their treachery with the face of peace, they make their bitterness seem sweet; they offer wickedness in the likeness of virtue.

God created these beings to be gods; his true day imbued them with the light of truth; and from the moment of their birth the glory of godhead enveloped them. Abandoning 290

in tenebras abiere suas; qui fonte relicto
inferni petiere lacus; qui veste decoris
exuti, vestem gemitus saccumque doloris
iniecere sibi; qui maiestate superna
295   deiecti sine fine sibi meruere ruinam.
     O gravis eventus, casus miser, unica pestis!
Iam servit qui liber erat, mendicat abundans
qui fuit, exilium patitur qui primus in aula
regnabat, patitur poenas a rege secundus.
300   Hoc casu fit gemma lutum, fit purpura saccus,
lux tenebrae, species confusio, gloria casus,
risus tristities, requies labor, alga iacinctus;
caelestis sic stella cadit, sic Lucifer ortus
nescius occasu premitur, sic civis Olympi
305   exulat eiectus nec temperat exulis omen
spes reditus: spes omnis abest ceditque timori.
     O fastus vitanda lues, fugienda Caribdis!
Culpa gravis, morbus communis, publica pestis,
ianua peccati, vitiorum mater, origo
310   nequitiae, semen odii, venatio pugnae!
Quae cadit ascendens, elata perit, peritura
erigitur, promota ruit, ruitura tumescit;
quae se ferre nequit, supra se lata, ruinam
infra se patitur nec sese sustinet, immo
315   mole sua premitur, proprio sub pondere lapsa.
Extra se cogit hominem se quaerere, dum se
exit homo, factusque sibi contrarius a se
discrepat oblitusque sui se nescit et ultra
transgrediens evadit adhuc, plus esse laborans
320   quam sit, nec propria contentus origine, sese

light, they departed into their shadowy realm; rejecting the
fountain of life they sought the lake of hell; putting off their
robes of glory, they threw over themselves the garments of
sorrow, the sackcloth of grief; outcast from the majesty of
heaven, they gained for themselves unending ruin.   295

O grievous fortune, wretched fate, ultimate curse! He
who was free is now a slave, he is a beggar who once was
wealthy, he who first held sway in the court of heaven suffers banishment, the king's very lieutenant suffers punishment. In this downfall a jewel is turned to mud, a purple   300
robe becomes sackcloth, light turns to shadow, form to confusion, glory to disaster, laughter to misery, rest to toil, the
hyacinth to a weed. Thus does a star fall from heaven, thus
Lucifer, forgetful of his rising, is forced to descend; thus he
who dwelt on Olympus is cast into exile, and no hope of re-   305
turn lightens the exile's doom: all hope is gone and he gives
way to terror.

O sickness of pride to be shunned! O Charybdis to be
fled! Grievous fault, disease common to all, plague of nations, gateway to sin, mother of vice, source of villainy, seed 310
of hatred, seeker of strife! Pride, which falls as it ascends,
perishes as it is exalted, is raised high only to be destroyed;
faces ruin as it is preferred, swells up to be cast down. Pride
which, raised above itself, cannot endure itself, suffers ruin
within itself, cannot sustain itself but rather is crushed by   315
its own bulk, helpless beneath the burden of itself. It drives
a man to seek himself outside himself, even as his manhood leaves him; once become the contrary of himself, he
is at odds with himself; forgetful of himself, he does not
know himself; and pressing further he goes still further
astray, striving to be more than he is, not content with his   320

351

esse cupit maior et se superare laborat;
quod petit amittens, perdens quod postulat, optans
quod sibi mentitur, falsum venatur honorem.

    Haec pestis rectum vitiat, deturpat honestum,
325 fermentat mores, iustum fugat, utile perdit;
haec saliunca rosas, haec nubes nubilat astra
virtutum, cuius tenebris patiuntur eclipsim.
Hac lue caelestis regni proscriptus ab aula,
delictum luit exilio poenaque reatum
330 angelus, a propria demissus sede tumore
fractus, deiectus fastu, livore solutus.

    Aëris excurso spatio, quo nubila caeli
nocte sua texunt tenebras, quo pendula nubes
in se cogit aquas, quo grandinis ingruit imber,
335 quo certant venti, quo fulminis ira tumescit,
aethera transgreditur Fronesis, quo gratia pacis
summa viget, quo grata quies, quo gratior aura
cuncta fovet, quo cuncta silent, quo purior aether
ridet et expellit fletum, quo nubilus aër
340 ingemit, et totus arcano lumine floret.

    Aethereae lucis superatis tractibus, illa
altius ingreditur spatium, quo splendor et ignis
iura tenent, lux grata micat, sed coniuga luci
lucis blanditias retrahit vis ipsa caloris.
345 Hic rerum novitas, rerum decus, unica rerum
forma, decor mundi visum demulcet euntis
virginis et cantus species nova debriat aurem,
sed parco tamen auditu sonituque minore

birthright; he longs to be greater than himself, struggles to rise above himself; losing what he seeks, squandering what he needs, hoping for what deceives him, he chases illusory honors.

This sickness makes the good man bad, defiles the man of honor, corrupts character, drives away the sense of right, de- 325 stroys common sense. This is the weed that overruns the rose, this cloud darkens the star of virtue, and in its shadow virtue is eclipsed. By this sickness an angel was banished the court of the heavenly kingdom, paid for his crime with exile, suffered torment for his sin, was cast out from his true 330 home, destroyed by his presumption, alienated by his scorn, undone by envy.

Having crossed the airy region, where the clouds fashion the darkness of their own night, where the low-hanging cloud gathers water into itself, where the showers of hail pour forth, where the winds do battle, where the wrath of 335 the thunderbolt swells, Fronesis travels across the ether. Here the blessing of complete peace prevails, here welcome quiet and a pleasant breeze give comfort everywhere, here all is still. Here the clear ether smiles, and drives away the tears that the cloudy atmosphere sheds, and all things flour- 340 ish in a mysterious light.

Rising beyond the region of ethereal light, Fronesis attains the higher place where brilliant light and fire hold sway, where the bright light is soothing, but the fiery heat wedded to the light takes away its pleasing effect. Here the novelty 345 and beauty of all things, the perfection of their form, the elegance of the cosmos charms the sight of the maiden as she passes, and a new sort of music intoxicates her ear, though she perceives the sound as barely audible and low in volume.

concipit illa sonum. Certa tamen imbibit aure,
350　qualiter hic sonitus citharae caelestis obesis
vocibus expirat, ubi Lunae sphaera remisso
suspirat cantu, rauce sonat, immo sonando
paene silet, languetque sonans, nervique iacentis
inferius gerit illa vicem, cordamque minorem
355　reddit et in cithara sedem vix illa meretur.
　　Hic videt explicito visu Prudentia Lunae
detrimenta vices cursus momenta labores,
quomodo iunctus ei Phoebus depauperat illam
luce vel econtra Phoebo furatur honorem
360　luminis et populos fallaci nocte timere
cogit et effigiem noctis sine nocte figurat.
Humores cur Luna parit, cur aequora Lunae
detrimenta luunt vel eadem divite gaudent;
quid notet in Luna lunae nota quidve notando
365　signet. Nec tenuem possit delere lituram
splendoris cumulus, dum fonti luminis instat
parva lues, nec ei dignatur cedere, cum quo
litigat et radio lucis magis umbra diescit.
　　Altius evadens virgo conscendit in arcem,
370　Sol ubi iura tenet, ubi Solis cereus ardet
et lucis scaturit fons vivus, vena caloris
manat splendorisque novi thesaurus habundat.
Illic virgo videt quae sit via semita cursus
Solis et unde sui sumat fomenta vigoris
375　aethereae lucis genitor fons pastor origo;
qualiter in stellis regnans artansque planetas
imperio servire suo, nunc stare meantes
cogit, nunc timidos sectari devia sola
maiestate iubet, nunc libertate meandi

Nonetheless she drinks in with a ready ear how the sound of 350
the celestial lyre issues forth in sluggish tones where the
Moon's sphere breathes out a languid song, plays harshly,
even falls nearly silent as it plays, grows faint as it plays. It
plays its role in a low tone, produces only a feeble note, and 355
scarcely deserves to have a place in this music.

Here Providence sees clearly the mishaps of the Moon,
her changes, course, movement, labors: how Phoebus,
though joined with her, robs her of light, or she, conversely,
steals from Phoebus the dignity of his light, and the false 360
darkness makes people fearful, presenting the image of
night in the absence of night itself. She sees why the Moon
gives rise to our temperaments, why the ocean suffers from
her wanings, and rejoices when she is full; what marks the
Moon with moon spots, and what this marking signifies. All 365
the Moon's splendor cannot wipe away this faint blemish,
for the tiny flaw withstands her fountain of light, disdains to
yield to her, quarrels with her; and its shadow is only made
clearer by her radiance.

Mounting higher, the maiden attains the height where
the Sun holds sway, where his lamp burns and a living stream 370
of light gushes forth, a stream of heat flows out, and a wealth
of new splendor is stored up. There the maiden sees the
road, the path, the course of the Sun, and whence this creator, fount, guardian and source of ethereal light draws the 375
food that sustains his energy; how he reigns among the stars,
and compels the planets to accept his dominion; how he
now compels them to cease their movement, now by his
majesty alone makes them timidly stray onto byways, now,

380 concessa, motus reddit sua iura planetis;
qualiter alternans vultus aetatis in ortu
fit puer inque die medio iuvenescit adultus,
mentiturque virum tandem totusque senescit
vespere. Sic varias species aetatis ad horam
385 Sol prefert unusque dies complectitur aevum.
   Iam Lunae sonitum fastidit virginis aures
quam dulcis meliorque sonus seducit inescans
aurem, nec cantus memorem sinit esse prioris.
Hunc cantum Syrena parit quae Solis adheret
390 motibus et citharam vocis dulcore fatetur.
Vox omnis miratur eam, veneratur adorans,
totiusque sonus citharae suspirat ad illam.
   Egrediens Solis regnum maturat in altum
gressus virgo suos, sed gressum praepedit ipse
395 limitis anfractus anceps, multaeque viarum
ambages; tandem superato calle laboris
pondere cautelae studio regione potitur
qua Venus et Stilbon complexis nexibus herent.
Illic praecursor Solis praecoque diei
400 Lucifer exultat, terris solatia lucis
praesignans, ortuque suo praeludit ad ortum
Solis et auroram proprio praedicit in ortu.
Gressibus his Stilbon comes indivisus adheret,
tamquam verna sui comitans vestigia Solis,
405 obnubensque comas radiis solaribus, ignes
temperat et Solis obnubilat astra galero.
Sphaeraque Luciferi motu levis, ocior aura,
motu parturiens sonitum, lascivit acuta
voce, nec in cithara Veneris plebea putatur
410 musa, sed auditus assensum iure meretur.

granting them freedom of movement, restores to the plan- 380
ets their rights. How, changing his apparent age, he is a boy
at his rising, at midday becomes a young man, then feigns
manhood, and finally grows old at sunset; thus hour by hour,
the Sun presents the appearance of different ages, and a sin- 385
gle day becomes a complete life.

Now the song of the Moon wearies the maiden's ears; a
finer, sweeter sound, satisfying to hear, attracts her, and will
not let her recall the earlier song. A Siren brings forth this
song; she follows closely the Sun's movements, and in the 390
sweetness of her voice that of the lute finds expression. Every voice marvels at hers, and honors her with adoration,
and at the sound of her voice the lute's every note becomes a
sigh.

Leaving the domain of the Sun, the maiden directs her
steps upward, but the winding, forking path and its many 395
circlings slow her pace; having finally mastered the pathway
by dint of effort and alert persistence, she attains the region
where Venus and Stilbon dwell in close embrace. Here Lucifer sallies forth, forerunner of the Sun and herald of dawn, 400
presaging to the world the comfort of daylight; by his rising he preludes the rising of the Sun, and in his own emergence he foretells the Dawn. Stilbon, inseparable companion, closely imitates the movement of the Sun, following in
his footsteps like a servant; concealing his locks within the 405
radiance of the Sun, he tempers his own fires, and hides his
star in the Sun's helmet. The sphere of Lucifer is quick in
movement, swifter than the wind; giving out a sound as it
moves, it revels in its high song. And let it not be thought
that a plebeian muse sounds in the lyre of Venus; she rightly 410
claims the approval of her audience. With a similar voice, in

Voce pari similique modo cantuque propinquo
Mercurii Syrena canit, Venerisque Camenam
reddit et ex aequo sonitu citharizat amico.
    Progreditur Fronesis flammata palatia Martis
415 ingrediens, stupet insultus irasque caloris
quem parit ille locus qui totus in igne vaporans
nil novit nisi fervores ignisque procellas.
Non ibi luget hyems, non veris gratia ridet,
non tumet autumnus, sed tantum fulminat aestas.
420 Imperat hic Mars igne calens, fecundus in ira,
bella serens, sitiens lites nostrique sititor
sanguinis, excutiens pacem foedusque recidens;
qui regni violare fidem, mutare potentes
gaudet, flammantis vestitus crine cometae;
425 qui parat arma viris, cogit sperare furentes,
seminat insultus, parit iras, laxat amores.
Quid gerat interius facies docet ipsa, rubore
praedicat interni rabiem pestemque furoris.
Tabe sua viciat comitem, sociumque planetam
430 vel saevum saevire magis, vel forte benignum
nequitia docet esse trucem, laeditque veneno;
cuius sphaera ruens torrentis more tonando
clamat et altiloquos resonat clamore boatus.
    Altius exclamat reliquis Syrena tonantis
435 Martis, sed cantus dulcedo remittitur ipsa
tempestate soni languens, minuitque favorem
asperitas, vocisque rigor fert damna favori.
    Et iam Lemniacos vomitus ignisque vapores
virgineus labor evadit nec flamma viantem
440 contigit aut eius ausa est contingere crinem.
Tunc Iovis innocuos ignes lucisque serenae

similar measure and consonant song, the Siren of Mercury sings, responding to the Muse of Venus in like manner, making music of a congenial tone.

Fronesis travels onward; entering the fiery palace of Mars, she is aghast at the reviling, the fiery rage to which this place 415 gives rise, a place wholly steeped in fire, which knows nothing but fury and firestorms. There is no gloomy winter there, no smiling spring, no bounteous autumn, only the blasting heat of summer. Here Mars is lord, goaded by fire, teeming 420 with rage, sowing the seeds of war, thirsting for battle and thirsty for our blood. Shatterer of peace, breaker of treaties, decked in the tail of a flaming comet, he rejoices to violate the kingdom's trust, to replace one ruler with another; he puts weapons in men's hands, goads madmen to hope, breeds 425 quarrels, gives rise to rage, makes love grow slack. His face reveals by its angry flush what inner thoughts he harbors: it tells of a raging, furious fever within. He infects companion bodies with his disease, and wickedly teaches a fellow planet, if cruel, to become more cruel; or if by some chance 430 benevolent, to become hostile; thus his poison wounds. His sphere, rushing like a torrent, roars thunderously, and resounds with deep-voiced bellowing.

The Siren of thunderous Mars cries out more loudly than the others, but the sweetness of her song is reduced, made 435 faint by a storm of sound whose harshness gives little pleasure, and the roughness of her voice destroys enjoyment.

And now the maiden has succeeded in avoiding the Lemnian eruptions and fiery vapors; no flame touches her as she passes, or presumes to disturb a hair of her head. She now 440 goes on to experience the harmless fires of Jove, the pleasure

laetitiam, risusque poli pertemptat eundo.
Hic regio stellae Iovialis lampade tota
splendet et eterno laetatur vere beata.
445 Hic sidus Ioviale micat mundoque salutem
nuntiat et Martis iram Martisque furorem
sistit et occurrit tranquilla pace furenti;
cui si stella mali praenuntia, praevia casus
iungitur, ille tamen inimicum sidus amicat,
450 alternansque vices, in risus tristia, planctum
in plausus, fletusque graves in gaudia mutat;
vel si forte Iovi societur stella salutis
nuntia, stella Iovis vultu meliore salutem
auget et eventus melioris duplicat omen,
455 foedus amans pacisque sator, nutritor amoris,
extirpans iras, proscribens bella, furores
compescens, delens lites Martemque refrenans;
qui motu generans sonitum, non verberat auram
obtuso cantu, sed dulcibus allicit aurem
460 cantibus. Et dulcem Philomenam reddit amoenans
musa Iovis, tantoque soni laetatur alumno
musica qui propriae thesauros aggerat artis.
    Ulterius progressa suos Prudentia gressus
dirigit ad superos. Superans Iovis atria cursu,
465 Saturnique domos tractu maiore iacentes
intrat et algores hyemis brumaeque pruinas
horret et ignavum frigus miratur in aestu.
Illic fervet hyems, aestas algescit et aestus
friget, delirat splendor, dum flamma tepescit.
470 Hic tenebrae lucent, hic lux tenebrescit et illic
nox cum luce viget et lux cum nocte diescit.
Illic Saturnus spatium percurrit avaro

of his serene radiance, his happy heaven. This entire region of the sky is brightened by the lamp of the Jovial star, and rejoices to be blessed with eternal spring. Here Jove's planet shines, announcing comfort to the world; he withstands the rage and madness of Mars, and meets his raving with untroubled calm. If a star foretelling evil, a harbinger of disaster, is joined to him, he befriends this unfriendly star; altering its condition, he changes its sorrow to laughter, its complaint to approbation, its bitter tears to joy. But if a star foretelling comfort should be joined with Jove, the star of Jove adds to this message its own propitious aspect, and so makes double the omen of a happy issue. Lover of agreement, sower of peace, fosterer of love, rooting out wrath, banishing war, curbing madness, ending quarrels, restraining Mars, he generates a sound as he moves which does not strike the air with a dull note, but entices the ear with sweet singing. Jove's charming muse echoes the sweet song of Philomela, and music rejoices in such a student of song, who enriches the treasury of her art.

Proceeding further, Providence directs her steps toward the high heavens. Passing beyond the halls of Jove, she enters the realm of Saturn, spread over a wider expanse, and is horrified by the wintry chill and frost, amazed by numbing cold amid glowing heat. Here winter is fiery hot, summer freezes, heat is cold, and brilliance becomes erratic as its fire cools. Here darkness is bright, light becomes shadow, here the night is alive with light, and daylight appears at nightfall. Here Saturn moves stingily through his orbit at a lumbering

motu progressuque gravi longaque dieta;
hic algore suo praedatur gaudia veris
475 furaturque decus pratis et sidera florum.
Algescitque calens, frigens fervescit, inundat
aridus, obscurus lucet iuvenisque senescit.
Nec tamen a cantu sonus eius degener errat,
sed comitum voces vox praevenit huius adulto
480 concentu, quem non cantus obtusio reddit
insipidum, cui dat vocis dulcedo saporem.
Hic dolor et gemitus, lacrimae discordia terror
tristities pallor planctus iniuria regnant.

Liber Quintus

Lucis inoffensae spatium fontemque nitoris,
quo radiant stellae, quo certant fulgure multo
astra poli propriumque diem sine fine perennant,
quo caeli faciem depingunt sidera, virgo
5 exhilarata subit, hausto pro parte laboris
pondere, laetaturque poli perflata sereno.
In stellis ibi praeradiant caeloque fruuntur
quos vel fama deos facto vel fabula verbo
effinxit, retinentque sibi sine numine nomen.
10 Hic novus Alcides caelo summittitur, illic
Perseus ardentis gladio metit ora Medusae;
illic ense carens, ensem mentitur Orion:
sub pugnae facie sine bello, bella minatur;
Emoniusque senex, arcu dictante, sagittam

pace, and his journey is long. Here with his icy chill he preys
on the joys of spring, and robs the meadows of the beauty of   475
their starlike flowers. He grows cold as he grows warm,
seethes while freezing, causes floods though he is arid; his
darkness shines and his youth grows old. Yet his sound is no
unworthy aberration from song; for his voice outdoes the
voices of his companions in its mature harmony, and no flat-   480
ness of tone reduces it to dullness, for the sweetness of the
voice lends it elegance. Here grief, sobbing, tears, confusion,
terror, misery, pallor, lamentation, and protest hold sway.

Book 5

The maiden is cheered as she enters a region of untroubled
light, a gleaming fountain, where the stars are radiant, where
the lights of the firmament compete in brilliance, and maintain an endless day, and the constellations adorn the face of
the heavens. The most burdensome part of her task is fin-   5
ished, and she rejoices, caressed by the serene air of the celestial sphere. Here those whom fame has made into gods
for deeds actual or legendary shine brilliantly in starry form
and enjoy a place in the heavens, preserving their renown,
though not their godlike power. Here a new Alcides is placed   10
in the sky. Here Perseus severs with his sword the head of
a glaring Medusa. Here Orion, deprived of his sword, pretends to wield a sword, and by his warlike appearance threatens war without the tools of war. The Haemonian ancient,

15 excitat ad motum: nullo tamen illa volatu
effugit, aut monitus arcus evadit eundo;
hic proles Ledea micat nec pignus amoris
quem prius in terris gessit deponit in astris.
Vertitur in sidus, stellatus sidere famae.

20 Hic cuius dono medicinae stella caducis
illuxit, contra morbos dans arma salutis;
ablatos redimit vultus et damna pudoris
Parrasis in caelum translata; repensat eidem
Iupiter ablatum florem, pro flore pudoris

25 aeterno largitus ei florere nitore.
　　Praeterea variis stellis inscribitur aula
caeli, quas vario titulavit nomine quondam
musa poetarum, veri sub imagine ludens.
Signorum duodena cohors praefulget in astris

30 excepto fulgore nitens, infraque relinquit
stellarum vulgus reliquasque supervenit astro.
Hic ardet Cancer, urit Leo, Virgo resultat,
aequat Libra diem, crudescit Scorpius, alget
Chyron, Capra riget, diffunditur Urna, madescunt

35 Pisces, exultat Aries vexilla gerendo
veris, preradiat Taurus Geminique Lacones.
Hanc caeli speciem Fronesis delibat ocellus,
quam penetrare nequit visus notamque requirit
materiem tantaeque stupet miracula lucis.

40 　　Postquam caelestes aditus caelique profundum
astrorumque vagos reditus emensa reliquit
inque supercilio mundi stetit anxia; mente
fluctuat, in varios motus deducitur. Haeret
mens animusque fluit, dubitat cum mente voluntas

aiming his bow, urges an arrow on its way, but the arrow 15
leaves without taking flight, evading the prompting of the
bow as it departs. Here the children of Leda shine, and do
not abandon among the stars the bond of love they had
maintained on earth. He by whose gift the star of healing 20
shone on mortal men, granting them arms of health to fight
against disease, is here transformed to a constellation, shining in the starlight of fame. The Arcadian maiden, translated
to the heavens, recovers her stolen form and ruined chastity; Jupiter recompenses her for the loss of this flower; in
place of the flower of purity he grants her the power to flour- 25
ish in eternal beauty.

In addition the court of heaven is inscribed with various
stars to which the muse of the poets long ago assigned various names, playfully creating imaginary truth. The twelvefold cohort of the Signs stands out among the stars, shining 30
with a special brilliance; they leave behind the common herd
of stars, and surpass the others in glory. Here Cancer blazes,
Leo burns, Virgo shimmers, Libra balances day and night,
Scorpio threatens, Chiron brings chill, Capricorn freezing
cold, the Urn pours forth, Pisces is drenched with rain, Ar- 35
ies rejoices, wielding the banner of spring, Taurus and the
Laconian Twins shine clearly. The eye of Fronesis drinks in
this heavenly spectacle, [but] her sight cannot fathom it; she
searches for familiar objects, and is stunned by the miracle
of so much light.

Having traversed the approaches of the sky, and the depth 40
of the celestial sphere, she leaves behind the wandering circlings of the stars, and stands at the summit of the universe,
uncertain; her thoughts are vacillating, and she is drawn in
different directions. Her mind hesitates, her spirit wavers,

45 ipsa nec in certo defigitur anchora mentis.
Namque timet dubitatque timens ambage locorum
seduci quos ulterius via porrigit anceps
quae nullos hominum gressus volucrumque volatus
noscit; ab incursu rerum strepituque viantum
50 funditus excipitur, nullo vexata tumultu.
Hic hominis gressus nutans peccaret eundo,
ebrius erraret pes ipse pedisque lucerna
otia visus hebens ageret, pedibusque negaret
ducatum, lumenque foret sub lumine caecum,
55 non quod regnet ibi noctis caligo, sed illam
emphaticae lucis splendor purgatus inignit.
Difficilis conscensus ad hanc facilisque recesssus,
accessus paucis, casus patet omnibus, in quam
vix aliquis transire valet, solet omnis ab illa
60 declinare via, quae paucis pervia, multis
clauditur, arta nimis virtuti, larga ruinae.
Non huc nobilitas generis, non gratia formae,
non gazae deiectus amor, non gloria rerum,
non mundanus apex, non virtus corporis, audax
65 improbitas hominis, praeceps audacia tendit,
sed solum virtus animi, constantia mentis
factaque nobilitas, non nata sed insita menti,
interior species, virtutum copia, morum
regula, paupertas mundi, contemptus honoris.
70 Difficiles igitur aditus facilemque ruinam
cum Fronesis videat, magno succenditur aestu
sollicitae mentis victique labore iugales
nec iuga ferre velint nec solvere iura magistrae
ignarique viae, callem mirentur ineptum
75 gressibus, et pedibus gradiendi iura negantem;

her will, like her mind, is doubtful, and the anchor of the 45
mind can affix itself to no certainty. For she is afraid and
doubtful, fearing to be misled by the confusing aspect of the
territory toward which the uncertain road ahead extends; a
road which has never known the footsteps of men or the
flight of birds, wholly exempted from the intrusion of the
world, the noise of travelers, troubled by no noisy confusion. 50
Here the uncertain tread of a mortal might make a false step,
the foot might stray as if drunk, and even sight, the foot's
lantern, might grow weak and inactive, deny the foot any
guidance, and its light become blind in the midst of light. It
is not that the gloom of night reigns here, but that the pure 55
splendor of so strong a light flames out at her. The ascent is
difficult, and falling back is easy; access is offered to few, but
failure to all; for scarcely any can pass over to this place, but
anyone is likely to stray from a path passable to few, closed 60
to many, so narrow for virtue, so open for disaster. No nobility of lineage can make way here, no bodily beauty, no base
love of riches, not worldly glory, not the height of worldly
power, not strength of body, not the impious boldness of 65
men, nor reckless bravery. Only virtuous purpose, constancy
of mind and achieved nobility, not inborn but instilled in the
mind, inner seemliness, abundant good qualities, moral discipline, worldly poverty, and a disdain for title.

When Fronesis considers the difficulty of access and the 70
likelihood of disaster, she is seized by a great turmoil of
troubled thoughts: that the horses, wearied by their labor,
may not wish to endure the yoke, or give obedience to their
mistress; that being ignorant of the path, they may marvel at
a roadway ill suited to their steps, and refusing to grant any 75

nec Ratio sursum deflectere possit habenas,
quas retinent instanter equi dominaeque repugnant
effrenes, ultraque negant servire iubenti.
    Dum mentem Fronesis anceps sententia motus
80   distrahit in varios, nec pertemptare locorum
abdita sola potest, nisi quis praemonstret eidem,
vel conducat eam, gressum moderatus euntis,
ecce puella poli residens in culmine, caelum
despiciens, sursum delegans lumina, quiddam
85   extramundanum toto conamine visus
vestigans, nil corporeum venata sed ultra
transcendens, incorporei scrutata latentem
causam, principium rerum, finemque requirens,
visibus offertur Fronesis, visumque nitore
90   luminis offendens, mentem novitate relaxat.
Nec mirum quoniam tanto fulgore decoris
praeminet ut stellas praeditet fulgure, lumen
lumine multiplicans et lucem luce, nec ipsi
lumen adoptivum largiri cesset Olimpo.
95   Nil terrestre gerens facie, nil ore caducum
insinuans, mortale nihil genitumque puellae
demonstrat facies, tantum caeleste quod offert
forma puellaris. Hanc argumenta decoris
esse deam monstrant; instantia nulla refellit
100   quod decor ipse probat faciesque simillima caelo.
    Inflammat diadema caput quod, lampade multa
gemmarum radians, auro flammatur et extra
scintillans, lapidum duodeno sidere fulget.
Librum dextra gerit, sceptrum regale sinistra
105   gestat, et ad librum plerumque recurrit ocellus,
sed raro redit ad virgam. Tandemque revertens

footing for their hooves; that Reason may be unable to direct them forward; for the horses pull vehemently against
the reins, fight their mistress unrestrainedly, and refuse to
serve any longer at her command.

While uncertain thoughts draw the mind of Fronesis in
different directions: she cannot essay this unknown situa-   80
tion alone; someone must instruct her or escort her, guiding her steps as she goes; behold! a maiden, seated at the
summit of the celestial sphere, surveying the heavens below,
then directing her eyes upward, searching with fully focused   85
sight for something not of this world; looking for something
not corporeal but transcendent, seeking the hidden causes
of incorporeal life, the first principle and final goal of existence. As she presents herself to the gaze of Fronesis, she
troubles her sight by her radiance, but this new spectacle   90
is calming to her mind. And no wonder, since the maiden
stands forth in such brilliant beauty that she outshines the
stars in brightness, adding radiance to radiance, light to
light, and she would not hesitate to bestow an adoptive light
on Olympus itself. There is nothing earthly in her aspect,   95
her face shows no hint of mortal nature; the girl's appearance declares her not of mortal birth; all that her youthful form reveals is celestial. Her beauty is a clear argument
that she is divine, and nothing about her gainsays what such   100
beauty and a face so like heaven itself declare.

A diadem glows brightly on her head; radiant with many
brilliant jewels, it gleams with gold, casting its light all
around, and glows with a twelvefold constellation of gems.
Her right hand holds a book, her left wields a royal scepter.
Her eye frequently turns to the book, but she rarely takes   105
note of the staff. Finally, though, her careful eye, redirecting

circuit ille manum sollers; ne laeva vacillet
succumbens oneri virgae, sceptrumque resignet.
   Claudit eam vestis auro perfusa, refulgens
110 argento, plus veste decens habituque decenti
gratior et puro caeli fulgentior astro,
quam divina manus et sollers dextra Minervae
texuit, ut formae nobis exponit honestas.
Hic arcana dei, divinae mentis abyssum
115 subtilis describit acus formaque figurat
informem, locat immensum monstratque latentem,
incircumscriptum describit, visibus offert
invisum. Quod lingua nequit pictura fatetur:
quomodo Naturae subiectus sermo stupescit
120 dum temptat divina loqui, viresque loquendi
perdit et ad veterem cupit ille recurrere sensum;
mutescunt soni, vix balbutire valentes,
deque novo sensu deponunt verba querelam;
qualiter ipse Deus in se capit omnia rerum
125 nomina, quae non ipsa Dei natura recusat;
cuncta tamen, mediante tropo, dictante figura
sustinet et voces puras sine rebus adoptat:
ens iustus sine iustitia, vivens sine vita,
principium sine principio, finis sine fine,
130 immensus sine mensura, sine robore fortis,
absque vigore potens, sine motu cuncta gubernans,
absque loco loca cuncta replens, sine tempore durans,
absque situ residens, habitus ignarus habendo,
cuncta simul sine voce loquens, sine pace quietus,
135 absque novo splendore nitens, sine luce coruscans.
Nec solum iustus vera ratione sed ipsa
iustitia est, non solum lucidus ipse, sed ipsa

its gaze, regards it; lest her left hand waver, succumbing to the weight of the staff, she lays the scepter aside.

A robe covers her body, suffused with gold and gleaming silver; it is comelier than any garment, more graceful than a 110 comely garment, more radiant than the pure starlight of the celestial sphere. It was woven by the divine skill and careful hand of Minerva, as the nobility of its shape makes clear to us. Here the subtle needle depicts the mysteries of God, the depth of the divine mind. It endows what is formless with 115 form, measures immensity, shows forth what is hidden describes the uncircumscribed, presents the invisible to sight. Painting proclaims what the tongue cannot utter: how language, being subject to Nature, is confounded when it tries 120 to speak of things divine; it loses the power to communicate, and longs to retreat to old meanings; sound is struck dumb, scarcely capable of a stammer, and words lay aside any dispute about new meaning. How God himself claims for himself the names of all things—those names that his divine na- 125 ture does not reject—all these names he bears, through the agency of metaphor and the rule of figuration, applying to himself the pure names without their worldly meanings. He is just without justice, living without life, beginning without beginning, end without end, immense without measure, 130 strong without strength, powerful without power, governing all things without motion, filling all space without occupying space, lasting without time, present without place, possessing though without possession, uttering all meanings without voice, tranquil without peace, splendid without 135 added splendor, shining without light. He is not only just but justice itself in its true meaning; not only is he radiant,

lux est nocte carens, nec solum nomine solo
dicitur immensus, verum mensura caduca
140 singula describens et certis finibus aptans.
Nec fortis sola dicti ratione sed ipsum
robur subsistit, aeterno robore nitens,
solus iure potens, qui summa potentia solus
cuncta potest, a quo procedit posse potentum.
145 Nec solum loca cuncta replet, sed singula solus
infra se claudit, quasi meta locusque locorum.
  Hic legitur tamen obscure tenuique figura
qualiter una manens simplex aeterna potestas,
fons splendor species via virtus finis origo,
150 ingenitus genitor, vivens Deus, unicus auctor,
unus in usia, personis trinus in uno,
unicus esse manet, quem trina relatio trinum
reddit et in trino manet unus, trinus in uno;
qua ratione Patris speculum lux splendor imago
155 Filius est a Patre Deo Deus unus et idem
principium de principio, de lumine lumen,
sol de sole micans, splendor productus ab igne,
a simili similis, a vero verus, ab uno
unus, ab aeterno nascens aeternus, ab aequo
160 aequalis, bonus a summo, sublimis ab alto;
qualiter ardor amor concordia forma duorum
Spiritus est, in quo propriae Pater oscula proli
donat et in Nato sese Pater invenit, in quo
se videt ipse parens, dum de se nascitur ipse
165 alter et in genito splendet gignentis imago.
  Cultibus his afflata poli regina caduca
deserit atque Dei secretum consulit. Haeret
divinis, mentem terrenis exuit, ipsam

he is the light itself that knows no night; not in name alone
is he declared "immeasurable," he is in truth measure, giving   140
shape to all mortal things and assigning them fixed limits;
Nor is he "strong" by virtue of a mere word; he is the substance of strength itself, glorying in eternal strength; he
alone is truly powerful who alone, by his supreme power, can
accomplish all things; from whom issues the power of the
powerful. Not only does he fill all space, but he alone con-   145
tains all things within himself, as if he were the boundary
and space of all spaces.

Here can be read, albeit obscurely and in tentative figuration, how a single, abiding, simple, eternal power, the fount,
glory, form, way, strength, end and beginning, the uncreated   150
creator, the living God, the one true author, one in substance, a trinity of persons in one, is forever the one true being, whom a triune relation makes three, yet he remains one
in three, three in one. By what law the mirror, light, splendor, image of the Father is the Son, God born of God the   155
Father, one and the same, first principle from first principle,
light of light, shining sun of the sun, radiance brought forth
from fire, like from like, true from true, one from one, eternal born of eternal, equal born of equal, good from supreme   160
good, high from the most high. How the ardor, love, harmony, form of these two is the Spirit, in whom the Father
bestows the kiss on his child, the Father discovers himself in
his Son, in whom the parent sees himself, since another self
is born of him, and the image of the begetter shines in the   165
begotten.

Inspired by these devotions, the heavenly queen leaves
mortal things behind, and seeks to know the hidden wisdom
of God. She is devoted to what is divine, has rid her mind of

haurit mente Noym, divini fluminis haustu
170 ebria, sed potius dicatur sobria, namque
ebrietas nascens ex tali nectare plena
sobrietate viget, nec mentem cogit ab usu
degenerare suo, verum generosius ipsam
erigit, elimans nostrae contagia sordis.
175 Hanc humili gressu, vultu submissa, modesta
gestibus assequitur Fronesis primoque salutem
delibans, tali pingit concepta loquela:
"O regina poli, caeli dea, filia summi
artificis, nec enim facies divina caducam
180 te docet, aut nostri generis deferre litturam,
quam probat esse deam vultus sceptrumque fatetur
reginam natamque Deo tua gloria monstrat,
cui superum sedes, caeli via, limes Olimpi,
extramundanus orbis regioque Tonantis
185 tota patent, soliumque Dei fatumque quod ultra est:
me moderare vagam, stupidam rege, siste timentem
indoctamque doce, fluitantem corripe, tristem
laetifica gaudens, peregrinae consule, coeptum
perfice, nutantem firma, succurre cadenti.
190 "Nam vaga sum, tremebunda, stupens, indocta laborans,
deficiens, ignara loci, peregrina fatiscens;
quae nitens superare polos sedesque supernas
invadens, penetrale Dei talamumque Tonantis
consiliumque Iovis nutans vaga sola pererrans
195 aggredior, caelique vias pertempto latentes.
Nec tamen inconstans praeceps improvida casu
praecipitante vias istos invado labores;

earthly things, draws Noys herself into her mind, drunk from drinking of the divine source; but she should rather be 170 called sober, for the drunkenness that results from such nectar has the power of total sobriety. It does not cause the mind to lapse from its normal functions but rather raises it to a greater nobility by removing all noxious traces of our foul existence.

With reverent step, lowered face, and modest bearing, 175 Fronesis approaches this maiden and, having first received her greeting, sets forth her thoughts in these words:

"O heavenly queen, goddess of heaven, daughter of the supreme creator—for your divine demeanor tells me that 180 you are not mortal, and do not lament the stain of our condition—, your face proves you divine, your scepter declares you a queen, and your glorious seat shows you to be a daughter of God, one to whom the dwelling of the higher powers, the paths of heaven, the gateway to Olympus, the superuniversal world and the realm of the Thunderer all are open, 185 and the throne of God, and the destiny that is beyond. Guide, direct, support me, wandering, bewildered, fearful as I am, teach one who knows nothing, take hold of one who wavers, in your joy make happy one who is sad, provide for a pilgrim, complete what is begun, steady one who falls, aid her who is fallen.

"For I am a wanderer, fearful, bewildered, laboring un- 190 guided, failing, ignorant of this place, exhausted by my journey. Having striven to pass beyond the spheres and enter the supernal realms, now, tottering, wandering, alone, uncertain of the way, I seek to enter the sanctuary of God, the chamber of the Thunderer, to know the wisdom of Jove, and the 195 hidden pathways of heaven. Yet I who undertake these labors am not capricious, reckless, careless, was not cast onto my

sed precibus cedens et tandem velle coacta
Naturae monitu, Virtutum numine, nutu
200 praecipue Rationis ad hoc ego mittor, ut ipsa
Naturae summo praesentem vota Tonanti.
    "In multis errasse manum Natura recordans,
erratum revocare volens culpasque priores
tergere, vel veteres operis novitate beati
205 excusare notas, hominem formare, beatum
cudere, perfectum complere, creare modestum
temptat, quo possit veteres velare reatus
erranti mundo dans de tot milibus unum,
qui rectum sibi defendat, scrutetur honestum,
210 damnet avaritiam, diffundat munera, vitet
excessus, medium teneat, proscribat abusus.
Nec sine consiliis nutu moderamine voto
Virtutum decernit opus, sed tota sororum
contio conceptus assensu nutrit eosdem.
215   "Sed quoniam tantum circa terrena potentis
Naturae viget officium, languetque potestas,
in superis nil iuris habens animamque creare
nescia, quam sola pictoris dextra superni
format et in nullo Naturae iura requirit,
220 hac ratione diu nitens multumque reluctans
huc agor, et superos perquiro sola recessus,
quo possim deferre Deo quod concipit ipsa
Naturae ratio, quod virtus optat; ut ipsum
velle Dei nostrum confortet velle, precesque
225 audiat et nostris aspiret gratia votis,
ut divina manus animam demittat ab alto
quae sit mente sagax, virtute referta, pudore

path by fate; but yielding to prayers, and drawn to acquiesce
by the urging of Nature, the power of the Virtues, and above
all the prompting of Reason, I have been sent on this mis-   200
sion, to present to the almighty Thunderer the appeal of
Nature.

"Nature, realizing that her hand has committed many errors, wishing to undo her mistakes and expunge her former
sins, or atone for the old blemishes on her work with a new
and divinely favored creation, now seeks to give shape to a   205
man, to forge a blessed being, to make one wholly perfect, to
create a man of virtue, whereby she may hide her former
wrongdoing by giving to the sinful world one man, out of so
many thousands, who may claim rectitude for himself, seek
out what is honorable, condemn avarice, be lavish in giving,   210
avoid excess, keep to the mean, condemn abuses. She has
not decided on this work without the advice, the assent, the
guidance, the favor of the Virtues; the entire sisterhood have
given life to this plan by their assent.

"But since the authority of powerful Nature has force   215
only in earthly affairs, and her power fails, having no rights
in the higher realms, and being incapable of creating a soul
(for only the hand of the supreme artist can form that, and
He has no need for the powers of Nature), for this reason,   220
then, after long striving and with much reluctance, I have
been brought hither. I alone seek out the secrets of heaven,
so that I may report to God what Nature's mind has conceived, what the Virtues hope for: that the will of God Himself may strengthen ours; that he may hear our prayers, and   225
his grace favor our desires; that the hand of God may send
down from on high a soul that will be wise in mind, replete

377

praedita, praesignita fide, pietate refulgens;
quae carnis vestita toga sic visitet orbem
230 quod facinus redimat pietas virtusque reatum
incestumque pudor, fraudem ius, gloria casum.
   "Quod superest—terrena domus, vis terrea, vestis
corporeae massae, corpus mortale—potentis
Naturae dicatur opus, sic dote beandum
235 multiplici, nullo fraudatum munere formae;
ut iam corporeum non dedignetur habere
spiritus hospitium nec tantus defleat hospes
hospitii tabem, sed carnis regnet in aula.
   "Ergo mihi describe viam qua callis ad arcem
240 superni Iovis erigitur ne devia passim
errabunda ferar, ne nostrum devius error
propositum perdat, viduans mercede laborem."
   His verbis gavisa, poli regina benigno
reddidit affatu quod se praeberet eunti
245 consortem callisque ducem gressusque magistram.
Sed soli Fronesi ducatum spondet et ipsi
consulit instanter, praecepti robur eidem
consilio miscens, ut currum deserat, ipsos
in caelo deponat equos comitemque relinquat
250 inferius, quae sit stabilis custodia tanti
depositi, currum sistens frenansque iugales;
ne, si currus equi Ratio nitantur in altum
tendere, nec talem dignetur habere viantem
semita caelestis, alios experta meatus,
255 erret equus, nutet Ratio currusque vacillet.
   Explentur praecepta deae votisque favetur.
Stat Ratio, sistuntur equi, quadriga quiescit.

with virtue, endowed with purity, adorned with the seal of faith, shining in piety; a soul which, once clothed in its fleshly garment, will sojourn in the world, that he may answer crime with piety, guilt with virtue, unchastity with purity, fraud with justice, death with glory.

"As to the rest, his earthly dwelling, his earthbound strength, the clothing of his bodily substance, his mortal body, let this work be assigned to the power of Nature, that he may thus be blessed with attributes of many kinds, deprived of no gift of form; that the spirit may not disdain to occupy a bodily dwelling, nor such a guest deplore so mean a lodging, but instead reign with the body as its court.

"Show me, then, the way, the path that leads upward to the palace of lofty Jove, lest I be drawn hither and thither, pathless and wandering; lest straying on a false path defeat my purpose, depriving my labor of reward."

Rejoicing at these words, the queen of the firmament responds with benevolence: she will offer herself as the traveler's companion, her guide on the path, directress of her steps. But she offers this guidance to Fronesis alone, and advises her earnestly, mingling with her advice the force of precept, that she abandon the chariot, leave the horses in the celestial region and leave her companion behind as well, that she may keep sure watch over this great trust, securing the chariot and tethering the horses. For if the chariot, the horses, Reason should attempt to move higher, the heavenly path would not deign to accept such travelers, having known only journeys of another kind; the horses would go astray, Reason would falter, the chariot would teeter.

The precepts of the goddess are carried out, and her wishes obeyed. Reason stays, the horses are secured and the

379

Omnibus exclusis, solum regina secundum
consorti concedit equum, qui parcius ipsum
260 admiretur iter nec multum deneget ipsos
ascensus, fractus freni melioris habena.
Fertur equo Fronesis, se fert regina; volatu
fertur equus, dea certat equo gressuque volantem
praevenit; et comiti praetemptat praevia gressum.

265 Hactenus insonuit tenui mea Musa susurro,
hactenus in fragili lusit mea pagina versu,
Phoebea resonante cheli. Sed parva resignans,
maiorem nunc tendo liram totumque poetam
deponens, usurpo mihi nova verba prophetae.

270 Caelesti Musae terrenus cedet Apollo,
Musa Iovi, verbisque poli parentia cedent
verba soli, tellusque locum concedet Olimpo.
Carminis huius ero calamus non scriba vel auctor,
aes resonans, reticens scriptoris carta, canentis
275 fistula, sculptoris scalprum vel musa loquentis,
spina rosam gestans, calamus nova mella propinans,
nox aliunde nitens, luteum vas nectare manans.

Summe parens aeterne Deus vivensque potestas,
unica forma boni, recti via, limes honesti,
280 fons vitae, sol iustitiae, pietatis asylum,
principium finisque modus, mensura, sigillum,
rerum causa, manens ratio, noys alma, sophia
vera, dies verus, lux nescia noctis, origo
summa, decor mundi perfectus, vita perhennis,
285 nata regens, ventura serens, nascentia servans,
omnia sub numero claudens, sub pondere sistens
singula, sub stabili mensura cuncta coercens;

chariot sits at rest. All else being left behind, the queen allows her companion only the second horse, who will be less wary of the road, and less resistant to the ascent, when broken to the control of a better bridle. Fronesis is borne by the horse, the queen goes unaided; the horse is lifted in flight, but the queen's speed rivals that of the horse, and her steps prove faster than his flight; she goes before, and tests the path for her companion.

Thus far my Muse has sung in a faint whisper, thus far my writing has indulged itself in feeble verse to the sound of Phoebus's lyre. But now, putting aside petty things, I tune a greater instrument: wholly abandoning the role of poet, I presume to claim for myself the new voice of a prophet. Earthly Apollo must give way to the heavenly Muse, the Muse herself to Jove; earthly words will yield in deference the words of heaven; earth will give place to Olympus. Of this song I will be the mere pen, not the scribe or author, a sounding brass, the writer's silent page, the singer's pipe, the sculptor's chisel, the muse of him who speaks, the thorny branch that bears the rose, a reed dripping with new honey, a night lit by another's light, an earthen vessel brimming with nectar.

Parent of all, eternal God, living power, sole true form of goodness, way of rectitude, path of honor, fountain of life, sun of justice, refuge of piety, beginning and end, mean, measure, seal, first cause of things, unchanging reason, nurturing mind, true wisdom, true light of day, light that knows no night, ultimate origin, perfect beauty of the universe, eternal life, ruling over things born, sowing the seeds of things to come, watching over things coming to birth, encompassing all with number, assigning place to all by weight, defining

260

265

270

275

280

285

qui rerum species et mundi sensilis umbram
ducis ab exemplo mundi mentalis, eundem
290   exterius pingens terrestris imagine formae;
qui veterem massam de vultus sorde querentem
investis meliore toga, formaeque sigillo
signans, excludis nexu mediante tumultum;
efficiens causa, dum rem producis ad esse,
295   formalis dum pingis eam, finalis in esse
dum rem conservans, certo sub fine coartas:
tu mihi praeradia divina luce meamque
plenius irrorans divino nectare mentem
complue, terge notas animi, tenebrasque recidens
300   discute, meque tuae lucis splendore serena;
tu repara calamum, purga rubigine linguam,
da blaeso tua verba loqui mutoque loquelam
praebe, da fontem sitienti, dirige callem
erranti, duc nauta ratem portumque timenti
305   dona, caelesti perflans mea carbasa vento.
     Iam Fronesis, dictante dea, superaverat arces
sidereas, callemque novum nodosque viarum
mirans, quae tantae quereretur pondera molis,
ni proprios visus rerum novitate foveret
310   et proprii partem ferret regina laboris.
Dum transit miratur aquas, quas foederat igni
indivisa loci series, nec flamma liquorem
impedit, aut flammae certat liquor ille repugnans,
sed potius sua deponunt certaminis arma;
315   nec iam nativos curant memorare tumultus
quos ligat assensus discors discordia concors,
pax inimica, fides fantastica, falsus amoris
nexus, amicitia fallax, umbratile foedus.

all by certain measure; you bring forth the shapes of things and the shadowy sensible world from the archetype of the mental world, depicting this model outwardly in the like- 290 ness of earthly form. You clothe the ancient mass, which complains of its ugliness, in a finer garment, stamping it with the seal of form, and eliminating its chaotic movement by a mediating bond; you are efficient cause, when you bring a creature into being; formal when you give it shape; final 295 when you maintain it in being, assigning it a fixed span of life. Shine your divine light upon me, fill my mind to the full with divine nectar, cleanse my thought of stains, cut through and dispel the darkness, make me glad with the splendor of 300 your light. Make ready the pen, purge the tongue of rust, give the stammerer power to speak your words, grant speech to the dumb, your waters to him who thirsts, show the way to the wanderer, be the navigator of the vessel of one who is afraid, and bring him to port, filling my sails with heavenly 305 wind.

Now Fronesis, guided by the goddess, has ascended be- yond the starry realms, wondering at the new pathway and astonished by its windings; she might have complained about the weight of such a heavy task, if she were not in- dulging her sight with the newness of everything, and if the 310 queen were not sharing in her toil. As she travels she won- ders at waters which the unbroken continuity of the place has united with fire: the flame does not disturb the liquid, nor does the liquid seek to reject the flame; instead they lay aside the weapons of their conflict. No longer do they care 315 to recall the tumult natural to those bound by a discordant accord, a concordant discord, a hostile peace, an imaginary trust, a false bond of love, a deceitful friendship, an illusory

Figit in his visum mentemque Sophia sagaci
320   perquirens animo quis pacem fecit adesse,
pax ubi nulla manet; quis Martem iussit abesse,
Mars ubi iura tenet; quis foedus nexuit illic,
foedus ubi nullum; quis pacem miscuit irae,
litigio foedus, liti coniunxit amorem.
325   Altius inquirit Fronesis, ferventius instans,
an liquor ille fluat, sibi quem vicina maritat
flamma poli flammaeque truces contemperat iras;
an nebulae faciem gestans formamque vaporis,
in speciem nubis expansus, in aethere summo
330   pendeat et donet sitienti pocula flammae;
an glaciem gerat in specie reddatque figuram
cristalli perdatque suum liquor ipse liquorem;
sed tamen a Fronesi viva ratione probatur
quod nullos illic possit torquere recursus
335   humor nec proprio valeat discurrere fluctu,
cum gremium nullus ibi praebeat alveus illi,
nec matrix terrena sinus expandat eidem,
nec centrum repetens, nativo pondere tractus
humor ad ima ruat, propriae gravitatis amicus;
340   descensum cum flamma neget sursumque manere
cogat aquas, supraque liget quasi carcere clausas.
(348)   Hac etiam ratione probat quod nullus ibidem
(349)   exhalat vapor in nebulas, nec pendulus umor
(350)   aethera velat aquis, ubi nullas evomit auras
345 (351)   terra, nec ignis ibi suspendit in aethere nubes.
(342)   Nam qui furtivo lapsu quasi nesciat ignis
(343)   a superis rorem descendere, somniat ille
(344)   philosophus, ratione caret falsumque prophetat,

compact. Sophia fixes on them both sight and thought, pon-   320
dering in her wise mind what power has caused peace to
appear where peace cannot abide; what power has ordered
Mars to withdraw where Mars holds sway; who has created agreement here where none agree; who could combine
peace with rage, conflict with truce, join together love and
strife. She probes deeper, eagerly questioning whether this   325
water, which the encroaching heavenly fire has joined to itself, remains fluid, and tempers the flame's fierce rage, or assumes the aspect of mist, and in the form of vapor expands
into the condition of cloud, hangs suspended in the lofty   330
ether, and bestows drink on the thirsty flames; or whether
the liquid takes on the form of ice, displays the appearance
of crystal, and wholly forsakes its liquid state. Yet it is evident to the lively reasoning of Fronesis that the water is not
able to turn back its course, nor can it flow along a course of   335
its own, since no channel offers it a bed, and no mothering
earth opens its recesses to it, nor may it rush downward,
seeking the center and drawn by its own weight, accepting
its natural tendency; for the flame will not let it descend,   340
compels the waters to remain still, and holds them confined
on high as if in prison. By the same reasoning she proves that
in this place no vapor is diffused into clouds, nor does its
moisture, suspended, bathe the ether with its waters, for the
earth sends up no vapors here, and fire does not hang clouds   345
in the ether. For any philosopher who imagines that dew
descends from above in a furtive showering, as if fire were
unaware of it, is devoid of reason, a false prophet, one who

(345)   otia sectatur, nubes et inania captat,
350 (346)   in scirpo nodum quaerens, in lumine fumum,
(347)   in plano scrupum fingens, in luce tenebras.
    Ex his concludit Fronesis quod caelicus humor
    cristalli retinet speciem glaciemque figurat
    quae glacies, ignara gelu nec conscia brumae,
355   aestatem magis agnoscit caelique calores,
    ad vultus ignis minime dignata liquari.
    Hoc solo magis illa stupet meliusque movetur,
    qua nexus mediante fide, quo foedere pacis
    frigida conveniant calidis, fluitantia pigris,
360   hic ubi nullus adest pacis mediator et omne
    foedus abest extrema ligans, quod pace reperta
    deleat hostiles rixas pugnamque recidat.
    deficit inquirens, quaerendo vincitur illa;
    quaesitu superata suo. Sed victa querelis
365   defectus queritur proprios; sic ista querela
    quaestio fit, Fronesi suspiria sola relinquens.
      Nec mirum si cedit ad haec Prudentia, quae sic
    excedunt matris Naturae iura, quod eius
    exsuperant cursus, ad quae mens deficit, haeret
370   intellectus, hebet ratio, sapientia nutat,
    Tullius ipse silet, raucescit lingua Maronis
    languet Aristoteles, Ptholomei sensus aberrat.
      Ulterius producit iter Prudentia, gressum
    informans gressu comitis, tandemque labore
375   magno, multiplici nisu, conamine multo
    ascendit loca laetitiae, loca plena favoris,
    caelesti loca grata Deo, loca grata Tonanti.
    Hic risus sine tristitia, sine nube serenum,
    deliciae sine defectu, sine fine voluptas,

pursues idle dreams, snatches at clouds and vanities, seeking 350
a knot in a bulrush, smoke in brightness, pretends that there
is a flaw in a smooth surface, shadow in light. From all of this
Fronesis concludes that water in the heavens has the appearance of crystal, and resembles ice, but ice which, knowing
nothing of cold or frost, is better adapted to summer and the 355
warmth of heaven, and does not at all deign to melt when
exposed to fire. This in itself astounds her, and she is moved
to ask further by what securely mediating bond, by what
pledge of truce cold can be reconciled with hot, liquid with
inert matter, here where no peacemaker is present and all 360
agreement is absent which might join these two extremes,
which, by establishing peace, might eliminate their angry
quarrels and terminate their war. Her inquiry falls short, she
is defeated in her search, what she seeks is beyond her. But
in lamenting her defeat she blames her own shortcomings, 365
so that complaint becomes self-doubt, and Fronesis is left
sighing.

It is no wonder if Providence gives way before these questions, which so exceed the powers of mother Nature; for
they are wholly beyond her sphere; before such questions
the mind fails, intellect is at a loss, reason grows dull, wis- 370
dom nods, Tully himself falls silent, the tongue of Maro
grows rough, Aristotle grows faint, Ptolemy's wits go astray.

Providence pursues her journey further, shaping her own
step by that of her companion. At last, with great labor, 375
many struggles, much effort she arrives in the region of happiness, a place greatly favored, a place dear to the god of
heaven, dear to the Thunderer. Here are smiles without sorrow, clear day without cloud, inexhaustible delights, endless

380   pax expers odii, requies ignara laboris,
            lux semper rutilans, sol veri luminis ortus
            nescius occasus, gratum sine vespere mane;
            hic splendor noctem, saties fastidia nescit;
            gaudia plena vigent, nullo respersa dolore;
385   non hic ambiguo graditur Fortuna meatu,
            non risum lacrimis, adversis prospera, laeta
            tristibus infirmat, non mel corrumpit aceto,
            aspera commiscens blandis, tenebrosa serenis,
            connectens luci tenebras, funesta iocosis,
390   sed requies tranquilla manet, quam fine carentem
            fortunae casus in nubila vertere nescit.
              Hic sua praeradiat caelestis regia solis
            quae sordes hominum, mundi contagia spernit.
            Extramundanus orbis mundique beata
395   portio, munda magis quam mundus, purior ipso
            puro, lucidior claro, fulgentior auro,
            quae blando splendore micat, quae fulgurat igne
            innocuo, fervore carens, fulgoris abundans,
            blanditias splendoris habens, fervoris abhorrens
400   nequitiam, splendore fovet nec verberat aestu.
            Hic ignis minus igne calet, plus igne nitescit,
            sicque manens unus minor est et maior eodem,
            sed quoniam totus scintillat in igne beato
            hic locus et flammae nutu blanditur amico,
405   censetur polus empireus, cui flamma benignis
            ignibus arridet aulamque nitoribus ornat.
              Hic habitant cives superi proceresque Tonantis,
            angelici coetus divinaque numina, mundi
            rectores, turmae caelestes, agmina caeli,

pleasure, peace immune to hatred, repose unmarked by toil, 380
light ever shining, sun whose true light has risen never to
set, fair morning without evening. Here brightness knows
no night, satiety does not breed disgust, joy waxes strong,
unshadowed by sorrow. Here Fortune does not stalk along 385
uncertain paths, to infect laughter with tears, prosperity
with adversity, happy with sad; does not taint honey with
gall, mingling bitter with sweet, clouds with fair weather;
joining shadow to light, dismal to merry; instead tranquil re- 390
pose abides, which has no end, and the accidents of fortune
cannot overcloud it.

Here the court of the heavenly sun spreads a radiance
that scorns the foulness of humanity, the contagions of the
world. This is a world wholly apart, a blessed portion of the 395
universe, more elegant than the cosmos, purer than purity
itself, clearer than clarity, brighter than gold, which gleams
with a mild splendor, glows with harmless fire, lacking in
heat but abounding in radiance; possessed of the tender-
ness of warm light but rejecting the annoyance of warmth, it 400
soothes with brightness but does not cause pain by its heat.
Here fire is less warm than fire but brighter than fire, so that
while remaining constant it is less and greater in one. But
since the whole place sparkles in this blessed fire, and is
soothed by the kindly nodding of its flame, it is clearly the 405
empyrean heaven. Fire smiles on it with gentle flames, and
adorns the court with its glow.

Here dwell the citizens of heaven, noble companions of
the Thunderer, the angelic hosts, divine powers, orderers of
the universe, the heavenly company, the legions of heaven,

410 excubiae nostri, varius quos dividit ordo
munus et officium, virtus diversa, potestas
plurima, dissimilisque gradus, distantia facti.
Hic ardent Seraphim, flammata calore supernae
lucis et eterni solis radiata nitore.

415 Divini fontis Cherubim satiata liquore,
plus sapiunt mentique Dei perfectius haerent.
Inque Tronis librata Dei censura resultat,
in quibus ipse Deus residens examina librat.
Nomen ab officio Dominantia numina sumunt,

420 quae sicut superis cedunt, sic ceditur ipsis
a reliquis, pariterque iubent parentque iubenti.
Princeps turma suos disponit in ordine cives
atque suis votis astringit vota suorum.
Aëris istius rectores, immo tyrannos

425 turba Potestatum vincit caelestibus armis.
Legibus occurrunt Naturae iuraque solvunt
Virtutes, formisque novis antiqua reformant.
Mistica denudat, aperit secreta, revelat
abdita quaeve magis latitant Archangelus orbi

430 nuntiat et caeli pandit mysteria terris.
Maior in obsequiis sed eo virtutibus impar,
Angelicae plebis exercitus omnibus istis
persolvit ius obsequii mundoque minora
praedicat et varios nobis discurrit in usus.

435 Hic cives habitant supremi regis in urbe.
civibus his servanda datur respublica caeli,
inter quos haec lex sancitur: ut imperet unus.
Hic operetur agens reliquis, obtemperet ille

our guardians. Differences in station, function, and duty ₄₁₀
distinguish them, different attributes, many different powers, distinctions of rank, differing tasks. Here the Seraphim
burn, fired by the heat of heavenly light and the radiant
splendor of the eternal sun. The Cherubim, drinking deeply ₄₁₅
of the divine fount, are wiser, and more perfectly aware of
the mind of God. In the Thrones, the balanced judgments
of God are expressed; God himself weighs his delibera-
tions while seated among them. The Dominations take their
name from their office: as they give way to their superiors, ₄₂₀
so the rest give way to them; they both give and obey orders. The host of Principalities arrange their subjects by
rank, and identify the wishes of their people with their own.
The throng of Powers control with celestial arms the gover-
nors—or better tyrants—of the lower air. The Virtues chal- ₄₂₅
lenge the laws of Nature, and suspend her power, transforming the old order of things with new forms. The Archangel
unveils mysteries, makes secret things known, reveals things
that are hidden or conceal themselves, announces them to
the world, and unfolds the mysteries of heaven to earthly ₄₃₀
beings. Greater in obedience, but unequal to him in virtue,
the army of common Angels perform the duty of obedient
service to all the other orders; they proclaim lesser tidings
to the world, and readily perform various tasks on our behalf. All these dwell as citizens in the city of the supreme ₄₃₅
king. It is the duty of these citizens to serve the republic of
heaven, and among them this law is sacrosanct: that one
should rule, that this one should exercise control over the
rest, and that all owe him obedience who learn their duty in

quilibet in libro divinae mentis agenda
440 discit ibique legit quae sint ventura, Deumque
consulit, in speculo deitatis singula cernens;
nec solus tantum sibi vindicat angelus urbem.
    Hic habitat quem vita deum virtusque beatum
fecit et in terris meruit sibi numen Olimpi,
445 corpore terrenus, caelestis mente, caducus
carne, Deus vita, vivens divinitus, extra
terrenum sapiens, intus divina repensans;
quem non erexit fastus, non gloria rerum,
non mundi deiecit amor, non lubrica fregit
450 luxuries, non luxus opum, non ardor habendi
succendit, non livor edax, non anxia foedae
pestis avaritie, non laudis caeca cupido,
sed potius demisit eum patientia, mundi
contemptus, rerum paupertas artaque victus
455 regula, despectus carnis, deiectio vitae;
qui calcavit opes animo victore, malignum
devicit carnemque sibi servire coegit.
Coetibus angelicis tales ascribit honestas
vitae, virtutis meritum mercesque laboris,
460 quos vel virgineus candor vel purpura vestit
martirii, vel doctoris sua laurea ditat,
vel quos aureolae munus non excipit, omnes
aurea communi fretos mercede coronat.
Cum sint diversi merito meritique resultet
465 splendor inaequalis, lux dispar, gaudia cunctis
aequa manent, risusque pares, ubi dissona merces.
Nec mirum si laetitiae par gratia cunctos
expectat, quibus una datur pro munere vita,

the book of the divine mind, read there what will come to 440
pass, and seek God's judgments, seeing all in the mirror of
the godhead. No single angel can claim so great a city for
himself.

Here too dwell those whose lives made them divine,
whose virtue beatified them and on earth earned for them
the status of Olympians. For they were earthly in body but 445
heavenly in mind, mortal in the flesh, but godly in spirit,
living godlike lives, wise beyond earthly wisdom, inwardly
meditating on things divine. No scornful pride stiffened
them, no worldly glory. The love of worldly things did not
debase them, no wanton luxury sapped their strength, no 450
sumptuous excess, no love of wealth inflamed them, no
gnawing envy or anxious fever of foul avarice tainted them,
no unthinking desire for glory. But patience made them submissive, and a disdain for worldly things, poverty in possession, an austere rule of diet, a contempt for fleshly appetite, 455
a humble way of life. Such a person trod riches underfoot
with heroic spirit, abased the hostile flesh and compelled it
to obey him. For their honorable life such people are en-
rolled among the angelic host, a fit reward for their virtue,
the wage for their toil; they are clad in the virgin's gleaming 460
white or the purple robe of the martyr, or the laurel of the
doctor crowns their heads; and if the honor of the aureole
does not set them apart, a golden crown is theirs, the common reward of all. Though they differ in merit, and so are
rewarded with unequal degrees of splendor, disparate luster, 465
yet the joy of all remains the same, though their rewards differ their joy is equal. And no wonder if the same gift of happiness awaits them all, for the life that is bestowed on all

in quibus ipse Deus est omnibus omnia, donum
470 et donans, dans uni plurima, pluribus unum.
    Hic superos cives proprio praecellit honore
Virgo quae proprium pariendi lege pudorem
non perdens, matris meruit cum virgine nomen;
in qua concordant duo nomina, lite sepulta,
475 quae secum pugnare solent litesque movere,
nec iam discordant mater virgoque, sed ipsis
litibus exclusis, se pacis ad oscula vertunt.
Hic Natura silet, Logicae vis exulat, omnis
Rhetoricae perit arbitrium Ratioque vacillat.
480 Haec est quae miro divini muneris usu
nata patrem natumque parens concepit, honorem
virgineum retinens nec perdens iura parentis,
in cuius ventris thalamo sibi summa paravit
hospitium deitas, tunicam sibi texuit ipse
485 filius artificis summi, nostraeque salutis
induit ipse togam, nostro vestitus amictu.
    Haec est stella maris, vitae via, porta salutis,
regula iustitiae, limes pietatis, origo
virtutis, veniae mater thalamusque pudoris,
490 hortus conclusus, fons consignatus, oliva
fructificans, cedrus redolens, paradisus amoenans,
virgula pigmenti, vinaria cella liquore
praedita caelesti, nectar caeleste propinans,
nescia spineti florens rosa, nescia culpae
495 gratia, fons expers limi, lux nubila pellens,
spes miseris, medicina reis, tutela beatis,
proscriptis reditus, erranti semita, caecis
lumen, deiectis requies, pausatio fessis.

is one and the same, God Himself is present in all of them, gift and giver, granting many things to each one, and one gift   470
to many.

Here a Virgin surpasses all the denizens of heaven in dignity, she who not sacrificing her chastity to the necessity of giving birth, earned the name of mother together with that of maiden. For in her the two names are harmonious, no longer at war, though they normally resist one another and   475
stir up quarrels. For here mother and maiden are not at odds, for their conflict has been cast aside, and they offer each other the kiss of peace. Here Nature falls silent, the power of Logic is banished, all the authority of Rhetoric is lost, and Reason grows faint. For this is the daughter who by the mi-   480
raculous exercise of a divine gift conceived her father, and gave him birth as her son, preserving her virgin honor without surrendering her claim to parenthood; in the chamber of her womb the supreme Godhead prepared a dwelling for himself, the son of the supreme artificer wove a garment for   485
himself, clothed himself in the robe of our salvation by assuming our [fleshly] coat.

She is the star of the sea, the way to life, the port of salvation, the standard of justice, the pathway of piety, the source of virtue, the mother of mercy and chamber of chastity, the walled garden, the sealed fountain, the fruitful olive tree,   490
the scented cedar, the paradise of delight, the painted staff, the wine cellar stored with heavenly liquor, proffering the nectar of heaven, the blooming rose that knows no thorn, grace that knows no guilt, fountain unmuddied, light that   495
banishes cloud, hope of the wretched, cure for the sinful, sure hope of the blessed, return for the exile, path of the wanderer, light of the blind, ease for the downtrodden, rest for the weary.

Haec est quae primos casus primaeque parentis
500 abstersit maculas, vincens virtute reatum,
diruta restituens, reddens ablata, rependens
perdita, restaurans amissa, fugata repensans,
post vespertinos gemitus nova gaudia donans,
post mortis tenebras vitae novitate relucens.
505 Cuius ad adventum redit aetas aurea mundo,
post facinus pietas, post culpam gratia, virtus
post vitium, pax post odium, post triste iocosum.
Ut rosa spineti compensat flore rigorem,
ut dulcore suo fructum radicis amarae
510 ramus adoptivus redimit, sic crimina matris
ista luit; matrem facit sua nata renasci
ut sic munda ream, corruptam virgo, pudica
effrontem, miseram felix humilisque superbam
abluat et vitae pariat sua filia matrem.
515 Huius ab imperio caelestis curia pendet,
huius ad imperium devota mente parata.
Cum qua caelestis regni moderatur habenas,
qui pater et proles eiusdem, natus et actor.
Cuncta regit, sine fine regens, quo rege triumphat
520 in caelo miles, in terra militat exul.
Hic est qui carnis intrans ergastula nostrae
se poena vinxit ut vinctos solveret, aeger
factus ut aegrotos sanaret, pauper ut ipsis
pauperibus conferret opem, defunctus ut ipsa
525 vita donaret defunctos, exulis omen
passus ut exilio miseros subduceret exul;
sic livore perit livor, sic vulnere vulnus,
sic morbus damnat morbum, mors morte fugatur,

This is she who absolved us of the first fall and wiped away the stain of our first parent, conquering sin by her virtue, raising up what was cast down, restoring what was stolen, making good what was destroyed, returning what was lost, redeeming what was banished, granting new joys after sorrow at nightfall, after the shadows of death bringing the brightness of new life. At her coming the golden age returned to the world, piety after wickedness, grace after guilt, virtue after vice, peace after hatred, laughter after sorrow. As the bloom of the rose compensates for the sharpness of the thorn, as the engrafted branch redeems by its sweetness the bitter fruit of the tree, so this one made payment for the mother's crime; the daughter caused the mother to be reborn, that the pure might cleanse the guilty, the virgin the sinful woman, the chaste the shameless; that the happy might cleanse the wretched, the humble the proud; that the daughter might give birth to the mother of life. The celestial court awaits her command, ready to obey her bidding with devoted mind.

He who is both her father and her child, her son and her creator, guides with her the reins of the heavenly kingdom. He governs all things, and his rule is without end. Under his reign the soldier triumphs in heaven, the exile wages war on earth. This is he who, entering the prison of our flesh, accepted the pain of defeat that he might free those who were defeated, became sick that he might heal the sick, poor that he might make the poor rich, died that he might bring to the dead the gift of life, underwent the doom of exile that by his exile he might lead the wretched out of exile. Thus envy dies through envy, our wound through his wounding. Thus sickness destroys sickness, death drives out death,

500

505

510

515

520

525

sic moritur vivens ut vivat mortuus, heres
530 exulat ut servos heredes reddat, egenus
fit dives pauperque potens, ut ditet egenos;
sic liber servit ut servos liberet, imum
summa petunt ut sic ascendant infima summum;
ut nox splendescat, splendor tenebrescit, eclipsi
535 sol verus languescit, ut astra reducat ad ortum;
aegrotat medicus, ut sanet morbidus aegrum;
se caelum terrae conformat, cedrus ysopo,
ipse gigas nano, fumo lux, dives egeno,
aegroto sanus, servo rex, purpura sacco.
540 Hic est qui nostram sortem miseratus, ab aula
aeterni patris egrediens, fastidia nostrae
sustinuit sortis, sine crimine criminis in se
defigens poenas et nostri damna reatus.

Liber Sextus

Postquam virgo Dei solium sedesque supernas
ingrediens voluit nova praelibare videndo,
offendit splendor oculos mentemque stupore
percussit rerum novitas. Defecit in illis
5 visus et interior mens caligavit ad illas.
Sic sopor invasit vigilem, sic somnus adulter
oppressit Fronesis animum, somnoque soporans
exstasis ipsa suo, mentem dormire coegit.
Et iam praecipitem pateretur lapsa ruinam,

thus the living dies that the dead may live, the heir suffers 530
exile that he may make heirs of slaves, the wealthy becomes
poor, the powerful a pauper, that he may make the poor rich.
Thus the free man enters servitude that he may free the
slaves, the most high plumb the depths that the lowliest may
ascend on high. That the night may be made splendid, splendor enters the darkness, the true sun suffers eclipse that he 535
may bring the stars to rise again. The physician becomes ill
that his illness may heal the sick. Heaven accepts the condition of earth, the cedar becomes a hyssop, the giant becomes
a dwarf, light turns to smoke, rich to poor, health to sickness, king to slave, the purple robe to sackcloth. This is he 540
who, pitying our condition, came forth from the court of
the eternal Father, endured the loathsomeness of our life,
though guiltless imposed on himself the penalty of the guilty,
the sentence for our ruin.

Book 6

When the maiden, entering the heavenly halls and approaching the throne of God, wished to sample these new
wonders by gazing, their splendor troubled her sight and
their novelty stunned her mind. Her sight failed before
them, and her thoughts within were clouded as she pon- 5
dered them. A dullness came over the watchful mind of
Fronesis, a strange sleep weighed on her spirit, a trance of
stupefying drowsiness compelled her to fall asleep. And
now as she sinks down she would fall headlong did not her

10　ni comes occurrens manibus complexa cadentem
　　sisteret, et blando complexu virginis artus
　　confortans, tantos lapsus eluderet, ipsam
　　mitibus aggrediens verbis mentisque stuporem
　　demulcens. Mens plena tamen non redditur illi,
15　sed postquam nulla valuit ratione stuporis
　　exstirpare malum totamque reducere mentem,
　　ut Fronesi ferat auxilium totumque soporem
　　excutiens, reddat mentem cogatque reverti,
　　sollicitat precibus propriam regina sororem,
20　quae superum solio residens caeleste profundum
　　scrutatur solisque Dei penetralibus heret;
　　cui Ratio nihil affirmat, cui sufficit ipsa
　　credulitas et sola Fides, ratione remota.
　　Ipsam namque Fidem Ratio non praevenit, immo
25　ipsa Fides hanc anticipat Fideique docenti
　　obsequitur tandem Ratio, sequiturque docentem
　　articulos Fidei, divinaque simbola cartis
　　inserit haec, scribens animo quod arundine pingit.
　　　Purpureis clavata notis niveumque colorem
30　intermixta rubet vestis candore represso,
　　qua mulier praedicta nitet, cultusque fatetur
　　arbitrium mentis, mens ipsa videtur in illo.
　　Picturae cedit vestis, quae tota figuris
　　scribitur et formam praetendit scripta libelli.
35　Hic renovat veteres vivens pictura magistros,
　　per quos nostra fides totum diffusa per orbem
　　claruit et laudum titulis praeclara refulsit.
　　Hic Abraham nostrae fidei pater, exuit actus
　　patris dum summo Patri parere libenti
40　contendens animo, nato pater esse recusat,

companion, reaching out her arms and embracing her as she   10
falls, support her. Steadying the maiden's limbs with a gentle
embrace, she prevents such a fall, and addresses her with
tender words to alleviate her faintness. Yet her mind is not
fully restored. But when the queen is unable by any means to   15
drive out this fit of dullness and wholly restore her senses, in
order to assist Fronesis and wholly eliminate her faintness,
restore her mind and effect her recovery, the queen appeals
in prayer to her own sister, who, seated close to the supernal   20
throne, searches deeply into things divine, and knows the
innermost thoughts of God. Reason can teach her nothing;
belief and faith alone suffice her, and Reason is set aside. For
Reason does not take priority over Faith; indeed Faith an-   25
ticipates her, and Reason finally submits to Faith's instruction, accepts her teaching of the articles of Faith, then sets
down on paper her sacred creed, inscribing on the mind
what she sets forth with the pen.

Faith's robe, furnished with purple stripes intermixed
with snowy white, has a ruddy glow, while the white remains   30
subdued. So clad the lady is beautiful, and her dress declares
the character of her thoughts; her very mind can be seen in
it. But the robe defers to its decoration, for it is wholly covered with images, and, thus inscribed, has the appearance of
a book. Here vivid painting gives new life to the teachers of   35
old, through whom our faith, spread throughout the world,
shone clearly, and sparkled with tokens of praise. Here Abraham, the father of our faith, casts off the role of father when,
striving with willing mind to show obedience to the supreme   40
father, he refuses to act as a father toward his son, while

in quo discordes Natura Fidesque duellum
exercent unamque trahunt in dissona mentem:
nam Natura docet genitorem parcere nato;
econtra stat firma Fides quae spernere natum
45   imperat, ut summo faveat Natura parenti;
quod non vult cupit ergo pater; nunc parcere temptans,
nunc offerre volens, tandem negat ipse quod optat;
ergo succumbit Fidei Natura, dolensque
cedit victrici, quod non vult velle coacta.
50   In robur Fidei, virtutum luce coruscat
Petrus et ipsius virtus splendescit in umbra.
Armatus vitae meritis et dote sophiae,
Blanditiis ratione minis virtutibus instat
Paulus et introitum fidei gentilibus offert;
55   nec solum signis, verum ratione rebelles
vincit nec satis est concesso calle meare:
plus cupit atque viam gaudet ratione parare.
Illic blanda minas ergastula verbera mortes
expugnat, Fidei clipeo protectus et armis
60   iustitiae superatque suos Laurentius ignes.
Par pugnae meritis et eisdem miles in armis
mundum devincens Vincentius omnia victor
calcat et in vivos pugnans in morte triumphat.
        Hunc habitum, quamvis scripturae pingat honestas,
65   nulla tamen vestem lascivia deprimit, immo
talis erat qualem matronae postulat aetas,
quae senii metas attingit plena dierum,
canitie respersa caput seniique pruina.
Nec tamen illius faciem matura senectus
70   exarat in sulcos; facies discordat ab aevo,

within him Nature and Faith are at odds and wage a duel, drawing his single mind into division. For Nature teaches the father to spare the son; Faith stands firmly opposed, and commands that he reject his son, that Nature defer to the 45 supreme parent. Thus the father desires what he does not will, now seeking to spare, now willing to offer, and finally refuses that for which he hopes. Thus Nature submits to Faith, and sorrowfully yields to the victor, forced to will what she does not wish. A pillar of Faith, Peter shines with 50 the light of virtue, and his virtue shows its splendor [even] in this shadowy form. Armed with his praiseworthy life and his legacy of wisdom, Paul challenges the nations with kindness, reason, threats, good works, as he offers them admission into Faith. He conquers rebellious spirits not only with sym- 55 bols, but with rational arguments, and it is not enough that they walk in the path they have accepted; he wants more, and his joy is in preparing the way with rational instruction. Here Lawrence, protected by the shield of Faith and the arms of justice, withstands entreaty, threats, prison, the lash, 60 and murder, and triumphs over his fiery death. Vincent, his equal in the merit of his warfare, overcoming the world fighting in the same arms, treads all beneath his feet as victor, and by withstanding the living triumphs in death.

Although a noble inscription adorns this garment, no 65 wantonness dishonors it; instead it is such as the age of the matron requires, for she is full of days and has crossed the boundary of old age; her head is strewn with gray and the hoar frost of age. Yet ripe old age has not plowed furrows in her face; her face argues against her age, indicating 70

quae iuvenile docet aevum, contraque loquuntur
cani, cum canis sic vultus gratia certat.
    Haec mulier, motu proprio precibusque sororis
tacta, movet gressus illuc ubi laesa sopore
75 letargi languet Fronesis mortisque figuram
exemplans, moritur vivens et mortua vivit.
Sed postquam veniens signis dictantibus illam
agnovit, vidit stupidam stupuitque iacentem,
hos casus miserata dolet, mentisque rigorem
80 exuit, in gemitus erumpens, fracta parumper
maiestas animi mollescere cogitur, exit
durities et sola tenet miseratio mentem.
Haec igitur magis accedit propiusque iacentem
visitat et quaerit languoris semina, temptat
85 cuncta locum tempus causam symptomata morbi
caute disquirens, cuius vestigia tandem
invenit et Fronesim letargi somnia passam
noscit, ut exterius languoris signa fatentur.
Inventa ratione mali morbique reperta
90 materie, disquirit adhuc quae causa salutis
languoris causas valeat secludere, pestem
perdere, supplantare luem morbumque fugare.
Ergo minis precibus pulsu clamore soporem
expugnare parat, sed talis somnus obaudit.
95   Nec mirum si morbus ad haec contemnit abire;
non erat iste sopor somni, sed mortis imago,
quae vitae tenebrat lucem vitamque soporat
plus somno, sed morte minus, maiorque sopore,
morte minor, sed fida tamen praefatio mortis.
100 Cum talis nequeat medicina refellere morbum
nec tantum valeat morbi superare vigorem,

youthful years, while her white hair offers an opposing argument. Thus the charm of her face competes with her hair.

This woman, prompted by her own instinct and the prayers of her sister, comes forth to where Fronesis lies listless, stricken by her drowsy lethargy and offering the appearance of death, living though dead, and dead though alive. But when Faith, approaching, recognizes the signs that indicate the maiden's condition, sees her lying in a stupor and is stupefied at the sight, she feels grief and pity for her plight. She casts off sternness of mind, bursting into tears; her sober spirit, suspended for a time, is compelled to soften; austerity vanishes and compassion alone occupies her mind. Accordingly she draws nearer, examines the fallen maiden more closely, and searches for the cause of her weakness. She explores every avenue, carefully seeking out the place, time, cause, symptoms of the illness, finally discovers its traces, and recognizes that Fronesis is suffering the trance of lethargy, as the outward signs of lassitude indicate. Having discovered the reason for her malaise and the nature of the illness, she still seeks a means of restoring health that will control the causes of her weakness, eliminate the infection, drive out the pestilence, banish the disease. Then with threats, prayers, stamping and shouts she prepares to make war upon drowsiness. But a trance of this kind is stubborn.

It is no wonder if the disease refuses to give way to her. This is not the drowsiness of mere sleep, but the image of death, which darkens the light of life, and suspends vital energy more than sleep, though less than death. More potent than sleep, but less so than death, it is nonetheless a reliable presage of death. Since such medicine is unable to repel the sickness, is not able to overcome its power, the languishing

caelesti confecta manu, condita sapore,
mellifluo gustu mellita, suavis odore,
secretas redolens species, terrena repellens
105   condimenta, novum caeli thymiama propinans,
exquisita datur languenti potio, totum
quae corpus peragrat, vitalia circuit, intrat
venas, disquirit nervos penetratque medullas.
Huius ad adventum Fronesis sibi redditur, ad se
110   dum redit, et totus mentis secluditur error.
Hic stupor ipse stupet medicinam posse; fugatus
miratur talem medicinae cedere morbum.

Sed quamvis oculus mentis resplendeat intra,
languescit tamen exterior, nec ferre nitorem
115   sustinet empireum nec tantum fulgor Olimpi.
Ergo suam sollers matrona recurrit ad artem
et praesigne decens rutilans immitabile tersum,
grandi diffusum spatio scriptumque figuris
praesentat Fronesi speculum, quo cuncta resultant
120   quae locus empireus in se capit, omnia lucent,
quae mundus caelestis habet; sed dissona rerum
paret in his facies: hic res, hic umbra videtur
hic ens, hic species, hic lux, ibi lucis imago.

Detinet hoc speculum mentem visumque Sophiae
125   sistit, ne maior oculis lux obviet, illos
offendens, visumque simul cum mente fatiget.
Hoc speculum mediator adest, ne copia lucis
empireae radians visus depauperet usum.
Visus in hoc speculo respirat, lumen amicum
130   invenit et gaudet fulgens in lumine lumen.
Cernit in hoc speculo visu speculante Sophia,
quidquid divinus in se complectitur orbis.

one is given a potion carefully conceived, prepared by heavenly hands, imbued with savor, honeysweet in taste, sweet smelling, redolent of secret essences but rejecting any earthly seasoning, offering a new, heavenly incense. It travels through her body, moves through her vital organs, enters her veins, tests her nerves and penetrates the marrow of her bones. As it enters her body Fronesis revives, recovers herself, and all error is banished from her mind. The stupor is itself stupefied at the power of the medicine; driven out, it is amazed that such an illness should yield to medication.

But while the eye of the mind within is once again illumined, Fronesis is still outwardly feeble. She cannot endure the bright light of the empyrean or the great brilliance of Olympus. Therefore the attentive matron returns to her art and presents Fronesis with a remarkable mirror, elegant, radiant, clearly reflective, polished, casting its reflection over a broad expanse, and inscribed with images. All that the empyrean encompasses is reflected here, all the brilliance that the heavenly world contains. But the appearance of things is altered in this mirror. Here are seen the thing itself, its being, its radiance; there the shadow, the shape, the reflection of that radiance.

This mirror engages the mind of Sophia and rests her sight, lest a light too strong strike her eyes and cause them harm, wearying both sight and mind. This mirror serves as a mediator, lest the abundant, radiant light of the empyrean deprive her of the use of sight. Sight is renewed in this mirror; it finds the light congenial, and its own shining light rejoices in this light. Sophia, letting her sight move over this mirror, sees in it all that the realm of God contains. As she

105

110

115

120

125

130

Dum nova quaeque videt, miratur ad omnia, gaudet
in cunctis, novitas rerum nova gaudia gignit.
135 Eius cum visu mens delectatur, et omnes
exuit erroris nebulas, et gaudia mentem
perfundunt; perit omne sui symptoma doloris.
Si qua minus plene cognoscit, plenius illam
assistens matrona docet suppletque minorem
140 intuitum panditque latens aperitque reclusum.
    Hic videt angelicae plebis superique senatus
militiam, palmamque simul dulcesque triumphos
sanctorum, meritum dispar fructusque laborum.
Virginis illius meritum miratur, adorat
145 partum quod peperit, non marcescente pudoris
flore, nec atrito fervente libidinis aestu;
conceptus partusque modum floremque pudoris
intactum stupet admirans, non invenit unde
sit mater que nulla viri commercia novit.
150 Confugit ad logicae leges: huic ergo parentis
iura negat, cui virginitas concedit honorem
virginis, a simili vult supplantare pudorem
virgineum matri, quam disputat esse parentem
partus, et ad matrem nativo iure refertur.
155 Ista tamen ratio nutat, cum virgine matrem
invenit, et logices videt argumenta iacere.
    Amplius admirans, magis haesitat, amplius haerens,
inquirit quo iure poli, qua lege beata
nata patrem, terrena Deum, casura manentem,
160 flos cedrum, sidus solem, scintilla caminum
proferat, et mellis desudet petra liquorem.
Miraturque Deum nostram vestire figuram,

beholds each new thing she marvels at all of them, is delighted by all of them, and each new sight produces new joy.
Her mind as well as her vision feels delight, and emerges   135
fully from the clouds of confusion. Joy fills her mind, and every trace of her suffering vanishes. If she does not fully understand something, the matron is at hand to provide a fuller
explanation, supplement her limited insight, reveal what lies   140
hidden and open what is closed.

Here she sees the ranks of the lesser angels, and the ranks
of the heavenly senate; the glory and the blessed triumphs
of the saints, their differing merit and the fruits of their labors. She is awed by the honor accorded the Virgin, adores
the child whom she bore while the flower of her purity re-   145
mained unwithered, unsullied by the raging heat of lust. Astonished, she wonders at the conception, the manner of the
birth, the bloom of a chastity still intact; she cannot discover how one who had had no intercourse with a man could
be a mother. She retreats to the laws of logic, and so denies   150
to this maiden the title of parent, for her virginity claims for
her the honored title of virgin; she likewise wishes to refute
the virgin purity of the mother, whose having given birth
argues that she is a parent, and in the way of nature pertains
to a mother. But this reasoning fails; she finds virgin and   155
mother to be the same, and sees that logical argument has
been overcome.

As her amazement grows, she hesitates the more, then,
more perplexed, she asks by what heavenly privilege, by
what blessed law a daughter brings forth her father, an
earthly creature God, a mortal an immortal, a flower a ce-   160
dar, a star the sun, a spark a furnace, how a stone should ex-
ude a stream of honey. She marvels that our likeness clothed

et nostras habitare casas flammantis Olimpi
rectorem, floremque rosae latitare sub alga,
165   et gemmam vestire lutum, violamque cicuta
velari, vitamque mori, tenebrescere solem;
qui gunfi, quae iuncturae, quis nexus et unde
connectant humana Deo, divina caduco
consocient hominique Deum, quis foederat ordo.
170   Singula dum Fronesis miratur et omnia temptat
vestigare suae rationis legibus, illam
assistens matrona monet, ne somniet illic
humanas leges mundanaque foedera, cursus
Naturae nostrasque vices; ubi nulla potestas
175   illius, sed cuncta silent decreta, pavescunt
leges, iura stupent, ubi regnat sola voluntas
artificis summi, quae vult a canone nostro
excipiens, ubi iura pavent et regula cedit
artifici canonque silet, dictante magistro.
180   Non Ratio sed sola Fides ibi quaeritur, illic
transcendit causas caelestis causa, minores
exsuperat leges lex summa et foedera legum.
Ergo Fides ubi sufficiat, disquirere cesset
hic Ratio, sistatque Fides Rationis habenas.
185   His monitis fert assensum Prudentia, cedit
doctrinae, sequiturque Fidem totumque superno
deputat auctori quod nostram vincere legem
cernit et excepti iuris ratione moveri.
His edocta viam maturius arripit, eius
190   informat regina gradum gressumque sigillat
incessu proprio. Sed ne locus abditus, anceps
callis, distortus limes, via dissona gressus
virginis impediat, comitem sibi destinat illam,

God, that the ruler of brilliant Olympus dwelt in our humble house, that the blooming rose should hide itself in weeds, a gem clothe itself in mud, a violet be veiled in hemlock, life 165 suffer death, the sun overshadow itself; she asks what, and from what source, are the fastenings, the jointure, the bonds that connect human existence with God, bring together divine and mortal, what pact unites God with man.

As Fronesis ponders these questions, and seeks to exam- 170 ine all by the laws of reason, the watchful matron warns her not to think idly in terms of human laws, the bonds of the universe, the workings of Nature and our own experience of change. For here these have no power; all dictates are si- 175 lenced, laws grow feeble, justice is confounded; for here the will of the supreme artisan reigns alone, and what he wills is exempt from our standards; here rights give way, rule yields to the creator, law falls dumb as the master speaks. Rea- 180 son is not needed here, but Faith alone; here divine causation transcends other causes, the supreme law supersedes lesser laws and legal bonds. Thus here where Faith suffices, let Reason cease to question; let Faith take the reins from Reason.

Providence gives her assent to this advice, accedes to this 185 teaching, follows the way of Faith and imputes to the supreme author all that she recognizes as defeating our laws, as governed by a mind whose right is exempt from them. Thus instructed, Fronesis takes to the road with more assurance; the queen guides her steps and stamps each step with 190 her own footprint. But lest hidden recesses, the forking path, the unevenness and windings of the roadway should hinder the progress of the maiden, the queen assigns as her

ANTICLAUDIANUS

quae Fronesi mentem proscriptam reddidit, eius
195 restituens visum, cui cessit abusio morbi,
quam via nulla latet, nullus locus abditur illi,
non delirus obest limes, non semita fallit.
His comitata viae Fronesis securius instat
ancipitesque vias transit, loca dissona, calles
200 ignotos; nec iam posset superare locorum
anfractus; sed nutanti soror utraque vires
suppeditat, firmatque gradum, gressusque recidit
pondus et extenuans poenam fastidia tollit.
Oblatum Fronesi visum defendit ab omni
205 luminis occursu speculum, ne debriet illam
caelestis splendor oculosque reverberet ignis.
    Tandem fessa tremens admirans virgo dietam
explet et aeterni suprema palatia regis
intrat, et expleti superata mole laboris
210 laetatur; sed cuncta stupet quae nuntius offert
in speculo visus, ubi nil mortale, caducum
deficiens terrestre micat solumque refulget
eternum caeleste manens immobile certum.
Hic videt ingenitas species, speculatur ideas
215 caelestes, hominum formas, primordia rerum,
causarum causas, rationum semina, leges
Parcarum, fati seriem, mentemque Tonantis:
cur Deus hos reprobat, illos praedestinat, istum
praeparat ad vitam, sua munera subtrahit illi;
220 cur alios humiles paupertas cogit, egenos
comprimit et solum lacrimis satiatur egestas;
cur aliis praedives opum pluit alveus omnes
divitias divesque natat fecundus in auro;

412

companion the one who had returned to Fronesis her banished mind, restoring her sight, the one to whom the afflict-   195
ing disease gave way, to whom no way is closed, from whom
no place is hidden, whom no eccentric path can hinder,
whom no byway deceives. Accompanied by these two Fronesis pursues her path in safety, passes over the forking
roads, confusing places, obscure paths; even now she could   200
not master the circuitous road, but both sisters provide ample support when she grows faint; they steady her steps,
lighten the weight her feet must bear, and by reducing her
suffering ease her discomfort. The mirror presented to Fronesis protects her sight from any encounter with light, lest   205
heavenly splendor dazzle her and its fire strike her eyes.

At last the maiden, weary, trembling, amazed, reaches the
end of her journey, and enters the lofty palace of the supreme
king. She is happy to have overcome the difficulty of her
now completed labor, but astounded at every message that   210
vision offers her in the mirror. For there nothing mortal,
transitory, perishable, earthly appears; all that shines forth
is eternal, heavenly, abiding, unalterable, sure. Here she
sees species still unborn, contemplates the divine ideas, the   215
forms of men, the first beginnings of creation, the causes of
causes, the seeds of order, the laws of fate, the destined
course of things, the mind of the Thunderer. Why God rejects these, predestines those, readies this one for life, but
withholds his gifts from another. Why poverty constrains   220
and humbles some, oppresses those in need, and their in-
digence can only be solaced by weeping. Why on others a
bountiful stream of wealth showers riches of all kinds, and
the rich man, well supplied, wallows in gold. Why wisdom

cur istos ditat sapientia, nubilat illos
225   sensus inops, animus pauper, mendica voluntas;
cur formae species purgata serenat Adonim,
Davus abusivam speciem gerit; Hector in armis
fulgurat, ingenii radio scintillat Ulixes;
cur Cicero rhetor, cur Tiphis nauita, pictor
230   Milo, pugil Pollux, rigidus Cato, Naso poeta.
   Nec haec sola favent Fronesis conspectibus; ultra
progrediens visus alia novitate videntem
demulcet, redituque suo miranda reportat.
Hic videt irrigui fontis radiare nitorem
235   qui praedives aquis, reliquo conspectior amne.
Sidera luce domat, praecellit mella sapore
cuius deliciis cedit paradisus, odore
balsama vincuntur, nardus summititur illi.
A quo procedens rivus non immemor horum
240   quae fons ille gerit, totum sibi fontis honorem
assumit, fontique pari respondet honore;
nec tamen irriguum minor afflat gratia fontem;
ergo fons rivum, rivus cum fonte fluentum
producit, retinens fontis rivique saporem;
245   cum sint distincti, fons rivus flumen in unum
conveniunt, eademque trium substantia, simplex
esse, sapor similis, color unus, splendor in illis
unicus et vultus horum conformis et idem.
   Ad speciem fontis sol vincens lumine solem
250   hic radium fundit quem sol mundanus adorat,
cui caelum stellaeque favent et supplicat orbis.
Occasum numquam patitur sol iste, nec ullam
sustinet eclipsim, nec nubis nubila sentit,

enriches these, while a lack of understanding leaves those in 225
darkness, poverty of mind, will without means. Why pure
beauty of form makes Adonis fair, while Davus has a carica-
ture for a face. Why Hector shines in war, Ulysses gleams
with the spark of ingenuity, Cicero is an orator, Tiphys a
sailor, Milo a painter, Pollux a boxer, Cato inflexible, Naso a 230
poet.

Nor is it only these that charm the sight of Fronesis; proceeding further, sight favors the viewer with still other novelty, bearing news of things marvelous as it returns to her.
Here she sees the gleam of a brimming fountain spreading 235
forth an abundant flow of water, more beautiful than any
stream. It exceeds the stars in brilliance, surpasses honey in
sweetness; Paradise must yield to such delights; in scent balsam is defeated by it, nard must give it place. Flowing forth
from the fountain is a stream; not unmindful of all that the 240
fountain produces, it appropriates all the dignity of the
fountain to itself, and matches the fountain with an equal
dignity, though no less charm enhances the brimming fountain. The fountain, then, produces the stream; stream and
fountain together produce a river, which retains the flavor
of fountain and stream. Though they are distinct, fount, 245
stream, and river combine into one. The substance of the
three is the same, their essence is uniform, their flavor is the
same, their color one, the same unique splendor inheres in
them, their face is conformed and the same.

Here too, like the fountain, a sun surpassing our sun in
light pours forth a radiance which our planetary sun wor- 250
ships, which heaven and stars applaud, to which the world
offers prayers. This sun is never made to set, never suffers
eclipse, never sees itself darkened by cloud. A ray of brilliant

a quo procedens radius splendoris adaequat
255   luce patrem loquiturque suo splendore parentem.
Idem sol, species eadem, lux una, coaevus
splendor, nequaquam proprio declivis ab ortu,
sol alius sed non aliud, sol unus et unum
cum gignente manens, lux luci consona, fulgor
260   fulgori splendorque sui non immemor ignis.
De se producit radius cum sole calorem
qui mulcens urit, urendo mulcebris ardens
mitigat, incendens demulcet, temperat urens;
iste calor siccat vitiorum flumina, sordes
265   purgat, et a vitio virtutis decoquit aurum;
iste calor perimit peccati frigora, flammas
irae, torporis hyemes Venerisque calorem.
Sic calor expugnat ignem, sic flamma repellit
flammam, sic aestus aestum splendorque caminum.
270   Pullulat in flores mens isto tacta calore,
et terram mentis virtutum flore beato
purpurat iste calor, dum ver caeleste reducit.
    Haec mirata diu Fronesis, multumque retractans
singula quae visus praegustat, freta sororum
275   ducatu summi regis conscendit in arcem,
qua residet rex ipse poli, qui cuncta cohercet
legibus imperii, qui numine numina celi
constringit, cuius nutu caelestia nutant.
Haec igitur vicina Deo vix sustinet eius
280   immortale iubar, ius maiestatis, inundans
expectat lumen, sed eam defendit ab isto
fulgure planities speculi, quam visibus offert
illa suis, lucem speculo mediante retardans.

light emanating from this sun is equal in brightness to the 255
father, and declares its parentage by its splendor. It too is
the same sun, identical in nature; their light is one, their
splendor coeval. The other sun is not other, in no way inferior to its source, abiding, one and the same with its parent,
its light in harmony with his, its brilliance with his, its splen- 260
dor not unmindful of his fire. His radiance produces with its
sunlight a fire that soothes as it burns, a fire intense but gentle which makes its burning mild, which comforts as it burns,
which is temperate in its burning. This fire dries up the rivers of vice, purges what is vile, and smelts the gold of vir- 265
tue out of viciousness. This fire destroys the chill of sin, the
flames of wrath, the winter of sloth, the heat of Venus. Thus
fire drives out fire, flame repels flame, heat extinguishes
heat, and splendor the glowing forge. The mind touched by 270
this fire bursts into bloom; this fire adorns the soil of the
mind with the blessed flowering of virtue, as it calls forth a
heavenly springtime.

Having marveled at these things for a long time, turning
over in her mind each new thing of which her sight gave her
a foretaste, and trusting to the guidance of the sisters, Fro- 275
nesis ascends to the hall where the king of heaven has his
seat, he who makes all things submit to the laws of his empire, who governs by his power the powers of heaven, whose
nod all heavenly things obey. Once in the presence of God
she can scarcely endure his immortal brilliance, the author- 280
ity of his majesty; she fears the overwhelming light, but the
surface of the mirror, which she keeps before her eyes, protects her from this flashing light, reducing its effect by its
mediating reflection.

Tunc virgo, genibus flexis et supplice vultu,
285 submissae vocis modulo gestuque timentis
supplicat aeterno regi, verbumque salutis
praelibat, mixtaque tremunt formidine verba.
Sed superum genitor reddens sua iura saluti
erigit hanc et stare iubet motusque timoris
290 sistere, ne terror animum vocemque retardet.
Erigitur mentemque regit partimque retardat
virgo metum, stat mens cum corpore, corporis aequat
mens erecta situm; sic vox submissa resumit
vires, et erectam mentem sua verba sequuntur.
295 Exit in has voces animus verbisque redundat:
    "Si nostros gemitus et nostrae taedia sortis,
mundanos casus mundanaque fata, caducos
ortus, instantes obitus vitaeque propinquos
lapsus et nostrae pensemus originis omen,
300 quae nostrum tantos fastus invadat ut ante
conspectum faciemque Dei praesumat habere
colloquium noctisque lues cum luce loquatur,
conveniat regem servus pauperque potentem,
factorique suo moveat factura querelam?
305 Sed quia te fontem pietatis novimus, a quo
livoris stimulum bonitas innata relegat,
cuius iustititie pietas adiuncta rigorem
temperat et multum discurrere non sinit illam,
ad te confugimus proscriptae quas fugat orbis
310 persequitur mundus, homo respuit, improbat omnis
vivens. Sicque tuis, si fas est dicere, mundus
legibus excipitur: dum nostri iura nefandis
actibus expugnat, etiam tibi bella minatur;
nam tua res agitur, paries cum proximus ardet.

418

Then the maiden, on bended knee and with suppliant face, in a quietly submissive voice and with evident timidity, prays to the eternal king. She first offers a salutation, in tremulous words pervaded by fear. But the creator of heaven, reciprocating her greeting, makes her rise. He orders her to stand and cease to be afraid, so that fear may not hinder her thoughts or her voice. The maiden draws erect and steadies her mind, and as her fear diminishes a little, her mind aligns itself with her body; her upright mind adopts the stance of her body. Now her subdued voice recovers its strength, and her words conform to the erect stance of her mind. Her thought issues into these words, and pours forth as she speaks:

"If we consider our grief, and the dreariness of our condition, the calamities of earthly life and its fate, our birth into mortality, the imminence of death, the ever-present dangers of life, and our ill-starred origin, which of us would assume such arrogance that she would presume, in the sight and presence of God, to conduct a colloquy? Should sinful darkness converse with light, can a poor slave address the almighty king, the creature bring complaints against its creator? But because we know that you are the fount of compassion, from whom essential goodness banishes the sting of envy, whose mercy, united with justice, tempers its severity and does not allow it free rein, we who are banished seek refuge in you, we whom the world has cast out, who are everywhere persecuted, whom humanity disdains, whom every living thing condemns. For the world, if it is right to say it, has exempted itself from your laws; when it seeks to destroy our authority by its wicked actions, it even threatens war against you; for your own affairs are at stake when a neighbor's house is aflame.

285

290

295

300

305

310

315 "Hos casus Natura videt lapsusque cadentis
mundi, virtutem vitio succumbere fraudi
foedus amicitiam liti pacemque furori.
Hos gemit excessus, errores luget, abusus
deplorat mundumque dolet sub nocte iacere.
320 In multis etiam damnat sua facta, reatus
excusare volens facto meliore novisque
artibus atque nova medicina tergere morbum.
Qualiter ergo malum superet morbumque recidat
putrida membra secet, ne pars sincera trahatur,
325 occurrat vitio, ne totum diruat orbem,
vix cognoscit adhuc, sed tandem freta sororum
colloquio, meliore via procedit, in istud
consilium veniens, ut totum viribus unum
cudat opus, per quod proprio succurrat honori,
330 quo veteres operum possit pensare ruinas.

"Vult hominem formare novum, qui sidere formae
et morum forma reliquos transcendat, et omnes
excesssu resecans, regali limite gressum
producat, mediumque tenens extrema relinquat,
335 ut saltem mundo sidus praefulguret unum
qui iacet errorum tenebrosa nocte sepultus;
ut sic respiret virtus, excuset in isto
errores Natura suos, et conferat uni
quod multis conferre nequit meritumque favoris
340 et laudum titulos saltem lucretur in uno,
quae iacet in multis damnata, suumque decorem
amittit, dum sola sui iam restat imago.

"Sed nullo firmata manent concepta tenore
ni tua conceptis applaudat gratia, coeptum
345 roboret atque tuo confirmet munere votum.

"Nature beholds these disasters, the misfortunes of a sin-   315
ful world, sees virtue succumb to vice, good faith to deception, friendship to strife, peace to madness. She weeps at
these excesses, she bemoans such error, deplores its abuses,
grieves that the world is buried in darkness. She blames her   320
own work for much of this, and wishes to atone for her guilt
with a finer work, to cure the disease with new arts and new
medicine. How she may overcome this evil, remove the disease, cut away the rotting limb lest the healthy part be infected, confront vice so that it may not destroy the world,   325
this she still hardly knows; but encouraged by a council of
her sisters, she has now embarked on a better course, having
arrived at this decision: that she must apply her powers to
forge a single complete work, through which she may redeem her honor, whereby she may compensate for the ruin   330
of her former works.

"She wishes to fashion a new man, who in the glory of his
form and the formation of his character will transcend all
others, and avoiding all transgression, will set his feet on the
royal path, keeping to the mean and distanced from the extremes. Thus at least one star will shed its radiance on this   335
world which lies buried in the shadowy night of error; thus
virtue may revive, and Nature atone in this way for her errors, bestow on one what she could not bestow on many, and
reap the reward of approbation and the honor of praise in at   340
least this one case. For now she lies afflicted by many wounds
and bereft of her beauty, and what remains is the shadow of
herself.

"But this proposal must remain without the assurance of
any direction unless your grace favor what is proposed, support the work, and by your power grant our prayer. Nature's   345

Naturae langueret opus penitusque iaceret
incultum, veteris retinens fastidia massae,
ni tua Naturae firmaret dextera factum
infirmamque manum regeret, conduceret huius
350   scribentis calamum, lapsum suppleret euntis.
Corporis effigiem sibi deputat, exigit a te
quod superest Natura bonum munusque quod ipse
solus habes, animamque petit, quae sola superni
postulat artificis sensum limamque requirit.
355   Nostras namque manus terrestris fabrica tamen
exposcit sed eas animae caelestis origo
ignorat, solique suum tibi deputat ortum.
       "Ergo tuo nutu, numen caeleste caduca
visitet et corpus caelestis spiritus intret.
360   In terra positus, in caelo mente beata
vivat et in terris peregrinet corpore solo.
Virtutum dives opibus, fecundus amore
caelesti, carnisque domet ratione tirannum,
teque tuum fateatur opus, quis fecerit actor
365   praedicet, artificemque suum factura loquatur.
Sic ad nos divinus homo descendat, ut ipsis
virtutum titulis aliorum moribus instet.
       "Te saltem moveant Naturae damna, pudoris
exilium, iactura boni, deiectio morum,
370   error honestatis, fidei proscriptio, legum
contemptus, nostraeque preces; si pondera rerum
vel momenta sumus, noli confundere dudum
confusas: fuimus et nos quandoque beatae.
Si te nulla movent rerum discrimina, saltem
375   te gratis moveat tua gratia, suscipe vota
quae damus, et precibus devotis pondera dona.

work would fail, indeed would lie wholly unformed, still retaining the hostility of ancient chaos, did your hand not lend support to her labor, control her uncertain hand, guide the pen with which she writes, make up for the failings of her 350 initiatives. Nature has assigned to herself the fashioning of the body, and seeks from you the good that remains, that gift which you alone possess: she asks for the soul, which alone demands the understanding of the supreme artisan and requires his skill. For the earthly frame calls for the work 355 of our hands, but the heavenly origin of the soul does not acknowledge these; its creation must be assigned to you alone.

"By your assent, then, let heavenly power enter mortal life, and a divine spirit assume a body. Though placed on 360 earth, let his blessed mind have its life in heaven, and let him sojourn on earth in body alone. Richly endowed with virtue, abounding in divine love, let him overcome by reason the tyranny of the flesh. Let your work reveal you, let it proclaim its maker, let the artifact declare the artisan. Let this divine 365 man descend to us, so that by the excellence of his virtue he may influence the characters of others.

"Be moved at least by the wounded state of Nature, the exile of purity, the casting down of goodness, the rejection of morality, the faltering of honor, the banishment of trust, 370 the disdain for law, and be moved by our prayers; if we are figures of consequence, of importance, do not disappoint us, who are already disappointed; we too once knew blessed happiness. If the crisis of your creation does not move you, let your mercy at least move you to grant us your grace; ac- 375 cept the appeal we make, and give consideration to our de-

Si nos a patriis proscriptas sedibus omni
destituis voto, desertae vincimur, omne
perdimus officium nostrasque relinquimus artes."
His precibus donat assensus arbiter aulae
caelestis, mentemque foras vox provocat ista:
"Virgo parens rerum, superum germana meique
filia, caelestis ortu, tamen incola terrae,
in terris quae sola sapis divina, meaeque
exemplum deitatis habes, fastidia mundi
quae relevas fletusque tuo solamine tergis,
non tua degenerat a summa mente voluntas:
nam patris ad votum suspirat nata, parentem
in voto sequitur patri non dissona proles.
"Hoc mihi iampridem Ratio dictavit ut uno
munere respicerem terras mundumque bearem
numine caelestis hominis, qui solus haberet
tot virtutis opes, tot munera digna favore,
tot dotes animae, quo saltem mundus aberrans
floreret, vitiis aliorum marcidus, immo
iam defloratus in flore resurgeret uno.
Si terrae vitium, scelus orbis, crimina mundi
ad meritum pensans, vellem persolvere poenas,
aut iterum terras velarem fluctibus, undis
vestirem montes iterum, totumque periret
diluvio genus humanum, nec fluctibus ullum
exciperet vitae meritum, nec viveret alter
Deucalion, alterque Noë conduceret archam,
sed potius mundus, qui crimine vivit in uno,
ad vitae meritum poena moreretur in una:
aut terrae delicta novus consumeret ignis,

380
385
390
395
400
405

voted prayers. If you leave us exiled from the dwelling of our
Father, bereft of all hope, we are utterly defeated, our authority wholly lost, and we must cease to pursue our arts."

The ruler of the court of heaven grants assent to these   380
prayers, and these words summon forth his mind:

"Maiden, parent of the world, sister of the higher powers
and daughter to me, heaven-born, though you dwell on
earth, you who, alone on earth, have intuition of things divine, and alone possess the image of my godhead, you who   385
give relief to an ailing world, and wipe away its tears by your
compassion, your will does not forget its origin in the divine
mind: for the daughter longs to realize the father's wish; a
child not unworthy of her father accords with her parent in
her prayer.

"Reason has long since advised me that I should look   390
kindly on the earth with a single gift, and bless the world
with the soul of a divine man, who alone would possess such
a wealth of virtues, so many praiseworthy attributes, so
many spiritual gifts, that at least in him the erring world
would flourish; though now blighted, even wholly deflow-   395
ered by the vice of others, it would be renewed in this one
flowering. If I were to weigh earthly vice, the guilt of a
wicked world as it deserves, and wished to impose a sufficient punishment, I might cover the earth with floodwaters
again, again cloak the mountains in waves; the whole human   400
race would perish in the deluge; nothing deserving of life
would be exempted from the flood, no second Deucalion
would survive, or a second Noah construct an ark. Instead
this world that lives in a single state of sin, would die, as its   405
way of life deserves, by a single punishment. Or a new holo-
caust might consume the world's crimes, enveloping [all]

involvens homines una sub clade, nec ullum
exciperet tantae generalis regula cladis;
aut scelerum pestes alia sub peste perirent.

410   "Sed quia iustitiae vincit miseratio normam,
iudiciique rigor cedit pietate remissus,
non poenas aequabo malis, non praemia culpis,
non ferro purgabo luem, non vulnere morbum.
Sed victus dulcore precum vestrique misertus
415 exilii, meliora dabo medicamina mundo.
Munere divino donis caelestibus auctus,
spiritus a caelo terrae dimissus in orbe
terreno peregrinus erit, carnisque receptus
hospitio, luteum tegmen novus hospes habebit.

420   "Hoc superest: ut vestra manus concedat honestum
huic animae thalamum; regi respondeat aula,
ne novus hospitii contagia sentiat hospes,
ne nucleum laedat testae putredo, saporem
corrupti vasis sibi res contenta maritet."

425   His hilarata magis propriumque oblita laborem
virgo, nec ulterius pondus conquesta viarum,
persolvit grates et caeli numen adorat.
Ipse Deus rem prosequitur, producit in actum
quod pepigit: vocat ergo Noym, quae preparet illi
430 numinis exemplar, humanae mentis ideam,
ad cuius formam formetur spiritus omni
munere virtutum dives, qui nube caducae
carnis obumbratus, veletur corporis umbra.
Tunc Noys ad regis praeceptum singula rerum
435 vestigans exempla, novam perquirit ideam.

mankind in a single disaster, and the law of such a universal slaughter would exempt none. Or this plague of wickedness might be destroyed by another plague.

"But because compassion prevails against the rule of justice, and harsh judgment yields when tempered by pity, I will not make punishment equal to wrongdoing, reward to guilt; I will not purge corruption with the sword, wounding to excise disease. Instead, swayed by the sweetness of prayer, and pitying your exiled state, I will grant the world a better medicine: a spirit, endowed by divine favor with heavenly powers will be sent down from heaven to earth, and be a pilgrim in the earthly world. Once received in the hospice of the flesh this new guest will possess a covering of earthly matter.

"What remains is that your skill must grant this soul an honorable dwelling; the court must be worthy of the king; the new guest must not suffer from any contamination of its home, the rotting shell must not infect the fruit within, what is contained must not take to itself the taint of an unclean vessel."

Rejoicing at these words, the maiden, forgetful of her own labor and no longer troubled by the difficulty of her journey, offers her thanks and reverence to the heavenly power. God himself takes up the task, and brings to realization what he has conceived. To this end he summons Noys, who prepares for him the spiritual exemplar, the idea of a human soul, on the model of which may be formed a soul endowed with every attribute of virtue, which will be enveloped in the cloudy darkness of mortal flesh, veiled by the shadow of a body. Then Noys, at the king's command searching through the models of individual creatures, seeks a new

410

415

420

425

430

435

427

Inter tot species speciem vix invenit illam
quam petit. Offertur tandem quaesita petenti,
in cuius speculo locat omnis gratia sedem:
forma Ioseph, sensus Iudithae, patientia iusti
440　Iob, zelus Finees Moisique modestia, Iacob
simplicitas Abrahaeque fides pietasque Thobiae.
　　Hanc formam Noys ipsa Deo praesentat, ut eius
formet ad exemplar animam. Tunc ille sigillum
sumit; ad ipsius formae vestigia formam
445　dans animae, vultum qualem deposcit idea
imprimit exemplo. Totas usurpat imago
exemplaris opes, loquiturque figura sigillum.
　　Adsunt factori Parcae cumulantque decorem
facturae, non invidiae livore retractae
450　a donis animae, sed multa dote salutant
ortam, felici claudentes omine fatum.
　　His donis ditans facturam, factor eandem
commendat Fronesi. Monet hanc et praecipit addens
praeceptis monitisque minas, ne tanta remisse
455　conservet commissa sibi, sed cautius illam
conducat, meliore via moderata meatum,
ne vel Saturni glaciali frigore tacta
sentiat algorem nimium, vel Martis in aestu
torreat, aut dulci pruritu laesa Diones
460　langueat, aut Lunae fluitet torrentibus acta.
Tunc Noys unguenti specie, quae funditus omnem
aëris insultum sistat morbique procellam,
frigus avaritiae, foedaeque libidinis aestum,

and ideal form, but among all these forms she can scarcely find what she seeks. At last what is sought is revealed to the seeker; in its mirror every mark of grace finds a home: the beauty of Joseph, intelligence of Judith, the patience of Job the just, the zeal of Phineas, the modesty of Moses, Jacob's simplicity, the faith of Abraham, the piety of Tobias.   440

Noys herself presents this form to God, that he may form a soul on this model. He then takes his seal, granting to the form of the soul the attributes of the model, and imprints on this copy the pattern that its ideal form demands. The image takes to itself all the endowments of its exemplar; its form declares its origin.   445

The Parcae attend the creator, and augment the beauty of the new creation; they do not enviously begrudge the soul its endowments, but greet the newly born with many gifts of their own, completing its destiny with a favorable omen.   450

Having endowed the new creation with these gifts, the creator entrusts it to Fronesis. He admonishes and instructs her, adding threats to his precepts and admonitions, lest she be careless in caring for the great thing entrusted to her; but he directs her carefully along a better path, making her journey easier, lest she should feel the cold too keenly when struck by the icy chill of Saturn, grow parched in the heat of Mars, become weak when assailed by the sweet itch of Dione, or be borne away by the tides of the Moon. Then Noys, showering the soul with heavenly dew, anoints it with a certain ointment which will wholly withstand any assault by the air, the storms of disease, the chill of avarice, and the   455   460

invidiaeque sedet stimulum, contemperet iram,
465   perfundens animam caelesti rore perungit.
       Ergo potens voti, caelo dimittitur alto
virgo; gradum properat illucque revertitur unde
venerat; in caelum stellis radiantibus ardens
pervenit. Occurrit Ratio votoque potitam
470   laudat et auctoris miratur dona superni.
Tunc comites, quarum ductu Prudentia sursum
evasit, reddens grates solvensque salutem
deserit, ad currum rursus solitumque recurrens
aurigam, veteremque viam gavisa resumit.
475   Tunc loca pertransit Saturno proxima, caute
decipit illa senem, gressum secludit et illi
se procul absentat fugiens, callemque remotum
intrat, ut illius queat expugnare furorem.
Saturnique tamen sensisset spiritus iram,
480   ni liquor unguenti contra pugnasset, et illum
vincens, fervorem superasset caelicus imber.
Sic Veneris pestes, sic Martis decipit aestus,
lunaremque globum. Quae tandem singula vincens,
immensum consummat iter votisque sororum
485   expectata diu Prudentia redditur. Offert
Naturae caeleste datum; miratur in illo
artificis Natura manum, munusque beatum
laudat et in dono laudatur gratia dantis.

seething of foul desire, allay the sting of envy and temper   465
anger.

Then the maiden, having accomplished her mission, descends from the height of heaven. She makes haste in returning to the place whence she had come, and enters the heaven that glows with radiant stars. Reason comes to meet her, praises her realization of their hopes, and marvels at the   470 gifts of the supreme author. Then Providence parts from the companions under whose guidance she had journeyed on high, offering thanks and bidding them farewell. Returning to the chariot and its familiar charioteer, she joyfully sets out on the well known road.

Crossing the region closest to Saturn, she cleverly de-   475 ceives the old man, concealing her passage and keeping herself at a distance from him; in her flight she follows a path far removed, in order to avoid his rage. Even so the soul would have felt Saturn's wrath, had not the ointment fought   480 against it, and the heavenly dew conquered and subdued its fury. In the same way she evades the plague of Venus, the heat of Mars, and the sphere of the Moon. Finally, having prevailed against all these, Providence, so long awaited, completes her great journey, and rewards the prayers of her   485 sisters. She presents the divine gift to Nature, who marvels at the skill of the artist in creating it. She praises this blessed gift, and in so doing praises the grace of the giver.

Liber Septimus

Occurrit Fronesi virtutum turba suoque
pendet in amplexu, collum ligat, oscula praebet.
Felicem laudat reditum, cum grata labori
reddatur merces, felici fine laborem
5   concludens, nec iam risus et gaudia vendat
spem timor offendens, cum res sperata timorem
sorbeat et longo succedant gaudia voto.
    Ergo sollerti studio Natura requirit
materiae summam, de qua praesigne figuret
10   hospitium, carnisque domum quam spiritus intret
caelestis radietque, suo domus hospite digna.
Excipit a terra quicquid purgatius in se
terra tenet, quidquid puri sibi vindicat humor,
quidve magis purum purus sibi destinat aër,
15   vel defaecatum retinet sibi purior ignis.
Dividit a toto, divisaque rursus in unum
colligit, in summam commiscens; dumque futurum
sic praelibat opus, humani corporis aptat
materiem, signans operis vexilla futuri.
20   Ergo materiem colere vis ignea donat,
quae quamvis soleat totam turbare quietem
corporis et bellum plus quam civile movere,
hic pacata iacet, nullos motura tumultos.
Materiam purus traducit ab aëre sanguis,
25   nec iam luxuriat proprio torrente superbus,
sed pacem servat reliquis humoribus humor
sanguineus nullasque movet cum fratribus iras.
Illis inferior infra decurrit aquosus

Book 7

The Virtues throng to greet Fronesis; they embrace her
closely, throw their arms around her neck, offer kisses. They
applaud her happy return, for her labor has gained a welcome reward, her work has come to a happy conclusion. No 5
longer may the anxiety which strikes down hope put a price
on joy and laughter, for the result hoped for suppresses fear,
and joy now takes the place of long held hopes.

Now Nature applies her mind to seeking the finest materials with which to form a distinguished hospice, a fleshly 10
home which a divine spirit may inhabit and illumine, a home
worthy of its guest. She draws from the earth whatever it
contains that is pure, such purity as water can claim for itself, whatever the pure air possesses that is purer, what fire, 15
purer still, harbors within itself that is wholly purified. She
separates these, then gathers them together again, combining them into a perfect substance; and anticipating in this
way the work to come, she readies the material for the human body, indicating the character of her future creation.
The energy of fire contributes the material of choler, which, 20
though it is accustomed to upset all bodily repose, and give
rise to wars more than civil, here rests at peace, creating no
disturbance. Pure blood draws its material from the air, and
the sanguine humor does not now proudly revel in its mighty 25
flow, but keeps peace with the other humors, and does not
stir up quarrels with its brothers. The watery humor, inferior

humor et in morbos iam declinare recusat,
30 quamvis germanae soleat putredinis esse
proximus et varias languoris gignere pestes.
Hic faex humorum faecem deponit et omnes
ingenitos mores melius morata recidit.
    Ex his materiem ductam Natura monetat
35 in speciem vultus humani corporis aptans
materiae, cuius miratur turba decorem,
parque suum stupet in terra decor ipse decorum.
Omnes divitias formae diffundit in illo
Naturae praelarga manus. Post munera pauper
40 paene fuit Natura parens, quae dona decoris,
formae thesauros vultu deponit in uno.
Spirat in hac forma Narcissus, et alter Adonis
spirat in hac specie, quam si Venus altera rursum
cerneret, in solitum decurreret illa furorem.
45 Hoc simul in signum speciei donaque formae
cedit quod nulla corpus pinguedine surgit,
sed magis in maciem tendit. Sic omnia iuste
possidet: in nullo decor eius claudicat, immo
nil maius conferre potest Natura vel ultra.
50 [Nil imperfectum, quia perfectissimus actor,
nec maius voluit quam quod satis omnibus esset,
nec decuit fecisse minus qui plus potuisset.]
Haec igitur species tantum praetendit honoris
quod sese possit tute committere laudi
55 Invidiae laudemque suo mereatur ab hoste.
    Postquam materiem Naturae dextra beavit
vultibus humanis, animam Concordia carni
foederat et stabili connectit dissona nexu.
Iunctura tenui, gunfis subtilibus aptat

434

to these, flows below, and refuses to deviate into disease,   30
though it is wont to be closely associated with rottenness,
and give rise to various enfeebling illnesses. Here the dirti-
est of the humors puts aside its dirt and eliminates all its inherent traits to become better behaved.

Nature stamps the matter drawn from the elements into
a form, applying the shape of the human body to her mate-   35
rial. The throng marvels at its beauty, and beauty itself is astonished to see its equal on earth. The bounteous hand of
Nature showers on it all her wealth of beauty. After such lar-
gess mother Nature is almost a pauper, for she bestows all   40
her graces, her treasury of beauty, on a single form. Narcissus lives and breathes in this form, and a second Adonis in
this body. If a second Venus were to behold this body, she
would quickly succumb to her wonted madness. Nature also   45
granted this mark of beauty and grace of form: nowhere
does the body swell to fatness; instead it tends to leanness.
Thus the body truly possesses all gifts; in no respect is its
beauty flawed; indeed Nature can confer nothing grander,
nothing more. [There is no imperfection, for the creator is   50
supremely perfect; He willed no more than would be wholly
sufficient, and to do less would not have befit one who could
have done more.] This beauty displays such nobility that it
could safely offer itself for praise to Envy herself, and would   55
win praise from an enemy.

After the hand of Nature has blessed her material with
human form, Concord joins soul to body, and links these disparate substances with a firm bond. With delicate jointure

60 composito simplex, hebeti subtile, ligatque
    foedere complacito, carni divina maritat.
    Sic nocti lucem connectit et aethera terrae;
    sic diversa tenent pacem, sic dissona litem
    deponunt propriam. Nec iam caro bella minatur,
65 spiritui cedens sed non sine murmure multo.
    Nec iam corpoream vestem fastidit abhorrens
    spiritus, hospitio tali laetatus et umbra.
        Ut melius concludat opus Concordia, virgo
    quae nobis numeri doctrinam spondet et illa
70 quae monstrat vocum nexus et vincla sonorum,
    assistunt operi coepto firmantque duorum
    connubium, numerisque ligant et foedere certo
    nectunt, ut carni nubat substantia caeli.
        Ergo novus formatur homo. Miratur in illo
75 se tantum potuisse potens Natura stupensque
    vix opus esse suum credit quod fecerat ipsa.
    Accumulat dotes praedictas Copia, pleno
    perfundens cornu Naturae munera, nullam
    mensurae metam retinens in munere tanto,
80 et cornu, quod nulla prius munuscula, nullum
    exhausit munus, totum diffunditur in quo
    se probat et quantum possit metitur in illo.
        Accedit Favor in dotem, ne tanta priorum
    munera perfectae perdant praeconia laudis.
85 His favet ergo Favor, donans ut dona placere
    possint et celeri perflat tot munera Fama,
    quae, quamvis soleat verum corrumpere falso,

and intricate fastenings she adapts simple to composite, 60
subtle to sluggish, and binds them together in an agreeable
union, marries the divine to the flesh. In this way she joins
night to day, heaven to earth. Thus disparate things maintain peace, thus incompatibles lay aside their hostility; the
flesh no longer threatens war, but gives way to the spirit, 65
though not without much grumbling. No longer does the
horrified spirit disdain its fleshly garment, but instead rejoices at such a dwelling and outward form.

That Concord may complete her work well, the maiden
who affirms for us the doctrine of numbers and she who 70
shows us the joining of voices and the pattern of notes join
in the task at hand, and make firm the marriage of the two
components; they bind them with numbers and impose a
clear marriage compact, that heavenly substance may be
wedded to earthly flesh.

Thus the new man is realized. Powerful Nature marvels
at having been capable of so much; in her amazement she 75
can scarcely believe that what she has created is her own
work. Abundance brings together the aforementioned gifts
of Nature, and pours them from her full horn, setting no
limit on the quantity of this great endowment. And the horn 80
which no previous gifts, small or great, had exhausted, now
pours forth all it contains, and shows how great a quantity it
is capable of giving.

Grace comes forward with her gift, lest the great gifts
granted before should be denied the voice of unstinting
praise. Grace therefore graces them, bestowing on them the 85
power to please, and commends this abundance of attributes to the breath of swift Fame. Fame, though accustomed
to contaminating truth with falsehood, in this case can

437

hic nescit nisi vera loqui; moresque vetustos
exuit, et de se retinet sibi nomina Famae;
90   non ibi laus sine re, non res sine laude, suamque
curat ab ypocrisi laudem res digna favore.
      Munera laetitiae largitur grata Iuventus,
et quamvis huius soleat Lascivia semper
esse comes, deponit eam moresque severos
95   induit atque senis imitatur moribus aevum:
in senium transit morum gravitate Iuventus.
Sic aetate viret iuvenis, quod mente senescit,
aetatem superat sensus, primordia floris
anticipat fructus et rivum praevenit amnis;
100   aevo concludit animus, dum dispare ritu
pugnant: hoc iuvenem loquitur, probat ille senectam.
      Risus adest, non ille tamen quem saepe maligna
gignit abortivum derisio, livor ab intus
parturit, aut extra falsi describit amoris
105   forma, vel instabilis crebro Lascivia pingit;
sed multum gravitatis habens vultumque modeste
inscribens, nullo deformans ora cacchino,
talis erat risus, nullo corruptus abusu,
qualem causa locus tempus persona requirit.
110   His Pudor accedit, longe fermenta relegans
Luxuriae, Veneris declinans dulce venenum,
incestusque sitim redeuntem grata Pudoris
extinguit saties, fluctusque libidinis a se
depellit, vincitque fuga, non Marte, Dionem.
115   Yppolitus redit in vitam, redit alter in orbem
Helyas veteremque Ioseph novus alter adaequat.

speak only truth. She abandons her traditional behavior, and keeps for herself only the title of Fame. Now no praise is 90 without substance, no real quality is denied praise; a subject truly worthy of applause cures her praise of hypocrisy.

Charming Youth bestows the gift of pleasure, and though Wantonness is commonly the constant companion of Youth, he now rejects her, assumes a serious character, and 95 emulates the conduct of a grave elder; in the gravity of his character Youth has passed into old age. Thus in years he is a vigorous youth, but because he has the mind of an older man his understanding exceeds his years; fruition occurs before the first flowering, the river before the stream. Mind argues 100 against years, though the two quarrel in differing fashions; one asserts his youth, the other seeks to prove his age.

Mirth is at hand, but it is not that misbegotten kind that malign mockery breeds, to which envy of itself gives birth; that which the outward appearance of false love portrays, or 105 giddy wantonness so often exhibits. Instead it is possessed of much gravity, alters his expression to a moderate extent, does not twist his mouth with jeering. This Mirth is not contaminated by abusiveness, but such as purpose, place, time, and personal dignity require.

Chastity joins them, setting the leaven of Lechery at a 110 distance, refusing the sweet poison of Venus. Chastity's pleasure in sufficiency quells the recurring thirst of unchaste desire, and keeps away the surges of lust. She conquers Dione by flight, not by attack. Hippolytus comes back to life, 115 another Elijah appears in the world, a new, second Joseph equals the Joseph of old.

Forma pudicitiae custosque Modestia dotes
apponit proprias et donum cetera vincens
dona, nec in dando mensuram deserit, immo
120   singula describit certi moderamine finis.
Totum componit hominem, contemperat actus
verbaque metitur, libratque silentia, gestus
ponderat, appendit habitus sensusque refrenat.
Admonet instanter ut nil agat unde pudendum,
125   unde pudor frontem signet mentemque reatus
torqueat, aut Famae titulos infamia laedat.
Demonstrat quae verba, quibus vel quando tacenda
quaeve loqui deceat, ne vel dicenda tacendo
strangulet, aut nimio largus sermone tacenda
130   evomat, atque seram diffuso subtrahat ori.
Describit gestum capitis faciemque venuste
suscitat ad recti libram, ne fronte supina
ad superos tendens, videatur spernere nostros
mortales, nostram dedignans visere terram,
135   vel nimis in terram faciem demissus, inhertem
desertumque notet animum. Moderatius ergo
erigitur, nec enim surgit vel decidit ultra
mensuram.
    Signans mentem Constantia vultus
scurriles prohibet gestus nimiumque severos
140   abdicat incesssus, ne vel lascivia scurram
praedicet, aut fastus nimius rigor exprimat usum.
Et ne degeneres scurrili more lacertos
exserat et turpi vexet sua bracchia gestu,
aut fastum signans ulnas exemplet in arcum,
145   admonet illa virum, vel ne delibet eundo
articulisque pedum terram, vix terrea tangens,

Modesty, the model and guardian of chaste conduct, makes her contribution, and gives one gift that surpasses all others; yet in giving it she does not exceed due measure, but rather subjects all other gifts to the control of a fixed limit. 120 She brings composure to the whole man, tempers his actions, measures his speech; gives weight to his silences, dignity to his gestures, gravity to his character; governs his senses. She sternly advises him against any shameful act, lest 125 shame leave its mark on his countenance, guilt torment his mind, or infamy damage his reputation. She shows him what words should not be spoken, and what words it is appropriate to speak, and to whom, and when, lest he suppress useful speech with silence, or speak too freely, spewing forth what should be kept silent, opening the door for loose talk. She 130 shows the proper carriage of the head, and gracefully raises his face to the proper level, lest by stretching toward the sky with head thrown back he should seem to scorn us mortals, disdaining to look upon our earth, or, by lowering his gaze 135 toward the ground, reveal a sluggish and dejected spirit. Thus his head is held modestly erect, not held inordinately high, not overly cast down.

Self-Possession, setting her seal on his mind, forbids buffoonish facial expressions, and denies him an overly solemn bearing, lest wantons declare him a clown, or too great severity 140 reveal a habitual arrogance. She warns him not to stretch forth unruly limbs in a clownish way, throw out his arms in unseemly gestures, or show scorn by setting his arms akimbo. And so that in walking he will not merely kiss the 145 earth with his toes, barely touching the ground, she trains

eius legitimo firmat vestigia gressu;
ne cultu nimio crinis lascivus adaequet
femineos luxus sexusque recidat honorem,
150 aut nimis incomptus iaceat, squalore profundo
degener et iuvenem proprii neglectus honoris
philosophum nimis esse probet, tenet inter utrumque
illa modum proprioque locat de more capillos;
non habitum cultus nimio splendore serenat,
155 nec squalore premit, mediocriter omnia pensat.
Ne vitanda foris oculus venetur et auris,
mellifluae vocis dulci seducta canore,
seducat mentem deceptaque naris odore
defluat in luxus, visum castigat et aurem,
160 frenat odoratum; vel ne dulcore saporis
desipiens, gustus mentem nimium sapiendo
decipiat, sensum gustus contemperat. usum
Tactus componit, ne devius erret et intus
mentem sollicitet, Veneris praeludia quaerens
165 exterius nostrae ferens vexilla Diones.
    Non minor in donis Ratio succedit et omne
diffundit munus, nunc primum prodiga donis,
iampridem quae parca fuit iam parcere dono
desinit, ipsa tamen redeunt cum faenore dona.
170 Illa monet iuvenem monitu seniore senisque
largitur mores iuveni. Docet ergo repente
ne quid agat subitumve nil praesumat, at omne
factum praeveniat animo, deliberet ante
quam faciat, primumque suos examinet actus,
175 dividat a falso verum, secernat honestum
a turpi, vitium fugiens, sectator honesti.
Promittat raro, det crebrius, immo petentem
munere praeveniat, ne sit res empta rogatu;

his feet to an appropriate gait. Lest he be too wanton in ar-
ranging his hair and approach feminine extravagance, de-
tracting from the honor of his sex, or lest it remain too un-   150
kempt, slovenly in its utter squalor, and this neglect of his
proper dignity prove the young man to be too much the philosopher, she adopts a mean between these two, and arranges his hair in her own way. She does not brighten the
style of his clothing with excessive splendor, or debase by   155
squalor, but maintains a tactful balance in all things. Lest his
eye seek out what it should avoid; and his ear, seduced by
the sweet tone of a mellifluous voice, seduce his mind, and
his nose be drawn to extravagance, deceived by sweet odors,
she disciplines sight and hearing, and trains his sense of   160
smell. And lest taste, dizzied by sweet flavors, should distract his mind by too much tasting, she restrains the exercise of this sense. She controls his use of touch, lest it go
astray and disturb the mind within by setting forth in search
of the games of Venus, bearing the standard of our Dione.   165

Reason follows, no less generous, and pours forth all her
gifts, now for the first time prodigal in her largesse. She who
has long been frugal now ceases to be frugal in giving, but
these are gifts that return with interest. She advises the   170
young man with an elder's admonition, and bestows on his
youth an elder's character. Thus she teaches him to do nothing abruptly, not to act on a sudden impulse, but to first
think about what he will do, to reflect before acting, to eval-
uate his acts in advance; to distinguish true from false, honor   175
from baseness, fleeing vice, pursuing what is honorable. He
should promise rarely but give often, and indeed anticipate
the petitioner with his gift, lest it should seem to have been

si quid promittat, promissum munus adaequet
180 vel superet, ne re maior spes gaudia vincat.
Promissum comitetur opus, ne tarda sequantur
munera, ne doni merito dantisque favori
detrahat et donum minuat dilatio dantis.
    Non fluat in motus varios, sed firmiter uni
185 insistat mens fixa bono, ne singula temptans
nil teneat, ne sic animus discurrat ubique
quod nusquam; ne planta recens translata frequenter
areat, aut varii temptans medicaminis usum,
invaleat morbus; ne mens sic omnibus assit
190 quod nulli, sic cuncta probet quod singula perdat.
    Nec petat impelli populari laude, nec ipsam
respuat oblatam, nisi sit velata colore
Ypocrisis, verbo quaerens emungere lucrum;
nam nimis austerum redolet qui despicit omnem
195 famam, mollescitque nimis qui singula Famae
blandimenta petit, populari deditus auri;
non animo facili, non aure bibente favorem
audiat ypocritas laudes, mendacia famae,
palponis faleras qui verba sophistica pingit
200 et dulci laudum sonitu citarizat in aure
divitis et vendit laudes ad pondera doni.
    Post Rationis opes et tantum munus, Honestas
thesaurum reserat proprium iuvenemque suarum
custodem decernit opum, deponit in illo
205 quidquid habet, ius omne sui transfundit in illum.

bought by begging. If he should make a promise, what is
given must equal or exceed what was promised, lest a hope 180
greater than the reality defeat enjoyment. And the performance must be the companion of the promise; the gift must
not follow later, lest the donor's delay detract from the value
of what is given and the kindness of the giver, and make the
gift seem insignificant.

He must not be drawn in several directions, but his mind
should stand firm, directed to a single good, lest in attempt- 185
ing many things he attain none, lest his mind, scurrying everywhere, should find itself nowhere; for a plant frequently
transplanted will wither; one who tests the value of several
medicines may lend strength to the illness; a mind that applies itself to everything may learn nothing, so eager to try 190
all that it fails at each.

He should neither seek the stimulus of popular acclaim,
nor scorn it when it is offered, unless it is veiled by the rhetoric of Hypocrisy, seeking to obtain money deceitful words;
for he who wholly despises reputation appears overly aus- 195
tere, while he who seeks every sweet caress of Fame, surrendering himself to the popular audience, is too easily swayed.
He must not listen with an eager mind, and an ear that grows
drunk on applause, to the praise of hypocrites, the deceptions of fame, the smooth charms of the flatterer who cleverly adorns his speech, serenades the the rich man with the 200
sweet sound of praise, and sells his praises according to the
weight of the reward.

After Reason's rich and generous gift, Honesty throws
open her treasury, and declares the young man the guardian
of her wealth. She gives him in charge all that she possesses, 205
makes over to him the right to all of it. She warns him to

Infames vitare monet, ne fama laboret,
ne vicina bonos laedant contagia mores.
Ut vitium fugiat, Naturam diligat, illud
quod facinus peperit damnans, quod prava voluntas
210 edidit, amplectans quidquid Natura creavit,
non homines sed monstra cavens et crimina vitans;
sic instans vitio, quod rerum parcat honori,
in commune bonus, ne lux abscondita parce
luceat et fructus det virtus clausa minores;
215 interius sibimet, ut pauci, vivat, et extra
ut plures, intus sibi vivens, pluribus extra;
ut mundo natum se credat, ut omnibus omnis
pareat, et sapiens sese cognoscat in illo,
ne loca denigrent famam, ne tempora reddant
220 suspectum vitaeque modus rerumque facultas.
   Praedictis succedit Honor, praedicta colorans
luce sua, nullamque sinit sentire lituram
dedecoris, sed cuncta suo perlustrat honore
muneris, et proprio cultu decus omnia vestit,
225 non minus irradians aliarum facta sororum
quam rosa cognatos flores, quam Lucifer ignes
sidereos lapidumque iubar carbunculus auget.
   Assistens Fronesis pluit omnia dona Sophiae.
Non illas largitur opes quae saepe potentum
230 excaecant animos et maiestatis honorem
inclinant, minuunt leges et iura retardant,
sed potius donat thesaurum mentis et omnes
divitias animi, quas qui semel accipit, ultra

avoid low company, lest his reputation suffer, lest close contact with contagion damage his good character. He must
flee from vice and devote himself to Nature, repudiating
whatever villainy has spawned, whatever a depraved will has   210
brought forth, embracing only what Nature has created,
shunning not men but their monstrous acts, and keeping
wickedness far off; standing so firm against vice that he
keeps honor alive in the world, a good man for the benefit of
all. His light must not be hidden and shine faintly, a clois-
tered virtue that yields little fruit. He must be among the   215
few who live inwardly for themselves, and live outwardly as
the many do, living inwardly for himself, outwardly for others. He must believe himself born [to serve] the world, to
show himself all things to all men, and wisely come to know
himself in so doing. No place he frequents must damage his
reputation, nor occasion, manner of life, or management of   220
his affairs bring doubt upon him.

Honor is next, and casts her light over all the previous
gifts. She will allow them to reveal no taint of impropriety,
but makes all shine by the honor of her gift. Its beauty in-
vests all with her own elegance, illumining the gifts of the   225
other sisters no less than the rose brightens the flowers
around it, or Lucifer intensifies the starry fires, or a carbun-
cle the gleam of precious stones.

Fronesis, standing forward, pours forth all the gifts of
wisdom. She does not bestow those riches that so often
darken the minds of the powerful, rob majesty of its dignity,   230
diminish the force of law and hinder justice, but instead bestows a treasury of thought and all the riches of the mind.
Whoever has once received these will never again lack them;

non eget, immo semel ditatus semper abundat;
235 quarum rectus amor, possessio nobilis, usus
utilis, utilior largitio, fructus abundans.
Haec est gaza poli, caeli thesaurus, inundans
gratia quae doctos ditat, quae prodiga largos
vult possessores et dedignatur avaros.
240 Clausa perit, diffusa redit; nisi publica fiat,
labitur et multas vires adquirit eundo.
Non istas depascit opes rubigo, nec ignis
devorat, aut furis minuit subreptio, mergit
naufragium, tollit praedo, depauperat hostis.
245   Nec solum Fronesis confert sua dona, sed ultra
procedit, iubet ancillas exponere quicquid
possunt et quodam certamine fundere dona.
Grammaticae doctrina prior praecepta Sophiae
complet et in iuvenem descendit tota, nec in se
250 fit minor, immo magis crescens, grandescit in illo;
omne quod ipsius discernit regula canon
praecipit et dictat artis censura magistrae,
in dotem iuvenis confert, ne verba monetet
citra grammaticam, ne verbo barbarus erret,
255 barbaries quem nulla notat; sic ergo loquendi
recte scribendique viam sectatur et artem
assequitur, damnat vitium toleratque figuram.
Perfundensque virum Pegasei nectare fontis,
turba poetarum docet illum verba ligare
260 metris et dulci carmen depingere rithmo.
   Succedit Logicae virtus arguta, nec alget
munere pigmaeo, verum contendit in illo
spargere divitias, et dandi laxat habenam.
Haec docet argutam Martem rationis inire

once so endowed he will always be wealthy. To cherish these   235
riches is right, to possess them is noble, to use them is profitable, to give them freely more profitable, and they produce
an abundant reward. This is the wealth of heaven, celestial
treasure, an abounding grace that makes rich those who are
wise, which, prodigal itself, wishes its possessors to be generous, and disdains the avaricious. Locked away it perishes;   240
spread abroad it repays the giver. If it is not made public it is
powerless; by going forth it gains great strength. No rust
feeds on these riches, no fire consumes them, the stealth of
the thief does not diminish them, shipwreck sink them, the
bandit carry them off, or enemies destroy them.

Not only does Fronesis bestow her gifts, she goes further,   245
and orders her handmaids to bring forth whatever they possess, and shower down gifts as if in competition. Grammar
is the first to comply with Sophia's instruction, and all of her
doctrine enters the young man's mind, yet in itself it is made   250
no less, but indeed increases, and achieves full growth in
him. All that her rules define, that her laws enjoin, that a
stern teacher of the art demands, she bestows on the youth,
lest he should coin words ungrammatically, or commit barbarous faults in speech, he in whom no taint of barbarism   255
appears. Thus he will follow the path of correct speech and
writing, study the art closely, condemn vice and be merely
tolerant of trope. The poetic host, showering him with the
nectar of the Pegasean font, teach him to link words in me-   260
ter and to fashion a song with sweet rhythm.

The keen force of Logic comes next. She does not coldly
offer a tiny gift, but strives to shower her riches upon him,
and gives free rein to her giving. She teaches him how to engage in the lively wars of reasoning, to construct arguments

449

265 adversae parti concludere, frangere vires
opposites partemque suam ratione tueri,
vestigare viam veri falsumque fugare,
scismaticos logicae falsosque retundere fratres
et pseudologicos et denudare sophistas.

270 Assunt Rethoricae cultus floresque colorum,
verba quibus stellata nitent et sermo decorem
induit, et multa splendescit clausula luce.
Has sermonis opes, cultus et sidera verbi
copia Rethoricae iactat iuvenisque loquelam

275 pingit et in vario praesignit verba colore.
Succincte docet illa loqui sensusque profundos
sub sermone brevi concludere, claudere multa
sub paucis nec diffuso sermone vagari,
ut breve sit verbum, dives sententia, sermo

280 facundus, multi fecundus pondere sensus;
vel si forte fluat sermo sub flumine verbi,
fulminet uberior sententia, copia fructus
excuset folii silvam, paleasque vagantes
ubertas grani redimat sensusque loquelam.

285 Donat opes ars illa suas, quae semina rerum,
foedera, complexus, causas et vincula certis
legibus inquirit, numeros vestigat et omnes
discutit effectus, quibus omnia fixa tenentur,
sub vicibus constricta suis numerisque ligantur

290 cuncta simul, pacemque tenent, cessante tumultu.
Ergo virum, sua denudans secreta Minervae,
heredem facit esse suum, iuvenique revelat
scibile quicquid habet, quicquid sua copia fundit:
quae ratio numeris, quae virtus quaeve potestas

against the contrary position, to break the force of the op- 265
posing argument, and to defend his own position with reasoning, to seek out the path of truth and put the false to
flight, to retaliate against schismatics, false friends and
pseudologicians, and expose sophistry.

At hand also are the elegances of Rhetoric and its flowers 270
of speech, through which words shine like stars, a discourse
acquires dignity, and a final phrase gives out a brilliant light.
The bounty of Rhetoric casts forth these riches of speech,
these graces and brilliants of language, adorns the young
man's speaking and dignifies his words with a variety of col- 275
ors. She teaches him to speak succinctly, to compress profound thoughts into a brief discourse, to convey many things
in few words, and not to stray into a rambling discourse. The
words must be brief, their meaning rich, the speech engag- 280
ing and charged with the weight of much thought. Or if a
discourse should flow into a river of speech, let a richer
meaning give it force, an abundance of fruit justify the leafy
forest, a rich harvest of grain atone for scattered straw, sense
for loquaciousness.

That art bestows its riches which seeks out the seeds of 285
things, their union, relation, causes and bonds, according
to fixed laws, explores number, and probes into the laws by
which all things maintain a fixed relation, confined to their
courses, and all are bound together by number and dwell in 290
peace, all tumult stilled. Now, unveiling the hidden depths
of her wisdom, she makes the youth her heir, and reveals to
him all the knowledge she possesses, all that her abundance
can pour forth: what is the nature of numbers, what quality

295 insit, et in numeris quae tanta potentia regnet,
     ut numeri nodo stabilis liget omnia nexus.
     Musica divitias aperit, sua munera multo
     plena favore viro concedit, adoptat eundem,
     omne suum velut heredi delegat eidem:
300 quae vox displiceat voci, quae consonet illi
     monstrat, amicitias vocum rixasque sonorum
     edocet, et quae vox turbet, quae debriet aurem.
     Explicitas in dona manus ars illa relaxat,
     quae terrae spatium, tractus maris, aëris altos
305 discursus, caeli fines metitur, et omne
     corpus sub certo describit fine nec altum
     impedit, immensum tardat retrahitque profundum.
     Illa virum docet in spatio concludere terram,
     aëra metiri, mare sistere, claudere caelum
310 finibus et teretem mundi describere formam.
     Astrorum doctrina suum componit in illo
     hospitium, quo nulla magis sibi complacet aula.
     Illa docet quis motus agit caelestia, stellas
     excitat, aut caeli quis spiritus incitat orbem.
315 Hoc doni titulo mundi Sapientia ditat
     praesignitque virum; sed eum divinius afflans,
     ars divina poli, veri via, nescia falsi,
     ars quae sola fide gaudet subnixa nec arte
     nititur, humanae fugiens rationis asilum,
320 gratius arrisit, animam cum caelicus ignis
     in superis retineret adhuc splendorque serenus
     aspiraret ei, nec nostras aëris imi
     pressuras pateretur adhuc nec taedia mundi.
     Illa docet caeleste sequi, vitare caducum,
325 vivere lege poli, sursum suspendere mentem,

and force is in them, why their governing power is so great   295
that a stable bond links all things with the bond of number.

Music presents her wealth, with great kindness grants all
her gifts to the man; she claims him as her own, and assigns
to him all that she has, as to an heir. She shows him how   300
one note jars unpleasantly with another, or how they complement one another. She teaches him about harmony and
dissonance among sounds, which disturb and which soothe
the ear.

The art that measures the breadth of the earth, the regions of the sea, the lofty expanses of the air, the bounds of   305
heaven, which assigns a definite size to every body, she
whom no height deters, no distance wearies, no depth withstands, extends her open hands in giving. She teaches the
man how to confine the earth in a definite space, to take the
measure of the air, to still the ocean, set boundaries around
the heavens, and to define the round shape of the universe.   310

The science of the stars makes its home in him, and no
palace could be more pleasing to her. She teaches him what
force drives the heavenly bodies, sets the stars in motion,
what spirit impels the celestial sphere.

With this array of gifts earthly Wisdom enriches and hon-   315
ors the man. But the divine art of heaven, the school of
truth that knows no falsehood, the art which rejoices to be
founded on faith alone, and relies on no human art, wholly
rejecting the aid of human reason, has gladly smiled on him,
granting him divine inspiration, while the fiery heaven still   320
held his soul on high, and its serene splendor infused him;
when he was not yet subject to the afflictions of our lower
air and the world's suffering. She teaches him to pursue the
divine, shun what is mortal, to live by heavenly law, elevate   325

fastidire solum, caelum conscendere mente,
corporis insultus frenare, refellere luxus
carnis et illicitos rationi subdere motus.
   Succedens Pietas se totam donat et offert
330 in munus, tantumque viro committit ut ipse
credatur Pietas, tantae pietatis alumnus.
Haec docet ut maculas animi complanet et omnes
deponat nubes odii, mens cerea fiat,
si respersa semel fuerit pietatis olivo,
335 sic tamen ut numquam firmae constantia mentis
deviet a recto ne, si pietate remissus
mollescat iuvenis, magnos effeminet actus
mollities, perdatque viri mens fracta rigorem.
Haec docet ut miseri lacrimas, incommoda, casus
340 iudicet esse suos, nec se putet esse beatum,
dum superesse videt in multis unde dolendum;
defendat viduas, miseros soletur, egenos
sustentet, pascat inopes foveatque pupillos.
   Adnectens sua dona Fides in munere multo
345 se probat esse Fidem, nec se sibi subtrahit, immo
monstrat et in dono se disputat esse fidelem.
Illa docet vitare dolos, contemnere fraudes,
foedus amicitie, fidei ius, pignus amoris
illaesa servare fide, nec nomine falso
350 pseudo- vel ypocritam simulare latenter amicum.
Praeterea monet illa virum ne quaerat amicos
Fortunae comites, cum qua mutentur et assint,
vel fugiant, casusque vices et fata sequantur,

his mind, scorn the earth, and ascend to heaven in thought, to restrain the impulses of the body, put down fleshly desire, and subject unlawful urges to reason.

Compassion follows. She makes a gift of herself and with this offer she entrusts herself to him so completely that he 330 too, nourished by such piety, could himself be called "Compassion." She teaches him to clear the stains from his spirit and dispel all the clouds of hatred; for his mind, once anointed with the oil of compassion, will become more tractable, though in such a way that the constancy of his stead- 335 fast mind will never stray from the right, and though the youth be softened by the influence of Compassion, this softness will not rob his actions of strength, nor a ruined character destroy his force of will. She teaches him to consider that the tears of the wretched, their hardships, their ill fortune 340 are his own, that he should not think himself happy while he can see that there remains much to lament in the lives of many. He must protect the widow, console those who grieve, give aid to those in need, feed the poor and show kindness to the orphan.

Good Faith too adds her gifts, and by her great generosity proves that she is indeed Good Faith, nor does she diminish 345 herself, but rather reveals, and in her giving strongly asserts, that she is good and faithful. She teaches him to avoid guile, to scorn deceitfulness, to be unfailingly trustworthy in preserving the bond of friendship, the duty of keeping faith, the pledge of love, and not to falsely pretend a friendship 350 that conceals pretense or hypocrisy. She further warns him not to seek as friends the companions of Fortune, who change, come and go as she does, and subject themselves to the accidents and vicissitudes of fate; who disappear with

qui cum Fortunae fugitivo vere recedant,
355   adversi casus hyemes et nubila vitent.
Haec iuvenem docet ut numquam mercetur amicum
munere, nec doni merito venetur amorem;
nam pretio quaesitus amor cum munere cedit,
et quantum durat largitio durat amicus;
360   prostat talis amor, mensuram muneris implens.
Non ibi vera Fides ubi munus donat amorem;
non donum largitur amor, dum pondus amoris
ponderat ipsa dati merces et copia doni,
sed precis et pretii venali lege relicta
365   quaerat quem vero sic complectatur amore
illaesaque fide quod amor lucretur amorem
alterius, referatque novos amor alter amores.
Sicque relativa dilectio, mutuus adsit
nexus amicitiae, quem nec Fortuna novercans
370   solvat, nec casus agitet, nec gloria frangat.
Quaerat cui possit se totum credere, velle
declarare suum totamque exponere mentem,
cui sua committat animi secreta latentis,
ut sibi conservans thesaurum mentis in illo,
375   nil sibi secretum quod non develet eidem,
ut suus in tali signo mensuret amicus
pondus amicitiae, quam lance rependat eadem.

    Subsequitur virtus quae gaudet fundere dona,
spargere divitias et opum diffundere massam,
380   quae census nutrire vitat vel pascere nummos,
nec sinit ignavam secum torpescere gazam,
nec bursam satiat nummis, sed cogit eandem
ad vomitum, si quid census absorbuit umquam.
Olim parca viris, nunc uni prodiga, sese

the fleeting springtime of Fortune, and avoid the winter 355
clouds of adversity. She teaches the young man that he
should never buy friendship with rewards, or seek love by
virtue of a gift. For love sought at a price ceases when gifts
cease, and the friendship lasts no longer than one's largesse.
Such love prostitutes itself in proportion to the amount of 360
the reward. There can be no true trust where a gift brings
love; for it is not love that bestows the gift if the quantity of
love is weighed against the price and amount of the gift. Instead she bids him leave behind the mercenary law of plead-
ing and paying, and seek one whom he may embrace in true 365
love, in untroubled assurance that it is love that gains the
love of another, and that the other's love brings a renewal of
love. Thus let affection be reciprocal, let the bond of friendship be mutually present, a bond that neither the perversity
of Fortune can break nor hardship threaten nor vainglory 370
destroy. He should seek a friend to whom he can wholly entrust himself, declare his desires and reveal his thoughts; to
whom he can impart secrets of his heart, thus preserving in
his friend the treasure of his own mind. There will be no se- 375
cret that he does not reveal to the other, that his friend may
gauge the weight of his friendship, and repay it in equal measure.

Next comes the virtue who rejoices to pour forth gifts, to
spread her riches abroad and disperse the bulk of her wealth;
who refuses to nurse her capital, or put her money out to 380
graze. She will not allow treasure to lie idle and grow fat in
her care; she does not glut her purse with coin, but forces it
to vomit whatever wealth it may have swallowed. Long stint-
ing to mankind, she now gives prodigally to a single man,

385 transcendit, viresque suas excedit in uno.
Haec docet ut mentem dono suspendat ab omni,
excutiatque manum nec opum succumbat amori.
Divitias animo calcans et mente triumphans,
sic conculcet opes ne conculcetur ab illis,
390 ne manus ad donum currat nexuque tenaci
viscus avaritie munus constringat adeptum,
neve relativam mercedem munera quaerant;
nec lucrum sitiat nec praemia munus adoret;
sed sine spe reditus fundantur munera sparsim.
395 Solaque nobilitas et simplex gratia mentis
informet munus et doni condiat usum.

Post alias sua dona libens et laeta dedisset
filia Fortunae, Casus cognata propinqui
Nobilitas, si quid proprium cessisset in eius
400 sortem, quod posset Naturae lege tueri.
Sed quia nulla potest nisi quae Fortuna ministrat,
nil sine consilio Fortunae perficit. Immo
matris adire domum disponit filia, gressum
aggreditur superatque viae dispendia cursu.

405 Est rupes maris in medio, quam verberat aequor
assidue, cum qua corrixans litigat unda,
quae variis agitata modis percussaque motu
continuo; nunc tota latens sepelitur in undis,
nunc exuta mari superas respirat in auras;
410 quae nullam retinet formam, quam singula mutant
in varias momenta vices, quae sidera florum
iactat et in multo laetatur gramine rupes,
dum leni Zephirus inspirat singula flatu;
sed cito deflorat flores, et gramina saevus
415 deperdit Boreas, ubi, dum flos incipit esse,

rises above herself, and exceeds her own powers in this one 385
instance. She teaches him to restrain thought in his giving,
stretch out his hand freely, and not succumb to the love of
wealth. Viewing riches with scorn and triumphant in mind,
let him trample upon wealth, lest it trample on him, lest his 390
hand be too quick to accept a gift, and the snare of avarice
seize the gift received in its tight grasp, lest his gifts should
seek a reward in return. A gift must not thirst for money or
appeal for a reward, but his gifts must flow forth freely with
no hope of recompense. Only a noble spirit and sheer be- 395
nevolence should prompt his gifts, and enhance the act of
giving.

   After the others Nobility, daughter of Fortune and near
kin to Chance, would readily and happily have offered her
gifts, if anything had fallen to her lot that she could claim by 400
the law of Nature. But since she possesses nothing except
what Fortune assigns her, she does nothing without consult-
ing Fortune. Thus the daughter decides to visit the home
of her mother; she sets out and soon conquers the winding
path.

   There is a rock in the midst of the ocean against which 405
the sea pounds tirelessly, which the quarrelsome waves assail, which is troubled in many ways and subject to continual
change. Now it is wholly hidden, buried by the waves, now it
emerges from the sea and breathes the air above. It retains 410
no single appearance, for each moment alters it in a different
way: it puts forth bright flowers, and rejoices in rich herbage
when Zephyrus inspires each living thing with his gentle
breath. But suddenly fierce Boreas blights the blossoms and 415

explicit, et florum momento sistitur aetas.
Sicque furens Aquilo praedatur singula, flores
frigoris ense metit et pristina gaudia delet.
    Hic nemus ambiguum diversaque nascitur arbor:
420   ista manet sterilis, haec fructum parturit; illa
fronde nova gaudet, haec frondibus orphana plorat,
una viret, plures arescunt, unaque floret,
efflorent aliae; quaedam consurgit in altum,
demittuntur humi reliquae; dum pullulat una,
425   marcescunt aliae. Varius sic alterat illas
casus et in variis alternant motibus omnes.
Multa per antiphrasim gerit illic alea casus:
pigmaea brevitate sedens demissaque cedrus
desinit esse gigas et nana mirica gigantem
430   induit: alterius sic accipit altera formam.
Marcescit laurus, mirtus parit, aret oliva,
fit fecunda salix, sterilis pirus, orphana fructu
pomus et in partu contendit vitibus ulmus.
Hic iaculis armata suis spineta minantur
435   vulnus et insultans manibus nocet hispida taxus.
Hic raro Philomena canit, citharizat alauda;
crebrius hic miseros eventus bubo prophetat,
nuntius adversi casus et praeco doloris.
    Hic duo decurrunt fluvii quos dividit ortus
440   dissimilis, dispar vultus, diversa coloris
forma, sapor varius, distans substantia fontis.
Praedulces habet alter aquas mellitaque donans
pocula, melle suo multos seducit et haustae
plus sitiuntur aquae. Potantes debriat, immo
445   dum satiat, parit unda sitim potusque sititur
amnis et innumeros ydropicat ille bibentes.

destroys the grasses; the flower concludes its life even as it begins, and its span is ended in an instant. Raging Aquilo preys on everything, cuts down the flowers with his icy sword, and destroys their former joys.

Here a strange grove and a diversity of trees are born: this 420 one remains barren, that produces fruit; this rejoices in new foliage, that is sad, bereft of its leaves; one flourishes, many are withered; one flowers, others are bare; one grows tall, the rest are low to the ground; while one burgeons, others 425 are blighted. Thus the shifts of chance affect them all; all in turn are subjected to the forces of change. A roll of the dice brings about many contradictory effects here: reduced to pigmean smallness a diminished cedar ceases to be a giant, and the dwarfish tamarisk assumes gigantic stature; each 430 tree assumes the shape of another. The laurel withers, the myrtle bears fruit, the olive is parched, the willow becomes fertile, the pear tree is sterile, the apple bereft of fruit, while the elm vies with the vine in bearing. Here thorn bushes, armed with their spears, threaten to wound, and the unruly, 435 bristling yew hurts one's hands. Here Philomela's song and the music of the lark are rare, but the owl, messenger of mischance and herald of sorrow, continually utters prophecies of dire events.

Two streams flow here, distinguished by their dissimilar sources, contrasting appearance, different color and taste, 440 and the differing character of their springs. One possesses waters of great sweetness, offering honeyed drafts; it entices many with its sweet flavor, and when its waters are swallowed one's thirst for them increases. It inebriates those who drink; indeed while the water is satisfying thirst it is pro- 445 ducing thirst; to drink of this stream is to become thirsty, and it renders countless drinkers dropsical. It ripples with a

Murmure lascivit tenui dulcique susurro
murmurat et placida rupem praeterfluit unda.
Amnis in ingressu multi sistuntur et ultra
450   non patet accessus, qui dulces fluminis undas
vix tangunt libantque parum, tantoque sapore
tacti plus cupiunt; immergi plenius undis
optant et totos perfundi fluctibus artus.
Procedunt alii quos alto gurgite mersos
455   plenior amnis habet et provehit altior unda;
quos tamen imbutos tanta dulcedine fluctus
ad ripam levis unda refert terraeque remittit.
   Praecipiti lapsu fluctus dilabitur alter
sulfureis tenebrosus aquis. Absintia gignit
460   unda sapore suo, reddit fervore caminum.
Sicque color visum, gustum sapor, impetus aurem
turbat et insipidum fastidit naris odorem.
Non has crispat aquas Zephirus, sed funditus illas
evertens Boreas in montes erigit, undis
465   indicens bellum cognataque proelia miscens.
Fluminis in ripa lacrimarum flumina multos
demergunt qui demergi torrentis abisso
amne furente timent et fluctus ferre tumultum.
Multus in hunc amnem populus descendit et altis
470   consepelitur aquis tumidoque impellitur amne.
Absorbet nunc unda viros, nunc evomit, istos
fluctibus immergit, hos respirare parumper
permittit; sed quamplures sic sorbet abissus
quod revocare gradum superasque evadere ad auras
475   non licet et reditus vestigia nulla supersunt.

gentle murmur, murmurs with a sweet whisper as it flows
over the rock. Many stand at the head of the stream, and
it is forbidden them to approach too near. They taste the   450
stream's sweet waters hardly at all, [yet] once affected by
such a taste they long for more. They yearn to be fully immersed in these waters and let the stream wholly cover their
limbs. Others go further: the swelling stream holds them
immersed in a deep eddy, and deeper water bears them   455
along; but the light current bears them, too, to the bank,
when they have filled themselves with the surpassing sweetness of the water, and leaves them on dry land.

The other stream, with dark and sulfurous waters, flows
over a steep waterfall. The water gives off the smell of worm-   460
wood, and its heat is like that of a furnace. The color troubles sight, the taste the mouth, the onrushing water the ear,
and the nose rejects the unpleasing smell. Zephyrus does
not wrinkle these waters, but Boreas, driving them upward
from their bed, raises them into mountains, declaring war   465
and making the waters battle among themselves. On the
bank of the river, rivers of tears drench the many who fear to
be immersed in the torrential abyss of the raging stream and
suffer the violence of its waters. But many people descend
into it, become buried in its deep waters and are borne along   470
by the swollen stream. At one moment the water draws men
down, at the next it spews them forth; some it submerges in
its flow, yet it allows others a moment to draw breath. But
most the abyss so engulfs that it is not granted them to retrace their steps and emerge into the air above, and no signs   475
of escape can be seen.

Hic fluvius, variis currens anfractibus, intrat
torrentem praedulcis aquae, cogitque fluentum
degenerare luemque suam partitur eidem;
nubilus obtenebrat clarum, fermentat amarus
480   praedulcem, tepidum calidus, fetosus odorum.

Liber Octavus

Rupis in abrupto suspensa minansque ruinam,
Fortunae domus in praeceps descendit et omnem
ventorum patitur rabiem caelique procellas
sustinet et raro Zephiri mansueta serenat
5   aura domum flatusque Nothi Boreaeque rigorem
parcius abstergit lenis clementia flatus.
Pars in monte tumet, pars altera vallis in imo
subsidet, et casum tamquam lapsura minatur.
Fulgurat argento, gemmis scintillat et auro
10   resplendet pars una domus; pars altera vili
materie deiecta iacet; pars ista superbit
culmine sublimi, pars illa fatiscit hiatu.
    Hic est Fortunae sua mansio, si tamen usquam
res manet instabilis, residet vaga, mobilis haeret;
15   cuius tota quies lapsus, constantia motus,
volvere stare, situs discurrere, scandere casus;
cui modus et ratio rationis egere, fidesque
non servare fidem, pietas pietate carere.
Haec est inconstans, incerta volubilis anceps,
20   errans, instabilis, vaga; quae dum stare putatur,

This river, after a variously winding course, flows into the stream of water surpassingly sweet, causing it to become impure and imparting to it its own filth: a cloud darkens the clear water, the bitter pollutes the sweet, the boiling hot 480 overwhelms the cool, the fetid the fragrant.

Book 8

Hanging on a steep cliff and threatening to fall, the home of Fortune extends steeply downward; it suffers the rage of the winds and stormy skies. Rarely does the gentle breeze of Zephyrus smile on the house; too seldom does his gentle, 5 pacifying breath banish the blasts of Notus and the severity of Boreas. Part of the building rises proudly on the mountain, the rest spreads downward into a deep valley and, apparently on the point of collapsing, seems to threaten disaster. One part of the building gleams with silver, sparkles with gems and shines with gold; the other is low-lying, and de- 10 meaned by material of poor quality. One part is proud of its lofty roof, the other's is collapsed and gaping.

It is here that Fortune has her home, if indeed a thing so unstable can ever remain still, a thing so restless be at rest, a thing ever moving sit fast. Total rest for Fortune is random 15 movement, stability is mobility, to be stationary is to whirl, to stand still is to rush about, to climb is to fall. Her method and plan is to have no plan, trust for her is breaking trust, loyalty is to be disloyal. She is capricious, unreliable, ever-changing, ambiguous, random, unsteady, giddy. When she 20

occidit et falso mentitur gaudia risu;
aspera blanditiis, in lumine nubila, pauper
et dives, mansueta ferox praedulcis amara,
ridendo plorans, stando vaga, caeca videndo,
25 in levitate manens, in lapsu firma, fidelis
in falso, levis in vero stabilisque movendo;
hoc firmum servans quod numquam firma, fidele
hoc solum retinens quod nesciat esse fidelis,
hoc solo verax quod semper falsa probetur,
30 hoc solo stabilis quod semper mobilis erret.
     Ambiguo vultu seducit forma videntem.
Nam capitis pars anterior vestita capillis
luxuriat, dum calvitiem pars altera luget.
Alter lascivit oculus, dum profluit alter
35 in lacrimas; hic languet hebes dum fulgurat ille.
Pars vultus vivit, vivo flammata colore;
pars moritur quam pallor habet, qua gratia vultus
expirat, languet facies et forma liquescit.
Una manus donat, retrahit manus altera donum;
40 ampliat haec munus, haec munera contrahit; illa
porrigit, haec aufert; haec comprimit, illa relaxat.
     Gressus inaequalis retrogradus ebrius errans
progrediens retrograditur multumque recedit
procedens, pariter velox et lentus eundo.
45 Nunc meliore toga splendet, nunc paupere cultu
plebescens Fortuna iacet, nunc orphana veste
prostat et antiquos lugere videtur honores.
     Praecipitem movet illa rotam motusque laborem
nulla quies claudit nec sistunt otia motum.
50 Nam cum saepe manum dextram labor ille fatiget
laeva manus succedit ei fessaeque sorori

seems stable she falls away, and feigns joy with a false smile. She is cruel in her kindness, shadow in light, poor and rich, gentle, fierce, sweet, bitter, laughing as she weeps, steadily unsteady, blind to what she sees, consistently capricious, certain to fall, reliably false, true to inconstancy, unvaryingly in motion; holding firmly to never being firm; trustworthy only in her inability to be trusted; truthful only in that she is always found to be false; stable only in being always unstable.

Her appearance deceives the viewer by its doubleness, for the front of her head is abundantly covered with hair, while the back bemoans its baldness. One eye roves wantonly while the other pours forth tears; one is dull and drooping while the other gleams. One side of her face is lively, infused with vivid color; the other is possessed by pallor and seems dead. Here all charm of expression has failed; the face droops and beauty dissolves. One hand gives, the other retracts the gift; one makes the gift bounteous, the other diminishes it; one holds it out, the other snatches it away; one hand clutches, the other lies open.

Her gait is unsteady, halting, drunken, wandering; moving forward she falls back, and she recedes as much as she proceeds. Her pace is at once swift and slow. At one moment she displays herself in a splendid robe, at the next she is cast down, demeaning herself with the rags of poverty; she next offers herself bereft of clothing, and seems to mourn her dignity of old.

She turns a swiftly revolving wheel; no rest brings the labor of turning to an end; the movement of the wheel does not cease. For as often as the task wearies her right hand, the left takes its place, relieving its weary sister and driving

succurrit, motumque rotae velocius urget,
cuius turbo rapax, raptus celer, impetus anceps,
involvens homines, a lapsus turbine nullum
55   excipit; et cunctos fati ludibria ferre
cogit et in varios homines descendere casus.
Hos premit, hos relevat, hos deicit, erigit illos:
summa rotae dum Cresus habet, tenet infima Codrus;
Iulius ascendit, descendit Magnus, et infra
60   Silla iacet; surgit Marius, sed cardine verso
Silla redit, Marius premitur. Sic cuncta vicissim
turbo rapit variatque vices Fortuna volutans.
    Fortunae loca praedicto signata paratu
Nobilitas festina petit matremque salutat
65   adveniens causamque viae praestringit eidem
sub brevibus verbis et matri supplicat, orans
ut si quid praesigne gerat dignumque favore,
quod deceat virtutis opus, quod competat ipsi
Naturae facto, non illud deneget illi
70   quem Natura creat, recreat nova gratia, formant
mores, informat virtus, Prudentia ditat,
praeditat Pietas, afflat Decus, ornat Honestas,
exornat Ratio, species praesignit et omnis
Virtutum cumulus eius concurrit in usum.
75   His dictis, modico risu Fortuna severos
exhilarans vultus, haec natae verba rependit:
"Actus Naturae, virtutis fabrica nostrum
non deposcit opus, nostro non indiget actu.
Tam celebris factura Dei, quam singula ditant
80   munera Naturae, divinaque dona beatam
efficiunt, nulloque caret virtutis honore.
Quid poterit casus ubi casu nulla reguntur?

the wheel's motion ever more swiftly. As it spins it grasps, its grasp is quick and its assaults unexpected; it overwhelms mankind, and exempts no man from its precipitous whirl; 55 it forces all men to endure the antics of fate and succumb to various misfortunes. It oppresses these, eases the lot of those, casts down these, raises up those: while Croesus holds the highest place on the wheel, Codrus has the lowest; Caesar rises, Pompey descends; Sulla lies below as Marius strives 60 upward, but at a turn of the wheel Sulla is restored and Marius is driven down. Thus the whirling captures all in turn, as the shifts of Fortune change their situations.

Nobility hastily travels to the abode of Fortune, distinguished by the condition described above; once arrived she greets her mother, explains to her in a few words the reason 65 for her journey, and appeals to her mother, asking, if she possesses anything excellent and praiseworthy, fit to adorn a work of virtue, fit to complement the handiwork of Nature, that she not withhold it from this being whom Nature is 70 creating, whom a new grace is recreating; whom character forms and virtue informs; whom Providence makes rich and Compassion richer still; whom Beauty imbues, Honor adorns, and Reason dignifies; whose form distinguishes him, and in service to whom all the host of Virtues collaborate.

Fortune, brightening her face with a gentle smile, re- 75 sponds to her daughter's speech in these words: "The work of Nature, the handiwork of virtue, does not require our aid, calls for no exertion on our part. So wonderful a creation of God, which all the bounty of Nature has endowed, which 80 divine gifts make blessed, lacks no quality of virtue. What can chance provide where nothing is subject to chance? Of

469

Quid mea mobilitas ubi rem Constantia servat?
Quid levitas ubi res stabilis? Quid mobile certa
85 res ubi quaeque manet? Ferro non indiget aurum,
non lumen tenebris; sic me non exigit actus
Naturae, virtutis opus, factura superni
artificis, nostraeque manus non postulat usum.
Sed ne livoris stimulus videatur in istud
90 desaevire bonum, vel me suspendere fastus,
dona feram, quaecumque tamen sint; illa negare
nolo, ne donans potius quam dona pudorem
sustineat, donique notae sint crimina danti.
Addam quae mea sunt, si quae tamen aut mea dici
95 aut me posse decet alii conferre,—quod absit
ut dem!—sed potius ad tempus praesto, nec umquam
ulla dedi nisi quae pro velle resumere possem.
Sed tamen hic nostros conabor vincere lapsus
et vires inferre mihi; mutabo propinquas
100 fraudes atque mei deponam taedia casus.
Me reddam stabilem, motum pro parte recidens;
incipiam sollers sapiens discretaque verax
et stabilis fieri, quae stulta improvida mendax
et praeceps hucusque fui; mutabo priores
105 excessus, nostrasque manus mirabor ad horam."
    Arripit ancipites post haec Fortuna meatus
et coeptum maturat iter. Comitatur euntem
Nobilitas sequiturque suae vestigia matris.
Ergo viam superans incerto limite, gressu
110 ambiguo, casu ductore, errore magistro,
Naturae Fortuna domum perquirit et illam
vix tandem forte vaga praeceps mobilis errans
invenit. Adventum cuius mirata stupescit

what use is my shifting where steadiness prevails, flightiness
where all is stable, or uncertainty where everything has been   85
made clear? As gold has no need of iron, nor light of darkness, so an act of Nature, a work of virtue, a creation of the
supreme artist, has no need of me, does not require the exercise of our skill. But lest it should seem that the goad of
envy is raging against this good thing, or that scorn holds   90
me back, I will contribute gifts, such as they may be; I do
not wish to refuse them, lest the one who gives rather than
the gifts should suffer shame, and the defects of the gift be
charged to the giver. I will contribute what is mine, if indeed
anything can fitly be called mine, or I be fit to bestow any-   95
thing on another—which far be it from me to give! I rather
lend for a time, and have never given anything that I might
not reclaim when I wished. Yet in this case I will try to overcome my failings and turn my powers against myself. I will
change my native deceitfulness and lay aside my tiresome   100
randomness. I will make myself stable, ceasing my movement for a while. I will begin to become serious, wise, judi-
cious, truthful, and stable, I who have hitherto been foolish,
careless, false and impulsive. I will change my old aberrant   105
ways and for a time marvel at my handiwork."

   After this Fortune sets out on her uncertain journey, and
moves quickly along the road. Nobility accompanies the
traveler, and follows the footsteps of her mother. Making
her way along an uncertain path, with faltering step, guided   110
by chance, instructed by error, Fortune—wandering, ungoverned, vacillating, lost—searches for the home of Nature
and finally, by the merest chance, discovers it. The court is
struck with wonder at her arrival, but although her motley

curia, sed quamvis habitus mutatio vultus
115 degener, inconstans gestus, terrere videntem
posset et a recto stupidam divertere mentem,
non tamen illa metu nutat, sed visa parumper
miratur nec mentis abest constantia firmae.
 Ergo Nobilitas dotes et munera profert,
120 Fortuna dictante modum, iuvenemque beatum
Naturae dono, virtutis munere, dote
caelesti, nulla peccati labe iacentem
afflat honore suo. Tamen huius dona minori
luce micant donis adiuncta prioribus immo
125 vix aliquid splendoris habent, dum luce premuntur
maiori. Sic flamma minor vicina camino
languescit, sic stella latet contermina Phoebo.
Confertur tamen ad laudem titulumque favoris
nobilitas augusta, genus praesigne, parentes
130 ingenui, libertas libera, nobilis ortus.
 Dum Fortuna parat alias apponere dotes,
assistit danti Ratio, ne forte priorum
munera fermentet unius munus et uno
depereat vitio multarum gloria rerum.
135 Non sinit adversis respergere prospera, maestis
gaudia, Fortunam se fallere cogit et aufert
hanc sibi, mendacem veram facit esse, fidelem
falsam, constantem fluidam caecamque videntem
reddit et ad tempus cogit cessare vagantem.
140 Ergo suas largitur opes Fortuna nec ultra
mensuram citrave sinit decurrere donum
Fortunae Ratio, sed opes metitur et omnes
librat divitias, ne si nimis effluat harum
alveus, in praeceps mentem deducat et illam

dress, uncouth appearance, and unstable behavior might   115
well terrify the beholder, and disorient a foolish mind, they
do not give way to fear, though surprised for a moment at
seeing her, and their steady presence of mind does not for-
sake them.

Then Nobility, at the behest of Fortune, offers her gifts
and endowments and imbues with her dignity this youth   120
blessed by the bounty of Nature, the power of virtue, the
favor of heaven, and debased as he is by no taint of sin. But
these gifts shine less brightly in the company of his earlier endowments; indeed they possess scarcely any brilliance   125
when overcome by this greater radiance. Thus a small flame
seems feeble, set beside a furnace; thus a star is obscured
when close to Phoebus. Nevertheless there is conferred
upon him, as a tribute and a sign of his privileged status, the
honor of nobility, an illustrious ancestry, freeborn parents,   130
the liberty of a free man, a noble upbringing.

As Fortune prepares to bestow other endowments, Reason attends the donor, lest the gift of this one contaminate
the gifts of the previous donors; lest the glory of so much
good be destroyed by a single vice. She does not allow For-   135
tune to intermingle her favorable gifts with adversity, joys
with sorrows; she makes Fortune betray herself, and makes
the other's power her own: she makes the false become true,
turns treachery to trust, flux to stability, blindness to sight,
and compels Fortune for a time to cease her erratic shifts.
Then Fortune bestows her largesse, and Reason does not al-   140
low her gift to exceed or fall short of due measure, but measures and weighs everything, lest too great a stream of riches
should pour forth, drawing his mind to recklessness, and a

145 mergat opum torrens, animum declinet in usus
     illicitos mentisque suos effeminet actus.
         Iam perfectus erat in cunctis caelicus ille
     et divinus homo; iam lubrica Fama per orbem
     Naturae clamabat opus. Iam rumor in aures
150 multorum dilapsus erat, cum tristis ad istos
     horruit Allecto rumores; non tamen illis
     praebuit assensus faciles, sed credere tandem
     cogitur invita, cum res et Fama peroret.
     Ergo dolos languere dolet gemitusque silere
155 ingemit atque suos luget torpescere luctus.
     Cum laetetur homo, plorat; cum rideat orbis,
     luget; languescit, cum mundus floreat; aret
     cum vireat virtus; cum res humana virescat,
     marcescit; cum regnet homo proscribitur illa.
160 Ergo suas pestes pestis praedicta repente
     convocat, ad cuius nutum glomerantur in unum
     Tartarei proceres, rectores noctis, alumni
     nequitiae, fabri scelerum, culpaeque magistri,
     Damna Doli Fraudes Periuria Furta Rapinae,
165 Impetus Ira Furor Odium Discordia Pugnae
     Morbus Tristities Lascivia Luxus Egestas,
     Luxuries Fastus Livor Formido Senectus.
     Is scelerum turbo, vitiorum turba, malorum
     conventus, numerosa lues et publica pestis
170 Tartareas ruit in sedes, ubi regnat Herinis,
     imperat Allecto, leges dictante Megaera.
         Postquam turba furens, gens dissona, contio discors
     plebs dispar, populus deformis sedibus illis
     insedit, dum murmur adhuc percurreret aures,
175 dans tumidas voces et verba loquentia fastum,

torrent of wealth overwhelm him, divert his thoughts to for- 145
bidden practices and weaken his manly strength of mind.

Now the man heavenly and divine has been made perfect
in all respects. Now swift-gliding Fame is proclaiming the
work of Nature to the world, and already rumor has reached
the ears of many, when grim Alecto hears the news with hor- 150
ror. She does not give it ready credence, but is finally forced
to believe it against her will, when fact and rumor plead
their case. Now she laments that treachery grows feeble,
grieves that grief is stilled, is pained that the pain she causes 155
has been dulled. When men are happy, she weeps; when the
heavens smile, she grieves; she falls ill when the world flourishes, and withers when virtue thrives. When human affairs
prosper, she pines away; when man rules, she is banished.

Therefore this plague rapidly summons her fellow 160
plagues. At her nod the lords of Tartarus, the rulers of night,
the children of wickedness, artisans of evil, masters of
wrongdoing come together: Disaster, Guile, Fraud, Perjury,
Theft, Robbery, Violence, Wrath, Fury, Hatred, Discord, 165
Quarrel, Illness, Sadness, Wantonness, Excess, Want, Extravagance, Scorn, Envy, Fear, Old Age. This storm of wickedness, this mob of vices, this assemblage of the wicked, this
multitude of plagues, this public plague swarms into the
halls of Tartarus, where Erinys rules, where Allecto com- 170
mands and Megaera dictates the laws.

After this raging mob, this tribe at odds with itself, this
discordant assemblage, motley multitude, deformed race
have taken their seats, while their murmur still reaches her
ears, Alecto, adopting a bombastic tone and words that 175

Allecto prorupit in haec: "quae iura, quis ordo
quis modus, unde quies, quae tanta licentia pacis
ut nostras Natura velit proscribere leges
et mundum servire sibi? Damnare nocentes,
180   et iustos salvare velit, cum nostra potestas
eius praeveniat vires, nostroque senatu
plebescat Natura minor. Totiensque subacta
legibus imperii nostri, muttire valebit
amplius et nostris subducere colla catenis?
185   Proh pudor! Incestus aberit, regnante Pudore?
Languescit Facinus, mundum Pietate regente?
Cedet Avaritia, si munera fundat ubique
hostis Avaritie? Fraudis censura silebit,
regna tenente Fide? Feret Ira silentia Pacis?
190   Ius nostrum Pax subripiet, quod tempore tanto
defendens nobis praescriptio vindicat, usus
confert et iusto titulo collata tuetur?

    "Sed pudeat nos iura sequi, quas vivere iuste
non decet, aut precibus uti. Pro legibus ergo
195   sumendae vires, vis pro virtute feratur.
Nos pro iure decet assumere robur et armis
res dictare novas et sanguine scribere leges.
In nos maturas aevo bellique potentes,
in numero plures, maiores viribus, unum
200   expertem belli puerum, virtute minorem
armavit Natura parens. Sic saevit in ursum
hinnulus, in quercus armatur virgula, vallis
in montes, lepus in catulos, in tigrida dammae.
Si forti fortem clavoque retundere clavum
205   vellemus, numquid uni concludere posset
e nostris unus, primo quem fovit ab evo

declare her disdain, bursts into speech: "What laws are
these, what order, what restraint, whence this quiet, this allowance of peace, such that Nature seeks to banish our laws,
and make the world obey her? She would condemn the
wicked and protect the just, though our might surpasses   180
hers, and she is small and insignificant in comparison with
our assemblage. Having submitted so often to the laws of
our empire, is she able to protest yet again, and free her neck
from our chains? For shame! Will lewdness give way and pu-   185
rity reign? Will Crime grow feeble, and Piety rule the world?
Must Avarice yield, if the enemy of Avarice strews her gifts
far and wide? Will the slanders of Fraud fall silent, if Trust
holds sway? Will Wrath endure the silence of Peace? Will   190
Peace snatch away our rights, rights to which an unimpeach-
able charter of such long standing justifies our claim, when
possession confers them upon us, and the conferral is made
sure by just title?

"But be it our shame to speak of rights, for it does not
befit us to live justly or appeal for our rights. Instead of laws,
then, we must take up arms; let force, not virtue, be upheld.   195
It becomes us to rely on strength rather than law, to impose
new conditions by force of arms, and write our laws in blood.
Against us, we who are mature in years, powerful in war, superior in numbers, greater in strength, parent Nature has
armed a mere boy, untested in war, lacking in strength. Thus   200
a young mule menaces a bear, a sapling takes up arms against
an oak, valley against mountain, hare against hounds, doe
against tiger. If we were to match strength against strength,
to drive out a nail with a nail, could not any one of us put   205

Thesiphone, quem lacte suo potavit Herinis?
Numquid Silla novus, alter Nero vertere posset
leges, antiquos rursus renovare furores
210 Rufinus, Katelina novus pervertere mundum?
"Sed melius gens nostra simul collecta novellos
Naturae teret insultus fastusque recentes
demittit, veteri reddens elata ruinae.
Ergo pari strepitu, concordi Marte, furore
215 aequali, lites et bella geramus in illum
qui solus puer et belli male conscius in nos
armatur cedrosque cupit delere mirica."
His dictis plebs tota suos clamore fatetur
assensus, dominamque sequi quocumque feratur
220 spondet et ad votum confestim facta sequuntur.
Prima sitit bellum Discordia, prima tumultus
appetit et primi praeludia Martis inire
praeparat. Assistunt famuli complentque iubentis
praeceptum, dominaeque parant insignia belli:
225 Livor equos, Rabies currus, Furor arma ministrat;
Impetus auriga, Lis armiger, Ira maniplus
praevenit incessum dominae, sed Terror euntis
assistit dextro lateri Damnumque sinistro
haeret, Defectus sequitur, Mors ultima gressus
230 arripit occiduos, et Mortis fidus Achates
Pallor, et assiduo Caedes comitata Dolore.
Hos comites trahit ad pugnam Discordia, cunctos
excitat et sociis infundit Martis amorem.
Post hos arma rapit, humili de plebe creata
235 Pauperies, facie deiecta, paupere cultu
incessu tristi gradiens; sed prodiga vitae,
non mortis concussa metu, non fracta timore

478

down this one, we whom Tisiphone has nurtured for so long, who drank the milk of Erinys? Could not a new Sulla, another Nero overturn the laws, Rufinus once again revive the 210 ancient madness, a new Catiline corrupt the world?

"But it is better that our race, drawn together, should eliminate this new presumption, this fresh arrogance on Nature's part, returning what has arisen to its ruinous condition of old. Therefore with common clamor, shared violence, equal madness, let us stir up strife and make war on 215 on one who, a mere boy ignorant of warfare, is sent in arms against us, a tamarisk seeking to destroy cedars."

To these words the whole host give their assent with a shout; they pledge to follow their mistress wherever she may lead them, and action immediately follows vow. Discord is 220 first to feel the thirst for battle, first to hunger for a skirmish, and prepares to initiate the first action of the war. Her servants are at hand to carry out the orders of their mistress, and make ready her trappings for war: Malice readies 225 the horses, madness the chariot, Fury provides arms; Violence is her charioteer, Strife her armor bearer, Wrath, on foot, heads his mistress's procession, but Terror stations herself on the right flank, Disaster holds the left, Revolt follows; Death, with deadly tread, brings up the rear, with her 230 faithful Achates, Pallor, and Slaughter is attended by unremitting Sorrow. These are the comrades Discord draws into battle, raising the spirits of all her companions and instilling in them a love of war.

Next to take up arms is Poverty, sprung from humble stock, marching with face cast down, in a pauper's rags and 235 with weary steps. But unconcerned for her safety, neither shaken by the threat of death nor enfeebled by fear, she

479

irruit et vendens in multo funere vitam,
plus audet, dum nescit inops pauperque timere.

240 It pedes innumera peditum vallante corona,
cuius in arma ruit plebeae turba cohortis:
Poena Labor Sitis Esuries Ieiunia Curae.

Subsequitur vallata suis Infamia monstris;
illius vexilla gerunt Contagia Vitae,

245 factaque digna notis et vita notabilis actu.
Despectus comitatur eam, Pudor haeret eunti,
serpit ibi Murmur, currunt Convicia, laudem
Fama per antiphrasim fundit risumque cacchinni.

Morbida maesta tremens fragilis longaeva Senectus

250 innitens baculo nec mentis robore firma,
bella movet bellique novo iuvenescit in aestu.
Debilitas Morbi Languores Taedia Lapsus
illius comitantur iter, qui Martis amore
succensi, pugna cupiunt incidere vitam.

255 Ardet in arma furens, scisso velatus amictu
Luctus et irrorans lacrimis arat unguibus ora.
Tristities Pressura Dolor Lamenta Ruinae
eius in obsequium fervent, dominique fatentur
militiam, belloque calent cum rege ministri.

260 Martis in ardorem nativos excitat ignes
ignea Luxuries, multo comitata cliente.
Eius in auxilium iurant Periuria, spondet
Falsus Amor, Levitas Animi, Lascivia mendax,
insipidus Dulcor, sapidus Dolor, aegra Voluptas,

265 Prosperitas adversa, Iocus lugubris, amara
Gaudia, Paupertas dives, Opulentia pauper.

charges ahead, ready to trade her life for the deaths of many others. She is more daring because, poor and destitute as she is, she has nothing to fear. She goes on foot, surrounded by a   240 wall of countless infantry. In her ranks a mob of rank and file rush forward: Pain, Toil, Thirst, Hunger, Starvation, Care.

Infamy surrounded by her monsters, follows. The Diseases of Life bear her standards: shameful deeds and a rep-   245 rehensible way of life. Contempt accompanies her, Shame follows her closely, Muttering creeps, Abuse hastens along, while Fame pours forth antiphrastic praise and sarcastic laughter.

Old Age—sick, grim, trembling, feeble, long drawn out, leaning on her staff and infirm in mind—, prepares for war,   250 and in her renewed eagerness for battle grows young again. Weakness, Illness, Weariness, Boredom, Failure march in her company, inflamed by the love of Mars, eager to end their life in battle.

Mourning, clad in a tattered garment, rages in his desire   255 to take up arms; pouring forth tears he gouges his face with his nails. Sadness, Depression, Sorrow, Lamentation, Ruin, eager to obey his orders, declare themselves soldiers of their master; these officers, like their commander, are afire for war.

Burning Extravagance, attended by a multitude of ser-   260 vants, quickens his inherent fires into a passion for War. Perjury vows to support him; False Love takes the oath, and Foolishness, traitorous Wantonness, sickly Sweetness, sweet-tasting Sorrow, exhausted Pleasure, perilous Prosper-   265 ity, tired Mirth, soured Joy, abundant Poverty, impoverished Wealth.

Post alios in bella furens et pronus in arma,
sublimi provectus equo gestuque superbus,
excedens habitu verboque superfluus actu
270 degenerans Excesssus adest, bellique furorem
praevenit, et cunctis bellandi suggerit iras;
quo duce signa gerit et bellum voce minatur
Ebrietas Fastus Iactantia Crapula Luxus.

Assiduus scelerum fomes carnisque tirannus,
275 peccati stimulus, delicti flamma, reatus
principium, praedo nostrae rationis et hostis,
in tantam pugnae rabiem, bellique furores
currit, in auxilium cuius movet arma Reatus,
Velle malum, Calor illicitus, damnosa Voluptas.

280 Stultitiam non turba minor, non rarior armat
conventus procerum; comes est Ignavia Ludi
Segnities Nugae Garritus Otia Somni.

Non minus Impietas saevit multoque superba
milite, maiori voto sitit arma nec ullam
285 gaudet habere viam, nisi fusi sanguinis unda.
Eius castra tenent illamque fatentur in armis
Nequitiae Strages Facinus Violentia Clades.

In pharetris sua tela gerens arcuque doloso
Fraus armata furit; comes est Fallacia duplex,
290 Calliditas, Dolus illiciens, Versutia fallax.

Peior Avaritiam comitatur turba clientum,
Cura frequens, Usura vorax turpisque Rapina,
quae vigili cura, studiosa mente recenset
qui nummi venantur opes, quis segnis in arca
295 pigritat et nullos domino deservit in usus.
Hanc Ignobilitas sequitur gressusque sequentis
Dedecus assequitur. Haeret Deiectio, Verber

After these degenerate Excess comes forward, astride a
tall steed, mad for war and quick to arm, haughty in bearing,
too richly attired, verbose and active to no purpose. He feels   270
already the madness of war, and imparts to all a rage for
fighting. Drunkenness, Scorn, Boasting, Dissipation, Luxury bear their leader's standards, and loudly threaten war.

The relentless spark of wickedness, the tyrant of the
flesh, the goad to sin, the inciter of crime, the beginning of   275
guilt, the thief and enemy of our reason, quickly succumbs
to the great madness of battle, the madness of war. Guilt,
Malevolence, unlawful Passion, ruinous Desire lend their
arms to her cause.

A host no smaller, no sparser a company of leaders form   280
the army of Stupidity. Her companions are Sloth, Frivolity,
Indolence, Triviality, Loose Speech, Idleness, Slumber.

Impiety, proud of her vast army, is no less fierce; above all
she thirsts to take up arms, and it is her joy never to advance   285
unless by a tide of spilled blood. Iniquity, Butchery, Crime,
Violence, Slaughter have joined her camp and acknowledge
her as general.

Well-armed Fraud rages, carrying her darts in a quiver
and bearing her stealthy bow. Her companions are twofaced
Falsehood, Craft, seductive Guile, false Cunning.   290

A throng of servants still worse accompany Avarice, in-
cessant Care, Voracious Usury, vile Robbery, who calculate
with wakeful worry and eager mind which of her monies are
stalking wealth, which lie idle in the strongbox and perform   295
no service for their mistress. Ignominy follows her, and Dishonor follows in the follower's footsteps. Dispossession is
close at hand, Scourge sits in attendance, Scarcity applauds

483

assidet, applaudit Angustia, Casus adhaeret,
quae, quamvis onerosa foret deiecta malignans
300   plus sibi conciliat Fortunae matris honorem;
plusque placet matri, tantoque remissior alget
Nobilitatis amor; et iam mutare priora
facta cupit Fortuna parens, prolique secundae
tota favet, temptatque prius decidere factum.
305   Nuntia Fama volat et veris falsa maritans,
in superos Furias, in caelum regna silentum
conspirasse refert; Manes Herebique tirannum
Tartareum reserasse chaos, fratrique negare
regna, nec ulterius pacem concedere mundo.
310   Monstraque mentitur, monstris maiora loquendo,
dum sceleri scelus accumulat Furiisque furorem
addit et Eumenides solito plus posse fatetur.
Thesiphones cumulat iras augetque Megaeram;
saevior assurgit Pluto; fit maior Herinis;
315   desinit esse triceps inferni ianitor, ora
mille rapit; proprios Allecto duplicat angues.
    Proposito stat fixa suo Natura nec ullo
concutitur vexata metu, sed mente timorem
expugnat; crescit animus bellique voluntas
320   surgit et affectus Virtutibus insidet idem.
Armatur caelestis homo superumque beata
progenies, quae tanta novi discrimina Martis
sola subit. Dant arma viro, viresque ministrant
Virtutes, unumque suis insignibus armant:
325   Pax ocreas donat, Probitas calcaria confert,
loricam Pietas, galeam Prudentia, telum
Vera Fides, ensem Ratio, Constantia scutum;
Spes largitur equos, castus Timor addit habenas,

and close at hand is Mischance, who, though burdensome, outcast and cruel, has sought to win to herself the favor of 300 her mother Fortune; and the more she pleases her mother, the more weak and tepid is Fortune's love for Nobility. Now Fortune seeks to change her former conduct, wholly favors her second child and attempts to cancel her earlier behavior.

Messenger Fame flies forth and, marrying truth to false- 305 hood, reports that the Furies are conspiring against the powers on high, the realm of the silent against heaven; that the Shades and the tyrant of Erebus have loosed Tartarean Chaos; that they reject the rule of Pluto's brother and will no longer allow the world to be at peace. Fame invents mon- 310 sters, speaks of creatures greater than monsters, piles crime upon crime, exaggerates the madness of the Furies, and declares that the Eumenides are more powerful than ever before. She expands the wrath of Tisiphone, magnifies Megaera; a fiercer Pluto now arises; Erynis becomes more huge; the infernal gatekeeper ceases to be three-headed, and 315 now possesses a thousand mouths; Allecto is doubling the number of her serpents.

Nature, steadfast, adheres to her plan; she is unmoved by any anxiety, but banishes fear from her mind. Her spirit swells, a wish to make war arises in her, and the same desire 320 inspires the Virtues. The heavenly Man is armed, the blessed progeny of heaven who will undergo alone the perils of a new kind of war. The Virtues provide arms to the Man, apply their powers and arm this single being with all their properties: Peace offers greaves, Probity presents spurs, Pi- 325 ety a breastplate, Prudence a helmet, Good Faith a spear, Reason a sword, Constancy a shield. Hope bestows horses,

armigeri gerit officium Concordia. Praeco
330 Fama canit cumulatque viri praeconia laude.
Militat a dextris Ratio, Constantia laevam
assequitur partem, totamque Modestia plebem
ordinat, et peditum strepitum Prudentia frenat.
Quaelibet a simili Virtus gerit arma viroque
335 iurat in auxilium; quae totum Martis honorem
dat iuveni, cui bella movet Natura, suamque
donat ei belli palmam pugnaeque laborem.

 Iam pestes Herebi, scelerum contagia, monstra
inferni, cives Plutonis, noctis alumni,
340 Tartareum chaos egressi, funduntur in orbem.
Iamque diem nostrum multa caligine noctis
involvunt mundique iubar delere laborant.
Insultus lux ipsa novos miratur et ipsam
noctem plus solito iam posse magisque morari,
345 nec proprias servare vices, nec cedere Phoebo.
Sed tamen hoc solo pensat sua damna quod illic
lux aeterna manet nullis decisa tenebris,
continuusque dies, ubi caelicus ille senatus
turmaque Virtutum, Naturae militat agmen.

350 Iam se prospiciunt acies, iam prospicit hostem
hostis et aspectus animos succendit in iras.
Ignescunt animi, mentes audacia maior
erigit, exsurgunt irae. Iam mente cohortes
se superant, animi iam mutua vulnera fingunt.
355 Mens ardore prius pugnat quam dextera ferro.

 Impatiens morae Vitiorum turba priores
arripit insultus pugnae primumque furorem
excitat, et magnis clamoribus intonat iras

486

Chaste Fear supplies the reins, Concord performs the office
of armor bearer. Fame gives the herald's cry and proclaims   330
the Man's praises again and again. Reason guards his right
flank, Constancy takes her place on the left. Modesty sets
the army in formation, and Prudence curbs the clamor of
the infantry. Each of the Virtues arms herself in a similar
way, and pledges her support to the Man. They bestow all   335
the glory of Mars on this youth whom Nature is sending into
battle; she will assign to him the palm of her victory, and the
task of fighting.

Already the plagues of Erebus, diseases of wickedness,
the infernal monsters, the subjects of Pluto, the children of
night, emerging from Tartarean chaos, overrun the earth.   340
Now they cover over our daytime with a dense layer of darkness, and seek to obliterate the light of the universe. Light
itself, amazed at these new insults, wonders that night has
such unusual power, delays longer, and does not keep to its   345
proper cycle or give way to Phoebus. Yet against this injury
she balances one certainty: that there abides an eternal light,
undiminished by any shadow, an endless day, there where
the heavenly assembly, the throng of Virtues, the army of
Nature wages war.

Now the armies survey one another, now enemy con-   350
fronts enemy, and the sight inflames their spirits with anger.
Their spirits burn, a greater boldness quickens their resolve,
their wrath swells. Now in thought the armies are conquering each other, minds imagine bloodshed on both sides. The
mind attacks with passion before the arm wields its sword.   355

Impatient of delay, the mob of Vices seize the initiative
with insults, and are first to stir up the madness of battle.
The whole army expresses its rage with great shouts, and

360 tota cohors, verboque prius consurgit in hostem
quam ferro. Verbis bellum praelibat et illi
gestu voce minis insultat. Nec tamen illum
gestus verba minae frangunt, sed fixus in alto
mentis proposito, iuvenis constanter ad ista
erigitur, vincitque metum constantia mentis.
365 Sed, postquam sua verba minae gestusque vigoris
nil habuere, locum dant verba, nec amplius illis
est locus, immo minis. Factum succedit et armis
cedunt verborum pugnae. Iam mistica bella
rem sapiunt, pugnas animi res ipsa fatetur.

Liber Nonus

Iam pedites in bella ruunt, iam sanguinis audent
fundere primitias, iam libamenta cruoris
prima dare affectant primaevaque funera belli.
Pulveris insurgunt nebulae, novus imber inundat
5 in terris, dum tela pluunt, dum pulveris imber
funditur, et caelum telorum nubila velant,
et ferri splendore novo nova fulgura lucent.
    Mente calens, fervens animo, flammata furore,
prima viro movet assultus Discordia, primum
10 aggreditur Martem, primo casura tumultu.
Impetus urget equos, Lis suggerit arma, sagittam
Ira ministrat ei, Furor arcum praeparat, ensem
Livor, et ad pugnam reliquis ferventius ardet.
Ergo sagitta volat, praenuntia Martis, et hostem

charges against the enemy with words before using their   360
swords. The Man's first taste of war takes the form of words,
as they assail him with gestures, shouts and threats. But
these gestures, words and threats do not shake him; with his
lofty purpose firmly in mind, he stands up to them unmoved,
and his steadfastness of mind conquers fear. But after their   365
words, threats, and gestures have had no effect, words give
way, there is no further place for them, nor indeed for
threats. Action follows, as the war of words yields to armed
conflict. Now their imagined warfare partakes of reality, and
actual war gives expression to the fighting of the mind.

Book 9

Now the infantry rush into battle, unafraid to pour out the
first offering of blood; now they strive to make the first
bloody libation, inflict the war's first deaths. Clouds of dust
rise, a new rain floods the earth as a shower of spears pours   5
down; a shower of dust is spread abroad, a cloud of weapons
covers over the sky, and a new lightning flashes out from
new and gleaming weapons.

Discord, her mind inflamed, her spirit seething, burning
with rage, is the first to attack the Man, shows the first war-   10
like aggression, and is destined to fall in the first skirmish.
Violence drives her horses; Strife readies her arms; Wrath
has charge of her arrows; Fury readies her bow, Malice her
sword; and she burns for battle more keenly than the others.
Therefore Discord lets fly an arrow, a declaration of war,

15 impetuosa petit, quam totis viribus actam
dirigit in iuvenem Discordia. Nec tamen ictus
dextrae mittenti respondet: parma sagittam
respuit et totos obiectus umbo refellit.
Tunc animi vires et totum robur in unum
20 colligit et Marti se totum devovet ille;
indulget freno iuvenis, calcaribus urget
cornipedem, nec segnis hebes, pigredine lassus,
lentescit sonipes, sed eodem Martis amore
militat, hostiles frangens cum milite turmas.
25 Adversas igitur partes invadit et ipsis
hostibus occurrens, vagina liberat ensem.
Nec tonat ille minis, sed solo fulminat ense,
ferro cuncta probat nec verbis disputat, immo
verberibus multisque modis concluditur hosti.
30 Excipit a reliquis illam quae prima furoris
causa fuit, quae prima dedit fomenta malorum.
Hanc igitur mucrone petens, a corpore vitam
extorquet, cogitque mori quam vivere mundo
mors erat, et mundi mortem mors una retardat.
35 Nec satis est vidisse mori, plus exigit hostis:
ense metens caput, a trunco diffibulat ora.
Et merito caput a trunco discordat in illa
per quam lis odium rabies dissensio rixa
prima fuit, per quam primo conflictus et irae
40 primaevique metus et belli prima cupido.
Ergo solo iacet exanimis quae reddidit olim
exanimes alios, sed ea moriente, suorum
emoritur virtus; unius poena redundat
in multos; morbus capitis discurrit in artus.
45 Iam Timor ipse timet, Lis subticet, Ira tepescit,

impulsively seeking out the enemy, propelled with all her 15
strength, and aimed at the youth. But the shot does not reward the hand that sent it forth: his buckler rejects the arrow, and his shield repels all that follow. Then the youth
musters all his force of mind and all his strength, and dedi- 20
cates himself totally to the fight. He looses the reins and
spurs forward his horn-footed steed. The loud-hooved animal, neither sluggish, lazy, nor burdened with too much
weight, is not slow of pace, but wages war with the same
martial ardor, breaking through the hostile melee together
with the knight. Now he invades enemy territory, and en- 25
countering the foe, draws his sword from its sheath. He does
not bellow threats, but makes a thunderbolt of his sword.
He proves everything with steel, disputes not with words
but rather with blows, and brings the enemy to conclusion
in many ways.

He singles out from the rest her who was the first cause 30
of the turmoil, who first provided the spark of evil. Then,
attacking her with his blade, he tears the life from her body,
and compels to die one whose life was deadly for the world;
a single death stays the world's death. Nor is it enough to 35
have seen her die; the enemy requires more: cutting off her
head with his sword, he disjoins head from trunk. And it is
fitting that the head should be discordant with the trunk of
her through whom strife, hatred, madness, dissension, quarrel first arose, through whom conflict, wrath, primeval fear 40
and the desire for war first came to be. Thus she lies lifeless
on the ground who for so long rendered others lifeless. But
with her death the courage of her allies also dies; the punishment of this one affects many; the sickness of the head
spreads into all the limbs. Now Fear himself is fearful, Strife 45

mutescit Rabies, cadit Impetus, occidit ipsa
Livor, languescit Odium, Furor arma resignat.
Assunt Virtutes iuveni, quae Martis eodem
succensae stimulo, reliquos armantur in hostes;
50 hos perimunt illosque fugant, bellatur in omnes.
Vera Fides Odium perimit, Concordia Litem,
Pax Iram, Rabiem Constantia Spesque Timorem.
    Non minor ad pugnam sed maior surgit in iras
Pauperies, non ense tonans, non fulgure teli
55 bella minans, nulla loricae veste refulgens,
nec clipeo munita latus, nec casside vultus.
Sed nodis variis callosa, nec arte polita,
sed vultus veteres retinens primamque figuram,
clava vicem gerit armorum, sed quod minus arma
60 dant, supplent animi, dat mens quod perdit in armis.
Pauperies ruit in iuvenem clavaque minatur
funera, librat eam, librata percutit. Ictum
ille stupet, tanto dum cassis subsidet ictu.
Sed tamen instantis ictus Constantia partem
65 eludit mucrone suo. Magis ergo furore
uritur et magno strepitu bacchatur Egestas,
dum videt incassum clavam saevire nec illam
respondere sibi. Tunc ictus duplicat, immo
multiplicat, sed clava suo nugatur in ictu.
70 Nam quotiens clave Paupertas obicit ictum,
argumenta suo Virtus mucrone refellit.
Sed postquam sua bella videt nil posse, ministros
acrius ad pugnam stimulat. Labor irruit, instat
Esuries, Sitis insultat, Ieiunia pugnant,
75 insurgunt vigiles Curae, dant arma Labori
glaeba lapis fustes, telum de stipite querno.

falls silent, Wrath cools, Madness becomes mute, Violence loses his strength, Malice dies away, Hatred becomes faint, Rage lays down his arms. The Virtues stand by the youth; fired with the same warlike spirit, they take up arms against the remaining enemy. Some they slay, others they put to flight, war is waged against all. Good Faith kills Hatred, Concord kills Strife, Peace Rage, Constancy Madness, Hope Fear. 50

Not inferior as a warrior, but greater, Poverty swells with wrath, threatening war with no clashing sword or gleaming spear, clad in no shining breastplate, her body defended by no shield, her head by no helmet. But a club, toughened by many knots and untouched by craft, still retaining its old appearance and original shape, serves the purpose of arms, and spirit supplies what armor does not provide; boldness provides what she lacks in the way of arms. Poverty charges the youth, and her club threatens death; she raises it, then strikes. He is stunned by the blow, while his helmet gives way to its great force. Constancy, however, partly fends off the imminent blow with her sword. Poverty then burns with greater fury, and rages with great roars, when she sees that her club has threatened in vain and not obeyed her. Then she doubles and redoubles her blows, but the club is robbed of its force. For as often as Poverty aims a blow of the club, the Virtue refutes her argument with her sword. But when Poverty sees that her war-making has no effect, she fiercely goads her attendants into battle. Toil rushes forward, Hunger takes his stand, Thirst hurls insults, Starvation joins the fight, wakeful Cares rush forward and provide weapons to Toil—clods, stones, sticks, an oaken spear. Hunger seizes 55 60 65 70 75

Esuries armata rapit carecta, ministrat
tela Siti, reliquae paribus bacchantur in armis.
   Sed iuvenis prior occurrit, prior obviat hosti.
80   Pauperiem prior aggreditur; celerique volatu
cornipedis pariterque suo conamine nitens,
accumulat vires hastae qua deicit illam,
quae terrae deiecta iacet. Petit ergo iacentem;
nec tamen illius scrutatur viscera ferro,
85   nec rotat ense caput, nec inhebriat arma cruore,
funere famoso dedignans claudere vitam
hostis et insigni leto pensare ruinam.
Sed conculcat eam, confundens ora iacentis,
deiectamque solo pedibus triturat equinis.
90   Cogitur ergo mori iamdudum mortua mundo
Pauperies. Nec Mors animum praedatur in illa,
sed potius mens una manet languetque repressa
Mors a mente minor, multumque diuque resistit
mens Morti, tandemque simul cum Morte recedit.
95   Dum sic in fatum concedit iuraque fati
Paupertas, proprium moriens depauperat agmen.
Coetus eget qui dives erat dum vixit Egestas.
Eius divitiae pereunt omnisque facultas
Pauperie pereunte perit. Coguntur egere
100 concives quos illa prius ditavit egendo.
Languescit Labor exhaustus, Sitis effugit, arma
deicit Esuries, fugiunt Ieunia, Curae
depereunt. Sic turba minor maiore ruina
deprimitur populusque perit pereunte magistro.
105 Ergo Quies Poenam, Saties Ieiunia, Curas
Pax fugat, Esuriem devicit Copia, languet
Ubertate Sitis et victa Carentia cedit.

pointed reeds, supplies these weapons to Thirst, and the rest
rush wildly on similarly armed.

But the youth moves forward first, and is first to confront
the enemy. He first assails Poverty: trusting equally in the   80
swiftness of his horn-footed steed and his own strength, he
gives extra force to the spear with which he strikes her, and
she lies overthrown on the earth. He approaches the fallen
body, but does not pierce her entrails with steel, or cause her   85
head to roll with his sword, or steep his weapons in gore, for
he disdains to conclude his enemy's life with a memorable
end, and balance her downfall with a distinguished death.
Instead he tramples her [body], disfiguring the face of her
corpse, and crushing the fallen one with the hooves of his
steed. Thus Poverty, long since dead to the world, is forced   90
to die. But Death does not steal away her spirit: for her mind
remains intact, and Death proves weak, resisted and diminished by mind. For a long time mind strongly withstands
Death, but finally departs in his company.

When Poverty has thus yielded to fate and its laws, her   95
death impoverishes her troop. Rich while Poverty lived, her
company is now poor. Their wealth is exhausted. and with
Poverty's death all their resources are gone. Her companions are forced to suffer want, companions whom she had   100
once enriched by being in want. Toil is weak and exhausted,
Thirst takes flight, Hunger throws down his weapons, Starvation flees, Care is in despair. The lesser folk are overwhelmed by the downfall of the greater; with the death of
their mistress the people too perish. Now Repose drives   105
away Pain, Sufficiency routs Starvation, Peace Care, Abundance Hunger; Thirst falls before Fruitfulness; Deprivation
is defeated and departs.

Tunc comitum supplere volens Infamia casus,
fortior assurgit, sociorum vendere mortes
110 temptat et hostili leto satiare dolorem.
Irruit in iuvenem, sed verbo praevenit ictum,
et verbis accuens convicia: "Proh pudor!" inquit,
"gens aevo sensu cautela viribus armis
pollens unius iuvenis succumbet inermi
115 militiae, nostraque feret de gente triumphum
iste puer?" Nec plura loquens, delegat in illum
telum, demonstrans facto quod voce minatur.
Missile decurrens cum verbo verberat auram,
nec vice legati pacem denunciat, immo
120 bella gerit, cursuque ruens Infamia telum
insequitur telo, cursu contendit et hostem
ense petit, mucrone volens succurrere telo,
ut, si forte viri deludant arma sagittam
vel modica teli rabies desaeviat ira,
125 teli mucro furens algentes suppleat iras.
Ergo sagitta, memor dextrae quae miserat illam,
insilit in frontem iuvenis, sed cassis euntem
sistit, eam retinet, gressum negat, obstat eunti.
Sed teli supplere volens Infamia lapsum,
130 succurrit telo, nudo mucrone, sed ictum
excipit a galea medius Favor, ensis ab ictu
decidit et comitis male supplet damna sagittae.
Sed postquam ducis insultus nil posse clientum
turba videt, magis in rabiem succenditur; ergo
135 fortius arma rapit. Pugnant Contagia, Murmur
irruit, insurgunt Convicia, Dedecus instat.
Sed iuvenis nec mente iacet, nec frangitur hoste,

Then Infamy, wishing to make up for her companions'
downfall, attacks more vigorously, seeking to avenge the
deaths of her allies, and assuage her grief with the deaths of 110
enemies. She rushes at the youth, but precedes her blow
with speech, her words lending bite to her abuse: "For
shame!" she says, "shall a tribe endowed with maturity, intelligence, shrewdness, and strength in arms succumb to the
feeble soldiery of a single youth? Will this mere boy enjoy a 115
triumph over our nation?" Without further words she sends
spear toward him, displaying in act what she threatens in
speech. The speeding missile strikes the air in company with
her words, but it does not serve as an ambassador and offer
peace. It is rather an act of war, and Infamy, racing forward, 120
and following one dart with another, strives to match its
speed. She thrusts at the enemy with her sword, eager to follow up the missile with her blade so that, if the Man's arms
should deflect the arrow, or if its madness should rage with
diminished wrath, the furious blade may make up for the 125
cooling of the missile's wrath. Thus the arrow, mindful of
the arm that had sent it forth, strikes at the forehead of the
youth, but the helmet resists its passage, holds it back, denies it entry, blocks its path. Infamy, wishing to compensate
for the failure of her missile, rushes to its aid with naked 130
sword. But Grace, intervening, draws the blow away from
the helmet; the sword fails to strike, and compensates poorly
for the downfall of its fellow shaft.

When the mob of followers sees that the assault by their
leader is of no effect, they are inflamed by greater madness,
and wield their arms more aggressively. Disease enters the 135
fray, Muttering charges, Abuse advances, Dishonor takes a
stand. But the youth is neither disturbed nor shaken by the

497

nec terrore pavet, nec vulnere laesus oberrat,
sed cornu quo Fama suae praeconia laudis
140   intonat, ad tempus Famae subducit et hostem
hoc mucrone ferit. Vires in vulnere multo
monstrat et egressus crebro reseratur in ictu.
Hostis in occasu Pudor occidit, arma reponit
Murmur, mutescunt Convicia, Dedecus iram
145   nescit, Contemptus moritur, Contagia cedunt.
Dedecus ergo Favor extinguit, Fama Pudorem,
Gloria supplantat Murmur, Convicia Laudes,
Contemptum praedatur Honor, Contagia Virtus.
    Quamvis pigra foret, quamvis ignava Senectus,
150   quamvis delirans, quamvis torpore fatiscens,
prona tamen calet in bello, iuvenescit in armis,
nec baculi iam quaerit opem suffulta furore.
Nec regimen poscit quae sustentatur ab ira,
debilitate potens, morbo robusta, dolore
155   dives, segnitie fortis, pigredine prompta.
Ergo propinqua neci, morti vicina propinquae,
florida canitie, rugis sulcata Senectus
oppositum ruit in iuvenem. Nec primitus instat
ense nec aggreditur telo, nec cuspide pulsat,
160   sed quadam luctae specie conatur ut illum
in terram demittat, equum subducat et armis
exutum liber gladius grassetur in hostem.
Sed monitu calcaris equus succensus in illam
irruit et terrae miseram deponit, at illa
165   exsurgens vires pariter cum mente resumit,
vertit ad arma manus et spem deponit in armis.
Sed cassis torpore iacet, squalore senescit,

enemy; he does not grow pale with fear, nor does any wounding blow make him stumble. Instead he borrows from Fame for the moment the horn with which Fame trumpets procla- 140 mations in praise of him, and with this as his sword strikes at the enemy. He shows his strength by inflicting many wounds, then opens a path of departure with continuing blows. As the enemy falls away Shame lies fallen, Muttering lays her arms aside, Abuse falls silent, Dishonor can rage no 145 longer, Contempt falls dead and Disease retreats. Grace eliminates Dishonor, Fame slays Shame, Glory and Praise displace Muttering and Abuse, Honor makes a prize of Contempt, Virtue of Disease.

However slow she may have become, however idle, however confused, however weary and decayed, Old Age is none- 150 theless ready and eager for war; when armed she grows young; having the support of madness, she now does not seek the aid of her staff. Sustained by wrath she has no need for guidance; she is powerful in debility, made sturdy by disease, rich in sadness, strong in weariness, alert in her lassi- 155 tude. Therefore, though on the brink of ruin, near neighbor to death, flourishing only in her white hair, furrowed by wrinkles, Old Age rushes against the youth opposing her. At first she does not come upon him with her sword, attack with a missile, or thrust with her lance, but tries by a kind of 160 wrestling to throw him to the ground and rob him of his horse, so that her sword may range freely over him, once deprived of his arms. But the steed, at the prompting of the spur, rushes upon her in fury and casts her wretched body to the ground. She, however, rises again, recovering both her 165 strength and her faculties, her hands now take up arms and she places her hope in them. But her helmet lies useless; it is

atque situ scabrae morsum rubiginis horret.
Parma suum multa rubigine computat aevum,
170   nec vetat ingressum nudata crate sagittis.
Loricae fragiles mordens rubigo catenas
dissuit et iunctis addit divortia squamis.
Pigritat affixus vaginae mucro nec extra
de facili prodit, longo torpore quiescens;
175   quem senium nudare parat; sed degener ensis
respuit egressus istos dextraeque monenti
denegat obsequium, malens torpore quietis
uti quam varios belli sentire tumultus.
Sed tamen a loculo tandem producitur ensis
180   segnis hebes squalore iacens nec iam memor irae
bellorum; pacemque magis quam bella requirit
hic mucro, si mucro tamen de iure vocari
debeat hic gladius et non mucronis ymago.
      Impetit ergo virum gladio munita Senectus.
185   Vulnus ab ense petit, sed vulneris immemor ensis,
incassum pulsans, aditus ad vulnera nescit,
sed stupet ad galeam, vario delirus in ictu.
Ergo Senecta, videns proprium nil posse furorem,
miratur seseque dolet sine vulnere vinci,
190   et quamvis esset morti vicina, propinquam
maturare volens, hostis sibi provocat ensem.
Sed iuvenis miseratus eam nec digna rependens
hosti pro meritis, nolenti vivere vitam
concedit fatumque negat sua fata volenti.
195   Sistit equum, frenum retinet, sermone Senectam
aggrediens animos truces et vota retardans,
prodit in haec: "cur fata paras, cui proxima fatur
mors finem, cui vita mori, cui vivere fatum?

old and filthy, and shudders at the ravages of its coating of
rust. Her shield, too, reckons its age by its accumulation of
rust; with its ribs laid bare, it can no longer deny entry to ar- 170
rows. Devouring rust has broken the fragile chains of her
breastplate, and brought divorce to its jointed scales. Her
sword lies idle, stuck fast in its scabbard, and will not come
forth easily, [having] lain so long in disuse. When the old one 175
prepares to draw it, the decrepit sword repels withdrawal,
and refuses to obey the prompting of her hand, preferring to
enjoy its tranquil idleness rather than undergo the violence
of war. Nevertheless the sword is finally withdrawn from its
resting place, dull, blunt, coated with filth; no longer mind- 180
ful of the rage of war, this sword is suited to peace, not war,
if indeed it should rightly be called a sword, and not the imitation of a sword.

Armed with this sword, Old Age assails the man. She
seeks a wounding blow from the sword, but the sword has 185
forgotten how to wound, thrusts in vain, finds no opening
for a wound, but grows dizzy as it strikes, confounded by
the [man's] helmet. Now Old Age is amazed, realizing that
her rage is of no avail, and grieves that she is being overcome without receiving a wound. And though she is close to 190
death, she seeks to hasten what is near at hand, and draw the
enemy's sword against herself. But the youth, pitying her,
does not repay the enemy according to her deserts; he grants
life to one who does not wish to live, and denies her fate to
one who longs for it. He stays his steed, reins him in, and as- 195
sails Old Age with speech. Curbing his hostile thoughts and
impulses, he speaks these words: "Why do you seek to determine your fate, you for whom imminent death is the destined end, for whom to die will be life, for whom to live is to

Cur quaeris tibi concessum? Cur poscis inepte
200   quod Natura parat, quod mors vicina minatur?
Utere que restat vita nec quaere propinquos
anticipare dies. Vitae compendia mortem
solentur, mortis dispendia vita repenset."
     Ergo victa fugit, belloque renunciat, ensem
205   deicit, expellit clipeum galeamque Senectus
exuit, et solo baculo contenta recedit.
Debilitas perdit vires belloque recedens
languescit Morbus, Languor fit morbidus, haeret
Lapsus, labuntur Defectus, Taedia languent.
210   Iam comites errare videns et cedere pugnae
Fletus adest, partemque suam succumbere bello
luget, et abscisso maeret velamine Luctus.
Utque erat impatiens, gressum maturat et hostem
impetuosus adit, galeaeque resolvere nodos
215   temptat, ut ad vultus ingressum preparat ensi.
Sed Risus succurrit ad haec, mucrone lacertum
dissuit a trunco, galeae manus hesitat, haerens
emoritur proprioque stupet privata vigore.
     Iam Gemitus sua damna gemit, iam Luctus inundans
220   assumit sibi se, Fletus lacrimatur et omnis
turba comes, maeret Planctus Lacrimaeque madescunt.
iam Dolor ipse dolet, perdens fomenta doloris;
deprimitur Pressura, cadunt Lamenta, Ruinae
depereunt omnisque perit violentia Luctus.
225   Gaudia Tristitiem, Pressuram Gloria, Planctum
Prosperitas, Lamenta Iocus, Felicia Casum
exsuperant, vincitque mali fastidia Risus.

be cursed? Why do you beg for what has been granted to you? Why do you foolishly demand what Nature has read-ied, what impending death threatens to impose? Enjoy the life that remains; do not seek to anticipate a day that is near at hand. What life has to offer is our consolation for death; life is what we gain at the price of death."

Then Old Age, defeated, takes flight; she renounces war, casts aside her sword, throws down her shield, removes her helmet, and departs, content with only her staff. [Now] Debility loses her strength; Sickness grows weary and with-draws from battle; Weariness falls ill, Failure falters; Revolt collapses, Boredom droops.

Now Weeping comes forward. Seeing his companions wandering and giving up the fight, he laments that his cause should accept defeat. Mourning [too] mourns, his garment rent. In his frustration he quickens his pace, recklessly ap-proaches the enemy, and seeks to loosen the knots of his helmet, and provide the sword with a pathway to his face. But Mirth comes to his aid, and with his sword severs Mourning's arm from his body. The hand still clings to the helmet; fixed thus it dies and grows stiff, deprived of its vital spirit.

Now Sobbing sobs at his loss; now Mourning, pouring forth tears, draws him to himself; Weeping weeps, and with him all the attendant throng. Complaint complains, and Tears flow. Now Sorrow himself sorrows at the loss of what nourishes sorrow. Depression is depressed, Lament grows faint, Ruin is cast down, and all the violence of Mourning dies away. Joy defeats Sadness, Glory Depression, Prosper-ity Complaint, Mirth Lament, Good Fortune Failure. Mirth overcomes the arrogant pride of evil.

503

At Venus ipsa furit, cui fortior ira nefasque
maius et insultus peior graviorque potestas.
230   Dum comitum languere manus, rarescere pugnam
luget, et hostiles animoque manuque catervas
crescere, iamque suos dolet expirare furores.
Ignitam tamen illa facem, qua fulminis ipsam
mentitur speciem, qua saxa resolvere cautes
235   extenuare solet, ferrum mollescere, rupes
inflammare, rapit instanter, vibrat in hostem.
Has pugnas, haec bella tremens, haec proelia vitans
expectare timet iuvenis; fuga consulit illi
consilioque fugae venientes effugit ictus.
240   Fax ignita cadit, expirat in aëre, vires
amittit, dum nulla manent fomenta caloris.
Hic tamen a tergo Parthorum more sagittam
dirigit in Venerem nec fallitur illa, sed ictum
primo proponit, assumit vulnus et inde
245   mortem concludit, nec ad haec instare Libido
argumenta potest, dum sic concluditur illi.

Sic iuveni sub Marte novo nova laurea cedit
dum fugit, ergo fugat; dum cedit, ceditur illi;
dum cadit, erigitur; vincit, dum vincitur; audet,
250   dum timet; expugnat, dum pugnam deserit; absens
instat et in bello praeventus, praevenit hostem.

Dum moritur sua fata stupet Cytherea, nec ipsam
credit adesse necem, quamvis Mors ipsa loquatur.
Cum per eam soleant alii succumbere leto,
255   vix credit se posse mori. Sed proxima tandem
fata videns, prorumpit in has moritura querelas:

But now Venus herself is enraged: her wrath is stronger, her sinfulness greater, her assaults more painful, her power more oppressive. As she mourns that her allies are growing 230 weak, and their attacks less frequent, and that the enemy force are gaining both courage and strength, she grieves that her furies are expiring. But suddenly she seizes and hurls at the enemy the flaming torch with which she imitates the thunderbolt, and often splits open boulders, pulverizes great 235 rocks, melts iron, and causes stone to burn. The youth, hesitant in the face of this battle, this war, shunning this combat, fears to await the torch; flight seems the wisest course, and by deciding to flee he evades the oncoming missile. The 240 fiery torch falls, it expires in the air, loses its force, since nothing is left to feed its flame. Then the youth, in the manner of the Parthians, aims an arrow at Venus as he retreats, and it does not miss its mark: it first proposes a blow, premises a wound, and thence draws the conclusion of her death. 245 Lust cannot adduce an argument against these, which thus conclude her.

Thus new laurels befall the young man, in a war of a new kind. As he flees, he puts the enemy to flight; as he gives ground the enemy is given to him; as he falls away, he is raised up; he conquers while he is conquered; he is bold even as he shows fear; he fights in abandoning the fight; while 250 withdrawing he is pressing forward; bested in battle, he yet bests the enemy.

As she is dying, Cytherea is stunned at her fate, and cannot believe that her own destruction is at hand, though Death himself should tell her so. Since others commonly succumb to death through her power, she can scarcely be- 255 lieve that she too can die. But finally, seeing her fate close at hand, on the point of death she puts forth this complaint:

"Heu! Totiens victrix uno delirat in actu
nostra manus, totiens vincens nunc fata fatiscit
quae falli nescit, quam nunc Fortuna fefellit!
260 Nunc alget meus ille calor, meus ille caminus
qui Solis flammas urit, succendit in undis
Neptunum, Bacchum bacchari cogit et ipsum
fulminat igne Iovem, superis furatur honorem
numinis et multos cogit servire potentes.
265 Nunc mea tela iacent, quibus olim victus Achilles
cessit, degeneri mentitus veste puellam;
inque colum clavam vertens, in pensa sagittas,
in fusum pharetras, Alcides degener armis
totus femineos male degeneravit in actus."
270 Haec ait et vitam pariter cum voce reliquit.
    Iam timet Excessus, iam bello cedere quaerit
iam mens alta cadit, iam mentis decidit ardor,
dum comitis videt occasum qui maxima belli
pars erat et prima totius Martis origo.
275 Hasta tamen vibrata volat, sed deviat, hostem
dum petit haec; mittensque manus male consulit illi
quae male dum regitur, errans declinat ab hoste,
nec saltem clipei partem praelibat eundo.
Tunc iuveni delegat opem Moderantia, ferrum
280 nudat et hostilem turbat frangitque catervam.
Pugnat in Excessum Moderantia, sobria Fastum
aggreditur Ratio, Poenam Tolerantia, Luxum
Sobrietas, sed pugna favet Virtutibus, harum
defendit partem Victoria. Vincitur ergo
285 Fastus, Luxus abit, cessat Gula, Crapula cedit.
    Tunc Carnis Stimulus furtivo Marte reluctans,
impetit a tergo iuvenem temptatque latenter

"Alas! Our power, so often victorious, has gone astray in this one action, is now undone by fate; Fortune at last deceives one who could not be deceived. Now this fire of mine grows cool, this furnace of mine which has caused the flames of the Sun to burn, made Neptune feel its heat in the depths of the sea, caused Bacchus to become a Bacchant, and struck Jove himself with its lightning, robbed the gods of their divine dignity, compelled the mighty to become slaves. Now my weapons lie idle, which once made Achilles acknowledge defeat, feigning girlhood in a dishonorable costume; Alcides, too, disgracing his arms, turned his club to a basket, his arrows to wool, his quiver to a spindle, and utterly degraded himself by assuming a woman's role." Thus she spoke, then gave up both voice and life.

Now Excess grows timid, and wishes now to give up the war; now his proud mind sinks, his ardent spirit ebbs, as he sees the downfall of a comrade who had the greatest role in battle, and was indeed the first cause of the entire war. Nevertheless his shining spear wings its way, but as it seeks out the enemy, it goes off course. The hand that sent it forth guided it badly, and since it is ill governed, it strays, falls away from the enemy, and does not so much as graze the edge of his shield as it passes. Then Moderation brings aid to the youth, bares her steel, scatters the enemy and breaks through their lines. Moderation battles against Excess, sober Reason attacks Scorn, Tolerance Pain, Sobriety Luxury; but the battle goes in favor of the Virtues: Victory fights on their side. Thus Scorn is defeated, Luxury withdraws, Gluttony falls idle, Dissipation surrenders.

Then Fleshly Appetite, in a stealthy counterattack, rushes on the youth from behind, and tries to assail him

insultare viro. Tamen istos provida sentit
insultus Ratio, nec torpet pigra, sed illi
290   obviat, indomitum retinet sistitque furentem.
Sed tamen ille diu Rationis viribus obstans,
ex aequo contendit ei multumque repugnat
luctans, et tandem victus submittitur hosti.
     Acrius in pugnam volat Imprudentia. Nullam
295   bellandi servat legem, sed turbine belli
turbida, nil animo retinet, nisi Martis amorem.
Mole sua fixum summa de rupe molarem
extorquere cupit, sub quo nutaret Achilles,
Alcides gemeret totusque fatisceret Atlas,
300   sed vires oneri cedunt, et pondere victa
vis hebet, atque gravem patitur sub mole ruinam.
Obstat ei Fronesis, et iam sub pondere victam
vincit et invitam feriari cogit ab armis.
Segnitiem superat Sollertia, Seria Ludum,
305   Utilitas Damnum, Studium fugat Otia, Sensus
Stultitiam damnat, Nugasque Silentia vincunt.
     Non ultra retinens iras mentisque tumultus,
Impietas sese bellando praedicat et se
rixando loquitur. Verbis rixatur et ictu
310   consummat rixas; probat ense quod ore fatetur.
Errat in errore Martis, bellique furore
plus furit, inque via Martis fit devia, legem
bellandi sine lege tenens, sine foedere foedus.
Dum minus in vulnus desaevit mucro, securim
315   arripit, ut redimat gladii delicta securi.
Ergo virum ferit et vires consumit in illo.
Sed iuvenis stat securus sub mole securis.

secretly. But prudent Reason suspects such an attack, and does not sit idle, but confronts him, curbs his fierceness and 290 withstands his rage. Yet for a long time he stands up to the power of Reason, striving to hold his own and putting up a strong resistance. Finally he is overcome and submits to the enemy.

Recklessness flies fiercely into battle. She keeps to no 295 method in fighting but, caught up in the whirlwind of battle, is aware only of her love of war. She seeks to wrench from atop a great rock a boulder held fast by its own weight, a boulder beneath which Achilles would totter, Alcides would groan, and Atlas be wholly exhausted. Her strength suc- 300 cumbs to her burden; overcome by the weight she grows faint, and falls heavily beneath its mass. Fronesis confronts and defeats her who is already defeated by her burden, and compels her unwillingly to rest from fighting. Alertness defeats Sloth, Seriousness defeats Frivolity, Benefit defeats 305 Disaster, Zeal drives away Idleness, Understanding defeats Stupidity, Silence overcomes Triviality.

Impiety, no longer restraining her wrath and the tumult in her mind, announces herself by fighting, and declares her-self with invective. She brawls with words and finishes the brawl with blows: she demonstrates with her sword what 310 she asserts in speech. Amid the confusion of war she is con-fused; she is more furious than the fury of war itself; follow-ing the path of Mars she is pathless; she observes a law of war that is without law, a code that is no true code. Since her sword is not fierce enough to wound, she seizes her 315 ax, so that with this she may make up for the failure of her sword. Now she strikes at the man, and exhausts her strength in doing so. The youth stands firm beneath the impact of

Assistens Pietas ferro non militat, immo
blanditiis precibusque cupit mollescere bellum.
320　　Sed tamen imbre precum gravius succenditur ardor
bellandi, donantque preces fomenta furori.
Sed postquam nil blanditiae, nil verba favoris,
nil valuere preces, Pietas mellita resignat
verba, rapit ferrum, bellumque refellere bello
325　　incipit et ferrum ferro; fallitque securim
obiectu clipei, variosque reverberat ictus.
Sed tamen proprio devicta labore, fatiscit
Impietas, Marti cedens, sine Marte subacta.
　　Quae restat? Fraus sola; sibi solatia pugnae
330　　quaerit et ad veteres latebras fraudesque recurrit.
Degeneri pugna, servili Marte, dolosa
insultu, belli furias molitur in hostem;
blanditiis, non blanda tamen, Fraus allicit illum.
Has ergo vomit illa preces et dulcibus afflat
335　　verbis et phaleris dictorum palliat artem:
"O iuvenis cui terra favet, cui militat aether,
cui Deus arridet, caelum famulatur, et omnis
applaudit mundus, et totus supplicat orbis,
reliquiis belli, quae vix et forte supersunt,
340　　parce, nec in victos desaeviat ira leonis.
Vincere cur victos temptas? Cur bella movere
quaeris in imbelles? Satis est potuisse; nec ultra
nobilitas animi quaerit, nisi vincere posse."
　　Dum blandis precibus mentitur verba precantis,
345　　evocat occulte gladium, maturius ensem
nudat, et ingeminans ictus, ad vulnera ferrum
invitat; sed cassis ad hoc contendit, et ensem
spernit, nec tali dignatur cedere ferro.

the ax. Compassion, coming to his aid, does not fight with a sword, but seeks to assuage the fierceness of war with gentle words and appeals. But Impiety's hot desire for battle is only made more intense by her gentle rain of pleas; such appeals only add fuel to the fury. But when her gentle speech, her goodwill and her appeals have had no effect, Piety abandons honeyed words; seizing her sword, she begins to answer war with war, steel with steel. She fends off the ax, blocking it with her shield, and deals out many resounding blows. But Impiety is finally overcome by her own toil, grows faint and gives up the war, surrendering without a battle. 320 325

Who is left? Only Fraud. She seeks to solace herself by fighting, and resorts to her old subterfuges and frauds. She labors to inflict the fury of war on her enemy by a dishonorable strategy, a base kind of warfare, a treacherous assault; she seeks to entice the man with gentle words which yet are not gentle. She spews forth these appeals, puffs them up with sweet words, and cloaks her strategy with the trappings of rhetoric: "Oh Youth whom earth favors, for whom heavenly powers wage war, on whom God smiles, whom heaven serves, whom all the world applauds, to whom the universe bows down, spare those who are left, who barely and by chance have survived the war. Let not the lion's wrath rage against the defeated. Why should you strive to conquer the conquered? Why seek to make war on the powerless? That you would be able to do this is enough; the noble mind seeks no more than to be capable of victory." 330 335 340

While she feigns the words of a suppliant with these tender appeals, she secretly reaches for her sword, quickly bares the blade, and striking repeatedly, calls on the steel to wound. But the youth's helmet counters this, and rejects the sword, not deigning to yield to such steel. Good Faith takes 345

Econtra gerit arma Fides, Fraudisque refellit
350   insidias, nudatque dolos et furta revelat.
Sed postquam nil posse dolos nec pallia fraudis
Fraus videt, exit bella, fugae committitur, arma
exuit et partem vitae lucratur eundo.

    Restat Avaritiae strepitus, cui tota furoris
355   incumbit rabies, tantique pericula Martis
solus habet, solusque furit, se pluribus offert
unus et in solo spem desperatio gignit.
Spicula, quae multus argenti splendor inignit,
in iuvenem vibrat et ad instar grandinis instant
360   tela; pluunt hastae nubemque sagitta figurat.
Ergo telorum silvam pluresque sagittas
plantat in hostili clipeo vestitque sagittis
pestis Avaritiae, sed telum parcius intrat
scutum nec clipeo sua spicula firmiter haerent.

365   Sed Virtus quae dona pluit, quae munera spargit,
nec sepelit nummos, nec opes incarcerat arca,
sed bene divitias fundit sine spe redeundi,
telorum nemus ense secat silvamque recidit.
Instat Avaritiae, pugnat constanter et ensem,
370   quam tenet illa, rapit. Armis hostilibus hostem
vincit et in dominam cogit saevire sagittas;
ergo victa fugit.

              Pugnae stat sola superstes
filia Fortunae, sed eam Fortuna repellit
a bello, natamque monet ne bella movere
375   intestina velit, ne rixam nata parenti
misceat, aut pugnam moveat germana sorori.
Ergo consilio matris concordat et hostem

up arms against Fraud, thwarts her treachery, lays bare her 350
guile and exposes her stealth. But when Fraud sees that neither guile nor veiled fraud can accomplish anything, she
abandons the battle, takes flight, throws away her arms, and
by her departure gains an extra portion of life.

There remains the roaring of Avarice. All the furious
madness now devolves upon her; she alone bears the danger 355
of this great conflict; She alone still rages, only she offers
herself on behalf of many; in her alone desperation gives rise
to hope. She hurls against the youth javelins afire with the
gleam of much silver, and the weapons descend upon him
like a hailstorm. Spears shower down, and what appears a 360
cloud of arrows. Plaguing Avarice plants a forest of spears
and many javelins in the enemy's shield, and covers it with
arrows, but the spears barely penetrate the shield and the
javelins do not fix themselves firmly.

But that Virtue who showers gifts, who scatters her 365
bounty abroad, who does not bury her moneys or lock up
her wealth in a chest, but rather pours out her wealth with
no concern for repayment, cuts through the thicket of weapons with her sword, hews down the forest. She challenges
Avarice, fights steadily, and snatches away the sword which 370
the other is holding. With this enemy weapon she overcomes the enemy, and makes her arrows fly fiercely at their
mistress, so that she flees, defeated.

The daughter of Fortune remains, the sole survivor of the
war, but Fortune draws her away from the battle, warning
her daughter that she must not seek to initiate a war against
kindred; that a daughter should not quarrel with her mother, 375
or sister make war on sister. Nobility accepts her mother's

deserit, ignorans cui iustius arma movere
possit: sic neutri cedens, famulatur utrique.

380   Iam scelerum superata cohors in regna silentum
arma refert, et se victam miratur, et illud
quod patitur vix esse putat. Nec creditur illi
quod videt, et Stigias fugit indignata sub umbras.
Pugna cadit, cedit iuveni Victoria, surgit
385 Virtus, succumbit Vitium, Natura triumphat,
regnat Amor, nusquam Discordia, Foedus ubique.
Nam regnum mundi legum moderatur habenis
ille beatus homo, quem non Lascivia frangit,
non superat Fastus, Facinus non inquinat, urget
390 Luxuriae stimulus, Fraudis non inficit error.

    In terris iam castra locant et regna merentur
Virtutes mundumque regunt. Nec iam magis illis
astra placent sedesque poli quam terreus orbis.
Iam caelo contendit humus, iam terra nitorem
395 induit aethereum, iam terram vestit Olimpus.
Nec iam corrigitur rastro, nec vomere campus
laeditur, aut curvi deplorat vulnus aratri,
ut tellus avido, quamvis invita, colono
pareat, et semen multo cum faenore reddat.
400 Non arbor cultrum querit, non vinea falcem,
sed fructus dat sponte novos et vota coloni
fertilitate premit. Spes vincitur ubere fructu.
Gratis poma parit arbor, vitisque racemos,
et sine se natas miratur pampinus uvas.
405 E tunicis egressa suis rosa purpurat hortos;

advice and withdraws from the hostilities, uncertain on whose behalf she might legitimately take up arms. By thus acceding to neither side, she does service to both.

Now the forces of wickedness are overcome, and carry 380 their arms back to the realms of the silent. They are amazed at their defeat; they consider that what they have suffered can hardly have happened. They give no credence to what they see, and flee, resentful, into the darkness. Battle ceases, Victory is awarded to the youth, Virtue is affirmed, Vice suc- 385 cumbs, Nature triumphs. Love rules: nowhere is there discord, but everywhere agreement. For that blessed Man now governs the world with the reins of law whom no wantonness unmans, who is not subject to arrogance, defiled by crime, goaded by lust or infected by the waywardness of 390 fraud.

The Virtues now establish themselves on earth, claim their rightful domains and govern the world. No longer are the stars and the halls of heaven more pleasing to them than the earthly sphere. Now our lands vie with heaven, now earth assumes a heavenly brightness, now Olympus adorns 395 the earth. No longer is the field cultivated by the hoe or wounded by the plowshare; no longer does it lament the wounds that the curved plow inflicts, so that the earth, though unwilling, may obey the greedy farmer, and repay his sowing with high interest. No tree requires the knife, no 400 vine the sickle, but they yield their new fruits unprompted, and exceed the hopes of the husbandman by their fertility. Hope is outdone by the abounding fruit. The tree bears its apples, the vine its clusters, as a gift; the vine marvels at grapes born without its help. The rose emerges from its 405 jacket and tints the garden with crimson; it shows no trace

nec spinam matrem redolet, sed sponte creata
pullulat, atque novos sine semine prodit in ortus.
Sic flores alii rident varioque colore
depingit terram florum primaeva iuventus.

* * *

410 O mihi continuo multum sudata labore
pagina, cuius adhuc minuit detractio famam,
vive! Nec antiquos temptes aequare poetas,
sed potius veterum vestigia semper adorans,
subsequere et lauris humiles submitte miricas.

415 Iam ratis, evadens Scillam monstrumque Caribdis,
ad portum tranquilla meat, iam littore gaudet
navita, iam metam cursor tenet, anchora portum.
Nauta tamen tremebundus adhuc post aequoris aestum
terrenos timet insultus, ne, tutus in undis,

420 naufragus in terra pereat, ne livor in illum
saeviat, aut morsus detractio figat in illo,
qui iam scribendi studium pondusque laboris
exhausit proprio concludens fine laborem.
Si tamen ad praesens fundit sua murmura livor,

425 et famam delere cupit laudesque poetae
supplantare novas, saltem post fata silebit.

of a mother thorn, but blooms spontaneously, and emerges into new flowerings without seed. Other flowers, too, flourish happily, and their fresh youth adorns the earth with many colors.

* * *

May you live, o my book, born of ceaseless and exhausting 410
toil, though even now detraction [seeks to] diminish your fame. Do not attempt to rival the ancient poets, but rather follow reverently in their footsteps, and let your humble myrtle defer to their laurels.

Now my vessel, having evaded Scylla and the monster 415
Charybdis, comes peacefully into port; now the sailor rejoices at the sight of land, now the runner attains the goal, now the anchor is set in the harbor. Yet the mariner, still trembling after storms at sea, now fears assaults on land, fears that after surviving the waves he may perish, ship- 420
wrecked, on shore, that envy may rage against him, or detraction fix its teeth in one who has now finished the heavy labor of the writer's task, bringing his work to a fitting conclusion. But even if envy still spreads her mutterings, seeking to destroy the reputation and belittle the praise of this 425
new poet, she will at least fall silent after his death.

UNDOING THE KNOT

1. Vix nodosum valeo nodum denodare,
   et indemonstrabile monstrum demonstrare,
   nudae volens Veneris vultum denudare,
   quae naturas hominum vult denaturare.

5
2. Huius arte magica quivis protheatur:
   Iovialis deitas per hanc humanatur,
   Mars in pace vincitur, Bachus debachatur,
   ipse Titan uritur, Triton inflammatur.

3. Haec prestando surripit, auferendo praestat:
10
   honestum depauperat, pauperem honestat,
   incastum castificat, pudorem incestat,
   blandiendo verberat, blandiens infestat.

4. Laeta maestis, mellea felleis adiungit:
   dum proponit dulcia, sanguinem emungit;
15
   allicit illiciens et inungens pungit;
   illicit alliciens, immo pungens ungit.

5. Verbera post ubera suis impertitur,
   blandiendo vulnerat, vulnerans blanditur,
   verum dicit mentiens et vera mentitur,
20
   rerum compos omnium nullis compotitur.

1. I am scarcely able to unknot a knotty knot, and demonstrate an undemonstrable monstrosity, seeking to lay bare the face of naked Venus, who seeks to denature the natures of men.

2. By her magical art one and all are transformed: The divinity of Jove is made human; Mars is conquered in time of peace; Bacchus rages as a Bacchant; Titan himself is burned; Triton is inflamed.

3. Venus steals even as she offers, offers as she steals; she makes the good man poor, the poor man good, the unchaste chaste, chastity unchaste. She strikes by caressing; her caress is an attack.

4. She joins happy with sad, honey with gall; even as she proposes delight she draws blood. She attracts one seductively, and stabs as she soothes; she seduces one attractively, but even as she stabs she soothes.

5. She offers first her breasts, then blows, to her thralls; she wounds as she caresses, her caress is a wound. She speaks the truth falsely and lies truthfully; controlling all, she is controlled by none.

6.   Dulce malum amor est, et dulcor amarus,
inimica caritas, inimicus carus,
ignara prudentia, sapiens ignarus,
praeavara largitas, largiens avarus,

25   7.   Ingrata temperies, mulcebris tempestas,
praepotens debilitas, debilis potestas,
libertina servitus, serviens libertas,
pauper affluentia, affluens paupertas,

8.   Poena delectabilis, tristis paradisus,
30   arridens tristities et contristans risus,
visionis caecitas, caecitatis visus,
odium amabile et amor invisus,

9.   Sitiens ebreitas, sitis debriata,
saties famelica, fames satiata,
35   virtuosum vitium, virtus vitiata,
inquietum gaudium, requies ingrata.

10.   Sub hac sola quaestio solet ventilari,
an amori virginum ioco puellari
matronalis debeat amor ancillari,
40   an eundem deceat privilegiari.

11.   Ecce vultum induat dubitationis
quaestio sophistica, umbra quaestionis,
cuius in vestibulo disputationis
excubat solutio, soror rationis.

45   12.   Quis, nisi mentis inops, hostis rationi,
fletum confert gaudio, risum passioni,
lutum gemmae conferens, noctuam pavoni,
flori faenum comparat, Tersitem Adoni?

6. Love is a sweet evil, a bitter sweetness, a hostile cherishing, a cherished enemy, an imprudent prudence, an unwise wisdom, a most greedy generosity, a generous greed,

7. an unpleasant calm, a soothing storm, a powerful enfeeblement, a feeble power, a freely chosen slavery, a servile liberty, an impoverished affluence, and affluent poverty,

8. a delightful pain, a sorrowful paradise, a smiling misery and a painful smile, the blindness of one who sees, a blind man's vision, an amiable hatred and a hateful love,

9. a thirsty drunkenness, a drunken thirst, a starving satiety, a sated starvation, virtuous vice, vitiated virtue, anxious joy, unwelcome repose.

10. On this subject one question is often raised: whether, when one plays with women, the love of matrons should be considered inferior to that of virgins, or should rightly take pride of place.

11. See how a sophistical question can assume the appearance of uncertainty, the illusion of doubt, while the dispute's solution, sister of reason, is waiting at the door!

12. Who that is not bereft of wit, an enemy to reason, compares tears with joy, laughter with suffering, mud with gemstones, the owl with the peacock? Compares straw to flowers, Thersites to Adonis?

13. Laborat in extasi mentis furiosae
50 qui cicutam lilio, saliuncam rosae
  comparat, vel purpuram clamidi pannosae,
  gloriam deglorians rei gloriosae.

14. Sed boni malitia non deflorat florem,
  nec veri depauperat falsitas honorem,
55 nec incestus nubila nubilant pudorem,
  neque Venus coniugis virginis amorem.

15. Malum bono proximum vilius vilescit,
  bonum in contrarii facie nitescit;
  in unius tenebris alterum lucescit,
60 unum in alterius luce tenebrescit.

16. Sicut bruma gratior dies est aestiva,
  floreque decrepito rosa primitiva,
  sic matronae Venus est quasi positiva,
  cum Venus virgunculae sit superlativa.

65 17. Floret Venus virginis nondum deflorata,
  cum sit nuce vilior Venus triturata.
  sic libata gratior res est illibata,
  fons signatus dulcior aqua publicata.

18. Dione virginea nequit fermentari,
70 nec in fraudis fabulas vult adulterari.
  huic pudor simplicitas gaudet gratiari,
  sub hac amans quilibet vult meridiari.

19. Nil hoc infelicius fellius errore,
  melius vel mellius nil hoc est amore,
75 gravius ingratius nil hoc est furore,
  ditius vel dulcius nil hoc est dulcore.

13. He who pairs the hemlock with the lily, the wild nard with the rose, a purple robe with a cloak full of patches, suffers from the disorientation of a raving mind, and robs a glorious object of its glory.

14. But malice cannot blight the flower of good, nor falsehood deprive truth of honor; the darkness of the unchaste cannot darken what is chaste, nor the love of a married woman the love of a virgin.

15. Evil placed beside good shows its baseness more basely; good faced with its opposite shines. One glows brightly amid the shadows of the other; one remains shadowed in the other's light.

16. Just as a summer day is more pleasing than a frosty one, the blooming rose than a flower that has withered, so the Venus of a matron might be called positive, while the love of a tender virgin is superlative.

17. Not yet deflowered, the Venus of a virgin flourishes; a Venus already threshed is worth less than a nut. For what is still untasted is more pleasing than what has been tasted; a fountain sealed is sweeter than a public well.

18. A virginal Dione cannot be corrupted, and has no wish to be polluted by false stories. Her chaste simplicity rejoices at receiving pleasure, and any lover willingly takes his ease with her.

19. Nothing is more unfortunate, more galling than this error; nothing finer, nothing sweeter than this love; nothing more grave, less pleasing than this madness; nothing richer, nothing sweeter than this sweetness.

20.   Primos flores virginis, prima rudimenta,
       ver primum decerpere prima sub iuventa
       veneris praeludia sunt delectamenta,
80   que minus luxuriae sapiunt fermenta.

21.   Si quis vero coniugis in amore perit,
       flores carpit hyemis, in arena serit,
       virorem in arido, mel in felle querit,
       publice se publicans viam tritam terit.

85   22.   A Natura principe lex est instituta
       ut sub certo tempore, sub aetate tuta,
       sub statuto canone, lege sub statuta,
       sua solvant Veneri virgines tributa.

23.   Sed nec leges postulant, nec ius protestatur,
90   nec Natura recipit, quamvis patiatur,
       ut a nupta Veneri vectigal solvatur,
       maritalis fibula quo diffibulatur.

24.   Virgo tributaria redditur amori,
       suo favoraliter favens amatori,
95   ut naturae solito morem gerat mori,
       precum contradicere nesciens dulcori.

25.   Dat amor amarior stimulum uxori,
       quae, ut gulae pabulum det inferiori,
       et ferventis clibani consulat fervori,
100   foedera defoederat maritalis thori.

26.   Amore pecuniae postquam inescatur,
       ad moechie facinus mulier armatur,
       dum moechando teritur, terendo moechatur,
       ut a moechi loculo nummus emungatur.

20. To enjoy the first flowers of virginity, the first testings, the first spring; these preludes to Venus in the youthful prime are delights that savor little of the ferment of lust.

21. But if one succumbs to the love of a married woman, he plucks wintry flowers, sows in sand, seeks verdure in dry ground, honey in gall; revealing himself to the world, he treads a well-worn path.

22. A law has been established by ruling Nature that at a certain time, at a proper age, according to established rule and law, virgins must pay their tribute to Nature.

23. But no laws demand, right does not insist, Nature does not require (though she permits) that tribute be paid to Venus by a married woman, such that the clasp of marriage is unclasped.

24. A maiden is offered as a tributary to love, that she may adapt her behavior to Nature's usual custom, pleasing her love with every pleasure, unable to deny the sweetness of his prayers.

25. A more bitter love goads the wife, who, to provide fodder for her lower gullet and allay the heat of her glowing oven, defiles the pledge of the marriage bed.

26. Once she is lured by the love of money, a woman is prepared for the crime of adultery. Though she is exhausted by adultery, she commits adultery to exhaustion that coin may be squeezed from the purse of her adulterer.

105   27.   Ille, postquam Veneris potu debriatur,
                     cogitur ad vomitum venter bursae satur.
                     Totus perit igitur, totus deplumatur,
                     et qui dives fuerat, iam philosophatur.

          28.   Miser est qui coniugis in incude cudit,
110   qui sub tali ludicro ludens se deludit,
                     cui si sophistica mulier alludit,
                     ex laeto principio flebile concludit.

          29.   Iam naturam Veneris nimis denaturat,
                     de complexu coniugis cuius cura curat,
115   quam flagello mentulae rusticus triturat,
                     quae sub tantis ictibus inconcussa durat.

          30.   Nullus qui sit sapiens talem ludum temptat,
                     tali gaudet gaudio, timor quem fermentat,
                     metus, horror, gemitus ubi se praesentat,
120   ubi se securitas penitus absentat,

          31.   Ubi saepe sompnio mortis soporatur
                     moechus, dum mechanice cum moecha
                           moechatur,
                     ubi saepe mentulae bursa sincopatur,
                     ubi saepe geminus frater decollatur.

125   32.   Cum in nupta Veneris sitis incandescit,
                     discurrit in facinus, in furorem crescit,
                     nil audere dubitat, nichil pertimescit,
                     natum mater abdicat, nata patrem nescit.

27. Once he is made drunk by the draft of Venus, the sated belly of his purse is forced to vomit. Then he is wholly lost, plucked wholly bare; and he who once was rich now plays the philosopher.

28. He who beats on the anvil of a married woman is wretched; playing such a ludicrous game he deludes himself. For if a woman practices sophistry on him he moves from a happy premise to a miserable conclusion.

29. A man is already too far denaturing the nature of Venus if he lets himself care for the embraces of a married woman, whom some mere peasant flails with the lash of his phallus while she remains unshaken by such blows.

30. No one who is wise attempts such sport, or takes pleasure in a pleasure which fear sours, where dread, horror, grief appear, where security is wholly absent,

31. where the adulterer is often drugged by the sleep of death as he mechanically commits adultery with his adulteress, where the purse of the phallus is often cut away, where often the twin brother is beheaded.

32. When in a married woman the thirst of Venus grows hot, she rushes into crime, bursts forth into madness, unhesitatingly dares anything, fears nothing; mother abandons child, daughter does not know father.

33. Quid pudor, quid pietas, nupta non attendit,
130 caminus luxuriae nuptam dum accendit;
  iura, leges, foedera turpiter offendit,
  castitatis immemor castitatem vendit.

34. Cum Venus ad facinus coniugem invitat,
  sincopare coniugis vitam non evitat:
135 ut moechie maculam melius admittat
  a mariti capite truncum demaritat.

35. In prolis perniciem Procne neronizans,
  Pasiphe luxuriae potum tantalizans,
  boveque sophistica bovem paralogizans,
140 istud verum approbat, vere sillogizans.

36. Potens probabiliter ad hoc disputare,
  ad hoc pactum Helena vult sillogizare,
  nam Troiae nobilitas adhuc posset stare,
  si novisset Phrigius melius amare.

145 37. Ergo non ulterius quaestio procedat,
  cum se parti virginum ratio concedat:
  ergo nupta virgini in amore cedat,
  et innupta mulier nuptam antecedat.

Explicit.

* * *

In Oxford, Bodl. Digby 166, ff. 91–93, the following verses are added (d'Alverny, *Alain de Lille,* 43):

Si Venus illicitum est adulterare,
magis est illicitum in matrem patrare,
et magis odibile Deo sic peccare
scelus indicibile femina vel mare.

33. The married woman cares nothing for chastity or loyalty when the furnace of lechery grows hot. She offends grossly against right, law, covenant; having forgotten chastity, she sells her chastity.

34. When Venus summons a wife to crime, she does not stop at cutting off the life of her spouse; that she may more readily accept the stain of adultery, she divorces her husband's body from his head.

35. Procne, Nero-like in the destruction of her child, or Pasiphae, straining like Tantalus to reach the cup for which she lusts, paralogizing the bull with the false premise of a cow, prove by sound arguments that this is true.

36. Helen is well able to argue plausibly on this point, and will offer proofs to corroborate this. For Troy could still be standing if the Phrygian had known a better love.

37. Therefore let the debate proceed no further, since reason places itself on the side of the virgin. And so let the married woman yield to the virgin in love, and let the unmarried woman be preferred to the married.

* * *

Oxford, Bodl. Digby 166, ff. 91–93:

> If adultery is an unlawful form of love, it is even more forbidden to perform it upon a mother (i.e., a married woman?); it is hateful to God to sin in this way, an unspeakable crime for woman or man.

5a Cernens tot erroneos ad hoc declinare,
    viam pulchram linquere luteam captare,
    crus spinosum petere, plumosum sufflare,
    rithmo, prosa, versibus duxi reuocare.

    Christe, finis omnium, amans castitatem
10a qui de seruis expetis cordis puritatem
    tolle sodomiticum, deprecor, abbatem
    qui tot tuos docuit tantam feditatem.

Epilogium fratris Walteri de Burgo super Alanum in opere
suo De planctu Nature contra prelatum sodomitam.

Observing that so many erring ones go astray in 5a
this regard, leave the fair road and take the muddy
one, grasp the spiny limb and scorn the downy one, I
have decided to call them back with rhyme, prose,
verses.

Christ, final hope of all, lover of chastity, who re- 10a
quire purity of heart in your servants, strike down, I
pray, the sodomizing abbot who has taught such vile-
ness to so many of your sons.

Epilogue of Brother Walter de Burgo upon Alan in his work
"The Complaint of Nature" against the sodomitical prelate.

ON THE INCARNATION

1.   *Grammatica*
      exceptivam actionem
          verbum Patris excipit,
      dum deludit rationem,
          dum naturam decipit.
5   Casualem dictionem
          substantivum recipit;
      actioque passionem
          in hoc verbo concipit.
              in hac Verbi copula
10   stupet omnis regula.

2.   *Logica*
      Inter locos locum nescit
      locus a contrariis;
      suum locum obstupescit
          exceptum ab aliis.
15   Fit elinguis, obmutescit,
          fallitur in propriis,
      et de suis erubescit
          logica fallaciis.
              In hac Verbi copula
20   stupet omnis regula.

1. *Grammar*

The Word of the Father performs an action that introduces an exception, when it mocks reason, when it deceives nature. A substantive receives a declinable name. In this Word active conceives passive.

In this joining of the Word, every rule is confounded.

2. *Logic*

Among topics the topic from contraries can find no place. It is dumbfounded to see its position excluded by others. Logic becomes speechless, it falls silent, it is mistaken as to its own procedures, it blushes at its fallacies.

In this joining of the Word, every rule is confounded.

3.   *Rhetorica*
     Peregrinat a natura
          nominis positio,
     cum in Dei transit iura
          hominis conditio.
25   Novus tropus in figura
          novus fit constructio;
     novus color in iunctura
          nova fit translatio.
               In hac Verbi copula
30   stupet omnis regula.

4.   *Arithmetica*
     Dum ab uno non recedit,
          alteratur unitas;
     dum in unum se concedit,
          unitur alteritas.
35   In diversum idem cedit,
          in idem diversitas,
     suum tamen non excedit
          limitem simplicitas.
               In hac Verbi copula
40   stupet omnis regula.

5.   *Musica*
     Dum Factoris et facture
          mira fit coniunctio,
     quis sit modus ligature
          quis ordo, que ratio,
45   que sint vincla que iuncture,
          qui gumphi, que unio,

538

3. *Rhetoric*

The defining power of the noun strays from its natural role when the condition of a man passes into the rule of God. A new figural troping takes place, a new construction; a new metaphorical joining, a new translation comes to pass.

In this joining of the Word, every rule is confounded.

4. *Arithmetic*

While it does not depart from oneness, unity is altered; when it lets itself become one, alterity is unified. Same yields to diverse, diversity becomes same, yet simplicity does not exceed its limit.

In this joining of the Word, every rule is confounded.

5. *Music*

When a wondrous joining of Workman and work takes place, what kind of joining is it, what ordering, what plan? What are the links, the joints, the fastenings, the union?

stupet sui fracto iure
musica proportio.
In hac Verbi copula
50   stupet omnis regula.

6.   *Geometria*
Sue artis in censura
geometra fallitur,
dum immensus sub mensura
terrenorum sistitur.
55   In directum curvatura
circuli convertitur.
Speram claudit quadratura
et sub ipsa clauditur.
In hac Verbi copula
60   stupet omnis regula.

7.   *Astronomia*
Solis lumen nube tectum
nubis sub velamine
nostre nubis fert obiectum,
nec hebet in lumine.
65   Nostrum vergit in defectum
sol ortus de Virgine,
in defectum dans effectum,
lumen in caligine.
In hac Verbi copula
70   stupet omnis regula.

Musical proportion is amazed at the breaking of her laws.

In this joining of the Word, every rule is confounded.

6. *Geometry*

Geometry's skill in judging is deceived, when the immeasurable is reduced to the measure of earthly things, when the curvature of the circle is converted into a line, when square contains sphere and is contained by it.

In this joining of the Word, every rule is confounded.

7. *Astronomy*

The light of the Sun covered by cloud, beneath its veil of darkness suffers the obscuring of our darkened state, but its light is not dimmed. The Sun born from the Virgin enters into our weakness, granting a remedy for our weakness, light amid our darkness.

In this joining of the Word, every rule is confounded.

THE BOOK OF CREATION

1. Omnis mundi creatura
   quasi liber et pictura
       nobis est in speculum;
   nostrae vitae, nostrae sortis,
5 nostri status, nostrae mortis
       fidele signaculum.

2. Nostrum statum pingit rosa,
   nostri status decens glosa,
       nostrae vitae lectio:
10 quae dum primo mane floret,
   defloratus flos effloret,
       vespertino senio.

3. Ergo spirans flos exspirat,
   in pallorem dum delirat,
15   oriendo moriens.
   simul vetus et novella,
   simul senex et puella,
       rosa marcet oriens.

4. Sic aetatis ver humanae
20 iuventutis primo mane
       reflorescit paululum.
   Mane tamen hoc excludit
   vitae vesper, dum concludit
       senii crepusculum.

1. Every thing in the created universe is like a book for us, a picture, a mirror, a truthful sign of our life, our destiny, our condition, our death.

2. The rose portrays our state, an apt gloss on our condition, a reading of our life: for while this flower flourishes early in the day, its blossoms become withered in the old age of evening.

3. Thus the flower expires as it draws breath, dying as it comes forth, moving haplessly toward the pallor of death. At once old and new, at once aged and a girl, it withers even as it blooms.

4. Thus the springtime of human life, flourishes for a brief time in the morning of youth. But the evening of life banishes this morning, extinguishing the dim light of old age.

5. Cuius decor dum perorat
eius decus mox deflorat
   aetas, in qua defluit.
Fit flos foenum, gemma lutum,
homo cinis, dum tributum
30   huic morti tribuit.

6. Cuius vita, cuius esse
poena, labor et necesse
   vitam morte claudere;
sic mors vitam, risum luctus,
35 umbra diem, portum fluctus,
   mane claudit vespere.

7. In nos primum dat insultum
poena mortis gerens vultum,
   labor, mortis histrio;
40 nos proponit in laborem,
nos assumit in dolorem,
   mortis est conclusio.

8. Ergo clausum sub hac lege
statum tuum, homo, lege,
45   tuum esse respice,
quid fuisti nasciturus,
quid sis praesens, quid futurus,
   diligenter inspice.

9. Luge poenam, culpam plange,
50 motus frena, fastum frange,
   pone supercilia;
mentis rector et auriga,
mentem rege, fluxus riga,
   ne fluant in devia.

5. When life's beauty approaches its peroration, age quickly deflowers its grace as it flows away. Flower becomes grass, gem turns to mud, Man is reduced to ashes as he pays the tribute due to death.

6. Man's life, man's existence is pain and toil, and it is inevitable that his life will conclude in death; for death is the end of life, grief of mirth, darkness of day; the swelling sea closes in the harbor, and day ends in evening.

7. It is pain that mocks us first, wearing the face of death; toil, playing death's role, submits us to labor and subjects us to suffering, and this ends in death.

8. Therefore, O man, consider your condition, bound by this law; contemplate your existence: examine closely what you were born to be, what you are now, what you will become.

9. Grieve for your suffering, mourn your guilt, curb your actions, break your pride, put down your arrogance. Be ruler and charioteer of your mind; govern your thoughts, restrain their course, lest they flow into error.

Note on the Texts

SERMON ON THE INTELLIGIBLE SPHERE

The text is that of the single manuscript, Paris, B. N. lat. 3572, 272v–73, ed. d'Alverny, Alain de Lille, 297–306.

THE PLAINT OF NATURE

Four complete editions of the *De planctu Naturae* exist. An incunabulum (1494) was printed by Arnold of Cologne at Leipzig. The text in the edition of Alan's works produced by Carolus de Visch (1654), which was incorporated into volume 210 (1855) of the *Patrologia latina,* follows a fifteenth-century manuscript, now Lille, Bibliothèque municipale, MS 591. The edition of Thomas Wright (1872) is apparently based on the de Visch edition and two fifteenth-century manuscripts which Häring tentatively identifies as London, British Library, MS Cotton Cleopatra B. V, and London, British Library, MS Additional 24361. The texts of both de Visch and Wright are seriously defective.

Häring's edition rests on the collation of thirty manuscripts but depends primarily on London, British Library, MS Stowe 37, a late-twelfth- or early-thirteenth-century manuscript from northern France. My text is that of Häring, with emendations suggested by Shanzer, "Parturition" (Sh), and Minkova, "Textual Suggestions" (M), as well as my own (W). In the notes to the text, the emendation is followed by Häring's reading (H).

Editions of the *Anticlaudianus* were published at Venice (1582) and Antwerp (1611). The text in the edition of Alan's works produced by Carolus de Visch (Antwerp 1654), which was incorporated into volume 210 (1855) of the *Patrologia latina,* is based on two manuscripts from the library of the Jesuit College of Louvain, one from the Abbey of St. Bertin at St. Omer, and two owned by the printer Balthasar Moretus of Antwerp. Polycarp Leyser published a text of *Anticlaudianus* 1 in his *Historia poetarum et poematum medii aevi* (1741). The edition of Thomas Wright (1872) is based on the *Patrologia* text and two manuscripts, London, British Library, MS Cotton Vespasian A.X, and London, British Library, MS Royal 15 B.XX (Gibson, Shanzer, and Palmer, "Manuscripts," 964–65, 971–72). The edition by Massimo Sannelli (2004) presents a version of Bossuat's text with normalized orthography and incorporates conjectures by Sheridan that often draw on variants cited in Bossuat's apparatus and others drawn from the commentary of Radulphus.

The edition of Robert Bossuat (1955) uses Paris, Bibliothèque nationale, MS lat. 3517 as a base text. The readings of this manuscript are completely different both from those of his other manuscripts and from those of others in the tradition, not because they are authentic and constitute a direct route back to Alanus's autograph, but because they are synonymous glosses, guesses, and readings culled from other sources, all gathered together in a single manuscript. The layers are to some extent distinguishable, but the reader cannot tell this, because Bossuat's apparatus does not distinguish primary readings from those of correctors and glossators. Bossuat's trust in this manuscript led him to adopt its readings even when they were patently wrong and relegate correct vulgate readings to the apparatus.

The textual tradition of the *Anticlaudianus* is extensive and heavily contaminated. While it is not difficult to establish precise stemmatic relations among later manuscripts, the earliest manuscripts (owing to contamination) are not susceptible to full stemmatization. That said, it has not been hard to find an exceptionally clean early witness to the text in London, British Library, MS Royal 13 B.VIII from Canterbury (= L). The DOML text is not a fully critical text; a critical edition would not have been possible within the parameters of the DOML series. The text is based on Bossuat's edition, but variants from L, perhaps the best early manuscript, have been introduced when they provide better readings. The punctuation has frequently been altered. All significant departures from Bossuat's text have been signaled. Throughout, Bossuat's erratic and idiosyncratic orthography has been normalized silently to aid nonspecialist readers.

UNDOING THE KNOT

The *Vix nodosum valeo,* though its form and style are those of twelfth-century "goliardic" poetry, is found only in manuscripts of the fourteenth and fifteenth centuries. In only one is it attributed to Alan, but in most it follows the *De planctu Naturae*. The poem was published by Leyser in 1721. My text is that of Häring with the emendations noted.

On the Incarnation

The edition I have used is that of Marie-Thérèse d'Alverny, "Alain de Lille et la *Theologia*," 123–28. D'Alverny reviews the complex manuscript and early print history of the text and notes that in one manuscript, Florence, Laur. Plut. XXIX.1, the first strophe of the poem is part of a repertory of pieces sung at Notre-Dame in Paris in the late twelfth and early thirteenth centuries.

I have presented d'Alverny's text intact and have listed the variant readings of a Citeaux manuscript, now MS London, BM Add. 15722, fols. 48v–49, an early thirteenth-century text of the poem which d'Alverny considers may represent a second redaction by Alan.

The Book of Creation

A note in the volume of the *Patrologia latina* devoted to Alan (*PL* 210.577) indicates that this text was appended to the "Rhythmus on the Liberal Arts and the Incarnation" in the manuscript used for the early edition reproduced there. My text is that of Dreves and Blume, for which no manuscript source is given. I have listed the variant readings of the *PL* text.

ORTHOGRAPHY

In twelfth-century orthography most manuscripts no longer distinguish *ae* or *oe,* using *e* for both. We have restored the diphthongs to their classical spelling. We distinguish consonantal *v* from vocalic *u,* and consonantal *j* from vocalic *i.* Words containing palatalized *ti- (gratia),* commonly spelled *ci- (gracia)* in the manuscripts, have been restored to classical spelling.

Notes to the Texts

Notes to the "Sermon on the Intelligible Sphere," the prose chapters of the *De planctu Naturae*, and the Prose Prologue to the *Anticlaudianus* refer to paragraph and line in the Latin text.

ABBREVIATIONS

Bo = Bossuat
H = Häring
L = London, British Library, MS Royal 13 B.VIII
Lo = London, British Library, MS Add. 15722
M = Minkova
P = Paris, Bibliothèque Nationale, MS Latin 3572
PL = *Patrologia latina*
Sh = Shanzer
Var = Variant reading(s) in Häring's apparatus
W = Wetherbee

SERMON ON THE INTELLIGIBLE SPHERE

12.1	exultant *P*
12.6	ycos ydos *P*
13.4	*As d'Alverny notes, Alan has apparently coined this verb from the Old French adjective* ord.
29.1	centrum *P*

DE PLANCTU NATURAE

Chapter 2

2.13	glaciali *Sh*: graciali *H*
5.2	inextinguibilis *Var*: inestimabilis *H*

553

18.5	fraternis *M*: supernis *H*
21.6	ciconia *Var*: avis concordiae *H*
21.11	Illic phasianus . . . orbes: *om. H*
25.6	multipharias *Var*: multiphariam *H*
28.7	discidium *Sh*: dissidium *H*

Chapter 4

1.2	splendiditatis *Var*: splendititatis *H*
2.4	coniunctis *Var*: coniugis *H*
4.10	non solum *Var*: *om. H*

Chapter 5

13	linquens *Sh*: linguens *H*
28	iubet *W*: iubens *H*
30	ore *Var*: orbe *H*
46	cum *Var*: Et *H*

Chapter 6

3.14	fluitantem *om. H M*
7.6	Illa *W*: Hec *H*
7.7	Hec *Var*: Ista *H*
7.8	Illa *W*: Hec *H*
7.10	Illa *Var*: Ista *H*
7.11	Haec *W*: Illa *H*
7.12	Illa *Var*: Ista *H*
7.13	Haec *W*: Illa *H*
8.5	praemio *Sh*: premii *H*
9.14	se *Var*: res *add. H*
10.18	Voluptas *M*: voluntas *H*
17.3	diminutivam *M*: diminutam *H*
17.5	deficiat *Var*: deficit *H*
19.1	Dum *M*: Cum *H*
21.3	audiendi *Var*: audendi *H*

Chapter 7

28   complens *Var*: comples *H*

Chapter 8

5.4   nunc coruscationibus illuminatur *om. H Var*
5.4   tonitrus *M*: tonitruus *H*
5.7   fluctus *Var*: fluxus *H*
17.1   vultum *Sh*: vultu *H*
17.7   altioris *M*: altiori *H*
17.16   exterioris *M*: exteriori *H*
21.2   infantiam *Sh*: infamiam *H*
30.10   singularum *Sh*: sigillarium *H*

Chapter 9

65   inungens *Var*: inungit *H*
66   Pungit *Var*: Pungens *H*

Chapter 10

1.10   strangulare *Sh*: transgulare *H*
6.6   usurpativa *Var*: usurpata *H*
6.15   cum *om. H Var*
6.15   philosophicae *Var*: etiam *add. H*
7.5   edocui *Var*: docendo *H*
9.2   incursu *Var*: incursus *H*
10.1   nobilitata *Sh*: nobilitate *H*
10.1   Venus *Sh*: Veneri *H*
10.2   Quae *W*: Quem *H*
12.2   eosdem *om. H Var*
13.14–15   Iste in deserta planicie figit tentoria. Illi vallis complacet nemo-rosa. *H Sh*
13.15   Ille *Sh*: Iste *H*
13.15   iste *Sh*: ille *H*
13.16   Ille *Sh*: Iste *H*

13.17   Iste *Sh*: Ille *H*
13.18   Ille *Sh*: Iste *H*
13.18   Iste *Sh*: Ille *H*

Chapter 12

7.4   cotidianum *Var*: cotidiano *H*
13.6   mens *Var*: mentis *H*
13.7   deliciosus *Var*: deliciosa *H*

Chapter 14

3.9   exterioris *Var*: exteriore *H*
4.5   aut *M*: autem *H*
6.9   signaculo *Sh*: speculo *H*
12.2   munus *Var*: nummus *H*

Chapter 15

28   Victi *Sh*: Victe *H*

Chapter 16

2.7   libramine *Var*: libamine *H*
5.2   incessum *W*: incessus *H*
13.10   exsculpsit *M*: exclusit *H*
16.8   excepit *Sh*: excepi *H*
17.4   castigatioris *Sh*: castigationis *H*
17.5   videbatur *Var*: hortabatur *H*
17.7   venerat patrocinium: venerari patronum *H*
23.2   eos: *add. W*
23.4   convivente *Var*: covivente *H*
29.3   exsculpserat *M*: excluserat *H*

Chapter 17

19   mentisque *Var*: mentique *H*

Chapter 18

7.12   deletionis *Sb*: delectionis *H*
10.2   patri *M*: patris *H*

ANTICLAUDIANUS

Prologue

1.1   expendere *L*: expandere *Bo*

Book 1

16   adhuc *L*: ad hec *Bo*
55–56   tractu longo *L*: longo Tractu *Bo*
72   gustus *L*: gustum *Bo*
77   rerum vulgus *L*: vulgus verum *Bo*
100   amnis *L*: humor *Bo*
128   ista *L*: illa *Bo*
157   vel *L*: et *Bo*
201   cana *L*: canis *Bo*
218   si n. *L*: si hanc n. *Bo*
219   quia *L*: quod *Bo*
248   laboris *L*: pudoris *Bo*
249–50   robur debet *L*: debet Robur *Bo*
263   suggit sibi gaudia luctu *L*: luctu sibi gaudia suggit. *Bo*
267   orantis *L*: orandi *Bo*
270   haec *L*: hoc *Bo*
281   siderei *Sb*: sydereum *Bo*
287   humeris *L*: humero *Bo*
305   illam *L*: illum *Bo*
341   cum *L*: cur *Bo*
343   aborsum *L*: abortum *Bo*
345   istud *L*: illud *Bo*
352   conceptus mentis honestae *L*: mentis conceptus honeste *Bo*
361   promovet *L*: permouet *Bo*
363   distans *L*: dispar *Bo*

557

371	caeli *L*: celum *Bo*
387	silere *L*: tacere *Bo*
388	nostra *L*: nostram *Bo*
421	profectos *L*: petitos *Bo*
450	speculi triplicis *L*: triplicis speculi *Bo*
473	sentit *L*: querit *Bo*
480	fit *L*: sit *Bo*
490	causis *L*: metis *Bo*
504	quid casu *L*: quia casu *Bo*

Book 2

11	gemmisque *L*: germinique *Bo*
23	mei *L*: meis *Bo*
38	assidue *L*: assiduo *Bo*
40	metam *L*: metas *Bo*
53	extinguere *L*: depellere *Bo*
63	haec *L*: hanc *Bo*
72	caducum *L*: caduca *Bo*
80	poterunt *L*: possunt *Bo*
85	quam *L*: quem *Bo*
110	vel . . . vol *L*: aut . . . vel *Bo*
111	possint caeli *L*: caeli possint *Bo*
112	cursus motu *L*: motu cursus *Bo*
113	contraque *L*: contra quem *Bo*
152	conatus *L*: cognatus *Bo*
165	Dum *L*: Cum *Bo*
180	foris aptata *L*: aptata foris *Bo*
189	temptat *L*: victat *Bo*
201	nec . . . nec *L*: non . . . non *Bo*
212	et *W*: in *Bo*
241	potans . . . potasset *L*: portans . . . portasset *Bo*
245	moveret *L*: moverent *Bo*
252	fluerent *L*: ruerent *Bo*
261	pacis normam *L*: normam pacis *Bo*

271	oberrat *L*: oberret *Bo*
295	optat *L*: instat *Bo*
300	veniet mentem *L*: mentem veniet *Bo*
356	Persius *Sh*: Perseus *Bo*
369	nubila sidera *L*: sydera, nubila *Bo*
375	Non *L*: nec *Bo*
379	depingit *L*: deponit *Bo*
380	axis *L*: axi *Bo*
387	perscribit *L*: proscribit *Bo*
396	solidus *L*: solidum *Bo*
398	resudat *L*: resultat *Bo*
415	his *L*: hec *Bo*
438	solaque figura *L*: solumque figure *Bo*
445	vindicat *Sh*: vendicet *Bo*
457	quod *L*: cur *Bo*
461	formamve *L*: formamque *Bo*
464	debita *L*: federa *Bo*
465	tacebit *L*: iacebit *Bo*
486	sculptura *L*: cultura *Bo*
486	recenti *L*: decenti *Bo*
511	admittit *L*: dimittit *Bo*
512	sed *L*: Si *Bo*

Book 3

9	afflasset *L*: perflasset *Bo*
11	respersa *L*: resparsa *Bo*
16	vigilasse *L*: vigilare *Bo*
19	non p. *L*: Nec p. *Bo*
20	finem *L*: crinem *Bo*
28	risum *L*: risus *Bo*
29	pungitur *L*: pungit et *Bo*
32	medium retinens *L*: mediumque tenens *Bo*
34	logicaeque *L*: logicesque *Bo*
36	tunicata *L*: truncata *Bo*

43	quid . . . quid . . . quid *L*: que . . . quid . . . que *Bo*
46	proprias *L*: proprios *Bo*
60	ipsa *L*: ista *Bo*
61	cum non *L*: non quod *Bo*
80	sibi *L*: sui *Bo*
96	cultum *L*: culmen *Bo*
149	quae *L*: quod *Bo*
157	vultus *L*: riuus *Bo*
161	altum *Sh*: imum *Bo*
167	induta *L*: inducta *Bo*
214	sumat *L*: firmat *Bo*
227	soli *L*: solus *Bo*
243	meditatur *L*: meditatus *Bo*
245	mediam *L*: medium *Bo*
253	externus *L*: extremus *Bo*
294	decore *L*: colore *Bo*
306	caducis *L*: caduco *Bo*
310	figuram *L*: figuras *Bo*
318	a primo . . . ortu *L*: ad primum . . . ortum *Bo*
347	ortum *L*: ortus *Bo*
348	nec *L*: non *Bo*
379	prpriae menti *L*: menti propriae *Bo*
384	factisque *L*: factoque *Bo*
409	meruit *L*: potuit *Bo*
418	variatque *L*: variasque *Bo*
421	gigantis *L*: gigantum *Bo*
445	diastemata *Sh*: diasymata *Bo*
451	esse *L*: illa *Bo*
458	exenia *L*: encenia *Bo*
478–79	claudit limitibus certis *L*: certis Limitibus claudit *Bo*
480	minuti *L*: minutim *Bo*
498	obtusove *L*: obtusoque *Bo*
517	materiem plumbi *L*: Plumbi materiam *Bo*
520	priores *L*: priorem *Bo*
521	priorum *L*: prioris *Bo*
533	ut *Sh*: et *Bo*

Book 4

8	tanto *L*: facto *Bo*
34	pingat *L*: pinguat *Bo*
38	aufugit *L*: Aut fugit *Bo*
38	fixus *L*: fluxus *Bo*
74	illis *L*: istis *Bo*
88	instruxit *L*: construxit *Bo*
98	hoc *L*: hec *Bo*
119	minor in specie *L*: specieque minor *Bo*
135	Iuno *L*: uiuo *Bo*
153	narisque ... satiatur *L*: naresque ... satiantur *Bo*
184	pro *L*: pre *Bo*
185	potu *L*: potus *Bo*
202	nimis *L*: magis *Bo*
206	secum *L*: secum: *om. Bo*
207	iacet *L*: viget *Bo*
256	nocivior *L*: nocentior *Bo*
289	perfudit, quos *L*: fudit et quos *Bo*
291	abiere *L*: adiere *Bo*
295	deiecti *L*: deiecta *Bo*
316	dum *L*: de *Bo*
335	certant venti *L*: venti certant *Bo*
350	hic sonitus *L*: iste sonus *Bo*
355	sedem *L*: sedere *Bo*
369	arcem *L*: altum *Bo*
375	pastor *L*: mater *Bo*
381	aetatis *L*: erroris *Bo*
394	gressum praepedit *L*: gressus impedit *Bo*
410	auditus *L*: auditis *Bo*
430	magis *L*: docet B
432	torrentis *L*: tonantis *Bo*
433	altiloquos *L*: altisonos *Bo*
459	aurem *L*: aures *Bo*
461	soni *L*: sono *Bo*
462	qui *L*: que *Bo*

| 471 | viget *L*: nitet *Bo* |
| 479 | huius *L*: eius *Bo* |

Book 5

9	numine *L*: munere *Bo*
30	excepto *L*: Ex quo *Bo*
36	Lacones *L*: Latones *Bo*
56	inignit *L*: inungit *Bo*
59	solet *Sh*: ualet *Bo*
76	nec *L*: Non *Bo*
85	conamine *L*: cognamine *Bo*
94	cesset *L*: censet *Bo*
106	redit *L*: tendit *Bo*
123	novo *L*: suo *Bo*
127	sustinet *L*: concipit *Bo*
175	humili *L*: humilis *Bo*
180	deferre *L*: defflere *Bo*
185	patent *L*: patet *Bo*
202	errasse *L*: errare *Bo*
210	vitet *L*: curet *Bo*
213	decernit *L*: discernit *Bo*
222	deferre *L*: conferre *Bo*
224	confortet *L*: confirmat *Bo*
234	dicatur *L*: ducatur *Bo*
234	beandum *L*: beatum *Bo*
240–41	ne . . . ne *L*: nec . . . nec *Bo*
256	praecepta *L*: mandata *Bo*
280	vitae *L*: veri *Bo*
294	dum *L*: qui *Bo*
299	recidens *L*: recindens *Bo*
329	expansus *L*: expassus *Bo*
337	expandat *L*: expendat *Bo*
359	conveniant *L*: connveniunt *Bo*
371	raucescit lingua *L*: mutescit musa *Bo*
375	conamine *L*: cognamine *Bo*

384 dolore *L*: labore *Bo*
387 infirmat *L*: infirmans *Bo*
417 librata Dei censura *L*: censura Dei librata *Bo*
449 deiecit *L*: deiectus *Bo*
451 foedae *L*: fedat *Bo*
453 demisit eum patientia *L*: donauit eum Prudencia *Bo*
457 devicit *L*: Deiecit *Bo*
463 aurea *L*: laurea *Bo*
486 vestitus *L*: uestibus *Bo*
507 iocosum *L*: iocundum *Bo*
524 ipsa *L*: ipse *Bo*
525 omen *L*: omne *Bo*

Book 6

1 supernas *L*: superbas *Bo*
27 cartis *L*: carnis *Bo*
54 gentilibus *L*: gentibus *Bo*
59 fidei clipeo *L*: clipeo Fidei *Bo*
110 secluditur error *L*: seducitur horror *Bo*
128 visus *L*: visum *Bo*
136 exuit erroris *L*: Eroris pellit *Bo*
149 mater *L*: matri *Bo*
150 huic *L*: hec *Bo*
183 Fides ubi sufficiat *L*: sufficiat Fides *Bo*
191 Sed *L*: sed *om. Bo*
221 comprimit *L*: opprimit *Bo*
262 ardens *L*: et ardens *Bo*
293 vox *L*: mens *Bo*
295 verbisque *L*: verbumque *Bo*
320 facta *L*: fata *Bo*
330 operum *L*: hominum *Bo*
334 producat *L*: perducat *Bo*
348 Naturae *L*: mature *Bo*
369 deiectio *L*: detractio *Bo*
380 precibus donat *L*: donat precibus *Bo*

393	tot m. *L*: quot m. *Bo*
394	aberrans *L*: oberrans *Bo*
403	conduceret *L*: concluderet *Bo*
407	ullum *L*: unum *Bo*
429	quod *L*: que *Bo*
439	Judithae *Sh*: Ytide Bo
439	patientia *L*: potentia *Bo*
444	sumit *L*: sumpsit *Bo*

Book 7

6	sperata *L*: superata *Bo*
13	puri sibi *L*: sibi puri *Bo*
31	languoris *L*: morborum *Bo*
37	terra *L*: terris *Bo*
43	specie *L*: facie *Bo*
45	simul *L*: magis *Bo*
48	in *L*: et *Bo*
55	suo *L*: suam *Bo*
77	Accumulat *L*: Dat iuueni *Bo*
110	accedit *L*: accessit *Bo*
114	Marte *L*: mente *Bo*
134	terram *L*: uitam *Bo*
135	terram faciem *L*: faciem terre *Bo*
148	nimio *L*: nimium *Bo*
178	ne *L*: nec *Bo*
183	detrahat et *L*: Detractet *Bo*
186	ne *L*: nec *Bo*
205	sui *L*: boni *Bo*
212	instans *L*: instet *Bo*
213	bonus *L*: bonum *Bo*
255	quem *L*: quam *Bo*
263	habenam *L*: habenas *Bo*
282	uberior *L*: ulterius *Bo*
302	turbet *L*: trahat *Bo*
308	spatio *L*: spacium *Bo*

313   agit *L*: agat *Bo*
314   excitat . . . insidet *L*: excitet . . . incitet *Bo*
322   ei *L*: eius *Bo*
322   aëris *Sb*: etheris *Bo*
340   nec *L*: ne *Bo*
360   prostat *L*: perstat *Bo*
378   fundere *L*: spargere *Bo*
379   spargere *L*: fundere *Bo*
386   docet *L*: monet *Bo*
403   domum *L*: locum *Bo*
404   cursu *L*: gressu *Bo*
416   sistitur *L*: fallitur *Bo*
435   insultans *L*: incautis *Bo*
452   tacti *L*: pasci *Bo*
453   perfundi *L*: perfundunt *Bo*
474   ad *L*: in *Bo*
477   praedulcis aquae *L*: preclusus aquis *Bo*

Book 8

7   tumet *L*: sedet *Bo*
9   scintillat *L*: splendescit *Bo*
40   haec munera *L*: nec munera *Bo*
50   fatiget *L*: fatigat *Bo*
64   festina *L*: festiua *Bo*
65   praestringit *L*: perstringit *Bo*
68   ipsi *L*: illi *Bo*
70   quem *L*: quod *Bo*
80   dona *L*: uota *Bo*
91   sint *L*: sunt *Bo*.
99   inferre *L*: conferre *Bo*
122   caelesti *L*: electi *Bo*
123   minori *L*: minore *Bo*
126   maiori *L*: Maiore *Bo*
153   peroret *L*: perorat *Bo*
164   Periuria *L*: penuria *Bo*

175	fastum *L*: fastus *Bo*
180	salvare *L*: servire *Bo*
183	muttire *L*: mutare *Bo*
208	vertere *L*: vincere *Bo*
221	Prima sitit bellum *L*: Arma sitit belli *Bo*
234	rapit *L*: capit *Bo*
240	vallante *L*: vallata *Bo*
247	ibi *L*: humi *Bo*
254	pugna *L*: pugne *Bo*
254	incidere *L*: impendere *Bo*
257	tristities pressura dolor lamenta *L*: tristicies lamenta dolor pressura *Bo*
267	pronus *L*: promptus *Bo*
274	scelerum fomes *L*: fomes scelerum *Bo*
285	fusi *L*: fusa *Bo*
290	illiciens *L*: illicitus *Bo*
294	venantur *L*: uenentur *Bo*
294	segnis *L*: nummus *Bo*
295	domino *L*: domine *Bo*
304	decidere *L*: descindere *Bo*
316	rapit *L*: capit *Bo*
333	strepitum *L*: strepitus *Bo*
345	proprias *L*: proprios *Bo*
347	nullis decisa *L*: nullisque decisa *Bo*
361	Nec *L*: Non *Bo*

Book 9

3	funera *L*: vulnera *Bo*
18	obiectus *L*: abiectus *Bo*
18	refellit *L*: repellit *Bo*
22	pigredine *L*: pinguedine *Bo*
28	verbis *L*: uerbo *Bo*
31	malorum *L*: laborum *Bo*
35	nec *L*: non *Bo*
44	multos *L*: multas *Bo*

44	discurrit *L*: descendit *Bo*
45	subticet *L*: subditur *Bo*
46	mutescit *L*: Mitescit *Bo*
51	Odium perimit *L*: perimit odium *Bo*
70	ictum *L*: ictus *Bo*
78	Siti *L*: Sitis *Bo*
84	nec *L*: non *Bo*
85	arma *L*: ora *Bo*
92	repressa *L*: repensa *Bo*
128	gressum *L*: gressus *Bo*
132	male supplet *L*: supplet male *Bo*
149	ignava *L*: longeua *Bo*
160	luctae specie *L*: specie lucte *Bo*
174	torpore *L*: tempore *Bo*
177	obsequium *L*: officium *Bo*
190	et *L*: sed *Bo*
195	retinet *L*: retinens *Bo*
216	ad haec *L*: ei *Bo*
218	vigore *L*: rigore *Bo*
226	Casum *L*: casus *Bo*
231	catervas *L*: caternas *Bo*
232	expirare *L*: expirasse *Bo*
234	qua *L*: que *Bo*
284	partem *L*: partes *Bo*
294	in pugnam *L*: in iuuenem *Bo*
312	furit *L*: ferit *Bo*
318	ferro non *L*: nec ferro *Bo*
327	proprio *L*: uario *Bo*
328	Marti cedens *L*: cedens Marti *Bo*
330	veteres latebras *L*: latebras veteres *Bo*
334	vomit *L*: movet *Bo*
340	victos *L*: vitulos *Bo*
353	partem vitae *L*: vite partem *Bo*
370	hostem *L*: illam *Bo*
379	possit *L*: posset *Bo*
380	silentum *L*: silenter *Bo*

567

393   terreus *L*: terrenus *Bo*
410   multum *L*: multo *Bo*

Vix nodosum valeo

3   nudae: Unde *H*
68   signatus: sic gratus *H*
73   errore: est rore *H*
126   crescit: exescit *H*
142   Helena: Helene *H*

Rithmus de Incarnatione Domini

25–28   *In Lo*:

> Novus color in iunctura
>   Nova fit coniunctio;
> Novus tropus in figura
>   Nova fit conversio.

42   mira: Una *Lo*
43   modus: nodus *Lo*
44   ordo: modus *Lo*
47   stupet: Nescit *Lo*
48   musica: Musice *Lo*
52   geometra: Geometer *Lo*
54   terrenorum sistitur: Nostre carnis capitur *Lo*
55   directum: diversum *Lo*
63   nubis: carnis *Lo*
65   versit in: in se fert *Lo*
67   defectum: defectu *Lo*

Omnis mundi creatura

3   in: et *PL*
4   sortis: mortis *PL*
5   mortis: sortis *PL*
24   Senii: Vitale *PL*
35   portum: pontem *PL*

Notes to the Translations

Notes to the "Sermon on the Intelligible Sphere," the prose chapters of the *De planctu Naturae,* and the Prose Prologue to the *Anticlaudianus* refer to paragraph and line in the translation.

ABBREVIATIONS

Anticl. = Anticlaudianus
DpN = De planctu Naturae
Martianus, *De nuptiis* = Martianus Capella, *De nuptiis Philologiae et Mercurii*
PL = Patrologia latina
Radulphus, *In Anticl.* = Radulphus de Longo Campo. *In Anticlaudianum Alani Commentum*
SIS = Sermon on the Intelligible Sphere
SQH = Summa "Quoniam homines"

SERMON ON THE INTELLIGIBLE SPHERE

The "hermetic" formula may be Alan's own. See Introduction, n. 15.

1.1–3   The reference is to Exodus 3:22; 12:35–36, which, largely on the basis of Augustine, *De doctrina christiana* 2.40, became a standard justification for appropriating pagan writings to Christian purposes.

1.5   The formula does not appear in the works of Cicero; "Tullius" was apparently a name to conjure with.

2.7   Martianus, *De nuptiis* 1.7. *Choe* is a corruption of *Psyche,* "the soul."

2.8–9	By a false etymology, impossible to convey in English, *diadema* becomes *duo demens.* Apparently Alan's invention.
3.3–6	Boethius, *De arithmetica* 2.30.
3.8–9	Cicero, *De inventione* 1.38.
3.10	"Mercury," "Hermes Mercury," "Mercury Trismegistus," the supposed author of the pseudo-Hermetic *Asclepius,* extremely influential for twelfth-century Platonism.
7.1–4	Plato, *Timaeus* 30B–D, 36D–E.
9.1–2	The sensible sphere is "formal" in that the formation of creatures occurs there; the imaginable is "deformed" in that here the native forms are subjected to differentiation and adaptation to mortality; the rational is "conformed" in that here the forms most resemble their ideal models; the intelligible is "unformed" in that the divine is above form. D'Alverny cites *Regulae* 75, where Alan speaks of three types of action, *informis, deformis,* and *formata,* but the two passages have little in common.
9.3–4	The point of these two sets of paired terms is apparently to contrast, first, the status of forms still suspended with that of forms joined to matter, second, the immutability of the divine with the alterity of created forms.
9.7	As d'Alverny suggests, *ychome* seems to have been invented by Alan so that each sphere would have its own type of form.
11.4	The "genial" kiss recalls the role of Genius as described in *DpN* 18, and the sentence as a whole recalls the account of the birth of Veritas, *DpN* 18.10.
12.1	I read *exulant* for the *exultant* of the manuscript; Alan emphasizes the gloom of this sphere and the desire of the forms to return above. Compare *Anticl.* 1.495–97, where forms destined for worldly existence are "sent into exile."
12.7	I have followed Dronke, *Fabula,* 149, in reversing *ycos* and *ydos.*
14.4	On *ingenium* as described here, see John of Salisbury, *Metalogicon* 1.11.
18.5	"Enlivening power" is the basic meaning of *vegetatio* in postclassical Latin.
20.9–11	On the division between "political" and "noetic" virtues, see Macrobius, *In Somnium Scipionis* 1.8. On "physical" virtue, rational adherence to the natural law established by God, see

d'Alverny, *Alain de Lille,* 304 n. 48, and Lottin, *Psychologie et morale,* 2.71ff.

21.12   Properly speaking, *paetus* denotes a tendency to blink or squint.

21.17   The "first powers" are sense and imagination.

25.1   As d'Alverny notes, Alain probably recalls Claudianus Mamertus, *De statu animae* 2.6 (*PL* 53.745B), and perhaps 1.25 (*PL* 53.733). Both passages discuss the signs of the Trinity that inhere in created things, but neither mentions the triangle.

27.1   The reference is to the *Asclepius,* but as d'Alverny notes, Alan is apparently quoting from memory both that text and the pseudo-Augustinian sermon "Against Five Heresies" now attributed to the fifth-century bishop of Carthage Quodvultdeus. Alan cites "Mercurius" on the Trinity again in *SQH* 2.31; *Contra haereticos* 2.3 (*PL* 210.404D–405A).

The Plaint of Nature

Chapter 1

3   On the syntax of line 3, see Gärtner, "Vier Anmerkungen," 273–74.

17–19   In terms of Alan's sexual grammar, male is to female as predicate to subject (Ziolkowski, *Grammar of Sex,* 15).

24   The opposition between "trope," or metaphor, and "vice" *(vitium)* is an important consideration in twelfth-century grammar and in the *DpN.* A certain freedom in the use of literary devices, or *figurae,* is excused when deemed necessary for stylistic purposes, but practiced too freely it becomes *vitium,* the equivalent of barbarism, or the misuse of particular words, in grammar.

25   The first of Alan's many metaphors from formal logic. "Conversion" in logic is the reversal of subject and predicate terms in a proposition. A "simple" conversion would change "All A is B" to "Some B is A."

27–30   Compare the joining of *Yle* with *Ydea* in the creative activity of Veritas, below, 18.10.

29   On earlier uses of the images of plow and hammer, see Pejenaute Rubio, "Dos aportaciones relacionadas con la metáfora gramatical."

31–32   The point of this difficult couplet seems to be that whereas an iamb is properly the joining of a long (masculine) with a short (feminine) syllable, men now exploit the relative freedom of the iamb by converting it to a spondee, which joins two long or masculine syllables. On this passage, and metrical metaphor in general, see the excellent discussion of Ziolkowski, *Grammar of Sex,* 22–27.

35   Tyndareus was king of Sparta, and real or putative father of Helen, Castor, and Pollux.

47–50   On lines 47–50 see Gärtner, "Vier Anmerkungen," 275–77; "Der Übertritt der Seele."

55–56   Thetis, fearing that her son Achilles would be recruited to fight at Troy, took him to the island of Lemnos, where he lived, disguised as a girl, among the daughters of King Lycomedes, one of whom, Deidamia, became the mother of his son, Pyrrhus or Neoptolemus. The story is told in Statius, *Achilleid* 1.

Chapter 2

1.11   I take *decusata* here as a form of *decusso,* "to divide crosswise," i.e., in the form of a ten (*decus,* X), though Alan also uses the medieval coinage *decuso,* "to adorn."

1.17   The point is evidently that the two "consequents," the gold of the comb and the gold of the hair, cannot be distinguished; neither follows logically from the other, and the result is a paralogism, a syllogism in which the conclusion does not follow from the premises.

4.5   Dione is the mother of Venus, but often, and in Medieval Latin poetry regularly, Venus herself.

6.9–11   As Sheridan notes, *petitio principii,* or begging the question, is the logical fallacy in which what is to be proven is implicitly taken for granted. Alan's point seems to be that the circling diadem is continually "seeking" what it is certain of finding.

7.7–8   The zodiac as diadem recalls the description of the crown of Sol in Martianus, *De nuptiis* 1.75.

8.3   *Antonomasia* is the rhetorical trope which substitutes another term for a person's name (Arbusow, *Colores Rhetorici,* 85).

8.6   Alan uses *pictura* repeatedly, not just of painting but of all kinds of visual art. In translating I have tried to use terms appropriate to the contexts in which they appear.

8.8   I take *audaciam* here as referring to altitude; compare the wild ass of 2.31, who roams through *montium audaciam,* and *Anticl.* 2.101: *praeceps audacia montis.*

8.14   Sheridan suggests Pisces, the faintest of the zodiacal constellations, but the sign opposite to Gemini is Sagittarius.

9.6–7   The youth is Ganymede.

9.13–14   Sagittarius, once the centaur Chiron, teacher of Achilles.

12.3–4   Plato's Timaeus had flatly refused to describe the dance of the planetary "gods" (*Timaeus* 40C), and Alan's paragraph, with its oddly prosaic final sentence, is entirely his own. On the sensual effects of music as a prelude to sleep, compare the lyric "Dum Dianae vitrea," *Carmina Burana* 62.

15.1   *Astrites* has not been identified. Martianus, *De nuptiis* 1.75 names it as one of the jewels in the crown of Sol.

15.2   Though *caloris* is the reading of nearly all the manuscripts, including the three oldest, as Minkova notes ("Textual Suggestions," 183), *calibis (chalybis),* the *lectio difficilior,* is clearly appropriate to Mars.

20.9–10   Juvenal, *Satire* 3.289. Shanzer ("Parturition," 141), questions Alan's authorship of this sentence, which lacks the periodic structure of the other sentences in this passage.

21.7–8   Sheridan cites Vincent of Beauvais, *Speculum Doctrinale* 15.153, for the tradition that the stork offers one of its offspring as tribute to the owner of the land where it has nested. Many manuscripts have *avis concordiae* in place of *ciconia,* though in a number of them *ciconia* has been inserted by a later hand.

21.11–13   The pheasant is omitted in the manuscripts on which Häring's edition is chiefly based.

21.14   I take *discrimen* in the sense of "turning point."

22.7   Alan apparently raises the question of whether the magpie has the same number of white as black feathers. J. Ziolkowski, ed., *Solomon and Marcolf* (Cambridge, Mass.: Harvard University Press, 2008), 208, quotes a brief *Streitgedicht* in which *Albedo* and *Nigredo* (White and Black) present rival claims to be the bird's defining color, but Nature concludes that her color is neither white nor black, but "unresolved" *(dubius)*.

22.8   The Pierides insolently challenged the Muses to a singing contest, and when defeated they were turned to magpies but retained their disputatiousness (Ovid, *Met.* 5.677–78).

24.2–5 The nightingale is Philomela, raped by Tereus, husband of her sister Procne, who cut out her tongue to prevent her revealing what he had done. Philomela wove her story onto a piece of cloth, from which Procne learned the truth. Procne then killed her son Itys, served his flesh to Tereus, and told him what he had eaten. When Tereus sought to kill the sisters, all three were turned to birds (Ovid, *Met.* 6.412–674). Philomela, as a nightingale, can now sing of the violation of which she could not speak.

24.10   *gumphi,* literally "nails," recalls Plato, *Timaeus* 43A, where the Demiurge connects the elements that compose the human body with "invisible rivets" *(aoratois gomphois)*. Calcidius transliterates the term in his Latin version of the dialogue. *Gumphus* is used of the relation of musical tones in *Rhythmus* 46. In *Anticl.* 4.79 Reason uses *gumfi* in joining the parts of the chariot of Prudence.

25.3   The seamless garment *(tunica inconsutilis)* recalls the robe of Christ, for which the soldiers cast lots (John 19:23–24), in the twelfth century widely accepted as having been woven by his mother, Mary.

26.18–21 The belief that the bodies of oysters grew and contracted with the waxing and waning of the moon is reported by Cicero, *De divinatione* 2.33; Horace, *Satire* 2.4.30; Pliny, *Naturalis historia* 2.41.109.

27.17   Ausonius (*Mosella* 85) mentions the tender flesh of the capito, whose name ("large-headed") appears in medieval glossaries. John of Garland, *Epithalamium* 8.51, notes that the *capito* swims slowly *pro pondere capitis.*

27.19   Both *haec* and *figurata* are very well attested, but it is not clear to me why they should be neuter here.

27.20   The reference to "sculpture" is in keeping with Alan's several references to pictures as writing or speech. Compare the indeterminate medium of the panorama of Virgil, *Aeneid* 1.453–93, and the carved *visibile parlare* of Dante, *Purgatorio* 10.95.

28.7–9   The torn garment recalls that of Boethius's Philosophy, rent by the different philosophical sects; *Consolatio* 1.pr.1.5; pr.3.7.

31.2–4   Whereas the leopard is proverbially unable to change his spots (Jeremiah 13:23), Nero is said by Tacitus (*Annales* 13.25) to have roamed the streets of Rome at night disguised as a slave, with companions who attacked those whom they encountered and stole goods set out for sale.

32.4   John 11:39.

Chapter 3

6   Adonium. Venus is said to have transformed the dead Adonis into this flower; its blossom is golden or dark red, as if from his blood.

18–19   The Herbal of "Apuleius Barbarus" mentions the *basilisca* or "royal flower" *(herba regia)*.

28   Favonius is Zephyrus, the mild west wind of early spring, thought to stimulate new growth.

Chapter 4

2.4   Peacocks.

2.12   The referent of *cuius* is unclear. A case could be made for *homo*.

4.5   The phrase echoes Lucan, *De bello civili* 1.2. Alan is doubtless thinking also of the great political metaphor of Virgil, *Aeneid* 1.148–56.

4.9   Thetis was actually the daughter of Nereus, and the mother of Achilles through her marriage to the mortal Peleus.

6.4   Flora is the Italian goddess of flowers, honored with a lavish annual festival which included obscene miming.

Chapter 5

3–4   *Ligustra* are probably primrose or cowslip.

25   Medieval mythography commonly identified Juno with the sublunar atmosphere.

39–40   Phrixus, son of the Boeotian king Athamas, fled with his sister,

Helle, from the jealousy of their stepmother, Ino, on the back of the ram whose golden fleece was later captured by Jason. Here the ram is identified with the constellation Aries; the season is the portion of March and April when the sun is passing through Aries, when Chaucer's "yonge sonne / hath in the ram his halve course yronne."

41   See above, 2.24.2–5n.

Chapter 6

1.6   Alan is apparently punning on *cognatam,* using it here to refer to "closeness" in a merely physical sense rather than the kinship which he does not yet recognize.

4.1–4   Nature's words echo the opening poem of the *Cosmographia* of Bernardus Silvestris, where Nature appeals to *Noys,* the creative wisdom of God, on behalf of the "infant universe," which cries out in its longing for form.

5.3   On *ingenium* see John of Salisbury, *Metalogicon* 1.11, and *SIS* 14.

10.12   As often in Alan, Providence is an alternate title for Wisdom. *Prudentia/Sapientia/Sophia* is the heroine of Alan's *Anticl.*

10.19   I have substituted the well-attested *voluptas* for *voluntas* here, in view of the role of the *renes* in the previous paragraph. See also Minkova, "Textual Suggestions," 188–89.

13.8–10 In *SQH,* Prol., this maxim is again attributed to Aristotle. In *Anticl.* 3.115–28, Alan explains the difficult language of Aristotle's logical writings as designed to conceal his wisdom from the multitude.

Chapter 7

13   Noys is the divine mind. In the *Cosmographia* of Bernardus Silvestris identified with Providence.

30   Minkova ("Textual Suggestions," 190), notes that in place of *mutas* two of the oldest manuscripts offer *muscas,* "flies" or "insects," which would then be with *uulgus* an object of *donas.*

Chapter 8

1.3–5   Each of these four subject phrases contains suggestive wordplay which I have found it impossible to recreate in translation.

2.1–2   *Talio,* a legal term, normally denotes punishment corresponding to the offense: an eye for an eye. The term appears in its legal sense in par. 13 below, but in 16.25 it is used of reciprocated affection.

3.13   *Professio* suggests submission to the rules of an order, the taking of a vow; compare the fish of par. 6.

3.16   A solecism is a grammatical irregularity, such as a confusion of genders, too serious to be "excused" as a "figural locution" (Thurot, *Extraits,* 459–60; Lausberg, *Handbuch,* 1.268–74).

8.6   Metaplasm is the corruption of a single word in a verse "out of metrical necessity" (Ziolkowski, *Grammar of Sex,* 22–23; Thurot, *Extraits,* 463–64; Lausberg, *Handbuch,* 1.259–60). Nature is presumably referring to the irregularities noted in lines 31–32 of the opening poem.

8.7–8   Tiresias encountered two snakes copulating, struck them with his staff, and was turned into a woman; eight years later he met them again; struck them again, and was turned back into a man (Ovid, *Metamorphoses* 3.323–31).

8.11   Analogy or "proportion" in grammar concerns the inflected endings of words and the correct linkages of person, number, and gender (*Regulae* 27; Martianus, *De nuptiis* 3.290–324; Lausberg, *Handbuch,* 1.254–55).

8.12   Anastrophe is a change in the regular order of words (Arbusow, *Colores Rhetorici,* 40, 80).

8.13–14   Synaeresis is the compression of two vowels into a single syllable, or two syllables into one (Lausberg, *Handbuch,* 1.263–64). Tmesis is the separation of a word by the insertion of another word (Lausberg, *Handbuch,* 1.253).

10.5–7   Wife of King Minos of Crete. Her passion for a snow-white bull led her to persuade the master artisan Daedalus to create a wooden cow within which she concealed herself. When the bull mounted the false cow, the Minotaur was conceived.

10.8   A paralogism is a false syllogism. In a valid syllogism "a conclusion derived from premises, by expressing what the premises demand, is stamped with their likeness" (*Anticl.* 3.49–50). Here the conclusion is "stamped" with the false premise that Pasiphae is a cow, a paralogism in its representation of her, a sophism in its deception of the bull.

10.11–12   Ovid, *Metamorphoses* 10.298–502.

10.12   Stepmotherly behavior is invariably malicious in Medieval Latin poetry. See 12.10.21n below. Medea killed her children by Jason in revenge for his abandonment of her to marry Creusa; Virgil, *Eclogue* 8.46–47; Ovid, *Metamorphoses* 7.394–97.

11.7   Heteroclite nouns vary in declension (e.g., *domus,* which varies between the second and fourth declensions; *vas/is,* which varies between the second and third).

11.13   I assume that the passive *praedicari* refers to one's becoming subject to "predication" or impregnation.

13.5–6   *Secretarius* can denote one granted special knowledge, the keeper of a sacred trust. Compare *SQH,* Prol.: *sicut olim philosophia cum familiari et secretario suo Boetio....*

13.6   In view of the legal language that follows, *querimoniale* must have the sense of a "plaint" delivered in court.

13.9   On *talio* see 8.2.1–2n above.

16.5   The Phrygian youth is Ganymede.

16.6–8   In this sentence *propositum,* literally "placed before," the status of Ganymede as wine steward, is balanced against *suppositum,* "placed under."

18.5–6   The image is of the gods as pupils of schoolmistress Venus; Juvenal, *Satire* 1.15.

23.2–4   See above, 2.28.7–9n.

24.9–10   Macrobius, *In somnium Scipionis* 1.2.17–19, observes that Nature resists "an open and naked display of herself," conceals herself beneath her creation, and reveals herself only to the wise, through "fabulous narratives." Macrobius then recalls Numenius, who published an account of the Eleusinian mysteries. In a dream the goddesses of Eleusis appeared to him at the door of a brothel, dressed as prostitutes, to rebuke him for profaning "the sanctuary of their purity."

24.11 *Integumentum* in the twelfth-century schools denotes a myth or image that conceals a deeper philosophical, moral, or spiritual meaning. See Introduction, n. 42.

26.17–18 Nature quotes Boethius, *Consolatio* pr.12 ad fin., who in turn is quoting Plato, *Timaeus* 29B.

28.4 I have translated *verbum* by "idea," as making Alan's meaning more readily accessible, but the use of the Latin term is noteworthy.

28.18–19 The elements.

Chapter 9

21 I.e., the opposite of miracles, prodigies of evil.

27 The poor soldiery of Paris was proverbial.

27 Alan recalls the Tydeus of Statius, *Thebaid* 8.739–66, who gnaws at the head of Melanippus, who had inflicted his death wound.

28 Melicerta was the son of Athamas and Ino. To escape the madness of Athamas, Ino threw herself into the sea with Melicerta in her arms; both were turned to sea gods through the intercession of Venus.

29 Thersites was originally a character in the *Iliad,* a common soldier, lame, ugly, and fearless in criticism of his commanding officers.

30 Davus is a common name for a slave in Roman comedy; in medieval school poetry an ugly man, as also at *Anticl.* 1.182; 2.14; 6.227.

31 For Virgil (*Eclogue* 5.11; 7.22) and Juvenal (*Satires* 1.2; 3.203), Codrus is a bad poet; in twelfth-century poetry he is a stock figure for poverty.

32 For Virgil (*Eclogue* 3.90), Bavius is a bad poet.

33 Ennius is conventionally supposed to have been a bad poet.

33 Marcus is Marcus Tullius Cicero.

35 Antaeus was a Libyan giant who defeated all comers in wres-

tling and then murdered them. Hercules, having discovered that Antaeus's strength was derived from contact with his mother, the Earth, succeeded in killing him after raising him into the air.

41   Aphaeresis is the shortening of a word by removal of the first letter or syllable.

47–48   See above, 8.10, and 8.10.12n.

49–50   Byblis, daughter of the king of Miletus, was seized with an incestuous desire for her brother Caunus. Rejected, she fled to Lycia, where she was transformed into a fountain (Ovid, *Metamorphoses* 9.448–666).

Chapter 10

1.18   I take *excrementum* here in the sense of "outgrowth" or "prominence."

2.26   "Truthful" *(propria)* description refers to the condition of a creature as originally created; in the case of man, his prelapsarian state.

4.3   I read *anomale* as an adverb.

4.6–7   *Evocatio* and *conceptio* are elaborate grammatical puns. "Evocation" is the use of the personal pronoun *(ego, nos, tu, vos)* to grant a noun (in principle third-person) the status of first or second person. A first-person noun so constituted can "evoke" a second-person noun, and the two together can evoke a third-person noun (Thurot, *Extraits,* 257–58). The relevance of *conceptio* can be illustrated by the comparison of the phrases "I read and Peter reads" *(ego lego et Petrus legit)* with "I read with Peter" *(ego cum Petro legimus).* In the latter phrase the first subject, joined to the second by the copulative *cum,* is understood to "conceive" the second, producing the relation indicated by the plural verb (Thurot, *Extraits,* 258–59).

4.9–11   I.e., trope can be legitimate *translatio* or unacceptable *vitium;* compare 1.17–24.

6.4   Twelfth-century discussions of *transitio* considered whether such constructions as "X sits at the door" *(Sor* [meaning, Socrates] *sedet ad portam*) could be considered transitive, since the preposition effects a transition *quodam modo* (Thurot, *Extraits,* 230–33). Alan's purpose in contrasting such dubious cases with *recta directio transitionis* is clear enough.

7.4   "Conclusion" here denotes the final term of a syllogism.

7.12   *Similia instantiarum* are "like cases" which can be cited to refute a proposition.

7.17   The "extremes" are the subject and predicate terms in the conclusion of a syllogism.

8.2–3 Analogous predication applies the same predicate to related but not synonymous subjects, thus admitting the kind of unorthodox predication to which Alan objects.

8.4   Conversion is the reversal of the terms of a proposition so that predicate becomes subject.

8.4–5 The fallacy of the consequent consists in deducing the truth of the antecedent from the consequent, leaving open the possibility of a failure of true connection, a *complexio terminorum inconsequens.*

11.4–7 The sudden and isolated reference to drink and food suggests that Alan had at one time planned to develop this theme here. They are mentioned again in par. 13, in terms that seem to assume that their role as a goad to desire has been discussed in some detail.

13.16–17 With Shanzer ("Parturition," 146), I have reversed these two phrases to preserve the symmetry of Alan's comparisons.

14.3   I take *emphaticam* as referring to the rhetorical figure which suggests or implies (by comparison, ambiguous suggestion, logical consequence) but stops short of definite assertion (*Rhetorica ad Herennium* 4.67; Lausberg, *Handbuch,* 1.298–99).

Chapter 11

5–8   Astraea, the last of the immortals to leave the earth at the onset of the Age of Iron (Ovid, *Metamorphoses* 1.149–50), was transformed into the constellation Virgo, and I assume that this is the *sidus* of line 7.

Chapter 12

3.9	Boethius's Philosophy uses this phrase of the "Siren" Muses of poetry in *Consolatio* 1. pr.1.11.
7.4	The collector is the stomach.
10.17	*Monetam* here is perhaps the eloquence itself, Cicero's stock in trade, his equivalent to money, perhaps the stamp or die that produces his eloquence.
10.19	For *mercenaria*, De Visch offers the strikingly apt variant *vicennarie* (i.e., twenty-year), for which I have no other evidence.
10.21–22	*Novercari*, "to behave with a stepmother's malice," appears again in *Anticl.* 7.369 and in other twelfth-century school poetry. A probable source is Sidonius, *Epistulae* 7.14.3. Hippolytus's stepmother is Phaedra, sister of Ariadne and successor to Hippolyta as wife of Theseus.
11.2–3	Lucan, *De bello civili* 3.108: "Omnia Caesar erat."
11.9–10	As Sheridan notes, these phrases parody the tricolon "Christus vincit, Christus regnat, Christus imperat," a formula of the liturgical *laudes regiae* that appears as early as the mid-eighth century; see Kantorowicz, *Laudes Regiae,* 21–31.
12.14	The "accidents" of words are the variations required by case, number, person, tense.

Chapter 13

7	The toga was not worn by soldiers and represented peace for Romans. Cicero, *In Pisonem* 30.73; *De oratore* 3.42.167.

Chapter 14

3.21	*Patrocinium* ("patronage") controls the potentially unruly *plebs* as the scissors control the bristling eyebrows.
6.7	*Concludo* is used here as if in reference to logical argument: "conclude," "infer," "argue."
6.8–9	The waters of Hippocrene, the fountain of the Muses, first caused to flow by the stamping of the hoof of Pegasus.

6.9   1 Corinthians 13:12.

9.14–16   In translating this sentence I have assumed that *inanias* is a verb
         and taken *demordeo* in the punning sense of "un-bite" rather than
         "bite back."

Chapter 15

5   A name of Bacchus: "relaxer," "deliverer from care."

Chapter 16

1.4–14   The description of Hymen recalls that of Boethius's Philosophy,
         Consolatio 1.pr.1.

11.11   I have tried to suggest the aspect of *circumcisio* most appropriate
         to Temperance, though in the biblical passage to which Alan
         probably alludes (Exodus 6:8), *incircumcisus* seems to indicate a
         lack of eloquence.

13.6–7   I have retained *natu,* the reading of nearly all manuscripts,
         though this word is normally used only with reference to age;
         Shanzer ("Parturition," 147), suggests *nature.* For *regulariter* I
         could see no alternative to paraphrase.

15.15–16 A main verb is clearly missing here, and was evidently never sup-
         plied, or was lost at an early stage in the transmission of the
         text.

17.12   Apocope is the omission of a letter or syllable at the end of a
         word.

21.7–8   Horace, *Epistle* 1.18.84; compare the remarkable echo of this line
         in Prudence's appeal to God, *Anticl.* 6.314.

24.7   *Carmen* here has the sense of "form" or "formula" in legal or reli-
         gious writing, not necessarily in verse.

26.7–8   *Consequentia* here is the relation of terms in a logical proposi-
         tion.

29.2   Häring's *excluserat* is clearly unsatisfactory. Shanzer ("Parturi-
         tion," 147), argues that "Nature as craftsman and the act of seal-
         ing require *excuderat,*" the reading of many manuscripts. Mink-
         ova ("Textual Suggestions," 199), prefers *exsculpserat,* also well

attested, on the grounds that the verb refers "not to pressing the seal, but . . . to the image engraved on the seal."

Chapter 17

34–37   Pentaphone, perhaps a neologism coined by Alan himself, apparently refers to polyphony in five voices.

41–43   Alan may be recalling the description of the battle of Actium on the shield of Aeneas, where Cleopatra is shown playing the *sistrum* to urge forward her fleet (Virgil, *Aeneid* 8.696); or the women celebrating the victory of Saul and David over the Philistines, I Samuel 18:6.

Chapter 18

1.8   My translation takes *Nature* as modifying the understood *curiam* of *decuriatam*.

1.12–13   1 Corinthians 5:6; Galatians 5:9.

2.1–2   As we will be told, the vice in question is Prodigality.

2.11   *Usia,* substance or being.

2.12   See Introduction, pp. xxv–xxvi.

6.1   For Alan "drama" is in effect "dialogue."

6.2   The ontological status of Genius is suggested by *resultatio,* used elsewhere of manifestations of the divine; see the definition of *epiphania* in the *Hierarchia Alani* (d'Alverny, *Alain de Lille,* 229).

6.6–7   Aphaeresis is the omission of a letter or syllable at the beginning of a word. Prothesis is the prefixing of a letter or syllable (Lausberg, *Handbuch,* 1.252, 260).

8.4   In Virgil's *Aeneid* Turnus is the valiant leader of the native Italian armies, archfoe of Aeneas and the invading Trojans.

8.5   Capaneus is one of the seven champions whose war against Thebes is narrated in Statius, *Thebaid.* Distinguished by his size and his hostility to the gods, he becomes a giant in the twelfth-century *Roman de Thèbes.*

9.12   In Virgil, *Aeneid* 2, the Greek soldier who, having let himself be captured by the Trojans, persuaded them to draw the wooden horse into Troy, ensuring the city's fall.

9.14–17   Alan apparently refers to an incident cited by Horace (*Satire* 2.3.60–62): In a play by Pacuvius a mother is awakened by the ghost of her murdered son. At one performance the actor playing the mother had been drinking, actually fell asleep, and missed his cue. The audience joined the ghost in repeating the opening words of the speech intended to awaken the sleeper.

10.4–8   On this passage, see Introduction, p. xxvi, and compare *SIS* 11.

10.15   Diaeresis is the resolution of one syllable into two, usually by giving separate value to the two vowels in a diphthong (Lausberg, *Handbuch*, 1.261–62).

10.16   "Pharisee" is derived from the Aramaic verb *perish* (Hebrew *parush*), "separate."

12.4   The use of *promiscui* is puzzling, and Shanzer ("Parturition," 200), noting that the word is used pejoratively elsewhere in the *DpN,* follows earlier editors in emending to *mystici.* But *promiscui* is so well attested that I have retained it, assuming that the "promiscuous" *cupido* of Nature and Genius is a normative desire for sexual propagation, "promiscuous" in that it is innate in everyone.

Anticlaudianus

Prose Prologue

4.7–10   "Literal sense," "moral doctrine," and "allegory" refer to three of the traditional four "senses or levels of meaning which exegesis aims to reveal in the text of the Bible." The fourth sense, the "anagogical" or mystical, is clearly implied by the later references to "celestial theophany" and the contemplation of "supercelestial form."

5.4   I take *gramatis theorema* to be the diagrammatic representations of geometrical theorems. Radulphus, *In Anticl.,* 66, glosses *gramma* as *linea,* "because geometry deals with linear proportions." In the Prologue to the *Regulae,* Alan glosses *ebdomades* as

NOTES TO THE TRANSLATIONS

dignitates, citing Boethius's use of this term to denote theological questions which are understood only by those who are worthy *(digni).*

5.5 *Emblema* for the followers of Gilbert of Poitiers denotes the rules or maxims of theology (here "theophany"); see Gilbert, *In Boecii De hebdomadibus* prol. 9, ed. Häring, *Commentaries,* 185.

Book 1

47–52 "Nobility," as used in the *Anticl.,* is not an attribute of character but a matter of external circumstance. In 8.63–88 we learn that she is the daughter of Fortune and has no part in the work of Nature and the Virtues.

119–86 On this passage see Ratkowitsch, *Descriptio Picturae,* 218–43.

120 Here as elsewhere in the poem Alan uses *pictura* and *scriptura* interchangeably, perhaps imagining something like the *visibile parlare* Dante discovers on entering Purgatory (*Purgatorio* 10.95). At *Anticl.* 1.187 he will speak of painting as *fabula* inscribed with a pen *(calamus),* as if to minimize the difference between verbal and graphic art, and at 2.415, the art of grammar is both "inscribed" and "described" on the robe of Grammar.

129–30 I.e., these arts can only represent or imitate truth in their own terms.

141 Tully *(Tullius)* is Marcus Tullius Cicero.

145 Alcides is Hercules, grandson of Alcaeus.

147 As Roman emperor (79–81), Titus built the Colosseum and staged lavish public spectacles.

148 See *DpN* 18.8.4 and n.

151 Cytherea Venus, in whose honor a sanctuary was maintained on the island of Cythera.

165–70 "Ennius" was identified by commentators as Joseph of Exeter, author of a Latin poem on the Trojan War. "Maevius" (for Virgil, *Eclogue* 3.90, a bad poet) is clearly Walter of Chatillon: "Gesta ducis Macedum" are the opening words of the first book of his *Alexandreis.* On the likely literary and historical context of these references, see Adkin, "Alan of Lille on Walter of Châtillon."

180   *in Venerem* is clearly the best attested reading (the *in Venere* of some manuscripts is unmetrical), but *in* is puzzling. Perhaps the point is that Paris has become so debilitated through lustful excess that he is a liability to Venus rather than her champion.

182   Davus is a common name for a slave in Roman comedy; in medieval school poetry a name for an ugly man, as also at 2.14, 6.227.

190–93   The language of lines 190–93 closely echoes the opening sections of the *Cosmographia* of Bernardus Silvestris.

194–95   "civilia bella" in line 194 and "fratrum rixas" in 195 allude to the themes of the *De bello civili* of Lucan and the *Thebaid* of Statius.

218   Here, as at several points in the poem, *Minerva* is used as to denote the mind or understanding of an individual. I have substituted "wisdom," except in cases where it occurs as one of the names of *Prudentia*/Prudence.

262   Tisiphone is one of the three Furies, also called Eumenides (3.404), originally agents of retribution for wrongdoing, especially the shedding of kindred blood, but for Alan, powers of evil. Alan later names the other Furies, Megaera (2.198, 8.171) and Alecto (8.151, 171).

264   Here, and again at 8.207, 314, Alan apparently thinks of "Erinys" as a single figure, mother of the Furies, rather than a collective name for them.

270–71   There is no modern English equivalent to *Prudentia,* and as Simpson notes (*Sciences and the Self,* 53–54), her role in the *Anticl.* is hard to define. She will bestow on the New Man active virtues devoted to the common good (*Anticl.* 7.228–44), but she is above all the personification of a human wisdom which encompasses not only the universal knowledge represented by the Liberal Arts but also theology. As such she is the *prudentia* of John of Salisbury, who is capable of ascent "to the hidden realm of pure truth and things divine" and becomes "to a certain degree exempt from the limits of mortality" (*Metalogicon* 4.17).

    Alan refers to her also as *Sapientia,* which I translate as "Wisdom"; she is often called *Fronesis* and occasionally *Sophia* or *Minerva,* which I retain where they occur, though sudden shifts from one name to another can be disconcerting, as at 2.329–33 and 363–65.

298–302 The changing height of Providence and the tears in her robe recall the description of Philosophy in Boethius, *Consolatio* 1.pr.1. On the relation of Providence to Philosophy, Courcelle, *Consolation,* 55–58.

310–15 The faint forms on the robe of Providence recall the description of Nature in *DpN* 2. Alan is attributing to Providence a latent capacity for the Adamic vision of the natural order, the loss of which the Nature of *DpN* laments.

333 Dante knew the *Anticl.* well, and this line is a likely source of the famous "trasumanar" of *Paradiso* 1.70.

Book 2

112–14 Compare. *DpN* 2.6.

126 Lucifer: "light-bringer," Venus as the morning star. Cyllenius: Mercury, said to have been born on Cyllene, a mountain in Arcadia.

132 Hesperus is Venus as the evening star.

134 Phoebe is goddess of the moon, sister of Phoebus Apollo.

185–93 In these lines Alan uses reflexive pronouns freely to indicate how two persons become one in friendship.

188–89 In one version of the story of Theseus and Pirithous, the two friends descend to Hades intending to carry off Persephone as a wife for Pirithous. They are captured, but Theseus escapes and later descends again to seek to free Pirithous.

191–93 In Statius's *Thebaid* Tydeus plays a major role in the campaign to gain the throne of Thebes for Polynices, who recalls their friendship in a moving speech on learning of Tydeus's death (*Thebaid* 9.49–73).

194–96 Virgil's young Trojan warriors and devoted friends, killed together while on a nighttime mission against the Latins (*Aeneid* 9.176–449).

197–99 Atrides is Orestes, grandson of Atreus. Pylades was the companion who helped him avoid the wrath of the Furies after his murder of his mother, Clytemnestra.

203 *Concludit* completes a metaphor from logic which begins with

sophismate in 203, and which I have not attempted to preserve in translation.

216–18 Atreus served to his brother Thyestes the flesh of sons conceived by Atreus's wife in adultery with Thyestes. The sun turned back in its course to avoid the polluting spectacle (Seneca, *Thyestes;* Hyginus, *Fabulae* 86–88).

219–20 Eteocles, elder son of Oedipus, who refused to yield the throne to his brother Polynices at the stipulated time, precipitating the war that led to the deaths of both.

221–23 See *DpN* 2.24.3n.

224 This line, which closely imitates Ovid, *Remedia amoris* 59, is omitted in most manuscripts. That it is a scribal insertion is argued by Shanzer, "How Long?" 235–36.

227–28 Crassus was a Roman general killed in battle by the Parthians, who are said to have filled his head with molten gold and sent it to their king. In medieval accounts he is made to drink the gold while still alive (Bernardus Silvestris, *Cosmographia* 1.3.237–38).

229 The point of *olim* in line 229 is perhaps to distinguish "authentic" from legendary history.

230 Ptolemy XIII of Egypt. Lucan, *De bello civili* 8.536–608, describes his ordering of the assassination of Pompey.

231 Apparently a reference to the slave revolt led by Spartacus in 73–71 BCE.

232–33 Lucan, *Phars.* 8.698–711.

237 "Caesar" here is Octavius, the future Augustus, who defeated Antony at Actium in 31 BCE.

239–41 Cleopatra.

316 *Tonans* is Jove or Jupiter, keeper of the thunderbolt. Alan refers to God several times by this title (5.184, 193, 201, 377, 407; 6.217; as Jove, 5.194, 240, 271).

343 Zeuxis was a Greek painter (fifth century BCE) from Heraclea. Cicero, *De Inventione* 2.1, reports that when commissioned to paint a picture of Helen he chose five girls as models, since all the qualities he sought to combine could not be found in one, "because in no single case has Nature made anything perfect and finished in every part." "Milo" is Myron, a famous sculptor

(fifth century BCE) from Eleuthera. "Milo" appears again, this time as a painter, in 6.229–30.

344   Fabius is Quintilian, Roman rhetorician (first century CE), whose nomen was Fabius. His *Institutio Oratoria* was known only in incomplete form until the fifteenth century. "Hermes" is probably Hermes Trismegistus, legendary philosopher and astrologist, supposed author of the *Asclepius*, an important text for twelfth-century Platonist thought.

345   The Samian is Pythagoras, born on the island of Samos.

346   Zeno of Elea refuted opponents by drawing contradictory conclusions from their premises.

346–47   Bryson of Heraclea attempted unsuccessfully to square the circle. "Crisias" is perhaps the Critias of Plato's *Timaeus* 20D–27B, a very old man who relates the history of the antediluvian greatness of Athens; perhaps the Critias (460–403 BCE), probably the grandson of the former, who was one of the Thirty Tyrants set over Athens by the Spartans after the Peloponnesian War; *studet* could refer to his work as a scholar and poet, though he was best known for treacherous and violent conduct in political controversy (Cicero, *Tusculanae disputationes* 2.40.96).

347   Argus had a hundred eyes. After he was slain by Mercury, Juno placed them in the tail of the peacock (Ovid, *Metamorphoses* 1.625–723).

348   Julius Caesar's reformed calendar was adopted in 45 BCE. Augustine, *De Civitate Dei* 18.8, reports the belief that Atlas's mythic role as upholder of the heavens arose from his fame as an astronomer. See also Servius, *ad Aen.* 1.741.

349   Alan here, as elsewhere in this passage, may simply be following Sidonius Apollinaris, *Epistulae* 4.3.05, a catalog of contributors to the arts, where Zethus is identified with *pondera*. Cicero refers several times to a now lost play of Pacuvius in which Zethus and his brother Amphion debate the value of philosophy; *De inventione* 1.50.94; *De Oratore* 2.37.155; *De republica* 1.18.30. André Loyen, ed. *Sidoine Appollinaire: Lettres,* 2 vols. (Paris: Belles Lettres, 1960), 2.226, suggests that Zethus may have learned about *pondera* in carrying on his back the stones with which Amphion built the walls of Thebes.

350   Chrysippus, prolific Stoic author, was identified with "numbers"
       by Sidonius, though known primarily as a logician.

352   Perdrix was the nephew of Daedalus and inventor of the com-
       pass. So identified by Sidonius.

353   The Lemnian is Vulcan, cast down from Olympus to the island
       of Lemnos.

354   Sidonius pairs Appius, who "dissuades," with Cicero, who per-
       suades. Appius is probably Appius Claudius Caecus, who in
       278/79 dissuaded the Roman Senate from accepting peace on
       the terms offered by Pyrrhus after the battle of Heraclea; Cic-
       ero, *Brutus* 14.55.

355   Cicero praises two Curios, father and son, as forceful orators,
       though neither had received any formal training (Cicero, *Brutus*
       58.210; 81.281).

356   *Perseus* in some manuscripts, but in this context of verbal art-
       istry *velat* probably refers to the obscure style of the Roman
       satirist Persius.

356–57 Alan follows Sidonius, who pairs Crassus *simulans* and Caesar
       dissimulans.

357   Sheridan suggests that Alan here tips his hat to Sidonius, whose
       nomen was *Solius.*

358   Naso is Ovid (Publius Ovidius Naso). Maro is Virgil (Publius
       Virgilius Maro).

360   Presumably the Mercury of Martianus Capella, god of elo-
       quence.

362   Solon's reforms freed the poor of Athens from the threat of slav-
       ery and possible transportation.

363–66 *Minerva* and *Sophiae* in 363 and *Sophia* in 366 must all refer to
       Prudence, who is clearly the subject of the verbs in 369–72.

371   The divine wisdom, providence. See *DpN* 7.13n.

405   Boxwood is a pale white wood. Ovid twice compares a pale face
       to boxwood (*Metamorphoses* 4.134; 11.417).

420   *vitium,* a grammatical or stylistic error. See *DpN* 1.24n.

440–41 Alan refers to elision, common in classical verse but almost en-
       tirely absent in his own.

454   I take *peregrine* as referring to the noun's use as metaphor.

457   With Sheridan I take "demonstration" as reference to a per-

son actually or implicitly present, i.e., the reference of first and second personal pronouns, of which Priscian observes that, not having a single root, they are not strictly speaking declined.

460–61   Concrete and abstract nouns.

467–69   The participle.

488   Fourth-century grammarian who taught St. Jerome. His *Ars minor* was the standard introductory grammar text throughout the medieval period.

495   Aristarchus (ca. 216–144 BCE) was head of the Alexandrian library and a pioneering grammarian and textual critic. The *noster* in 495 might imply a modern writer (compare *noster Ennius*, almost certainly Joseph of Exeter, in 1.165–66). But "our apostate" in line 500 is certainly Priscian, so that *noster* may imply only a fellow grammarian's familiarity with Aristarchus. One thinks of Dante nodding to Thales and Empedocles in Limbo.

498–99   Didymus was a pupil of Aristarchus and a prolific writer on many subjects, including grammar. Radulphus, *In Anticl.*, 120, credits him as the first Latin (!) writer to define the parts of speech: "and thus he gathered and conjoined many distinct things in a single definition."

500   Priscian (fifth–sixth century CE) dedicated his *Institutiones Grammaticae* to a "Julianus" who was later confused with Julian the Apostate, giving rise to the belief that Priscian had renounced his Christian faith in return for patronage. *pertractat* perhaps has something of the force of *pertrahit*, "drags out," "prolongs," in reference to the length of Priscian's major work.

Book 3

25–26   Flower and scorpion recall Martianus, *De nuptiis* 4.328, and imply logic's power for good or ill.

42   In logic a topic is a form or strategy of argumentation, or the principle that confirms the argument produced by this strategy.

43   In logic a maxim or axiom is a self-evident proposition that is always true, e.g., the law of noncontradiction.

54   *Aphaeresis* in logic is the removal of a part, here the absence of a middle term in a syllogism. *Syncope,* or "cutting short," apparently refers to what Aristotle calls a *semeion,* or "sign," the indication of one thing by another when the second is in some way more evident than the first. Both are forms of induction.

55–56   An inductive argument infers a general claim from a number of instances. It is inferior to deduction in that it can be invalidated by the adding of an instance or premise for which the original instances do not allow.

58–59   An induction must allow for all cases to induce its proof, whereas one or more cases "cut off" from the induction constitute an example.

60–62   Lines 60–62 seem intended as humor, playing on the difference between topic, or *locus,* and the Aristotelian spatial category of "place," *locus* or *locum.*

72–76   The use of logic strengthens the demonstrative power of the other arts.

110–12   Porphyry's *Isagoge* was considered an important aid to understanding Aristotle's works on logic, the enigmatic character of which is emphasized in 114–22.

125–26   Lines 125–26, borrowed from the *Lapidarius* of Marbod of Rennes, are omitted in many manuscripts, and are unlikely to be Alan's; see Shanzer "How Long?," 234–35. On the maxim and its association with Aristotle, see *DpN* 6.13.8–10n.

129–30   Or perhaps "king and commander of the Sophists." Zeno is said to have been a major influence on Gorgias.

134–36   Boethius, translator of Aristotle's *Organon* and the *Isagoge* of Porphyry, and author of commentaries on logical writings of Aristotle, Porphyry, and Cicero.

171   With Radulphus, *In Anticl.,* 138, I take *causa* as referring to the *materia* or *instrumentum* of rhetoric.

199   *Quaestio* is the central point at issue between the two sides.

202–4   These lines refer to the "assumptive" issues defined by Cicero, *De inventione* 1.11.15.

230   Tullia was the name of Cicero's daughter.

231–32   Teacher of rhetoric, bishop of Pavia 514–21.

236   Senator and champion of the cause of pagan religion in later fourth-century Rome.

240   Fifth-century bishop of Clermont, author of poems and letters which emulate classical style.

288   Sheridan identifies this table as the abacus. Radulphus, *In Anticl.*, 176, describes it as a chessboard with numbers in place of chessmen; each number has a value based on "certain proportions" and can "take" others, as in chess, until "someone finally says 'mate.'" Lines 290–93 may allude to this game.

292   Probably, as Sheridan suggests, "rebel numbers" are numbers that could not be systematically ordered.

302   The "limits" are powers of ten; Martianus, *De nuptiis* 7.746.

313–15   Alan is perhaps Christianizing the reflections of Martianus's *Geometria* on the mysterious properties of the monad (*De nuptiis* 6.706–7).

316   The abstract number with which we count and the actual number inherent in the things counted.

317   Alan's terms are explained by Radulphus, *In Anticl.*, 177, who distinguishes "collective" (Socrates and Plato are two) from "distributive" (Socrates is one, Plato is another).

318   "Roots" are the lowest common denominators.

319–20   An odd number, which cannot be equally divided as an even one can, is therefore "stronger" and hence masculine. The virgin number is the heptad; Martianus, *De nuptiis* 7.738.

321–24   The elaborate contrast of male and female in lines 321–24 is evidently Alan's own. Radulphus does not comment on these lines, but observes, *In Anticl.*, 177, that the divisibility of even numbers expresses the susceptibility of the female and the resistance of the male to corruption and change. Boethius, *De arithmetica* 2.27, contrasts the odd number, which by its nature partakes of unchanging substance, with the even, which is "of a wholly different nature."

325   The point, *"cuius pars nihil est"* (Martianus, *De nuptiis* 6.708), is unity, the beginning of dimension but not itself dimension.

329–30   Perfect and imperfect numbers: Martianus, *De nuptiis* 7.753; Boethius, *De arithmetica* 1.19.

333–34   Boethius, *De arithmetica* 1.46. Squares: $a_2 : ab :: ab : b_2$. Cubes: $a_3 :$ $a_2 b :: ab_2 : b_3$.

375–76   Author of an introduction to arithmetic (ca. 100 CE) which was translated by Apuleius and used by Boethius in his *De arithmetica*.

377–78   Radulphus, *In Anticl.*, 187, reports the story that the great mathematician "Gilbert" (i.e., Gerbert, later Pope Sylvester II, ca. 940–1003) trafficked with the devil, who gave him a false solution to a problem: the resulting gap in Gerbert's system was known traditionally as the *saltus fallax,* or *saltus Gerberti.*

383–85   See Book 2.350n.

432–33   Martianus, *De nuptiis* 9.955–56, discusses these three *genera modulandi.*

437–38   Martianus, *De nuptiis* 9.933–34; Boethius, *De musica* 1.7–10.

439–45   On the *lemma,* or semitone, Boethius, *De musica* 2.28; on the *comma,* a minute interval between tones, *De musica* 3.4–10. On the *diastemata,* which Boethius calls *schismata, De musica* 3.8.

448–49   Radulphus, *In Anticl.,* 197, sees the transformation of stone to bronze as a figure for the transforming of arithmetic into music.

457   Timotheus, a famous lyre player and poet (ca. 450–360 BCE). The effect of his music is reported by Boethius, *De musica* 1.1.

464–66   Pope Gregory I, supposed inventor of Gregorian chant.

467–68   Aristotle uses one *Michalus Musicus* as the middle term in describing a flawed form of syllogism (*Prior Analytics* 1.47B). Alan could have found the name in Boethius's translation. I have found no other reference to this *doctor.*

499–505   Radulphus, *In Anticl.,* 204–7, provides proofs of the problems set in lines 499–505.

506   *Eleufuga,* translated by Radulphus, *In Anticl.,* 207, as *fuga miserorum,* "flight of the wretched," was the name given to the fifth proposition of Euclid, which was considered the first problem difficult enough to cause beginning students to abandon geometry.

526–29   Among other legendary feats of pioneering geometry, Thales is reputed to have calculated the heights of the pyramids by the length of their shadows.

Book 4

11–14   The planisphere.

29–31   Martianus, *De nuptiis* 8.823, 832–33. The Greek *kolouros* means "dock-tailed."

40–42   Martianus, *De nuptiis* 8.844–49; Radulphus, *In Anticl.*, 226–27.

47–48   Martianus, *De nuptiis* 8.848–49, refutes the false belief that all the planetary orbits have the earth as their center.

62–64   Abu Ma'shar (787–885/86), Persian astronomer and astrologer, whose astrological writings transmitted knowledge of Aristotelian physics to twelfth-century Europe.

66–70   On Atlas as astronomer, see above, Book 2.348n.

79   On *gumfis* see above, *DpN* 2.24.10n.

91–92   The horses are the five senses and appear in traditional hierarchical order: Sight, Hearing, Smell, Taste, Touch. See Dronke, "La personnification des cinq sens," 120–25.

111   Pyrous (Pyrois) is one of the horses of the Sun, as is Eous (133). Ovid, *Metamorphoses* 2.153; Ethon (205) is also named by Ovid, but Alan is also likely to be recalling Claudian, *De raptu Proserpinae* 1.284–85, where Aethon is one of four horses who draw the chariot of Pluto. Meier, "Die Rezeption des Anticlaudianus," 475, suggests that the sires of the horses of Prudentia correspond broadly to the elements: Pyrois would then represent fire; Eous perhaps the ether or upper atmosphere; Zephyrus, air; Triton, water; Ethon (as named by Claudian), earth.

186   Triton is the son of Neptune, a sea god who stirs up or calms the sea by blowing through a conch shell (Ovid, *Metamorphoses* 1.330–338).

234   My translation assumes that *reditu* in 234 refers to the soul of the new man which it is hoped Providence will obtain.

273–74   These spirits are discussed by Apuleius, *De Deo Socratis* 11–13; Augustine, *De Civitate Dei* 9.1–3; Bernardus Silvestris, *Cosmographia* 2.7.10.

389   Macrobius, *In Somnium Scipionis* 2.3, explores the cosmological and religious implications of the claim of Plato's Er that each planetary sphere has its "Siren" (*Republic* 10.617b).

398   Stilbon is Mercury. Martianus, *De nuptiis* 8.850–51, discusses the Greek terms for the planets. "Lucifer" here is not the fallen angel of line 303, but Venus as the morning star.

Book 5

14–15   Sagittarius, once the "Haemonian" (Thessalian) centaur Chiron; Ovid, *Metamorphoses* 2.81.

17–18   Castor and Pollux, the Gemini.

20–21   Ophiucus, the snake holder, in life Aesculapius.

22–23   Callisto, now the Great Bear; Ovid, *Metamorphoses* 2.401–507.

29–31   I take *astro* here as connoting the glory associated with the immortal figures who in stellar form populate the *aula celi.*

83–84   Though she is assigned no explicit role, the *puella* at the summit of the sphere is surely theology. Simpson (*Sciences and the Self,* 37–38) cites Alan's sermon on the liberal arts, which refers to theology as "the celestial queen" (d'Alverny, *Alain de Lille,* 275). The maiden, with her crown and book, is repeatedly called "queen," the only figure in the *Anticl.* to receive this title.

112   Here Minerva is the divine wisdom.

119–21   Compare *SQH,* Prol.: "When words are transferred from natural to theological [reference], they marvel at their new meanings, and seem to beg for their old ones."

123–27   These lines encapsulate the "negative" theology that Alan inherits from the tradition of Pseudo-Dionysius the Areopagite and the school of Gilbert of Poitiers.

162   The kiss is the *osculum* of Canticles 1.1, the archetype of every creative act.

185   "The destiny that is beyond" is presumably the innermost, inscrutable will of God. I translate *fatum* as "destiny," but perhaps Alan is suggesting that Prudence, still imperfectly enlightened, can only imagine it as fate. On the limited knowledge of

Fronesis, compare 6.170–82. On "the fate beyond," compare 6.214–30.

261   The "better bridle" which will control the second horse, which represents hearing, is the higher authority of Theology, who has replaced Reason as guide.

273   Nature, unlike Alan, will be accorded the status of "scribe" in Prvovidence's prayer to God, 6.349–50.

275   Alan will be the "muse" of divine speech in the sense that he will be the medium through whom divine inspiration generates poetry, a muse with no inherent power but that of the verbal arts.

342–51   I have followed Shanzer in reordering lines 342–51. Lines 342–47 of earlier editions are here 346–51, and 348–51 have become 342–45. The "hac . . . ratione" of 342 continues a line of thought begun in 333.

405   The empyrean (literally "fiery") heaven, Dante's *cielo di fiamma* (*Convivio* 2.3.8), is imagined as a kingdom or city ruled by God. As Peter Lombard observes (*Sententiae* 2.2.4), it is called *empyreum,* not for its heat (*ardore, calore),* but for its brilliant light (*splendore).*

426–27   The Virtues are empowered to perform miracles.

Book 6

58–60   Lawrence (d. 258) is traditionally believed to have been roasted to death on a gridiron.

61–63   Vincent is thought to have died during the persecution of the early fourth century. An elaborate account of his martyrdom is Prudentius, *Peristephanon* 5.

77   My translation assumes that the *signis dictantibus* are signs of Prudence's illness rather than her identity.

94   *Obaudit* can hardly mean "obeys" here; Alan has perhaps been uncharacteristically misled by the prefix to assume that the word denotes resistance.

122–23   Despite the repetition of *hic* in lines 122–23, *res, ens,* and *lux* clearly denote the reality of the *locus empireus,* while *umbra, spe-*

cies, and *lucis imago* are the *dissona facies* of these heavenly phenomena reflected in the mirror.

227   I take *abusivam* in its rhetorical sense. *Abusio,* or catachresis, is a misuse of terms, often in metaphor, and often to unintentionally comic effect; *Rhetorica ad Herennium* 4.33.45; Cicero, *De oratore* 27.94.

229   Tiphys was the pilot of the Argo.

248   *Conformis* recalls Romans 8:29: "For those whom he foreknew he also predestined to be conformed to the image of his Son."

254–55 Alan's description here recalls Bernardus Silvestris, *Cosmographia* 1.4.5.

314   This outrageous bit of advice comes verbatim from Horace, *Epistle* 1.18.84.

391   *respicerem* is a Hebraism, which recalls God's "looking on" the earth as effecting beneficent change or bestowing favor, as in Numbers 6:24–26, and in several Psalms. Ambrose uses this verb to describe the gift of grace in his hymn "*Aeterne rerum conditor*" 27.

403   Deucalion is the Greek counterpart to Noah. After Zeus has destroyed the rest of humankind with a flood, Deucalion and his wife, Pyrrha, repopulate the earth by casting stones over their shoulders (Ovid, *Metamorphoses* 1.163–413).

440   Phineas is apparently the priest of Numbers 25:7–8 who caused a plague to be removed from the people of Israel by killing an Israelite and the Midianite prostitute he had visited.

448–51 The Fates, traditionally three sisters, Clotho, Atropos, and Lachesis, thought to govern the course of human affairs.

Book 7

50–52   Lines 50–52 are omitted in several good manuscripts. Their subject is clearly God (the *qui* of 52), and they intrude on the account of Nature's handiwork to no purpose.

62–65   Lines 62–65, with their rather cheerful final touch, are as close as Alan comes to the quasi-dualism of Bernardus Silvestris.

116   Nothing in Elijah's story seems to indicate exemplary chastity.

Alan is perhaps recalling the prophet's hostility to the wicked queen Jezebel (1 Kings 18–19). Sheridan identifies Joseph here as the spouse of Mary, but Alan is more likely to be thinking of the Joseph who rejected Potiphar's wife (Genesis 39).

285–90 Arithmetic.

329 *Pietas* here is neither the Virgilian virtue nor simply "pity." Perhaps the best gloss is Dante's characterization of *pietà* as a noble disposition of mind apt to receive "charitable emotions" (*Convivio* 2.10.6).

474 Alan quotes verbatim Virgil, *Aeneid* 6.128, from the Sibyl's speech to Aeneas on the dangers of descending to the underworld.

Book 8

58 Croesus was king of Lydia (mid-sixth century BCE), famous for his great wealth. For Codrus see *DpN* 9.31 and n.

60 Sulla was a Roman general (138–79 BCE), who twice invaded Rome, establishing himself as dictator in his last years. Marius (157–86 BCE) was first the commanding officer and later the rival of Sulla.

151 On Alecto, see Book 1.262n.

170–71 On "Erinys" and Megaera, see Book 1.262n, 264n.

210 Rufinus is the antihero of Claudian's *In Rufinum,* an important model for this portion of the *Anticl* . . . See Introduction, p. xxix. Catiline was a Roman soldier and politician (d. 62 BCE). Frustrated in seeking high office, he formed a conspiracy that was exposed and denounced by Cicero in four famous orations.

230 Achates, the trusted companion of Aeneas in Virgil's *Aeneid,* is several times called *fidus* (6.158; 8.521, 586; 10.332; 12.384).

274 Lust.

306 *Silentes* is an ominous term for the dead in classical poetry. Virgil invokes the *umbrae silentes* together with the gods of the underworld in preparing to narrate the journey of Aeneas and the Sibyl (*Aeneid* 6.264).

308 Pluto's brother is Jupiter, Jove.

368–69   *mistica bella* and *pugnas animi,* which denote the wholly mental and verbal nature of the warfare thus far, also allude to the *Psychomachia* of Prudentius, on which the battle of Book 9 is largely modeled.

Book 9

28–29   In lines 28–29 I have aimed to preserve some sense of the terms of logic, *probat . . . disputat . . . concluditur.*

188–91   Old Age, in effect, regrets being Old Age, fated to die of natural causes.

237–39   Retreat, for Alan, is the only way of withstanding sexual desire; see 7.110–114, and the concluding lines of *DpN* 9.

260–61   I.e., Venus has caused Apollo the sun god to fall in love.

265–66   See *DpN* 1.55–56n.

267–69   Conduct imputed to Hercules in his infatuation with the Thessalian princess Iole (Ovid, *Ars Amatoria* 2.217–22; *Heroides* 9).

312–13   Thinking of *foedus* in line 313, I assume that the *lex* here is the "laws of war," in an ethical sense, whereas in 295 it refers to a way of fighting.

383   This echoing of the final line of Virgil's *Aeneid* begins a pattern of Virgilian allusion which is continued by what amounts to the dismantling of the world of the *Georgics,* where *labor improbus* amounts to a kind of postlapsarian burden, in lines 396–400, and ends with lines which are redolent of the golden age of *Eclogue* 4.

412–13   Lines 412–13 echo Statius's expression of reverence for the "divine" *Aeneid* in the concluding lines of his *Thebaid* (12.816–17).

Undoing the Knot

8   Titan is the sun, Apollo. Triton is Neptune.

63   As opposed to comparative or superlative.

139   A paralogism is a false syllogism. See above, *DpN* 8.10.8n.

7a   In *sufflare* I assume a puffing out of the cheeks and a discharge of breath to express scorn. One might read *petere* and *sufflare* as governed by *revocare* and see Walter as seeking to recall his brothers from a soft life to a more austere one.

ON THE INCARNATION

5–6   I.e., absolute being becomes subject to change. Thurot (*Extraits,* 384–85) cites Peter Helias and Alexander de Villa Dei concerning the use of words *materialiter,* the imposition of grammatical terms on nouns, as in "hoc nomen homo," so that "the word represents itself; it is imposed to refer to itself." But it can no longer do so if it is placed in a larger grammatical construction and changes case; then "it does not represent itself as it is." Here the Word has accepted changeable mortality and yet remains its unchanging self.

9   Thurot, *Extraits,* 218, quotes an anonymous treatise which defines *pura copula* as the joining of a verb in the present indicative with a nominative term, as in "sor (meaning, Socrates) est albus." Alan speaks of a *copula* that would be beyond the capacity of syntax.

11–14 These lines depend on our taking *locus* in two senses: as "topic," or ground of inference, and as the Aristotelian category of physical or literal place. The topic *e contrariis* or *a contrariis* (Cicero, *Top.* 3.17, 11.47–49) is rendered meaningless in a situation in which two contraries, divine and human, become one.

46   On *gumphi,* see *DpN* 2.24.10n.

57–58 This paradox appears also in *SIS* 28.

THE BOOK OF CREATION

40–42 The verbs *proponit, assumit,* followed by *conclusio* give these lines the structure of a syllogism.

52–54 This ultimately Boethian image of self-governance appears also in *SIS* 21; *DpN* 2.28. Alan's prototype is the divine *ratio* who guides Nature's chariot, *DpN* 4.2.

Bibliography

WORKS OF ALAN OF LILLE

Anticlaudian. Translated by William H. Cornog. Pennsylvania Dissertations 150. Philadelphia, 1935.

Anticlaudianus. Venice: Sebastiano Combi, 1582.

Anticlaudianus. Edited by Robert Bossuat. Textes Philosophiques du Moyen Âge 1. Paris: J. Vrin, 1955.

Anticlaudianus, Archivio medievale. Edited by Massimo Sannelli. Lavis (Trento): La finestra, 2004.

Anticlaudianus, or the Good and Perfect Man. Translated by James J. Sheridan. Toronto: Pontifical Institute of Mediaeval Studies, 1973.

Cyclopaediae Anticlaudiani. Antwerp: Trognaesius, 1611.

De planctu Naturae. Edited by Nicholas M. Häring. *Studi Medievali* ser. 3, 19 (1978): 797–879.

Distinctiones dictionum theologicalium. PL 210.685–1012.

Leyser, Polycarp. *Historia poetarum et poematum medii aevi.* Halle, 1741. Contains *Anticlaudianus,* Book 1 (pp. 1022–43); the verse passages from the *De planctu Naturae* (pp. 1045–61); and the *Vix nodosum valeo* (pp. 1092–97). Bologna: Forni, 1967.

"Omnis mundi creatura." In *Ein Jahrtausend Lateinischer Hymnendichtung,* vol. 1, edited by G. M. Dreves and Clemens Blume, 288. Leipzig, 1909. Repr. Bologna: Forni, 1969.

Opera. Edited by Carolus de Visch. Antwerp: 1654. Repr. in *PL* 210.

The Plaint of Nature. Translated by James J. Sheridan. Toronto: Pontifical Institute of Mediaeval Studies, 1980.

Regulae Caelestis Iuris. Edited by Nicholas Häring. *Archives d'histoire doctrinale et littéraire du moyen âge* 48 (1981): 97–226.

"Rhythmus on the Incarnation." Edited by Marie-Thérèse d'Alverny. "Alain de Lille et la *Theologia*." In *L'homme devant Dieu: mélanges offerts au père Henri de Lubac,* vol. 2, 126–28. Paris: Aubier, 1964.

"Sermon on the Intelligible Sphere." In *Alain de Lille: Textes inédits.* Études de Philosophie Médiévale 52, edited by Marie-Thérèse d'Alverny, 295–306. Paris: J. Vrin, 1965.

Summa "Quoniam homines." Edited by P. Glorieux. *Archives d'histoire doctrinale et littéraire du moyen âge* 28 (1953): 113–289.

Tractatus de virtutibus et vitiis. In *Psychologie et morale aux xiie et xiiie siècles,* vol. 6, edited by Odon Lottin, 27–92. Gembloux: Duculot, 1948–60.

Universalis doctoris Alani de planctu nature liber. Leipzig: Arnoldum Coloniensem, 1494.

"Vix nodosum valeo." Edited by Nicholas Häring. "The Poem *Vix Nodosum* by Alan of Lille." *Medievalia* 3 (1978): 165–85.

Wright, Thomas, ed. *Anglo-Latin Satirical Poets of the Twelfth Century.* Rolls Series 59. London, 1872. Contains the *Anticlaudianus* (vol. 2, pp. 268–428) and *De planctu Naturae* (vol. 2, pp. 429–522).

Primary Sources

Adam de La Bassée. *Ludus super Anticlaudianum.* Edited by Paul Bayart. Lille: R. Giard, 1930.

Bernardus Silvestris. *Cosmographia.* Edited by Peter Dronke. Leiden: Brill, 1978.

———. *The Cosmographia of Bernardus Silvestris.* Translated by Winthrop Wetherbee. Records of Civilization: Sources and Studies 89. New York: Columbia University Press, 1973.

Boethius. *De institutione arithmetica* and *De institutione musica.* Edited by Godefredus Friedlein. Leipzig: Teubner, 1867.

Ellebaut. *Anticlaudien.* Edited by Andrew J. Creighton. Washington, D.C.: Catholic University of America Press, 1944.

Gilbert of Poitiers. *Commentaries on Boethius.* Edited by Nicholas Häring. Toronto: Pontifical Institute of Medieval Studies, 1966.

Henri d'Andeli. *The Battle of the Seven Arts.* Edited and translated by L. J. Paetow. Berkeley: University of California Press, 1914.

John of Garland. *De triumphis Ecclesiae.* Edited by Thomas Wright. London, 1856.

———. *Parisiana Poetria.* Edited and translated by Traugott Lawler. New Haven: Yale University Press, 1974.

John of Salisbury. *Metalogicon.* Edited by C. C. J. Webb. Oxford: Clarendon Press, 1929.

Liber XXIV philosophorum. Edited by Françoise Hudry. Paris: J. Vrin, 2009.

Martianus Capella. *De nuptiis Philologiae et Mercurii.* Edited by James Willis. Leipzig: Teubner, 1983.

Ochsenbein, Peter. "Das Compendium Anticlaudiani." *Zeitschrift für deutsches Altertum und deutsche Literatur* 98 (1969): 81–109.

Peraldus, Guilelmus. *Summa de vitiis et virtutibus.* Cologne, 1629.

Peter of Compostella. *De consolatione Rationis.* Edited by P. Blanco Soto. Beiträge zur Geschichte der Philosophie des Mittelalters 8.4. Münster: Aschendorff, 1912.

Radulphus de Longo Campo. *In Anticlaudianum Alani commentum,* edited by Jan Sulowski. Źródła do dziejow nauki i techniki 13. Wrocław: Polskiej Akademii Nauk, 1972.

Rastatter, Paul H, ed. "*Ludus-Anticlaudien.*" Ph.D. diss., University of Oregon, 1966.

Westra, Haijo, ed. *The Commentary on Martianus Capella's De Nuptiis Philologiae et Mercurii attributed to Bernardus Silvestris.* Toronto: Pontifical Institute of Medieval Studies, 1986.

Secondary Sources

Adkin, Neil. "Alan of Lille on Walter of Châtillon: *Anticlaudianus* 1.167–70." *Classica et Mediaevalia* 43 (1992): 287–315.

Alain de Lille, le Docteur universel: Philosophie, théologie et littérature au XIIe siècle. Edited by Jean-Luc Solère, Anca Vasiliu, and Alain Galonnier. Turnhout: Brepols, 2005.

Alford, John A. "The Grammatical Metaphor: A Survey of Its Use in the Middle Ages." *Speculum* 57 (1982): 728–60.

d'Alverny, Marie-Thérèse. *Alain de Lille: Textes inédits.* Études de Philosophie Médiévale 52. Paris: J. Vrin, 1965.

———. "La Sagesse et ses sept filles." In *Mélanges F. Grat.,* vol. 1, 245–78. Paris: En dépot chez Mme Pecquer-Grat, 1946–49.

———. "Variations sur un thème de Virgile dans un sermon d'Alain de

Lille." In *Mélanges d'archéologie et d'histoire offerts à André Piganiol,* vol. 3, 1517–28. Paris: S.E.V.P.E.N., 1966.

Arbusow, Leonid. *Colores Rhetorici. Ein Auswahl rhetorischer Figuren und Gemeinplätze als Hilfsmittel für Übungen an mittelalterlichen Texten.* Edited by Helmut Peter. 2nd ed. Göttingen: Vandenhoeck & Ruprecht, 1963.

Arduini, Maria Lodovica. "'. . . et ratio mensura boni . . .': Die Fähigkeit der 'ratio' zur Schöpfung und Prophetie bei Alanus ab Insulis." *Recherches de Théologie ancienne et médiévale* 51 (1984): 20–41.

Bartola, Alberto. "Filosofia, teologia, poesia nel *De planctu Naturae* e nell'*Anticlaudianus* di Alano di Lilla." *Aevum* 62 (1988): 228–58.

———. "'Lacrimae' et 'planctus' in Alano di Lilla." In *Lachrymae: Mito e metafora del pianto nel Medioevo,* edited by Francesco Mosetti Casaretto, 145–89. Alessandria, Italy: Edizioni dell'Orso, 2011.

Callay, Brigitte L. "Jean de Meun's *Romance of the Rose* and the Polemic on the Theological Method: A Key to Meaning?" In *De la Rose,* 21–40.

Chenu, M.-D. "Involucrum: le mythe selon les théologiens médiévaux." *Archives d'histoire doctrinale et littéraire du moyen âge* 30 (1955): 75–79.

———. *La théologie au douzième siècle.* Études de Philosophie Médiévale 45. Paris: J. Vrin, 1957.

Chiffoleau, Jacques. "*Contra naturam.* Pour une approche casuistique et procédurale de la nature médiévale." *Micrologus* 4 (1996): 265–312.

Ciotti, Andrea. "Alano e Dante." *Convivium* 28 (1960): 257–88.

Cotts, John D. *The Clerical Dilemma: Peter of Blois and Literate Culture in the Twelfth Century.* Washington, D.C.: Catholic University of America Press, 2009.

Courcelle, Pierre. *La Consolation de Philosophie dans la tradition littéraire: Antécédents et Posterité de Boèce.* Paris: Études Augustiniennes, 1967.

De la Rose: Texte, Image, Fortune. Edited by Catherine Bel and Herman Braet. Dudley, Mass.: Peeters, 2006.

Delhaye, Philippe. "La vertu et les vertus dans les oeuvres d'Alain de Lille." *Cahiers de civilisation médiévale* 6 (1963): 13–25.

Dronke, Peter. *Dante and Medieval Latin Traditions.* Cambridge: Cambridge University Press, 1986.

———. *Fabula: Explorations into the Uses of Myth in Medieval Platonism.* Mittellateinische Studien und Texte 9. Leiden: Brill, 1974.

———. "Metamorphoses: Allegory in Early Medieval Commentaries on

Ovid and Apuleius." *Journal of the Warburg and Courtauld Institutes* 72 (2009): 21–39.

———. "La personnification des cinq sens: la cité de l'imaginaire." In Dronke, *Forms and imaginings: from Antiquity to the Fifteenth Century,* 113–28. Storia e Letteratura 243. Rome: Edizioni di Storia e Letteratura, 2007.

———. "Thierry of Chartres." In *A History of Twelfth-Century Western Philosophy,* edited by Peter Dronke, 358–85. Cambridge: Cambridge University Press, 1988.

Economou, George D. *The Goddess Nature in Medieval Literature.* Cambridge, Mass.: Harvard University Press, 1972.

Eley, Penny. "Sex and Writing: Hue de Rotelande's *Ipomedon* and Alan of Lille's *De planctu Naturae.*" In *Courtly Literature and Clerical Culture,* edited by Christoph Huber and Henrike Lähnemann, 93–103. Tübingen: Attempto, 2002.

Elswijk, H.C. van. *Gilbert Porreta: Sa vie, son oeuvre, sa pensée.* Louvain: Spicilegium sacrum Lovaniense, 1966.

Erismann, Christophe. "Alain de Lille, La métaphysique érigénienne, et la pluralité des formes." In *Alain de Lille, le Docteur universel,* 19–46.

Evans, Gillian R. *Alan of Lille: The Frontiers of Theology in the Later Twelfth Century.* Cambridge: Cambridge University Press, 1983.

Finckh, Ruth. *Minor Mundus Homo: Studien zur Mikrokosmos-Idee in der mittelalterlichen Literatur.* Palaestra 306. Göttingen: Vandenhoeck & Ruprecht, 1999.

Galand, Perrine. "Les 'beaux' signes: un 'locus amoenus' d'Alain de Lille." *Littérature* 74 (1989): 27–47.

Ganz, Peter F. "Minnetrank und Minne: zu *Tristan,* Z. 11 707f." In *Formen mittelalterlicher Literatur: Siegfried Beyschlag zum 65. Geburtstag,* edited by Otmar Werner, 63–75. Göppingen: A. Kümmerle, 1970.

Gärtner, Thomas. "Der Eros-Exkurs in 'De planctu Naturae' (VIII 247–IX 20) und seine Stellung in dichterischen Gesamtwerk des Alanus ab Insulis." *Mittellateinisches Jahrbuch* 33 (1998): 55–65.

———. "Der Übertritt der Seele beim Kuss. Nachtrag zu den literarischen Quellen des Alanus ab Insulis im Einleitungsgedicht zu *De planctu Naturae.*" *Filologia Mediolatina* 10 (2003): 123–26.

——. "Vier Anmerkungen zum Einleitungsgedicht von *De planctu Naturae*." *Filologia Mediolatina* 6–7 (1999–2000): 273–78.

Gibson, M. T., D. R. Shanzer, and N. F. Palmer. "Manuscripts of Alan of Lille, 'Anticlaudianus' in the British Isles." *Studi Medievali,* ser. 3, 28 (1987): 905–1001.

Glendenning, Robert. "Eros, Agape, and Rhetoric around 1200: Gervase of Melkley's *Ars poetica* and Gottfried von Strassburg's *Tristan*." *Speculum* 67 (1992): 892–925.

Godman, Peter. *The Silent Masters. Latin Literature and Its Censors in the High Middle Ages.* Princeton, N.J.: Princeton University Press, 2000.

Gonzalez-Haba, Maria. *La Obra 'De Consolatione Rationis' de Petrus Compostellanus.* Munich: Verlag der Bayerischen Akademie der Wissenschaften, 1975.

Green, Richard Hamilton. "Alan of Lille's *Anticlaudianus:* Ascensus mentis ad Deum." *Annuale Medievale* 8 (1967): 3–16.

——. "Alan of Lille's *De Planctu Naturae*." *Speculum* 31 (1956): 649–74.

Gregory, Tullio. *Platonismo medievale: studi e ricerche.* Istituto storico italiano per il Medio Evo: Studi storici, fasc. 26–27. Rome: nella sede dell'Istituto, 1958.

Häring, Nicholas. "Manuscripts of the *De planctu Naturae* of Master Alan of Lille." *Cîteaux: commentarii cistercienses* 29 (1978): 93–115.

Huber, Christoph. *Die Aufnahme und Verarbeitung des Alanus ab Insulis in Mittelhochdeutschen Dichtungen.* Munich: Artemis, 1988.

Hudry, Françoise. "Prologus Alani *De planctu Naturae*." *Archives d'histoire doctrinale et littéraire du moyen âge* 55 (1988): 169–85.

Huizinga, Johan. "Über die Verknüpfung des Poetischen mit dem Theologischen bei Alanus de Insulis." In Huizinga, *Verzamelde Werken,* vol. 4, 3–84. Haarlem: H. D. Tjeenk Willink, 1948–53.

I, Deug-su. "'Novus homo' in Alano di Lilla." In *Gli Umanesimi Medievali,* edited by Claudio Leonardi, 231–38. Florence: SISMEL, Galluzzo, 1998.

Jaeger, C. Stephen. *Medieval Humanism in Gottfried von Strassburg's Tristan und Isolde.* Heidelberg: Winter 1977.

Jeauneau, Edouard. "L'usage de la notion d'integumentum à travers les gloses de Guillaume de Conches." *Archives d'histoire doctrinale et littéraire du moyen âge* 32 (1957): 35–100.

Johnson, Michael A. "Reading the Sex out of Ovid in Alan of Lille's *The Plaint of Nature*." *Florilegium* 22 (2005): 171–90.

Jolivet, Jean. "La figure de Natura dans le *De planctu Naturae* d'Alain de Lille: une mythologie chrétienne." In *Alain de Lille, le Docteur universel*, 127–44.

Jordan, Mark D. *The Invention of Sodomy in Christian Theology*. Chicago: University of Chicago Press, 1997.

Jung, Marc-René. *Études sur le poème allégorique in France au moyen âge*. Romanica Helvetica 82. Bern: Francke, 1971.

Kantorowicz, Ernst. *Laudes Regiae*. Berkeley, Calif.: University of California Press, 1946.

Kelly, Douglas. *The Arts of Poetry and Prose*, Typologie des Sources du Moyen Âge Occidental 59. Turnhout: Brepols, 1991.

———. "Les visions du paradis chez Jean de Meun et Alain de Lille: contraires choses?" In *De la Rose*, 3–20.

Köhler, Johannes. "'Aus der Herrin wird eine Dienstmagd': Über den Wandel im Verständnis der Philosophie bei Alain de Lille." In *Was ist Philosophie im Mittelalter? Akten des X. Internationalen Kongresses für mittelalterliche Philosophie*, edited by Jan A. Aertsen and Andreas Speer, 468–74. Berlin: de Gruyter, 1998.

Krayer, Rudolph. *Frauenlob und die Natur-Allegorese. Motivgeschichtliche Unterschungen. Ein Beitrag zur Geschichte des antiken Traditionsgutes*. Heidelberg: Winter, 1960.

Krewitt, Ulrich. *Metapher und tropische Rede in der Auffassung des Mittelalters*. Mittellateinisches Jahrbuch, Beiheft 7. Ratingen: Henn, 1971.

Krochalis, Jeanne Elizabeth. "Alain de Lille: *De planctu Naturae:* Studies toward an Edition." PhD diss., Harvard University, 1973.

Landgraf, Artur M. *Introduction à l'histoire de la littérature théologique de la scolastique naissante*. Montreal: Institut d'études médiévales, 1973.

Lausberg, Heinrich. *Handbuch der literarischen Rhetorik*. 2nd ed. 2 vols. Munich: Hueber, 1973.

Leach, Elizabeth Eva. *Guillaume de Machaut: Secretary, Poet, Musician*. Ithaca, N.Y.: Cornell University Press, 2011.

Le Goff, Jacques. *Les intellectuels au moyen âge*. Paris: Éditions du Seuil, 1957.

Lemoine, Michel. "Alain de Lille et l'école de Chartres." In *Alain de Lille, le Docteur universel,* 47–58.

Lomperis, Linda. "From God's Book to the Play of the Text in the *Cosmographia.*" *Medievalia et Humanistica* 16 (1988): 51–71.

Luckner, Andreas. "'Prudentia' und die Schulung des Menschen: Der *Anticlaudianus* des Alain de Lille." *Philosophisches Jahrbuch* 111 (2004): 113–39.

Luttrell, Claude. *The Creation of the First Arthurian Romance: A Quest.* Evanston, Ill.: Northwestern University Press, 1974.

Maffia Scariati, Irene. "La 'descriptio puellae' dalla tradizione mediolatina a quella umanistica: Elena, Isotta e le altre." In *A Scuola con Ser Brunetto: indagini sulla ricezione di Brunetto Latini dal Medioevo al Rinascimento,* edited by Irene Maffia Scariati, 437–90. Florence: Edizioni del Galluzzo, 2008.

Maioli, Bruno. *Gilberto Porretano. Dalla grammatica speculativa alla metafisica del concreto.* Rome: Bulzoni, 1979.

Marshall, Linda E. "The Identity of the 'New Man' in the *Anticlaudianus* of Alan of Lille." *Viator* 10 (1979): 77–94.

Meier, Christel. "Zum Problem der allegorischen Interpretation mittellateinischer Dichtung." *Beiträge zur Geschichte der deutschen Sprache und Literatur* 99 (1977): 250–96.

———. "Die Rezeption des Anticlaudianus Alans von Lille in Textkommentierung und Illustration." In *Text und Bild: Aspekte des Zusammenwirkens zweier Kunste im Mittelalter und früher Neuzeit,* edited by Christel Meier and Uwe Ruberg, 408–549. Wiesbaden: L. Reichert, 1980.

———. "Wendepunkt der Allegorie im Mittelalter: Von der Schrifthermeneutik zur Lebenspraktik." In *Neue Richtungen in der hoch- und spätmittelalterlichen Bibelexegese,* edited by Robert E. Lerner and Elisabeth Müller-Luckner, 39–64. Schriften des Historischen Kollegs: Kolloquien 32. Munich: R. Oldenbourg, 1996.

———. "Zwei Modelle von Allegorie im 12. Jahrhundert: Das allegorische Verfahren Hildegards von Bingen und Alans von Lille." In *Formen und Funktionen der Allegorie,* edited by Walter Haug, 70–89. Symposion Wolfenbüttel 1978. Stuttgart: J. B. Metzler, 1979.

Méla, Charles. "'Poetria Nova' et 'Homo novus.'" *Littérature* 74 (1989): 4–26.

Minkova, Milena. "Textual Suggestions and Corrections to *De planctu Naturae* by Alan of Lille." *Filologia Mediolatina* 12 (2005): 180–81.

———. "Toward a New Edition of Alan of Lille's *Anticlaudianus:* Corrections and Suggestions for Improvement of the Text." *Filologia Mediolatina* 17 (2010): 215–55.

Moos, Peter von. "Was galt im lateinischen Mittelalter als das literarische an der Literatur? Eine theologisch-rhetorische Antwort des 12. Jahrhunderts." In *Literarische Interessenbildung im Mittelalter,* edited by Joachim Heinzle, 431–51. Stuttgart and Weimar: J. B. Metzler, 1993.

Murray, Alexander. *Reason and Society in the Middle Ages.* Oxford: Clarendon Press, 1978.

Neuberger, Andreas. "Les écrits dionysiens et le néoplatonisme d'Alain de Lille." In *Alain de Lille, le Docteur universel,* 3–18.

Ochsenbein, Peter. *Studien zum Anticlaudianus des Alanus ab Insulis.* Europäische Hochschulschriften, Reihe 1: Deutsche Literatur und Germanistik 114. Bern: Herbert Lang, 1975.

Pabst, Bernhard. *Prosimetrum. Tradition und Wandel einer Literaturform zwischen Spätantike und Spätmittelalter.* 2 vols. Ordo 4. Cologne: Böhlau, 1994.

Pejenaute Rubio, Francisco. "Dos aportaciones relacionadas con la metáfora gramatical en el *De planctu naturae* de Alain de Lille." *Faventia* 21 (1999): 105–16.

Pollmann, Leo. *Das Epos in den romanischen Literaturen.* Stuttgart: Kohlhammer, 1966.

Post, Gaines. *Studies in Medieval Legal Thought: Public Law and the State, 1100–1322.* Princeton, N.J.: Princeton University Press, 1964.

Quilligan, Maureen. *The Language of Allegory: Defining the Genre.* Ithaca, N.Y.: Cornell University Press, 1979.

Ratkowitsch, Christine. *Descriptio Picturae. Die literarische Funktion der Beschreibung von Kunstwerken in der lateinischen Grossdichtung des 12. Jahrhunderts.* Wiener Studien, Beiheft 15. Vienna: Österreichische Akademie der Wissenschaften, 1991.

Raynaud de Lage, Gaston. *Alain de Lille: Poète du XIIe siècle.* Publications de l'Institut d'Études Médiévales 12. Montreal: Institut d'Études Médiévales, 1951.

Rodriguez, Vera. "Nature et connaissance de la nature dans le *Sermo de sphaera intelligibili* et dans les *Glosae super Trismegistum.*" In *Alain de Lille, le Docteur universel,* 169–90.

Roques, René. *Libres sentiers vers l'érigénisme.* Rome: Edizioni dell'Ateneo, 1975.

Rossi, Luciano. "De Jean Chopinel à Durante: la série *Roman de la Rose—Fiore.*" In *De la Rose,* 273–98.

——. "La tradizione allegorica: da Alain de Lille al *Tesoretto,* al *Roman de la Rose.*" *Letture Classensi* 37 (2008): 143–79.

Scanlon, Larry. "Unspeakable Pleasures: Alain de Lille, Sexual Regulation and the Priesthood of Genius." *Romanic Review* 86 (1995): 213–42.

Shanzer, Danuta R. "Alan of Lille, Contemporary Annoyances, and Dante." *Classica et Mediaevalia* 49 (1989): 251–69.

——. "How Long Was Alan of Lille's 'Anticlaudianus'?" *Mittellateinisches Jahrbuch* 18 (1983): 233–37.

——. "Parturition through the Nostrils? Thirty-Three Textual Problems in Alan of Lille's 'De Planctu Nature.'" *Mittellateinisches Jahrbuch* 26 (1991): 140–49.

Simpson, James. *Sciences and the Self in Medieval Poetry: Alan of Lille's Anticlaudianus and John Gower's Confessio Amantis.* Cambridge: Cambridge University Press, 1995.

Siri, Francesco. "I classici e la sapienza antica nella predicazione di Alano di Lilla." In *L'Antichità classica nel pensiero medievale. Atti del convegno della Società Italiana per lo Studio del Pensiero Medievale (SISPM). Trento, 27–29 settembre 2010,* edited by A. Palazzo, 149–70. Textes et Études du Moyen Âge 61. Turnhout: Brepols, 2011.

Speer, Andreas. "Kosmisches Prinzip und Mass menschlichen Handelns. *Natura* bei Alanus ab Insulis." In *Mensch und Natur im Mittelalter,* edited by Albert Zimmerman and Andreas Speer. Vol. 1, 107–28. Miscellanea Medievalia 21. Berlin: de Gruyter, 1991.

Thurot, Charles. *Extraits de divers manuscrits latins pour servir à l'histoire de doctrines grammaticales au Moyen-Age.* Paris, 1869. Repr. Frankfurt: Minerva, 1964.

Tilliette, Jean-Yves. *Des mots à la parole: Une lecture de la Poetria nova de Geoffroy de Vinsauf.* Geneva: Droz, 2000.

Vasoli, Cesare. *Otto saggi per Dante.* Florence: Lettere, 1995.

Wetherbee, Winthrop. "Latin Structure and Vernacular Space: Chaucer,

Gower and the Boethian Tradition." In *Chaucer and Gower: Difference, Mutuality, Exchange,* edited by R. F. Yeager, 7–35. ELS Monograph Series 51. Victoria, B.C.: University of Victoria, 1991.

———. *Platonism and Poetry in the Twelfth Century.* Princeton, N.J.: Princeton University Press, 1972.

White, Hugh. *Nature, Sex, and Goodness in a Medieval Literary Tradition.* Oxford: Oxford University Press, 2000.

Whitman, Jon. "Twelfth-Century Allegory: Philosophy and Imagination." In *The Cambridge Companion to Allegory,* edited by Rita Copeland and Peter T. Struck, 101–15. Cambridge: Cambridge University Press, 2010.

Wilks, Michael. "Alan of Lille and the New Man." In *Renaissance and Renewal in Christian History,* edited by Derek Baker, 137–57. Studies in Church History 14. Oxford: Blackwell, 1977.

Wollin, Carsten. "Beiträge zur Werkchronologie und Rezeption des Matthäus von Vendome." *Sacris erudiri* 45 (2006): 327–52.

———. "Der 'Floridus Aspectus' D des Petrus Riga: Erstausgabe nach der Handschrift Douai 825 (Teil I)." *Mittellateinisches Jahrbuch* 43 (2008): 355–91.

Woods, Marjorie Curry. *Classroom Commentaries: Teaching the Poetria Nova across Medieval and Renaissance Europe.* Columbus: Ohio State University Press, 2010.

Ziolkowski, Jan M. *Alan of Lille's Grammar of Sex: The Meaning of Grammar to a Twelfth-Century Intellectual.* Cambridge, Mass.: Medieval Academy of America, 1985.

Index of Names

The spelling of proper names in the manuscripts varies widely. They are listed here in their classical forms. The works are abbreviated as follows: *Anticl. (Anticlaudianus), DpN (De planctu Naturae), SIS* ("Sermon on the Intelligible Sphere"), *VNV (Vix nodosum valeo).*

Abraham, *Anticl.* 6.38, 6.441

Achates, *Anticl.* 8.230

Achilles, *Anticl.* 9.265, 9.298; *DpN* 4.4

Adonis, *Anticl.* 6.226, 7.42; *DpN* 1.35, 2.20, 3.6, 9.30; *VNV* 48

Aegyptius, *SIS* 1

Aeneas, *DpN* 9.26

Aeolus, *DpN* 4.4

Aeternitas, *SIS* 2

Aethon, *Anticl.* 4.207

Ajax, *Anticl.* 1.178, 4.173; *DpN* 9.34

Albumasar, *Anticl.* 4.63

Alcides, *Anticl.* 1.145, 5.10, 9.268, 9.299

Alecto, *Anticl.* 8.151, 8.171, 8.176, 8.316

Amphion, *Anticl.* 3.407; *DpN* 12.10

Angelus, *Anticl.* 5.442

Antaeus, *DpN* 9.35

Antigenius, *DpN* 10.11, 10.13

Antonius, *Anticl.* 2.238

Aphrodite, *DpN* 18.10

Apollo, *Anticl.* 5.270; *DpN* 8.16

Appius, *Anticl.* 2.354

Aquilo, *Anticl.* 7.417; *DpN* 4.3

Archangelus, *Anticl.* 5.429

Argus, *Anticl.* 2.347

Aries, *Anticl.* 5.35; *DpN* 2.10

Aristarchus, *Anticl.* 2.495

Aristoteles, *Anticl.* 1.132, 3.112, 3.116, 5.372; *DpN* 6.13, 8.19, 10.7, 12.13, 14.2, 18.8

Arius, *DpN* 8.19

Asclepius, *SIS* 27

Astraea, *DpN* 2.11

Atlas, *Anticl.* 2.348, 4.67, 9.299

Atrides, *Anticl.* 2.197

Atropos, *DpN* 10.7, 10.11

Augustinus, *SIS* 27

Auster, *Anticl.* 4.260

Avaritia, *Anticl.* 8.187–88, 8.291, 9.354, 9.363, 9.369

Bacchilatria, *DpN* 12.4
Bacchus, *Anticl.* 9.262; *DpN* 8.16, 12.4–6, 15.6, 15.10; *VNV* 7
Bavius, *DpN* 9.32
Boethius, *SIS* 3
Boreas, *Anticl.* 1.69, 2.172, 4.105, 4.262, 7.415, 7.464, 8.5; *DpN* 5.2
Bryson, *Anticl.* 2.347
Byblis, *DpN* 9.50

Caesar, *Anticl.* 2.229, 2.235, 2.237, 2.348; *DpN* 12.11, 14.11
Camena, *Anticl.* 4.412
Cancer, *Anticl.* 5.32; *DpN* 2.8
Capaneus, *DpN* 18.8
Capricornus, *Anticl.* 5.34; *DpN* 2.9
Carentia, *Anticl.* 9.107
Carnis Stimulus, *Anticl.* 9.286
Castitas, *DpN* 16.9
Casus, *Anticl.* 7.398, 8.298, 9.226
Catilina, *Anticl.* 8.210
Cato, *Anticl.* 2.355, 6.230; *DpN* 18.8
Caunus, *DpN* 9.50
Chaos, *Anticl.* 1.191, 1.469, 8.303
Charybdis, *Anticl.* 3.466, 4.270, 4.307, 9.415; *DpN* 9.3, 10.14, 12.6
Cherubim, *Anticl.* 5.415
Chiron, *Anticl.* 5.34
Choes, *SIS* 2
Chrysippus, *Anticl.* 2.350, 3.383
Cicero, *Anticl.* 3.228, 6.229
Claudianus, *SIS* 25
Clio, *Anticl.* Vprol. 2

Codrus, *Anticl.* 8.58; *DpN* 9.31
Concordia, *Anticl.* 1.33, 2.166, 2.209, 4.77, 7.57, 7.68, 8.329, 9.51
Constantia, *Anticl.* 7.138, 8.327, 8.331, 9.52, 9.64
Contagia, Vitae, *Anticl.* 8.244, 9.135, 9.145, 9.148
Contemptus, *Anticl.* 9.145, 9.148
Convicia, *Anticl.* 8.247, 9.136, 9.144, 9.147
Copia, *Anticl.* 1.34, 7.77, 9.106
Crapula, *Anticl.* 8.273, 9.285
Crassus, *Anticl.* 2.228, 2.356
Crisippus, *Anticl.* 2.350, 3.383
Critias, *Anticl.* 2.347
Croesus, *Anticl.* 8.58; *DpN* 9.31, 14.6
Cupido, *Dpn* 8.10, 8.31, 8.32, 8.33, 9.21, 9.53, 10.1, 10.13, 15.17–18, 15.28
Curae, *Anticl.* 8.242, 8.292, 9.75, 9.102, 9.105
Curio, *Anticl.* 2.355
Cyclops, *Anticl.* 2.353
Cyllenius, *Anticl.* 2.126
Cypris, *DpN* 2.22, 8.10, 10.3, 10.5, 10.9, 18.9
Cytherea, *Anticl.* 1.151, 9.252; *DpN* 10.10, 16.4

Daedalus, *Anticl.* 2.352
Damnum, *Anticl.* 8.228, 9.305
Daphne, *DpN* 16.8
David, *Anticl.* 2.185
Davus, *Anticl.* 1.182, 2.14, 6.227; *DpN* 9.30

Decus, *Anticl.* 1.40, 7.224, 8.72

Dedecus, *Anticl.* 8.297, 9.136, 9.144, 9.146

Demosthenes, *Anticl.* 2.360

Deucalion, *Anticl.* 6.403

Deus, *Anticl.* 2.73, 2.109, 4.288, 5.124, 5.150, 5.155, 5.278, 5.418, 5.446, 5.469, 6.218, 6.428, 9.337; *DpN* 6.3, 6.9, 7.1, 8.19, 8.28; *SIS* 3, 22, 23, 25

Didymus, *Anticl.* 2.499

Dione (Venus), *Anticl.* 7.114, 7.165; *DpN* 2.4, 2.17, 2.22, 8.8, 8.11, 10.6, 10.12; *VNV* 69

Dione (Venus, planet), *Anticl.* 6.459

Dis, *Anticl.* 3.404

Discordia, *Anticl.* 8.165, 8.221, 8.232, 9.9, 9.16, 9.386

Dolor, *Anticl.* 8.231, 8.257, 8.264 (sapidus), 9.222

Dolus, *Anticl.* 8.164, 8.270

Dominantia, *Anticl.* 5.419

Donatus, *Anticl.* 2.488; *DpN* 12.13

Driades, *DpN* 5.10

Egestas, *Anticl.* 8.166, 9.66, 9.97

Endelichia, *SIS* 2

Ennius, *Anticl.* 1.166; *DpN* 9.33, 18.9

Ennodius, *Anticl.* 3.232

Eous, *Anticl.* 4.133

Epicurus, *DpN* 8.19

Erebus, *Anticl.* 8.307, 8.338

Erinys, *Anticl.* 1.264, 8.170, 8.207, 8.314

Esuries, *Anticl.* 8.242, 9.74, 9.77, 9.102, 9.106

Euclides, *Anticl.* 2.351, 3.531; *DpN* 12.12

Eumenides, *Anticl.* 3.404, 8.312

Euryalus, *Anticl.* 2.194–95

Excessus, *Anticl.* 8.270, 9.271, 9.281

Fabius, *Anticl.* 2.344

Facinus, *Anticl.* 8.287, 9.389

Falsitas, *DpN* 18.11

Fama, *Anticl.* 7.86, 7.89, 7.126, 8.148, 8.153, 8.248, 8.305, 8.330, 9.139–40, 9.146

Fastus, *Anticl.* 8.167, 8.273, 9.281, 9.285, 9.389

Favonius, *DpN* 3.28, 4.3

Favor, *Anticl.* 1.35, 7.83, 7.85, 9.131, 9.146

Felicia, *Anticl.* 9.226

Fides, *Anticl.* 6.23–25, 6.27, 6.41, 6.44, 6.48, 6.50, 6.59, 6.180, 6.183–84, 6.186

Fides (natural virtue), *Anticl.* 1.41, 7.344–45, 7.361, 8.189, 8.327, 9.51, 9.349

Figura, *Anticl.* 2.422

Fletus, *Anticl.* 9.211, 9.220

Flora, *DpN* 4.6

Foedus, *Anticl.* 9.386

Fortuna, *Anticl.* 1.51, 5.385, 7.352, 7.369, 7.398, 7.401–2, 8.2, 8.13, 8.46, 8.62, 8.63, 8.75, 8.106, 8.111, 8.120, 8.131, 8.136, 8.140, 8.142, 8.300, 8.303, 9.259, 9.373; *DpN* 18.1, 18.3

Fraus, *Anticl.* 8.164, 8.188, 8.289, 9.329, 9.333, 9.349, 9.352, 9.390

Fronesis, *Anticl.* 2.147, 2.296, 2.329, 4.222, 4.229, 4.272, 4.336, 4.414, 5.37, 5.71, 5.79, 5.89, 5.176, 5.246, 5.262, 5.306, 5.325, 5.333, 5.352, 5.366, 6.7, 6.17, 6.75, 6.87, 6.109, 6.119, 6.170, 6.194, 6.198, 6.204, 6.231, 6.273, 6.453, 7.1, 7.228, 7.245, 9.302

Furiae, *Anticl.* 3.405, 8.306, 8.311

Furor, *Anticl.* 8.165, 8.225, 9.12, 9.47

Gemini, *Anticl.* 5.36

Genius, *DpN* 1.59–60, 16.23, 16.25, 18.6, 18.10, 18.12–13, 18.15–16, 18.19

Geometria, *Anticl.* 3.469–533

Gilbertus, *Anticl.* 3.378

Gloria, *Anticl.* 9.147, 9.225

Grammatica, *Anticl.* 2.421, 2.487, 2.489, 2.492, 2.494, 2.498, 2.500, 7.248

Gregorius, *Anticl.* 3.465

Haemonius, *Anticl.* 5.14; *DpN* 2.9

Hebraeus, *SIS* 1

Hector, *Anticl.* 4.173, 6.227; *DpN* 12.10

Helena, *DpN* 18.8; *VNV* 142

Helias, *Anticl.* 7.116

Hercules, *DpN* 12.10, 14.6, 18.8

Hermes, *Anticl.* 2.345

Hermes Mercurius, *SIS* 3, 27

Hesperus, *Anticl.* 2.132

Hippolytus, *Anticl.* 1.150, 7.115; *DpN* 1.42, 12.10, 14.6, 16.8

Homerus, *DpN* 14.6

Honestas, *Anticl.* 1.39, 2.294, 7.202, 8.72

Honor, *Anticl.* 7.221, 9.148

Humilitas, *DpN* 16.18–19

Hymeneus, *DpN* 8.31, 10.11–12, 16.6–7, 16.20, 16.29, 18.1

Hypocrisis, *Anticl.* 7.193

Idaeus, *DpN* 2.9

Impetus, *Anticl.* 8.165, 8.226, 9.11, 9.46

Impietas, *Anticl.* 8.283, 9.308, 9.328

Imprudentia, *Anticl.* 9.294

Infamia, *Anticl.* 8.243, 9.108, 9.120, 9.129

Invidia, *Anticl.* 7.55; *DpN* 14.5

Ira, *Anticl.* 8.165, 8.189, 8.226, 9.12, 9.45, 9.52

Jacob, *Anticl.* 6.440

Jejunia, *Anticl.* 8.242, 9.74, 9.102, 9.106

Job, *Anticl.* 6.440

Jocus, *DpN* 10.12, 10.13

Jonathan, *Anticl.* 2.185

Joseph, *Anticl.* 6.439, 7.116

Jovialis, *Anticl.* 2.289, 4.443, 4.445; *DpN* 2.14, 4.3, 5.29; *VNV* 6

Jovis, *Anticl.* 4.113, 5.194, 5.271, 9.263; *DpN* 1.39, 4.3; *VNV* 6

Jovis (planet), *Anticl.* 2.116, 4.46, 4.441, 4.452–53, 4.461, 4.464, 5.240, 5.271; *DpN* 2.14

Judith, *Anticl.* 6.439
Julius, *Anticl.* 2.356, 8.59
Juno, *Anticl.* 4.135; *DpN* 4.2, 4.3, 5.25
Jupiter, *Anticl.* 5.24; *DpN* 8.16; *SIS* 2
Juventus, *Anticl.* 1.35, 7.92, 7.96

Labor, *Anticl.* 8.242, 9.73, 9.75, 9.101
Lacones, *Anticl.* 5.36
Largitas, *DpN* 16.15–17, 18.1, 18.2, 18.4, 18.5
Lascivia, *Anticl.* 7.93, 7.105, 8.166, 8.263, 9.388
Laudes, *Anticl.* 9.147
Laurentius, *Anticl.* 6.60
Ledaea, *Anticl.* 5.17; *DpN* 2.8
Lemniacus, *Anticl.* 4.438
Lemnius, *Anticl.* 2.353, 3.88
Leo, *Anticl.* 5.32; *DpN* 2.8
Liaeus, *DpN* 15.5, 15.9, 15.11
Libido, *Anticl.* 9.245
Libra, *Anticl.* 5.33; *DpN* 2.11
Lis, *Anticl.* 8.226, 9.11, 9.45, 9.51
Livor, *Anticl.* 8.167, 8.225, 9.13, 9.47
Logica, *Anticl.* 3.36, 3.40, 3.42, 3.70, 3.117, 3.136, 5.478, 7.261; *SIS* 11
Lucanus, *Anticl.* 2.361
Lucifer, *Anticl.* 2.45, 4.303
Lucifer (planet), *Anticl.* 2.126, 2.132, 4.400, 4.407, 7.226; *DpN* 3.14, 7.4, 11.5
Lucretia, *DpN* 12.10, 16.8
Luctus, *Anticl.* 8.256, 9.212, 9.219, 9.224
Ludus, *Anticl.* 8.281, 9.304

Luna, *Anticl.* 2.133, 4.351, 4.356, 4.362, 4.364, 4.386, 6.460
Luxuries, *Anticl.* 8.167, 8.261, 9.390
Luxus, *Anticl.* 8.166, 8.273, 9.282, 9.285

Macedo, *Anticl.* 1.168
Maevius, *Anticl.* 1.167
Magnanimitas, *DpN* 6.10, 6.11, 18.1, 18.3
Magnus (Pompey), *Anticl.* 2.232, 8.59
Manes, *Anticl.* 8.307
Manichaeus, *DpN* 8.19
Marcus, *Anticl.* 3.227; *DpN* 9.33
Marius, *Anticl.* 8.60–61
Maro, *Anticl.* 2.86, 2.358, 4.171, 5.371; *DpN* 9.32; *VNV* 7
Mars, *Anticl.* 2.234, 3.508, 5.321–22, 7.114, 7.264, 8.214, 8.222, 8.233, 8.253, 8.260, 8.322, 8.335, 9.10, 9.14, 9.20, 9.23, 9.48, 9.247, 9.274, 9.286, 9.296, 9.311, 9.312, 9.328, 9.331, 9.354; *DpN* 17.42; *VNV* 7
Mars (planet), *Anticl.* 2.117, 4.44, 4.414, 4.420, 4.435, 4.446, 4.457, 6.458, 6.482; *DpN* 2.15
Martianus, *SIS* 2
Medea, *DpN* 8.10, 9.47
Medusa, *Anticl.* 5.11
Megaera, *Anticl.* 2.198, 8.171, 8.313
Melicerta, *DpN* 9.28
Mercurius, *Anticl.* 2.360
Mercurius (planet), *Anticl.* 4.44, 4.412; *DpN* 2.17

Michalus, *Anticl.* 3.467
Midas, *Anticl.* 1.176
Milesius, *Anticl.* 3.457; *DpN* 12.12
Milo, *Anticl.* 2.343, 6.230
Minerva, *Anticl.* 1.218, 1.363, 1.393,
2.8, 2.363, 3.15, 3.320, 4.82, 5.112,
7.291
Moderantia, *Anticl.* 9.279, 9.281
Modestia, *Anticl.* 1.37, 7.117, 8.332
Morbus, *Anticl.* 8.166, 8.252, 9.208
Mors, *Anticl.* 8.229–30, 9.93–94,
9.253
Moyses, *Anticl.* 6.440
Murmur, *Anticl.* 8.247, 9.135, 9.147
Musa, *Anticl.* 4.410, 4.461, 5.265,
5.270, 5.271; *DpN* 1.9
Musica, *Anticl.* 3.413, 3.418, 3.424,
3.430, 3.467, 7.297
Myrrha, *DpN* 8.10, 9.51

Napaeae, *DpN* 4.6
Narcissus, *Anticl.* 2.14, 7.42; *DpN*
1.36, 3.11, 8.10, 14.6
Naso, *Anticl.* 2.358, 6.230
Natura, *SIS* 11; *VNV* 85, 90
Neptunus, *Anticl.* 9.262
Nereus, *DpN* 4.4
Nero, *Anticl.* 1.171, 8.208; *DpN* 2.31,
9.26; *VNV* 137
Nestor, *DpN* 2.20, 9.28
Nicomachus, *Anticl.* 3.375
Niliacus, *Anticl.* 2.411
Nisus, *Anticl.* 2.194–95
Nobilitas, *Anticl.* 1.47, 7.399, 8.64,
8.108, 8.119, 8.129, 8.302
Noë, *Anticl.* 6.403

Notus, *Anticl.* 1.70, 8.5
Noys, *Anticl.* 2.371, 5.169, 5.282,
6.429, 6.434, 6.442, 6.461; *DpN*
7.13, 18.2
Nugae, *Anticl.* 8.282, 9.306
Nummulatria, *DpN* 12.10

Oceanus, *Anticl.* 4.252
Odium, *Anticl.* 8.165, 9.47, 9.51
Oedipus, *Anticl.* 3.114
Olympus, *Anticl.* 3.529, 4.304, 5.94,
5.183, 5.272, 5.444, 6.115, 6.163,
9.395
Ops, *Anticl.* 4.210
Organum, *SIS* 11
Orion, *Anticl.* 5.12
Orpheus, *Anticl.* 2.351; *DpN* 8.8,
12.10
Otia, *Anticl.* 8.282, 9.305
Ovidius, *Anticl.* 2.361

Pacuvius, *DpN* 18.9
Parcae, *Anticl.* 6.217, 6.448; *DpN*
8.31, 10.2, 10.7, 10.10
Paris, *Anticl.* 1.179; *DpN* 1.52, 8.10,
9.27, 9.29, 18.9
Parrasis, *Anticl.* 5.23
Parthi, *Anticl.* 9.242
Pasiphae, *DpN* 8.10; *VNV* 138
Paulus, *Anticl.* 6.54
Pauperies/Paupertas, *Anticl.* 8.235,
8.266, 9.54, 9.61, 9.70, 9.80, 9.91,
9.96, 9.99
Pax, *Anticl.* 1.33, 3.410, 8.189–90,
8.325, 9.52, 9.106
Pegaseus, *Anticl.* 7.258

Pelides, *DpN* 1.55

Penelope, *DpN* 12.10, 16.8

Perdix, *Anticl.* 2.352

Periuria, *Anticl.* 8.164, 8.262

Perseus, *Anticl.* 5.11

Persius, *Anticl.* 2.356

Petrus, *Anticl.* 6.51

Philomena, *Anticl.* 4.460, 7.436;
   DpN 2.24, 5.41, 17.13

Phineas, *Anticl.* 6.440

Phoebe, *Anticl.* 2.134

Phoebus, *Anticl.* Vprol. 7, 2.351,
   5.267; *DpN* 1.40, 16.8

Phoebus (sun), *Anticl.* 2.217, 4.251,
   4.358–59, 8.127, 8.345; *DpN* 4.3,
   5.27, 5.33, 5.37, 5.39

Phrixeus, *DpN* 5.40

Phrygius, *DpN* 1.51, 8.16; *VNV* 144

Pietas, *Anticl.* 1.41, 2.295, 7.329,
   7.331, 8.72, 8.186, 8.326, 9.318,
   9.323

Pirithoüs, *Anticl.* 2.188

Pisces, *Anticl.* 5.35; *DPN* 2.10

Planctus, *Anticl.* 9.221, 9.225

Plato, *Anticl.* 1.134, 2.345; *DpN* 14.6,
   18.8

Pluto, *Anticl.* 8.314, 8.339

Poena, *Anticl.* 8.242, 9.105, 9.282

Pollux, *Anticl.* 6.230

Polynices, *Anticl.* 2.192, 2.219

Porphyrius, *Anticl.* 3.110, 3.113

Potestates, *Anticl.* 5.425

Pressura, *Anticl.* 8.257, 9.223, 9.225

Priamus, *Anticl.* 1.166

Princeps, *Anticl.* 5.422

Probitas, *Anticl.* 8.325

Procne, *Anticl.* 2.221; *VNV* 137

Proserpina, *DpN* 4.6

Prosperitas, *Anticl.* 9.226, 9.265

Prudentia, *Anticl.* 1.271, 1.319, 1.324,
   1.383, 1.435, 1.439, 2.97, 2.160,
   2.310, 2.332, 4.71, 4.239, 4.245,
   4.356, 4.463, 5.367, 5.373, 6.185,
   6.470, 6.484, 8.71; *DpN* 6.10,
   12.14, 18.1

Prudentia (natural virtue), *Anticl.*
   1.40, 8.326, 8.333

Ptholemaeus, *Anticl.* 1.137, 5.372;
   DpN 12.12

Pudor (vice), *Anticl.* 8.246, 9.143

Pudor (virtue), *Anticl.* 1.37, 7.110,
   7.112

Pylades, *Anticl.* 2.198–99

Pyramus, *DpN* 1.54

Pyrois, *Anticl.* 4.111

Pythagoras, *Anticl.* 3.288, 3.379;
   DpN 12.13

Quintilianus, *Anticl.* 3.233

Rabies, *Anticl.* 8.225, 9.46, 9.52

Rapina, *Anticl.* 8.212

Rhetorica, *Anticl.* 3.172, 3.227, 5.479,
   7.270, 7.274

Risus, *Anticl.* 1.36, 7.102, 9.216,
   9.227

Rufinus, *Anticl.* 8.210

Ruinae, *Anticl.* 8.257, 9.223

Samius, *Anticl.* 2.345

Sapientia, *Anticl.* 2.321; *DpN* 6.11,
   12.13–14, 18.3

Saturnus (planet), *Anticl.* 2.115,
    2.445, 2.465, 2.472, 4.45, 4.465,
    6.457, 6.475, 6.479; *DpN* 2.13
Saties, *Anticl.* 9.105
Satyra, *Anticl.* 2.362
Scorpio, *Anticl.* 5.33; *DpN* 2.11
Scylla, *Anticl.* 9.415; *DpN* 9.25,
    10.15, 15.1
Segnities, *Anticl.* 8.282, 9.304
Seneca, *Anticl.* 1.135, 2.354
Senectus/Senecta, *Anticl.* 8.167,
    8.249, 9.149, 9.157, 9.184, 9.188,
    9.195, 9.205
Seraphim, *Anticl.* 5.413
Severinus, *Anticl.* 3.134
Sidonius, *Anticl.* 3.240
Sinon, *DpN* 18.9
Siren, *Anticl.* 1.92, 3.466, 4.389,
    4.412, 4.434; *DpN* 2.26, 12.3, 17.8
Sitis, *Anticl.* 8.242, 9.74, 9.78, 9.101,
    9.107
Sobrietas, *Anticl.* 9.283
Socrates, *Anticl.* 2.346
Sol, *Anticl.* 2.121, 2.126, 2.130, 4.208,
    4.374, 4.389, 4.402, 9.261; *DpN*
    2.16; *SIS* 2
Solius, *Anticl.* 2.357
Solon, *Anticl.* 2.362
Sophia, *Anticl.* 2.331, 2.363, 2.366,
    4.221, 5.319, 6.124, 6.131, 7.228,
    7.248
Spes, *Anticl.* 8.328, 9.52
Sphinx, *Anticl.* 3.114
Statius, *Anticl.* 2.358
Stigiae, *Anticl.* 9.383
Stilbon, *Anticl.* 4.398, 4.403

Stultitia, *Anticl.* 8.280, 9.306
Sulla, *Anticl.* 8.60–61, 8.208
Superbia, *DpN* 14.5
Symmachus, *Anticl.* 3.236

Tantalus, *DpN* 13.10
Tartareus, *Anticl.* 8.162, 8.170,
    8.308, 8.340; *DpN* 4.6
Taurus, *Anticl.* 5.36; *DpN* 2.10
Temperantia, *DpN* 16.12–13
Terror, *Anticl.* 8.227
Thales, *Anticl.* 3.526
Thebanus, *Anticl.* 2.219
Thersites, *DpN* 9.29, 18.9; *VNV* 48
Theseus, *Anticl.* 2.189
Thetis, *DpN* 4.4, 15.11
Thisbe, *DpN* 1.53
Threicius, *Anticl.* 3.403
Throni, *Anticl.* 5.417
Tindaris, *DpN* 1.35, 1.51, 8.10
Tiphys, *Anticl.* 6.229
Tiresias, *DpN* 8.8
Tisiphone, *Anticl.* 1.262, 8.207, 8.313
Titan, *VNV* 8
Titus, *Anticl.* 1.147; *DPN* 14.6
Tobias, *Anticl.* 6.441
Tolerantia, *Anticl.* 9.282
Tonans, *Anticl.* 2.316, 4.432, 5.184,
    5.193, 5.201, 5.377, 5.407, 6.217
Tristities, *Anticl.* 8.166, 8.257, 9.225
Triton, *Anticl.* 4.186, 4.188; *VNV* 8
Troia, *Anticl.* 2.225; *VNV* 143
Tullia, *Anticl.* 3.230
Tullius, *Anticl.* 1.141, 2.344, 3.229,
    5.371; *DpN* 12.10, 12.13, 18.8;
    SIS 1, 3

Turnus, *Anticl.* 1.148; *DpN* 14.6, 18.8

Tydeus, *Anticl.* 2.191; *DpN* 9.27

Tyrius, *Anticl.* 3.406

Ubertas, *Anticl.* 9.107

Ulixes, *Anticl.* 1.145, 4.170, 6.228; *DpN* 9.33, 12.10, 18.8

Urna, *Anticl.* 5.34

Usia, *DpN* 12.2, 18.2, 18.17

Usura, *Anticl.* 8.292

Venus (planet), *Anticl.* 2.122, 4.44, 4.398, 4.409, 4.412, 6.482

Veritas, *DpN* 18.10–11

Victoria, *Anticl.* 9.284, 9.384

Vincentius, *Anticl.* 6.62

Virgilius, *Anticl.* 1.142, 2.362; *DpN* 12.10

Virgo, *Anticl.* 3.313, 5.472, 6.144

Virgo (constellation), *Anticl.* 5.32

Virtus, *Anticl.* 9.148, 9.285

Virtutes, *Anticl.* 5.199, 5.213, 5.224, 8.74, 8.320, 8.324, 8.349, 9.48, 9.283, 9.385, 9.392; *DpN* 16.27

Virtutes (angels), *Anticl.* 5.427

Voluptas, *Anticl.* 8.264, 8.279; *DpN* 6.10

Zeno, *Anticl.* 2.346, 3.129; *DpN* 12.13

Zephyrus, *Anticl.* 1.79, 1.430, 4.156–57, 4.264, 7.413, 7.463, 8.4; *DpN* 5.1

Zethus, *Anticl.* 2.349, 3.129

Zeuxis, *Anticl.* 2.343

Zodiac, *DpN* 2.7